HOMO NECANS

HOMO NECANS

The Anthropology of Ancient Greek Sacrificial Ritual and Myth

by

WALTER BURKERT

Translated by

PETER BING

UNIVERSITY OF CALIFORNIA PRESS

Berkeley Los Angeles London

Originally published in German by Walter de Gruyter & Co., Berlin, under the title *Homo Necans* (1972).

University of California Press
Berkeley and Los Angeles, California

University of California Press, Ltd.
London, England

Library of Congress Cataloging in Publication Data

Burkert, Walter, 1931–
Homo necans.

Translation of: Homo necans.
Bibliography: p.
1. Rites and ceremonies—Greece. 2. Sacrifice.
3. Mythology, Greek. 4. Greece—Religion. I. Title.
BL788.B8713 1983 292'.38 77-93473
ISBN 0-520-03650-6

Printed in the United States of America

1 2 3 4 5 6 7 8 9

For Reinhold Merkelbach

καὶ ταῦτ᾽ ἐστι τὰ μυστήρια, συνελόντι φάναι· φόνοι καὶ τάφοι

Clement of Alexandria

et nos servasti———sanguine fuso

Mithraic inscription, Santa Prisca, Rome

Contents

Translator's Preface

Walter Burkert's style is often suggestive rather than explicit, his descriptions are vivid (at times almost visionary) rather than dryly academic, and he does not hesitate to use colloquialisms so as to make a point more forcefully. In the process of translation, such features inevitably undergo a certain levelling. I have tried, however, to maintain the drama and drive of Professor Burkert's prose. In the German, *Homo Necans* is remarkable for being both an exemplary piece of scholarship and just plain good reading. It is my hope that it remains so in the English.

Among the many friends and colleagues who helped me at various stages in this translation, special thanks are due to James Fanto, Professor Bruce Frier, Professor Ludwig Koenen, Charlotte Melin, Professor William Owens, and Professor Susan Scheinberg. I was privileged to spend several enjoyable and productive days revising the manuscript with Professor Burkert in Uster. Finally my thanks to Doris Kretschmer of the University of California Press who entrusted this project to me and politely, but firmly, kept my nose to the grindstone.

PHILADELPHIA, NOVEMBER 1982

Peter Bing

Preface to the English Edition

It is with some hesitation that I present this book, conceived in the sixties, to an Anglo-American public of the eighties. An holistic synthesis in the field of anthropology may appear preposterous and inadequate at any time; and changes in approach, method, and interest, which have been especially marked in these decades—be it through progress in the individual branches of study, be it through changes of paradigms or even fashions—make such an attempt all the more questionable. When this book appeared in German in 1972, it could claim to be revolutionary in various respects. To a field still dominated largely by philological-historical positivism or by the residue of the Tylorian approach in Nilsson and Deubner, it brought a comprehensive and consistent application of the myth-and-ritual position; it introduced, after Harrison's *Themis*, functionalism to the study of Greek religion; it used a form of structuralism in interpreting the complexes of mythical tales and festivals; and it made a first attempt to apply ethology to religious history. In the English-speaking world, ritualism and functionalism had made their mark long before, and much more on all these lines has been worked out, disseminated, and discussed in the last decade. What was originally novel and daring may thus soon appear antiquated. The social aspect of religion in general and the central role of sacrifice in ancient religion are taken for granted today. Much of the credit goes to the school of Jean-Pierre Vernant and Marcel Detienne in Paris. René Girard's *Violence and the Sacred*, which appeared in the same year as *Homo Necans* and may be seen as largely parallel in intent (cf. I.5.n.1), was also instrumental. More generally, we have seen the swift rise of semiology and structuralism, which, though judged by some to be already past their apogee, still command attention and discussion. We have likewise witnessed the emergence of sociobiology, which aspires to a new synthesis of natural and social sciences. To keep up with all these developments and integrate them into *Homo Necans* would virtually require another book replacing the tentative essay that now constitutes my first chapter.

Chapters II through V appear less problematical. They elaborate basic ritual structures reflected in myth, demonstrating correspondences and integrating isolated pieces into a comprehensive whole. As a description this will prove valid in its own right. The attempt, however, to extrapolate from this an historical-causal explanation of the phenomena—that is, to derive sacrifice from hunting and religion from sacrificial ritual—could be condemned by the stern rules of many a methodology. Yet I have decided to run this risk rather than limit my perspectives by preestablished rules.

In so doing, I have inevitably made use of various hypotheses concerning prehistory, sociology, and psychology that are open to error and to the possibility of attack and falsification in the course of further research. There is no denying that a decisive impulse for the thesis of *Homo Necans* came from Konrad Lorenz's *On Aggression*, which seemed to offer new insight into the disquieting manifestations of violence, which are so prominent in human affairs and not least in the ancient world. Lorenz's assertions about the innate roots of aggression and its necessary functions have come under vigorous attack by progressive sociologists. Some overstatements no doubt have been corrected, but some of the criticism and subsequent neglect may be viewed as part of the schizophrenia of our world, which pursues the ideal of an ever more human, more easygoing life amid growing insecurity and uncontrolled violence. Fashionable psychology attempts to eradicate feelings of guilt from the human psyche; ideas of atonement appear old-fashioned or even perverse. The thrust of *Homo Necans* runs counter to these trends. It attempts to show that things were different in the formative period of our civilization; it argues that solidarity was achieved through a sacred crime with due reparation. And while it has no intention of thwarting modern optimism, it tries to warn against ignoring what was formerly the case.

Great advances have been made in prehistory and especially in primatology. We now know there are hunts with subsequent "distribution of meat" among chimpanzees (see I.2.n.23)—showing them to be more human than had been suspected; a chimpanzee "war" has been observed, and there are reports of intentional killing by gorillas and orangutans (see I.6.n.5). The picture of evolution has become ever richer in details but increasingly blurred in its outlines. In reaction to the "hunting hypothesis" of Robert Ardrey and others, specialists are now reluctant to lay claim to knowledge of the importance of hunting behavior. What had been taken to be the earliest evidence for sacrifice has been called into question again (see I.2.n.6). Yet the historian of religion still insists that religion must have come into existence at some specific point—chimpanzees are apparently irreligious—and that it first becomes discernible with funerary and hunting ritual. In view of all this it is essential to note that the course of historical development as delineated in *Homo Necans* does not at any stage require that "all" men acted or experienced things in a certain way—e.g., that all hunters feel sympathy for their quarry or remorse over their hunting—but only that some did indeed institute forms of behavior that became traditional and had a formative influence on the high cultures accessible to historical investigation. For the strange prominence of animal slaughter in ancient religion this still seems to be the most economical, and most humane, explanation.

In dealing with tradition, *Homo Necans* takes a stance that is hardly popular: it restricts the role of creative freedom and fantasy; it reduces "ideas" to the imprinting effect of cultural transfer. On the other hand, modern insistence on "creativity" may simply be an attempt to compensate for the enormous anonymous constraints at work in our society. Nobody wants to question the spiritual achievements of mankind, but these may have strange and opaque substructures. In pointing them out it is perhaps wisest not even to shun the accusation of reductionism, for, though from a structuralist-semiotic perspective one may well describe religion as the relations between men and gods, with sacrifice mediating between them, the term *gods* nonetheless remains fluid and in need of explanation, while sacrifice is a fact.

The thesis that those groups united by religious ritual have historically been most successful seems to conflict with the modern version of the theory of evolution. That theory now discards the concept of group selection and insists, rather, on the self-perpetuation of the "selfish gene" (see I.3.n.9). It may be pointed out once more that this is a predictable modern perspective reflecting the disintegration of our society. Whether it applies to the history of culturally determined groups is another question. The thesis of *Homo Necans* does not hypothesize about genetic fixation of "human nature." It seeks, rather, to confront the power and effect of tradition as fully as possible. In this sense it is radically historical, and factual.

In preparing the translation, I have only been able to rework the bibliography and notes to a limited extent. They still largely reflect the state of the relevant scholarship in 1972. I have, however, taken the opportunity to refer to more recent specialized studies and standard works and to make the documentation more complete and up-to-date.

It remains to thank the University of California Press and Peter Bing, the translator, for their untiring efforts.

USTER, JULY 1982

Walter Burkert

List of Illustrations

Introduction

It is not so much the limits of our knowledge as the superabundance of what can be known that makes an attempt to explain man's religious behavior an almost hopeless enterprise. The mass of available data and interpretation has long exceeded the limits of what an individual can grasp and assimilate. Perhaps this stream of information will soon be ordered and surveyed through a collective effort using computers, but as long as intellectual independence prevails and an individual must seek to orient himself within his own world, he may—indeed, he must—take the risk of projecting a model of his situation and reducing a confusing multiplicity into a comprehensible form.

A philologist who starts from ancient Greek texts and attempts to find biological, psychological, and sociological explanations for religious phenomena naturally runs the risk of juggling too many balls at once and dropping them all. And if it is strange for a philologist to venture beyond scrupulous discussion of his texts, psychology and sociology are just as reluctant to burden their analyses of contemporary phenomena with an historical perspective stretching back to antiquity and beyond. There is a danger that important biological, psychological, and ethnological findings be overlooked, just as can happen with archaeological finds, and it is hardly possible for the non-specialist to give the Near Eastern evidence the expert treatment it requires. Yet we must not assume that all subjects fit neatly within the limits of a particular discipline. Even philology depends on a biologically, psychologically, and sociologically determined environment and tradition to provide its basis for understanding. And just as biology acquired an historical dimension with the concept of evolution,[1] so sociology, like psychology before it, should accept the notion that

[1] H. Diels, *Internationale Wochenshrift* 3 (1909), 890, discussed the "historicizing of nature" through Darwin's theory.

human society is shaped by the past and can be understood only by examining its development over long periods of time.

Of course, the act of understanding itself presents us with problems that have been widely discussed. If by "understanding" we mean that the outside world will ultimately correspond to our expectations and thought structures, then we admit that the diversity of that world is perceived as though through a predetermined filter and that there will be different kinds of understanding, distinguished according to individuals and groups. But if reality were not anthropomorphically or at least intellectually determined, then understanding in a personal sense would be altogether impossible. The possibility remains of using our consciousness, fully aware of these problems, to unravel the course of received tradition,[2] and to adapt the structures of understanding to the ever-new realities with which we are confronted and to which man, whether he likes it or not, remains tied. Our task is to seek the perspectives that give us the broadest and clearest view, to project a model that accounts for the various areas of experience as comprehensively as possible and that is susceptible to frequent factual verification. We cannot hope that our model will be a finished product; it is merely an attempt set forward for discussion, with full knowledge of its tentative nature.

Every religion aspires to the absolute. Its claims, when seen from within, make it self-sufficient. It establishes and explains, but needs no explanation. Within this sphere of power, any discussion about religion will almost automatically become a religious pronouncement, especially as the essence of religion is an attempt at expression and communication. In this way, however, religion becomes the agent and the medium of communication rather than its subject. This is precisely why religious discussion about religion is effective, for it finds resonance in nearly everyone. Thus, even when the seriousness of religious practice is replaced by the ambiguous and non-binding "as if" of emotional understanding, this mode of discourse remains entirely respectable even in a secularized society.

The opposite extreme in the study of religion is likewise generally accepted and carries no risk: this is the lexicographical documentation and arrangement of the details that have been observed and transmitted to us from the past. And yet a lexicon will not give us an understanding of the language if the grammar is unknown or disregarded and if the practice under discussion has not been under-

[2]For the fundamental philosophical treatment see H. G. Gadamer, *Wahrheit und Methode* (1965)[2].

stood. Thus, precisely because religious phenomena seem more and more to elude the modern world's grasp, mere gathering of material can shed no more light on them than can the uncontrolled resonances of emotional understanding.

Especially when dealing with foreign or extinct religions, an outsider finds himself confronted, as it were, with a strange and unknown language: to understand it, he must translate it. This means first of all that there should be no ambiguity about the language into which one translates. To vacillate between transformation and imitation will produce the kind of misunderstandings that do, in fact, dominate many controversies in the study of religion. If one tries to translate one religion into the language of another, one finds, just as in working with ordinary languages of different nations, that this is only possible to a limited degree. Equivalent expressions will frequently be lacking, due to the respective differences in religious practice and in living conditions. If we take up foreign words such as *totem*, *tabu*, and *mana*, their meaning remains unclear or changes according to the interpreter's intent. If we invent new concepts such as *vegetation spirit* or *Year Daemon*,[3] their legitimacy remains a matter of dispute, especially if it is unclear at what point the concept becomes a new myth itself.

The language that has proved the most generally understood and cross-cultural is that of secularized scholarship. Its practice today is determined by science in its broadest sense, its system of rules by the laws of logic. It may, of course, seem the most questionable endeavor of all to try to translate religious phenomena into this language; by its self-conception, a religion must deny that such explanations are possible. However, scholarship is free to study even the rejection of knowledge and repudiation of independent thought, for scholarship, in attempting to understand the world, has the broader perspective here and cannot abstain from analyzing the worldwide fact of religion. This is not a hopeless undertaking.[4] However, a discussion of religion must then be anything but religious.

---

[3] W. Mannhardt, *Die Korndämonen* (1868); Harrison (1927) 331–34. Especially dangerous is the little word *is*, which confounds translation, allegory, classification, and ontological or psychological realization. See, for instance, Nilsson (1906) 27: "wenn der Stier des Zeus Sosipolis ein Korngeist ist, muss der des Zeus Polieus es auch sein."

[4] E. E. Evans-Pritchard, *Theories of Primitive Religion* (1965), offers a survey with penetrating criticism that leads to the conclusion that the "believer" is superior to the "nonbeliever" (121). Still fundamental, however, is E. Durkheim's *Les formes élémentaires de la vie religieuse* (1912). Psychoanalytical enterprises—most recently La Barre (1970)—are also to be taken seriously.

We shall examine religion as an historical and social phenomenon, as the medium of tradition and communication among men. This contradicts the common assumptions, if not the practical reality, of the dominant religious tradition in the West, i.e., Christianity, which views the individual's encounter with the one God, and his subsequent salvation, as the only relevant facts. This perspective has determined the common scholarly definition of religion as, for instance, "man's experiential encounter with the sacred and his action in response to the sacred."[5] And yet individual religions exist in typical and persisting forms precisely because very little unforeseen spontaneity and innovation occur in them. To the extent that we find a "personal encounter with the sacred," it is performed according to a traditional method and with pedagogical intent. Only those who can attest to a genuine encounter are accepted. The pre-Christian religions proclaimed with the utmost conviction that only ancestral tradition could guarantee the legitimacy of religion. Thus, through his oracle, the Delphic god always sanctioned rites "according to the custom of the city"; and the Boeotian was speaking for many when he remarked, in regard to a strange fish-sacrifice at Lake Copais, "There is just one thing I know: that one must maintain the ancestral customs and that it would be improper to excuse oneself for this before others."[6]

Ancient Greek religion is distinguished neither by extreme antiquity nor by a great wealth of source material. It is far younger than either the Egyptian or Sumerian tradition, and in terms of accessibility it cannot even begin to compete with a living religion. In spite of this, the general problems in the study of religion have been repeatedly linked to research on the religion of the Greeks. This can hardly be a coincidental offshoot of the once-ubiquitous humanistic tradition. If, rather, we take both age and accessibility into account simultaneously, the ancient Greek religion assumes a unique position after all: among the most ancient forms of religion, it is still the most comprehensible and the one that can be observed from the greatest number of perspectives. For it never disappeared entirely, but remained

[5] G. Mensching, *Die grossen Nichtchristlichen Religionen unserer Zeit* (1954), 13; *RGG*³ V 961; cf. F. Heiler, *Erscheinungsformen und Wesen der Religion* (1961), 562: "Umgang mit dem Heiligen."

[6] Agatharchides, Ath. 297d; *νόμῳ πόλεως* Xen. *Mem.* 1.3.1, 4.3.16, and cf. Hes. fr. 322; Eur. *Bacch.* 201–204; Plat. *Leg.* 738b–d; Cotta in Cic. *Nat. deor.* 3.5, 9; Cic. *Leg.* 2.40; Cic. *Har. resp.* 18–19. Likewise, early Christianity felt obliged to its ancestors: *οὐκ ἀρεῖς τὴν χεῖρά σου ἀπὸ τοῦ υἱοῦ σου ἢ ἀπὸ τῆς θυγατρός σου, ἀλλὰ ἀπὸ νεότητος διδάξεις τὸν φόβον τοῦ θεοῦ* (*Didache* 4.9).

active, even if in strange transformations, from superstition and literary tradition to liturgical practice and Christian theology. Only in ancient Greek religion do we find an uninterrupted tradition of the greatest antiquity in a highly refined culture, unsurpassed in its intellectual and artistic achievement. It was due to this union of antiquity with sophistication that the Greeks were the first systematically to call religion into question. Seen from that distance and from changing perspectives, the phenomenon may come into sharper relief.

In the following studies, the Greek tradition will hold center stage, though it is hoped that we will illuminate important stages in the mainstream of human development as well. We will not try to explain phenomena by amassing "primitive" material for comparison, stripped of its context and hence all the more difficult to understand. Rather, we shall proceed from a consistent historical perspective stretching back to man's beginnings. We will not place great weight on the individuality of Greek culture, regardless of how praiseworthy it may be; the anthropological aspect outweighs the humanistic. But it is precisely here that both the primeval roots and the lucidity of the Greek material becomes evident. It can serve, as it were, as a mirror in which the basic orders of life, lying far behind us, become visible with an almost classical clarity.

We shall try to combine this consistent historical perspective with a functional one. Within historical reality, religion is a stabilizing factor of the first order in society. As such it appears in its enduring aspect, always a given tradition which is modified time and again but never replaced by something entirely new. As it unfolds within the many-faceted play of social forces, various traditions unite, thereby asserting and perpetuating themselves or languishing and dying out. In this respect, religion, while tied to social reality, does not simply reflect that reality; it takes little account of society's swift changes, especially those regarding economic conditions. Rather, it seems to deal with more fundamental layers of communal human life and with its psychological preconditions, which have changed only slightly from the earliest times until now. If religious forms have often provided a focal point for new social and economic developments, they were more a prerequisite than a consequence of these developments.[7]

At the core of our study are the rituals, together with the mythic

---

[7]Max Weber, in his famous study, demonstrated the influence of Calvinism on capitalism (*Die protestantische Ethik und der Geist des Kapitalismus, Ges. Aufsätze zur Religionssoziologie* I [1920], 17–206), but Calvinism cannot conversely be explained by way of capitalism.

traditions relating to them. Our aim is to identify and to understand relationships and structures that recur in various guises but always bind certain elements together in the same way.[8] We shall consciously refrain from trying to arrange the material according to a mathematical model. The elements are, on the one hand, so complex and, on the other, so directly understandable that it would be wrong to reduce them to a yes/no pattern, thus making them so complicated that they would be obscured. Killing and eating, virgins, mothers and fathers —these basic configurations of human life are more easily grasped through experience than through logical analysis, just as the structure of a ritual and of a mythic tale unfolds in linear time and cannot be represented by a system of reversible permutations. Thus, the sacrificial ritual moves from preparation through the "unspeakable" central point to the act of "setting up" an order, a pattern which can be repeated but not reversed.

The first chapter deals with basic principles and could stand on its own, although it would then probably seem too dogmatic and speculative. It pulls together the various threads that appear in the case studies of the subsequent chapters. By spelling out the consequences, it lays the foundation that is then assumed for the rest of the book. The hypothesis and the application confirm one another, even though neither is quite self-sufficient. Following this attempt to analyze the complex of hunting, sacrifice, and funerary ritual both historically and functionally, we turn to an interpretation of groups of Greek festival rites under various aspects. We examine, on the one hand, the divisions and interactions of individual groups at the sacrifice of a ram and, on the other, the sequence of dissolution and restoration of the order of life, from the city festivals to the Dionysiac orgies. The sacrificial structure of guilt incurred and subsequent restitution also appears in the consumption of wine at the oldest festival of Dionysus; and the mysteries of the grain goddess Demeter appear to be likewise organized by the rhythm of the sacrificial rites. This sequence is not to be understood as historical stratigraphy. It is increasingly difficult to separate Mediterranean, Near Eastern, and Eurasian elements, and to distinguish Greek from pre-Greek. The structures are perhaps too basic to follow ethnic distinctions.

The aim of our presentation is to set out the phenomena in a per-

---

[8]The following analyses were begun and conducted largely without reference to C. Lévi-Strauss's *Anthropologie structurale* (1958; *Mythologiques* I–IV [1964–1971]; *Anthropologie structurale deux* [1973]). For a closer look at structuralism, see Burkert (1979) 5–14.

spicuous and understandable form. This requires a practicable brevity and limitation of scope, a selective treatment of the boundless mass of material. It would be impossible to discuss all questions in detail or refer exhaustively to all specialized secondary literature. We have attempted instead to refer to what is basic and what is new. The most important sources are cited, but the list is by no means exhaustive. We refer the reader to the standard works of Preller-Robert, Deubner and Nilsson, Farnell and Cook for more complete documentation.

The aspects of Greek religion and of humanity that emerge in this study are not those which are particularly edifying, not the ideal or the most likable traits of Greek culture. Yet we can invoke the Delphic god's injuction that mankind should see itself with absolute clarity, no illusions: *Γνῶθι σαυτόν.*

I. SACRIFICE, HUNTING, AND FUNERARY RITUALS

1. *Sacrifice as an Act of Killing*

Aggression[1] and human violence have marked the progress of our civilization and appear, indeed, to have grown so during its course that they have become a central problem of the present. Analyses that attempt to locate the roots of the evil often set out with shortsighted assumptions, as though the failure of our upbringing or the faulty development of a particular national tradition or economic system were to blame. More can be said for the thesis that all orders and forms of authority in human society are founded on institutionalized violence. This at least corresponds to the fundamental role played in biology by intraspecific aggression, as described by Konrad Lorenz. Those, however, who turn to religion for salvation from this "so-called evil" of aggression are confronted with murder at the very core

[1] S. Freud pointed the way in *Das Unbehagen in der Kultur* (1930), *Ges. Schriften XII* (1934), 27–114 = *Ges. Werke XIV* (1948), 419–506. K. Lorenz (1963) is basic from the standpoint of the behaviorist. The sometimes spirited criticisms of his approach—for instance, M. F. Ashley-Montagu, ed., *Man and Aggression* (1968); A. Plack, *Die Gesellschaft und das Böse* (1969[4]); J. Rattner, *Aggression und menschliche Natur* (1970)—did indeed correct some particulars but sometimes also displayed wishful thinking and partisanship; cf. Eibl-Eibesfeldt's (1970) defensive posture. For application to religious studies see P. Weidkuhn, *Aggressivität, Ritus, Säkularisierung. Biologische Grundformen religiöser Prozesse* (1965).

of Christianity—the death of God's innocent son; still earlier, the Old Testament covenant could come about only after Abraham had decided to sacrifice his child. Thus, blood and violence lurk fascinatingly at the very heart of religion.

From a classicizing perspective, Greek religion appeared and still appears to some as bright and harmlessly cheerful. Yet those who maintain that the skandalon of the Cross (I Cor. 1:23) is on another level altogether overlook the deeper dimension that accompanies the easy life of the gods as portrayed by Homer. If a man is able to draw near to the gods, as the priest Chryses with Apollo or as Hektor or Odysseus with Zeus, he can do so because he has "burnt many thigh-pieces of bulls" (*Il.* 1.40, 22.170; *Od.* 1.66), for this is the act of piety: bloodshed, slaughter—and eating. It makes no difference if there is no temple or cult-statue, as often occurs in the cult of Zeus. The god is present at his place of sacrifice, a place distinguished by the heap of ashes left from "sacred" offerings burnt there over long periods of time, or by the horns and skulls of slaughtered rams and bulls, or by the altar-stone where the blood must be sprinkled. The worshipper experiences the god most powerfully not just in pious conduct or in prayer, song, and dance, but in the deadly blow of the axe, the gush of blood and the burning of thigh-pieces. The realm of the gods is sacred, but the "sacred" act done at the "sacred" place by the "consecrating" actor consists of slaughtering sacrificial animals, *ἱερεύειν τὰ ἱερεῖα*.[2] It was no different in Israel up to the destruction of the temple.[3] It is prescribed that daily "burnt offering shall be on the hearth upon the altar," "all night until the morning" (Lev. 6:2); these offerings, the remnants of two one-year-old lambs cut into pieces, are "a pleasing odor to the Lord." Thus the principal sin of Antiochus Epiphanes against Jerusalem was that he ordered that "the continual burnt offering [be] taken away" (Dan. 8:11). Augustus built an altar to

---

[2]On Greek sacrifice see Stengel (1910), (1920) 95–155; Eitrem (1915); F. Schwenn, *Gebet und Opfer* (1927); L. Ziehen, *RE* XVIII (1939), 579–627, III A (1929), 1669–79; Meuli (1946); Burkert (1966); Nilsson (1955) 132–157; Casabona (1966); E. Forster, "Die antiken Ansichten über das Opferwesen," Diss. Innsbruck, 1952; E. Kadletz, "Animal Sacrifice in Greek and Roman Religion," Diss. University of Washington, 1976; Detienne and Vernant (1979). For the pictorial tradition see G. Rizza, *ASAA* 37/38 (1959/60), 321–45; Metzger (1965) 107–118. On sacrifice generally see W. R. Smith (1894); H. Hubert and M. Mauss, "Essai sur la nature et la fonction du sacrifice," *Année Sociologique* 2 (1898), 29–138 = M. Mauss, *Oeuvres I* (1968), 193–307; A. Loisy, *Essai historique sur le sacrifice* (1920); R. Money-Kyrle, *The Meaning of Sacrifice* (1930) (psychoanalytical); E. M. Loeb, "The Blood Sacrifice Complex," *Mem. Amer. Anthr. Assoc.* 30 (1923); E. O. James, *Sacrifice and Sacrament* (1962); Burkert (1981).

[3]R. de Vaux, *Les sacrifices de l'Ancien Testament* (1964); cf. n. 42 below.

celebrate the establishment of world peace and, together with his family, appears on the reliefs of this Ara Pacis as a sacrificer, preceded by servants carrying the sacrificial axe. Thus, the most refined Augustan art provides a framework for the bloody sacrifices at the center.

Sacrificial killing is the basic experience of the "sacred." *Homo religiosus* acts and attains self-awareness as *homo necans*. Indeed, this is what it means "to act," *ῥέζειν*, *operari* (whence "sacrifice" is *Opfer* in German)—the name merely covers up the heart of the action with a euphemism.[4] The bliss of encountering divinity finds expression in words, and yet the strange and extraordinary events that the participant in the sacrifice is forced to witness are all the more intense because they are left undiscussed.

Thanks to the descriptions in Homer and tragedy, we can reconstruct the course of an ordinary Greek sacrifice to the Olympian gods almost in its entirety. The path that leads to the center of the sacred experience is complex. The preparations include bathing and dressing in clean clothes,[5] putting on ornaments and wreaths;[6] often sexual abstinence is a requirement.[7] At the start, a procession (*πομπή*),[8] even if still a small one, is formed. The festival participants depart from the everyday world, moving to a single rhythm and singing. The sacrificial animal is led along with them, likewise decorated and transformed—bound with fillets, its horns covered with gold.[9] Generally it is hoped that the animal will follow the procession compliantly or even willingly. Legends often tell of animals that offered themselves

---

[4]The basic meaning of *θύειν* is "to smoke." Concerning the ancients, Plutarch writes (following Theophrastus?) *ταραττόμενοι καὶ δειμαίνοντες "ἔρδειν" μὲν ἐκάλουν καὶ "ῥέζειν," ὥς τι μέγα δρῶντες, τὸ θύειν ἔμψυχον*, *Q. conv.* 729 f.; *πονεῖσθαι* *Il.* 2.409, cf. 1.318; *Hy. Merc.* 436. Likewise in Hebrew and Hittite, the verb *to do* is used in the sense of "to sacrifice"; cf. Casabona (1966) 301–304, who warns against generalizations.

[5]E.g., *Od.* 4.759; Eur. *El.* 791 and J. D. Denniston's *Commentary* (1939), *ad loc.*; Poll. 1.25; Wächter (1910) 11–12; R. Ginouvès, ΒΑΛΑΝΕΥΤΙΚΗ; *Recherches sur le bain dans l'antiquité grecque* (1962), 299–318.

[6]Xen. *Anab.* 7.1.40; Aeschines 3.77; etc.; J. Köchling, *De coronarum apud antiquos vi atque usu* (1913); K. Baus, *Der Kranz in Antike und Christentum* (1940); L. Deubner, *ARW* 30 (1933), 70–104; Blech (1982).

[7]Fehrle (1910), esp. 155–58; for the Coan inscription on the sacrifice of a bull for Zeus Polieus see now *SIG*^{3} 1025 = *LS* 151 A 41–44.

[8]E. Pfuhl, *De Atheniensium pompis sacris* (1910); Wilamowitz (1932) 350–54.

[9]*Od.* 3.432–38. This survived in folk custom until modern times; see U. Jahn, *Die deutschen Opferbräuche bei Ackerbau und Viehzucht* (1884), 136–37, 315–17, on the proverbial "ox at Pentecost"; Megas (1956) 17. On the meaning of *ἱερεῖον τέλειον* see Arist. fr. 101; Plut. *De def. or.* 437a; Schol. A. *Il.* 1.66; Eust. 49.35.

up for sacrifice,[10] apparent evidence of a higher will that commands assent. The final goal is the sacrificial stone, the altar "set up" long ago, which is to be sprinkled with blood. Usually a fire is already ablaze on top of it. Often a censer is used to impregnate the atmosphere with the scent of the extraordinary, and there is music, usually that of the flute. A virgin leads the way, "carrying the basket" (*κανηφόρος*),[11] that is, an untouched girl holding a covered container (see figures 1 and 2). A water jug must be there as well.

First of all, after arriving at the sacred place, the participants mark off a circle; the sacrificial basket and water jug are carried around the assembly, thus marking off the sacred realm from the profane.[12] The first communal act is washing one's hands as the beginning of that which is to take place. The animal is also sprinkled with water. "Shake yourself," says Trygaios in Aristophanes,[13] for the animal's movement is taken to signify a "willing nod," a "yes" to the sacrificial act. The bull is watered again,[14] so that he will bow his head. The animal thus becomes the center of attention. The participants now take unground barley grains (*οὐλαί*), the most ancient agricultural product, from the basket. These, however, are not meant for grinding or to be made into food: after a brief silence, the solemn *εὐφημεῖν*, followed by a prayer out loud—in a way, more self-affirmation than prayer—the participants fling the barley grains away onto the sacrificial animal, the altar, and the earth.[15] They are after

[10] *ϑεηλάτου βοὸς δίκην* Aesch. *Ag.* 1297; see Burkert (1966) 107 n. 43; Dio Chrys. *Or.* 12.51 (Olympia); Porph. *Abst.* 1.25 (Gadeira, Kyzikos); Plut. *Pel.* 22 (Leuktra); Apollon. *Mir.* 13 (Halikarnassos); Arist. *Mir. Ausc.* 844a35 (Pedasia); Philostr. *Her.* 8 p. 294 (Rhesos), 17 p. 329 and Arr. *Peripl.* 22 (Leuke); Ael. *Nat. an.* 10.50 (Eryx), 11.4 (Hermione); especially for human sacrifice see Neanthes *FGrHist* 84 F 16 (Epimenides), Serv. *Aen.* 3.57 (Massalia), Paus. 4.9.4 (Messenia); Isaac, according to Hellenistic tradition, see Jos. *Ant. Jud.* 1.232; IV Macc. 13:12, 16:20. Cf. J. Schmitt, *Freiwilliger Opfertod bei Euripides* (1921).

[11] J. Schelp, *Das Kanoun, der griechische Opferkorb* (1975); for reproductions see, e.g., Simon (1969) 193; Deubner (1932) pl. 11.1; Nilsson (1955) pl. 32.1.

[12] E.g., Aristoph. *Pax* 956–58, Eur. *Iph. Aul.* 1568; Eitrem (1915) 7–29.

[13] Aristoph. *Pax* 960; *ὅ δ' ἑκούσιον ἂν κατανεύσῃ* . . . Porph. *Abst.* 2.9 = Parke and Wormell (1958) II #537; Plut. *Q. conv.* 729 f., *De def. or.* 435b–c, 437a; Schol. *Il.* 1.449; Schol. Aristoph. *Pax* 960; Schol. Apoll. Rhod. 1.425; cf. Meuli (1946) 254, 266; J. G. Frazer, *Pausanias' Description of Greece*, 1898, on Paus. 10.5.7; Ginouvès, ΒΑΛΑΝΕΥΤΙΚΗ, 311–18.

[14] Bull-sacrifice for dithyrambic victory: see, e.g., the Munich stamnos 2412 = *ARV*^{2} 1036, 5 in Stengel (1920) pl. V.

[15] A. W. H. Adkins, "Εὔχομαι, Εὐχωλή and Εὖχος in Homer," *CQ* 19 (1969), 20–33: "asserting his existence, his value, and his claims" (33); this characteristic, a given in Homeric usage, conforms exactly to the position of prayer in the sacrificial ritual, although the prayer qua request can, as Oriental texts show, be far more elaborate.

another kind of food. The act of throwing simultaneously as a group is an aggressive gesture, like beginning a fight, even if the most harmless projectiles are chosen. Indeed, in some ancient rituals stones were used.[16] Hidden beneath the grains in the basket was the knife, which now lies uncovered.[17] The leader in this incipient drama, the *ἱερεύς*, steps toward the sacrificial animal, carrying the knife still covered so that the animal cannot see it. A swift cut, and a few hairs from the brow are shorn and thrown into the fire. This is another, though more serious, act of beginning (*ἄρχεσθαι*),[18] just as the water and the barley grains were a beginning. Blood has not yet been spilled and no pain whatsoever has been inflicted, but the inviolability of the sacrificial animal has been abolished irreversibly.

Now comes the death blow. The women raise a piercing scream: whether in fear or triumph or both at once, the "Greek custom of the sacrificial scream"[19] marks the emotional climax of the event, drowning out the death-rattle. The blood flowing out is treated with special care. It may not spill on the ground; rather, it must hit the altar, the hearth, or the sacrificial pit. If the animal is small it is raised over the altar; otherwise the blood is caught in a bowl and sprinkled on the altar-stone. This object alone may, and must again and again, drip blood.[20]

The "act" is over; its consequences are the next concern. The animal is carved up and disembowelled. Its inner organs are now the main focus, lying revealed, an alien, bizarre, and uncanny sight, and yet common in the same form to men as well, as is known from seeing wounded soldiers. The tradition specifies precisely what must

---

[16] *Οὐλοχύτας ἀνέλοντο / προβάλοντο Il.* 1.449/458, 2.410/421, and cf. *Od.* 3.447; *χέρνιβα τ' οὐλοχύτας τε κατάρχεσθαι Od.* 3.445; cf. Aristoph. *Pax* 961–67. For *οὐλαί* as the most ancient grain see Theophrastus in Porph. *Abst.* 2.6 and Schol. *Il.* 1.449b; Schol. *Od.* 3.441; *Suda* o 907; Eust. 132.25, 133.12, and cf. Eust. 1859.48; as an expression of *πολυπληθεία* and *εὐφορία* see Schol. A *Il.*1.449, Schol. *Od.* 3.441. *Ψηφῖσιν . . . ἀντὶ οὐλῶν χρώμενοι* Paus. 1.41.9 (cf. III.4 below). For ritual stone-throwing around the altar of Poseidon at the Isthmian sanctuary see O. Broneer, *Hesperia* 28 (1959), 303. Cf. L. Ziehen, *Hermes* 37 (1902), 391–400; Stengel (1910) 13–33; Eitrem (1915) 261–308, who recognized the equivalence with *φυλλοβολία* and *καταχύσματα*; Burkert (1966) 107, n. 46.

[17] Plat. Com. fr. 91 (*CAF* I 626); Aristoph. *Pax* 948 with Schol.; Eur. *El.* 810, *Iph. Aul.* 1565; Philostr. *V. Ap.* 1.1

[18] *Od.* 3.446, 14.422; Eur. *Alc.* 74–76, *El.* 811; Eitrem (1915) 344–72—who, however, erroneously makes the "beginning" into a "selbständige Opfergabe" (413).

[19] *Ἑλληνικὸν νόμισμα θυστάδος βοῆς* Aesch. *Sept.* 269; *Od.* 3.450; Aesch. *Ag.* 595, 1118; Hdt. 4.189; L. Deubner, "Ololyge und Verwandtes," *Abh. Berlin* (1941), 1.

[20] *Αἱμάσσειν τοὺς βωμούς* Poll. 1.27; Porph. *Abst.* 1.25; cf. Bacch. 11.111; Aesch. *Sept.* 275. For vase-paintings see n. 2 above; *ἀμνίον Od.* 3.444 (cf. Schol.) = *σφαγεῖον* Poll. 10.65. In place of the altar (*βωμός*), the hearth (*ἑστία, ἐσχάρα*) or sacrificial pit (*βόθρος*) can receive the blood; cf. II.2.n.18 below. Cf. Stengel (1910) 105–125.

be done with each piece.[21] First of all, the heart, sometimes still beating, is put on the altar.[22] A seer is present to interpret the lobes of the liver.[23] In general, however, the *σπλάγχνα*—the collective term for the organs—are quickly roasted in the fire from the altar and eaten at once. Thus the inner circle of active participants is brought together in a communal meal, transforming horror into pleasure. Only the bile is inedible and has to be disposed of. Likewise, the bones are not to be used for the subsequent meal, so they are "consecrated" beforehand. The bones, above all the thigh-bones (*μηρία*) and the pelvis with the tail (*ὀσφύς*), are put on the altar "in the proper order."[24] From the bones, one can still see exactly how the parts of the living animal fit together: its basic form is restored and consecrated. In Homer, a "beginning," i.e., a first offering, consisting of raw pieces of flesh from every limb, is put on the bones as well, indicating the entirety of the slaughtered animal.[25] The purifying fire then consumes all these remains. The skulls of bulls and rams and goat-horns are preserved[26] in the sacred place as permanent evidence of the act of consecration. The flow of blood is now replaced in its turn by the offerings of the planter, pouring libations of wine into the fire and burning cakes.[27] As the alcohol causes the flames to flare up, a higher reality seems present. Then, as the fire dies down, the pleasing feast gradually gives

---

[21] Stengel (1910) 73–78; Meuli (1946) 246–48, 268–72; *συσπλαγχνεύειν* Aristoph. *Pax* 1115; Eup. fr. 108 (*CAF* I 286); Ath. 410b.

[22] Galen *Plac. Hipp. et Plat.* 2.4 p. 238 K; cf. Cleanthes in Cic. *Nat. deor.* 2.24; *Suda* κ 370 (*An. Bekk.* I 275.10; *Et. M.* 492.12); Hsch. *καρδιοῦσθαι*, *καρδιουλκίαι*, and cf. Luk. *Sacrif.* 13; *LSS* 121.7.

[23] G. Blecher, *De extispicio capita tria* (1905); for the Near Eastern tradition see J. Nougayrol, "Les rapports des haruspicines étrusque et assyro-babylonienne," *CRAI* (1955), 509–18.

[24] *Εὐθετίσας* Hes. *Th.* 541. Meuli (1946) 215–17 proved that the *μηρία* mentioned regularly in Homer are the bare thigh-bones; *ὀστέα λευκά* Hes. *Th.* 540, 557. The comic poets normally mention *ὀσφύς* and gall; cf. Men. *Dysc.* 451–52 and cf. fr. 264, *Sam.* 399–402; Eub. fr. 95, 130 (*CAF* II 197, 210); *Com. adesp.* fr. 1205 (*CAF* III.606). Vase-paintings (see n. 2 above) portray the *ὀσφύς* and tail of the sacrificial animal on the altar; cf. Aristoph. *Pax* 1054 with Schol.

[25] *'Ωμοθέτησαν* *Il.* 1.461, 2.424; *Od.* 3.458, 12.361, 14.427; Dion. Hal. *Ant.* 7.72.17; Meuli (1946) 218, 256, 262.

[26] Theophr. *Char.* 21.7; Schol. Aristoph. *Plut.* 943; Eitrem (1917) 34–48; Nilsson (1955) 88, 145. For the accumulation of goat-horns in the temple of Apollo at Dreros see S. Marinatos, *BCH* 60 (1936), 224–25, 241–44. On the Keraton of Delos see Dikaiarchus fr. 85 W. = Plut. *Thes.* 21; Callim. *Hy. Ap.* 58–64; E. Bethe, *Hermes* 72 (1937), 191–94.

[27] *Od.* 3.459–60; *κ]αὶ ἐπιθύει ἀλ[φίτων ἡμίεκτον* . . . *LS* 157 A, and cf. 151 A 20 *ἐπιθύειν*.

way to everyday life.[28] The skin of the sacrificial victim is generally sold to benefit the sanctuary, to purchase new votive offerings and new victims: in this way, the cult insures its own continuance.[29]

This rite is objectionable, and was already felt to be so early on, because it so clearly and directly benefits man. Is the god "to whom" the sacrifice is made any more than a transparent excuse for festive feasting? All he gets are the bones, the fat, and the gall bladders. Hesiod says that the crafty Prometheus, the friend of mankind, caused this to be so in order to deceive the gods, and the burning of bones became a standard joke in Greek comedy.[30] Criticism that damned the bloody act per se was far more penetrating. Zarathustra's curse applies to all who lust for blood and slaughter cattle.[31] "I have had enough of burnt offering of rams and the fat of fed beasts; I do not delight in the blood of bulls or of lambs or of he-goats," says the Lord through Isaiah.[32] In the Greek world, the Pythagoreans and Orphics demanded that the lives of all creatures with souls be spared, and Empedokles was the most vehement of all in attacking the cannibalistic madness of the traditional sacrificial meal, as also in expressing the desire for a realm of non-violent love on the path toward "purification."[33] Philosophy then took up the criticism of blood-

---

[28] Often everything must be eaten on the spot (*οὐ φορά*): see Burkert (1966) 103 n.36; *LSS* 88, 94.

[29] Stengel (1920) 116–17; esp. *IG* II[2] 1496 *τὸ περιγινόμενον ἀναλίσκειν εἰς ἀναθήματ[α* *SIG*[3] 1044, 47 = *LSAM* 72, 47; cf. *LSS* 61, 62–67, 23b4; *SIG*[3] 982, 23–28; *LS* 69, 85. An exception: *τὸ δέρμα ἁγίζετ[αι* *LS* 151 D 16; *LS* 18 Γ 11 *τὸ δέρμα καταγίζ(εται)*, Δ 11 *δέρμα καταιγίζε(ται)* meaning "is burned" (Sokolowski) or "is torn apart" (Hsch. *καταιγίσας* and *αἰγίζει*, *Suda* *αι* 44; G. Daux, *BCH* 87 [1963], 630)?

[30] See n. 24 above; A. Thomsen, "Der Trug des Prometheus," *ARW* 12 (1909), 460–90; J. Rudhardt, "Les mythes grecs relatifs à l'instauration du sacrifice," *MH* 27 (1970) 1–15. The basis of the criticism is the concept that *τὸ θύειν δωρεῖσθαί ἐστιν τοῖς θεοῖς* (Plat. *Euthyphr*. 14c). Accordingly, tables were set up for the gods (*τράπεζαι*); *σκέλος τô πράτο βοὸς παρθέντο τôι θιôι* *IG* IV 914 = *SIG*[3] 998 (Epidaurus, fifth century B.C.); cf. L. Ziehen, *RE* XVIII 615–16; S. Dow and D.H. Gill, "The Greek Cult Table," *AJA* 69 (1965), 103–114. Yet it is possible to slaughter a wild boar "for Zeus and Helios" and then throw the cadaver into the sea (*Il*. 19.197/268 and cf. 3.104/310; for tortuous hypotheses to save the "offering"-interpretation see Stengel [1910], 19–23). Likewise in the Latin *mactare*, "glorify," the god's glory and exaltation derive from the subjection of the *victima*.

[31] Esp. Yasna 32.8, 12, 14 (G. Widengren, *Iranische Geisteswelt* [1961], 155; H. Humbach, *Die Gathas des Zarathustra* [1959], I 97–99). It is unclear, however, to what extent blood-sacrifice was rejected on principle, since it continued in practice: see M. Boyce, *JRAS* (1966), 110; G. Widengren, *Die Religionen Irans* (1963), 66, 92, 109.

[32] Is. 1:11; cf. 66:3.

[33] The Pythagorean tradition is divided, with *ἐμψύχων ἀπέχεσθαι* against *δικαιότατον*

sacrifice—above all, Theophrastus, in his influential book *On Piety*. This book explained animal-sacrifice as having replaced cannibalism, which, in turn, had been forced on men because of difficult times.[34] After this, a theoretical defense of sacrificial custom was virtually hopeless.[35] Both Varro and Seneca were convinced that the gods do not demand blood-sacrifice.[36] Judaism in the Diaspora spread more easily because cult practices had become concentrated in one temple in Jerusalem, thus virtually making Judaism outside Jerusalem a religion without animal-sacrifice.[37] This also helped form Christian practice, which could thus take up the traditions of Greek philosophy. On the other hand, it gave the idea of sacrifice a central significance and raised it to a higher status than ever before.[38] The death of God's son is the one-time and perfect sacrifice, although it is still repeated in the celebration of the Lord's Supper, in breaking the bread and drinking the wine.

Folk custom, however, managed to defy even Christianization and was subdued only by modern technological civilization. The German expression *geschmückt wie ein Pfingstochse* ("decked out like an ox at Pentecost") preserves the memory of the ritual slaughter of an ox at the church festival (see n. 9 above). In Soviet Armenia the slaughter of a sheep in front of the church is still a feature of regular Sunday service. Isolated Greek communities in Cappadocia celebrated the ancient sacrificial ritual well into the twentieth century: opposite the conventional altar in the chapel of the saint would be a sacrificial altarstone, upon which incense was burned when candles were lit; during prayers, it would be decked with wreaths. The sacrificer would bring the animal—a goat or a sheep—into the chapel, leading it three

---

θύειν (Iambl. *V. Pyth.* 82). Cf. J. Haussleiter, *Der Vegetarismus in der Antike* (1935), 79–163; W. Burkert, *Lore and Science in Ancient Pythogoreanism* (1972), 180–83; Empedokles B 136–39.

[34] Porph. *Abst.* 2.27; J. Bernays, *Theophrastos' Schrift über Frömmigkeit* (1866), 86, 116; W. Pötscher, *Theophrastos Περὶ εὐσεβείας* (1964), 174–75.

[35] One way out was to posit inferior, more bloodthirsty demons: see Xenokrates fr. 23–25 Heinze.

[36] *Dii veri neque desiderant ea neque deposcunt* Varro in Arnob. 7.1; *deum . . . non immolationibus nec sanguine multo colendum* Sen. fr. 123 = Lact. *Div. inst.* 6.25.3. Cf. Demonax in Luk. *Dem.* 11; the Sibyl in Clem. *Pr.* 4.62; (Just.) *Coh. ad. Gr.* 16.

[37] With the exception of Passover celebrations; cf. J. Jeremias, *Die Passahfeier der Samaritaner* (1932); Th. H. Gaster, *Passover: Its History and Traditions* (1958).

[38] Τὸ πάσχα ἡμῶν ἐτύθη Χριστὸς I Cor. 5:7. For the rest, I refer the reader to H. D. Wendland and E. Kinder, *RGG*[3] IV 1647–56. The Christian Jews still made Paul partake in a sacrifice in Jerusalem (Num. 6:13–21) and finance it; cf. Acts 21:23–26. On the other hand, "Petrus" (Clem. *Hom.* 2.44.2) declares that the sacrificial laws of the OT are forgeries.

times around the sacrificial stone while children threw grass and flowers onto it. As the priest stood at the altar, the keeper of the animal would make a sign of the cross with his knife three times and then slaughter the animal while praying. The blood was supposed to sprinkle the stone. After this, outside the chapel, the animal would be carved up and the feast prepared. The priest, like his ancient counterpart, received the animal's thigh and skin, as well as its head and feet.[39] Christianity is here no more than a transparent cover for the ancient form that underlies it: that is to say, for the sacred act of blood-sacrifice.

Animal-sacrifice was an all-pervasive reality in the ancient world. The Greeks[40] did not perceive much difference between the substance of their own customs and those of the Egyptians and Phoenicians, Babylonians and Persians, Etruscans and Romans, though ritual details varied greatly among the Greeks themselves.[41] One peculiarity of Greek sacrifice presents a problem for the modern historian: the combination of a fire-altar and a blood-rite, of burning and eating, corre-

[39]Megas (1956) 15, and cf. 17, 84, 87, 224. (The name of the sacrifice, *γουρπάνι*, comes from Islam: Arabic *qurbān*). For animal sacrifice to "Zeus" in Albania see Cook III (1940) 1168–71. See now G. N. Aikaterinides, Νεοελληνικὲς *αἱματηρὲς θυσίες* (Athens, 1979).

[40]Theophrastus (Porph. *Abst.* 2 and cf. n. 34 above), in his study of the development of sacrifice, found it natural to include Egyptians, Syrians, Carthaginians, Etruscans, Thracians, and Scythians. The tradition that the Cyprians invented sacrifice (Tatian. 1, pp. 1, 6 Schwartz) goes back to Asklepiades of Cyprus, *FGrHist* 752 F 1 = Neanthes, *FGrHist* 84 F 32 = Porph. *Abst.* 4.15.

[41]The antithesis between Olympian and Chthonic cult is often regarded as fundamental (Rohde [1898] 148–52; Harrison [1922] 1–31; less schematically, Meuli [1946] 188–211, and cf. Nilsson [1955] 132–33). The antithesis between heavenly gods and gods of the underworld is frequently attested starting with Aeschylus (*Hik.* 24, 154, *Ag.* 89); a familiar distinction is that between *ἐναγίζειν*, "to make tabu," or *ἐντέμνειν*, "to slaughter into the sacrificial pit" for heroes and the dead, and *θύειν* (F. Pfister, *Der Reliquienkult im Altertum* II [1912], 466–80; Casabona [1966] 204–208, 225–29). On the different ways of slaughtering see Schol. Apoll. Rhod. 1.587, *Et. Gen.* p. 115 M = *Et. M.* 345.24–26; H. v. Fritze, *JdI* 18 (1903), 58–67. Yet besides the sacrificial pits (*βόθροι*) there are different kinds of altars (*βωμοί, ἐσχάραι*, Porph. *Antr.* 6; Schol. Eur. *Phoen.* 274; Serv. *Buc.* 5.66; Yavis [1949] 91–95), and the complex of *θυσίαι ἄγευστοι* (Stengel [1910] 105) does not correspond to the realm of the chthonic: sacrificial meals are familiar to us from the cult of the *θεοὶ χθόνιοι* (Stengel [1910] 131–133), especially *δεῖπνα* from hero-cults (A. D. Nock, *HThR* 37 [1944], 141–66). Likewise, *σφάγιον* and *θοίναμα* do not mutually exclude each other: see Eur. *Or.* 815. In the cult of the dead, the meal during which the dead man is offered blood (*Il.*23.29–34; *αἱμακουρία*, cf. I. 6 below) is juxtaposed to a rite of burning (*Il.* 23.166–76). Burnt offerings alone are rare: they often function as a preliminary, e.g., *LS* 151 A 29–36 (cf. burnt-offering/thank-offering in I Sam. 10:8, 13:9), just as a single sanctuary will often have both the grave of a hero and the altar of the god: i.e., we are dealing with an antithesis within the ritual, not with two fundamentally different and separate things. Cf. Burkert (1966) 103 n. 36.

sponds directly only with the burnt offerings (*zebah, šelamim*) of the Old Testament[42]—although the details of Ugaritic and Phoenician sacrificial cults are uncertain—and these differ markedly from Egyptian and Mesopotamian, as well as Minoan-Mycenaean, rites, all of which have no altars for burning whole animals or bones.[43] And yet, whatever complexities, layers, and changes in cultural tradition underlie the individual peculiarities, it is astounding, details aside, to observe the similarity of action and experience from Athens to Jerusalem and on to Babylon. A detailed Babylonian text of which several copies were made describes the sacrifice of a bull whose skin was used as the membrane of a tympanon in the temple:[44] an untouched black bull would be chosen for the secret ceremony, which took place in a room enclosed on all sides by curtains. The complicated preparations included scattering grain, offering breads and libations, and sac-

---

Likewise, in the Egyptian realm, sacrifice for the dead and that for the gods have common roots: see W. Barta, *Die altägyptischen Opferlisten von der Frühzeit bis zur griech.-röm. Epoche* (1963), 153. On roasting/boiling see II.1.n.29.

[42]R. K. Yerkes, *Sacrifice in Greek and Roman Religions and Early Judaism* (1952); R. Schmid, *Das Bundesopfer in Israel* (1964), therefore assumed that Israeli burnt offering was a Mycenaean import via Ugarit (92), but cf. D. Gill, *Biblica* 47 (1966), 255–62: Homer's familiar *μηρία καίειν* is absent from Mycenaean.

[43]Demostrated by Yavis (1949); cf. K. Galling, *Der Altar in den Kulturen des Alten Orients* (1925). On Mesopotamia see G. Furlani, "Il sacrificio nella religione dei Semiti di Babilonia e Assiria," *Mem. Linc. VI* 4 (1932), 103–370; F. Blome, Die *Opfermaterie in Babylon und Israel* (1934); Y. Rosengarten, *Le régime des offrandes dans la société sumérienne d'après les textes présargoniques de Lagas* (1960). On Egypt see H. Kees, "Bemerkungen zum Tieropfer der Ägypter und seiner Symbolik," *NGG* (1942), 71–88; Ph. Derchain, *Rites égyptiens I: Le sacrifice de l'oryx* (1962), concerning which cf. J. Zandee, *Bibl. Or.* 20 (1963), 251–53; W. Barta, *Die altägyptischen Opferlisten* (n.41 above). On Ugarit see B. Janowski, *Ugarit-Forschungen* 12 (1980), 231–59.

For a sacrificial list from Alalakh see D. J. Wiseman, *The Alalakh Tablets* (1953), 126. For a monumental altar for bull-sacrifice at Myrtou Pygades on Cyprus, including horn-symbols, a watering place for cattle, and bull statuettes (ca. 1700/1200 B.C.) see *AA* (1962) 338–39, fig. 84. For a depiction of bull-sacrifice at Pylos see *The Palace of Nestor II* (1969) pl. 119.

The "hearth-house," out of which the Greek temple developed, is a type known already in Helladic times: see H. Drerup, *Archaeologia Homerica* O (1969), 123–28. M. H. Jameson, *AJA* 62 (1958), 223, refers to sacrifice at the hearth in Mycenaean times. Open-air sites for burnt offering—ash-altars consisting of piles of ashes and bones—are abundantly attested both for Greece (Nilsson [1955], 86–88; cf. II.1 below on Lykaion, II.2 on Olympia) and for bronze-age Europe (W. Krämer, "Prähistorische Brandopferplätze," in *Helvetia antiqua, Festschr. E. Vogt* [1966], 111–22). It does not seem possible at this time to organize the various forms of sacrifice at the "hearth-house," the stone altar, and the ash-altar into an historical system.

[44]*ANET* 334–38. The main text is Seleucid; others were copied in the seventh century B.C. from older Babylonian models. They thereby attest to the survival of the ritual over the centuries. On the tympanon and the Kalu-priest (= Sum. *galu*), who "laments" "in

rificing a sheep. The bull stood chained on a rush mat until it was time for its mouth to be washed. After this, incantations would be whispered into both its ears, after which it was sprinkled with water, purified with a torch, and surrounded by a circle of grain. Following prayer and song, the bull was killed, the heart burned at once, and the skin and left shoulder sinew removed to string the tympanon. After further libations and offerings, the priest would bend down to the severed head and say, "This deed was done by all the gods; I did not do it." One version of the text says that the cadaver would be buried; an older one forbids at least the head priest from eating the meat. Fifteen days later, in a largely parallel ceremony, with preparatory and closing rites, the newly covered tympanon was brought into the center in place of the bull, thus inaugurating it into its function.

Not even the religious revolution in the Near East, i.e., the emergence of Islam, could eliminate animal-sacrifice. The high point in the life of a Moslem is the pilgrimage to Mecca[45] which still today draws hundreds of thousands of worshippers annually. The central point occurs on the ninth day of the holy month, in the journey from Mecca to Mount Arafat, where the pilgrims stay from noon till sundown praying "before God." This is followed by the Day of Sacrifice. On the tenth day, in Mina, the pilgrim must throw seven pebbles at an old stone monument and then slaughter—usually with his own hands—a sacrificial animal—a sheep, a goat, or even a camel—which is driven up and sold to him by Bedouins. He eats some of the animal, though usually giving most of it away or simply leaving it. Saudi Arabia has resorted to bulldozers to remove the carcasses. After this, the pilgrim is allowed to cut his hair again and remove his pilgrim's robes. Likewise, sexual abstinence ends after his return to Mecca. It is the consecrated man who kills and the act of killing is made sacred. "In the name of Allah" and "Allah is merciful" are the Moslem formulas that accompany even profane slaughter.

Daily routine inevitably made the sacrificial ritual an empty formality.[46] Therefore, in order to stress its importance, especially in the ancient Near East, ordinances were created stipulating countless observances. The Greeks seem to have given most care to the "begin-

---

the language of the female," see E. Dhorme, *Les religions de Babylonie et d'Assyrie* (1949²), 207–209, 217.

[45] *Enzyklopädie des Islam II* (1927), 208–213; *Encyclopédie de l'Islam* III (1965), 33–40 *s.v.* *HADJDJ*; ibid. for the proof that the basic elements of the pilgrimage are pre-Islamic.

[46] A sacrificial list from Uruk notes 50 rams, 2 bulls, 1 ox, and 8 lambs, among many others, as the daily sacrifice: *ANET* 344. Croesus had 3,000 animals sacrificed at Delphi: Hdt. 1, 50; 154 cows were bought for a festival on Delos: *IG* II/III² 1635, 35. King Seleukos gave 1,000 ἱερεῖα (sheep) and 12 cows for a sacrifice at Didyma: *OGI* 214, 63.

ning" stages (ἄρχεσθαι), as if trying to distract attention from the central point, which nonetheless remained permanently fixed. Hubert and Mauss[47] aptly characterized the structure of sacrificial ritual with the concepts of "sacralization" and "desacralization"; that is to say, preliminary rites, on the one hand, and closing rites, on the other, framing a central action clearly marked as the emotional climax by a piercing scream, the "Ololygé." This act, however, is the act of killing, the experience of death. Thus, a threefold rhythm becomes evident in the course of the sacrifice,[48] moving from an inhibited, labyrinthine beginning, through a terrifying midpoint, to a scrupulously tidy conclusion. Vegetable offerings frequently come at the beginning and again at the end of the ceremony, when libations are also especially characteristic. But the offerings can overlap and multiply, enlarging the pattern until a triad of sacrificial festivals emerges which yet adheres to the same unchangeable rhythm: the preliminary sacrifice, the terrifying sacrifice, and the victorious, affirming sacrifice. The core is always the experience of death brought about by human violence, which, in turn, is here subject to predetermined laws. And this is nearly always connected with another human—all too human—action, namely, eating: the festive meal of those who share in the sacred.

2. *The Evolutionary Explanation: Primitive Man as Hunter*

Karl Meuli's great essay on "Griechische Opferbräuche" (1946)[1] added a new dimension to our understanding of sacrifice. He noted striking similarities in the details of Greek sacrifice and the customs of

[47] See n. 2.

[48] Corresponding to the special case of the initiation rite, as established by Harrison (1927) 15: *παιδοτροφία–σπαραγμός–ἀναβίωσις*.

[1] Nilsson's "durchschlagender Einwand" (1955), 145 n. 2, "dass nur gezähmte Tiere, fast nie wilde geopfert werden," applies only to a problem of historical change (cf. I.5

hunting and herding societies, mostly in Siberia. Moreover, he pointed out prehistoric discoveries that seemed to attest to similar customs by Middle Palaeolithic times. This powerful step backward about 50,000 years in time admittedly seems to explain *obscurum per obscurius*. Whether the prehistoric evidence may be taken to indicate belief in a supreme being—a kind of primordial monotheism—is a moot question. It seemed less risky to state: "Sacrifice is the oldest form of religious action."[2] But much of the oldest evidence remains controversial.

Meuli relied on the "burial of bears" of Neanderthal times, as described by Bächler and others:[3] they claimed that they had found bears' skulls and bones, especially thigh-bones, carefully set up in caves, and that these corresponded to the "skull- and long bone sacrifice" observed among Siberian hunters, who used to deposit the bones and skulls of their quarry in sacred places.[4] In Greek ritual, too, it is the bones, especially the thigh-bones, that belong to the gods. The bear's special role further appears in the "bear festivals" of northern Eurasian tribes, from the Finns to the Ainus and on to America.[5] Yet the findings of Bächler have come under serious attack: chance

---

below) and not to Meuli's basic argument. To be sure, the latter completely overlooked the Neolithic Near Eastern component by making an all-too-direct connection between the Indo-Germanic Greeks and the Eurasian hunters and herders. Against Meuli's allegedly magical interpretation, Müller-Karpe (1966) 227–28 proposes a religious one that proceeds from the experience of a "transcendental power"; but this is precisely what the ritual communicates, and any interpretation of it—even self-interpretation—is secondary (cf. I.3 below).

[2]H. Kühn, "Das Problem des Urmonotheismus," *Abh. Mainz* (1950), 22, 17, whose interpretation follows P. W. Schmidt, *Der Ursprung der Gottesidee VI* (1935), 444–54, as well as A. Vorbichler, *Das Opfer auf den heute noch erreichbaren ältesten Stufen der Menschheitsgeschichte* (1956), and Müller-Karpe (1966) 228.

[3]E. Bächler, *Das alpine Paläolithikum der Schweiz* (1940); Meuli (1946) 237–39. For additional finds in Central Franken, Silesia, and Siberia, see Müller-Karpe (1966) 226; in Hungary, see I. Trencsényi-Waldapfel, *Untersuchungen zur Religionsgeschichte* (1966) 19 n.17.

[4]U. Holmberg, "Uber die Jagdriten der nördlichen Völker Asiens und Europas," *J. Société Finno-Ougrienne* 41 (1925). A. Gahs, "Kopf-, Schädel- und Langknochenopfer bei Rentiervölkern," *Festschr. P. W. Schmidt* (1928), 231–68; I. Paulson, "Die Tierknochen im Jagdritual der nordeurasischen Völker," *Zeitschr. f. Ethnologie* 84 (1959), 270–93; I. Paulson, Å. Hultkrantz, and K. Jettmar, *Die Religionen Nordeurasiens und der amerikanischen Arktis* (1962).

[5]A. I. Hallowell, "Bear Ceremonialism in the Northern Hemisphere," *American Anthropologist* 28 (1926), 1–175; J. M. Kitagawa, "Ainu Bear Festival," *History of Religions* 1 (1961), 95–151; I. Paulson, "Die rituelle Erhebung des Bärenschädels bei arktischen und subarktischen Völkern," *Temenos* 1 (1965), 150–73.

assemblage of bones cannot be excluded as an explanation of the alleged bear-burials.[6] It is safer to rely on the evidence of the Upper Palaeolithic, the epoch of homo sapiens. At this period, hunters' customs, including the manipulation of animals' bones and skulls, are clearly attested; Meuli's insight about the antiquity of Siberian hunting ritual is basically confirmed, even if still more ancient layers remain in the dark. There are places where stag skulls and deer skeletons were gathered, as well as the bones of bison and mammoths.[7] At a site in Siberia, twenty-seven mammoth skulls were found set up in a circle around a central point where a female statuette lay buried beneath a pile of bones and partially worked tusks.[8] This recalls a frequently reproduced gold ring from Mycenae, on which a row of animal skulls borders the procession to the seated goddess.[9] A stylized pair of horns is the common and omnipresent religious symbol of Minoan-Mycenaean culture. Much earlier, in the household shrines of Çatal Hüyük, there are genuine cow-horns set up in rows or inserted in plaster heads.[10] Upper Palaeolithic deer hunters had attached a reindeer skull to a pole near a place where they used to throw young roes into the water, weighted down with stones—a "sacrifice of immersion."[11] There is a life-size clay statue of a bear in the cave of Montespan, which had been covered with a genuine bearskin, including the skull.[12] Similarly, hunters in the Sudan covered a clay figure with the skins of slaughtered lions or leopards, just as farmers in southern Abyssinia did with the skin of a young sacrificial bull. Hermes the cattle-thief and cattle-killer stretched out on a rock

---

[6] Against Bächler's theory, see F. E. Koby, *L'Anthropologie* 55 (1951), 304–308; H. G. Bandi in *Helvetia antiqua* (1966), 1–8; cf. the discussion in J. Maringer, "Die Opfer der paläolithischen Menschen," in *Anthropica* (1968), 249–71; M. Eliade, *Histoire des croyances et des idées religieuses* I (1976), 23–27, 393f.

[7] Müller-Karpe (1966) 225–26.

[8] Jelisejevici: see Müller-Karpe (1966) 225.

[9] *Corpus der minoischen und mykenischen Siegel*, ed. F. Matz and H. Biesantz, I (1964) #17; Nilsson (1955) pl. 17.1; Simon (1969) 181–83. Even if these were meant to represent animal-headed vessels (Simon), they are a further, symbolizing development of the ancient sacrificial structure (see IV.2.n.39).

[10] Mellaart (1967) 140–41, 144–55, 181.

[11] Müller-Karpe (1966) 224–25, pl. 199.45.

[12] Müller-Karpe (1966) 205 pl. 107.1; A. Leroi-Gourhan, *Préhistoire de l'art occidentale* (1965), 313, figs. 646–47. For parallels from the Sudan see L. Frobenius, *Kulturgeschichte Afrikas* (1933), 83; from Abyssinia see A. Friedrich, *Paideuma* 2 (1941), 23–24; Meuli (1946) 241; cf. I. Paulson, *Temenos* 1 (1965), 160–61, on statues of bears as substitutes for actual dead ones, "the soul's residence."

the skins of the cows he had slaughtered. This, too, is "one of the many sagas about the origin of sacrifice."[13]

One could, of course, try to cut through these correspondences with conceptual distinctions, and separate hunting and sacrifice on principle.[14] In the hunt, one might argue, killing is not ceremonial but practical and subject to chance; its meaning and goal, both quite profane, lie in obtaining meat for food; a wild beast must be seen in opposition to a tame domestic animal. And yet the very similarity of hunting and sacrificial customs belies such a distinction. Killing can become ceremonial even among hunters. A tame bear, for instance, would have to perform at the bear festival. We also hear of a complete mammoth skeleton found on a high crag, a place to which it could only have been driven by men.[15] On the other hand, the hunting situation is often evoked and acted out in later civilizations, as if one had to catch a wild beast so as to sacrifice it at a predetermined place. Thus, Plato combines the hunt and sacrifice in a semi-barbarous context, his fictitious Atlantis,[16] and in fact bull-hunts are attested in the marginal areas of Greek culture.[17] An Attic myth tells how Theseus subdued the wild bull of Marathon so that it let itself be led to the sacrifice—and this is said to be the legendary origin of the local festival in Marathon, the Hekaleia.[18] Among the Sumerians, a "wild bull" was considered the most eminent sacrificial animal, even though it had long been extinct in Mesopotamia. The consecrated horns in the sanctuaries of Çatal Hüyük were, however, still obtained from genuine wild bulls; bull- and stag-hunting appear on the very impressive wall-paintings there (see Figure 3).[19] The way in which the leop-

---

[13] W. R. Smith (1894) 306.2; πέτρῃ ἐπ' ἠλιβάτῳ *Hy. Merc.* 404, hence probably to be read 124 ἐπὶ (Cdd. ἐνὶ) πέτρῃ. In the myth, the skins apparently turned to stone, like the skin of Marsyas at Kelainai (Hdt. 7.26; Xen. *Anab.* 1.2.8). The rite was no longer practiced; cf. I.1.n.29 above.

[14] See Nilsson's objection, n. 1 above. On the interrelation of hunt and slaughter in Africa see Straube (1955) 199–204.

[15] Müller-Karpe (1966) 225 (Gravettien).

[16] Plat. *Critias* 119d–e; H. Herter, *RhM* 109 (1966), 140–42.

[17] For *ταυροθηρία* in Thessaly see *IG* IX 2528, 531–37; *Arch. Deltion* 16 (1960), 185, *REG* 77 (1964), 176; *AP* 9.543; on this and on the *ταυροκαθάψια* in Asia Minor see L. Robert, *Les gladiateurs dans l'Orient grec* (1940), 318–19, who also treats the remaining *κυνηγέσια* and *θηρομαχίαι* (309–331). For a *ἱερὸν κυνηγέσιον* in Athens see *Hypoth. Dem.* 25.

[18] Soph. fr. 25 P.; Callim. fr. 259–60; 264; Plut. *Thes.* 14 following Philochoros, *FGrHist* 328 F 109; Paus. 1.27,10. For vase-paintings see Brommer (1960) 192–96.

[19] On Sumerian wild bulls see Müller-Karpe (1968) II 338; on Çatal Hüyük see Mellaart (1967) 200–208, pl. 54–57, 61–64; cf. n. 9 above.

ard men swarm around the bull and the stag in these paintings is perhaps almost more suggestive of a dance than of hunting. In Egypt, the sacrifice of bulls and hippopotami, performed by the pharaoh, was entirely stylized as a hunt.[20] In many parts of Greece, the animals chosen for sacrifice were "set free for the god," almost as if they were wild beasts on sacred land until the time appointed for the bloody "act."[21]

The continuity between the hunt and sacrificial ritual appears most forcibly in the ritual details that leave no tangible archaeological trace; these have been set out in detail by Meuli. The correspondences extend from the preparations, with their purifications and abstinences, to the closing rites, involving bones, skulls, and skins. In hunting societies accessible to ethnological study, hunters are said to have expressed clear feelings of guilt with regard to the slaughtered animal. The ritual provides forgiveness and reparation, though frequently taking on a scurrilous character which prompted Meuli to coin the phrase "the comedy of innocence." The ritual betrays an underlying anxiety about the continuation of life in the face of death.[22] The bloody "act" was necessary for the continuance of life, but it is just as necessary for new life to be able to start again. Thus, the gathering of bones, the raising of a skull or stretching of a skin is to be understood as an attempt at restoration, a resurrection in the most concrete sense. The hope that the sources of nourishment will continue to exist, and the fear that they will not, determine the action of the hunter, killing to live.

---

[20] H. Kees, "Bemerkungen zum Tieropfer der Ägypter und seiner Symbolik," *NGG* (1942), 71–88.

[21] Babrius 37 (*μόσχος ἄφετος* in antithesis to the plow-ox). For herds of Hera in Croton see Livy 24.3.2, and cf. Nikomachos in Porph. *V. Pyth.* 24, Iambl. *V. Pyth.* 61. For the cattle of Argive Hera see III.2.n. 25 below; for Διὸς *βοῦς* at Miletus see Hsch. *s.v.*; for a donkey sacrificed to the winds at Tarentum see Hsch. *ἀνεμώτας*; for the sheep of Helios at Apollonia/Epirus see Hdt. 9.93; for bulls of Dionysus at Kynaithos see Paus. 8.19.2; for sacred sheep, goats, cattle, and horses at Delphi see *OGI* 345, 15–19; for sacred sheep at Delos see *IG* II/III^2 1639, 15; for cattle of "Herakles" in Spain see Diod. 4.18.3; for cattle of the "Meteres" in Sicily see Diod. 4.80.6; for "Persian Artemis'" (Anahita) herds on the Euphrates see Plut. *Luc.* 24; for *τὰ θρέμματα τῆς θεοῦ* at Kleitor see Polyb. 4.19.4; Scillus, Xen. *Anab.* 5.3.9; for the herds of Persephone of Kyzikos see Plut. *Luc.* 10. Cf. further, in myth, Apollo's cattle in Thessaly, *Hy. Merc.* 70–72; and Helios' cattle, *Od.* 12. For Atlantis see Plat. *Critias.* 119d, and cf. *Prot.* 320a, Aesch. *Prom.* 666. Similarly, for the Indian Aśvamedha a horse is "set free": see W. Koppers, *Wiener Beitr. z. Kulturgeschichte* 4 (1936), 306.

[22] Meuli (1946) 224–52; H. Baumann, "Nyama, die Rachemacht," *Paideuma* 4 (1950), 191–230. For a psychiatric perspective see R. Bilz, "Tiertöter-Skrupulantismus," *Jahrbuch f. Psychologie und Psychotherapie* 3 (1955), 226–44.

These customs are more than mere curiosities, for the hunt of the Palaeolithic hunter is not just one activity among many. The transition to the hunt is, rather, one of the most decisive ecological changes between man and the other primates. Man can virtually be defined as "the hunting ape" (even if "the naked ape" makes a more appealing title).[23] This statement leads to a second indisputable fact, namely, that the age of the hunter, the Palaeolithic, comprises by far the largest part of human history. No matter that estimates range between 95 and 99 percent: it is clear that man's biological evolution was accomplished during this time. By comparison, the period since the invention of agriculture—10,000 years, at most—is a drop in the bucket. From this perspective, then, we can understand man's terrifying violence as deriving from the behavior of the predatory animal, whose characteristics he came to acquire in the course of becoming man.

Our conception of primitive man and his society will always be a tentative construct; still, there are some social and psychological preconditions that cannot have been absent from the situation of the early hunters. The primate's biological makeup was not fit for this new way of life. Man had to compensate for this deficiency by a tour de force of ingenious technology and institutions, that is to say, by his culture, although that culture itself quickly became a means of selection. Of primary importance was the use of weapons, without which man poses virtually no threat to beasts. The earliest weapon that was effective at a distance was the wooden spear hardened by fire.[24] This presupposes the use of fire; earlier, bones had served as clubs.[25] Man's upright posture facilitated the use of weapons. But perhaps more important than all this was the development of a social order leading to sharp sexual differentiation, which has even become a part of our inherited biological constitution. Among human beings, hunting is

---

[23]Morris (1967) 19–49, and cf. C. F. Hocket and R. Ascher, "The Human Revolution," *Current Anthropology* 5 (1964), 135–47, with discussion 148–68; A. Kortlandt, *Current Anthropology* 6 (1965), 320; La Barre (1970) 69–92; R. Ardrey, *The Hunting Hypothesis* (1976). Important points were anticipated by R. Eisler, *Man into Wolf* (1951). In the meantime, organized hunting, with sharing of meat, has been observed in chimpanzees: G. Teleki, *Scientific American* 228/1 (1973), 32–42, and cf. P. J. Wilson, *Man* n.s. 10 (1975), 5–20. Chimpanzees are more human than expected—cf. also A. Kortlandt and M. Kooij, *Symp. Zool. Soc. London* 10 (1963), 61–88—yet they do not use weapons and cannot attack big game.

[24]Müller-Karpe (1966) 148; Burkert (1967) 283–87. See generally K. Lindner, *La chasse préhistorique* (1950).

[25]R. A. Dart, *Adventures with the Missing Link* (1950), 191–204; cf. 109–19, "The Antiquity of Murder."

man's work—in contrast to all animal predators—requiring both speed and strength; hence the male's long, slender thigh. By contrast, since women must bear children with ever larger skulls, they develop round, soft forms. Man's extraordinarily protracted youth, his *neoteny*, which permits the development of the mind through learning and the transmission of a complicated culture, requires long years of security. This is basically provided by the mother at home. The man assumes the role of the family breadwinner—an institution universal to human civilizations but contrary to the behavior of all other mammals.[26]

The success of the "hunting ape" was due to his ability to work cooperatively, to unite with other men in a communal hunt. Thus, man ever since the development of hunting has belonged to two overlapping social structures, the family and the *Männerbund*; his world falls into pairs of categories: indoors and out, security and adventure, women's work and men's work, love and death. At the core of this new type of male community, which is biologically analogous to a pack of wolves, are the acts of killing and eating. The men must constantly move between the two realms, and their male children must one day take the difficult step from the women's world to the world of men. Fathers must accept their sons, educating them and looking after them—this, too, has no parallel among mammals. When a boy finally enters the world of men, he does so by confronting death.

What an experience it must have been when man, the relative of the chimpanzee, succeeded in seizing the power of his deadly enemy, the leopard, in assuming the traits of the wolf, forsaking the role of the hunted for that of the hunter! But success brought its own dangers. The earliest technology created the tools for killing. Even the wooden spear and wedge provided man with weapons more dangerous than his instincts could cope with. His rudimentary killing inhibitions were insufficient as soon as he could kill at a distance; and males were even educated to suppress these inhibitions for the sake of the hunt. Moreover, it is as easy, or even easier, to kill a man as it is to kill a fleeing beast, so from earliest times men slipped repeatedly into cannibalism.[27] Thus, from the very start, self-destruction was a threat to the human race.

If man nonetheless survived and with unprecedented success

---

[26] Morris (1967) 37–39; La Barre (1970) 79–83. On the role of man as breadwinner see M. Mead, *Male and Female* (1949), 188–94.

[27] On the "gesicherten Tatsache von Ritualtötungen" in Palaeolithic times see Müller-Karpe (1966) 240 (Ofnet cave), 232–33 (Monte Circeo), 230 (Peking Man). Cannibalism is probable: see La Barre (1970) 404–406, 134 n.30; M. K. Roper, "A Survey of Evidence for Intrahuman Killing in the Pleistocene," *Current Anthropology* 10 (1969), 427–59.

even enlarged his sphere of influence, it was because in place of his natural instincts he developed the rules of cultural tradition, thus artificially forming and differentiating his basic inborn behavior. Biological selection rather than conscious planning determined the educational processes that helped form man, so that he could best adapt himself to his role. A man had to be courageous to take part in the hunt; therefore, courage is always included in the conception of an ideal man. A man had to be reliable, able to wait, to resist a momentary impulse for the sake of a long-range goal. He had to have endurance and keep to his word. In these matters men developed behavior patterns that were lacking in anthropoid apes and were more closely analogous to the behavior of beasts of prey.[28] Above all, the use of weapons was controlled by the strictest—if also artificial—rules: what was allowed and necessary in one realm was absolutely forbidden in the other. A brilliant accomplishment in one was murder in the other. The decisive point is the very possibility that man may submit to laws curbing his individual intelligence and adaptability for the sake of societal predictability. The educative power of tradition attempts to bind him in an irreversible process analogous to biological "imprinting."[29]

On a psychological level, hunting behavior was mainly determined by the peculiar interplay of the aggressive and sexual complexes, which thus gave form to some of the foundations of human society. Whereas research on biological behavior, at least in predatory animals, carefully distinguishes intraspecific aggression from the behavior of hunting and eating,[30] this distinction obviously does not hold for man. Rather, these two became superimposed at the time when man unexpectedly assumed the behavior of predatory animals. Man had to outdo himself in his transition to the hunt, a transition

---

[28] A. Kortlandt, *Current Anthropology* 6 (1965), 323: "The evolution of the specifically human type of culture required the combination of the manual dexterity of an arboreal fruit eater with the long-term foresight and perseverance of a highly specialized carnivore." On the human tendency to submit to authority see Eibl-Eibesfeldt (1970) 120–23.

[29] On the biological fact of imprinting see K. Lorenz, "Über tierisches und menschliches Verhalten," *Ges. Abh.* I (1965), 139–48, 270–71 (orig. 1935); E. H. Hess, *Science* 130 (1959), 133–41, who makes the remarkable finding that "the administration of punishment or painful stimulation increases the effectiveness of the imprinting experience" (141) in contrast to the learning process. For the problem of applicability to man see H. Thomae, "Entwicklung und Prägung," *Hdb. d. Psychologie* III (1959), 240–311 (which, as it deals with secular man, ignores religious ritual).

[30] Lorenz (1963) 40; Eibl-Eibesfeldt (1970) 7–8, with a polemic against R. A. Dart (n. 25 above). On the other hand, La Barre (1970) 130, for instance, speaks of the obviously "necessary aggression of hunting."

requiring implementation of all his spiritual reserves. And because this sort of behavior became specific to the male sex, that is to say, "men's work," males could more easily adapt themselves to the intraspecific aggression programmed for courtship fights and the impulses of sexual frustration (see I.7).

It is not easy for adult males to cooperate, and especially the "naked ape," whose sexuality clearly grew out of proportion in order to bind men to women and thus insure that the family would be supported.[31] The heightened aggressiveness thus aroused could be turned to the service of the community by means of redirection, as has been described by Konrad Lorenz;[32] for it is precisely group demonstration of aggression toward outsiders that creates a sense of close personal community. The *Männerbund* becomes a closed, conspiratorial group through the explosive potential of aggression stored internally. This aggression was released in the dangerous and bloody hunt. The internal and external effects of aggression mutually enhanced the chances of success. Community is defined by participation in the bloody work of men. The early hunter soon subdued the world.

Because the hunter's activity was reinforced by behavior aimed originally at a human partner—that is, through intraspecific aggression—in place of a biologically fixed relationship of beast and quarry, something curious occurred: the quarry became a quasi-human adversary, experienced as human and treated accordingly. Hunting concentrated on the great mammals, which conspicuously resembled men in their body structure and movements, their eyes and their "faces," their breath and voices, in fleeing and in fear, in attacking and in rage. Most of all, this similarity with man was to be recognized in killing and slaughtering: the flesh was like flesh, bones like bones, phallus like phallus, and heart like heart,[33] and, most important of all, the warm running blood was the same. One could, perhaps, most clearly grasp the animal's resemblance to man when it died. Thus, the quarry turned into a sacrificial victim. Many observers have told of

---

[31] Morris (1967) 50–102; putting some limitations on his theses, cf. Eibl-Eibesfeldt (1970) 149–87, esp. 170–72.

[32] Lorenz (1963) 251–318; Eibl-Eibesfeldt (1970) 187–90.

[33] Human and animal σπλάγχνα bore the same names from the earliest times, but whereas the animal's were well known from slaughter, human entrails became visible only in those wounded in war or during human sacrifice. Their visible presence was basic for the consciousness of one's own "subjectivity"—heart, diaphragm, and gall in Greek; liver and kidneys as well in other languages (cf. R. B. Onians, *Origins of European Thought* [1951], esp. 21–43 and 84–89).

the almost brotherly bond that hunters felt for their game,[34] and the exchangeability of man and animal in sacrifice recurs as a mythological theme in many cultures besides the Greek.[35]

In the shock caused by the sight of flowing blood[36] we clearly experience the remnant of a biological, life-preserving inhibition. But that is precisely what must be overcome, for men, at least, could not afford "to see no blood," and they were educated accordingly. Feelings of fear and guilt are the necessary consequences of overstepping one's inhibitions; yet human tradition, in the form of religion, clearly does not aim at removing or settling these tensions. On the contrary, they are purposefully heightened. Peace must reign within the group, for what is called for outside, offends within. Order has to be observed inside, the extraordinary finds release without. Outside, something utterly different, beyond the norm, frightening but fascinating, confronts the ordinary citizen living within the limits of the everyday world. It is surrounded by barriers to be broken down in a complicated, set way, corresponding to the ambivalence of the event: sacralization and desacralization around a central point where weapons, blood, and death establish a sense of human community. The irreversible event becomes a formative experience for all participants, provoking feelings of fear and guilt and increasing desire to make reparation, the groping attempt at restoration. For the barriers that had been broken before are now all the more willingly recognized. The rules are confirmed precisely in their antithetical tension. As an order embracing its opposite, always endangered yet capable of adaptation and development, this fluctuating balance entered the tradition of human culture. The power to kill and respect for life illuminate each other.

With remarkable consistency, myths tell of the origins of man in a

---

[34] Meuli (1946) 248–52, and cf. H. Baumann, *Paideuma* 4 (1950), 198, 200; Meuli (1967) 160.

[35] For an animal substituted for a man see the story of Abraham and Isaac in Gen. 22:13; Iphigenia in Aulis, Apollod. *Epit.* 3.22; virgin and goat at Munichia, Zen. Athous 1.8 p. 350 Miller; Paus. Att. ε 35 Erbse; for Veiovis *immolatur ritu humano capra* Gell. 5.12.11. The reverse situation, that a man dies instead of a sacrificial animal, is a beloved motif in tragedy: see Burkert (1966) 116. Substitution, however, also occurs in ritual: see the *βουθυσία* instead of human sacrifice at Salamis/Cyprus, Porph. *Abst.* 2.54; for the frequent substitution of child- and animal-sacrifice at Carthage see G. Charles-Picard, *Les religions de l'Afrique antique* (1954), 491; for children designated as calves and sacrificed see Luk. *Syr. D.* 58; for a calf treated as a child and sacrificed see Ael. *Nat. an.* 12.34 (Tenedos).

[36] For folkloristic material see H. L. Strack, *Das Blut im Glauben und Aberglauben der Menschheit* (1900[7]); F. Rüsche, *Blut, Leben und Seele* (1930); J. H. Waszink, *RAC* II (1954),

fall, a crime that is often a bloody act of violence.[37] The Greeks speculated that this was preceded by a golden age of modest vegetarianism, ending in the "murder" of the plow-ox. Accordingly, anthropologists once saw the peaceful gatherers, or even the planters, as the original form of human civilization. The study of prehistory has changed this picture: man became man through the hunt, through the act of killing. "The greatest danger to life is the fact that man's food consists entirely of souls," said an Eskimo shaman,[38] just as Porphyrios characterized the state of mankind, divorced from the gods and dependent on food, by quoting Empedokles: "Such are the conflicts and groanings from which you have been born." As one of the Old Testament myths seems to tell us, men are the children of Cain. Yet killing, if it was a crime, was salvation at the same time. "You saved us by shedding blood," the Mithraists address their savior-god, Mithras the bull-slayer.[39] What has become a mystic paradox had been just fact in the beginning.

3. *Ritualization*

Although sacrifice began in the hunt, it appeared at its most meticulous and brilliant in the ancient city cultures, and at its most gruesome in Aztec civilization. It maintained its form and perhaps even

---

459–73. For a psychological perspective on the shock caused by blood see G. Devereux, *Mohave Ethnopsychiatry and Suicide* (1961), 14, 42–45.

[37] For man being created from the blood of a rebellious god see the Enuma Eliš VI, *ANET* 68, and cf. *ANET* 100; for man's *παλαιὰ* Τιτανικὴ *φύσις* see Plat. *Leg*. 701c, probably following the Orphic myth. Aratus 130–34 links the transition to the Iron Age, the flight of Dike, and the sacrifice of the plow-ox. Cf. W. R. Smith (1894) 306–308; B. Gatz, *Weltalter, goldene Zeit und sinnverwandte Vorstellungen* (1967), 165–71.

[38] Cited by Meuli (1946) 226; Empedokles B 124.2 in Porph. *Abst*. 3.27 (*ἔκ τε νεικέων* Porph., *ἔκ τε στοναχῶν* Diels, following the parallel tradition). Plut. *Conv. sept. sap.* 159c–d: *ᾧ δ'ἄνευ κακώσεως ἑτέρου τὴν αὑτοῦ σωτηρίαν ἀμήχανον ὁ θεὸς πεποίηκε, τούτῳ τὴν φύσιν ἀρχὴν ἀδικίας προστέθεικεν*. A. E. Jensen's treatment, "Über das Töten als kulturgeschichtliche Erscheinung," *Paideuma* 4 (1950), 23–28 = *Mythos und Kult bei Naturvölkern* [1951], 197–229, is fundamental and rich in source material. His thesis that this is the expression of man's basic realization that he is dependent on organic food can be made more specific from an historical perspective: it is the ideology of the hunter, still maintained in the planter's culture. Cf. Straube (1955) 200–204.

[39] *Et nos servasti* [. . .] *sanguine fuso*: inscription in the Mithraeum of Santa Prisca, Rome: M. J. Vermaseren and C. C. van Essen, *The Excavations in the Mithraeum of the Church of*

acquired its purely religious function outside the context in which killing was necessary for life. For the action to be thus redirected and maintained, there had to be ritualization.

The concept of *ritual* has long been used to describe the rules of religious behavior. Biology's recent usurpation of the term appears, however, to confuse the concept, mixing the transcendent with the infra-human. But perhaps these two do indeed meet within the fundamental orders that constitute life. Thus, we deliberately start from the biological definition of ritual, and from there we will soon be led deep into the nature of religion.

Since the work of Sir Julian Huxley and Konrad Lorenz,[1] biology has defined *ritual* as a behavioral pattern that has lost its primary function—present in its unritualized model—but which persists in a new function, that of communication. This pattern in turn provokes a corresponding behavioral response. Lorenz's prime example is the triumph ceremony of a pair of graylag geese, which is no longer prompted by a real enemy. The victory over a nonexistent opponent is meant to demonstrate and draw attention to the couple's solidarity and is confirmed by corresponding behavior in the partner, who understands the ritual communication because of its predetermined stereotypy. In the triumph ceremony, communication is reciprocal and is strengthened by the reactions of each side. But it can also be one-sided, as, for example, when a threatening gesture is answered by ritual submission, which thus upholds a hierarchy. This communicating function reveals the two basic characteristics of ritual behavior, namely, repetition and theatrical exaggeration. For the essentially immutable patterns do not transmit differentiated and complex information but, rather, just one piece of information each. This single piece of information is considered so important that it is reinforced by constant repetition so as to avoid misunderstanding or misuse. The fact of understanding is thus more important than what is understood. Above all, then, ritual creates and affirms social interaction.

Santa Prisca in Rome (1965), 217–20. In the lacuna, *eternali* had been read, but this cannot have been there: S. Panciera in U. Bianchi, ed., *Mysteria Mithrae* (1979), 103ff.

[1] Sir Julian Huxley, *Proc. Zool. Soc.* (1914), 511–15 on "ceremonies" of the Great Crested Grebe; Lorenz (1963) 89–127; "A Discussion on Ritualization of Behavior in Animals and Man," *Philos. Trans. Roy. Soc. London* B251 (1966), 247–526, with articles by Huxley, Lorenz, and others; Eibl-Eibesfeldt (1970) 60–70; P. Weidkuhn, *Aggressivität, Ritus, Säkularisierung* (1965). In defining ritual as "action re-done or pre-done," J. Harrison (*Epilegomena to the Study of Greek Religion* [1921], xliii) recognized the displacement of behavior but not the communicatory function. Now E. R. Leach, for example, finds that "communicative behavior" and "magical behavior" in ritual are not basically different (*Philos. Trans. Roy. Soc. London* B251 [1966], 403–404).

Aggressive behavior evokes a highly attentive, excited response. Pretended aggression thus plays a special role in ritual communication. Raising one's hands, waving branches, wielding weapons and torches, stamping the feet while turning from attack to flight, folding the hands or lifting them in supplication, kneeling and prostration: all these are repeated and exaggerated as a demonstration whereby the individual proclaims his membership and place in the community. A rhythm develops from repetition, and auditory signals accompanying the gestures give rise to music and dance. These, too, are primordial forms of human solidarity, but they cannot hide the fact that they grew out of aggressive tensions, with their noise and beating, attack and flight. Of course, man has many modes of expression that are not of this origin and that can be ritualized. But in ethology, even laughter is thought to originate in an aggressive display of teeth.[2] Gestures of disgust or "purification" are not far removed from the impulses of aggression and destruction. Some of these ritual gestures can be traced with certainty to the primates, from waving branches and rhythmic drumming to phallic display and raising the hand in supplication.[3]

It is disputed to what extent ritual behavior is innate or learned.[4] We will have to wait for further ethological research. There is even a possibility that specific learning or formative experiences may activate innate behavior. Universal modes of behavior suggest an innate stock from which they are drawn. Yet, building upon these, cultural education creates special forms delimiting individual groups almost as if they were "pseudo-species." Fortunately, in studying the effect of rituals as communication in society, the question of their biological roots is comparatively unimportant.

Ever since Emile Durkheim, sociologists have been interested in the role of rites, and especially of religious rituals in society. "It is through common action that society becomes self-aware"; thus "the collective feelings and ideas that determine [society's] unity and character must be maintained and confirmed at regular intervals."[5] A. R.

---

[2]Lorenz (1963) 268–70; cautiously, Eibl-Eibesfeldt (1970) 197.

[3]Burkert (1979) 39–45. On drumming see Eibl-Eibesfeldt (1970) 40; on phallic display see I.7 below; on the outstretched hand see Eibl-Eibesfeldt (1970) 204–205; Morris (1967) 157, 166.

[4]On the socially learned behavior of the primate see, for instance, L. Rosenkötter, *Frankfurter Hefte* 21 (1966), 523–33, and cf. I.1.n. 1 above.

[5]E. Durkheim, *Les formes élémentaires de la vie religieuse* (1912; 1960[4]), 598: "c'est par l'action commune qu'elle [sc. la société] prend conscience de soi"; 610: "entretenir et raffermir, à intervalles réguliers, les sentiments collectifs et les idées collectives qui font son unité et sa personnalité."

Radcliffe-Brown has been the most thorough in developing this functional perspective: a society can exist only by means of common concepts and feelings which, in turn, are developed through society's effect on the individual. "The ceremonial customs of a society are a means by which the sentiments in question are given collective expression on appropriate occasion."[6] Today one would perhaps replace the term *sentiment* with *thought structure and behavior pattern* but on the whole, ethology has confirmed and reinforced this view. The ritual actualizes social interaction; it dramatizes the existing order. We may call it "status dramatization,"[7] although this is not to say that a rite cannot establish and define a new status.

Besides this functional-behavioristic approach, and apparently contradicting it, is the psychoanalytic concept of ritual based on empirical observation of compulsive behavior. Here, too, we find set behavior patterns that have lost their primary, pragmatic function. In this view, neurosis becomes a kind of private religion, and sacred ritual becomes collective neurosis. Through ritual, the psyche tries to avoid anxieties, fleeing to a world of its own making from a reality it cannot accept and thus negates. Oppressed and wounded by that reality, it seeks to escape utter madness. Thus, religion is seen as an irrational outburst, a "ghost dance."[8]

The contrast, however, is more one of perspective than of substance. Just as in biology one may, on the one hand, observe the formation of a mutation and its physiological effects in terms of causality, while, on the other, gauging its relative advantage or disadvantage from a different environmental perspective, so, too, in studying the formation of private rituals, the sociological-functional approach provides a necessary complement to psychology. We cannot grasp religion as a fixed form if it is merely personal; it becomes a formative construct only over the course of generations. Sacrificial rituals, in any case, are impressive evidence for a continuity spanning thousands of years, and even if they exist only because of certain psychological influences, the continuity is surely due to other factors, factors of biological and social selection.

The first of these factors is negative. A ritual can persist in a com-

---

[6]A. R. Radcliffe-Brown, *The Andaman Islanders* (1933[2]) 234.

[7]For the term see F. W. Young, *Initiation Ceremonies: A Cross-Cultural Study of Status Dramatization* (1965).

[8]It is sufficient to refer to La Barre's comprehensive treatment (1970). See S. Freud, "Zwangshandlungen und Religionsübungen," *Ges. Schr.* 10 (1924), 210–20 = *Ges. Werke* 7 (1941), 129–39.

munity only so long as it does not threaten that community with extinction. Some religious developments have indeed tended in this direction. The swift fall of most Gnostic movements and the final fall of Manichaeism were undoubtedly caused by their negation of life, just as the monks of Mount Athos, who were maintained by the outside world's consciousness of sin, are dying out today. If, however, practically all human cultures are shaped by religion, this indicates that religious ritual is advantageous in the process of selection, if not for the individual, then at least for the continuance of group identity.[9] Religion outlives all non-religious communities; and sacrificial ritual plays a special role in this process.

Furthermore, those rituals which are not innate can endure only when passed on through a learning process. The impulse for imitation, which is highly developed in man and especially in children, is decisive here, and it is encouraged by the theatricality of ritual. Children act out weddings and funerals again and again. This alone, however, cannot preserve the form of ritual, which remains rigid and unchanging over long periods of time. For this, the rite must be established as sacred. A religious rite is almost always "serious": some danger is evoked arousing anxiety, which then heightens attentiveness and lifts the subsequent proceedings out of the colorful stream of daily experience. Thus, the learning process leaves an ineradicable impression. By far the greatest impression is made by what terrifies, and it is just this that makes aggressive rituals so significant.

But even this is not enough to guarantee the permanence of the ritual: deviations are corrected by elimination. Ritual was evidently so important for the continuance of human society that it became one of the factors of selection itself for innumerable generations. Those who will not or cannot conform to the rituals of a society have no chance in it. Only those who have integrated themselves can have influence and affect action. Here, the serious character of religious ritual becomes a very real threat. The psychological failure to meet this threat causes personal catastrophe. For instance, a child who consistently laughs during solemn occasions will not survive in a religious community. Apollonios of Tyana once declared such a boy to be possessed by a demon, but luckily the evil spirit quickly left the frightened young

---

[9] So already O. Gruppe, *RML* Suppl., "Geschichte der klassischen Mythologie und Religionsgeschichte" (1921), 243. Group selection is not accepted by the modern theory of evolution—see R. Dawkins, *The Selfish Gene* (1976)—but it is still granted that "a grudger's strategy" is "evolutionarily stable": ibid. 199–201.

rascal.[10] In the Middle Ages, abbots fought the devil with very real cudgels, and up until modern times, a consecrated "devil's whip" always lay ready. This helps to account for the durability of aggressive ritual.

The biological-functional view of ritual has a consequence that is seldom realized, because it seems to go against the intention of humanism, which sees its mission in pursuing a phenomenology of the mind or soul and in disclosing a world of concepts or ideas. Ever since Wilhelm Mannhardt and Robertson Smith, the study of religions has focused on ritual. The evidence of the literary tradition no longer satisfied, since it had become evident that it was secondary. Thus, scholars looked for its roots in "deeper," "more primitive ideas."[11] It was, and is, considered self-evident that ritual, especially religious ritual, must depend on an antecedent "idea,"[12] even though it always turns out that those people whom history has been able to observe still practicing ritual "no longer" understand its "deeper meaning." After the rationalistic bias in the concept *idea* was exposed, scholars looked instead to "experience" or "deep perception"[13] for the roots which, as a creative response, produced ritual. Sociology, however—and, in this case, history—long ago revolutionized this perspective. Ideas do

---

[10] Philostr. *V. Ap.* 4.20. On the *Teufelspeitsche* see A. Jacoby, *Schweiz. Archiv f. Volkskunde* 28 (1928), 81–105. Cf. the story of the "witch's child" in Gottfried Keller's *Der grüne Heinrich* (1854), I, ch. 5.

[11] For instance, Mannhardt (1875) 603 states his conclusion as follows: "Als Überlebsel der primitivisten Entwickelungszustände des menschlichen Geistes hat sich . . . die Vorstellung von der Gleichartigkeit des Menschen und des Baumes gerettet. Die Überzeugung 'der Baum hat eine Seele wie der Mensch,' und der Wunsch zu wachsen und zu blühen wie ein Baum, sind . . . die Eltern eines weitverzweigten Glaubens und mannigfacher Gebräuche gewesen"; that is, the conception and wish give rise to the custom. W. R. Smith speaks of the ideas expressed in the ritual tradition, "Ideen, die im traditionellen Ritual zum Ausdruck kommen" ([1894], 20, etc.) and of the fundamental idea of the conception grasped in the ritual (439). H. Usener (*Götternamen* [1895, 1948³], 330) sought behind the varying names "eine Geschichte der Vorstellungen" as the building blocks of an "Entwicklungsgeschicte des menschlichen Geistes."

[12] E.g., Nilsson (1955) 2: "Es gibt Glaubenssätze . . . aus ihnen entspriessen . . . die religiösen Handlungen"; we are obliged "die allgemeinen Vorstellungen zuerst auf Grund der religiösen Handlungen herauszuarbeiten."

[13] H. Usener, *Vorträge und Aufsätze* (1907), 42, for instance, spoke of "religiöser Empfindung," which finds expression "in Vorstellungen und in Handlungen." Likewise Meuli looks to "den natürlichen, spontanen Ausdruck," "die lebendige Empfindung" as the "Grundlage," "Vorbild" and "Formgeber" of the custom ([1946], 202, and cf. 250; *Schweiz. Archiv f. Volkskunde* 43 [1946], 91–109, in which, however, he is fully aware of the rite's demonstrative character).

not produce ritual; rather, ritual itself produces and shapes ideas, or even experience and emotions. "Ce ne sont pas des émotions actuelles, ressenties à l'occasion des réunions et des cérémonies, qui engendrent ou perpétuent les rites, mais l'activité rituelle qui suscite les émotions."[14] "A specific practice or belief . . . never represents a direct psychological response of individuals to some aspect of the outer world. . . . The source of their beliefs and practices is . . . the historic tradition."[15] It is this, by transmitting the custom as custom, that produces ideas, shapes experiences, excites desires.

This change in perspective, of course, takes us back to a basic assumption of primitive religion which religious studies constantly try to transcend: the source of religious custom is the "ways of our ancestors."[16] Ever since the pre-Socratics, people have stubbornly asked how mankind came to have its religious ideas; and they have done so although all men of the historical era, and certainly countless prehistoric generations, were taught their religious beliefs by the generation immediately preceding them. Plato expressed it thus: children come to believe in the existence of the gods by observing how "their own parents act with utmost seriousness on behalf of themselves and their children" at sacrifice and prayer.[17] Even the most radical innovations in the history of religion proceed from this basis.

To be cautious, let us say that all human action is accompanied by ideas, surrounded by images and words. Tradition embraces language as well as ritual behavior. Psychoanalysis even speaks of "unconscious ideas." But to what extent these ideas, which are then raised after all into the realm of linguistic presentation, are just hermeneutic accessories or factors that exercise a demonstrable causality is a difficult question, at best answerable only in the context of psychology itself. By means of interpretation, one can attribute ideas to any action. Ritual has an understandable function *within* society—of course, it often has many, and changing, functions, for, as we know, biological selection favors multiple functions. Human beings can usually understand ritual intuitively, at least in its constituent parts. Thus, ritual makes sense in two ways. It is quite right to speak of "ideas" or "insights" which are "contained" in ritual and which it can

---

[14] C. Lévi-Strauss, *Le totémisme aujourd'hui* (1962) 102f.

[15] A. I. Hallowell, *American Anthropologist* 28 (1926), 19. M. Mead, *Male and Female* (1949), 61, stresses that even childhood experiences bear the stamp of the adult world, "a process of transmission, not of creation."

[16] Cf. Preface n. 7.

[17] Plat. *Leg*. 887d.

express and communicate—as, for instance, the reality of a higher, transcendent power or the sacredness of life. However, it is more problematic to say that ritual has some "purpose," since we know that its course is predetermined and that a superimposed purpose cannot change it but can at most provoke it as a whole. There is no justification for viewing the "idea," even in its linguistic manifestation, as anterior to or decisive for ritual. In the history of mankind, ritual is far older than linguistic communication.[18] Neither the ideas and insights that can be extracted as a partial clarification by interpreting the ritual nor the emotions and explanations expressed by participants in the cult are the basis and origin of ritual; they simply accompany it. Thanks to its theatrical, mimetic character and the deep impression that its sacred solemnity can impart, ritual is self-perpetuating.

4. *Myth and Ritual*

Ritual, as a form of communication, is a kind of language. It is natural, then, that verbalized language, man's most effective system of communication, should be associated with ritual. Although the accomplishment of language resides in communicating some content and in projecting a model of reality, it is at the same time an extremely social phenomenon: it brings about reciprocal personal contact and preserves it; it determines who belongs to the group; indeed, the special peculiarities of grammar and phonetics almost seem made to keep the circle of members small. In many cases, that which is said seems less important in everyday life than that something is in fact said.[1] Being together in silence is almost unbearable.

Doubtless for this reason, ritual and language have gone hand in

[18] There is the thesis that Neanderthal man could not yet produce articulate speech in our form due to his physiology. See Ph. Lieberman, "On the Evolution of Human Language," *Proc. Seventh Int. Congr. Phonetic Sciences* (Leiden, 1972), 258–72; see also Ph. Lieberman, E. S. Crelin, and D. H. Klatt, *American Anthropologist* 74 (1972), 287–307; "Origins and Evolution of Language and Speech," *Annals New York Acad. Sciences* 280 (1976). Yet there was hunting, cannibalism, and burial—but no pictorial art—in the Lower Palaeolithic: this points to a human society based on ritual before the final evolution of language. Lieberman's thesis, though, is controversial.

[1] See Morris (1967) 202–206 on "grooming talk."

hand since language began. Any number of forms are conceivable for such a combination, and many are indeed attested; from a responsion of expressive cries during the ritual, to naming that which seems present in it and invoking it,[2] to a more or less direct account of what is happening there. This leads us to the problem of myth.

The theme of myth and ritual is still the subject of great controversy. While some see the ritual backdrop of a myth as the only acceptable meaning for something that at first appears absurd, others champion the cause of free fantasy and speculation. After Robertson Smith had determined "the dependence of myth on ritual," which Jane Harrison then distilled into the theory that myth is often just "ritual misunderstood,"[3] S. H. Hooke postulated on the basis of ancient Near Eastern and biblical material that there was a unity, a necessary connection between myth and ritual: myth is "the spoken part of the ritual."[4] The occasional claims that this thesis resolved the question absolutely have caused a variety of strong reactions,[5] but these

---

[2]The divine names Paian (L. Deubner, "Paian," *NJb* 22 [1919], 385–406; Nilsson [1955] 543; see already the Mycenaean *pa-ja-wo-ne*, Gérard-Rousseau [1968] 164–65) and Iakchos (Foucart [1914] 111; Deubner [1932] 73; Nilsson [1955] 664) arose out of the cultic cries *ἰήιε Παιάν* and "Ιακχ' ὦ "Ιακχε.

[3]W. R. Smith (1894) 17–20; for "absurd mythology" seen as "ritual misunderstood" see J. Harrison, *Mythology and Monuments of Ancient Athens* (1890), xxxiii. Cf. Harrison (1927) 327–31, where the meaning of myth is recognized once again: "the myth is the plot of the dromenon" (331). The connections between myth and ritual were already stressed by F. G. Welcker (*Die aeschylische Trilogie Prometheus und die Kabirenweihe zu Lemnos* [1824], esp. 159, 249–50) and Wilamowitz (e.g., *Euripides Herakles* I [1889], 85; "Hephaistos," *NGG* 1895, 234 = *Kl. Schr.* V 2, 23–24).

[4]S. H. Hooke, ed., *Myth and Ritual* (1933), 3: myth is "the spoken part of the ritual," "the story which the ritual enacts." As early as 1910, A. van Gennep stated that myth is "eine Erzählung . . . , deren Bestandteile sich in gleicher Sequenz durch religiös-magische Handlungen (Riten) äussern" (*Internationale Wochenschrift* 4, 1174). In the meantime, empirical ethnology had arrived on the scene: B. Malinowski, *Myth in Primitive Psychology* (1926). For an attempt at an overview see D. Kluckhohn, "Myths and Rituals: A General Theory," *HThR* 35 (1942), 45–79; also S. H. Hooke, *Myth, Ritual and Kingship* (1958); and Th. H. Gaster, *Thespis: Ritual, Myth and Drama in the Ancient Near East* (1950, 1961[2]). Lord Raglan, *The Origins of Religion* (1949), and A. M. Hocart, *Social Origins* (1954), went so far as to reconstruct an Ur-ritual, rooted in ancient Near Eastern kingship.

Alongside this debate—carried on almost exclusively among English-speaking scholars—are parallel attempts in the early work of G. Dumézil (*Le crime des Lemniennes* [1924]; *Le problème des Centaurs* [1929]) on the one hand, and, on the other, in Germany where W. F. Otto, *Dionysos* (1933), 44, spoke of the "Zusammenfall von Kultus und Mythos," and O. Höfler (1934) derived the sagas about hordes of wild men and about werewolves from ritual.

[5]H. J. Rose, *Mnemosyne* n.s. 3 (1950), 281–87; M. P. Nilsson, *Cults, Myths, Oracles and*

have been unable to dampen the fascination occasioned by the myth-and-ritual theory. Because the concept of myth is even more vague than that of ritual, a solution satisfactory to all is virtually hopeless.

A radical way out is to say that the defining feature of myth, as opposed to saga, fairytale, and folktale, is its connection with ritual.[6] But empirical facts argue against this: stories that are obviously identical are sometimes accompanied by ritual, sometimes not. Likewise, in both ancient and modern cultures there are rituals without corresponding, explicatory myths.[7] And although one could attribute the lack of a correspondence in antiquity to incomplete documentation preserved by chance, it is hard to attack the proofs brought forward by ethnology.[8] One could, of course, argue that myths without rituals derive nonetheless from lost rituals, that myth is so much easier to transmit and takes so much less expense that it could spread and grow on its own. But this hypothesis cannot be verified. Ritual is far older in the history of evolution, since it goes back even to animals, whereas myth only became possible with the advent of speech, a specifically human ability. Myth, however, cannot be documented before the era in which writing was invented, although it was obviously present long before. Somewhere in between, in the vast reaches of the unknowable, are the "origins." We are left with the fact that stories are something new in relation to biologically observable ritual. To this extent, myth does not grow directly out of ritual. On the other hand, even critics do not dispute that ritual and myth came to be closely allied.

According to the broadest definition, a *myth* is a traditional tale.[9] This is already enough to dispose of the opinion, held from Xenopha-

---

Politics in Ancient Greece (1951), 10, and cf. Nilsson (1955) 14n.; A. N. Marlow, *Bull. J. Ryland Libr.* 43 (1960/61), 373–402; Fontenrose (1959); idem, *The Ritual Theory of Myth* (1966); Kirk (1970) 12–29. In the surveys by J. de Vries, *Forschungsgeschichte der Mythologie* (1961), and K. Kerényi, *Die Eröffnung des Zugangs zum Mythos* (1967), the ritual theory appears only marginally. Cf. Burkert (1980).

[6]According to Harrison, Hooke, and Kluckhohn (nn. 3 and 4 above) and E. R. Leach, *Political Systems of Highland Burma* (1954), 13; for an opposing view see Kirk (1970) 28: "Myths and rituals overlap rather than being interdependent."

[7]Particularly in ancient Egypt: see E. Otto, "Das Verhältnis von Rite und Mythus im Ägyptischen," *SB Heidelberg* (1958), 1; C. J. Bleeker, *Egyptian Festivals, Enactments of Religious Renewal* (1967), 19.

[8]Kirk (1970) 25–28.

[9]For Kirk (1970), the "traditional tale" is in any case the framework within which the "myth" must be located (28, 73–75, 282); the distinction between myth and "folktale" remains hazy (41).

nes up through modern classicists, that myths were created by the poet's fancy, if not in historical times, then in prehistory.[10] Regardless of its origin, myth is characterized by its suitability for telling and retelling. Although it does not derive from empirical observation or individual experience and can be only partially verified, at best, myth is extraordinarily lucid. Its themes are often surprisingly constant, in spite of the many fantastic and paradoxical motifs that shape its unmistakable identity; even though slightly distorted, they return again and again. For this reason, psychoanalysis sees myth as a projection of specific structures in the soul, an elaboration of inborn psychological dispositions.[11] From a strictly evolutionary standpoint, however, we must suppose that even these archetypes, like valleys hollowed out by ancient streams, were created by a process of selection between various ways of life open to Palaeolithic man. And if the ways of life were determined by rituals, then from the very start they shaped the mythic patterns.

This is speculation. We can be certain, however, that myths and rituals successfully combine as forms of cultural tradition. There is no need for the myth itself to be part of the ritual, as the strict orientation of the myth-and-ritual school would have it. Continuous stories appear in ritual only exceptionally. The ritual can be discussed outside its own context, either in preparation or to explain it afterward; in this way, the Greeks connected almost every ritual with a story explaining in each case why a questionable custom was established.[12] Only the opposite question, whether in turn all Greek myths refer to rituals, is

---

[10] "Der Mythos . . . entsteht in der Phantasie des Dichters," Wilamowitz (1931) 42, a thesis restated programatically by E. Howald, *Der Mythos als Dichtung* (1937). To be sure, it is perfectly legitimate to investigate each particular individual manifestation of a myth, but it is no less legitimate to search for the underlying themes which are the given for every poet historically known to us.

[11] C. G. Jung, *Eranos-Jb.* (1938), 403–10, on archetypes as "Funktionsformen"; idem, *Man and His Symbols* (1964); J. Jacobi, *Komplex, Archetypus, Symbol in der Psychologie C. G. Jungs* (1957). Following A. E. Jensen (*Das religiöse Weltbild einer frühen Kultur* [1948], 131ff.), even Kerényi (1967) xxiii–xxxiii has now distanced himself from Jung. Regarding the problem of myth and history, W. F. Jackson Knight stated: "Myth . . . is used as a mental container to hold the facts of some new event. The container can be called an archetypal pattern" (*Cumaean Gates* [1936], 91).

[12] The earliest examples are Hesiod's Prometheus story (*Th.* 556–57), the possibly interpolated verses *Il.* 2.546–51, among the *Homeric Hymns* primarily those to Apollo (D. Kolk, *Der pythische Apollonhymnus als aitiologische Dichtung* [1963]), to Demeter (F. Wehrli, *ARW* 31 (1934], 77–104), and to Hermes (cf. I.2 at n. 13 above). On cultic etiologies in tragedy see W. Schmid, *Geschichte der griech. Literatur* I/3 (1940), 705.7, 776.8. Cf. Nilsson (1955) 27–29.

disputed. There have been attempts, of course, to distinguish etiological myths referring to cult from "genuine" myths,[13] but the distinction falls apart as soon as one can show in even a few cases that indisputably genuine old myths are subordinate to cultic action, as, for instance, the myth of Pelops is to the festival at Olympia. Nor is it generally true that the Greeks saw a correspondence between speech and action, λεγόμενα and δρώμενα, only in mystery cults.[14] Piety was indeed in the Greek view a matter of ritual, but myth was nonetheless ubiquitous. The two were transmitted together because they explained and strengthened each other.

This is not to say that ritual is a theatrical dramatization of myth.[15] Nor can it be seen as arising from magical ideas with an alleged purpose. The relationship of the two becomes clear if we take ritual for what it is, if we accept that its function is to dramatize the order of life, expressing itself in basic modes of behavior, especially aggression. In its own way, too, myth clarifies the order of life.[16] As is well known, it frequently explains and justifies social orders and establishments,[17] and in so doing it is related to ritual, which occurs by means of social interaction. The most exciting themes in myth come from the realm of sexuality and aggression, and these are also prominent in ritual communication. The most fascinating stories concern the perils of death and destruction. These have their counterpart in sacrificial killing.

---

[13]E.g., A. E. Jensen, "Echte und ätiologische (explanatorische) Mythen," in K. Kerényi, *Die Eröffnung des Zugangs zum Mythos* (1967), 262–70 = *Mythos und Kult bei Naturvölkern* (1951), 87–91, 97–100, in which "mythical truth" is the criterion for what is genuine; cf. I.2.n. 38 above.

[14]Thus Nilsson (1955) 14n. It is true that the general terms (ἱερός) λόγος (Hdt. 2.47, 2.51, 2.81) or λεγόμενα and δρώμενα (Paus. 1.43.2, 2.38.2, 2.37.2, 9.30.12, 9.27.2) come up precisely in situations where the content of the story and ritual may not be described, that is, in the mysteries. So also, for instance, Euseb. *Praep. Ev.* 15.1.2 τελεταὶ καὶ μυστήρια σύμφωνα τοῖς τῶν προτέρων μυθικοῖς διηγήμασιν; Lact. *Div. inst.* 1.21.39 *quidquid est gestum in abscondendo puero, id ipsum per imaginem geritur in sacris* (mysteries of Kuretes); Steph. Byz. *s.v.* Ἄγρα . . . μίμημα τῶν περὶ τὸν Διόνυσον. But the correspondence is not limited to these cases: on sacrifice generally see Firm. *Err.* 16.3: *ut acerbarum mortium casus cottidiano victimarum sanguine recrudescant*. Ach. Tat. 2.2.2 τῆς ἑορτῆς διηγοῦνται πατέρα μῦθον.

[15]See Fontenrose (1959) 464, who correctly states: "Whenever myth precedes ritual, then drama is produced."

[16]On the parallel functions of ritual and myth see Kluckhohn, "Myths and Rituals" (n. 4 above); Leach, *Political Systems*.

[17]Following Malinowski, *Myth in Primitive Psychology*, on "charter myths" see Kirk (1970) 154–57.

"The myth is the plot of the dromenon."[18] The mythical tale, as communication between participants within a single ritual tradition, does not, of course, provide an objective behavioral description of what occurs there. It names that which the ritual intends. Rituals are redirected patterns of behavior, with a displaced referent. Thus, the mythical naming, because it follows the original orientation and so fills the space left vacant, creates a quasi-reality which cannot be perceived with the senses but is directly experienced in the ritual. Human speech naturally refers to some subject, and thus ritual communication gives rise to mythical subjects. In hunting and then in sacrifice, aggressive modes of behavior between men are diverted onto animals; in the myth, on the other hand, is a human victim.[19] Fears are displayed in the preparatory rituals; the myth names someone who is to be feared. The ritual is shaped by gestures of guilt and submission; the myth tells of some stronger being and of his power. The myth develops what the gestures contain *in nuce*: a threatening gesture becomes murder, sorrow acted out becomes genuine mourning, erotic movements become a story of love and death. The as-if element in the ritual becomes mythical reality; conversely, the ritual confirms the reality of the myth. In this way, by mutually affirming each other, myth and ritual became a strong force in forming a cultural tradition, even though their origins were different.

To some extent myth can even supplant ritual, especially in its function of expressing the unity and organization of the group. Speech is far superior to ritual in its precision and dexterity. One word, one cry can replace a complicated war dance. But because of its very flexibility, language is also fickle. It can easily be abused or used to deceive. Therefore society always returns to ritual, even though it runs contrary to the rational acceleration of communication.[20] An agreement can be expressed quickly and clearly in words, but it is only made effective by a ritual gesture: open, weaponless hands stretched toward one another, grasping each other in a mutual handshake—a mutual display of aggression—sealing what had previously been merely spoken. Similarly, it may be possible to conceive of a religion without myths, but not of a religion using myth without ritual practice. There has yet to be a community without ritual.

---

[18] Harrison (1927) 331.

[19] See I.2.n.35 above; cf. at n. 2 above.

[20] A. Portmann, *Das Tier als soziales Wesen* (1964), 340: "Das Ritual bleibt auch in Zukunft das gewaltige Instrument des Überindividuellen in allem höheren, d.h. sozialen Leben." On shaking hands see Eibl-Eibesfeldt (1970) 203–206.

5. *The Function and Transformation of Ritual Killing*

Hunting behavior became established and, at the same time, transferable through ritualization. In this way it was preserved long after the time of the primitive hunter. This cannot be explained simply by the psychological mechanisms of imitation and imprinting, whereby customs are inherited. These rituals were indispensable because of the particular thing they accomplished. The only prehistoric and historic groups obviously able to assert themselves were those held together by the ritual power to kill. The earliest male societies banded together for collective killing in the hunt. Through solidarity and cooperative organization, and by establishing an inviolable order, the sacrificial ritual gave society its form.

As ethology has shown, a sense of community arises from collective aggression.[1] A smile can, of course, establish contact, and a crying child touches our hearts, but in all human societies "seriousness" takes precedence over friendliness and compassion. A community bound by oaths is united in the "sacred shiver" of awe and enthusiasm—the relic of an aggressive reflex that made the hairs bristle[2]—in a feeling of strength and readiness. This must then be released in an "act": the sacrificial ritual provides the occasion for killing and bloodshed. Whether in Israel, Greece, or Rome, no agreement, no contract, no alliance can be made without sacrifice. And, in the language of the oath, the object of aggression that is to be "struck" and "cut" becomes virtually identical with the covenant itself: *foedus ferire*, *ὅρκια πιστὰ τέμνειν*.[3] Families and guilds[4] organize themselves into

[1]Lorenz (1963) esp. 249–318. For criticisms, see I.1.n.1; Eibl-Eibesfeldt (1970) 145–48, 187–90 is somewhat reluctant; his example of the sudden effect of a smile in war (113–14) shows how shaky these other kinds of bonding are. A new theory of how human community is founded on aggression has been set out by Girard (1972); his model is not the hunting pack but the scapegoat complex (cf. Burkert [1979] 59–77) and Dionysiac *σπαραγμός*—a combination which is questionable. The practice of eating in sacrifice is not taken into account by him.

[2]On the "sacred shiver" of awe see Lorenz (1963) 375–77.

[3]As a formula, see *Il.* 3.73 and 19.191; *Od.* 24.483; R. Hirzel, *Der Eid* (1902); Stengel

sacrificial communities; so too cities at a festival, as well as gatherings of larger political groups. The inhabitants of the Peleponnesus, the "island of Pelops," meet at Pelops' grave for sacrifice at Olympia; the islanders celebrate in Delos; the Ionian cities slaughter a bull to Poseidon at Mykale.[5] In the time of Cicero, the cities of the Latin League still had the right "to demand their portion of meat"[6] from the sacrifice of a bull to Jupiter Latiaris. The Ionian League headed by Athens first met at Delos; later, Athens exacted a phallus for the procession at the Dionysia at Athens, and a cow for the Panathenaia.[7] It is in the sacrificial procession that the empire's power becomes manifest.

The closer the bond, the more gruesome the ritual. Those who swear an oath must touch the blood from the accompanying sacrifice and even step on the testicles of the castrated victim.[8] They must eat the meat of the victim as well, or at least the *σπλάγχνα*.[9] It was generally believed that conspiracies practiced human sacrifice and cannibal-

---

(1920) 136–38; Nilsson (1955) 139–42. On the Semitic "cutting" of a covenant see E. Bickermann, "Couper une alliance," *Archives d'Histoire du Droit Orientale* 5 (1950/51), 133–56. A special case of the encounter with death is passing through the severed halves of the sacrificial victim: see S. Eitrem, *Symb. Oslo* 25 (1947), 36–39; for the Hittites see O. Gurney, *RHR* 137 (1950), 5–25. On the sacrifice of the *fetiales* with the sacred *silex* see Latte (1960) 122–23; R. M. Ogilvie, *A Commentary on Livy* I (1965), 112; Burkert (1967) 287. Calling down a curse on oneself (Livy 1.24; Nilsson [1955] 139) does not explain the details of the ritual; the essential point is that the act, during which the one who swears raises himself above annihilation, is irrevocable. This can be shown, for instance, by sinking metal bars in the sea: Hdt. 1.165; Arist. *Ath. Pol.* 23.5. For this reason the *σπονδή* can take the place of blood sacrifice (cf. I.6.n.26 below).

[4] The phratries are constituted at the sacrifices of the *μεῖον* and *κούρειον* at the Apaturia: see Deubner (1932) 232–34. Amasis allowed the Greek merchants to construct "altars and sacred precincts for the gods" at Naukratis (Hdt. 1.178)—the permanent establishment of a trading company; cf. late Hellenistic Delos.

[5] Hdt. 1.148; Strabo 8 p. 384; 14 p. 639; *Marm. Par.*, *FGrHist* 239 A 27; G. Kleiner, P. Hommel, and W. Müller-Wiener, "Panionion und Melie," *JdI Erg.-H.* 23 (1967); F. Sokolowski, *BCH* 94 (1970), 109–112; on Pelops see II.2 below.

[6] Livy 32.1.9, 37.3.4; Cic. *Planc.* 23. Cf. Latte (1960) 144–46; A. Alföldi, *Early Rome and the Latins* (1965), 19–25.

[7] Delos: Thuc. 1.96.2. For the phallus see *IG* II/III^2 673. *βô[ν καὶ πανοπ]λ[ίαν ἀπάγειν ἐς Παναθ]ένaια τὰ με[γάλα] hαπάσας* *IG* I^2 63 = R. Meiggs and D. Lewis, *A Selection of Greek Historical Inscriptions* (1969), #69, 55ff.; #46, 41; cf. *IG* I^2 10 = *SIG*^{3} 41; Schol. Aristoph. *Nub.* 386.

[8] Stengel (1910) 78–85; *Hermes* 59 (1924), 311–21; *στὰς ἐπὶ τῶν τομίων* Demosth. 23.68, and cf. Dion. Hal. *Ant.* 7.50.1; Paus. 3.20.9, 4.15.8, 5.24.9. Cf. I.7 below.

[9] Thus Demaratos adjures his mother at the sacrifice: Hdt. 6.67, *ἐσθεὶς ἐς τὰς χεῖράς οἱ τῶν σπλάγχνων*. Cf. Stengel (1920) 136, 14; Aristoph. *Lys.* 202 with Schol.; Antiphon 5.12; Aeschines 1.114; Isaeus 7.16; Lyk. *Leokr.* 20.

ism.[10] And, in a secularized form among Athenian hetairiai, collective killing was an expression of loyalty.[11] Here, the *sacrilegium* normally contained in the *sacrum* no longer remains within the confines of ritual.

In a sacrifice the circle of participants is segregated from the outside world. Complicated social structures find expression in the diverse roles the participants assume in the course of the ritual, from the various "beginnings," through prayer, slaughter, skinning, and cutting up, to roasting and, above all, distributing the meat. There is a "lord of the sacrifice" who demonstrates his *vitae necisque potestas* (actually only a *necis potestas*, but it seems *e contrario* to include the power of life). And as for the rest, each participant has a set function and acts according to a precisely fixed order. The sacrificial community is thus a model of society as a whole, divided according to occupation and rank. Hence, the hierarchies manifested in the ceremony are given great social importance and are taken very seriously. An ancient epic, the *Thebaid*, relates that Oedipus cursed his sons because he was given the wrong piece of sacrificial meat.[12] Harmodios murdered Hipparchos, the Peisistratid, because his sister had been denied the honor of being a "basket carrier" in the Panathenaia.[13] And the Corinthians turned against the Corcyrans not least of all because "in their common festivals they would not allow them the customary privilege of founders and, at their sacrifices, they did not perform the rites of 'beginning' for a man of Corinth, as the other colonies did": this ultimately resulted in the Peleponnesian War.[14]

The sacrificial meal is particularly subject to sacred laws that reg-

---

[10] On the Catilinarians see Sall. *Cat.* 22; Plut. *Cic.* 10.4; Dio Cass. 37.30.3. On the rebellious βουκόλοι in Egypt in A.D. 172 see Dio Cass. 71.4.1. The *Phoinikika*, a novel by Lollianos, contains a detailed description of such a gruesome sacrifice: A. Henrichs, *Die Phoinikika des Lollianos* (1972); cf. Henrichs, "Pagan Ritual and the Alleged Crimes of the Early Christians," in *Kyriakon, Festschr. J. Quasten* (1970), 18–35.

[11] Thuc. 8. 73.3 Ὑπέρβολον . . . ἀποκτείνουσιν, πίστιν διδόντες αὐτοῖς; cf. Plat. *Apol.* 32c on the request of the Thirty to Socrates, βουλόμενοι ὡς πλείστους ἀναπλῆσαι αἰτιῶν. The mutilation of the herms was a similar πίστις, Andoc. 1.67—and likewise a symbolic castration (Aristoph. *Lys.* 1094, Schol. Thuc. 6.27). Cf. also Diod. 1.21.2.

[12] *Thebais* fr. 3 Kinkel/Allen—even the Grammarian who cited the passage (Schol. Soph. *OC* 1375) found this motivation utterly primitive, τελέως ἀγενῶς. Cf. the διμοιρία ἐν ταῖς θοίναις for the Spartan king, Xen. *Ages.* 5.1; the double portion for Hanna, Samuel's later mother, I Sam. 1:5.

[13] Thuc. 6.56.

[14] Thuc. 1.25.4 οὔτε Κορινθίῳ ἀνδρὶ προκαταρχόμενοι. The situation is explained by Andoc. 1.126: sacrificers bring the victim to the altar and ask the priest κατάρξασθαι.

ulate social interaction in distributing, giving, and taking. The very fact that eating became ceremonial clearly distinguishes human behavior from animal. Once the deadly knife has been used on the victim, intraspecific aggression must be set aside. This is accomplished through an eating inhibition evoked by rituals that excite anxiety and guilt. Since a hunting society must support women and children, abstinence becomes an excuse: we killed for the sake of others. Thus, there is often a rule that the killer, the sacrificer himself, must refrain from eating. And this is not so only in human-sacrifice;[15] Hermes, the cattle-killer, must also obey this rule, and similarly the Pinarii were excluded from the meal in the sacrifice at the Ara Maxima. Sometimes there is a rule that sacrificial meat must be sold at once;[16] in this way, the ritual inhibition becomes an economic factor. The tabu makes social interaction all the more intense.

The shock felt in the act of killing is answered later by consolidation; guilt is followed by reparation, destruction by reconstruction. Its simplest manifestation is in the custom of collecting bones, of raising the skull, the horns, or the antlers, thereby establishing an order whose power resides in its contrast to what went before. In the experience of killing one perceives the sacredness of life; it is nourished and perpetuated by death. This paradox is embodied, acted out, and generalized in the ritual. Whatever is to endure and be effective must pass through a sacrifice which opens and reseals the abyss of annihilation.

---

[15] For Mexico see E. Reuterskiöld, *Die Entstehung der Speisesakramente* (1912), 93; for cannibals sèe E. Volhard, *Der Kannibalismus* (1939), 443–44; for Persian youngsters, Strabo 15 p. 734, and cf. G. Devereux, *Mohave Ethnopsychiatry and Suicide* (1961), 42–43; J. P. Guépin, *The Tragic Paradox* (1968), 161–62. See *Hy. Merc.* 130–33; likewise at the Attic Buphonia, the *βουτύπος*, who flees and does not reappear, is excluded from the sacrificial meal (cf. III.1 below). On the sacrifice at the Ara Maxima see Latte (1960) 213–21. On Pinarii see Cic. *Dom.* 134; Verg. *Aen.* 8.269–70 and Serv. on 269; Dion. Hal. *Ant.* 1.40; Diod. 4.21.2; Macr. *Sat.* 3.6.14. On the sacrifice to Pelops at Olympia see II.2 below. On Egyptian customs see Hdt. 2.48.1.

[16] *IG* I^2 188 = *LS* 10 C 18, 21; *LSAM* 54, 1–3; Hdt. 2.39; Serv. *Aen.* 8.183 *de hoc bove immolato Herculi carnes carius vendebantur causa religionis, et inde alter redimebatur*—this is not just an expansion of Vergil's phrase *perpetui bovis* (Latte [1960] 217, 2) but, rather, evidence of a custom whose function it is simultaneously to insure exchange and continuity. The Manichaeans transfer the principle of exchange and assertions of innocence to all food, even vegetables: *οὔτε σε ἐγὼ ἐθέρισα οὐδὲ ἤλεσα οὔτε ἔθλιψά σε οὔτε εἰς κλίβανον ἔβαλον, ἀλλὰ ἄλλος ἐποίησε ταῦτα καὶ ἤνεγκέ μοι. ἐγὼ ἀναιτίως ἔφαγον* (Hegemon. *Acta Archel.* 10.6; cf. A. Henrichs and L. Koenen, *ZPE* 5 [1970], 146–54). E. Durkheim, *Les formes élémentaires de la vie religieuse* (1912), interpreted totemism as a system of reciprocal collaboration and supplementation.

Building-sacrifices, for example, are for this reason widespread.[17] A house, a bridge or a dam will stay strong only if something lies slaughtered beneath it. One of the most detailed Latin descriptions of a sacrifice depicts the erection of a border-stone.[18] A sacrificial animal would be slaughtered in a pit and burned together with offerings of incense, fruits, honey, and wine. The stone was then placed on top of the remains while they were still hot. Thereafter, neighbors would return regularly on the anniversary of that sacrifice to repeat it. Similarly, altars and statues can be set up over a victim in the course of a ritual.[19] Any new creation, even the birth of music, requires ritual killing. Underlying the practical use of bone-flutes, turtle-shell lyres, and the tympanon covered with cowhide is the idea that the overwhelming power of music comes from a transformation and overcoming of death.[20] Thus, a slain man is easily made a hero or even a god, precisely because of his horrible end.[21] In any case, apotheosis is always preceded by death.

---

[17] Hock (1905) 75–83; Nilsson (1955) 404, 10; Müller-Karpe (1968) 336, 351, 361; K. Klusemann, *Das Bauopfer* (1919); cf. F. S. Krauss, *Volksglaube und religiöser Brauch der Südslaven* (1890), 158–64; B. Schmidt, *Das Volksleben der Neugriechen* (1871), 196–99. According to the *Enuma Eliš*, Ea kills his father Apsu and builds his temple upon him: *ANET* 61. However, animal sacrifice is rare, and human sacrifice unattested, for a building-sacrifice in the ancient Near East: see R. S. Ellis, *Foundation Deposits in Ancient Mesopotamia* (1968), 35–45.

[18] Gromatici ed. Lachmann I 141: *lapides in solidam terram rectos conlocabant . . . unguento velaminibusque et coronis eos coronabant. in fossis . . . sacrificio facto hostiaque immolata atque incensa facibus ardentibus in fossa cooperta* (Lachmann; -i Cdd.) *sanguinem instillabant eoque tura et fruges iactabant, favos quoque et vinum . . . consumptisque igne omnibus dapibus super calentes reliquias lapides conlocabant.* On the festival see Ov. *Fast.* 2.639–78.

[19] See the oracle ordering the construction of a statue of Apollo to ward off the plague: Kaibel, *Epigr.* 1034. K. Buresch, *Klaros* (1889), 81–86: a ram and a sheep are slaughtered in the sacrificial pit and burned; the fire is extinguished with wine and sea-water; the statue is then set up on the remains.

[20] *Hy. Merc.* 38 *ἢν δὲ θάνῃς τότε κεν μάλα καλὸν ἀείδοις*; Soph. *Ichn.* 281–93. On the tympanon see I.1.n.44 above. On the *νόμος πολυκέφαλος* see Pind. *Pyth.* 12.4–24. On Itylos see III.4 below. On the head of Orpheus see III.7 below. The death of the lyre-player—not just Orpheus but Linos as well—was a favorite theme in Greek art (Brommer [1960], 84–85); cf. Aegisthus with the lyre on the Boston Oresteia-crater: E. Vermeule, *AJA* 70 (1966), 5, pl. 4.

[21] Thus Agamemnon, when murdered, becomes an *ἀνὴρ θεῖος*: Aesch. *Ag.* 1547; and Rhesos becomes an *ἀνθρωποδαίμων*, Eur. *Rhes.* 962–73. Among the Hittites, "to become a god" is the normal expression for the death of the king: see Otten (1958) 119. The murder and deification of Caesar is historically the most significant example: see Burkert, *Historia* 11 (1962), 356–76; H. Gesche, *Die Vergottung Caesars* (1968), with A. Alföldi's review in *Phoenix* 24 (1970), 166–76.

Sacrifice transforms us. By going through the irreversible "act" we reach a new plane. Whenever a new step is taken consciously and irrevocably, it is inevitably connected with sacrifice. Thus, when crossing frontiers or rivers, there are the *διαβατήρια*;[22] when opening an assembly, there are strange purifications;[23] when passing into a new age group or on entering an exclusive society, there will be sacrifice.[24] Before the sacrifice there is a period of abstinence, and if, after it, new barriers are erected as a sort of reparation, their limits can give new definition to life. If it is followed by a predetermined *βίος*, or lifestyle, the sacrifice becomes an initiation. Those who have undergone the unspeakable are both exonerated and consecrated, as expressed in the Greek word *ὁσιωθείς*.[25] Thus, the new lifestyle and the sacrifice at its inception are almost complementary: omophagy is followed by vegetarianism. Killing justifies and affirms life; it makes us conscious of the new order and brings it to power.

Following Rudolf Otto,[26] students of religion have used the following concepts to describe the experience of the Holy: terror, bliss, and recognition of an absolute authority, *mysterium tremendum*, *fascinans*, and *augustum*. The most thrilling and impressive combination of these elements occurs in sacrificial ritual: the shock of the deadly blow and flowing blood, the bodily and spiritual rapture of festive eating, the strict order surrounding the whole process—these are the *sacra* par excellence, *τὰ ἱερά*.[27]Above all, the young must confront the

---

[22] *Il.* 11.726–30. For the special importance of these rituals for Spartans see Thuc. 5.54–55, 116; Pritchett (1979), 68–72. At the crossing of the Hellespont, Xerxes burned incense, poured libations, and sank valuable objects in the sea: Hdt. 7.54. Alexander made numerous sacrifices to the same end: Arr. *Anab.* 1.11.5–7.

[23] Demosth. 54.39 *τοὺς ὄρχεις τοὺς ἐκ τῶν χοιρίων, οἷς καθαίρουσι ὅταν εἰσιέναι μέλλωσιν. . . .* Cf. Harp. *καθάρσιον*; Schol. Aeschines 1.23; Schol. Aristoph. *Eccl.* 128.

[24] See n. 4 above; V.2 below.

[25] Eur. fr. 472.12–15 *τάς τ' ὠμοφάγους δαῖτας τελέσας μητρί τ' ὀρείῳ δᾷδας ἀνασχὼν καὶ κουρήτων βάκχος ἐκλήθην ὁσιωθείς*; cf. Wilamowitz, *Berliner Klassikertexte* V/2 (1907), 77, 1 (reading *μετὰ* instead of *καὶ*). J. Bernays, *Theophrastos' Schrift über Frömmigkeit* (1866), 160, thought *τελέσας* corrupt. On *ὅσιος* see Harrison (1922) 504; M. van der Valk, *Mnemos.* III/10 (1942), 113–40; *REG* 64 (1951), 418; H. Jeanmaire, *REG* 58 (1945), 66–89. On the Delphic *ὅσιοι* who were consecrated through a sacrifice performed by a *ὁσιωτήρ* see II.5.n.47 below. There was presumably a similar contrast between the egg tabu (Plut. *Q. conv.* 635e) and ritual egg-swallowing among the Orphics (Mart. Cap. 2.140; P. Boyancé, *Mél. d'Arch.* 52 [1935], 112; Burkert [1968], 104n.25).

[26] R. Otto, *Das Heilige* (1917; 1929[17–23]); thereafter G. Mensching, *Wesen und Ursprung der Religion: Die grossen nichtchristlichen Religionen* (1954), 11–22.

[27] See P. Weidkuhn, *Aggressivität Ritus Säkularisierung* (1965), 62: "Gipfelpunkt der Faszination . . . ist das Opfer seiner selbst. Gipfelpunkt des Tremendum . . . ist die Opferung des Nächsten."

Holy again and again so that the ancestral tradition will become their own.

Although we can understand the persistence of sacrificial ritual through its social function, this by no means excludes change as an explanation. Ritual is a pattern of action redirected to serve for communication, and this means that the terms of expression are open to substitution, i.e., symbolization—this occurs even in the insect world, when a resourceful male offers his bride a white balloon or veil instead of an edible wedding gift.[28] Every communication is symbolic inasmuch as it does not use the real object it wants to communicate, but substitutes a sign that is familiar to and, hence, understood by the addressee. The object serving as sign is exchangeable. If the sender and the receiver are sufficiently familiar with one another, the complex of signs can be greatly reduced. On the other hand, when in competition with rival communications, the sign is exaggerated and heightened. Substitute signs thus used—whether consisting of natural or artificial objects, pictures, cries, or words—may be called *symbols* in a pregnant sense. They are not chosen arbitrarily, but are taken from a continuous tradition; they are neither independent nor self-evident, but bound to the system in which they function. Their richness of meaning coincides with the complex effects they produce in predetermined interactions.[29]

In ritual aggression, the ends and the means of aggression are exchangeable. Even mammals tear up tufts of grass or shred tree bark when performing the threatening rituals that both introduce and postpone a fight.[30] The triumphant cries of the greylag goose are directed toward a purely imaginary interloper. In human ritual, too, the aggressive gesture can become so important that its object is unessential. The wildest form of destruction, that of tearing an object to pieces (*σπαραγμός*), can be carried out on an ivy plant,[31] and instead of a deadly club, a safe and flexible narthex stalk can be used.[32] Spiri-

[28] Lorenz (1963) 99–101.

[29] This is not far removed from the basic meaning of *σύμβολον* (on which see also W. Müri, "Symbolon," *Beil. z. Jahresbericht des Städt. Gymn. Bern* [1931]); the biological and traditional roots should not be lost sight of in the more sublimated use of the concept—see, for instance, P. Tillich, *Symbol und Wirklichkeit* (1962).

[30] Morris (1967) 153–55.

[31] Plut. *Q. Rom.* 291a *αἱ γὰρ ἔνοχοι τοῖς βακχικοῖς πάθεσι γυναῖκες εὐθὺς ἐπὶ τὸν κιττὸν φέρονται καὶ σπαράττουσι δραττόμεναι ταῖς χερσίν.*

[32] On the mock combat of the *ναρθηκοφόροι* see Xen. *Cyrop.* 2.3.17; Ath. 631a. In myth, the thyrsos becomes a terrifying weapon: see Eur. *Bacch.* 762.

tual forces thus find release in a harmless game which heightens the sense of social ordering by means of dramatization.

Yet the theatrical character of the ritual may become so obvious here that it imperils its necessary function. In groups shaped by aggression, especially in the younger generation, forces that question the acceptance of tradition become active. Willfulness stands in the way of the impulse to imitate. Thus, along with its theatricality, human ritual must always have a strong underlying component of seriousness, and this means that time and again there is a regression from symbolism to reality. A non-instinctive ritual, transmitted by human beings, can fulfill its communicatory function only if it avails itself of a pragmatism that is unquestionably real.

In the hunting ritual, aggression between men was redirected toward an animal quarry which was thereby raised to the status of a personality, a blood-relation, even a father.[33] It became the object of a "comedy of innocence," but because of the necessity of food, the hard underpinning of reality was never questioned. This all changed when mankind took its most important step, its mastery of the environment, in the Neolithic Revolution, the invention of agriculture, some 10,000 years ago.[34] Thereafter, hunting was basically dispensable. Characteristically, however, it was retained even in advanced cultures, as a ritual status symbol.[35] The pharaoh was celebrated as a

---

[33]See I.2.nn.33–35 above; I.8 below.

[34]Earlier cultural historians thought that an era of nomadic shepherds formed an intermediate stage between hunters and farmers, but this has been made dubious by prehistoric finds, especially the discovery of Near Eastern Neolithic sites. Nomads seem, rather, to be offshoots of farming and city culture—see Müller-Karpe (1968) 20–21. Likewise, there is no archaeological support for the position—still held by some, and usually argued in connection with the theory of a matrilineal system (cf. P. W. Schmidt, *Das Mutterrecht* [1955])—that the cultivation of bulbous plants must have preceded grain-growing; cf. Müller-Karpe (1968) II.21–22, 249, and P. J. Ucko and G. W. Dimbleby, eds., *The Domestication and Exploitation of Plants and Animals* (1969). In this respect, the outlines of a universal history such as A. v. Rüstow's *Ortsbestimmung der Gegenwart* I (1951) and A. Weber's *Kulturgeschichte als Kultursoziologie* (1935; 1950²) have been rendered obsolete.

G. Childe coined the term *Neolithic revolution* (*Man Makes Himself* [1936], ch. V), cf. S. Cole, *The Neolithic Revolution* (1959; 1963²). The term is, however, controversial: see R. Pittioni, *Propyläen-Weltgeschichte* I (1961), 229; Ucko and Dimbleby, *Domestication*.

[35]For Egypt see E. Hornung, *Geschichte als Fest* (1960), 15–17; E. Otto, *JNES* 9 (1950), 164–77; *SB Heidelberg* (1958), 1, 20–21. For Assyria/Persia see B. Meissner, "Assyrische Jagden," *Der Alte Orient* 13 2 (1911). For the reliefs of Assurbanipal see *ANEP* 626; for the animal parks (παράδεισοι) see Xen. *Anab.* 1.2.7, *Hell.* 4.1.15; on the sarcophagus of Alexander, etc., see F. Orth, *RE* IX (1914) 558–604; J. Aymard, *Essai sur les chasses romaines* (1951); K. Schauenburg, *Jagddarstellungen in der griechischen Vasenmalerei* (1969); generally, cf. J. Ortega y Gasset, *Über die Jagd* (1956); W. Frevert, *Das jagdliche Brauchtum* (1969¹⁰).

hunter, as were his counterparts in Babylon and Nineveh; the Persian kings maintained animal parks for hunting, and Alexander followed in their footsteps. Of course, it was no longer a question of catching one's dinner, but purely a demonstration of the ruler's power to kill. Thus, the most prestigious quarry was the beast of prey. Through this emphasis the sport remained pragmatic and serious. Herakles, the bearer of the club, was more popular as a lion-killer than as the tamer of the bull.

We find a transitional phase documented at Çatal Hüyük.[36] The most important religious symbol in this farming town where goat and sheep had long been domesticated was a pair of horns from the wild bull, and wall paintings contain clear, thrilling depictions of the ritual hunt of a band of leopard men. We can even trace the gradual extinction of wild cattle in Çatal Hüyük, though not the critical step that followed: in place of the dwindling bands of wild animals, domestic ones were now used for sacrifice. The power of the traditional ritual to bind thus remained intact. The animal must, of course, now be removed from the everyday world; it must become sacred. Hence the adornment and the procession, and, sometimes, the animal being set free and recaptured.[37] Hence, too, the many steps of "beginning," the incense and the music. In addition to the "action," which is no longer dangerous or even difficult, there are also words: prayers to the "stronger" powers and myths that tell of them. The reality of death and flowing blood is an unmitigated presence, perhaps all the more intense because the reaction is now inspired by a domestic animal, a familiar member of the household. The rapture attendant on eating game in the sacrificial meal is no less real now. Moreover, the domestic animal is a possession which must be given away;[38] thus, in addi-

---

[36] Cf. I.2.nn. 10, 19 above; Mellaart (1967) 268. On domestication see R. E. Zeuner in C. Singer, E. J. Holmyard, and A. R. Hall, *A History of Technology* I (1954), 327–52; F. E. Zeuner, *A History of Domesticated Animals* (1963), *Geschichte der Haustiere* (1967); Ucko and Dimbleby, *Domestication*. The oldest domestic animals are—apart from the special case of the dog—goats and sheep; shortly thereafter, the pig appears, followed in the seventh millennium by the cow. E. Hahn's thesis (*Die Haustiere* [1896], and cf. Ebert, *Reall. d. Vorgesch.* V 218) that the domestication of the cow occurred from the very start for sacral reasons, i.e., for sacrifice, has recently been resurrected: see E. Isaac, *Science* 137 (1962), 195–204; C. A. Reed in Ucko and Dimbleby, *Domestication*, 373. It remains an open question to what extent the ritual of human sacrifice had developed before animal-sacrifice. The evidence for ritual sacrifice of men in the Palaeolithic age is overwhelming: see I.2.n.27 above.

[37] See I.2.n.21 above.

[38] In this way, ceremonies of bartering and buying developed. On Cos, the owner presents the sacrificial bull for Zeus Polieus "to the Coans," and Hestia, i.e., the coffers of the state, gets the proceeds of the sale; see *LGS* I 5 = *SIG*³ 1025 = *LS* 151 A 23–27.

tion to the old fundamental ambivalence of life and death in the sacrifice, there is now also renunciation and gratification. Even more than before, a sacred order is presumed and confirmed in this critical situation. In any case, with the integration of animal-sacrifice into agricultural society, a very stable socio-religious structure was established, which was to survive many thousands of years.

No less important was the expanded symbolism brought about by the newfound sources of food from farming—barley, wheat, the fruit of the vine—and added to the themes of ritual killing. The ritual pattern was so strong and inflexible that a festival meal without the preliminary horror of death would have been no festival at all. The farmer had to be just as reliable, enduring, and farsighted as the hunter. In particular, it was no mean task to overcome the inclination to eat the seed grain rather than throw it on the ground in the mere hope that something would grow. Here, too, the individual's desire for immediate profit could be controlled by the sacred tradition of the hunting ritual, which established the old order in a new context: renunciation and abstinence for the sake of long-range success, and with it a new order. Thus, the harvest is celebrated in a hunting festival and in sacrifice.[39] Gathering and storing at the sacred place now took on a new reality. Most importantly, the seed grain could not be touched as long as it was stored in sacred granaries, those mysterious, half-buried depositories of wealth.[40] At the same time, aggres-

---

"Shepherds today in Crete will dedicate one of their animals to the village saint, selling it by auction on the Saint's Day to give the proceeds to the saint's church": S. G. Spanakis, *Crete, a Guide to Travel, History and Archeology*, Iraklion (n.d.) 291. Those who sacrifice a goat on the island of Leuke must deposit the buying price in the temple of Achilles: Arr. *Perip.* 22, and cf. n. 16 above.

[39] The researches of Wilhelm Mannhardt (*Roggenwolf und Roggenhund* [1865]; *Die Korndämonen* [1868]; *Wald- und Feldkulte* [1875/77]; thereafter *GB* VII/VIII), who developed the idea of the "Vegetationsdämon," are basic. The fact that it is precisely the "Vegetationsdämon" who is killed time and again in the ritual has been explained in various ways: the drowning is weather-magic for rain ([1875] 214, 417), the immolation is a purification (607–608), the burying is intended for sowing and germination (419–21), the whole process stimulates the annual cycle of the death and rebirth of vegetation. Indeed, in this case the rite cannot be derived from any attested or hypothetical mythology (I.3–4 above). The sacrificial rites are a given: no matter how great the hopes for increase and harvest are, the ritual can give form only to death and destruction.

[40] For sacred circular structures functioning as granaries ever since Arpachija see Müller-Karpe (1968) 336. The myth of Trophonios and Agamedes (*Telegony*, p. 109 Allen; Charax, *FGrHist* 103 F 5; Egyptianized in the story of Rhampsinit's treasure house, Hdt. 2.121) deals with such a ϑησαυρός which can be opened only "secretly," accompanied by sacrifice. Cf. the underground ϑησαυρός at Messene: Plut. *Philop.* 19; Livy 39.50.3 (following Polybius).

sion had to look for new objects. Consequently, farming implements assumed the character of weapons. After all, a plow, a sickle, and a pestle were all used for chopping, cutting, and tearing apart. Cutting the wheat could thus become a symbolic substitute for castration; grinding the grain and pressing the wine could take the place of tearing up an animal in the hunt or sacrifice. Plowing and sowing could be seen as preliminary sacrificial renunciations.[41]

We have already shown how, in hunting ritual, death gives way to a new order of life. In agriculture, the victory of life can be felt with even greater immediacy. The vine that has been pruned will bear all the more fruit; the grain that was buried in the earth sends up new shoots toward the light. The sacrificial ritual's power to bind is preserved on this level as well. Contracts are sealed with libations of wine (*σπονδαί*), and weddings are celebrated by cutting up cake or bread; cutting or breaking must still precede eating,[42] just as slaughtering precedes the eating of meat. The symbolism could easily become detached were it not for a counterforce guiding it back to the frightening reality. This occurs first of all in the myth, for the most gruesome tales of living creatures torn apart and of cannibalism are presented in conjunction with the achievements of civilized life. But the myth is not enough. Blood-sacrifice must be made at the harvest festival and at the preparations for it. Here the savagery beneath the seemingly civilized exterior is exorcized. In Greece, as far back as we can see, the victims were animal. But in the tropics, the very regions that had more favorable climates, the planters regressed to regular human sacrifice, to cultic cannibalism. Only in this way, it was said, could the seed grow and the fruit ripen.[43] Civilized life endures only by giving a ritual form to the brute force that still lurks in men.

---

[41] See IV and V below.

[42] Of course, apportioning presupposes a division, and it is precisely the latter act that is emphasized: taking/praying/breaking (I Cor. 11:24). Among the Hittites, breaking bread is one of the most common sacrificial ceremonies (*ANET* 345–51, 360–61); at an Attic wedding, the groom cuts (*κόψαι*) a sesame cake (Aristoph. *Pax* 869 with Schol. = Men. fr. 910) and divides it up (Men. *Sam.* 74, 125, 190; Phot. *σήσαμον*). On the *confarreatio* see V, 3 below.

[43] Polynesian myths, especially the myth of Hainuwele from West-Ceram, about a being that was killed and out of which grew edible plants, "Dema," made a great impression: J. van Baal, *Dema: Description and Analysis of Marind Anim Culture* (1966); A. E. Jensen, *Hainuwele* (1939); *Das religiöse Weltbild einer frühen Kultur* (1948) = *Die getötete Gottheit. Weltbild einer frühen Kultur* (1966); C. G. Jung and K. Kerényi, *Einführung in das Wesen der Mythologie* (1941), 183–90. As applied to ancient myths and rituals, see A. Brelich, "Quirinus," *SMSR* 31 (1960), 63–119, followed by I. Chirassi, *Elementi di culture precereali nei miti e riti Greci* (Rome, 1969). The notion that this represents a pre-agricultural

Thus, aggression is once again directed toward human beings. Although the male societies that had been superimposed on the family structure lost their ostensible function when the hunt was abandoned, they were reestablished among planters as secret, or mask, societies.[44] At the center was a secret sacrifice, and if the aggression there did not suffice, it was worked out within the society itself. The contrast between the sexes was now played up—*Männerbund* versus female power—the more so because women now shouldered the main burden, supporting the family according to the new agricultural method. Likewise, the conflict between the generations became highly dramatized in the initiation rituals. Deprived of its hunting quarry, the secret society makes the initiand himself into a victim.[45] The group's aggression becomes focused on this man and he is forthwith killed—symbolically, of course; a sacrificial animal is substituted at the last minute. However, the bloodshed and the refined methods of torture are very real and guarantee the seriousness of the ritual. The gruesome "evil" at work in the ritual fulfills a function, i.e., to preserve a social structure over the course of generations. Once again, life rises up from the peril of death. Indeed, the individual experiences in himself how, after life had been endangered, there is a resurrection, a rebirth.

To some extent, this too was still a game, a show. With the progressive growth of consciousness, civilization came to demand absolute seriousness—one could no longer *pretend* to kill men. For this reason the death penalty became the strongest expression of governmental power,[46] and, as has often been shown, the criminal's execu-

---

stage has, however, been superseded through the excavations at Jericho and Jarmo: see n. 34 above.

[44] H. Schurtz, *Altersklassen und Männerbunde* (1902); H. Webster, *Primitive Secret Societies* (1908); Höfler (1934); W. E. Peuckert, *Geheimkulte* (1961).

[45] Aristoph. *Nub.* 257, and cf. V.3.n.16 below; Livy 10.38.9 *admovebatur altaribus magis ut victima quam ut sacri particeps* at the initiation into the *legio linteata* of the Samnites. On initiation rites generally see M. Eliade, *Birth and Rebirth* (1958).

[46] On the ancient evidence see K. Latte, *RE* Suppl. VII 1599–1619; on its sacrificial character see Th. Mommsen, *Römisches Strafrecht* (1899), 900–904, 918; for an opposing view see Latte, *RE* Suppl. VII 1614–17; K. v. Amira, "Die germanischen Todesstrafen," *Abh. München* 31/3 (1922); L. Weiser-Aall, *ARW* 30 (1933), 209–27; Guépin (1968) 84. A traitor dies, according to the "law of Romulus," ὡς θῦμα τοῦ καταχθονίου Διός, Dion. Hal. *Ant.* 2.10.3.

There are clear elements of a comedy of innocence in the "last meal" before an execution and in the expectation of goodwill; cf. also the executioner's mask. For the use of criminals in sacrificial ritual on Leukas, see Strabo 10 p. 452; on Rhodes (Kronia), Porph. *Abst.* 2.54; on Massalia, Petron. fr. 1 Buecheler; Schol. Stat. *Theb.* 10.793; on the Druids, Caes. *BGall.* 6.16.

tion at a public festival corresponded to a sacrificial ritual. In ancient times, the death penalty was not so much aimed at profane murderers as at those who entered an "untouchable" sacred precinct, went into a house of the mysteries unconsecrated, or laid a branch upon the wrong altar.[47] The tabu almost became an excuse to find a victim for releasing the sacred impulses of aggression.

There is another, far more serious, way to divert aggression toward the outside world: by integrating large groups of men in a common fighting spirit, i.e., war.[48] History, as far back as we can trace it, is the history of conquests and wars. Ever since Thucydides, historians have tried to understand the necessity of these events and, if possible, make them predictable. But it is precisely the irrational, compulsive character of this behavior mechanism that confronts us more clearly today than ever before. War is ritual, a self-portrayal and self-affirmation of male society. Male society finds stability in confronting death, in defying it through a display of readiness to die, and in the ecstasy of survival. Such modes of behavior are so bound up with the governmental systems and values of our society that even today, when modern military technology has made war so distant that its absurdity is patent, when it is beginning to be the source of discord rather than of solidarity, still final emancipation from war lies far in the future.

For the ancient world, hunting, sacrifice, and war were symbolically interchangeable. The pharaoh and Herakles could be lord of the hunt, lord of the sacrifice, and warrior. On grave reliefs, Greek youths appear as hunters, warriors, or athletes. The emphasis may well have varied according to the social reality. A farmer, for instance,

---

[47] On the Lykaion precinct see II.1.n.7 below; on Eleusis see Livy 31.14, and V.1 below; Kallias the Daduchos claimed that it was *νόμος . . . πάτριος, ὃς ἂν θῇ ἱκετηρίαν μυστηρίοις, τεθνάναι* (cf. V.4.n.45 below), Andoc. 1.110–16.

[48] A "World History of War" such as L. Frobenius (1903) attempted could hardly be accomplished today. On the earliest evidence, that of Palaeolithic (?) drawings in Spain, see F. Cornelius, *Geistesgeschichte der Frühzeit* I (1960), 54, pl. 3. Today there are an enormous number of sociological and psychological studies on the problem of war: for instance, B. L. Richardson, *Arms and Insecurity: The Causes of War* (1960); G. Bouthoul, *Les guerres* (1951). K. R. Eissler, *Psyche* 22 (1968), 645, among others, stated that war is "the revenge of the elder generation on the younger." On Greece, see J. P. Vernant, ed., *Problèmes de la guerre en Grèce ancienne* (1968); on the distancing of modern historians from Thucydides see A. Momigliano, "Some Observations on the Causes of War in Ancient Historiography," in *Studies in Historiography* (1966), 112–26. On the cultic aspects see F. Schwenn, *ARW* 20 (1921), 299–322; 21 (1922), 58–71; 22 (1923/24) 224–44; and A. Brelich, *Guerre, agoni e culti nella Grecia arcaica* (1961). For the Hebrew term *to consecrate war* = to begin war, see W. R. Smith (1899) 122–23. On ceremonial war in Egypt and among the Aztecs see E. Hornung, *Geschichte als Fest* (1966).

would put more weight on sacrificial ritual, whereas the nomadic animal breeder, wary of slaughtering his proud possessions, would become a conquering warrior.

Among the Greeks, a military expedition was prepared and ended by sacrificial ritual. There was sacrifice before setting off, then adornment and crowning with wreaths before battle—all as if it were a festival. A slaughtered victim introduced the subsequent deadly action which, in Homer, is simply called *ἔργον*. Afterward, a monument, a tropaion, was set up on the battlefield as a consecrated, enduring witness. This was followed by the solemn burial of the dead, a privilege the victor could not deny his defeated enemy. The burial, almost as important as the battle itself, was far more lasting in its consequences, for it left an enduring "monument." It almost seems as though the aim of war is to gather dead warriors, just as the Aztecs waged war in order to take prisoners to use as sacrificial victims.[49] The erected and consecrated monument is what endures, and it embodies the duty of the following generation. For war, necessary yet controlled because it is ritual, has this function above all: it must integrate the young into the patriotic community. The *senatus* resolves; the *iuventus* must fight. As a rule, the Greeks' *σπονδαί* were for a period of thirty years at most. Each generation has the right and the obligation to have its war.

6. *Funerary Ritual*

It is a peculiarity of the human race that it cares for its dead. Hence, burials have been among the most important finds from prehistory. Along with the use of fire and tools, they testify to the process, starting in the early Palaeolithic era, by which man became man. Frequent attempts have been made to describe the extraordinary spiritual and intellectual step underlying this process, sometimes even

[49] See I.7 below. On decoration see Hdt. 7.208–209; Plut. *Lac. inst.* 238 f.; on the *σφάγια* see Stengel (1910) 92–102, (1920) 132–33; Casabona (1966) 180–93; Pritchett (1979) 83–90; *ἔργον* *Il.* 4.470, etc.; on burial see Thuc. 2.34. On human sacrifice among the Aztecs see Hornung, *Geschichte*, 43. For the metaphor of sacrifice applied to war see, for instance, Pind. fr. 78. On the Delphic oracle for king Philip see Parke and Wormell (1956) #266 = Diod. 16.91; Paus. 8.7.6.

to interpret it as a first move toward a metaphysical, transcendent realm.[1] It is somewhat more certain that we are dealing with a human action which may vary from culture to culture but within a single community proceeds according to the same scheme with great constancy over many generations. Behind every burial there is a funerary ritual.[2]

However, the Palaeolithic era, in which burial evolved, was also the age of hunting. Thus, the ritual of hunting and sacrificing accompanied the funerary ritual from the start, each influencing the other. In prehistory and ethnology it generally holds true that dead men and dead animals are treated alike:[3] both rituals basically deal with death. It makes little difference whether one says that the quarry is treated like a dead man or whether a dead man is treated like the sacrificial quarry. Homo sapiens is also homo necans and homo sepeliens. Both rituals are, of course, complex, and one can hardly hope to discover the origins of each detail. Nevertheless we can observe that essential elements of funerary ritual derive from the ritual of hunting and sacrificing, inasmuch as the necessary functions deal with hunting rather than with the death of a member.[4] Did man come to understand death through the paradox of killing?[5] One's own death always seems far

---

[1] Müller-Karpe (1966) 229 speaks of a "metaphysischen Dimension." The Pavianes do not acknowledge death: see G. Devereux, *Symb. Oslo* 42 (1967), 85, 4.

[2] We can here give only a brief indication of the enormous complex of funerary rites. On prehistory see Maringer (1956) passim; Müller-Karpe (1966) 229–42, (1968) 348–71. For Greece see Rohde (1898) 216–58; Nilsson (1955) 174–99, 374–84; A. Chudzinski, *Tod und Totenkultus bei den alten Griechen* (1907); J. Wiesner, *Grab und Jenseits* (1938); M. Andronikos, "Totenkult," in *Archeologia Homerica* W (1968); J. Pini, *Beiträge zur minoischen Gräberkunde* (1968); A. Schnaufer, *Frühgriechischer Totenglaube* (1970); on cremation see n. 17 below. On the particularly complex problem of how belief and ritual are related in funerary custom see R. Moss, *The Life after Death in Oceania and the Malay Archipelago* (1925), who concludes that the two coexist largely without being related, but that ritual will sooner influence belief than vice versa. K. Meuli's "Entstehung und Sinn der Trauersitten," *Schweiz. Archiv f. Volkskunde* 43 (1946), 91–109, is also of fundamental importance.

[3] Meuli (1967) 160 on tree-burial; no less remarkable is the similar bone-interment, using red ochre, and the special treatment of the skull. See also H. Baumann, *Paideuma* 4 (1950), 198, 200.

[4] See Müller-Karpe (1968) 367 on cremation; in general, Girard (1972) 352–55. Baudy (1980) 102 stresses that in the wild, dead bodies are eaten by scavengers. Hence the fantasies of how the dead are eaten in the underworld, by Eurynome in Paus. 19.28.7; and by Hecate in a vase-painting, Vermeule (1979) 109. Modern hunters have the "great Halali" sounded at the burial of a hunter as at the end of a hunt: W. Frevert, *Das jagdliche Brauchtum* (1969[10]), 76.

[5] See B. M. F. Galdikas, *National Geographic* 157 (1980), 832, on an adolescent orangutan,

off and uncertain. But, when another dies, the frightening confrontation with death and the pleasurable shock of survival leave a deep impression.

The most widespread element in funerals—so obvious it may seem hardly worth mentioning—is the role played by eating, i.e., the funerary meal. Ethnology and religious studies have dwelt mainly on the bizarre and more or less unsuccessful attempts to feed the dead themselves, but it is more often the real and festive meal of the living "in honor of" the dead that is of primary importance. Thus, even while mourning the death of Patroklos, Achilles permits his companions to "feast the heart-pleasing burial."[6] This unabashed statement refers to behavior that is offensive to anyone concerned merely with the dead individual, yet has not been expunged to this day, namely, that in an environment of grief, pain, and tears, the pleasure of the festive meal will thrive. At first the necessary combination of death and eating appeared only in the hunt. Starting here, the ritual meal functioned as a bond within the community.[7] This is not to say that cannibalism was the earliest form of honoring the dead.[8] The ritualization of hunting behavior made possible a twofold transferral: the dead could take the place of the quarry—a substitute more serious than what it replaces—but in the subsequent feast, his place could in turn be taken by the sacrificial animal.[9]

Sugito, who drowned his younger foster-sister, Doe: "Sugito . . . was staring off into space with a funny look that I had never seen before. He studiously avoided looking into Doe's direction. After some time . . . he slowly approached. Then, standing on two legs, he raised both arms over his head and brought them down, fluttering, in front of him . . . [like] a shaman . . . performing rituals of obsequiousness to his god. . . . Sugito . . . knew perfectly well that Doe was dead. He had killed her." On intraspecific killing with gorillas, see D. Fossey, *National Geographic* 159 (1981), 508–512.

[6] *Il.* 23.29, and cf. 24.801–804; *Od.* 3.309. For eating at the tomb in Geometric times see J. Boardman, *JHS* 86 (1966), 2–4; cf. M. Murko, "Das Grab als Tisch," *Wörter und Sachen* 2 (1910), 79–160. Gregory of Nazianzus rails against eating and drinking in churches at the tombs of the martyrs: *AP* 8.166–69, 172, 175. After the burial, people met for the festive meal of the *τρίτα, ἔνατα, τριακάς, ἐνιαύσια*: *An. Bekk.* 268.19 *τῇ τριακοστῇ γὰρ ἡμέρᾳ . . . οἱ προσήκοντες ἅπαντες . . . συνελθόντες κοινῇ ἐδείπνουν ἐπὶ τῷ ἀποθανόντι. καὶ τοῦτο καθέδρα ἐκαλεῖτο.*

[7] Besides this there is the psychological explanation that the sense of loss is compensated for, in a form of oral regression, by eating. This sense of loss could, however, manifest itself just as well through fasting; it is the ritual constraint that causes Niobe to eat after ten days: *Il.* 24.602–13.

[8] Allegedly the custom among the Massagetai; see Hdt. 1.216, *Dissoi Logoi* 2.14.

[9] S. Freud, *Totem und Tabu*, *Ges. Schr.* 10 (1924), 66–88 = *Ges. Werke* 9 (1940), 66–88, developed the idea of the ambivalence between love and aggression in relationship to the dead man.

The funerary meal for Patroklos shows very clearly that although feasting follows death, the death must be repeated immediately before the feast, through ritual killing. After the mourners circled the corpse three times while crying out in grief and swearing vengeance, many cows, sheep, goats, and pigs were slaughtered and "blood poured from the cups flowed all around the dead man." [10] The corpse could hardly be placed more emphatically at the center of a bloody act which, however, at the same time also signals a pleasing meal for 10,000 Myrmidons. So too in Athens it was customary to eat at the grave; Solon was the first to forbid that cows be slaughtered there.[11] There was no thought of burning or burying such a cow whole, for the meat belonged to the living, while the dead man "took his fill" of the blood. The idea that the dead delight in blood obviously emanates from the reality of the ritual: the pattern of hunting calls for the bloody "act" at the place of death. Because death becomes killing, and the participant, a killer,[12] death itself becomes an act of the will, subject to performance and repetition. For this very reason it can be overcome through the festive meal, which confirms the survivor's will to live.

The sacrificial analogies extend to the actions that precede and follow as well. There is a period of preparation, in which the corpse lies in state and is washed and adorned; a procession marks the transition from indoors to out. This is then followed by wild, ecstatic behavior, bloodshed, and a hearty meal.[13] The location in which the action takes place remains sacred forever after—distinguished by a monument as the realm of the extraordinary—whereas at home, the ordinary order is restored.

The most striking resemblances between hunting and funerary customs can be seen in the treatment of the bones. The funeral cere-

---

[10] *Il.* 23.34. For funerary sacrifice already in the Moustérien see Müller-Karpe (1966) 231–33. For horse-sacrifice in, and bull-sacrifice at, the royal tomb at Archanes (Crete), see *Archaeology* 20 (1967), 278–79.

[11] Plut. *Solon* 21.5; A. Martina, *Solone* (1968), #465–70; and cf. n. 6 above. For *αἱμακουρία* see II.2 below.

[12] The central act in the great funerary festival of the Dajak on Borneo (Tiwah) is the killing of a buffalo—in earlier times, it was a man—whom each participant had to stab with a spear: F. Grabowsky, *Internat. Archiv f. Ethnographie* 2 (1899), 199; H. Schärer, *Der Totenkult der Ngadju Dajak in Süd-Borneo* I (1966), 20.

[13] A somewhat different, though no less characteristic, sequence is noted by Herodotus among the Thracians (5.8): *τρεῖς μὲν ἡμέρας προτιθεῖσι τὸν νεκρὸν καὶ παντοῖα σφάξαντες ἱερήια εὐωχέονται προκλαύσαντες πρῶτον. ἔπειτα δὲ θάπτουσι κατακαύσαντες ἢ ἄλλως γῇ κρύψαντες, χῶμα δὲ χέαντες ἀγῶνα τιθεῖσι.* On the agon see n. 23 below.

mony often centers not so much on the corpse as on the bones from individual limbs. These are collected and solemnly deposited. The rhythm of the hunting ritual is, thus, repeated: death/tearing apart/restoration. In Çatal Hüyük, as among the Parsees, bodies were set out for scavenging birds, after which the bones were carefully deposited in household shrines at the feet of the Great Goddess.[14] Often a corpse was intentionally torn apart, only to be put back together again. In Egypt, the roots of the mummification ritual are much the same.[15] It was a widespread custom during the Neolithic to sever the head and preserve it in a sanctuary, like a Bukranion; head and thighbones are buried separately at Ugarit.[16] Until modern times, ruling houses of Europe used to bury certain parts of their dead in different sacred places. With the development of artisan skills, it became possible to substitute a symbol for the skull: the Roman *lararium*, for instance, preserved only the masks of the ancestors.

Among the Greeks and Romans, even cremation[17] was used for the avowed purpose of obtaining the bones quickly. The most sacred duty for the next-of-kin is to gather the bones (*ὀστολογεῖν; ossa legere*) from the ashes of the pyre. The fire that burns the corpse is described as a beast of prey, "tearing apart" the dead man with "a furious jaw."[18] The remains are then united forever in an urn. This act is at once a joining together and a foundation, as in the Latin word *condere*. When, as early as Homer's description of the death of Achilles, we find the wine jar of Dionysos serving as an urn,[19] it is merely the transforma-

---

[14]Mellaart (1967) 241–45.

[15]A. Hermann, "Zergliedern und Zusammenfügen," *Numen* 3 (1956), 81–96.

[16]On burying the skull see Maringer (1956) 67–70, 78–86, 122–28, 220–22; Müller-Karpe (1966) 231–34, 239–40; (1968) 365–66. The skulls from pre-ceramic Jericho that have been formed into portraits are particularly impressive: see *Arch. f. Orientforsch.* 16 (1953), 384; Müller-Karpe (1968) 349. On skull-burial at Archanes (Crete) see *Archaeology* 20 (1967) 276–77; cf. Hdt. 4.26 on the Issedonians. For Ugarit see H. Th. Bossert, *Altsyrien* (1951), on nr. 354.

[17]For post-Mycenaean cremation in Greece, see Müller-Karpe (1968) 351, 366–67; G. Mylonas, *AJA* 52 (1948), 56–81; V. R. d'A. Desborough, *The Last Mycenaeans and Their Successors* (1964^2), 71; Schnaufer, *Totenglaube*, 36–45. Cremation is found among the Hittites, Hurrians, Troy VI, etc., by the second millennium: see Otten (1958) 5; U. Schlenther, *Brandbestattung und Seelenglaube* (1960); Pini, *Beiträge*, 19–21, 58–62.

[18]*Δάπτειν Il.* 23.183; *πυρὸς μαλερὰ γνάθος* Aesch. *Cho.* 325. *'Οστέα λέγειν* already in *Il.* 23.239, 252; *συνθείς* Eur. *Hik.* 1126. According to Andron of Halikarnassos, *FGrHist* 10 F 10 = Schol. A *Il.* 1.52, Herakles at Troy was the first to use cremation, burning the body of the dead Argeios so as to be able to carry "him" back to his father: see *Il.* 7.334–35 (contradicted in Schol. A *ad loc.*); Thuc. 2.34.

[19]*Od.* 24.73–75. Cf. the Dionysiac bronze-crater from Derveni, which served as an urn:

tion of sacrificial ritual into that of the plant realm. The produce gathered by the farmer replaces the hunter's quarry; thus, gathering bones acquires new meaning.

There are, of course, aspects of funerary ritual that cannot be traced to the hunt. It is then all the more characteristic that these elements have frequently been taken up in the sacrificial ritual. Above all, lamentation[20]—weeping and wailing, tearing one's clothes and hair, scratching the face and beating the breast; then defiling oneself, *μιαίνεσθαι*—smearing one's face, strewing one's head with clay, dirt, and ashes. The large part that aggression plays in these rites is evident.[21] It is an inevitable group reflex to offer to protect an endangered member against a hostile force by means of aggressive threats. When faced with the fact of death, this reflex aggression strikes out into a vacuum and hence returns in upon itself. With no enemy near, the hand raised to strike comes down upon one's own head.

Men, of course, often seek some external substitute as the butt of their rage: hence those funerary sacrifices that are and intend to be merely destructive. When a Hittite king died, for example, a plow ox was sacrificed while the king was invoked: "What you have become, this too shall become."[22] Achilles slaughters countless sacrificial animals, four horses, nine dogs, and twelve Trojans at the bier of Patroklos. Once again, death is mastered when the mourner becomes a killer. For this reason there is often no clear-cut distinction between merely destructive sacrifice and the sacrifice of the funerary meal (cf. n. 13).

Unbounded rage can be vented in a life-affirming form through fighting, through an agon. Karl Meuli demonstrated the extent and inner necessity of the connection between funerals and competitive contests:[23] it remains to say that an agon can accompany not only a

---

BCH 87 (1963), 802, pl. XVI–XX. Bones (unburnt) had been deposited in clay vessels already at Neolithic Lerna: see Müller-Karpe (1968) 365.

[20] E. Reiner, *Die rituelle Totenklage der Griechen* (1938); E. de Martino, *Morte e pianto rituale nel mondo antico* (Turin, 1958). On *μιαίνεσθαι* see, for instance, the law at Iulis (Keos), *SIG*[3] 1218 = *LS* 97, 24–31; Hdt. 6.58.1.

[21] On destructive rage in funerary customs see Meuli (1946) 201–207; *Antike* 17 (1941), 193–97; *Schweiz. Archiv f. Volkskunde* 43 (1946), 106–108.

[22] Otten (1958) 19; *Il.* 23.166–76, and cf. *Od.* 24.65–66. On bloody sacrifice at the interment and "opening of the mouth" in Egypt, see A. Wiedemann, *ARW* 22 (1923/24), 72–86.

[23] "Der Ursprung der Olympischen Spiele," *Antike* 17 (1941), 189–208; *Der griechische Agon: Kampf und Kampfspiel im Totenbrauch, Totentanz, Totenklage und Totenlob* (1968; orig. Habilitationsschrift Basel, 1926).

deposition ceremony for human bones but animal sacrifice as well. The Greek agon of historical times was a sacrificial festival. In Rome, the ancient sacrifice of the October-Horse was followed by a ritual battle between two groups. Similarly, the Macedonians would pretend to fight a battle after the dog-sacrifice at their Festival of Purification, the Xandika.[24] Myth applies the same pattern to the hunt, raising it to tragic seriousness in the story of the war between the Aetolians and the Curetes after the Calydonian Boarhunt.[25] Here, too, as soon as the quarry was killed, the warriors' accumulated energy struck into a vacuum; moreover, their bad conscience made them willing to suffer for their "action."

Even more prominent in funerary ritual than in sacrifice is the willingness to assume and recognize a pattern of renunciation after the fact. This willingness is primarily shown by offering food in the form of libations, *χοαί*. Milk, honey, oil, and wine, the precious commodities of a society familiar with dearth and hunger, were poured away irretrievably; similarly, grain was mashed into pap so it could drain into the ground. In southern regions, even water is a precious commodity and hence played a part in some libations. Like the sacrificial ritual, libation would have occurred outside the confines of everyday reality. There would have been a procession, then the restrained attitude of prayer, and finally the ecstatic cry (ὀλολυγή) at the moment of the libation.[26] No other act of destruction can be expressed by gestures so noble and sublime: Achilles pouring wine for his dead friend Patroklos, an unforgettable poetical image.[27] The artfully shaped libation vessels stress the grandeur of the proceedings. By renouncing personal profit, man can uplift himself; by humbling himself in spite

[24] On Olympia see II.2 below; on the Isthmia see III.7 below; on the October-Horse see Latte (1960) 119–21; U. W. Scholz, *Studien zum altitalischen und altrömischen Marsmythos* (1970); on the fight for the head see Festus 190 L. On the Xandika see Nilsson (1907) 404–406, who correctly compares the Platanistas-fight of the Spartan ephebes (406–407), which also occurred in connection with a dog-sacrifice (Paus. 3.20.8, 14.8–10).

[25] "For the head and the tufted hide of the boar," *Il.* 9.548; Apollod. 1.70–71; etc. H. Usener, the first to collect the ancient evidence for ritual combat (*ARW* 7 [1904], 297–313 = *Kl. Schr.* IV [1913], 435–47), saw in it a fight between Winter and Summer; objections already in Nilsson (1906) 413–14. The mock-battle among the Hittites (H. Ehelolf, *SB Berlin* [1925], 269–70; A. Lesky, *Ges. Schr.* [1966], 310–17) occurs in the context of a sacrifice, which, however, was not discussed by the editor.

[26] Aesch. *Cho.* 22–163, esp. 149 ff.; *Pers.* 610–18; for additional evidence see Stengel (1910) 178–86, (1920) 103–105; Casabona (1966) 231–97.

[27] Homer *Il.* 23.218–20; "Giesse, Myrmidone, den funkelnden Wein ins Land," Gottfried Benn, *Ges. Werke* I (1960), 129. See also Lucr. 3.434 f.

of his needs, he displays his wealth or at least his freedom. Alexander the Great acted in this way in the Gedrosian desert when he emptied into the sand a helmet filled with water.[28]

Here, the social significance of renunciation ritual and, for that matter, funerary ritual altogether, is clear. By keeping a space empty artificially, one can prevent grasping, greedy, aggressive individuals from clashing, or at least pretend to do so. The pleasure of inheriting possessions has to be masked and at least part of the dead man's property renounced. By playing out the breakdown of the social order, even in the easily neutralized act of self-defilement, that very order can be gotten under control. Such actions preserve the basic structure of society, because death is not perceived as an ending. Now, human culture needs continuity: to be able to go on, there has to be an authority recognized through the course of generations. Man's neoteny, the long period of time he spends in the process of learning, forged a new relationship between young and old, above all between son and father, in which the catastrophe of death became especially disturbing and dangerous. And the very elements that funerals took over from hunting and sacrificial ritual were the ones able to mend the rift, transforming death into killing, celebration into an eruption of aggression followed by reparation. In this way, there arose a posthumous duty toward the dead. A swing of the pendulum transformed symbolic parricide into an obligation to worship one's ancestors. Thus, fathers, chiefs, and kings have the most magnificent funerals; and a pile of stones, the monument left by collective stoning, will grow until it becomes a pyramid.[29]

Funerary ritual alone may almost be enough to confirm and insure continuity in the community. Indeed, among some peoples all else pales by comparison. Among the Greeks, rulers characteristically expected their vassals to participate in funerals as a sign of loyalty; the Spartans demanded it of the Messenians, the Corinthians of the Megarians.[30] But a funeral is dependent on circumstance and chance, whereas ritual requires repetition and regularity. Thus, funerary ritual can be repeated through funerary sacrifice. The act of killing re-

[28] Arr. *Anab.* 6.26 . . . *ὥστε εἰκάσαι ἄν τινα ποτὸν γενέσθαι πᾶσιν ἐκεῖνο τὸ ὕδωρ τὸ πρὸς Ἀλεξάνδρου ἐκχυθέν.*

[29] Among the Kabylai, a great hunter is buried beneath a pile of rocks, upon which new rocks are always thrown: see H. Baumann, *Paideuma* 4 (1950), 192; and cf. Plat. *Leg.* 873b; B. Schmidt, *NJb* 39 (1893), 369–95; Baudy (1980) 148f.

[30] Tyrtaios fr. 5.4 Diehl = Prato; Schol. Pind. *Nem.* 7.155b = Demon, *FGrHist* 327 F 19; Hippias of Erythrai, *FGrHist* 421 F 1.

establishes the context of death;[31] the dead man becomes the focus of attention once again, and thus his power is recognized and renewed. Inversely, the Greeks set a funerary monument at almost every place of sacrifice, a tomb that may or may not have been real: the hero had, then, his place at sacrifice beside the recipient god, the sacrificial pit beside the altar, the chthonic aspect beside the Olympian.[32] We see here how deeply sacrificial and funerary ritual permeated one another. By joining together to honor the dead, the survivors, and especially the young, would have been initiated, integrated into the continuity of the society, and educated in the tradition all at once. The rituals of sacrifice, funeral, and initiation are so closely related that they can be interpreted through the same myths and may even partially overlap. The myth tells of death and destruction, while in sacrifice an animal is killed. By encountering death as symbolized in word and ritual, succeeding generations are molded into successors. In this way society is consolidated and renewed.

Plutarch provides us with the most detailed description of a funerary sacrifice in Greece.[33] It concerns those who died at Plataea. The cult was active till the end of antiquity, and Plutarch was obviously an eyewitness: just before dawn, a procession was formed leading from the center of town to the outside, from the marketplace to the cemetery. The atmosphere was aggressive and warlike; a trumpeter gave the signal for war. But the wagons were loaded with myrtle branches and wreaths; a black bull trotted along in the middle of the procession. The young men carried amphoras with wine and milk, jugs of oil and salves. The archon of the city brought up the rear. As head of the civil authorities, he would normally have been forbidden to carry weapons and would always have worn white robes. But on the day of the sacrifice he was dressed in a purple mantle and was carrying a sword in his belt. Something extraordinary had replaced the everyday order, and bloodshed was imminent. The archon himself brought a water jug from the Bouleuterion. Thus, the procession

---

[31] Just as "blood is purified through blood," so funerary sacrifice (with an agon) counts as expiation for killing: Hdt. 1.166–67. Clytaemnestra alone celebrates the Day of Death in open triumph, with sacrifices (Soph. *El.* 277–81); otherwise, the more profound ambivalence (n. 9 above) is concealed in gestures of propitiation toward the dead (*μειλίσσειν, ἱλάσκεσθαι*). Sometimes it is indeed the dead enemy who becomes a hero: Hdt. 5.114.2; Plut. *Cimon* 19.5.

[32] See, for example, Pelops-Zeus (II.2 below), Pyrrhos-Apollo (II.5 below), Erechtheus-Athena (III.1 below), Epopeus-Athena (II.5 below), Palaimon-Poseidon (III.7 below).

[33] Plut. *Aristides* 21, and cf. Thuc. 3.58.4; Paus. 9.2.5; Nilsson (1906) 455–56; on the penteteric agon Eleutheria see Paus. 9.2.6; Philostr. *Gymn.* 8.24.

moved toward the cemetery. No slaves were permitted: the archon himself drew water from a nearby well, then washed and anointed the steles rising up from the graves of the dead. The myrtle branches and wreaths were also evidently used to decorate the steles. These monuments had been set up over the men who fell in battle, and they were treated like guests of honor in the sacred ceremony.[34] The remaining participants had likewise come to the festival washed, anointed, and wreathed. In the time of Thucydides, robes were also brought for the dead and presumably laid upon the steles before being burned, for we know that a pyre was built in the center—though Pausanias also mentions an altar and statue of Zeus Eleutherios. Libations of milk introduced the sacrifice: children's food, in contrast to what followed.[35] Swiftly drawing his sword, the archon slit the black bull's throat so that the blood flowed onto the pyre. After this, he called the fallen warriors to supper, to "take their fill" of blood (*αἱμακουρία*). The remaining participants presumably ate their fill of the meat, but Plutarch does not say. Whatever was finally burnt on the pyre,[36] there were always libations of wine at the end. The archon mixed a krater of wine from the amphoras that were brought along, and, in all likelihood, poured it over the pyre, which had by now burned to the ground. He did so, as he announced, "for the men who died for the freedom of the Hellenes." In just this way, the lord of the sacrifice poured wine on a flaming altar, and Achilles extinguished the pyre of Patroklos.

Both battle and burial were reenacted in the bloody ritual. Death and victory alike were present in the act of killing. The Plataeans evidently had already experienced their victory as a sacrifice in the year of the battle: the votive offering they presented at Delphi after 479 was a bull.[37] The ritual celebrating the defeat of the Persians is therefore not a creation of the historical event but, rather, a traditional form assimilating that event. A unique occurrence was thereby given universal significance and transformed into an enduring obligation that lasted through centuries. Of course, this could not prevent the de-

---

[34] See *AP* 11.8; I.5.n.18 above.

[35] On milk libations see Serv. *Aen.* 5.78; K. Wyss, *Die Milch im Kultus der Griechen und Römer* (1914); Eisler (1925) 357–93; W. Deonna, *Deux études de symbolisme religieux* (1955), 21–31.

[36] For garments and seasonal fruits (*ὡραῖα*) see Thuc. 3.58.4, and cf. *Od.* 10.523 = 11.31. See in general Luk. *Merc. cond.* 28 on *ἐναγίσματα: καταχέαντες μύρον καὶ τὸν στέφανον ἐπιθέντες αὐτοὶ πίνουσι καὶ εὐωχοῦνται. . . .*

[37] Paus. 10.15.1, 16.6.

struction of Plataea in 427, but the victors built a sanctuary of their own for observance of the cult.[38] The actors are interchangeable; the ritual remains.

7. *The Sexualization of Ritual Killing: Maiden Sacrifice, Phallus Cult*

If the themes of killing and eating are so intensely enacted in ritual that they are able to grip, move, and transform human personality, it is inconceivable that the most powerful human impulse, sexuality, would play no part. On the contrary, sexuality is always intimately involved in ritual. There is no social order without a sexual order; but, even so, sexuality always retains the quality of something extraordinary and strange.

Even among primates, sexual behavior is ritually redirected to demonstrate power and differences in rank. Among some primates, the male delimits his territory by facing outward and displaying his erect phallus. Rump-presentation as an invitation to mate is a gesture of submission inhibiting an aggressive response from the stronger partner.[1] It is astounding how corresponding behavior recurs in human ritual: the function of the phallus is "apotropaic." The Babylonians made their boundary stones in the shape of a phallus; the Greeks marked their territory with herms.[2]

Human sexuality was not alone in experiencing inordinate growth, even from the standpoint of externals.[3] Rather, it was part of a new tension brought about by the polarity of human existence. The

[38] Thuc. 3.68.3.

[1] On phallic display see Fehling (1974) 7–28; Burkert (1979) 39–41. On rump-presentation see Lorenz (1963) 203–204; Morris (1967) 158, 167–68; Eibl-Eibesfeldt (1970) 201–202; Fehling (1974) 28–38.

[2] F. X. Steinmetzer, *Die babylonischen Kudurru* (1922), 114–15. On the herms see H. Herter, *RE* XIX 1688–92, *s.v.* Phallos; ibid. 1733–44, on the apotropaic phallus.

[3] Morris (1967) 9 and passim.

family's supporter had to be emotionally bound to his wife, though regularly having to tear himself away from her to go out into the unknown and hunt. Separation and bonding are thus two aspects of a single situation. Sexuality defines the specifically male role just as much as does hunting and warring behavior. It does so, first, in the expectations and educative impulses of society in which women play no small part, and, second, in the psychological makeup that the male developed in this context. Hunting is, of course, fueled in part by the powers of aggression, which had their original function in mating fights. That is to say, from the very start it included an undercurrent of sexual motivation. Male aggression and male sexuality are closely bound up with one another, stimulated simultaneously and almost always inhibited together.

The actions of banging[4] and stabbing, thrusting and piercing thus all become ambivalent in deed just as they do in language. There is no need to enumerate the ubiquitous military metaphors for the sexual organs and activity. In ancient literature the *Cento nuptialis* by Ausonius takes pride of place, consisting as it does of nothing but Vergilian battle sequences patched together so as to describe a deflowering in great detail. Whether it be a stick or a club, a spear or a sword, a gun or a cannon, as a symbol of masculinity the weapon has been equivalent to and almost interchangeable with the sexual organs from Stone Age drawings[5] to modern advertising.

Thus, when enthusiastic, aggressive tension reaches its peak, particularly at the moment of success, it may suddenly turn sexual. If an opponent is defeated, this tension strikes into a vacuum and must find release in some other way. Therefore in hunting rituals, sacrifice, warlike fighting, and even in funerary cult, there are frequent periods of license during which sexual impulses stimulated earlier can express themselves freely.[6] Such practices, which have been observed by ethnologists, were of course already suppressed in the Greek ur-

[4]See, for instance, Ov. *Fast.* 2.425–46, and the evidence that Mannhardt (1875) 251–303 (esp. 256) assembles under the title "Schlag mit der Lebensrute."

[5]For the associations male/spear, female/being wounded, see A. Leroi-Gourhan, *Préhistoire de l'art occidental* (1965), 119; La Barre (1970) 78, 170. For hunting as "making love to the animal" among modern primitives, see G. Reichel-Dolmatoff, *Amazonian Cosmos* (1971), 220. African hunters fear that the dying animal's revenge could affect their masculinity—they cover their genitals and perceive the symbolic castration in initiation as an anticipatory sacrifice to their prey: L. Frobenius, *Kulturgeschichte Afrikas* (1938), 71–79.

[6]Thus, after the gruesome sacrifice of the Tiwah festival (I.6.n.12 above): F. Grabowsky, *Internat. Archiv f. Ethnographie* 2 (1899), 199–200.

ban culture, but the ambiguity of the extraordinary could not be altogether suppressed. The girl losing her virginity at a sacrificial festival became a stock motif in comedies and novels[7]—an almost predictable fall. When leaving office, the Boeotian polemarchs were said to sacrifice to Aphrodite, the not-altogether-legitimate wife of Ares.[8] In depicting the fall of Troy, archaic artists portray Menelaus attacking Helen with a drawn sword, but everyone knew that he threw his sword away the moment Helen bared her breast in supplication. Thus, what would otherwise have ended in death became the start of a happy marriage.[9] Another especially well-loved scene portrays Aias, heavily armed, tearing the virgin Cassandra away naked from the altar and statue of Athena, the virgin goddess. An apocryphal variant of the myth tells how he raped her as well. It is the ambivalence in the confrontation between warrior and virgin that makes both pictorial and narrative accounts so thrilling.[10]

Suppliants at a sanctuary are inviolable, especially at an altar, precisely because that is the place where blood must be spilled. In a similar vein, Greeks were strictly prohibited from "having intercourse in a sanctuary."[11] The very ritual that gives expression to the realm of the extraordinary also painstakingly controls it.

Such prohibitions correspond to the pattern at the beginning and the end of sacrificial ritual. Precisely because the act of killing is sexually charged, sexual abstinence is frequently a part of preparing for

---

[7]For example, Men. *Sam.* (Adonia); *Epit.* (Tauropolia).

[8]Xen. *Hell.* 5.4.4; cf. III.1.n.118 below.

[9]Depicted already on the pithos relief from Mykonos (ca. 670 B.C.), Schefold (1964) T.35b; *Little Iliad* fr. 17 Allen = 14 Bethe; Aristoph. *Lys.* 155; the Kypselos-chest, Paus. 5.18.3; Brommer (1960) 291–97; further elaborated by Stesichoros (201 Page) and Ibykos (296 Page). L. Ghali-Kahil, *Les enlèvements et retours d'Hélène* (1955), 71–98.

[10]*Iliu Persis* p. 108, 2–6 Allen; Alkaios, *ZPE* 1 (1967) 81–95; Schefold (1964) 41–42, pl. 77; Brommer (1960) 282–84; the Kypselos-chest, Paus. 5.19.5; *PR* II, 1266–74. For the rape see Callim. fr. 35; Lycoph. 348–62; Apollod. *Epit.* 5.22; *PR* II, 1267–68; C. Robert, *Röm. Mitt.* 33 (1918), 35–42.

[11]Hdt. 2.64. Myths frequently tell of shocking exceptions: Atalanta with Melanion, Apollod. 3.108, or with Hippomenes in the grotto of Meter, Ov. *Met.* 10.686–704; Laocoön in the temple of Thymbraic Apollo, Euphorion fr. 70 Powell; Melanippos and Komaitho in the temple of Artemis Triklaria at Patrai, Paus. 7.19.3; Poseidon and Medusa in the temple of Athena, Ov. *Met.* 4.798–803; the begetting of Theseus through Poseidon and Aigeus in the sanctuary of Athena, Hyg. *Fab.* 37; etc. The background is determined in part by hieros-gamos rituals (A. Klinz, "Hieros Gamos," Diss. Halle, 1933; on the ancient Near Eastern tradition see H. Schmökel, "Heilige Hochzeit und Hohes Lied," *Abh. f. d. Kunde des Morgenlandes* 32/1 [1956]; S. N. Kramer, *The Sacred Marriage Rite* [1969]).

sacrifice, for war, and for the hunt. Artemis is both huntress and virgin; her servant Hippolytus makes chastity the guiding principle of his life. And yet, Aphrodite triumphs in his fall, and her temple stands beside his sanctuary and grave.[12] In the growth of the individual, life's necessary polarity, the far-swinging movement between renunciation and fulfillment, is in constant danger of becoming one-sided and absolute. Before an agon, which was itself also a sacrificial festival, athletes had to go on a vegetarian diet and abstain from sex; victory and sacrifice at the altar were frequently followed, according to mythic fantasy, by a wedding festival.[13] Many mysteries required sexual abstinence for a certain period preceding initiation; some form of sexuality then would accompany the blissful shock of the concluding ceremony.[14]

The preliminaries correspond to the order reestablished in the closing rituals. And just as the realm of the extraordinary—the experience of hunting, sacrifice, and death—is sexualized, so the everyday order is desexualized by the tool of civilization, that is, by ritual. In all human societies, even among "primitives," there is some kind of sexual tabu, though observers of foreign cultures may at first notice only the violation of tabus that they share. Above all, the prohibition against incest is universally recognized by mankind and is the basis

---

[12] Paus. 2.32.1–3. For the sanctuary of Ἀφροδίτης ἐπὶ Ἱππολύτῳ in Athens see Eur. *Hipp.* 30 with Schol., *IG* I² 324.69, 190, 310.280; W. S. Barret, *Euripides Hippolytos* (1964), 3–10. For Hippolytus as a vegetarian and Orphic see Eur. *Hipp.* 952–54, a *crux interpretum* (cf. Barret *ad loc.*; Dodds [1951] 148, 169.86; D. W. Lucas, *CQ* 40 [1946] 65–69), actually only a special accentuation of the hunter paradox. For the hunter's sexual abstinence see *GB* III, 191–200; also *Handwörterbuch dt. Aberglaubens* IV, 579. The necessary break between the hunter and the alluring woman is also manifested through the Potiphar motif in the myth of Peleus (Hes. fr. 208–209 M.-W.; Apollod. 3.164–66); an unsuccessful break, in the myth of Kephalos and Prokris—there, instead of killing a beast, the hunter kills the woman who has pursued him (see Pherekydes, *FGrHist* 3 F 34, and cf. Parthenios 10; "Plut." *Par. min.* 310e). The animals flee Enkidu after he makes love to the whore: see the epic of Gilgamesh I, *ANET* 74–75. For sexual abstinence before war see I Sam. 21:6; W. R. Smith (1899) 123; Amphitryon, Apollod. 2.55; before sacrifice, see I.1.n.7 above.

[13] On abstinence see Philostr. *Gymn.* 22; Paul in I Cor. 9.25; on the agon and the wedding, see the Argonauts on Lemnos, Simonides 547 Page, Pind. *Pyth.* 4.253 with Schol., Pind. *Ol.* 4.23–31; for the Danaids, see Apollod. 2.22; Paus. 3.12.2; for Penelope, see Paus. 3.12.1; for Marpessa, see Bacchyl. 20 A, Schol. Pind. *Isthm.* 4.92; for Thebes (Asia Minor), see Dikaiarchus fr. 52 W.

[14] Fehrle (1910) 137–38 (Demeter/Ceres), 159 (Bacchanalia), 136–37 (Isis); Schol. Nik. *Alex.* 410. Diod. 4.6.4 *ἔν τε ταῖς τελεταῖς οὐ μόνον ταῖς Διονυσιακαῖς, ἀλλὰ καὶ ταῖς σχεδὸν ἁπάσαις οὗτος ὁ θεὸς* (scil. Πρίαπος Ἰθύφαλλος) *τυγχάνει τινὸς τιμῆς, μετὰ γέλωτος καὶ παιδιᾶς παρεισαγόμενος ἐν ταῖς θυσίαις.*

for our concept of the family.[15] On the other hand, aggression plays a prominent part in erecting these barriers, in providing motivation—primarily that of jealousy—and in the methods of regulating them. Mockery plays a special role here. Man cannot afford to expose himself in an aggressive society as out of control and helpless, "the beast with two backs." Therefore, all permissible and necessary sexual activity is restricted to a permanently defined area which is, in turn, consecrated and tabu, almost as though the wild outdoors were present within: such is the immovable bed of Odysseus,[16] built into a wild tree rooted in the earth, the *lectus iugalis*. Marriage is a θεσμός, an institution, and, once instituted, it endures in its sacredness and cannot be abrogated.

Of course, this order will be violated again and again, only to be reinstituted. The older generation dies out and the younger one takes its place. Here, too, sacrificial ritual is the means of reestablishing an order of the extraordinary. Even marriage, as initiation, is the product of sacrificial rites.[17] The sacrificial meal that seals the new bond is permeated by rituals making the bride and groom the butt of make-believe aggression. By hurling flowers[18] and smashing pots, outsiders come to grips with the couple's new status. Above all, the bride must suffer the male act. Defloration turns into sacrifice mainly because of the exclusively human phenomenon of shedding blood in first intercourse. The bride's alienation and anxiety can be eased through temporary ritual substitutes. In Rome, for example, a spear was used to part the bride's hair, a spear that had dripped with blood and had killed men.[19] Greek brides had to make a sacrifice called a προτέλεια, in which they apparently appeased the anger of the virgin Artemis,

---

[15] M. Mead, *Internat. Encycl. Social Sciences* 7 (1968), 115–22 with lit.; La Barre (1970) 69, 559.

[16] *Od.* 23.184–204, 296 λέκτροιο παλαιὸν θεσμόν. Θεσμός is likewise the name for sacrificial remains which have been deposited: see *LS* 154 B 17 = *Abh. Berlin* (1928), 8, 22. Deubner (1932) 44 derives the name θεσμοφόρος from the latter meaning, the ancient tradition from the former. Yet in the act of securing the order the two virtually coincide.

[17] On wedding rites see K. F. Hermann and H. Bluemner, *Lehrbuch der griech. Privataltertümer* (1882³), 268–78; V. Magnien, "Le mariage chez les Grecs," *Mél. Cumont* (1936), 305–20; M. P. Nilsson, "Wedding Rites in Ancient Greece," *Opuscula* III (1960), 243–50; L. Deubner, "Hochzeit und Opferkorb," *JdI* 40 (1925), 210–23. This is not the place to give more than a few references; see also I.5.n.42 above.

[18] On καταχύσματα and related topics see E. Samter, *Familienfeste der Griechen und Römer* (1901), 1–14; his animistic interpretation, however, is not compelling: cf. I.1.n.16 above.

[19] *Caelibaris hasta*: see Festus 62–63 M.; Ov. *Fast.* 2.560; Plut. *Rom.* 15.7; *Q. Rom.* 285a–d; Arnob. 2.67.

giving her a life for a life.[20] In the cult of Aphrodite, deflowering occurred in the sanctuary itself—admittedly a custom that remained foreign to the Greeks.[21] And if, on this occasion, virgins had to spend their first night with total strangers, this too served to remove responsibility in a way familiar to us, once again, from sacrificial ritual. Sometimes it was the groom, in disguise, who assumed the stranger's role. Reparations followed the wedding "sacrifice," just as they do in a normal sacrifice. After the fact, the husband brought gifts and started supporting the new family.[22] Thus here too the new order was based on sacrifice. The rituals do not mitigate the transition; rather, they stress it by creating inhibitions and guilt. It is unimportant whether or not an individual leads a placid existence, as long as the continuance of society is guaranteed by a durable structure. And the human soul is suited to such structures precisely because of its capacity for inhibition and resigned obedience.

To succeed in the tension between the indoor and outdoor worlds, man must practice renunciation. In renouncing love, one's frustration can be transformed into aggressive ability.[23] The only activity that cannot under any circumstances be renounced in a hunting society is the hunt itself, and yet hunting is not innate—it has to be taught. Each

---

[20]Poll. 3.38 ἡ δὲ πρὸ γάμου θυσία προτέλεια . . . and cf. Plat. *Leg.* 774e; Men. fr. 903 Koerte; Hsch. γάμων ἔθη; for Artemis see Eur. *Iph. Aul.* 433 and cf. 718 προτέλεια σφάττειν; depending on local customs, Hera, Aphrodite, nymphs, and local heroines can also be recipients of the preliminary wedding sacrifice. Sacrificing the bride's hair is common: at Troizen (Hippolytus), see Eur. *Hipp.* 1423–27; at Delos (Opis and Hekaerge), see Hdt. 4.34, Paus. 1.43.4; at Megara (Iphinoe), see Paus. 1.43.4, and cf. Paus. 2.33.1 (Troizen), 2.34.12 (Hermione); Plut. *Am. narr.* 772b (Haliartos); Plut. *Aristides* 20 (Plataea); Agathocles, *FGrHist* 472 F 1 (Praisos); Procl. *In Tim.* III 176.26 Diehl (Athens). Likewise, the ἀρκτεία for Artemis of Brauron and a parallel rite in Munichia are preliminary wedding sacrifices: see Harp. ἀρκτεύειν = *FGrHist* 342 F 9, Brelich (1969) 240–79; with a goat as substitute victim see I.2.n.35 above. Characteristically, προτέλεια can also mean "preliminary sacrifice" generally (see Harp. *s.v.*, *An. Bekk.* 293.5, *LS* 4.2), especially for the mystery initiation (Kratinos fr. 180, *CAF* I 67).

[21]In Greece per se, only in southern Italian Lokroi: see Klearchos fr.43 a W., Just. 21.3; H. Prückner, *Die Lokrischen Tonreliefs* (1968), 8–13, who connects the votive reliefs (fifth century) with the cult of Aphrodite, and also considers whether the Ludovisi and Boston thrones might belong to this temple of Aphrodite (89–91). See also the legend of the hero of Temesa, Paus. 6.6.7–11. On Cyprus see Hdt. 1.199; Justin. 18.5.4; Nilsson (1906) 365–67; Fehrle (1910) 40–42. On the presentation to strangers see also S. Freud, *Das Tabu der Virginität, Ges. Schr.* 5 (1924), 212–31 = *Ges. Werke* 12 (1947), 161–80.

[22]'Ανακαλυπτήρια: see Pherecydes *VS* 7 B 2; A. Brückner, *Anakalypteria* (84. Winckelmannsprogr. 1909); *AM* 32 (1907), 79–122.

[23]J. Dollard, ed., *Frustration and Aggression* (1939); L. Berkowitz, *Internat. Encycl. Social Sciences* 1 (1968), 168–74.

new generation must be forced to hunt, just as, much later, with the "progress" of civilization, each is forced into military service. Hunting and war are sanctioned by social custom as tests of manhood, and they take precedence over courtship and marriage. Man declines to love in order to kill: this is most graphically demonstrated in the ritual slaughter of "the virgin," the potential source both of a happy union and of disruptive conflict within the group. In the maiden-sacrifice, all the tensions—the jealousy of the elderly, the strivings of the young—are released. An irreparable act transforms an erotic game into fighting fury. Desperate "searching" turns into "hunting." In the period of preparation, maiden-sacrifice is the strongest expression of the attempt to renounce sexuality. It comes at the start of fighting expeditions and war, and it precedes the great sacrificial institution in farming, namely, the harvest festival.[24] In hunting myth, the sacrificed virgin becomes the bride of the quarry, whether it is a bear, a buffalo, or a whale;[25] in agricultural myth, she is connected with the seed that must go beneath the earth in order to insure the return of the crops. In any case, as a preliminary, maiden-sacrifice stands in contrast, and provides a balance, to the main sacrifice that supplies the food. It is a ritual of giving in order to get: in the main sacrifice, fulfillment comes in the *sparagmos*, in cutting up and eating; during the preliminaries, however, there is an anticipatory self-denial which consequently requires other forms of destruction—submerging in water, hanging from trees.[26]

---

[24] For the sacrifice of a virgin before fishing see *GB* II 147 (Algonquins and Hurons), II 158 (Guinea), II 149 (India), II 151–52 (Egypt; cf. E. Mader, *Die Menschenopfer der alten Hebräer und der benachbarten Völker* [1909], 26–27); before the harvest, see *GB* VII 237 (Mexico), and cf. the virgins sent to the dragon at Lanuvium, Prop. 4.8.3–14. The sacrifice of a virgin appears atavistically especially during famine and drought. It may be conducted symbolically or in actuality: see Mannhardt (1875) 327–33, and cf. the legend of the Παρθένοι Κορωνίδες, Korinna and Nikander in Ant. Lib. 25, and Ov. *Met.* 13.692–99; for Λέω κόραι see n. 33 below. See, in general, D. Wyss, *Strukturen der Moral* (1968), 136ff., on "die Verschränkung von Inzestverbot und Opfermythologem."

[25] On the bride of the bison, a myth of the Blackfoot Indians concerning the origin of the bison dance, see J. Campbell, *The Masks of God.* I: *Primitive Mythology* (1959), 183–86. On the bride of the whale, a myth of the Chukchis, see I. Trencsényi-Waldapfel, *Untersuchungen zur Religionsgeschichte* (1966), 28–29. In a similar way Andromeda and Hesione are given to the sea monster.

[26] C. Gallini, "Katapontismos," *SMSR* 34 (1963), 61–90; cf. III.7–8 below. On Ἄρτεμις ἀπαγχομένη see Paus. 8.23.6–7; Callim. fr. 187; a hanged woman becomes Hekate, Callim. fr. 461; on Helena Dendritis (Rhodes) see Paus. 3.19.10; on Ariadne hanged see Plut. *Thes.* 20.1; on goats hanged in the ritual in which the myth tells of the maiden's suicide (Melite) see Ant. Lib. 13.7.

Ethnology has shown that maiden-sacrifice occurred, with disconcerting frequency, from Mexico to Polynesia. Perhaps it was not unknown even among the Greeks, although usually a symbolic (animal) substitute was used here as well. Maybe that is how we must understand the early Palaeolithic submersion sacrifices:[27] a young doe, after being killed and weighted down with rocks, would be pushed into the water in springtime. In Greece, the maiden would be represented by a goat for Artemis, a pig for Demeter.[28] The myths, however, call them Iphigenia and Kore and, at least in some rituals (initiation and mystery rites), the substitution is made explicit.

The great sacrifice that followed, the departure for hunting and war, could thus be psychologically motivated as a punitive expedition, as vengeance for the maiden's death. The maiden-sacrifice provided the basis and the excuse for the subsequent killing, and the restitution that followed referred mainly to her "disappearance": she returned, symbolically and ritually restored, as the focus of the company of youths brought together by the double sacrifice. For this reason, a city goddess could also serve as "the virgin."[29]

Among the Greeks, preliminary maiden-sacrifice is for the most part a prelude to war.[30] When beginning their military service, for example, the Attic ephebes marched in a procession and made sacrifice in honor of Artemis, the "goddess of the outdoor world," Artemis Agrotera;[31] they swore an oath in the sanctuary of Aglauros, a king's daughter who met with a mysterious death.[32] We know no details of

---

[27] Maringer (1956) 138–42 on the prelude to the hunt; cf. Müller-Karpe (1966) 224–25.

[28] Cf. n. 20 and I.2.n.35 above; V.2 below.

[29] Thus, a myth about the sacrifice of a virgin was linked to the Tyche of Antioch and the city goddess of Laodikeia: see Paus. *FGrHist* 854 F 10; Porph. *Abst.* 2.56; cf. Paus. 3.16.8.

[30] Myths about the (willing) sacrifice of a maiden are mainly connected with particular sanctuaries and their rites: Agesilaos sacrificed at Aulis (Xen. *Hell.* 3.4.3; Plut. *Ages.* 6; *Pelop.* 21; on the ritual see Paus. 3.9.4, 9.19.6–7). On the sacrifice for the "Leuktrian maidens," where a colt was substituted for the maiden, see Xen. *Hell.* 6.4.7; Diod. 15.54; Plut. *Pel.* 21–22; Paus. 9.13.5, 14.3; "Plut." *Am. narr.* 774d. For the sacrifice of the virgin Makaria see Eur. *Heracl.* 408–601; Schol. Plat. *Hp. Mi.* 293a. For the sacrifice of a virgin at Thebes see Paus. 9.17.1 (in conjunction with the pre-wedding ritual, n. 10 above); during the Messenian War, see Paus. 4.9.4 (following Myron). Cf. also the tearing apart of a dishonored woman as a call to war: OT Judges 19:29.

[31] *Θύσαντες ταῖς ἐγγραφαῖς . . . ἐπόμπευσαν τῇ Ἀρτέμιδι τῇ Ἀγροτέρᾳ*, *IG* II/III^2 1006.6–9, 1008.7, 1011.7, 1028.8, 1029.6, 1030.5; *Hesperia* 34 (1965), 256; 36 (1967), 66; Deubner (1932) 209.

[32] Philochoros, *FGrHist* 328 F 105; Plut. *Alc.* 15.7; on the ephebic oath see L. Robert, *Etudes épigraphiques et philologiques* (1938), 296–307.

the sacrifice that surely accompanied the oath. Before setting off for war, moreover, the army sacrificed at the sanctuary of the Hyakinthides, who, in mythology, were often portrayed as king's daughters who had been killed: in the war between Erechtheus, first king of Athens, and Eleusis, Erechtheus' daughters, of their own free will, offered themselves up for sacrifice.[33] Their death, which was repeated in sacrifice before setting off for war, guaranteed success in the subsequent bloodshed and victory in battle. And again, immediately before battle, animals were slaughtered in great numbers as the enemy looked on.

The Spartans sacrificed a female goat to Artemis Agrotera:[34] thus began the deadly activity that then continued in the human slaughter of battle. A victory meant there had to be restitution, so a stake made of oak would be set up and adorned with a captured helmet, shield, and spear. Through this tropaion,[35] a monument to the enemy's flight, those who were conquered were made to attest to their adversary's victory. So, too, hunters already hung up their "hunting trophies"—horned skulls and, above all, skins—on a tree or a stake.[36] By adding to the tropaion the skin of the goat, the *aigís*, which had been slaughtered before battle, the stake came to represent the goddess Athena with her helmet, shield, and aegis.[37] The "virgin" thus came into

---

[33] See Eur. *Erechtheus*, in C. Austin, *Nova Fragmenta Euripidea*, fr. 65.65–89, on annual cattle-sacrifice with choruses of maidens, burnt offering without wine at the start of a war. In addition see Phanodemos, *FGrHist* 325 F 4; Philochoros, *FGrHist* 328 F 12. The third group of heroic sisters at Athens is that of the Λέω κόραι, honored at the Leokoreion; the motivation for their willing sacrifice was a plague (cf. n. 24): Kock, *RE* XII 2000–2001.

[34] Xen. *Lak. Pol.* 13.8; *Hell.* 4.2.20; Plut. *Lyc.* 22.2; for the most part, the brief reports do not even mention a divinity. In this context the art of the seer is of decisive importance: see Hdt. 9.38.1, 41.4, 45.2; Thuc. 6.69.2; Eur. *Phoen.* 173–74, 1109–11; Stengel (1910) 92–102.

[35] K. Woelcke, *Bonn. Jbb.* 120 (1911), 127–235; F. Lammert, *RE* VII A (1939), 663–73; Cook II (1925) 108–13; A. J. Janssen, *Het antieke tropaion* (1957). On depictions in art see Metzger (1965) 115–17. The tropaion is called Διὸς βρέτας, Eur. *Phoen.* 1250, Διὸς ἀγάλματα, Gorg. *VS* 82 B 6, because Zeus bestows victory (cf. the inscription from Selinus, *IG* XIV 268).

[36] Meuli (1967) 159–60; Callim. fr. 96; Verg. *Aen.* 9.407; etc. For depictions in art and epigrams, see I.2 above.

[37] This must have already arisen in prehistoric times; it is symbolically reproduced in the Palladion (G. Lippold, *RE* XVIII 2, 189–201; on a gold ring from Mycenae, see Nilsson [1955], T.17.1 = *Corpus der minoischen und mykenischen Siegel* I [1964], #17; Simon [1969] 183; on a stucco dish from Mycenae, see Simon [1969] 181). The old cult-statue of Athena Polias at Athens is different, as it is seated (A. Frickenhaus, *AM* 33 [1908], 17–32; C. J. Herington, *Athena Parthenos and Athena Polias* [1955], 16–27; Simon [1969]

being through the battle, just as her symbolic substitute had been slaughtered in the preliminary sacrifice. Similarly, there were tales telling how the statue of Athena, the Palladion, fell from heaven during the primordial war between the gods and the giants,[38] and how Pallas was named after a creature of that name whose skin had been removed to serve as her attire.[39] In the paradox that both the god of the hunt and the god of war were "virgins" we observe the sexual tensions, the frustration and symbolic substitution, upon which hunting and warring behavior feeds.

If the preliminaries and the aftermath of the great experience correspond, the sequence of guilt and atonement can be reversed, that is, the sacrifice of a maiden or woman can follow the battle. This occurs mainly in funerary ritual, although there are analogies in sacrificial ritual. The demands of the dead man may, for instance, be recognized through an irrevocable act of renunciation, which may in turn have a symbolic substitute. In this way, feelings of guilt and readiness to atone can be expressed, just as death previously had been given the form of killing, of an aggressively and sexually motivated act. If the sacrifice of Iphigenia precedes the Trojan War, the sacrifice of Polyxena follows it. That is how Achilles gets his share of the captured women. A dead father can demand renunciation from his son; his wishes are carried out by youths, *νέοι*.[40] The most detailed description of a cremation with maiden sacrifice was given by an Arab emissary to the Rus on the Volga. There, before being strangled on the dead man's bier, the victim, a volunteer, had to offer herself to all the participants in the funeral.[41] Does the name *Polyxena* point to similar practices?[42] A period of license gives vent to the extraordinary; another act of killing ends and transforms it into an order of renunciation.

Sexually colored fighting and killing can give rise to yet another

---

194); different too is Athena's head-birth, which is linked to the sacrifice of a bull (Cook III [1940], 556–739).

[38] Phylarchos, *FGrHist* 81 F 47; F. Vian, *La guerre des géants* (1952), 279.

[39] For *αἰγίς* as the skin of Gorgo after she had been killed in the gigantomachy see Eur. *Ion* 987–97; Diod. 3.70.3–5 = Dionysios Skytobrachion, *FGrHist* 32 F 8 (*Αἰγίς* as a fire-breathing monster like the *Χίμαιρα*). For Athena killing her father Pallas, who wanted to rape her, and putting on his skin, see Cic. *Nat. deor.* 3.59; Clem. *Pr.* 2.28; Schol. Lyk. 355; Firm. *Err.* 16.2; Kerényi (1952) 57–64. For Pallas as a maiden slain by Athena and reconstituted as a *ξόανον*, see Apollod. 3.144–45.

[40] *PR* II 1276–79; Ibykos fr. 307 Page; Simonides fr. 557 Page; Sophocles fr. 522–28 Pearson; Eur. *Hec.* 107–582 (*νεανίαι* 525); Brommer (1960) 298–99.

[41] Ahmad ibn Fodlan, quoted by Jaqut, English transl. in *Antiquity* 8 (1934), 58–62.

[42] *Πολύξεναι νεάνιδες*, Pind. fr. 122.1.

cycle of destruction and reparation. When stimulated by sexual jealousy, the destructive rage operating in the battle of man against man will turn against the adversary's masculinity: when killed, a warrior is immediately castrated. This has occurred regularly in wars up until recent times,[43] and it appears to be a basic element in man's fighting instinct. It can also, without further ado, be translated into the hunter's "battle" with his quarry.[44] In mammals, the significance of the male reproductive organs is obvious. They stimulate aggression and hence are accorded special treatment when the quarry is cut up and distributed. It is certain that castration rituals play an important role in sacrifice,[45] but because they largely belong to the "unmentionables," the *ἄρρητον*, we hear of them only exceptionally or by chance. For instance, only by virtue of a gruesome joke in Martial[46] do we know that the goat sacrificed to Dionysus was castrated by an assistant at the very moment it received its death-blow. The pseudo-explanation that in this way the meat would be freed of its goat odor and thus be made edible, simply shows that the procedure was the same at every he-goat sacrifice, whether to Dionysus or to Aphrodite. Thus, Clement of Alexandria gives prominence to an apocryphal myth telling of the ram's castration;[47] and the frequent association of a

---

[43] The interpretation of Tyrtaios fr. 7 Diehl/Prato proposed by F. Dümmler, *Philologus* 56 (1897), 13, has not stood up to criticism (Wilamowitz, *Die Ilias und Homer* [1916], 95.1; F. Jacoby, *Hermes* 53 [1918], 24, 1; R. Nierhaus, *JdI* 53 [1938], 90–113), but the non-Greek evidence is clear, especially that from Egypt (Nierhaus 90); for the OT see I Sam. 18:25–27; cf. A. E. Jensen, ed., *Altvölker Süd-Äthiopiens* (1959), 327. For castration in connection with torture and the death penalty see, for instance, Plat. *Gorg.* 473c; in conjunction with lynch law see William Faulkner, *Light in August*.

[44] "As any big game hunter knows, at the moment of death a male animal's sexual organ becomes tumescent and emits semen," writes G. Devereux in *Mnemosyne* 4, 23 (1970), 299, though there is no detailed verification. At the great elephant-sacrifice among the Pygmies, cutting off and burying the procreative organ plays a large role: R. P. Trilles, *Les Pygmées de la forêt équatoriale* (1933), 460; *UdG* IV 88–90, 95–100; O. Eberle, *Cenalora* (1954), 80–82, 88–90, 109–110; see also Meuli (1946) 247–48, 256. During the festival of the bull at Drömling (Mark Brandenburg), the genitals of the slaughtered village bull were hung from the loft: A. Kuhn, *Märkische Sagen und Märchen* (1843), 368–69.

[45] During the sacrifice at an oath and funerary sacrifice: Stengel (1910) 78–84, and I.5.n.8 above. During purification sacrifice: I.5.n.23. The *vires* of the sacrificial victim are kept and carried in a kernos at the Taurobolion and the Kriobolion of the Meter cult: *CIL* XII 1567, XIII 510, 522, 525, 1751; Hepding (1903) 190–93.

[46] 3.24 . . . *stabat moriturus ad aras hircus . . . quem Tuscus mactare deo cum vellet haruspex / dixerat agresti forte rudique viro / ut cito testiculos et acuta falce secaret / taeter ut immundae carnis abiret odor.* For a phallus with a he-goat's legs at the Dionysia on Delos see *BCH* 31 (1907), 500–501.

[47] Clem. *Pr.* 2.15.2; V.4.n.44 below.

sacrificial ram and the phallic Hermes is surely no accident. Thus, too, when the October-Horse was sacrificed and its tail carried bleeding to Regia from the Campus Martius, we may suspect that the "tail" represented the genital organ; and our suspicions are raised to the level of probability by the fact that a horse's tail has too little blood to be of use in the ceremony.[48] Donkeys are sacrificed to the phallic god Priapos, and one etiological myth clearly states that the donkey's death is due to its remarkable and proverbial lust.[49] Pindar incorporates such associations into his description of the Hyperborean donkey sacrifice: Apollo laughs at seeing the animals' "upright presumption."[50]

The ritual reparation corresponding to ritual castration evidently consisted of an especially striking, provocative custom. A single phallus was set up for worship and carried through the city as if in a triumph. If this worship entailed submission, the worshipper was forced to assume a female role and appearance—padding his body, presenting his rump. Just such practices are known to us from Dionysiac processions.[51] Scholars have sought an easy explanation for

[48] G. Devereux, *Mnemosyne* IV 23 (1970), 297–301, and cf. Eitrem (1917) 28–34; H. Wagenvoort, *Serta Philologica Aenipontana* (1962), 273–87; U. Scholz, *Studien zum altitalischen und altrömischen Marskult und Marsmythos* (1970), 126–40, but cf. C. Bennet Pascal, *HSCP* 85 (1981), 276, 282. For worship of a horse's phallus, *Völsi*, in the Edda, see F. Genzmer, *Edda* (1979[5]), 185 nr. 31; A. Heusler, *Zeitschr. f. Volkskunde* 13 (1903), 25–39.

[49] "Erat." *Cat.* p. 90 Robert = Schol. Germ. p. 70–p. 129; Lact. *Div. inst.* 1.21.28, quoting from Philiskos (fr. 2, *Tragicorum Graecorum Fragmenta* p. 819 Nauck[2]); Ov. *Fast.* 1.391–440, 6.319–48; H. Herter, *De Priapo* (1932), 78–85, 264–67.

[50] Pind. *Pyth.* 10.33–36; Callim. fr. 186.10, 492; Simmias and Boios in Ant. Lib. 20; Apollodorus, *FGrHist* 244 F 126. Aristeas' "Arimaspeia" may possibly have been Pindar's source. This work may have connected the horse-sacrifice of Asiatic rider-nomads—which has been linked to the *Equus October* and the Aśvamedha (W. Koppers, *Wiener Beiträge zur Kulturgeschichte und Linguistik* 4 [1936], 279–411; for sources see *UdG* IX 278–96)—with the donkey-sacrifices of Asia Minor. During the castration of an animal, the Moi-Sedang (Vietnam) habitually laugh (unpubl. note by G. Devereux).

[51] For the one Attic black-figure bowl with a phallic procession see Deubner (1932) pl. 22, Nilsson (1955) pl. 35, a new photograph in Pickard-Cambridge (1962) pl. IV (Florence 3897). For the figures on the phallus (one of them *κύβδ' ἀποθυμαίνων τινί*, like the description of a similar satyr's gesture in Soph. *Ichn.* 122), see Luk. *Syr. D.* 28 *φαλλοὺς ὅσοι Διονύσῳ ἐγείρουσιν, ἐν τοῖσι φαλλοῖσι καὶ ἄνδρας ξυλίνους κατίζουσι, ὅτευ μὲν εἵνεκα ἐγὼ οὐκ ἐρέω*, with a clear allusion to the female role (cf. Herter, *RE* XIX 1706, 62; "aufgesetzt," but this does not necessarily mean that the figures are portrayed in a seated position). For the rest, see Herter, *RE* XIX 1673–81, 1701–23.

On the pygal symbolism of the padded dancers (who are precisely *not* ithyphallic) see E. Buschor, *AM* 53 (1923), 105–106; L. Breitholz, *Die dorische Farce im griechischen Mutterland vor dem 5. Jahrhundert* (Göteborg, 1960), 149–54, who is too quick, however, to posit "magic" in place of the purely biological-physical factors. In the rite with the

these phallic processions in the term *fertility rites*, leaving open the question of whether this fertility is animalic or vegetal, or both at once. The act which alone produces fruit, that is, the union of male and female, is precisely what the phalluses do not indicate: they do not stand with their heads in the earth but, rather, upright. They are "erected," "aroused,"[52] impressive rather than reproductive. It has caused some puzzlement that those carrying the phallus are not ithyphallic, that Dionysus riding the lewd donkey is soft and effeminate. This polarity is understandable, even necessary, in view of the tensions and inhibitions contained in sacrificial ritual. The phallophoria presupposes sacrificial castration and assumes the character of a restoration and reparation consonant with the transition from seriousness to merriment, the period of license.

The etiological myth clearly shows that setting up the Dionysiac phallus is a restoration after some kind of death. Dionysus himself, as the archetype of his worshippers, promised Prosymnos that he would submit to him like a woman. Returning from the dead when Prosymnos had died, the god set up a phallus made of figwood. Once again, Clement of Alexandria exposed this myth in a polemic,[53] but Lukian clearly alludes to it, and his allusion is explicitly substantiated in sixth-century vase-paintings of the *phallophoria*.

Inscriptions from the Delian Dionysia have provided us with a

---

elephant's phallus, the Pygmy chieftain is dressed as a bride (cf. n. 44 above). At the Aśvamedha, the queen lies with the horse which had been killed; see also I.8.n.15 below. A phallic rite was observed at the Altaic horse-sacrifice: D. Zelenin, *Internat. Archiv f. Ethnographie* 29 (1928), 83ff.; *UdG* IX 399–413. It takes place partly before, partly after the sacrifice.

[52] Φαλλοὺς ἐγείρειν: see Luk., n. 51 above; cf. the black-figure lekythos, Athens 9690 (*ABV* 505.1) in Metzger (1965) 51–52, pl. 26, where satyrs dance around a phallus as they would for an ascending goddess (cf. Metzger [1965] 50). Cf. W. Wickler, *Stammesgeschichte und Ritualisierung* (1970) 253 on the herms: "keine Fruchtbarkeits-, sondern soziale Drohsymbole."

[53] Clem. *Pr.* 2.34, and cf. Paus. 2.37.5 (Πόλυμνος Cdd.); Tzetz. ad Lyk. 212 (Πολύυμνος); Schol. Luk. p. 187 (Κόροιβος). Dionysus *ἐπὶ μέσης* (scil. *τῆς συκῆς*) *διέβη* *Et. M.* 455.25. There is a different etiology for the phallus-cult in the legends about Archilochus (Archilochus-monument E[1]III, *Arch. Eph.* [1952], 42–43; M. Treu, *Archilochos* [1959], 47–48; J. Tarditi, *Archilochus* [1968], 6–7), Pegasus of Eleutherai (i.e., city Dionysia; cf. Schol. Aristroph. *Ach.* 243, Paus. 1.2.5), or Ikarios (Schol. Luk. p. 211.14–212.9; 280.1–12): the god punishes those who scorn his prophet by making them ithyphallic, a condition that ends only with the production of artificial phalluses. That which rises out of the unconscious as something overwhelming and oppressive for man is rendered "do-able" in the rite and is thereby overcome. The third, Egyptianizing, etiology—since Isis cannot find Osiris's organ, she erects artificial phalluses (Plut. *Is.* 358b; Diod. 1.22.7; Euseb. *Praep. Ev.* 2.1.21)—situates the phallus-cult squarely in the context of restitution following the act of tearing apart.

rather detailed picture of the ritual. A large phallus would be built from a beam, painted with wax colors, and equipped with large wooden wings. The phallus-bird has long been known to us from an often-reproduced votive offering on Delos and from the art of Attic vase-painters. In the Delian ritual, however, it was driven on a lead-weighted wagon down to the "river"; while the wagon sank in the water, the phallus-bird floated out to sea and out of sight.[54] This phallagogia is clearly a closing ritual, for the act of worship includes disposing of the object of worship. In the mythological version, the same events occur in the fate of Thoas, son of Dionysus and king of Lemnos: after the Lemnian women had exterminated all other men, Thoas was brought down to the beach in a Dionysiac procession and set afloat in a wooden coffin.[55] There is an even earlier example of a phallus floating away on the sea in Greek mythology. When Kronos, at Earth's instigation, castrated the father of the heavens, he threw the severed portions behind him into the sea—plainly a ritual gesture embedded in a speculative myth, even though we are no longer able to localize the ritual.[56]

The larger the phallus, the greater the element of humor, of the *γελοῖον*. For man, the inventor of serious weapons, the lighthearted threats in obscene gestures are all too transparent. Aggression dis-

---

[54]The decisive contribution is R. Vallois, "L'agalma des Dionysies de Délos," *BCH* 46 (1922), 94–112. G. M. Sifakis, *Studies in the History of Hellenistic Drama* (1967), 7–13, gives an overview of the Delian Dionysia. He is hasty, however, in speaking of the god's "epiphany" (12), and overlooks the phallus swimming away. The inscriptions clearly show that the cart remains and is repaired from time to time, but that the winged agalma is produced anew every year. The topography is uncertain; the inscriptions mention the "Leukothion" and a "river."

For the votive offering of Karystios see *BCH* 31 (1907), 504, fig. 18; for an archaic depiction of the phallus-bird see Ch. Dugas, "Les vases de l'Héraion," *Délos* X (1928), 12, #28; cf. C. Bérard, *AK* 9 (1966), 93–96; E. Vermeule, *AK* 12 (1969), pl. 11.4/5.

[55]Val. Flacc. *Arg.* 2.242–302; a red-figure bowl, Berlin 2300 = *ARV*² 409.43; Burkert (1970) 7–8; III.6 below. Megas (1956) 117–18 reports from Tyrnabos/Thessaly that, after a festival meal on a mountain, a "king" is consecrated and led, sitting on a donkey backward, with a phallus through the village, and that in the evening he is dumped into the water. The *πλοιαφέσια* in the cult of Isis (Apul. *Met.* 11.17; L. Vidman, *Isis und Sarapis bei den Griechen und Römern* [1970], 76–87) are probably a sublimated version of the same ritual.

[56]Hes. *Th.* 176–200. Both Anatolian and Cypriot ritual may be in the background; the passage presupposes the sacrifice of a goat for Aphrodite (cf. n. 46 above) like those for Aphrodite *ἐπιτραγία* (cf. Simon [1969] 252; for an archaic depiction from Argos see *BCH* 93 [1969], 999). On the strange clay figurine from Perachora, a bearded Aphrodite growing up out of testicles (675/50 B.C.), see H. Payne, *Perachora* I (1940), 231–32, pl. 102; W. Sale, *TAPA* 92 (1961), 508–21. Cf. also G. Devereux in *Echanges et communications, Mél. Lévi-Strauss* (1970), 1229–52.

solves into laughter. It is characteristic that rituals requiring seriousness could once again symbolically substitute a weapon for the phallus—the weapon of the hunted animal, the horns of the goat or bull. According to the myth, for instance, Herakles broke off the horn of the bull-shaped Acheloos while fighting for his bride Deianeira.[57] The broken-off horn turned into the "horn of plenty," brimming with flowers and fruit (it is hardly accidental that, in one instance, phalluses rather than fruits project from Herakles' *cornu copiae*).[58] Already in the Upper Palaeolithic representation of the Venus of Laussel, the goddess is holding a horn in her hand.[59] And perhaps it is significant that on Corinthian vases, Dionysiac padded dancers so often carry horns from which they drink wine. This too is a horn of plenty; sacrificing a bull is after all also part of the dithyramb.[60]

Sexual reproduction and death are the basic facts of life. Mutually determinant and interwoven, both are acted out in the sacrificial ritual, in the tension between renunciation and fulfillment, destruction and reparation. The stele built on a grave can take the form of a phallus.[61] Orgies and death are close neighbors. Thus, ritual itself serves in the process by which the group perpetuates its existence through death.

8. *Father God and Great Goddess*

Trying to reconstruct the ideas or concepts of preliterate ages is a game in which nothing can be verified. The earliest pictorial repre-

[57] Archilochus fr. 181 Bergk = Hsch. μουνόκερα; Diod. 4.35.4; Apollod. 2.148; Ov. *Met.* 9.1–92; cf. H. P. Isler, *Acheloos* (1970), 11–28, 115–19.

[58] *Gazette Archéologique* 3 (1877), pl. 26; P. Baur, *AJA* 9 (1905), 159; Furtwängler, *RML* I 2176.

[59] Müller-Karpe (1966) 252, T. 93.1.

[60] See n. 51 above; III.7 below. For the sacrifice of a bull see Pind. *Ol.* 13.19; Simonides fr. 79 Diehl; Burkert (1966) 98.

[61] For Asia Minor see G. Perrot and Ch. Chipiez, *Histoire de l'art* V (1890), 48–51; Herter, *RE* XIX 1728–33; F. Poulsen, *Delphische Studien* (1924), fig. 8; *AA* (1939), 171–74. For Scandinavia see E. Mogk, *Reallexikon der germanischen Altertumskunde* III, 415.

sentations allow us to draw only uncertain conclusions about visual concepts in early times, and these are no older than Upper Palaeolithic. But already in Lower Palaeolithic finds there is evidence of ritual activity in hunting and funerary custom. Under these circumstances, any attempt to discover the *Ursprung der Gottesidee* will simply reflect one's own assumptions; it will be an act of faith. The only certainty appears to be that from the very start, the rites of hunting, sacrifice, and funerals played a decisive part.

Students of religion have long attempted to grasp and reconstruct a stage of religion without gods, a pre-deistic level; belief in gods would be preceded by animism and this, in turn, by a pre-animism characterized by formless notions of Mana and "simple" magical rites. "God is a latecomer in the history of religion."[1] It has since become clear that the assumption on which this theory is based comes from modern preconceptions. Scholars saw their own religion as the culmination of a development, as though it contained no primitive elements, and assumed that this development proceeded from "the simple" to the complex—as though life, even in its earliest stages, were not a vast and intricate system of balances. Against these tendencies, Wilhelm Schmidt[2] gathered impressive evidence for his theory that there was a belief in a single, father-like god at the very start of human evolution, as it appears among the most primitive hunters. He did not see how this coincided with Sigmund Freud's theory, developed almost contemporaneously, which likewise posited a father-like god at the beginning of man's development. Of course, what Schmidt saw as a primordial revelation, Freud viewed as a primordial catastrophe: patricide.

---

[1]G. van der Leeuw, *Phänomenologie der Religion* (1933), 87; cf. the survey in Nilsson (1955) 36–67. The theory of animism goes back to E. B. Tylor's *Primitive Culture* (1871) and affected the study of Greek religion primarily through J. Harrison's first great book (1922; 1st ed. 1903). The thesis of pre-animism was formulated by R. R. Marett (see "The Tabu-Mana Formula as a Minimum Definition of Religion," *ARW* 12 [1909], 186–94) and was followed by Nilsson (see esp. [1955] 47–60, 68–71), Deubner (see I.4.n.2 above; *NJb* 27 [1911], 321–35; in Chantepie de la Saussaye, *Lehrbuch der Religionsgeschichte* II[4] [1925], 421–30); Latte ([1959] 12–13). The position drew protest from Walter F. Otto (*Die Götter Griechenlands* [1929]) and his school. Recently, La Barre (1970) still supposes that the belief in god came late and was preceded by shamanism (10; 439, etc.).

[2]*UdG*; applied to prehistory by H. Kühn, *Das Problem des Urmonotheismus* (Abh. Mainz, 1950), 22; criticized by R. Pettazzoni, "Das Ende des Urmonotheismus?" *Numen* 3 (1956), 156–59; 5 (1958), 161–63. The concept of an Urmonotheism is suspect, but the belief in a supreme god is more widespread and older than the proponents of evolution had supposed.

Freud's fascinating construct, developed mainly in his book *Totem and Tabu*,[3] proceeds from Darwin, on the one hand, and from Robertson Smith's description of sacramental sacrifice, on the other. Among the primitive hominid hordes, brothers joined together to kill and eat their father because he jealously prevented them from sharing his women. Yet, this crime was avenged by an inner compulsion within these now-human brothers. Obedient to the dead man, they submitted to the newly created order of renunciation and sexual tabu. The father became mightier than before and was worshipped as a god. Freud sees the reenactment of this primordial crime in sacrificial and funerary ritual. So, too, within the individual's soul, repressed within his subconscious, stirs the desire to commit the crime of Oedipus: to kill his father and marry his mother.

Regardless of the psychological significance of the Oedipus complex, Freud's construct is, as has long been recognized, a myth, impressive but unverifiable,[4] and, in this form, under no circumstances correct. Even if one assumes matricide or infanticide as the primordial crime, the same basic problem remains: a unique occurrence, no matter how gruesome, could not assume such formative significance, stretching over thousands of generations, if there were no genetically predetermined tendency for such imprinting, and this can be understood in biological terms only as an adaptation within a long evolutionary process. Patricide assumes the existence of fatherhood and father-bonding, although both are specifically human, civilized innovations. It is characteristic of modern biases about man that Freud and his school did not even consider the area where killing had a necessary function—a function which in fact determined the course of evolution. It was at the time when Australopithecine primates were killing and eating baboons, and sometimes even one of their own,[5]

---

[3](1912/13); *Ges. Schr.* 10 (1924), 1–194 = *Ges. Werke* 9 (1940); enthusiastically taken up by J. Harrison, *Epilegomena to the Study of Greek Religion* (1921), xxiii; see also Karl Meuli, *Der griechische Agon* (1968; written 1926), 20; criticized by A. L. Kroeber, *American Anthropologist* 22 (1920), 48–55.

[4]See R. Money-Kyrle, *The Meaning of Sacrifice* (1930), 194; A. L. Kroeber, "*Totem and Taboo* in Retrospect," *American Journal of Sociology* 45 (1939), 446–51; R. Fox, "*Totem and Taboo* Reconsidered," in E. R. Leach, ed., *The Structural Study of Myth and Totemism* (1967), 163–75. In conscious conflict with the teachings of biological heredity, Freud found himself constrained (*Ges. Werke* 16 [1950], 200–208) to postulate some archaic heritage in man, "Erinnerungen an das Erleben früherer Generationen" (206). J. W. M. Whiting considered the desire for matricide, rather than patricide, to be central (Fox, "*Totem*," 173), whereas G. Devereux demonstrates "The Cannibalistic Impulses of Parents" (*Psychoanalytic Forum* 1 [1966], 113–24) in conjunction with actual cases of infanticide. Are the aggressive impulses more constant and hence earlier than their object?

[5]See I.2.nn.25, 27 above.

that spiritual and social structures began to evolve which made killing the foundation of cultural order.

In hunting, intraspecific aggression focuses on the hunted animal and is thus deflected from man. But in order for this aggression to achieve its goal, instincts that inhibit aggression—namely, responses to female sexuality and infant behavior[6]—have to be blocked. In the hunter's imagination and in mutual acts of encouragement, the quarry could not appear as woman or child but, rather, had to seem "big" and "masculine," even when it was only a rabbit. The fact that the most profitable game was the largest mammals—cows, bears, mammoths—and that the largest, though not the tastiest, specimens in each case were male, plays into this as well.[7] The hunter's aggressiveness was, however, modified in a remarkable way. It was not his aim to drive the quarry away or destroy it, but, rather, to catch it and make it his own. Thus, in a sense, the "big" and "masculine" prey was part of the group, φίλος in the basic sense of the word.[8] Masculine, big, both a member of the family and doomed to die, the quarry becomes a kind of father, a father-symbol, a father-substitute. Conscious killing is a kind of patricide.

Such stylized hunting behavior became very significant, because the outwardly directed societal activity combined here with its inner tensions in a special way. Man's neoteny, the long period of dependency and learning, caused grave tensions, especially since masculine aggressiveness was cultivated at the same time. Yet boys must learn from and identify with their fathers if they are to be able to perpetuate the achievements of culture as dictated by tradition. The human tendency to respect authority offsets aggressive impulses, as does the older generation's head start, which allows it, at least temporarily, to assert its power. The rising generation's latent rebelliousness, however, and its Oedipal inclinations toward patricide are deflected and ritually neutralized in the hunt, sacrifice, and war. Freud's intuition that a patricide stands at the start of human development is thus to some extent confirmed, although not in the sense of an historically fixed crime but, rather, in the function of ritual symbols and the corresponding structures in the soul.

For ritual emphasizes and guides individual fantasies. In the

---

[6] Lorenz (1963) 180–95, 201–204; Eibl-Eibesfeldt (1970) esp. 135–38.

[7] Animal friezes on archaic Greek vases frequently contain confrontations between predatory animals (mainly lions) and their prey; the prey (cow, sheep, goat, boar) is almost always clearly depicted as masculine, the predator as sexless.

[8] On φίλος as possessive pronoun see M. Landfester, *Das griechische Nomen "philos" und seine Ableitungen* (1966).

hunter's "comedy of innocence," the quarry is frequently invoked and appeased as "father."[9] Ritual restitution includes expressing one's bad conscience and renewing renunciation, submission, and worship; preparatory ritual includes anticipatory renunciation and giving things away in the hope of success. The gestures—kneeling, prostration, folding or raising one's hands, solemn presentation, sighing, crying, and wailing—are taken from behavior found in human interaction. Their particular function is in relation to one's fellow man, promoting unity and trust rather than aggressive tension. As ritual, as demonstrative communication, they are severed from any real object and instead oriented toward something imaginary. This conduct is consolidated and grows with the urge to imitate and with the pressures of tradition: people act collectively as though an invisible, quasi-human being were present whom they must worship.[10] The experience of a transcendent power is mediated by the community. At the same time, in worshipping this power the individual acquires a special freedom and independence from his fellow men, since the inescapable confrontations that result from selfish interests are replaced by a collective orientation. When language comes to name this imaginary object and attempts to describe it, there is at least a rudimentary "conception of god," based on the experience shaped by the ritual.

Yet, by describing the ritual experience through language, by consciously rendering it concrete, great problems arise. It was certain that the god was intimately linked to sacrifice; in classical antiquity this is self-evident in the complex of *ἱερόν/ἱερεῖον*, *sacer/sacrificare*. It was possible to play with the idea that the god and the sacrificial animal were identical; accordingly, the god would be killed, eaten,[11] destroyed, and yet later, when the ritual was repeated, miraculously be present once again. The closing rituals could be staged as a resurrection or revivification.[12] Certain Greek myths indeed give some indica-

---

[9] E.g., the elephant among the Pygmies (I.7.n.44 above); "lieber Vater Nilpferd, lieber kleiner Vater, lass dich von deinen Kindern fressen" (Abyssinia, *Paideuma* 2 [1941], 25).

[10] Morris (1967) 178–81 thinks that when the cooperative hunting society reduced the actual superiority of the individual father, it created the concept of an almighty Father as a substitute—a reprise of Freud's ideas rendered harmless. M. Mauss wrote: "La création de la divinité est l'oeuvre des sacrifices antérieurs": *Oeuvres* I (1968), 288.

[11] The idea of a god eaten as a sacrament was spread primarily by J. G. Frazer (*GB* VIII 48–108), following W. R. Smith (1894). The provocative problem in this context was, of course, the relationship to the Christian communion; cf. E. Reuteskiöld, *Die Entstehung der Speisesakramente* (1912).

[12] The focus of myth and ritual is characteristically the death—i.e., the sacrifice—whereas the "resurrection" is seldom explicit: cf. Dumuzi/Attis, and Adonis/Osiris; on Aqhat see II.4.n.34 below; on Dumuzi see V.2.n.30 below. Even in the Gospels, the reports of the resurrection are mere appendices to the Passion.

tion that the god is identical with his sacrificial animal. Zeus, for instance, transforms himself into a bull,[13] Dionysus into a kid.[14] Behind the story that Pasiphaë copulated with an exceptional sacrificial bull are rituals in which a woman offers herself sexually to the victim.[15] Is Pasiphaë to be seen as identical with Europa mating with Zeus in form of a bull? The women of Elis call upon Dionysus to appear as a bull:[16] the real bull is doubtless present in the sacrificial meal. But the assertion that the father-like god was related to the patricidal character of sacrifice provoked strong resistance, especially in an extremely patriarchal society such as that of ancient Greece. Honoring one's father was central to the conscious morality, patricide almost unthinkable. Thus, the crime of Kronos against Uranos entered official Greek literature only once under the impact of an Orientalizing fashion.[17] The complementary character of extraordinary and ordinary behavior could otherwise be expressed only in the context of secret societies and secret myths, that is to say, in the mysteries. Hence, it was simpler to style the sacrificial animal an "enemy of the god." The goat is killed for Dionysus because it gnaws at the vine;[18] Hera's anger drives Io the cow away. But in characteristic contrast to the Egyptians, for example, the Greeks were not consistent in this ideology of designating the victim as an enemy: Io was simultaneously the priestess of Hera, representing the goddess herself, and Artemis killed the she-bear Kallisto who was, however, considered the "most beautiful" and hence the perfect likeness of Artemis, the "most beautiful."[19] In the pictures showing the god and his sacrificial animal side by side in almost inner communion, we recognize that heartfelt ambivalence of

---

[13]For the Europa myth, see the large amount of evidence in Cook III (1940) 615–28; see also W. Bühler, *Europa* (1968).

[14]Apollod. 3.29; Διόνυσος Ἔριφος at Sparta, Hsch. *εἰραφιώτης*.

[15]Eur. *Cretans;* C. Austin, *Nova Fragmenta Euripidea* (1968), fr. 82; Apollod. 3.8–10, where Poseidon himself made the bull emerge from the sea as a sacrifice for Poseidon; Türk, *RML* III 666–73; *PR* II 361–64. Cf. the ritual of the queen at the Vedic Aśvamedha, I.7.n.51 above.

[16]Plut. *Q. Gr.* 229b = 871 Page (*Poetae Melici Graeci*); cf. Ath. 476a. On the bull-Dionysus see also Eur. *Bacch.* 100, 920, 1017; Soph. fr. 959 Pearson; Euphorion fr. 14 Powell; Horace *Carm.* 2.19.30; *βουγενής* Plut. *Is.* 264 f. (Argos-Lerna).

[17]On the long-discussed relation between Kumarbi and Kronos (*ANET* 120, Hes. *Th.* 154–200), see M. L. West, *Hesiod Theogony* (1966), 18–31; Kirk (1970) 214–20.

[18]Leonidas of Tarentum, epigr. 32 Gow-Page = *AP* 9.99; Euenos, *AP* 9.75 (for a Near Eastern parallel see M. L. West, *HSCP* 73 [1969], 116–17); Eratosthenes fr. 22 Powell.

[19]On Io see III.2 below. On Kallisto and Artemis Kalliste (Paus. 8.35.8) cf. already K. O. Müller, *Prolegomena zu einer wissentschaftlichen Mythologie* (1825), 75; *PR* I 304–305; II.1.n.18 below. On the theme of the murdered maiden = goddess see also I.7.nn.26, 39 above.

sacrifice which made it possible for the Greeks to create tragedy.[20] Strangely, mythology often reversed the crime of Oedipus so that the father sacrificed his own son and even ate him, due to some gruesome madness. In reality, child-sacrifice is attested with frightening frequency[21] as a horrible but easy form of substitution, as a deadly solution to the conflicts arising from the generational gap. Myth itself sometimes seems to indicate uncertainty: was Athamas or Phrixos, the father or the son, the sacrificial victim for Zeus Laphystios?[22] In reality, some kind of substitute, a perfect—and, according to myth, golden—ram, was given to Zeus "the glutton."

The succession of male generations is characterized by conflict and death, and yet culture needs a continuity that can survive catastrophe. In order to attain such continuity and demonstrate it, ritual, starting in the Upper Palaeolithic, apparently found a special device: the symbolizing of the feminine.

Besides sacrificial and burial rites, remarkable evidence for the continuity between the age of the hunt and the agricultural era is provided by the female statuettes that have come to be known as "Venus statuettes," although that name has long been recognized to be inappropriate. They make their appearance in the Upper Palaeolithic from Siberia to Spain and continue, sometimes in further developed variations, sometimes in quite "primitive," simple form, throughout the Neolithic and on into the high cultures.[23] At that point they are not easy to interpret, and it is even harder to postulate a unity or clarity of meaning and function for them during the Palaeolithic. In Siberia

---

[20] See also E. Buschor, *Phidias der Mensch* (1948), esp. 47–50, 52–56 on the "gemeinsamen geistigen Raum" in the look and the gesture of the Phidian fighters involved in single combat.

[21] See Devereux, "Cannibalistic Impulses." It is characteristic that Empedokles (*VS* 31 B 137) describes in detail the eating up of the son, not of the father.

[22] See II.4.n.27 below.

[23] Müller-Karpe (1966) 249–52, 216–19; (1968) 289–301, 380–95; F. Hancar, *Prähistor. Zeitschr.* 30/31 (1939/40), 85–156; K. J. Narr, *Antaios* 2 (1961), 132–57; R. Levy, *The Gate of Horn* ([1948] = *Religious Conceptions of the Stone Age* [1963]), 54–63, 78–81; Maringer (1956) 193–201. On the Greek Neolithic see C. Zervos, *Naissance de la civilisation en Grèce* II (1963), 565–68, 575–79. For the Near East see E. D. van Buren, *Clay Figurines of Babylonia and Assyria* (1930); J. B. Pritchard, *Palestinian Figurines in Relation to Certain Goddesses Known through Literature* (1943); J. Thimme, "Die religiöse Bedeutung der Kykladenidole," *AK* 8 (1965), 72–86, criticized by K. Schefold, ibid., 87–90; P. J. Ucko, *Anthropomorphic Figurines of Predynastic Egypt and Neolithic Crete with Comparative Material from the Prehistoric Near East and Mainland Greece* (1968), contests the interpretation of the figurines as mother-goddesses and argues for a plurality of functions and meanings. W. Helck, *Betrachtungen zur Grossen Göttin* (1971), sees her primarily as a goddess of female sexuality.

these idols are a part of the female realm, but they are also connected with hunting quarry, as indicated above all in a statuette found at the center of a circle of skulls of mammoths.[24] Further, in Çatal Hüyük there are large plaster statues of a goddess, or sometimes two goddesses, set up in household shrines over the bones of the dead. The goddess is portrayed with her legs spread wide so as to give birth; next to her, bull horns and boar skulls dominate the room.[25] In several instances, bull skulls—and, in one case, a ram's skull—are emerging from between her thighs.[26] She is the mother of the beasts[27] that are hunted and sacrificed, a life-giving power governing the dead. On the murals, men clothed in leopard skins swarm around a stag or a bull; in a statuette, the goddess appears flanked on either side by a leopard:[28] she is attended by the hunting community, the *homo necans*, assimilating himself to a beast of prey. The iconography leads directly to the image of Kybele sitting upon her throne between two lions. Could the young boy who is intimately connected with the great goddess at Çatal Hüyük perhaps be a predecessor of Attis/Adonis?[29]

In the Neolithic and Bronze ages, the female idols became in many ways more developed and differentiated. One cannot simply equate the statuettes from Sesklo and Lerna, the beautiful marble statues from Cycladic graves, and the consummately splendid statues of goddesses from Minoan palace shrines. But it can hardly be doubted that they reflect a continuity and differentiation growing from a common root. The goddesses of Greek polytheism, so different and complementary, are, nonetheless, consistently similar in appearance at an earlier stage, with one or the other simply becoming dominant in a

---

[24]See I.2.n.8 above; on the female realm see I. Paulson, Å. Hultkrantz, and K. Jettmar, *Die Religionen Nordeurasiens und der amerikanischen Arktis* (1962), 309–10.

[25]Mellaart (1967) 133–34, 139, 144–45, 236; cf. (1970) I 166–85.

[26]Mellaart (1967) 116–33 (sanctuary, VII 1), 140–41 (VI B 7), 144–46 (VI B 14), 147–48 (VI B 8), 148–50 (VI B 10, ram); summary on 106–107. For the goddess on her throne giving birth to a boy see pl. IX (V.4.n.75 below). Müller-Karpe ignores the animal births [(1968) 382–83], so as to contest the identification of the figure as a goddess.

[27]It is primarily the Eskimos who have a mother of hunting prey, namely, Sedna, Mother of Seals, a sacrificed maiden in the myth (F. Boas, *Sixth Annual Report of the Bureau of Ethnology, 1884–5*, [1888], 583–91; K. Rasmussen, *Thulefahrt* [1925], 69–73), as well as a mother of reindeer (Rasmussen, *Thulefahrt*, 245–46; I. Paulson, *Schutzgeister des Wildes (der Jagdtiere und Fische) in Nordeurasien* [Uppsala, 1961], 266–69), a mother of the whales among the Chukchis (Paulson, *Schutzgeister*, 64–65). For Rhea/Demeter as mother of the horse see Paus. 8.8.2 (Nestane).

[28]Mellaart (1967) pl. 67/68; IX and pl. 54/55, 61/63.

[29]The statuette of the goddess and the boy from Hacilar (*Anat. Stud.* 11 [1961], 59) does not, however, depict sexual intercourse; cf. Mellaart (1970) I 170.

sanctuary or city. Each is the Great Goddess presiding over a male society; each is depicted in her attire as Mistress of the Beasts,[30] and Mistress of the Sacrifice, even Hera and Demeter. Artemis enjoys the closest ties to the hunt, but at the same time Artemis of Ephesus is very much like Asiatic Kybele.[31] Aphrodite[32] recalls Oriental origins, the naked goddess, who was herself a transformation of the ancient "Venus statuettes," becoming more sexual and less dangerous in the course of civilization. The goddess Ištar, however, remained a goddess of war, and Venus could bring victory to a Sulla or a Caesar.[33]

Bachofen's ingenious but fantastic theory of a prehistoric matriarchy has hindered the understanding of these female deities. Female dominance is no more possible in Neolithic farming cultures than it is among Upper Palaeolithic hunting societies.[34] Moreover, these goddesses are characteristically savage and dangerous: they are the ones who kill, who demand and justify sacrifice.

---

[30] On the Potnia Theron (*Il.* 21.470) see F. Studniczka, *Kyrene* (1890), 153–65; Nilsson (1955) 308–309; E. Spartz, "Das Wappenbild des Herrn und der Herrin der Tiere," Diss. München, 1964; Ch. Christou, *Potnia Theron* (Thessaloniki, 1968). Argive Hera appears as mistress of the beasts (Simon [1969] 41–45; Hera Argeia with an animal park among the Veneti—Strabo 5 p. 215), as does Hera Lakinia (I.2.n.21 above), Artemis Orthia (R. M. Dawkins, *The Sanctuary of Artemis Orthia*, *JHS* Suppl. 5 [1929]), Demeter of Phigalia, the Despoina of Lykosura, or Athena Alea (R. Stiglitz, *Die grossen Göttinnen Arkadiens* [1967], 125, 36, 90), etc.; Pandora (Hes. *Th.* 578–84).

At least in Greece, the Master of the Beasts is less prominent (J. Chittenden, "The Master of Animals," *Hesperia* 16 [1947], 89–114); one ought not to call him in pseudo-Greek *πότνιος θηρῶν (*sic* Nilsson [1955] 309–10). See generally H. Wozak, "Herr und Herrin der Tiere in Vorderasien" Diss. Wien, 1967; Å. Hultkrantz, ed., *The Supernatural Owners of Nature* (Uppsala, 1961); Paulson, *Schutzgeister*; La Barre (1970) 163–69, 189–91.

[31] On Artemis of Ephesus see Ch. Picard, *Ephèse et Claros* (1922), 451–538 (who hypothetically posits an origin in the "earth-goddess").

[32] G. Contenau, *La déesse nue babylonienne* (1914); H. Herter in *Eléments orientaux dans la religion grecque ancienne* (1960), 61–76; Nilsson (1955) 519–21.

[33] On *Venus victrix* see C. Koch, *RE* VIII A 860–64. For the Near East see M. Th. Barrelet, "Les déesses armées et ailées," *Syria* 32 (1955), 222–60. For an armed Aphrodite see Paus. 2.5.1, 3.15.10 (Sparta: cf. Plut. *Lac. inst.* 239a); Paus. 3.21.1 (Kythera). The special cult of Aphrodite at Lokroi (I.7.n.21 above) was established in thanks for a victory in war.

[34] See I.5.n.34 above. See also S. Pembroke, "Women in Charge: The Function of Alternatives in Early Greek Tradition and the Ancient Idea of Matriarchy," *Journal of the Warburg Inst.* 30 (1967), 1–35; F. Cornelius, *Geistesgeschichte der Frühzeit* I (1960), 67–71, 178–79, sees the priority of the patrilineal farmer, but wants to fit matrilinearity in as a later transitional stage (83–86). One does well to remember that in spite of their tremendous honor for the mother of god, both Eastern and Western forms of Catholicism are purely male organizations.

It is the hunter's job to support the family. He acts for the sake of his wife and his mother. When this merges with feelings of anxiety and guilt, it is comforting to shift responsibility to another, higher will. The hunter sets out to do his deadly work "for the sake of the Mother." For the time being, this long-range objective forces him to abstain from sexual intercourse. When sexual frustration is added to the hunter's aggressivity, it appears to him as though a mysterious female being inhabits the outdoors. Thus, this higher will to which he submits becomes consolidated in the conceptions and artistic reproductions, even already in language, as the figure of the Great Goddess, the wife and mother, the bearer of children, the giver of life, but the one who demands death; in her hands, she holds the broken-off Horn of Plenty.[35] Primitive man saw and realized that the mysterious process of birth, a woman releasing new life from her womb, could shut the jaws of death. Thus, it was the woman who insured continuity beyond death. Blood sacrifice and death provided the necessary complement. Next to the goddess was her dying partner, the sacrificial animal. Beside the anthropomorphic goddess in Çatal Hüyük[36] and in Minoan Crete is the bull representing masculinity, the bull that must die. While Isis represents the permanence of the throne, the pharaoh takes office as Horus, but always dies as Osiris.[37] Man, the paradigm of mankind in a male society, enters the permanent order as a young man, ritually and symbolically transformed into "his mother's bull," as we learn from one of the pharaonic epithets,[38] and sooner or later he must die, just like the sacrificial animal. Thus, myth provides the Great Goddess with a chosen companion who is both her son and lover; he is known as "father" Attis,[39] whom the goddess loves, emasculates, and kills.

The unspeakable sacrifice follows the maiden-sacrifice and is thus simultaneously a restitution of the maiden according to the Great

---

[35] See I.7.n.59 above.

[36] Mellaart (1967) 215 and passim.

[37] On Isis and the throne see H. Frankfort, *Kingship and the Gods* (1948), 43–45; *The Intellectual Adventure of Ancient Man* (1946), 26. The priest of Sarapis is changed annually, whereas the priestess of Isis holds office for life; L. Vidman, *Isis und Sarapis bei den Griechen und Römern* (1970), 48–51.

[38] Kamutef: see Frankfort, *Kingship and the Gods* (1948), 177–80. The "marriage of the mother" after the father's murder is a routine motif of succession in a Babylonian myth: see W. G. Lambert, *Kadmos* 4 (1965), 64–72 = *ANET* 517–18.

[39] For the evidence see Hepding (1903); M. J. Vermaseren, *The Legend of Attis in Greek and Roman Art* (1966). On the children's word "atta," "daddy," see P. Chantraine, *Dictionnaire étymologique de la langue grecque* I (1968), *s.v.*

Goddess's will. The mother and the maiden, Kore, stand side by side, meeting in the course of the secret rituals of the *Männerbund*. In mythology, the two may become indistinguishable and overlap,[40] in which case the Great Goddess is maiden, lover, and mother at once. But the maiden has her share of sacrifice as well: the ram, an animal considered a kind of father, was sacrificed to Kore.[41] Thus, what appears, when following up the myth by logic, to cause the most severe contradiction, actually has a necessary function in the drama of human society in the counterpoint of familial bonds and male activity.

In the religious ritual and the resultant worship of a god, the cohesiveness and continued existence of a group and its culture are best guaranteed through one supreme and permanent authority. The ritual provides the orientation that transforms confrontation into unity. In the storm of history, it was always those societal organizations with religious foundations that were finally able to assert themselves: all that remained of the Roman Empire was the Roman Catholic Church. And there, too, the central act remained the incredible, one-time and voluntary sacrifice in which the will of the father became one with that of the son, a sacrifice repeated in the sacred meal, bringing salvation through admission of guilt. A permanent order thus arose—cultural progress that nonetheless preserved human violence. All attempts to create a new man have failed so far. Perhaps our future chances would be better if man could recognize that he still is what he once was long ago, that his existence is defined by the past.

---

[40] Hekate (at Ephesus) comes into existence when Artemis puts her own ornaments on a hanged girl: see Callim. fr. 461 (I.7.n.26 above). So, too, in the Eskimo myth, Sedna is made a sacrificed maiden. For the sacrifice of a virgin for the Great Goddess see Steph. Byz. *s.v.* Lemnos.

[41] See V.4.n.40 below.

II. WEREWOLVES AROUND THE TRIPOD KETTLE

In the first chapter we tried to see man's basic condition from a biological, psychological, and sociological perspective, as indicated in Greek sacrificial ritual. However, in spite of the evidence adduced from prehistory and folklore, we were unable to proceed without hypothetical supplements and generalizations; moreover, since the examples used to illustrate the thesis were chosen selectively, doubts could be raised as to our methodology. The following chapters reverse the procedure. We will examine various individual cult-complexes as exhaustively as possible, then ask to what extent the details fit the perspective developed in Chapter I. If in so doing we find ourselves confronted again and again by sacrificial ritual with its tension between encountering death and affirming life, its external form consisting of preparations, a frightening central moment, and restitution, then we may see in this a confirmation of our hypothesis.

Ancient Greek rituals were bound to permanent local groups and hence to specific localities as well, i.e., the sanctuaries and altars that had been set up for all time. Yet, in studying such complexes, one always discovers similarities to other rituals in other places, just as various myths often reflect a single structure. Thus, related rituals can be grouped; they need by no means invoke or worship the same gods in order to be considered similar. By comparing related phenomena we shall find that details will illuminate each other, that we can bridge gaps in the transmission and surmise certain lines in the tradition which do not always correspond to ethnic or linguistic categories.

First of all, we shall examine a complex that appears especially ancient, since it reflects the ideology of the predatory animal pack at its sacrificial meal, and this in spite of the fact that cooking in a kettle, a clearly cultural achievement, is an essential part of the rite. Antitheses and tensions are the stuff of ritual—hence, individual rituals cannot be explained by their momentary aims; rather, we must understand them in the larger context. Not just the religious cult, but the order of society itself takes shape in sacrifice.

1. *Lykaia and Lykaion*

When the wave of Sea Peoples and Dorian migrations destroyed Mycenaean culture, only the mountainous region of Arcadia was able, as a retreat, to assert its pre-Dorian individuality. Later, too, it was slow to join in the rise of the city cultures; it developed an urban center only after 371, at the newly founded city of Megalopolis. The Arcadians themselves were as aware of the antiquity of their race and customs as were their neighbors: long before the Hellenistic Age discovered pastoral Arcadia as the setting for its romantic yearnings, the Arcadians had been known as "acorn eaters" and "older than the moon."[1]

Rumors of terrible, primitive activity especially surrounded the main Arcadian festival to Zeus,[2] celebrated in the mountains of Lykaion in the heart of Arcadia. There were tales of human sacrifice, cannibalism, and werewolves. Plato is the first source we know who mentions this as a current story (*mŷthos*) "that is told of the sanctuary of Lykaian Zeus in Arcadia, namely, that he who tastes of one bit of human entrails minced up with those of other victims is inevitably transformed into a wolf."[3] Plato compares this eerie metamorphosis with the development of a tyrant who, once having killed, can no longer stop. Bloodshed has its consequences. The pseudo-Platonic

[1] Βαλανηφάγοι: see the oracle (#31 Parke and Wormell [1958]) in Hdt. 1.66; ἄκρον χεῖμα Lyk. 483 with Schol.; Verg. *Ecl.* 10.20; Plut. *Es. carn.* indicates a festival: ἐχορεύσαμεν ὑφ' ἡδονῆς. Προσέληνοι: see Hippys, *FGrHist* 554 F 7; Eudoxos fr. 41 Gisinger = Schol. Apoll. Rhod. 4.264; Schol. Aristoph. *Nub.* 397; Callim. fr. 191.56 and Pfeiffer *ad loc.*; Lyk. 482 with Schol.; etc.

[2] W. Immerwahr, *Die Kulte und Mythen Arkadiens* (1891), 1–24; Nilsson (1906) 8–10; (1955) 397–401; Farnell I (1894) 41–42, 144–46; Cook I (1914) 63–99; Schwenn (1915) 20–25; Joh. Schmidt, *RE* XIII (1927), 2248–52; G. Piccaluga, *Lykaon, un tema mitico* (1968).

[3] *Resp.* 565d.

Minos[4] mentions human sacrifice at the "Lykaia festival" as certain fact, and Theophrastus[5] compares the sacrifice "at the Lykaia in Arcadia" with Carthaginian sacrifices to Moloch.

Pausanias saw and described the altar of Zeus at the summit of Mount Lykaion, but he did not participate in the festival, for the sacrifice there took place "in secret." To this Pausanias remarks: "I could see no pleasure in delving into this sacrifice; let it be as it is and as it was from the beginning."[6] Pausanias also named and described the other cult sites of Zeus Lykaios: the mysterious precinct where none may enter, on the mountain slope somewhat below the summit—anyone going in would have to die,[7] and inside he would cast no shadow; then the Cave of Rhea and the precinct called Kretaia on the mountain where, it was told, Zeus was born, and fed and cared for by the Arcadian nymphs;[8] finally, the Stadium, the Hippodrome, and the sanctuary of Pan further down the mountain.[9] This is where the athletic competitions took place during the Lykaia festival. Other literary sources supplement Pausanias' indications, and excavations have confirmed and expanded our knowledge. Votive offerings dating back to the seventh century B.C. have come to light near the altar of Zeus, a simple mound of earth and ash.[10]

But what Pausanias piously concealed in his description of the altar of Zeus, he mentioned in relating the story of Damarchos of Parrhasia, who won the boxing competition at Olympia in about 400 B.C.[11] It was claimed that he "turned into a wolf at the sacrifice to Zeus

---

[4] 315c.

[5] In Porph. *Abst.* 2.27.

[6] 8.38.7; cf. 8.2.6, 4.22.7; Kallisthenes, *FGrHist* 124 F 23; Pind. *Ol.* 13.108.

[7] Paus. 8.38.6; cf. Theopompos, *FGrHist* 115 F 343 = Polyb. 16.12.7; Architimos, *FGrHist* 315 F 1 (cf. Jacoby III B Notes p. 48 n. 8) = Plut. *Q. Gr.* 300a–c; Schol. Callim. *Hy. Zeus* 13; Strabo 8 p. 388; Pliny *NH* 4.21; n.33 below; Schol. Theocr. 1.123e–f *τὰ εἰσερχόμενα ζῷα ἄγονα γίνεσθαι*, and cf. Schol. Callim. *Hy. Zeus* 13. On the results of the excavations see *RE* XIII 2240–41; Cook I (1914) 83; the measurements are approx. 60 × 130 m.

[8] *Κρηταία*: Paus. 8.38.2. *Σπήλαιον τῆς Ῥέας*: Paus. 8.36.3; cf. 8.31.4; Callim. *Hy. Zeus* 10–14 (the scholion confuses the precinct of Rhea with the *ἄβατον*: see n. 7 above). Cf. *RE* XIII 2243. On the spring, Hagno, and rain-magic see Paus. 8.38.3–4.

[9] Paus. 8.38.5; *RE* XIII 2237–40; Cook I (1914) 82.

[10] K. Kourouniotis, *Eph. Arch.* (1904), 153–214; (1905), 161–78; *Praktika* (1909), 64, 185–200; Cook I (1914) 63–99; cf. E. Meyer, *RE* XIII (1927), 2235–44; G. Mylonas, *Classical Studies in Honour of W. A. Oldfather* (1943), 122–33. On the type see W. Krämer, "Prähistorische Brandopferplätze," in *Helvetia antiqua* (1966), 111–22.

[11] 6.8.2; L. Moretti, *Olympionikai* (Rome, 1957), #359. The name appears as Demainetos (i.e., Damainetos) in Skopas (?), *FGrHist* 413 = Varro in Pliny *NH* 8.82; Aug. *Civ. Dei* 18.17.

Lykaios, and changed back into a man again in the tenth year thereafter." The condition for being transformed and changed back is just that: "someone was always turned into a wolf at the sacrifice to Zeus Lykaios, but not for his whole life; if he refrained from eating human flesh while he was a wolf, they say he would turn back into a man in the tenth year; but if he ate it, he remained a beast forever." [12] Pausanias probably found the legend of Damarchos in a local Hellenistic history; but if it is tied to the victory at Olympia, it goes back beyond Plato.

The accompanying myth is found already in the Hesiodic catalogues [13] and reflects the ritual in a particularly transparent way. What was only a vague rumor among Plato's contemporaries is told here as the crime of the ancestral king of the Arcadians; he is related to the wolf even in his name, Lykaon. Once upon a time, the gods, including Zeus himself, came to visit him and be entertained in a common sacrificial meal. But the sacred meal turned into cannibalism, for Lykaon slaughtered a young boy upon the altar at the summit and poured out his blood on that altar; then he and his helper "mixed the boy's entrails in with the sacrificial meat and brought it to the table." [14] Of course, divine punishment followed. Zeus overturned the table, graphically putting an end to the newly formed community, and hurled a bolt of lightning into Lykaon's house; most importantly, Lykaon himself turned into a wolf. In another, frequently told version, the gruesome sacrifice was followed by a flood that destroyed most of the human race, [15] yet Lykaon's descendants, the Arcadians, survived to come together at the altar again and again for secret sacrifice.

Opinions differed as to the identity of the boy whose entrails were sliced into the sacrificial meat. The *Library* of Apollodoros speaks of an anonymous "native" boy; Ovid calls him a "hostage"; Lycophron gives him the name "Nyktimos," the "night-like," [16] and makes him Lykaon's own son; the Eratosthenic *Katasterismoi*, by contrast, invoking Hesiod as its precedent, [17] say that he was "Arkas," the eponymous hero of the Arcadians, who was Lykaon's grandson. His mother was

---

[12] Paus. 8.2.6.

[13] Hes. fr. 163 M.-W., and cf. fr. 354; Apollod. 3.96–97; Eumelos, *FGrHist* 451 F 8 = Apollod. 3.100; Lyk. 480–81 with Schol.; a tragedy by Xenokles, *TGF* p. 770; Ov. *Met.* 1.198–239; Clem. *Pr.* 2.36.5; Nonnus 18.20–24; *RML* II 2165–68; *PR* I 127–29; Piccaluga, *Lykaon*, 29–98.

[14] Apollod. 3.98; cf. Nikolaos, *FGrHist* 90 F 38.

[15] Apollod. 3.98–99; Tzetz. ad Lyk. 481; Ov. *Met.* 1.240 ff.; Hyg. *Fab.* 176.

[16] Apollod. 3.98; Ov. *Met.* 1.227; Lyk. 481.

[17] Fr. 163 M.-W. = *"Eratosth." Catast. Fragmenta Vaticana*, ed. Rehm (1899), p. 2.

Kallisto, Lykaon's daughter, who during her amorous encounter with Zeus was turned into a bear.[18] Thus, the Arcadian par excellence is the "son of a bear," on the one hand, and a victim at the altar of Zeus, on the other. This death does not end the story, for both Arkas and Nyktimos were included in the genealogies as ancestral Arcadian kings.[19] Zeus brought his victim back to life,[20] according to the myth, only to have him come full circle and return to the sacrificial situation: Arkas was brought up by a goatherd, but upon becoming an ephebe he turned to hunting. Once, while in the region of Mount Lykaion, he came on the track of his own mother. According to one text, he hunted her down; according to another, they mated.[21] These mythical variants attest once more to the ambivalence of weapons and sexuality in hunting behavior. The gruesome act occurred in that very precinct on the mountain into which none could enter. For this reason, Arkas and the bear had to be sacrificed again "according to the custom" at the altar of Zeus Lykaios. At this point the myth fades, allowing the victims to be translated to heaven as stars. The ritual, however, goes on in the same place, and in the circuit of time, it is to form an important junction in the lives of the Arcadians.

Some curious details were reported by a Hellenistic author called Euanthes,[22] who was read by Varro. Admittedly, his concern is not with the Arcadians as a whole but with a single family descended from Anthos, whom the author seems to count as one of his own ancestors. A young boy of the family would regularly be selected by lot and led to a lake. He had to strip, hang his clothes on an oak tree, and swim across the lake; thereupon he would disappear in the wilderness and turn into a wolf. He would have to live as a wolf among wolves for eight years, after which time, if he had abstained from human meat, he could return to the lake, swim across it, take down his clothes from the oak tree, and turn into a human again, though he was now nine years older and a grown man. Thus far, Euanthes. This

---

[18] R. Franz, "De Callistus fabula," *Leipz. Stud.* 12 (1890), 235–365; *RML* II 931–35; *RE* X 1726–29; W. Sale, *RhM* 105 (1962), 133–41; 108 (1965), 11–35.

[19] Paus. 8.3–4, 8.24.1.

[20] *"Eratosth." Catast.*: *πάλιν ἀναπλάσας ἄρτιον ἔθηκεν.*

[21] "Erat." *Cat.* 1 pp. 52–53 Robert *ὑπὸ δὲ τοῦ ἰδίου υἱοῦ διωκομένην . . . ; ἀγνοήσας τὴν μητέρα γῆμαι* in *Fragmenta Vaticana* (see n. 17), where the last word is written between the lines; *matri inscius vim ferre voluit* Schol. Germ. p. 64.21 Breysig.

[22] *FGrHist* 320 = Varro in Pliny *N.H.* 8.81; Aug. *Civ. Dei* 18.17. For the Arcadians being descended from the oak see Lyk. 480; Plut. *Q. Rom.* 286a; for Dryas as the wife of Arkas see Paus. 8.4.2.

is not identical with the versions reported by the earlier authors.[23] Any link with the pan-Arcadian festival, the Lykaia, is missing; there is selection by lot instead of the sacrificial meal. But the combination of a transformation into a wolf, a nine-year period, and an injunction to abstain makes the connection very close. Did pan-Arcadian werewolf practices and familial customs run a parallel course? It is more likely that some sort of development took place. With the founding of Megalopolis, urban culture arrived in Arcadia, and there in the agora Zeus Lykaios was given the most prominent temple.[24] Thus, the Lykaia festival was now organized here, and although, as Pausanias tells us, the Arcadians still sacrificed upon the altar on the mountain, it is safe to assume that some aspects of the cult were changed at that time and, to some extent, civilized. After this reform, the old ways could no longer be carried on officially, but only in the tradition of a particularly conservative family. Plato's testimony comes from before this time, as does the legend of the boxer Damarchos. Regardless of how we conceive of the relationship between family customs and pan-Arcadian rituals, Euanthes' report at least gives us some idea of how such wolf-metamorphoses were accomplished.

Both Pausanias and Pliny considered these werewolf stories to be clear examples of shameless braggadocio and the shameful gullibility of the masses,[25] and when Plato uses the word *mŷthos* he is already expressing a certain skepticism. Paradoxically, the modern researcher cannot assume the same critical, enlightened stance. There is no doubt that werewolves existed, just like leopard men and tiger men, as a clandestine *Männerbund*, a secret society, wavering between demonic possession and horseplay, as is common in such a *Männerbund*. In Europe, there is at least one case of a "werewolf" on record in sixteenth-century Livland. There, the werewolvish activity consisted for the most part of breaking into other people's cellars at night and drinking any beer found there.[26] More dangerous and perhaps more ancient were the bands of leopard men in Africa, who conspired to assassinate others and practice cannibalism. Leopard men appear on the

[23] Stressed by Nilsson (1906) 9, (1955) 400; cf. Cook I (1914) 73.

[24] Paus. 8.30.2.

[25] Paus. 8.2.6; Pliny *N.H.* 8.80.

[26] Höfler (1934) 315ff.; L. Gernet, "Dolon le loup," *Mél. Cumont* (1936), 189–208 = *Anthropologie de la Grèce antique* (1968), 154–71; W. E. Peuckert, *Geheimkulte* (1961), 100–117; R. Eisler, *Man into Wolf* (1951); I.2 above. See also B. Lindskog, *African Leopard Men* (Uppsala, 1954). For werewolves in Wallis still in the eighteenth century see H. G. Wackernagel, *Schweiz. Arch. f. Volkskunde* 35 (1936), 1–12; 46 (1949), 74. For "dog-men" in Hittite ritual texts see *ANET* 360. On the *Hirpi Sorani* see Serv. *Aen.* 11.785.

murals in Çatal Hüyük as well,[27] and their costumes recall those of the later Greek centaurs and satyrs, those "wild men" who fell upon wine jars much like the werewolves in Livland. The leopard, one of the great cats and a climber, was the primate's arch-enemy. By training himself in the ways of the wolf, man became a hunter and lord of the earth. Could it be that these bands of leopard men and wolf men were the direct result of this decisive step? Werewolves are, in any case, attested in antiquity not only in fairytales but in a doctor's clinical report. Markellos of Sidon treated cases of "lykanthropy" as a mental disorder,[28] a special form of melancholy, by the cure-all of letting blood. He knew patients who "run out at night imitating wolves and dogs in every way and gadding about for the most part in cemeteries until dawn." Their legs usually bore the scars of dog bites. Strangely, these fits of madness occurred with great regularity, according to the calendar, in February, the month of the Lupercalia: even in late antiquity, then, the so-called mental disorder was regulated through ritual.

By combining rumors about Arcadian sacrifice with local mythology, we arrive at a description of an entirely real, institutionalized ritual. At its center was the secret sacrificial festival at the ash-altar of Zeus Lykaios. We gather from the name, Nyktimos, that it occurred at night. The entrails of many sacrificial animals were, so they say, sliced in together with those of a man, so that what each person ate was seemingly a matter of chance. Apparently, everything would be stirred together in a large tripod kettle[29] and each person had to fish

---

[27] See I.2.n.19 above; I.8.n.28. For Indians hunting in wolf's clothing see F. E. Zeuner, *Geschichte der Haustiere* (1967), 54.

[28] In Aët. Amid. 6.11 (Oribas. 8.9; Paul. Aeg. 3.16; *Physiognom. Graeci* II 282), cf. W. H. Roscher, *Das von der Kynanthropie handelnde Fragment des Marcellus von Side*, Abh. Leipzig 17.3 (1897); Galen XIX 719 Kühn; *περὶ Λυκάονος ἢ λυκανθρώπου* Paul. Aeg. 3.16. "Lykanthropy" no longer plays a role in modern psychiatry (*contra* Piccaluga, *Lykaon*, 58): it was culturally determined.

[29] Because Homeric descriptions of sacrifice, and most depictions on vases, present only the act of roasting on a spit, boiling has gone largely unnoticed; there is nothing about it, e.g., in Stengel (1910; 1920). On the other hand, the significance of the sacred tripod has been studied (K. Schwendemann, *JdI* 36 [1921], 151–85; P. Guillon, *Les trépieds du Ptoion* [1943], 87–174), but without considering its use as a pot for cooking. Both roasting with spits and cooking in a kettle are represented on a Caeretan hydria, Villa Giulia, *ASAA* 24/26 (1946/48) pl. 4, Detienne and Vernant (1979) pl. I–IV; cf. a fragment from the Acropolis, Graef and Langlotz nr. 654. *Ὄπτησις σπλάγχνων, κρεῶν ἕψησις* in the decree of the Milesian *Molpoi SIG*[3] 57 = *LSAM* 50.35; for boiling at the sacrifice to the Horai see Philochoros 328 F 173. "Partially boiling and partially roasting" is a standard motif in stories of gruesome banquets: Lykaon, Ov. *Met.* 1.228–29; Thyestes, Accius 220–22, Sen. *Thy.* 765–67; Harpagos, Hdt. 1.119; Tereus, Ov. *Met.* 6.645–46; Dionysus, *OF* 35 = Clem. *Pr.* 2.18; Eur. *Cyclops* 243–46, 358, 403–404. Cf. the Orphic taboo *ἑφθὸν*

out his portion with the sacred fork (the trident?) (see Figure 4).[30] For all must partake of the sacred object; no participant was allowed to decline. The sacrificial meal separated the "wolves" from the "sons of the bear," the Arcadians, just as Lykaon had divorced himself from the circle of the gods. Excavators at Mount Lykaion, however, have discovered no human bones among the sacrificial detritus. Yet, even by daylight it is hard to distinguish a piece of human heart, liver, or kidney from that of an equally large mammal; modern surgeons have even pondered the feasibility of transplants. In the flickering flames at night, only the innermost circle of sacrificial servants could know what was really floating about in the kettle. The power of suggestion comes from tradition, from social constraints. Human entrails may well have been thought to be present. The proof lay in their effects on the participants: each time one or more would be struck with "wolf's frenzy," whether spontaneously or because they were somehow manipulated. The "eaters" and the "slaughterers" were not the same. The "wolves" disappeared into the dark and had to avoid human settlements for years. By the time the dawning rays of sunlight hit the golden eagles on top of the columns east of the altar, the sacrifice was long over.

The wolf metamorphosis, as described by Euanthes, can easily be seen as an initiation ritual, for stripping off one's clothes and swimming across a lake are clearly rites of passage. If Damarchos won an Olympic victory after his time as a wolf, he could have been no older than 16 at the time of his transformation. Now it is surely the novice, the first-time participant in the nocturnal festivities, who would be most susceptible to suggestion, and hence to the shocking realization that he had eaten human flesh. From this we surmise that the separation of the "wolves" from the "sons of the bear" reflected a division according to age. The myth always speaks of a "young boy" to be sacrificed, that is, a representative of precisely that age-class which the

---

μὴ ὀπτᾶν, Arist. *Probl. ined.* 3.43 Bussemaker (Paris, 1857), and cf. Iambl. *V. Pyth.* 154; Ath. 656b; Detienne (1977) 163–217. For boiling a ram see *IG* XII 7, 515.78; for its place in Roman ritual see Varro *Ll.* 5.98; for the boiling of meat in Germanic sacrifices see J. de Vries, *Altgermanische Religionsgeschichte* I (1956^2), 416–20; for the Hittites see *ANET* 348/49; for reference in the OT see n. 30 below. It is not certain whether the invention of boiling presupposes the invention of ceramics; boiling is also possible in stretched-out hides, into which hot stones would be thrown to heat the water.

[30] For the trident as a fork for meat see I Sam 2:13 (cf. Exod. 27.3); E. D. van Buren, *Symbols of the Gods* (1945), 138. The trident also appears as a harpoon: Aesch. *Sept.* 131; cf. Bulle, *RML* III 2855; Simon (1969) 82; J. Boardman, *CR* 21 (1971), 143; III.8.n.21 below.

ephebes must leave. The boy must die if they are to enter the sphere of manhood. But expulsion has to precede inclusion. Life as a wolf in the wilderness, occurring, as we see, roughly between the ages of 16 and 25, was thus analogous to the Spartan Krypteia which, in turn, later corresponded to military service.[31] According to Myron in his history of the Messenian War,[32] Arcadian warriors carried the skins of wolves and bears instead of shields. This behavior, wild and primitive though it was, was enough to preserve Arcadian independence.

In discussing the preparations for the sacrificial festival, the myth makes mention of the precinct "that none may enter." Because both Arkas and the bear went in, they had to be sacrificed.[33] Those who break the tabu are damned and consecrated at once, destined for sacrifice. Predatory animals, it was said, would not follow their quarry past this line.[34] Thus, within this small area they were free although caught in an inescapable trap, for the wolves were waiting just outside. The tabu was evidently created only as an excuse and justification for the sacrificial killing. Presumably the sacrificial animals were set free only to be caught all the more certainly when they would cross the line "of their own free will." The Arcadians' own name may indicate a "bear festival," which would easily fit the well-known type.[35] It is, of course, doubtful whether bears still lived in Arcadia in historical times; perhaps a shaggy ram could have been used as a substitute quarry.

It is clear that women would have been excluded from the Arcadians' nocturnal sacrifices. Instead, there is a female realm that is closed to men. Only "consecrated women" could enter the cave where Rhea bore Zeus,[36] for they represented the Arcadian nymphs who took care of him. Whereas the men gathered for sacrifice, for the "act" of killing, the women attended to newborn life. Thus, the polarity of

---

[31] Jeanmaire (1939) 550–69. Alcaeus, in exile, calls himself λυκαιμίαις (130.25 LP).

[32] In Paus. 4.11.3; cf. Verg. *Aen.* 8.282, Stat. *Theb.* 4.303 f.

[33] "Erat." *Cat.* 1 pp. 52–53 Robert.

[34] Ael. *Nat. an.* 11.6, who mentions an Αὐλή of Pan at Mount Lykaion; it is presumably identical with the ἄβατον nn. 7, 33 above, in accordance with the parallel of the sanctuary of Apollo Hylatas at Kurion (Cyprus). Cf. Ael. *Nat. an.* 11.7: there, too, the dogs do not pursue the ἔλαφοι into the sacred grove, and whoever touches Apollo's altar is thrown from a cliff; cf. Strabo 14 p. 683. Anyone who entered the precinct on Mount Lykaion was considered a "deer": see Plut. *Q. Gr.* 300a–c (n. 7 above).

[35] See I.2.n.5 above; ἄρκος rather than ἄρκτος already in *LSS* 115 B 16 (fourth century B.C.), not just since the Septuagint (thus Frisk, Chantraine *s.v.*).

[36] Paus. 8.36.3 (n.8 above).

the sexes bound together the course of life and assured perpetuity in the face of death.

Thus, too, there must be a new unity corresponding to the rift in male society due to the sacrifice: following the sacrifice at the altar on the summit, there was the inevitable agon further down the mountain. According to Xenophon, Xenias the Arcadian "performed the Lykaion sacrifice and held an agon"[37] even in foreign lands. In enumerating the Greek agonistic festivals, Pindar mentions the "festive gathering of Zeus Lykaios," "the race-track of Zeus," several times.[38] It is even called the oldest of all Greek agons.[39] The prize there was a bronze implement, probably a tripod, a constant reminder of that nighttime festival. Those who had turned into "wolves" were of course not allowed to participate in the agon, but those who had returned after nine years' abstinence were permitted to enter. Thus, for Damarchos, his time as a wolf was a time of preparation for the agon, and even for the Olympic victory which he then won—the victory that lifted him out of his Arcadian context, bringing him pan-Hellenic fame. In the agon following the sacrifice, societal roles were reassigned. The expulsion of some and the new start for others went together. The younger members of the rising generation had to be forced away into the wild "outdoors" while the twenty-five-year-olds, now marriageable, entered athletic competitions.[40] They were now true Arcadians, "acorn-eaters" as opposed to carnivorous beasts of prey. They had found their way and might now participate in the sacrifice without danger, taking their wreaths from the altar and dedicating their bronze tripods.

Strange to say, there was another god besides Zeus who was involved in the agon—Pan, the lewd goat-like god. His sacred grove and sanctuary were next to the stadium,[41] and the eponymous official organizing the Lykaia was alternately a priest of Zeus, then a priest of Pan.[42] Arcadian coins, moreover, display Zeus's head on one side and

---

[37] Xen. *Anab.* 1.2.10 *τὰ Λύκαια ἔθυσε καὶ ἀγῶνα ἔθηκε.*

[38] *Ol.* 9.96; *Nem.* 10.45–48; *Ol.* 7.83–84, 13.107–108.

[39] Paus. 8.2.1; Pliny *NH* 7.205. For a prize of *χαλκός* see Pind. *Nem.* 10.45; Polemon Schol. Pind. *Ol.* 7.153d (*σκεύη* 153c); cf. Pind. *Ol.* 7.84; Arist. fr. 637; *Marm. Par.*, *FGrHist* 239 A 17; Kleophanes, *Περὶ ἀγώνων* Schol. Pind. *Ol.* 9.143a. For inscriptions see *IG* V 2.463, 549, 550, IV 428, 673, IV 1² 629, II/III² 993 (new foundation ca. 215 B.C.). For coins with the superscription ΛΥΚΑΙΑ see Imhoof-Blumer (1886) 105.

[40] For agon and wedding see I.7.n.13 above.

[41] Paus. 8.38.5 ("Zufall," Nilsson [1906], 444.2); *μαντεῖον Πανός* Schol. Theocr. 1.123c.

[42] *IG* V 2, 550.

Pan's on the other.[43] In genealogical myths, Arcadian Pan is said to be the son of Zeus and, hence, the brother or half-brother of Arkas.[44] Similarly, when it is told that Arkas was raised by a "goatherd,"[45] it evidently reflects the role played by the cult of Pan in the life of a growing boy. It is thus the polar opposite of the world of the huntress Artemis, to which Arkas' mother, Kallisto, belongs. Zeus and Pan almost seem to embody the antithesis between aggression and sexuality, or at least between order and wild living. The serious sacrifice that divides the group is the antithesis of the unification during a period of license. But the details of the program, and its sequence in time, escape us.

A strange abundance of antitheses is thus impressed upon the celebrants at the Arcadian ritual: predatory animals/sacrificial animals, wolves/bears, wolves/stags, meat-eaters/acorn-eaters; night/day, sacrifice/agon, Zeus/Pan; the old/the young, men/women, killing/giving birth. Characteristically, these antitheses do not merely collapse into a uniform duality. They are, rather, generally transformed, each into the other, like night into day: the hunter becomes the hunted, the cannibal turns ascetic, the living are killed, the dead come back to life—the "secret sacrifice" reveals the primordial situation of the hunt.

2. *Pelops at Olympia*

Although they were of the greatest antiquity, the Lykaia remained a basically provincial, purely Arcadian event. They were clearly eclipsed by the Olympic games, held every four years on the banks of the Alpheios, at the foot of the Hill of Kronos, in the sacred grove of Zeus.[1]

---

[43] Cook I (1914) 68–70. On the statue of Pan in the sanctuary of Zeus Lykaios at Megalopolis see Paus. 8.30.2–3; for altars of Zeus Lykaios and Pan at Tegea see Paus. 8.53.11.

[44] Epimenides, *FGrHist* 457 F 9 = Schol. Theocr. 1.3–4c, and cf. Schol. Theocr. 1.123b; Aristippos, *FGrHist* 317 F 4. For Pan as the son of Aither, see Ariathos, *FGrHist* 316 F 4; as the son of Hermes, see Pind. fr. 100. For Pan as the inventor of astronomy, i.e., putting an end to the primitive *προσέληνοι* see Schol. Lyk. 482.

[45] *"Eratosth." Catast.*, p. 2 = Hes. fr. 163; according to another version ("Erat." *Cat.* p. 52 Robert), the she-bear and her baby are caught by *αἰπόλοι*.

[1] E. N. Gardiner, *Olympia, Its History and Remains* (1925); W. Hege and E. Rodenwaldt,

These games were the most important expression of unity above all in the Peloponnesus, but also for all of Greece. Their enormous importance in giving the Greeks a sense of identity in sports and politics, and even in their spiritual existence, is well known. Long after Pindar, the Greeks were still aware that this athletic event was simultaneously a religious festival, even if only through the Zeus of Phidias, which was considered the most important expression of their conception of god. But the fact that both the religious experience and the socio-athletic event were imbedded in a ritual with a striking resemblance to the Lykaia, a sacrificial ritual that centered on the precinct of Pelops and the altar of Zeus, received far less notice and hence has come down to us only in scattered fragments.[2]

Although there are signs of a pre-Doric tradition, the history of the sanctuary at Olympia[3] seems to start in the Protogeometric era. From then on, the significance of the games constantly grows. It is probably just chance that the list of victors begins in the year 776, for it was about then that the Greek alphabet was introduced.[4] Pisa and Elis fought to possess the famous site over many generations until, in the sixth century, Pisa was destroyed and the pan-Hellenic organization of the Hellanodikai was established, with Elis presiding.[5] Thanks to the excavations, we have detailed knowledge of the sanctuary's glorious architectural history, as well as its decline in late antiquity until the emperor Theodosius abolished the games.[6] But it is far easier to

---

Olympia (1936); L. Ziehen and J. Wiesner, *RE* XVIII (1939), 1–174; A. Mousset, *Olympie et les jeux grecs* (1960). On the excavations see E. Curtius and F. Adler, *Olympia* (1890–97); W. Wrede and E. Kunze, *Bericht über die Ausgrabungen in Olympia* 1–5 (1944–64); E. Kunze, *Olympische Forschungen* 1ff. (1944ff.). For the lists of victors see L. Moretti, *Olympionikai* (Rome, 1957).

[2] A. B. Cook, "Zeus, Jupiter, and the Oak," *CR* 17 (1903), 268–78, interpreted the ritual as a battle between the young and the old priest-king; he was followed by F. M. Cornford in Harrison (1927) 219–29. L. Drees, *Der Ursprung der Olympischen Spiele* (1962) sees "pre-Doric fertility cults."

[3] F. Mezö, *Geschichte der Olympischen Spiele* (1930); for a hypercritical account see U. Kahrstedt, "Zur Geschichte von Elis und Olympia," *NGG* (1927), 157–76; cf. F. Jacoby, *FGrHist* III B: Kommentar 221–28.

[4] L. H. Jeffery, *The Local Scripts of Archaic Greece* (1961), 20–21.

[5] The tradition is late, confused, tendentious, and unverifiable; Paus. 6.22.3–4 (destruction of Pisa after 588), 5.9.4; Strabo 7 p. 355 (cf. F. Bölte, *RE* VII A 196–97): destruction of Pisa by Elis and Sparta after the (Second?) Messenian War. On the discus of Iphitos and Lykurgus, see Arist. fr. 533, and cf. F. Jacoby, *Apollodors Chronik* (1902), 116 n. 30, 122–26.

[6] On the prohibition against pagan cults see *Cod. Theod.* XVI.10.10–12 (391/92); the last Olympic games took place in 393.

sift through the archaeological layers than to organize and evaluate the literary evidence for the cults and games at Olympia, for here the most diverse traditions have become superimposed: pre-Doric and Doric, Pisan and Elean, local and pan-Hellenic. Moreover, they are frequently distorted by local patriotism or politics or because genealogies have become systematized.[7] We can often do no more than combine those items that necessarily belong together because of their function.

In so doing, however, we must omit the most famous foundation myth of the Olympic games. Although the story of Pelops' abduction of Hippodameia from her father, Oinomaos, in the chariot race and Oinomaos' death in the process was already a part of the pseudo-Hesiodic Great Ehoiai and appeared on the Kypselos chest about 570 B.C., and although the pedimental sculpture on the eastern side of the great temple of Zeus depicted the preparations for this chariot race,[8] the myth only became important for Olympia once chariot-racing had become the most prestigious and costly sport and thus become the focal point of the games. However, according to the Olympic victory lists, chariot-racing was only introduced in the twenty-fifth Olympiad, that is, in 680 B.C.[9] Until then, only victors in the foot-race were recorded. There are, admittedly, reproductions of war chariots among the votive offerings long before 680—as there are in other Greek sanctuaries as well—and perhaps even the name of the wily charioteer, Myrtilos, can be traced to Hittite roots, which might then be related to the introduction of the war chariot in the middle of the second millennium B.C.[10] But all this does not touch upon the heart of the Olympic festival. Rather, in its details the myth of Hippodameia reflects the strange tabus of Elean animal-husbandry rites;[11] and the fact that it penetrated to Olympia testifies to growing Elean influence in the sev-

[7] In what follows we will not deal with the traditions that attribute the founding of the games to Endymion (Paus. 5.1.4, 5.8.1, 6.20.9), Peisos (Phlegon, *FGrHist* 257 F 1), Herakles the Idaean dactyl (Paus. 5.7.6, 5.8.1, 5.13.8, 5.14.7), or Zeus after his victory over Kronos (Paus. 5.7.10, 8.2.2).

[8] *PR* II 206–17; Hes. fr. 259 M.-W.; Paus. 5.17.7. On the pedimental sculptures see M. L. Säflund, *The East Pediment of the Temple of Zeus at Olympia* (1970). There is perhaps already an allusion at *Il.* 2.104 Πέλοπι πληξίππῳ.

[9] Paus. 5.8.7; doubted by L. Deubner, *Kult und Spiel im alten Olympia* (1936), 26–27, on account of the votive offerings.

[10] H. R. Hall, *JHS* 29 (1909), 19–22; cf. F. Schachermeyr, *Anzeiger für die Altertumswissenschaft* 19 (1966), 16.

[11] G. Devereux, "The Abduction of Hippodameia as 'Aition' of a Greek Animal Husbandry Rite," *SMSR* 36 (1965), 3–25; Hdt. 4.30; Plut. *Q. Gr.* 303b; Paus. 5.5.2.

enth century. But the Hippodrome was located far from the Altis of Zeus, in the plain of the Alpheios. The stadium, by contrast, was inside the sacred precinct and oriented toward the altar of Zeus.[12] The preeminent agon at Olympia was the foot-race in the stadium, and it alone had a sacral function.

The altar of Zeus, the stadium, and the precinct of Pelops are the cultic centers of the sanctuary at Olympia. It goes without saying that the cultic activity consisted mainly of sacrifice. Of course, in such a highly frequented sanctuary there would be a considerable diversity of rituals current at any one time: private, occasional sacrifice; daily and annual state sacrifice—important because the city administration of Elis was intimately involved in running Olympia; and finally, once every four years, all the sacrifices at the great festival. And yet, to the extent that they concerned the same hero or god at the same site, we may assume that there was some analogy between the smaller sacrifices and the larger ones, the frequent and the rare; they would express essentially the same thing, whether abbreviated or elaborated.

"The Eleans honored Pelops as much more than the other heroes at Olympia as they honored Zeus more than the other gods," says Pausanias.[13] And already Pindar describes his unique status: "Now he is drenched in glorious blood-offerings, lying by the ford of the Alpheios, with his busy tomb right next to the altar which the most people come to visit."[14] The altar of Zeus is the true center of the Altis, remaining until the very end nothing more than a primitive heap of earth and ash, though it had risen to an impressive height through the sacrifices of countless visitors.[15] Not far off, toward the west, was the precinct of Pelops, enclosed by a circle of stones. Before sacrificing to Zeus, one sacrificed to Pelops,[16] who thus got the same number of sacrifices even if they were not as large. In both cases, only white poplar wood could be used, and it was regularly provided by a specially appointed sacrificial servant, the woodman (ξυλεύς).[17] Whereas

[12] E. Kunze, 5. *Bericht über die Ausgrabungen in Olympia* (1956), 10–12; *AJA* 52 (1948), 492–93. *Πάντα προσθήκη πλὴν τοῦ δρόμου* Plut. *Q. conv.* 675c; cf. Paus. 5.8.6, 8.26.4; Philostr. *Gymn.* 12.

[13] 5.13.1.

[14] *Ol.* 1.90–93 *νῦν δ' ἐν αἱμακουρίαις ἀγλααῖσι μέμεικται, 'Αλφεοῦ πόρῳ κλιθείς, τύμβον ἀμφίπολον ἔχων πολυξενωτάτῳ παρὰ βωμῷ.*

[15] Paus. 5.13.8–11, 14.1–3; cf. Thuc. 5.50.1. On the type, see II.1.n.10 above.

[16] Schol. Pind. *Ol.* 1.149a *καὶ πρὸ τοῦ Διὸς αὐτῷ τοὺς 'Ηλείους θύειν*. On the Pelopion, see Paus. 5.13.1–3.

[17] Paus. 5.13.3, 14.2; for *ξυλεύς* in inscriptions see *Olympia* V (1896), #62, 64, 121, 122, 124.

the entrance to the precinct of Pelops is in the west, the altar of Zeus was approached from the stadium, i.e., from the east. Whereas blood was poured into the sacrificial pit[18] for Pelops, that is to say, downward, the altar of Zeus grew higher and higher. Thus, the two sacrificial recipients were united in a polar tension. The hero and the god went together like night and day. The name *Pelops* can be interpreted to mean "dark-face,"[19] the antithesis of the god of daylight. The agon took place in the daytime and could not be continued into the night.[20] When the schedule started to get too long, the pentathlon and the horse-racing were moved up, to be followed by the sacrifices,[21] which were, in turn, followed by the foot-race in the stadium. Thus, the preparatory sacrifice to Pelops occurred at night. "When the Eleans had slaughtered the sacrificial victim according to their custom, its consecrated parts would lie on the altar, though not as yet set on fire. The runners would stand at a distance of one stade from the altar, in front of which there was a priest signalling the start with a torch. And the winner would set fire to the consecrated parts and then depart as an Olympic victor." Thus, following ancient sources, Philostratus[22] describes the foot-race to the altar; one stade long, hence *stadium*. And in fact, the early stadium ended at the altar.

Philostratus also connects the double course with sacrifice: "When the Eleans had finished their sacrifice, all the Greek envoys present had to sacrifice. But in order that their procession not be delayed, the runners ran one stade away from the altar, calling on the Greeks to come, then turned and ran back as if to announce that all Greece was present rejoicing. So much for the double course."[23] It started at the altar and returned there in the end. Pausanias describes the altar more exactly: "The custom is to slaughter victims in the lower part of the altar, the so-called prothysis. Then they take the thighs up to the very highest point of the altar and burn them there. . . . But only men may climb up from the prothysis to the top."[24] Thus, the foot-race

---

[18] *Εἰς τὸν βόθρον* Paus. 5.13.2.

[19] J. B. Hofmann, *Etymologisches Wörterbuch des Griechischen* (1950), *s.v. πελιτνός*; *RE* Suppl. VII 849. Even if Pelops were—as is more probable—the eponym of a people, Πέλοπες (like Δόλοπες, Δρύοπες), the association would not be without significance.

[20] Paus. 5.9.3.

[21] Paus. 5.9.3: 472 B.C.

[22] *Gymn.* 5. Cf. Eumenes' foundation at Delphi, *LSS* 44.15 *ὁ δὲ δρόμος γινέσθω . . . ἄχρι ποτὶ τὸν βωμόν, ὁ δὲ νικέων ὑφαπτέτω τὰ ἱερά.*

[23] *Gymn.* 6.

[24] Paus. 5.13.9–10.

presupposes the bloody act of killing; likewise Pelops was "drenched with blood" in the preliminary sacrifice. The end of the race, its goal, is the top of the ancient heap of ash, the place where fire must blaze and burn up the thigh-bones. The race marks the transition from blood to purifying fire, from encountering death to the joyful satisfaction of surviving as manifested in the strength of the victor. Thus, the most important agon at Olympia is part of a sacrificial act moving between the Pelopion and the altar of Zeus.

The proper victim for Zeus is a bull;[25] for Pelops, however, it is a black ram—this, too, stresses the dark side of the ceremony. Pausanias describes the annual sacrifice offered to Pelops by the Elean officials: "From this sacrifice the prophet gets no share; rather, it is customary to give only the ram's neck to the so-called woodman. . . . Anyone, whether Elean or foreign, who eats the meat of the victim sacrificed to Pelops is not allowed to go in to Zeus"[26]—that is, he may not enter his precinct or draw near to the altar. Pausanias states this rule in a general way; it was surely not restricted to the annual sacrifice but applied to every Pelops sacrifice preceding a sacrifice to Zeus, especially during the great penteteric festival.

Characteristically, the sacrifice of a ram is also present in the myth linking Pelops to Oinomaos and Hippodameia. Oinomaos, so it is told, used to sacrifice a ram, letting the suitor get a head start until the "consecrated" parts of the victim were burned; thereupon he would chase after the fleeing suitor and, upon catching up with him, kill him.[27] A series of vase-paintings depicts the sacrifice of a ram, based on scenes from tragedy;[28] admittedly, these rams are white, but this is probably just an iconographical shift caused by some intervening factor. Even the tale is quite far removed from ritual; yet, in the seventh century, those who told the myth were moved to combine Pelops with a race and the sacrifice of a ram, just as these had been combined in ritual until the time of Pausanias and Philostratus.

---

[25] Dio Chrys. *Or.* 12.51. On Milon's sacrifice of a bull at Olympia see Ath. 412–13a; Phylarchos, *FGrHist* 81 F 3.

[26] Paus. 5.13.2. Cf. the sacrifice of a ram at the Babylonian New Year Festival. There, the priests and those who do the slaughtering must leave Babylon: *ANET* 333.

[27] Diod. 4.73.4 ὁ μὲν Οἰνόμαος ἔθυε κριόν . . . ἁγισθέντων δὲ τῶν ἱερῶν τότε ἄρχεσθαι τοῦ δρόμου.

[28] Brommer (1960) 370: Calyx-crater *BM* F 271 = D 6, Cook I (1914) pl. 5; amphora *BM* F 331 = D 7, Cook I (1914) pl. 3; bell-crater in Naples H. 2200 = Cook I (1914) 409 = B 3 = *ARV*² 1440.1, *FR* III 151, Harrison (1927) 218; amphora at Ruvo = Cook I (1914) 408 = D 14, *Annali* 23 (1851), pl. QR. For Etruscan urns see *EAA* V 115f. Zeus appears as the recipient of the sacrifice on D 7, Artemis on B 3.

The sanctuary of Pelops was no ordinary grave. It was said that his bones were preserved in a chest not far from the sanctuary of Artemis Kordax;[29] an outsized shoulder blade, however, was kept separately for display, though it no longer existed during Pausanias' lifetime.[30] Pelops' severed shoulder blade belongs, of course, with that other gruesome myth of Pelops which Pindar mentioned in his first *Olympian Ode*, only to reject it indignantly as a malicious invention of the poets.[31] This myth runs directly parallel to the myth of Lykaon: with Zeus leading the way, the gods came to visit Tantalos for a festive meal. Tantalos, however, for whatever reason, turned the divine banquet into cannibalism: he slaughtered his own son Pelops and offered him to the gods as food; and Demeter, unaware because of her intense mourning for Kore, took the shoulder and ate it. Here, too, the justice of Zeus was quick to follow, even though there is little agreement as to the form it took. In any case, Pelops' limbs were put back together in the sacrificial kettle and he was brought to life once more; only the missing shoulder had to be replaced by a piece of ivory.[32]

After Pindar, the Greeks often changed the setting of this cannibalistic banquet of the gods to Sipylos in Asia Minor.[33] Modern mythologists think that the myths of Tantalos and Lykaon must have influenced each other. But because both clearly depict a sacrificial act, from cutting the victim up and cooking him in a kettle, to the typical closing "revival" by putting together his bones, both are therefore bound to a specific locality through ritual. Pelops' shoulder was displayed at Olympia, not in Asia Minor. And just as the Pelopion, the altar of Zeus, and the stadium were all very close to each other, so too the only woman allowed to enter the stadium was the priestess of De-

---

[29] Paus. 6.22.1.

[30] Paus. 5.13.4–6, cf. Lykcoph. 52–56 and Schol. 54; Apollod. *Epit.* 5.10–11; Schol. LV *Il.* 6.92; Dionysios, *FGrHist* 15 F 3; Firm. *Err.* 15.1. Pelops' shoulder guaranteed the victory of the Pelopids over Troy.

[31] Pind. *Ol.* 1.26–27, 47–53.

[32] *PR* II 290–92; Bacchyl. fr. 42; Eur. *Iph. Taur.* 386–88; Lyk. 152–55; Apollod. *Epit.* 2.2–3; etc. F. M. Cornford in Harrison (1927) 243–51 interpreted the myth as belonging to an initiation and New Year's festival. The "knife of Pelops" was kept in the Sikyonian treasury: see Paus. 6.19.6, and cf. Pind. *Ol.* 1.49. There may be a depiction of Pelops in the tripod kettle on metope 32 from the Heraion at the river Sele: see E. Simon, *JdI* 82 (1967), 281–86. The myth of Medea, Pelias, and the ram in the kettle is far more popular (for vases see Brommer [1960] 348–49); there, Medea appears as the priestess of "Artemis" (Diod. 4.51; Hyg. *Fab.* 24), i.e., of Hekate, the nocturnal leader of dogs.

[33] Pind. *Ol.* 1.38, and cf. *PR* II 286.

meter Chamyne, who took her place at the games upon an altar opposite the Hellanodikai.[34] Thus, the Olympic ritual combines the very gods that went together in the myth—Pelops, Zeus, and Demeter. The cannibalistic myth of Pelops that so shocked Pindar clearly refers to the Olympic festival.

The hero's mythical fate is strangely connected with the ram slaughtered in the Pelopion—on account of that same shoulder blade. In Greece, as elsewhere, a ram's shouder blade played a special part in the sacrifice of a ram. In such a sacrifice for Poseidon on Mykonos, it is expressly stated that "the back and the shoulder blade should be cut up, the shoulder blade sprinkled with wine"[35]—i.e., destruction first, then sacred honors. In Slavic and German folk-religion, a ram's shoulder blade is used for making predictions,[36] while at Olympia a seer would have been present at the sacrifice for Pelops. We do not know what was actually done with ram's bones in historical times. Philostratus was content to avoid the problem by simply saying that they did "whatever was customary there"[37] and we too must be satisfied with the realization that, in both the sacrifice of the ram and the myth of Pelops, the traces of ancient hunting and sacrificial customs shine through precisely in the way in which the bones are treated.

One thing is certain—and once again this connects the sacrifice at Olympia with the Lykaia—the big tripod kettle was extremely important in these sacrificial customs. At least part of the sacrificial meat would be collected in such kettles (λέβητες) and prepared in them, although at first without fire. This is apparent from a legend current in the time of Peisistratos and retold by Herodotus: Hippokrates, the father of the future Athenian tyrant, "as yet held no public office, when a great marvel happened to him while he was at Olympia to see the games. When he had offered the sacrifice, the tripod kettles, which were full of meat and water, began to boil without fire and to overflow."[38] Hippokrates was evidently one of those envoys who, according to Philostratus, would sacrifice after the double course. The fact that the kettles began to boil by themselves was a sign of the vic-

---

[34] Paus. 6.20.9, 6.21.1; *8. Bericht über die Ausgrabungen in Olympia* (1967), 69–74.

[35] *SIG*³ 1024.5 = LS 96.7 *νῶτογ καὶ πλάτη κόπτεται, ἡ πλάτη σπένδεται*. Tearing off the arm together with the shoulder blade plays a special role in the *σπαραγμός*; see Eur. *Bacch.* 1125–27; Theocr. 26.22; cf. Hdt. 4.62.

[36] F. S. Krauss, *Volksglaube und religiöser Brauch der Südslaven* (1890), 166–67.

[37] Philostr. *Gymn.* 5.

[38] Hdt. 1.59. According to the bequest of Kritolaos, *IG* XII 7.515 = *LSS* 61, 78, a sacrificial ram is cooked and prepared so as to be eaten after the games.

torious strength emanating from Hippokrates, a sign of the future tyranny of his son, who had yet to be born. Such was the importance of cooking in a tripod kettle at the pan-Hellenic festival at Olympia. It is no surprise, then, that—as the excavations have shown—great numbers of tripods were dedicated there from the tenth century on.[39] And when, in the fifth century, the great temple of Zeus was constructed, the architects chose for the acroteria this very symbol of Olympic sacrifice, namely, the tripod.[40] Between the tripods was the battle of the Lapiths and the Centaurs, and the start of the chariot race between Pelops and Oinomaos.

Just as Arkas was the ancestor of the Arcadians, so Pelops was the eponymous hero of the whole "island of Pelops" (Peloponnesus). Just as the Arcadians gathered for the festival of Zeus Lykaios, so the inhabitants of the "island of Pelops" and, later, all of Greece gathered for the Olympic festival "in the wooded valleys of Kronos in Pelops' land."[41] And just as the sacrifice for Zeus Lykaios divided Arcadian society, thereby shedding light on its workings, so too the sacrificial ritual at Olympia accentuated the distribution of roles in society. The division is most noticeable in those participating in the sacrifice of the ram to Pelops. This chthonic, dark, nocturnal sacrifice is for eating, but the "eaters" must subsequently shun the daytime sky god, Zeus; their expulsion is comparable to that of the werewolves of Lykaion. Of course, age groups and initiations were no longer part of the pan-Hellenic festival; thus, perhaps the meat was given to any social outcasts who happened to be there. There was one person of sacred status who ate of the ram, namely, the "woodman"; consequently he was permanently barred from the precinct of Zeus. The others were probably allowed to purify themselves and return, as in the parallel case, cited by Pausanias, of a purificatory bath in Pergamon.[42] Nevertheless, the "woodman" supplied the wood for burnt offerings to Zeus whereby the ash-altar grew ever higher—a typical distribution of roles in a comedy of innocence. In sacrificing the ram, fasting was definitely required of the seer taking part, and was also required of the athletes. We know with certainty that at least until the late sixth

[39] F. Willemsen, "Dreifusskessel von Olympia," *Olympische Forschungen* 3 (1957), 161, reports that the older pieces found were remarkably numerous around the Pelopion; H.-V. Herrmann, "Die Kessel der orientalisierenden Zeit," *Olympische Forschungen* 6 (1966); 11 (1979).

[40] Paus. 5.10.4.

[41] Pind. *Ol.* 3.23.

[42] 5.13.3. On the ξυλεύς see n. 17 above.

century, athletes had to undergo a thirty-day period of preparation with a strict vegetarian diet of cheese and figs. This was likewise a time of sexual abstinence.[43] Such renunciation and focusing of one's strength was meant to lead all the more certainly to a final goal, to the competition, to victory, and to sacrifice. For many kinds of sacrifice followed on a victory, with banquets at the state's expense; the victory celebration also included an evening procession; and in the story that Artemis Kordax was given her name[44]—a name that reflects a lascivious dance—because Pelops' companions held their procession within her precinct, we get some indication of the sexual urges that, having built up inside, would now break out into the open in the festival celebration. Yet, Pelops' bones were kept in the precinct of Artemis Kordax—that is, sacrifice underlay this uninhibited celebration. After this, military symbolism would mark a return to order: trumpets instead of flutes, armor instead of athletic nudity;[45] this was the norm for all Greek men.

Women, though not virgins, were barred from the Olympic games, under threat of death.[46] The festival divided the family in order to illuminate its relationships. At Olympia, the women had to play their part before and after the games. On an evening at the start of the festival, the women, weeping and wailing, would gather in the gymnasium for sacrifice: this was said to be in honor of Achilles,[47] though it may just have been a secondary motivation for the comedy of innocence preceding the sacrifice. After the games, they had an athletic festival of their own, the Heraia.[48] The temple of Hera was built much earlier than that of Zeus, not because Zeus was any less important but, rather, because the men gathered around the site where killing took place, the ash-altar, whereas the goddess of women stayed at home, in her *ναός*. On the other hand, the men were barred from the sacred cave of Zeus Sosipolis and Eileithyia on the slopes of the Hill of

---

[43] *Τυρὸν ἐκ τῶν ταλάρων* Paus. 6.7.10, until the victory of Dromeus (#188 Moretti, *Olympionikai*, 484 B.C.), for whom the sculptor Pythagoras of Rhegion made a statue; thence, perhaps, the tradition that Pythagoras of Samos introduced a diet of meat rather than cheese, Porph. *V. Pyth.* 15 (from Antonios Diogenes), Iambl. *V. Pyth.* 25. *Ἀφροδισίων ἀπέχεσθαι* see Philostr. *Gymn.* 22; cf. I.7 at n. 13 above. For the thirty-day period see Philostr. *V. Ap.* 5.43; Johannes Chrysostomos, Migne *PG* 51, 76. For a training period of ten months, see Paus. 5.24.9, 5.21.13, 6.24.3.

[44] Paus. 6.22.1; cf. Schol. Aristid. III 564, 10 Dindorf *ὅτι ἐν τῇ Πέλοπος κρεουργίᾳ ὠρχήσατο ὁ Πᾶν*.

[45] Philostr. *Gymn.* 7; Plut. *Q. conv.* 639e; Artemidorus 1.63.

[46] Paus. 5.6.7, 6.7.2; Ael. *Nat. an.* 5.17; Philostr. *Gymn.* 17 (II 270 ed. Teubn.).

[47] Paus. 6.23.3.

[48] Paus. 5.16.2; Nilsson (1906) 62; on Hera at Olympia see Simon (1969) 36–38.

Kronos.[49] An aged priestess and a virgin chosen each year, the "loutrophoros," were responsible for ministering to the cult of the divine child in the room of Eileithyia. The child's name seems to have been of little importance. Olympia was unable to establish itself as the birthplace of Zeus even though Pindar had mentioned the "Idaean Grotto,"[50] and a temple was built for the mother of the gods in the fifth century. Yet it was evidently not so much a question of the child's name as the expectation expressed in the ritual act, that the incessant killing in the male sphere where Pelops was "drenched" with blood must have its counterpart in the female sphere in the mysterious birth in the cave. How else could the "city be saved," as the name *Sosipolis* suggests? Thus, Rhea's cave on the slopes of Mount Lykaion has its necessary counterpart at Olympia. By combining those aspects which the festival divides, the power of men and the power of women, the circle of life is sealed.

These connections were no longer so obvious when the games grew into a highly organized business and when sport became important for its own sake, yet the two managed to survive side by side for a thousand years. An Olympic victory was a unique societal event, but the victor's status and the order in which the participating cities were ranked became visible mainly in the sacrifice. The winner of the foot-race would be the first to light the sacrificial fire, after which the envoys would sacrifice in a specific order set by the Judges of the Hellenes. Pride in individual achievement, and divine glory radiating from the sanctuary, were inseparably united. The participating communities demonstrated their renewed strength each time in the festive competition, the race between the "dark" sacrifice to Pelops and the fire of Zeus, past death to the sovereign order of life.

3. *Thyestes and Harpagos*

The third and most famous, indeed, proverbial, cannibalistic meal in Peloponnesian mythology is directly preserved only in liter-

---

[49] Paus. 6.20.2–4, 6.25.4. On the archaeological problem of the sanctuary see R. Hampe, *Studies for S. M. Robinson* I (1950), 336–50.

[50] Pind. *Ol.* 5.18, and cf. Schol. 42a.

ary sources: it is the feast of Thyestes (Θυέστεια δεῖπνα).[1] Thyestes and Atreus were sons of Pelops, and the parallels to the crime of Tantalos were drawn already in tragedies. Unfortunately, the *Atreus* of Sophocles and the *Thyestes* tragedies of Sophocles and Euripides have not survived, nor have the imitations by Ennius and Accius;[2] only the late version of *Thyestes* by Seneca remains, along with allusions in surviving tragedies, above all in Aeschylus' *Agamemnon* and in the *Electra* and *Orestes* of Euripides.[3] On the basis of quotations, it is clear that the myth appeared already in ancient epic, in the *Alkmaionis*, and in early mythography, in Pherekydes of Athens.[4]

The essential part of the "act" is the same in all versions; variation occurs only in the preceding sections and in the motivation. The two brothers struggled for the throne of Mycenae; Atreus slaughtered Thyestes' infant sons and served them up for dinner, so that Thyestes unsuspectingly ate the flesh of his own children. Of the brothers, one was a killer, the other an eater, but the worse pollution belonged to the eater. After this meal—all versions agree in this detail as well—Thyestes had to abandon the throne forever and flee the land: thus Atreus became, or remained, the Mycenaean king. Another set detail in the story is that Thyestes had previously committed adultery with his brother's wife, Aerope, whence the motivation for Atreus' dreadful deed: the "eater" could not restrain himself sexually either. Therefore, Atreus, the killer, hurled his unfaithful wife into the sea.[5]

It is clear once again how the myth repeats the course of the sacrificial ritual and adds gruesome details. It is hard to tell how much in Seneca's fantastic description derives from ancient tradition—the children were sacrificed, according to the letter of the ritual, in a secret sacrificial grove in an obscure corner of the palace grounds[6]—thus, effective theatrical pathos springs from the religious *mysterium tremendum*. According to Apollodorus,[7] the children fled to the altar of Zeus, only to be torn away and slaughtered. It is certain that the

[1] *PR* II 293–98; Cook I (1914) 405–409; Θυέστεια δεῖπνα Achill. Isag. p. 55.18 Maass = *VS* 41.10, and cf. Eur. *Or*. 1008.

[2] Sophocles pp. 91–94 and fr. 247–69 Pearson, Eur. fr. 391–97; Ennius *Scaen*. 340–65 Vahlen², Accius vv. 197–234c Ribbeck.

[3] Aesch. *Ag*. 1090–97, 1185–93, 1217–23, 1583–1602; Eur. *El*. 699–736; *Iph. Taur*. 812–17; *Or*. 811–15, 997–1010.

[4] *Alkmaionis* fr. 6 p. 77 Kinkel, and Pherekydes, *FGrHist* 3 F 133 = Schol. Eur. *Or*. 995. Cf. Apollod. *Epit*. 2.10–12.

[5] Soph. *Aias* 1295–97, Schol. 1297 = Euripides, *TGF* pp. 501–502.

[6] Sen. *Thy*. 641–788.

[7] *Epit*. 2.13.

feast of Thyestes followed the form of a sacrifice, as did any meal with meat. In Aeschylus, Atreus serves Thyestes his meal "under the pretense of happily celebrating a feast day" (*κρεουργὸν ἦμαρ*), a name clearly taken from sacrificial ritual.[8] At this unusual meal, Thyestes sits alone at his own table, as do all the others, "man for man." It was in just this way that the men of Aegina sacrificed to Poseidon as "solitary eaters," and this separation of the participants recurs at the Pitcher Feast in Athens.[9] Some of the entrails were roasted, and the majority were boiled in a bronze kettle, according to Accius and Seneca.[10] Here, then, as at Mount Lykaion and Olympia, the tripod kettle makes its appearance. Lykaon, too, it is said, prepared the meat of his human victim partially by roasting, partially by boiling. The head and feet were kept intact, and that is how the father later realized what he had eaten. This special treatment of the head and feet, recurring several times in Greek sacrificial ritual,[11] evidently goes back to primitive hunting customs. Finally, Thyestes overturns the table, just as happened after Lykaon's crime.[12] But the most transparent link between sacrifice (*θύος*) and the man who ate this feast, with which he remained proverbially associated, is his very name, Thyestes.

This dreadful sacrifice stirred the powers of the cosmos: the sun reversed its course. During the height of fifth-century speculation about nature, this wondrous change was variously rethought and rationalized. These interpretations assume that at that time the sun began to follow the course which it demonstrably follows today; the world was organized differently beforehand.[13] Thus, the crime as-

---

[8] Aesch. *Ag.* 1592, and cf. Fraenkel *ad loc.*; ἡ Πέλοπος κρεουργία Luk. *De salt.* 54; II.2.n.44 above.

[9] Aesch. *Ag.* 1595, and cf. IV.2.n.23 below.

[10] Accius 220–22 Ribbeck; Sen. *Thy.* 765–67; II.1.n.29 above.

[11] Head and feet for the god, see *SIG*[3] 1042 = *LS* 55.10; for the priests, see *LSS* 115, B 16; for the king, see Demon, *FGrHist* 327 F 1. Cf. Porph. in Euseb. *Praep. Ev.* 4.9.7; Hsch. *ἔνδρατα*, *Hy. Merc.* 137; Luk. *Syr. D.* 55; *LSS* 40 B 2; *LSS* 121; Eitrem (1917) 43–48; Stengel (1910) 85–91. For this practice in hunting customs see Meuli (1946) 241; A. Gahs, *Festschrift P. W. Schmid* (1928), 240; *UdG* IX 287.

[12] See II.1.n.14 above; Aesch. *Ag.* 1601. On Lesbos, there are as the parents of Dionysus *ἐνόρχης* the couple Thyestes and Daito ("sacrifice" and "meal"): Schol. Lyk. 212.

[13] Oinopides, *VS* 41.10; Plat. *Soph.* 269a *μαρτυρήσας ἄρα ὁ θεὸς Ἀτρεῖ μετέβαλεν αὐτὸ ἐπὶ τὸ νῦν σχῆμα*; Sophocles, *AP* 9.98; Hyg. *Fab.* 88; Serv. *Aen.* 1.568; Schol. Stat. *Theb.* 4.306; cf. also Hdt. 2.142. For the sun travelling from west to east see Eur. *Or.* 1001–1004, and cf. Schol. 812; Apollod. *Epit.* 2.12. For the scientific reinterpretation that Atreus, as an astronomer, discovered the sun's retrograde motion in the zodiac see Eur. fr. 861; Polyb. 34.2.6 = Strabo 1 p. 23; Soph. fr. 738 Pearson; Schol. Eur. *Or.* 998; Serv. *Aen.* 1.568.

sumes an almost cosmogonic function: ever since that unspeakable sacrifice, and because of it, the sun has kept to its familiar and reliable course. Just so, the Old Testament covenant followed the crime and the flood to guarantee the order of "seed-time and harvest, cold and heat, summer and winter, day and night." [14] The kingship of Mycenae was legitimized by the sun; Thyestes had to flee. The great feast took place at night; the next day at dawn the miracle had occurred. Once again, the transition of night into day—the Greek conception of time always follows this order—corresponds to the dark and the light sides of sacrifice. And just as we saw at Olympia,[15] the man who eats the meat at night is forced to leave; at dawn, the other man, even if he killed, becomes the victor.

From the very start, in the *Alkmaionis*, the myth relates the brothers' quarrel to an animal, a sacrificial animal—the golden ram or golden lamb. Ever since Euripides, this lamb was referred to in the feminine, reflecting a familiar tendency in the Greek language;[16] the likelihood that it should, rather, be a ram—referred to once in this context with the archaic word *ἀρνειός*[17]—is suggested by its counterpart at Olympia. Possession of the crown depends on this golden lamb. By rights it belonged to Atreus, and it was considered the most beautiful animal in his herd. It had, of course, been intended for sacrifice, but Atreus secretly strangled it instead and hid it in a chest (*λάρναξ*).[18] However, with the help of the unfaithful Aerope, Thyestes seized the lamb and showed it as his own at a great feast. Later versions struggled to connect the story of the lamb with the feast of Thyestes, and already in Aeschylus this gave rise to the curious doublet that Thyestes was banished twice.[19] Starting with Euripides,[20] the wondrous change in the course of the sun was moved to the first act. Thus, Thyestes, who had wanted to seize the crown by stealing the lamb, was overthrown and expelled by the evidence of the sun; it was only when he returned that Atreus served him that gruesome meal. Yet according to the older versions, and by the nature of the myth itself, the change in the sun's course and the unspeakable sacrifice go hand in hand: what appear as successive events in the story collapse into a single act as soon as the ritual-symbolic equivalence of animal and man in the sacrificial ritual is recognized. Indeed, the brothers'

---

[14] Gen. 8:22. [15] See II.2.n.26 above.

[16] Eur. *El.* 699–736; *Iph. Taur.* 813; *Or.* 812, 998.

[17] Schol. Eur. *Or.* 998; *aries* Sen. *Thy.* 226; Schol. Stat. *Theb.* 4.306.

[18] Apollod. *Epit.* 2.11; Schol. Eur. *Or.* 811. [19] Aesch. *Ag.* 1586/7.

[20] Eur. *El.* 699–736.

actions are exactly the same in both acts: Atreus kills something and hides it; Thyestes greedily snatches it up and exposes what had been hidden. Similarly, we saw that the Tantalos myth reflected the sacrifice of a ram at Olympia and that the Arcadian myth was a gruesome elaboration of the sacrifice on Mount Lykaion. There are two roles at this sacrifice, kept strictly apart yet closely related; in the Argive myth, they are played by two hostile brothers. The nocturnal "sacrificer" wins only a temporary victory, for the sunrise determines who has won the day: his is a mediating role at an exceptional time. Already in the *Iliad*—even though heroic epic abhors ritual atrocities—Thyestes' reign is seen as merely provisional. Agamemnon, though known to all as the son of Atreus, did not receive the king's scepter from his father; rather, it came to him via Thyestes.[21] Thus, the societal rift caused by sacrifice helps to achieve the succession between the generations—and what happened at Mount Lykaion and at Olympia was no different.

Whereas Argive mythology became literary early on, Argive cults sank into oblivion. The only indication that Thyestes was anything more than a character in tragedy in the Argolid is given by Pausanias, who describes "the grave of Thyestes" on the road from Mycenae to Argos. "A stone ram stands on top of it, because Thyestes took possession of the golden lamb." People called the site "the rams" (*κριοί*), even though there was only one stone ram. Could the multiple rams in the name point to a custom still in practice, consisting of repeated ram-sacrifice at Thyestes' grave? In the same context, a bit further on toward Argos at the crossing of the river Inachos, Pausanias mentions an altar of Helios.[22] Sacrificing a ram at night, crossing a river, and then sacrificing to Helios at dawn: the conjunction of these acts would be most attractive. But there is no proof.

Other sources, however, point to an Argive sacrificial festival that was named after a lamb, and even lent its name to a summer month: the "days of the lamb," *Ἀρνηίδες ἡμέραι*, in the month Arneos.[23] The festival began with the mourning cries of women and girls—just as the women and girls gathered for lamentation at the gymnasium on

---

[21] *Il.* 2.106–108; cf. Schol. A 106, where Aristarchus argues against Likymnios that Homer did not "yet" know of the fraternal strife between Atreus and Thyestes.

[22] Paus. 2.18.1–3. Crossing the river would correspond to swimming across the lake; cf. II.1.n.22 above.

[23] For the month Ἄρνηος see Schwyzer 90.3; *SEG* 3 (1929), #312.3; Nilsson (1906) 435–38; Callim. fr. 26–31; Konon, *FGrHist* 26 F 1 #19; Paus. 1.43.7, 2.19.8; Ov. *Ibis* 573 with Schol. The story of Poine and Koroibos (Paus. 1.43.7–8; *AP* 7.154) belongs to the Agrionia-type: see III.3 below.

the evening before the Olympic games. The refrain of their lament, the *αἴλινον*, gave rise to the myth of the death of the young boy, Linos. According to the tale, he was Apollo's son by Psamathe, the daughter of king Krotopos, and grew up among the lambs of the royal flock. But he was torn apart by the hounds of his grandfather Krotopos. The *αἴλινον* lament is sung in his honor at the Festival of the Lamb, which is held to commemorate his name and "his youth among the lambs."[24] It is, of course, only an appealing conjecture that the main sacrificial victim at this festival was a lamb, but an ancient Argive tradition speaks of a "lamb-singer," *ἀρνῳδός*, so called because he was awarded the sacrificial lamb as a prize.[25] Thus, it was not Argive dignitaries but a wandering stranger who would eat the victim. Callimachus, at least, apparently made the connection between this lamb-singer and the Festival of the Lamb.[26] But another aspect of the festival made a far greater impression and hence became the focus of our sources: "If a dog happened to enter the marketplace, they would kill it."[27] The myth explained this as vengeance for Linos; the proponents of nature-allegory saw it as a symbolic battle against the deadly heat of the dog-star, Sirius; the "dog-days" coincide with the "days of the lamb"—which are close, too, to the time of the Olympic games. Yet how are we to understand the peculiar role of the boundaries of the marketplace, in that a dog would be killed only if it crossed them? This is not an event in nature but a social ordinance. The market of Argos stood under the protection of Apollo, worshipped here as "Lykeios," a name which was taken to mean "wolf-like"; in this context Sophocles calls him the "wolf-killer," λυκοκτόνος,[28] possibly a direct allusion to that "day of dog-killing" (the close affinity of dogs and wolves needs no elaboration). Apollo the "wolf-like" was Linos' father; the boy—the lamb—was torn apart; therefore the greedy predators were henceforth barred from the kingdom of men, that is, from Apollo's agora. Likewise, Sophocles tells us in his *Electra* that Orestes, protected by Apollo the "wolf-like," killed Aegisthus, Thyestes' son, at Argos, and the impious Aegisthus had also been a provisional king, between Agamemnon and Orestes.

In his history of the Persians, Herodotus constructed a story in the Median-Persian milieu that corresponds in all its details to the feast of Thyestes. Just as Atreus had taken dreadful vengeance on Thyestes, so Astyages avenged himself on Harpagos, for the latter

[24] Konon, *FGrHist* 26 F 1.19. [25] Dionysios of Argos, *FGrHist* 308 F 2.

[26] Fr. 26.1–5. [27] Ael. *Nat. an.* 12.34 (on Klearchos, fr. 103 W.); Ath. 99e.

[28] Soph. *El.* 6, and cf. 645, 655, 1379.

had not obeyed his orders to kill Cyrus, the child of Mandane. Therefore, Astyages sent for Harpagos' thirteen-year-old son, whom he subsequently slaughtered, tearing him limb from limb; some of his flesh he boiled, some he roasted. He then served it to Harpagos at his special table while the others—significantly—ate lamb. The head, hands, and feet were covered in a basket which Harpagos himself had to uncover at the end of the meal.[29] The details of the story were probably taken from the feast of Thyestes, for we know that Herodotus was preceded by the versions in the *Alkmaionis*, Pherekydes, and Aeschylus' *Agamemnon*. But the gory feast is typically connected with the theme of the dog, or, rather, the wolf, even in this Median-Persian milieu: Cyrus, the king's son, was brought up by Kyno, "the bitch"—i.e., almost exactly like Romulus and Remus.[30] Moreover, the wolf-boy was helped in carrying out his appointed tasks by Harpagos, "the rapacious," i.e., the wolf, as his name must have been understood by the Greeks. They knew him as the Persian general who relentlessly subdued the cities of Asia Minor, a terrifying character on whom fitting stories would be fastened. The "wolf-like" man had become the eater of human flesh, and this meal transformed him, if only inwardly, invisibly: for under the mask of the devoted servant, he was henceforth the inexorable enemy of the king, unwilling to rest until Astyages had been overthrown. "By reason of that banquet," according to Herodotus (1.129), the Median empire fell to the Persians. The parties were divided through the sacrificial meal, and their division determined the dynastic succession.

4. *Aristaios and Aktaion*

On the island of Keos there was an animal-sacrifice to ward off the deadly power of Sirius, "the dog." Our evidence dates from the fourth and third centuries B.C. and is provided by Aristotle and his students and by the poets Callimachus and Apollonios.[1] The rite

---

[29] Hdt. 1.108–19.

[30] Hdt. 1.110–11; Just. 1.4.10–14; G. Binder, *Die Aussetzung des Königskindes* (1964), 17–23, 45–57.

[1] Theophr. *De ventis* 14, and cf. Arist. fr. 511, 611.27; Heraclides fr. 141 Wehrli = Cic. *div.*

was not accompanied by the sort of myth that would be used in tragedy, but only by a foundation legend: once, when the people of the Aegean islands were threatened by drought, they sought the advice of an oracle, which ordered them to summon the priest and prophet Aristaios, son of Apollo. When he came, he brought with him Arcadian priests, descendants of Lykaon,[2] and built an altar on a mountaintop to Zeus Ikmaios, "Zeus the rain god";[3] then he sacrificed to the dog-star and to this Zeus. Suddenly the cooling north winds began to blow, just as they do today in July, the "Etesian" winds that make the summer heat in Greece bearable.

Aristaios' activity has been interpreted as weather-magic,[4] and it is easy to empathize with a passionate, desperate yearning for coolness and moisture in the arid Greek summers. But the corresponding cult is not mere wish-fulfillment or symbolic rain-making; it is, rather, a sacrifice in traditional Arcadian style, by "the descendants of Lykaon." Its special form derives from a ritual handed down since ancient times. Even in the little we know of the Kean festival we can recognize analogies to the Lykaia.

Like the Lykaia, the Kean sacrificial ritual moves between two poles, oriented on the one hand toward the dangerous "dog," on the other toward Zeus; the one brings searing heat, the other coolness and rain. The dog-star first appears in July, just before dawn. The sacrificers waited on the mountaintop for this, the brightest star, to rise.[5] Thus, the ritual began at night and would have been continued in the morning and into the day. The first sacrifice was for the dog; thereafter, for Zeus. But only Zeus had an altar.[6] Accordingly, the preliminary sacrifice to the "dog" would have used a sacrificial pit, a *βόϑρος*. And since Aristaios was commonly portrayed as a shepherd—specifically, as Agreus and Nomios,[7] hunter and herdsman,

---

1.130; Callim. fr. 75.32; Apoll. Rhod. 2.516–27 with Schol. 498; Diod. 4.82.1–3; Clem. *Strom.* 6.29; Schol. Pind. *Pyth.* 9.115; Nonnus 5.269–79. For the head of Aristaios, a star, and a dog on coins from Keos, see *HN*² 484; Cook III (1940) 270. Cf. Nilsson (1906) 6–8. Aristaios appears in myth already in Hes. fr. 216/7 M.-W.

[2] Apoll. Rhod. 2.521 and Schol. 498. For a cult organization of Ἀριστηαστή (= Ἀριστaιασταί) in Boeotia see *ZPE* 23 (1975), 251f.; 25(1977), 135f.

[3] Apoll. Rhod. 2.522 and Schol. 498; Ἴκμιος Callim. fr. 75.34; Schol. T *Il.* 14.19.

[4] Cook III (1940) 265–70; *GB* VI 35.

[5] Ἀντολέων προπάροιϑε Apoll. Rhod. 2.527, and cf. Schol. 498a/w; Heraclides fr. 141.

[6] Apoll. Rhod. 2.522—but a sacrifice "for Sirius and for Zeus." "For Zeus, Apollo, Poseidon and the Winds" Nigidius fr. 99 Swoboda.

[7] Pind. *Pyth.* 9.65. For sacrifice of a black lamb for a typhoon, see Aristoph. *Ran.* 847.

killer and keeper—we must presume that his sacrificial victim for the raging dog-star would have been, once again, a ram. Nonnus, on the other hand, mentions a bull-sacrifice at the altar of Zeus, and a honey mixture.[8] Aristaios had "discovered" oil and honey in Keos—so it was told—and libations of oil and honey were clearly linked to the sacrificial ritual, even though we know nothing of the order—so important for understanding the ritual—in which they occurred. In any case, the ritual's nighttime aspect was followed by a daytime aspect, analogous to the polarity of Pelops and Zeus at Olympia; and just as Lykaon's sacrifice provoked a flood, and the feast of Thyestes made the sun change its course, so the sacrifice of Aristaios set cosmic powers in motion: the supremacy of the "dog" was overturned and the rising winds renewed the forces of life. The Keans awaited the appearance of the dog-star and the sun "in arms."[9] It was the men of arms-bearing age who became conscious of their solidarity and identity at this sacrificial festival; they would naturally have identified with the daytime order, the winds that dispelled the danger. And they conceived of their tiny island as the center of the world: the Keans claimed that they celebrated the festival, which Aristaios founded, "for all the Greeks."[10]

Lykaon sacrificed an Arcadian boy, his son or nephew, as a wolf; similarly, Aristaios, the herdsman who discovered oil and honey and established the sacrifice for the "dog,"was the father of Aktaion, who was torn apart by dogs. This leads us from ritual back to myth, to one of the most famous of all Greek myths, a frequent subject in art from archaic times.[11] As is often the case, the motivating forces in the story are unclear. The only certainty is in what Aktaion suffered, his πάθος, and what Artemis did: the hunter became the hunted; he was transformed into a stag, and his raging hounds, struck with "wolf's frenzy" (λύσσα), tore him apart as they would a stag. The regal anger of an offended goddess is at work here, demanding a victim. Her wrath was stirred by an oversight with regard to sacred laws, by trespassing

[8] 5.270–73. For the invention of oil and honey on Keos see Schol. Apoll. Rhod. 2.498b.

[9] Schol. Apoll. Rhod. 2.498a/w.

[10] Diod. 4.82.2.

[11] *PR* I 458–61; Hes. *Th.* 977; a new fragment of Hesiod's *Catalogues* in T. Renner, *HSCP* 82 (1978), 282; Stesichorus 236 Page = Paus. 9.2.3; Akusilaos, *FGrHist* 2 F 33; Aesch. *Toxotides* fr. 417–24 Mette; Eur. *Bacch.* 339; Callim. *Hy.* 5.110–15; Diod. 4.81.4; Apollod. 3.31, etc. For depictions in art see P. Jacobsthal, *Marburger Jahrb. f. Kunstwiss.* 5 (1929), 1–23; Brommer (1960) 336–37. On Polygnotus' depiction see Paus. 10.30.5. ΛΥΣΑ appears with a wolf's-head cap on the Boston bell-crater 00.346 = *ARV*[2] 1045.7.

on an "untouchable" precinct, by sexual desires, or, from an ethical perspective, by behaving presumptuously toward a divinity.[12]

The stag-metamorphosis recalls the"untouchable" precinct on Mount Lykaion: all who entered were forthwith regarded as stags to be hunted and killed.[13] Even the Delphic god ordered such a "stag" to be given up to its pursuers. And, according to mythic fantasy, Arkas and his mother mated in that very precinct[14]—the same motifs, the same excuses are always superimposed on the act of killing. The fact that in stories and art this stag-metamorphosis is often enacted by Artemis throwing a stag's skin over Aktaion[15] is perhaps not so much a rationalization as a feature of ritual, a mask, though of course completely serious for the masked participant. Whereas the Greek examples show a man disguised as a stag being attacked by real hounds, the wall paintings at Çatal Hüyük depict the masked leopard men surrounding a realistically painted stag.[16]

In fact, there is something peculiar about Aktaion's dogs as well. It is probable that already Hesiod gave a catalogue of their names, thus making them virtually individuals;[17] and the end of the myth, as told by the mythographers, has a particularly ancient quality: "When Aktaion was dead, his dogs searched and howled for their master. Their search took them to the cave of Cheiron; and he made an image of Aktaion which stilled their grief."[18] This description of the dogs' behavior doubtless goes beyond anything that could be observed in nature; real dogs cannot be comforted by an image. Rather, these animals are performing a human ritual of the sort we find attested again

---

[12] According to Hesiod (new fragment), Stesichorus, and Akusilaos, Aktaion wanted to marry Semele; according to Eur. *Bacch.* 339 he boasted that he was a better hunter than Artemis (cf. Soph. *El.* 569). There is no certain attestation before Callimachus that Aktaion saw Artemis naked.

[13] Architimos, *FGrHist* 315 F 1 = Plut. *Q. Gr.* 300a–c; II.1.nn.7, 34 above.

[14] See II.1.n.21 above.

[15] Stesichorus 236 Page; Jacobsthal, *Marburger Jahrb.*, fig. 6 = *ARV*² 287 24, fig. 8 = *ARV*² 285.1, fig. 9 = *ARV*² 552.20; cf. the metope from Selinus, fig. 11. Similarly, in Dionysios' *Bassarika*, the god clothes the victim, who is to be torn apart, in the skin and horns of a newly slain stag; cf. D. L. Page, *Literary Papyri* (1941), 536–40 = fr. 19.9 Heitsch. For deer-masquerades among the Bukoliastai in Sicily see Schol. Theocr. pp. 3.6, 7.14, 14.25 Wendel; cf. an early Greek gem in D. Ohly, *Griech. Gemmen* (1957), fig. 24; for Ἀκταίων κερασφόρος as a theater mask see Poll. 4.141.

[16] See I.2.n.19, I.8.n.28 above, and Figure 3.

[17] See Apollod. 3.32; Aesch. fr. 423 Mette; Ov. *Met.* 3.206–224; Hyg. *Fab.* 181.

[18] Apollod. 3.31; *POxy* 2509, going back to Hesiod. Cf. A. Casanova, *RFIC* 97 (1969), 31–46.

and again: the "search" for a torn-up victim ending in a symbolic restoration.[19] Aktaion's death is a sacrificial ritual of the hunt, consecrated by the Mistress of the Beasts and performed in the form that had been standard since Palaeolithic times. The actors are dogs struck mad by "wolf's frenzy," werewolves whose shrine is in a mountain cave. One mythographer even identifies Aktaion's dogs with the Rhodian Telchines,[20] the magical bronze-smiths; in so doing, he equates one secret society with another.

The literary myth probably combines various local cultic traditions. Aktaion's death, for instance, is situated at the spring Gargaphia near Mount Kithairon;[21] the cave of Cheiron, however, is on Mount Pelion in Thessaly. Almost by chance, a few details about the cave of Cheiron in Thessaly happen to have come down to us in a note by the Hellenistic periegete Heraclides: "On the heights of Mount Pelion, there is a cave, the so-called cave of Cheiron, and a shrine of Zeus Aktaios. At Sirius' rising, which is the time of the greatest heat, the most prominent citizens, those in the prime of their lives, climb up to the cave. They are chosen by the priest and girded with fresh, thrice-shorn sheepskins. This shows how cold it must be on the mountain!"[22] What the witty author considers a geographical curiosity is obviously a sacred ritual performed by the ruling class of Magnesia. It was introduced by the sacrifice of a sheep or ram; every participant had to slaughter an animal. Then came the strangest part of the ritual: each man put on the skin of his victim, and thus the procession climbed the mountain to the cave of Cheiron and the shrine of Zeus. The sacrificer identifies with his victim to the point of wearing its skin, tries in effect to undo his own deed; yet he remains a wolf in sheep's clothing. With its expiatory character, the journey to Cheiron's cave following the sacrifice obviously corresponds to the journey of Aktaion's dogs to the mysterious mountain cave where they found comfort in the restored image of their victim. The connection with Aktaion would be direct if the transmitted text, which names "Zeus Aktaios," were reliable; but the inscriptions from Magnesia near Mount Pelion speak only of "Zeus Akraios," "Zeus of the heights."[23]

---

[19] See I.2.n.12 above, IV.6 below.

[20] Armenides, *FGrHist* 378 F 8; Eust. 771.59.

[21] Vib. Sequ. 172, and cf. Stat. *Theb.* 7.274 with Schol; *RE* VII 757; for "on Kithairon" see Apollod. 3.30.

[22] Herakl. 2.8 (F. Pfister, *Die Reisebilder des Herakleides* [1951], 88). On hunters masquerading in animals' skins see Baudy (1980) 403 n.102.

[23] 'Ακτέων, 'Ακτάων-Zeus Aktaios, like Lykaon-Zeus Lykaios. For Zeus Akraios as su-

They do, however, mention a cult of Pan in the cave of Cheiron, and there were even rumors of human sacrifice.[24] Thus, the parallels to the Lykaia become closer.

The sacrifices on Mount Lykaion, Keos, and Mount Pelion have long been connected from the standpoint of weather-magic.[25] The proverbial "prayer of Aiakos" at the altar of Zeus Hellanios on the highest mountain in Aegina, said to bring storms and rain,[26] falls into this category as well, as does the sacrifice to Zeus Laphystios in the myth of Phrixos and the golden ram.[27] In order to prevent famine, king Athamas (whether in Orchomenos or Thessalian Halos) wanted to sacrifice his son to Zeus Laphystios. When he was already standing at the altar, the "cloud," Nephele, suddenly came down and a golden ram appeared. Thereupon both Phrixos and the ram vanished. The old connection with the Argonauts, and the removal of Phrixos and the ram to Aietes, more likely reflect a poetic combination than a cult legend. But even in this version of the myth, the ram is sacrificed, and all that remains is the golden fleece.

Herodotus tells us that a similar human sacrifice faced the descendants of Phrixos (that is, Athamas) in Thessalian Halos down to his own time.[28] The crucial step was characteristically left to the victim in a comedy of innocence: if the eldest member of the family set foot in the "Leiton," the prytaneum, he had to die. Once again, entering a place not to be entered is used as an excuse for sacrifice. If the victim manages to flee but happens to be caught later on, he is led back into

---

preme god and god of oaths see *IG* IX 2.1103, 1105, 1108, 1109.54, 71, 1110, 1128. For Διόνυσος Ἀκταῖος on Chios see *CIG* 2214e (II 1030); for Ἀπόλλων Ἀκταῖος see Strabo 13 p. 588, Steph. Byz. Ἄκτιον.

[24] "Erat." *Cat.* 40 p. 184 Robert; Monimos in Clem. *Pr.* 3.42.4. The "Pan Painter" couples his famous depiction of Pan with Aktaion's death; see Boston 10.185 = *ARV*[2] 550.1.

[25] Nilsson (1955) 395–401.

[26] Isocr. 9.14–15; Diod. 4.61; Paus. 2.29.6–8; Clem. *Strom.* 6.28. On Cos there was a *κοινὸν τῶν συμπορευομένων παρὰ Δία Ὑέτιον*: see *SIG*[3] 1107. Ἱερείων ἀνάβασις on Mount Olympus in Thessaly, with an ash-altar: see Plut. fr. 191 Sandbach = Philop. *CAG* XIV 1.26–27. For an alleged human sacrifice for Zeus Ombrios at Elis, see Lyk. 160 with Schol.

[27] Türk, *RML* III 2458–67; *PR* II 41–51; Schwenn (1915) 43–46; Cook I (1914) 414–19; Hes. fr. 68/9, 254–56, 299; Hekataios, *FGrHist* 1 F 17; Pherekydes, *FGrHist* 3 F 98/9; Hellanikos, *FGrHist* 4 F 126; Soph. "*Athamas*" fr. 1–10 Pearson; Eur. *Phrixos* I and II, *Nova Fragmenta Euripidea*, ed. C. Austin (1968), pp. 101–103. The myth of Phrixos is linked to two sanctuaries of Zeus Laphystios, at Halos in Thessaly (Eur. *Phrixos* I; Hdt. 7.197; cf. Strabo 9 p. 433; Schol. Apoll. Rhod. 2.513) and at Orchomenos in Boeotia (Eur. *Phrixos* II; Paus. 9.34.5, 1.44.7; Hellanikos, *FGrHist* 1 F 126).

[28] Hdt. 7.197, and cf. Plat. *Minos* 315c.

the "Leiton" to start the sacrificial procession according to the rules. The descendent of Phrixos, "completely covered with woolen fillets," would be led to the shrine of Laphystian Zeus. The equation with the ram could hardly be more obvious. Presumably, a ram would normally take the place of a human victim for Zeus Laphystios, as it would for other deities. But here, too, the motif of the wolf accompanies the myth of human sacrifice: Athamas became, just as the oracle had proclaimed, a companion in the meal of the wolves, before he ascended the Thessalian throne.[29]

The motivation for sacrificial ritual in weather-magic must have seemed quite convincing to early farming and urban communities always living in the shadow of famine. But the element of the werewolf cannot derive from this source, nor the ritual's persistence, given the undoubtedly frequent failure of the weather to cooperate. Wherever we can grasp details, we see that the festival accentuates and restructures the distribution of societal roles; there are hints of this in the domestic tragedy behind the Phrixos myth—women against men, father against son, brother and sister against everyone else. What actually sets the "unspeakable sacrifice" in motion is not nature but the order of the community and its spiritual life. The sacrifice causes such a shock that the cosmos might well seem to move to the rhythm of the sacred action.[30]

Scholars have tried to relate this weather-magic surrounding Zeus to the concept of an Indo-European storm god, but the parallels lead rather toward Asia Minor and the Semitic realm. A strange sheep-sacrifice, attested for Cyprian Aphrodite, has been the subject of detailed study by Robertson Smith: "They sacrifice sheep together, while they are themselves covered with sheepskins";[31] then there is a sacrifice of wild pigs, which is seen as vengeance for Adonis, who was killed by a boar. Thus, the preliminary sheep-sacrifice, in which the participants disguise themselves so strangely, probably repeats the death of the Great Goddess's "lord" and lover. At Hierapolis, in the temple of the "Syrian Goddess"—another place where the Adonis legend was at home—a worshipper's preliminary sacrifice consisted in slaughtering a black sheep, then prostrating himself on its skin, with the head and feet wrapped around his body.[32] But the Great Goddess can bring about a wolf-metamorphosis as well. Gilgamesh's

---

[29] Schol. Plat. *Minos* 315c; Apollod. 1.84.

[30] Thus, Seneca, *Thy.* 696, has the earth quake during the sacrifice of Atreus.

[31] Lydus *Mens.* 4.65 p. 119.19–22 Wuensch; Smith (1894) 469–79.

[32] Luk. *Syr. D.* 55, and cf. Porph. *V. Pyth.* 17 (Idaean cave, Crete).

complaint against Ištar has long been known: "Because you loved the herdsman, the keeper . . . you smote him and changed him into a wolf: now he is hunted by his own shepherd boys and his dogs bite his ankles."[33] Although the distribution of roles is somewhat different, the context is reminiscent of both Adonis and Aktaion. In Ugaritic mythology, there is the story of Aqhat the hunter, who was torn apart by birds of prey, at the bidding of the goddess Anat, who wanted his bow; his father managed to retrieve from the belly of the vulture-mother his remains—bones and fat—and to bury them.[34] It would be tempting to equate the names Aktaon, Akteon, Aktaion with Aqhat,[35] but even in the Babylonian and Ugaritic versions we are nowhere near the "origins" of the myth. The wall painting at Çatal Hüyük has already been mentioned:[36] here, some four to five thousand years earlier, we find the leopard men, servants of the Great Goddess, a *Männerbund* and mask society, dancing around their victim, the stag. By changing himself into a predatory animal, a hunter, man single-handedly guaranteed the continuance and development of the human race in Palaeolithic times; he lived on in this form through the Neolithic period in the rituals that shaped society, and on into classical Greece in the sacrificial rites and myths about the stag and the werewolf.

5. *The Delphic Tripod*

The first sanctuary that comes to mind in considering the sacred tripod is, of course, Pytho, the Delphic sanctuary, the far-famed oracle of Apollo which, simultaneously, was the center of the Pylaic Amphictiony and site of the Pythian games. Delphi played such a significant role in Greek religious, intellectual, and political life that it is impossible to do justice in a few pages to the Delphic phenomenon as

---

[33] Gilgamesh VI i, 58–63, *ANET* 84.

[34] *ANET* 149–55. It has been postulated time and again that Aqhat is revived—*ANET* 155; Th. Gaster, *Thespis* (1961²), 323—but the heart of the myth consists of death by being torn apart, "collecting," and burying; cf. I.8.n.12 above.

[35] Astour (1965) 163–68.

[36] See above at n. 16.

a whole.[1] Moreover, like Olympia—or even more so, because of its great popularity—the sanctuary was repeatedly entangled in political and military disorders, and each Sacred War brought new forms of administration which influenced the function and sense of identity of Apollo's servants. Thus, as at Olympia, various traditions became superimposed, and disentangling them is no mean task. The most significant break probably came with the first Sacred War, shortly after 600 B.C., in the course of which the Pylaic Amphictiony of Anthela took over the supervision of Delphi from the inhabitants of Krisa and, above all, organized the Pythian games, starting in 586.[2] Nonetheless, the oracle's authority was undiminished by the crisis. The cult of the Delphic priesthood was virtually untouched, just as, later, it would survive the sanctuary's sudden decline in late Hellenistic times—Strabo called Delphi "the poorest sanctuary"[3] of his time. Yet the detailed information about the cult, which we find primarily in Plutarch, consistently corresponds to more ancient allusions or indications. Thus, we may conclude that the Delphic rituals maintained essentially the same forms at the same place for at least eight hundred years.

Delphi was set apart from the normal Greek polis: since it was isolated on a steep mountain six hundred meters above the valley of the Pleistos, nestled by the Castalian spring between the grandiose Phaedriadic cliffs, Delphi could never be a farming community. Already the *Homeric Hymn to Apollo*[4] states in no uncertain terms that the Delphians had lived for, as well as from, the sanctuary ever since the most ancient times. There may be some truth to the tradition that the Delphians originally came from Lykoreia,[5] inasmuch as it is possible for a community to exist there on the large plateau above the

[1]See Nilsson (1906) 150–62, 283–88, 461–62; (1955) 170–74, 625–53; Farnell IV (1907) 179–218, 291–95; H. Pomtow, *RE* IV 2517–2700; *RE* Suppl. IV 1189–1432; F. Schober, *RE* Suppl. V 61–152; G. Daux, *Pausanias à Delphes* (1936); P. Amandry, *La mantique apollinienne à Delphes* (1950); J. Defradas, *Les thèmes de la propagande delphique* (1954); M. Delcourt, *L'oracle de Delphes* (1955); Parke and Wormell (1958); G. Roux, *Delphi: Orakel und Kultstätten* (1971). On the myth see Fontenrose (1959); on the results of the excavations see *Fouilles de Delphes* (1902 and after).

[2]The most accurate tradition is to be found in the hypothesis to Pindar's *Pythian Odes*, Schol. Pind. II.1–5 Drachmann, based on the archival researches of Aristotle and Kallisthenes at Delphi, *SIG*[3] 275 = *FGrHist* 124 T 23.

[3]Strabo 9 p. 420 *νυνί γέ τοι πενέστατόν ἐστιν τὸ ἐν Δελφοῖς ἱερὸν χρημάτων γε χάριν*. Cf. Plut. *De Pyth. or.* 405c, in whose time the Pythia was the daughter of poor farmers.

[4]See n. 7 below.

[5]See n. 22 below.

Phaedriadic cliffs between the Korykian cave and Mount Parnassus, but already before 600 B.C. Delphi was governed by Krisa down on the gulf of Corinth, for the envoys who came to the isolated slopes seeking the counsel of the god generally came by ship. Delphi was the only Greek community to make religion its main occupation; the basis for this unique role was the oracle's pan-Hellenic and even international fame. It was this, too, that prompted the intervention of the Amphictiony. And the Pythian games were all the more glorious because they were connected to the sanctuary. The god spoke at Delphi: here, piety was firmly imbedded in the transcendental world. However, the worldly action that gave rise to the oracle, and which we can grasp, was a special form of sacrificial ritual. The site of the oracle, the place of pronouncements and liberating purifications, was first and foremost a place of sacrifice, outdoors, high on the mountain.

The excavators of the temenos found "the earth fat with organic remains mixed with ash and burnt bones, and filled with countless Mycenaean sherds and terra-cottas."[6] Houses were even built in this terrain that would normally have been considered unfit for habitation. The *Homeric Hymn to Apollo* describes how the god himself built his sanctuary among the crags of Mount Parnassus and in the form of a dolphin personally led his priests, the Delphians, from Crete. "How shall we live now?" they ask in fright on seeing the temple high up on the slope. But the god comforts them with a smile: "Each of you should carry a knife in your right hand and slaughter sheep continually; for they will be there in abundance. . . . But guard my temple and receive the tribes of men."[7] Thus, Apollo's worshippers brought their sheep up from the fertile plain to the mountain to be slaughtered with the assistance of the priests with their knives. These priests were then allowed to enjoy themselves at the meal. The sacrifice was accomplished in a most peculiar way: "Whenever someone enters the sacred precinct to sacrifice to the god, the Delphians surround the altar, each of them carrying a knife. And when the lord of the sacrifice has slaughtered the victim, skinned it, and removed its entrails, then all those standing around cut off as much as they can for themselves and go away with it; thus, the sacrificer himself is often left empty-handed."[8] For this reason, a verse from comedy be-

[6]Nilsson (1955) 339.

[7]*Hy. Ap.* 528–38; *μηλοδόκῳ* Πύθωνι Pind. *Pyth.* 3.27.

[8]For the legend of Aesop see *POxy* 1800 fr. 2 col. II 32–46 = *Aesopica*, ed. B. E. Perry (1952), Test. 25 p. 221, and cf. Schol. Flor. Callim. fr. 191.16–25; Schol. Pind. *Nem.* 7.62a; Pherekydes, *FGrHist* 3 F 64; in addition see Achaios fr. 13, *TGF* p. 749 = Ath. 173d; Burkert, *Gnomon* 38 (1966), 439–40.

came proverbial: "When you sacrifice at Delphi, you will have to buy extra meat for yourself to eat."[9] The Delphic knives were made in a special form which we are unable to reconstruct with certainty in spite of numerous ironic allusions.[10] In any case, rather than a transcendental piety, the Delphic sheep-sacrifice exhibited all-too-human traits. "Like flies around a goatherd or like Delphians at sacrifice:"[11] this is a picture of shameless obtrusion. But no one ever tried to reform what actually took place in the sacred precinct, for it was an unchangeable, sacred custom.

Precisely this form of Delphic sacrifice is reflected in the heroic myth that reconstructs the action as a human tragedy: Neoptolemos-Pyrrhos, the son of Achilles, suffered a horrible death at Apollo's hearth in Delphi, and his grave in the sacred precinct was always pointed out.[12] The motivation for the act varies according to whether or not the specific version presents Pyrrhos in a good light. Some make him a temple robber whom the god justly punishes;[13] others describe him as a pious worshipper of the oracle who was perniciously killed by Orestes.[14] What actually happened there, the "act" itself, remains unchanged. Neoptolemos sacrificed to Apollo at the "hearth" in his temple; there he was surrounded by Delphians and, in the confusion of carving and snatching up the sacrificial meat, he was killed with a Delphic knife.[15] Thus, in sacrificing, he himself became the victim in this specifically Delphic ritual. The genealogies call the murderer "Machaireus," "the knife-man," son of Daitas, "the feaster"; and, far from making him a criminal, they give him priestly status. His descendant is Branchus, the founder of the other famous oracle of Apollo, at Didyma near Miletus.[16] As for Neoptolemos-Pyrrhos, he is

---

[9] *Com. adesp.* 460; *CAF* III 495 = Plut. *Q. conv.* 709a; App. Prov. 1.95, *Paroem. Gr.* I 393.

[10] Arist. *Pol.* 1252b2 and in Hsch. Δελφικὴ μάχαιρα, Prov. Coisl. 105 = App. Prov. 194, *Paroem. Gr.* I 393. The knife is also mentioned in *Hy. Ap.* 535 and Aristoph. fr. 684.

[11] Callim. fr. 191.26–27.

[12] J. Fontenrose, *The Cult and Myth of Pyrros at Delphi* (1960); M. Delcourt, *Pyrrhos et Pyrrha* (1965); J. Pouilloux and G. Roux, *Enigmes à Delphes* (1963); L. Woodbury, *Phoenix* 33 (1979), 95–133. For the tomb see Paus. 10.24.6, 1.4.4; Schol. Pind. *Nem.* 7.62c; J. Pouilloux, *Fouilles de Delphes II: La région nord du sanctuaire* (1960), 49–60. For the myth see Pind. *Pae.* 6.116–20; *Nem.* 7.40–47 with Schol. 58, 62; Eur. *Andr.* 49–55, 1122–57; Eur. *Or.* 1654–57; Soph. *Hermione* pp. 141–43 Pearson; Pherekydes, *FGrHist* 3 F 64; Asklepiades, *FGrHist* 12 F 15; Apollod. *Epit.* 6.13–14. On the Ruvo crater (Jatta 239) see J. Pouilloux and G. Roux, *Enigmes à Delphes* (1963) 119.3, and cf. G. Roux, *AK* 7 (1964), 30–41.

[13] Strabo 9 p. 421; Schol. Pind. *Nem.* 7.58, 150a; and cf. Paus. 1.13.9, 4.17.4.

[14] Eur. *Andr.* 995–98, 1090 ff.

[15] Μαχαίρᾳ Pind. *Nem.* 7.42.

[16] Asklepiades, *FGrHist* 12 F 15; Callim. fr. 229.7; Strabo 9 p. 421.

honored eternally precisely because he died: he now has a place in the sanctuary, "seeing to law and justice in the heroes' processions amid much sacrifice."[17] Pindar assures us that it was necessary for such a hero to be situated in the sanctuary. Admittedly, the excavators did not find at the site a grave consecrated to Neoptolemos-Pyrrhos, but, rather, a Mycenaean pithos, filled with ashes and the remains of bones.[18] This is, however, a place of sacrifice, with its double aspect of killing and renewing life. Just as Zeus was united with Pelops, so Delphic Apollo is associated with his chosen victim, whom the poets made into the son of Achilles. His death occurs in the sacred precinct in a violent ritual which the Delphians regularly repeat.

Once again, two groups confront each other in the sacrifice: Apollo's worshipper coming from afar, and the native Delphians. The one brings a sacrificial animal and slaughters it, the others "steal" the meat and eat it. Thus, man searches for god in the wilderness, far from the world of peaceful communities and farms, and there he encounters the god's wild servants, a group of greedy gluttons. The first inhabitant of the ravines of Mount Parnassus to be attested in Greek literature is none other than Autolykos, the "werewolf." His grandson was Odysseus, whom he taught how to hunt, and it was there that Odysseus suffered the wound that was to reveal his identity.[19] The Delphians pointed out the site of the boar hunt, and the place where Odysseus received his wound, in their gymnasium[20] not far from the Castalian spring.

This early legend is not the only link between Delphi and the wolf. "The Delphians worship the wolf" was Aelian's straightforward pronouncement[21] in reference to the bronze statue of a wolf that the Delphians set up as a votive gift beside the great altar; moreover, there was a story that a wolf caught and killed a temple robber. If Neoptolemos-Pyrrhos was a temple robber, he suffered the same fate at the hands of the Delphians. In any case, in stealing the sacrifice, their behavior was distinctly wolf-like. The name of the wolf is linked primarily with Lykoreia, the place where the Delphians were said to have originated. The name was taken to mean "howling of the wolves," though "wolf-mountain" would be etymologically more accurate. According to the legend, the first human beings, Deucalion and Pyrrha, landed on Mount Parnassus after the great flood and,

---

[17] Pind. *Nem.* 7.44–47. [18] Pouilloux, *Fouilles II*, 57–59.

[19] *Od.* 19.393–466.

[20] Paus. 10.8.8. On Apollon Lykeios at Delphi, see J. Bousquet, *BCH* 90 (1966), 91.

[21] *Nat. an.* 12.40; Paus. 10.14.7, and cf. Plut. *Pericl.* 21.

guided by "howling wolves," they founded their city and named it accordingly.[22] The Delphians, or at least the most prominent Delphic families, traced their ancestry back to Deucalion;[23] in a sense, they were still following the footsteps of the wolf in the ritual of robbing the sacrifice. There was even a story that Apollo was borne by a she-wolf;[24] and modern scholars dispute whether the name Apollo *Lykeios* has to do with Lycia, "light" or the "wolf"[25]—most Greeks, in any case, took it to mean "wolf."

Opposing the she-wolf's son was the son of the "ram": one tradition claimed that the Pythian games were established because Apollo killed a robber from Euboea, the son of Krios.[26] Here, the sacrifice of a sheep in Apollo's precinct has become part of the legend almost undisguised. By contrast, the official myth, which became widespread no later than the first Pythian games in 586 when Sakadas included it in his performance of the "Pythian nome,"[27] names Python, the earth-born dragon, as Apollo's opponent and victim.[28] But already Plutarch noticed that the fight against the dragon has very little to do with Delphic ritual.[29] Rather, it is a favorite motif of the Orientalizing era, a period with a distinct preference for such monsters, and it was probably transposed to Delphi by the poets without affecting the cult or entirely supplanting rival traditions. Still more ancient, and immensely popular, is the story of how Herakles fought Apollo for the Pythian tripod.[30] This may or may not reflect the memories of a Dorian invasion and the take-over of a pre-Dorian cult-site; in any case, the fact that two polarized groups arose in the Delphic ritual, each struggling

---

[22] Paus. 10.6.2, and cf. *Marm. Par.*, *FGrHist* 239 A 2, 4; Andron, *FGrHist* 10 F 8; Callim. fr. 62; Strabo 9 p. 418; Ἀπόλλων Λυκωρεύς Callim. *Hy.* 2.19; Apoll. Rhod. 4.1490; Euphorion fr. 80.3 Powell.

[23] See n. 47 below.

[24] Arist. *Hist. an.* 580a18; Ael. *Nat. an.* 10.26; cf. Ant. Lib. 35. The meaning of Apollo Λυκηγενής, *Il.* 4.101, was disputed even in antiquity.

[25] Cook I (1914) 63–68, who argues for "light."

[26] Paus. 10.6.6.

[27] Paus. 2.22.8–9; Poll. 4.78; cf. Strabo 9 p. 421.

[28] For the most detailed discussion see Fontenrose (1959); in the *Hymn to Apollo*, the dragon is female and nameless.

[29] Plut. *De def. or.* 417f–418a.

[30] There are reliefs and vase-paintings with the fight for the tripod starting in Geometric times, but the identification of Herakles and Apollo becomes a certainty only in the sixth century: see S. B. Luce, *AJA* 34 (1930), 313–33; E. Kunze, *Olympische Forschungen* 2 (1950), 113–17; F. Willemsen, *JdI* 70 (1953), 93–99; Brommer (1960) 30–38; Schefold (1964) T.4b.

for the sacrificial meat—which, of course, would have been kept in the tripod—and the fact that the "robbers" in this ritual were those who were truly obedient to the god are good indications that the ritual provided the story's basic structure and that it was not just a product of chance. Transcending the sacrificial struggles, however, Apollo's order prevailed.

Together with the tripod, the act of cutting up the ram links Delphi to the Lykaia and Olympia. As at Olympia, moreover, a foot-race was held in the stadium. The temple's special function, however, was unique to Delphi, as was the role of the Pythia, the woman consecrated to Apollo. Inside, there was the famous hearth (*ἑστία*), home of the eternal flame[31]—a very ancient feature,[32] alien to the ordinary Greek temple. The tripod was kept in the temple's innermost area, the adyton,[33] which was open to only a few. Those who came for advice could probably have seen what was happening only from a distance; they would have seen the consecrated woman sitting on the tripod, would have heard her altered voice and thus have known that Apollo's word was passing through her lips. The Stoic "pneuma" doctrine gave rise to the theory—eagerly taken up by rationalists—that vapors rising from the depths of the earth in the adyton would have induced the Pythia's trance and her prophetic powers. But this theory has not stood up to archaeological examination:[34] there is simply no trace of a chasm or any volcanic activity whatsoever beneath the temple at Delphi. There were, of course, vapors surrounding the tripod as the Pythia entered the adyton and took her place on the sacred seat: laurel leaves would have been burned, with barley grains[35] and

---

[31] Paus. 10.24.4; Plut. *Numa* 9.12; *Aristides* 20.4; *De E* 385c. For the Amphictionic oath see *SIG*[3] 826 C 14 Θ[έμις τε] καὶ Ἀπόλλων Πύθιος καὶ Λατὼ καὶ Ἄρτεμι[ς καὶ] Ἑστία *καὶ πῦρ ἀθάνατον καὶ θεοὶ πάντες καὶ πᾶσαι*; and cf. *Hom. Hy.* 24; Aesch. *Cho.* 1037; the hymn of Aristonoos, pp. 164–65 Powell.

[32] Yavis (1949) 59–70; S. Marinatos, *BCH* 60 (1936), 239–40; F. Oelmann, *Bonn. Jb.* 157 (1957), 11–52; E. Drerup, *Archaeologia Homerica* O: *Griechische Baukunst in geometrischer Zeit* (1969), 123–28.

[33] Paus. 10.24.5; *ἄδυτον* Hdt. 7.141; Eur. *Iph. Taur.* 1256; Aristonoos I 13 p. 163 Powell; *οἶκος, ἐν ᾧ τοὺς χρωμένους τῷ θεῷ καθίζουσιν* Plut. *De Def. or.* 437c. The exact arrangement of the interior of the temple is not certain: see Roux (1971) 91–115.

[34] Cic. *Div.* 1.115, and cf. 38, 79; Diod. 16.26 (late Hellenistic source, E. Schwartz, *RE* V 682); Strabo 9 p. 419; Lucan 5.165; Ps.-Long. 13.2; Callim. *Hy.* 4.178, with text and interpretation uncertain. Cf. Nilsson (1955) 172.3.

[35] Plut. *De Pyth. or.* 397a; *De E* 385c; chewing the laurel is mentioned by Lyk. 6 and Tzetz. *ad loc.*, Luk. *Bis acc.* 1.

perhaps other sorts of incense. But it was simply subjective opinion and traditional belief that the tripod rocked and shook in the murky room, that a power from the depths was at work when the Pythia spoke or, rather "sang" and "screamed."[36] The tripod and the vapors rising from a fire go hand in hand in any case; at Olympia, too, we encountered the tale of the tripod mysteriously starting to boil.[37]

The Delphic tripod had a cover, on which the Pythia sat.[38] It is no wonder that all sorts of rumors circulated as to its secret contents, but all of them pointed basically in one direction: the remains of some slaughtered creature were gathered inside—"the bones and the teeth of the Python snake,"[39] according to one version in keeping with the official myth of the fight and death at Delphi. An apocryphal tradition, by contrast, inverted the victor and his victim: "Apollo was the son of Silenus; he was killed by Python; his remains were deposited in the so-called tripod."[40] The majority, however, also unofficial and related to sectarian mysteries, spoke of Dionysus slain: "When the Titans had torn apart Dionysus, they gave his limbs to his brother, Apollo, having thrown them into a kettle, but he preserved them close to the tripod."[41] This was surely not Callimachus' own invention. We find his statement confirmed by Plutarch: "The people of Delphi believe that the remains of Dionysus rest with them beside the oracle, and the Hosioi offer a secret sacrifice in Apollo's shrine whenever the Thyiades wake Liknites [sc. Dionysus]."[42] Thus, Plutarch places this tradition in the context of a sacrificial ritual.

Starting with Aeschylus' *Eumenides*, there is a great deal of evi-

---

[36] Pythia *τὸν τρίποδα διασεισαμένη* Luk. *Bis acc.* 1; Schol. Aristoph. *Plut.* 213 *πλησίον τοῦ τρίποδος δάφνη ἵστατο, ἣν ἡ Πυθία, ἡνίκα ἐχρησμῴδει, ἔσειεν*; cf. Aristonoos I 10, p. 163 Powell; *ἀείδουσα* Ἕλλησι *βοάς* Eur. *Ion* 92.

[37] See II.2, p. 100 above.

[38] Ὅλμος Zenob. Par. 3.63, *Paroem. Gr.* I 72; Schol. Aristoph. *Plut.* 9; *Vesp.* 238; *ἐνόλμιος* Soph. fr. 1044 Pearson. For the Pythia "sitting" see Eur. *Ion* 92 (correspondingly, Apollo, Eur. *Iph. Taur.* 1254; *Or.* 955–56); Diod. 16.26–27. For vase-paintings see Willemsen, *JdI* 70 (1955), 85–88. The "raving" (*μανεῖσα*) of the Pythia is mentioned by Plat. *Phdr.* 244a. Amandry, *Mantique*, 19–24, disputed the Pythia's ecstasy; cf. R. Flacelière, *Revue des Etudes Anciennes* 52 (1950), 306–24; Parke and Wormell (1958) I 34–41.

[39] Serv. auct. Aen. 3.360 and cf. 3.92, 6.347; Eust. ad Dion. Per. 441; *δράκων ὑπὸ τῷ τρίποδι φθέγγεται* "Luk." *Astr.* 23.

[40] Porph. *V. Pyth.* 16, following Antonios Diogenes.

[41] Callim. fr. 643 = Schol. Lyk. 207; Callim. fr. 517 in *Et. Gen.* = *Et. M.* 255.14–16; Philochoros, *FGrHist* 328 F 7; Euphorion fr. 13 Powell; Clem. *Pr.* 2.18.2.

[42] Plut. *Is.* 365a, and cf. *De E* 389c.

dence that not only Apollo was worshipped at Delphi, but Dionysus as well.[43] The Leningrad vase-painting on which Apollo offers his hand to Dionysus at Delphi has often been used as an illustration. The pediments of the fourth-century temple presented Apollo in the circle of the Muses in the east, Dionysus among the Thyiades in the west[44]—a studied antithesis of morning/evening, light/darkness, the two were in fact conceived of as brothers. Plutarch[45] testifies that three winter months were consecrated to Dionysus, but Apollo resumed power in the month Bysios in spring. This pairing has been seen as a result of a religious-historical process, a shrewd balance, permitting the Delphic priesthood to assimilate the religious movements of the sixth century and at the same time to soften their impact.[46] There is undoubtedly some truth to this. But it is not a question of diplomatic compromise or give-and-take, but, rather, of a polarity in which the contrary elements determine each other, like east and west, day and night. It comprises savagery versus clarity, lack of inhibition versus awareness of limitations, female versus male, proximity to death versus affirmation of life: this is the circular course that sacrificial ritual charts again and again, renewing life by encountering death. The circle of the "werewolves" around the tripod kettle is a form of the ritual especially rich in antitheses. In the Delphic context, *Dionysus* is more likely a new name or accentuation of the one pole than a foreign intruder; in the sacrificial ritual, the polar tension is present from the outset.

Plutarch mentions two rituals, simultaneously performed and mutually determinant, that he associates with the dismemberment of Dionysus. The Hosioi would offer an "unspeakable" sacrifice in the

---

[43] Aesch. *Eum.* 22, 24; Soph. *Ant.* 1126; Eur. *Ion* 550–53, 714–18, 1125; *Iph. Taur.* 1243; *Phoen.* 226 with Schol.; *Bacch.* 306–309; *Hypsipyle* fr. 752; Aristoph. *Nub.* 605; Philodamos p. 165 Powell.

[44] Leningrad crater, St. 1807 = *ARV*^{2} 1185.7, Metzger (1951) T.25.3; for the pediment see Paus. 10.19.4. The sixth century temple was different: see *FD* IV 3; P. de la Coste-Messelière, *Art archaïque: sculptures des temples* (1931), 15–74; J. Dörig, *Festschr. K. Schefold* (AK Beih. 4, 1965), 105–109. For "Delphos" the son of Apollo and Thyia see Paus. 10.6.4; cf. the Vienna crater 935 = *ARV*^{2} 1441; Metzger (1951) pl.22.4: Aphrodite, Apollo, Omphalos, Thyiad.

[45] Plut. *De E* 389c; for the identification of Dionysus with Apollo see Menander *Rhet. Gr.* III 446 Spengel, and cf. Aesch. fr. 86 Mette and Philodamos. On Dionysus as the first to give oracles see Schol. Pind. *Pyth.* p. 2.7, 13 Drachmann. See also Ἀπόλλων Διονυσόδοτος at Phlya, Paus. 1.31.4; in Asia Minor see Apollo and Marsyas (linked with the sacrifice of a ram in the Louvre statue 542).

[46] Rohde (1898) II 54–55; cf. H. Jeanmaire, *Dionysos* (1951), 187–91.

shrine; and the Thyiades would "wake" the child in the winnowing fan.[47] The Hosioi were the most distinguished social group at Delphi, direct descendants of Deucalion. By undergoing a special, seemingly ancient, initiation sacrifice, they attained the status of "the purified" and were hence able to deal with "the unspeakable" on a regular basis. This probably entailed a sacrificial dismemberment. Euripides combines a similar "consecration" with omophagy in Crete.[48] The *Männerbund* is juxtaposed to the company of "raving" women; the act of killing in the shrine corresponds to caring for the newborn child in the female realm, a secret action performed in the mountain wilderness, as on Mount Lykaion or at Olympia. The Thyiades would have roamed Mount Parnassus in ecstasy during the winter;[49] accordingly, the Hosioi must have offered their unspeakable sacrifice at this time. Plutarch indicates, as clearly as one possibly could with something "unspeakable," that the sacrifice corresponded to the dismemberment of Dionysus. Thus, it probably followed the main lines of Dionysiac myth, i.e., tearing apart, gathering, and preserving in a sacred container. This in turn corresponds to the ancient closing rite in hunting and sacrificial ritual. The myth tells us that Arkas and Pelops emerged from the sacrificial kettle revived. And at Delphi, the advent of Apollo marked the close of the Dionysiac period. Apollo's birthday falls on the seventh day of the month of Bysios in the spring,[50] which likewise signals Apollo's return to power. "In ancient times" the oracle spoke only on this day. Death, as embodied in the previous unspeakable sacrifice, was finally overcome by renewed divine life when the Pythia took her place on the covered tripod. Ecstasy is a phenomenon sui generis, but its place is fixed by the sacrificial ritual.

Yet another sacrifice had to be made before the Pythia might enter the adyton—this time, a goat-sacrifice. Before it could be slaughtered, however, its entire body had to be made to shudder;[51] therefore

---

[47] Plut. *Is.* 365a; cf. *De def. or.* 438b; *Q. Gr.* 292d.

[48] Eur. fr. 472.12–15; cf. I.5.n.25 above. Lyk. 207 alludes to a secret sacrifice to Dionysus at Delphi.

[49] Plut. *Prim. frig.* 953d; *De mul. vir.* 249e–f; Paus. 10.4.2–3 (every second year), and cf. 10.32.7; Hdt. 7.178; Philodamos 21–23, p. 166 Powell; Aristonoos I 37, p. 163 Powell; Catullus 64.390–93. On Liknites see Nilsson (1957) 38–45.

[50] Plut. *Q. Gr.* 292e–f, with reference to Kallisthenes, *FGrHist* 124 F 49.

[51] Plut. *De def. or.* 435c, 437b τὴν αἶγα; τῶι ϑεῶ[ι χρηστήρ]ιον . . . αἶγα κ[αλλι]στεύοντα *LSS* 41.21. For a goat's head on Delphic coins see *HN*² 340; Hsch. ὀμφαλὸς Αἰγαῖος is corrupt; cf. Steph. Byz. Αἰγά. On the shudder of the sacrificial animal see I.1.n.13 above.

it was doused with cold water. When the goat then quivered, it was not taken as a nod of consent—as would normally be the case in a comedy of innocence—but, rather, as a sign of quaking fear. Legends speak of how Aix, the "goat," mourned its father, Python,[52] but also of how goats discovered the oracle when they were driven insane by the mantic vapors.[53] Thus, the goat is clearly made to correspond to the Pythia herself. When the Pythia mounted the tripod, she was offering herself up to death in an expiatory act of mourning for the previous killing. It made no difference whether the victim was called Python or Dionysus or even Apollo himself. The Pythia, a mature woman, yet dressed and adorned like a virgin,[54] the only woman in a male society—for no other woman was permitted to approach the oracle—was led to the tripod almost like a sacrificial victim herself. She too would shudder, her entire body would quake, but the divine presence welled up out of the anguish and fear: Apollo would be there and would speak.

Christian polemics tried to denigrate the image of the woman sitting atop rising vapors by embroidering it with sexual details.[55] Even a pagan like Pausanias called the Sibyl "the god's consecrated wife," as Aeschylus had made Apollo's relation to Kassandra a sexual encounter;[56] similar ideas were applied to the Pythia consorting with Apollo.[57] Yet, in the context of sacrifice, offering oneself up to the god is simultaneously an encounter with death. The "virgin" awakens the reproductive powers in what had been dead and, being possessed by it, makes this new life manifest. After the unspeakable sacrifice of winter performed in the shrine beside the hearth and the tripod, the buds of spring mark the advent of Apollo, the embodiment of divine wisdom and clarity, the source of potentially crucial guidance.

Besides the hearth and the tripod, and even more prominent, was the omphalos, the "navel of the earth," the sacred symbol of the

---

[52] Plut. *Q. Gr.* 293c.

[53] Diod. 16.26; Plut. *De def. or.* 435d.

[54] Diod. 16.26; *γυνή* Eur. *Ion* 91; *γραῦς* Aesch. *Eum.* 38; *ἁγνὴ διὰ βίου* Plut. *De def. or.* 435d, 438c.

[55] Orig. *Cels.* 7.3 *δέχεται πνεῦμα διὰ τῶν γυναικείων κόλπων*; Joh. Chrysost., Migne *PG* 61.242, followed by Schol. Aristoph. *Plut.* 39, Suda π 3140; cf. Fehrle (1910) 7–8, 75–76; K. Latte, *HThR* 33 (1940), 9–18.

[56] Paus. 10.12.2; Aesch. *Ag.* 1203–12. The prophetess at Patara is shut into the temple at night: Hdt. 1.182.2. See also *Pap. Gr. Mag.* 1.291.

[57] Plut. *De Pyth. or.* 405c, and cf. *De sera* 566d; Ps.-Long.13.2 *ἐγκύμονα τῆς δαιμονίου καθισταμένην δυνάμεως*.

Delphic sanctuary.[58] The actual omphalos was probably located in the adyton of the temple, next to the tripod. It was covered with a net-like fabric made of raw wool.[59] Both in antiquity and today, there have been numerous interpretations of this symbol. The concept of a center of the world, expressed anthropomorphically in the image of the navel, characteristically designates a place where sacred actions occur; every sanctuary is in some sense a "center."[60] Nevertheless, the function of the Delphic stone was a matter for debate. Was it a grave monument, for Python,[61] for instance; was it a chthonic altar?[62] Whatever the standard interpretations or designations may have been, the omphalos had one primary function in the ritual: it was the stand over which the woolen net was draped. In just this way Palaeolithic hunters spread a bearskin over a clay model, and Hermes laid out the cowskins on the rocks.[63] The omphalos, as a sacrificial monument, belongs in the category of ritual restoration, a practice spanning the time from the ancient hunter through Greek sacrificial ritual. Slaughtering the victim at the "hearth" and tearing it apart like wolves are combined with "gathering" the pieces into the tripod kettle and spreading the fleece, or the goatskin, out on the stone: in the temple at Delphi, the symbols of the oracle are Hestia, the tripod, and the omphalos. The stone set up for sacrifice is the center of the world.

Every eighth year there was a festival at Delphi, which Plutarch alone describes in all its curious details.[64] However, because both

---

[58] See Harrison (1922) 396–406; Cook II (1924) 169–93; Fontenrose (1959) 376–77; H. V. Herrmann, *Omphalos* (1959); J. Bousquet, *BCH* 75 (1951), 210–23. There is rich comparative material in the essays of W. H. Roscher, *Abh. Leipzig* 29.9 (1913), 31.1 (1915); *Ber. Leipzig* 70.2 (1918).

[59] Its name could be *αἰγίς*, Ael. Dion. α 48, Paus. Att. α 40, but J. Harrison called it *ἀγρηνόν* with reference to Poll. 4.116: *BCH* 24 (1900), 254–62.

[60] Cf. M. Eliade, *Das Heilige und das Profane* (1957), 22–29. The omphalos appears as the center of the world in the myth of the two birds who come from either end of the world and meet there; cf. Pind. fr. 54 = Strabo 9 p. 419; Paus. 10.16.3; Plut. *De def. or.* 409e.

[61] Varro *L.l.* 7.17; Hsch. Τοξίου βουνός. For frescoes from the house of the Vettii see *RML* III 3407; Fontenrose (1959) 375; Harrison (1927) 424; *EAA* VI 335. For the "tomb of Dionysus" see Tatian 8 p. 9.17 Schwartz (cf. n. 41 above).

[62] Herrmann, *Omphalos* (n. 58 above).

[63] See I.2.n.13 above.

[64] The main source is Plut. *De def. or.* 417e–418d; see also *Q. Gr.* 293c; *De mus.* 1136a; Ephoros, *FGrHist* 70 F 31b = Strabo 9 p. 422; Theopompos, *FGrHist* 117 F 80 = Ael. *VH* 3.1; Callim. fr. 86–89, 194.34–36; cf. B. Snell, *Hermes* 73 (1938), 439 on Pind. *Pae.* 10;

Ephorus and Theopompus allude to it, we know that the festival had, by the fourth century, long been in existence; it was evidently even older than the first Sacred War, for it was closely linked to the Pythian games, which were also originally held in every eighth year until in 586 they began to be celebrated every fourth. The ritual establishes a striking relationship between Delphi and the valley of Tempe in Thessaly. It was from there that the sacred laurel branch was brought which was used to crown the victor at the Pythian games. In the course of the long pilgrimage on the "sacred" route, a large group of tribes and cities would be summoned to the common festival, to the agon, which was preceded by the festival which Plutarch called the "Septerion,"[65] the festival of "dread" or "flight." One might consider whether or not this was actually a festival of the Pylaic Amphictiony, since it was originally centered at Thermopylae, considerably closer to the valley of Tempe. The eight-year period, however,[66] cannot have been introduced into Delphi at the time of the first Sacred War, for it was then that the four-year interval was established. There may have been a more complicated overlapping, based on the foundations of an essentially ritual structure, for even the rare and exceptional Septerion fits the structure of the normal Delphic sacrificial ritual: there, too, we find a sacrifice to incur guilt, marked by flight, expiation, and the return of the god.

For this festival, a wooden building, a "hut" (σκηνή), which, however, "looks like an imitation of a king's or a tyrant's palace," was built on the "threshing floor" (ἅλως), the circular space a short distance down from the temple terrace.[67] We do not know what went on inside the hut, but the climax came when the building was completely destroyed. Torches in hand—that is, at night—the members of the Labyadai phratry silently led a young boy to attack the hut; inside, they overturned the table, set fire to the wooden structure, and fled without turning around until they reached the entrance of the

---

H. Usener, *ARW* 7 (1904), 317–28 = *Kl. Schr.* IV (1913), 451–58; Nilsson (1906) 150; Harrison (1927) 425–28; Jeanmaire (1939) 387–411; Fontenrose (1959) 453ff.

[65] *Q. Gr.* 293c Σεπτήριον Mss., Στεπτήριον Bernardakis; Hsch. *σεπτηρία· καθαρμός, ἔκθυσις* (incorrectly listed after *σεσωσμένος*); Hsch. *στεπτήρια· στέμματα, ἃ οἱ ἱκέται ἐκ τῶν κλάδων ἐξῆπτον.* A. Mommsen argued for *σεπτήρια*, Nilsson (1906) 151.1 for *στεπτήριον*, following W. H. Roscher, *Neue Jb.* 49 (1879), 734–36, before the new Teubner edition by J. B. Titchener (1935).

[66] Plut. *Q. Gr.* 293c; Ael. *VH* 3.1; cf. M. P. Nilsson, *Die Entstehung u. religiöse Bedeutung des griech. Kalenders* (Lund, 1962²), 46–48; (1955) 644–47.

[67] Plut. *De def. or.* 418a. For the ἅλως in Delphic inscriptions see *SIG*³ 672 = *LS* 80.58; *LS* 81.7; *LSS* 44.9.

shrine. The attack was called the Dolonia,[68] and the "dangerous cunning" in this name recalls the cunning and murderous exploit of Odysseus and Diomedes at Troy, when they slew Rhesus, the barbarian king, guided by the information wrested from Dolon, who was clothed in a wolfskin. Thus, at Delphi, a young boy whose parents are still alive, who has not as yet faced the spectre of death, is made the instrument of destruction. Mythographers tried to link this ritual to Apollo's victory over the Python dragon,[69] but, as Plutarch noted, the details are incongruous. If there was a table inside the "king's building," there was surely a meal on top of it, a sacred meal at a festival in the sanctuary—i.e., a sacrifice—a meal which was then violently destroyed and obliterated so that no trace remained to attest to its existence. The act of overturning a table, documented here in ritual, appears in the myths of Lykaon and Thyestes.[70] Lykaon's "act" is followed by the all-consuming flood; and Delphi is the other site linked to the myth of the flood.[71] An exceptional period, and an unspeakable sacrifice, end suddenly and radically in ritual fire.

But the ritual here is only beginning; it must still travel a wide arc before it can finally overcome the catastrophe and reestablish divine purity in the sanctuary. Thus, the young boy sets out with his retinue in the long procession to the valley of Tempe. His journey is an "erratic wandering," "a slave's work," but at the same time an "orgiastic" march through the land[72]—this could mean something like armed dances or torch-waving. It was then taken up in the Python myth. According to the story, the wounded monster fled from Apollo; the god chased it to the valley of Tempe, where he finally killed it.[73] It is a "sacred route," uniting the Thessalians, Pelasgians, Oitaeans, Anians, Malians, Dorians, and Locrians. Finally, there was a "splendid" sacrifice at an altar on the Peneios in the valley of Tempe, together with purificatory rites, as if a terrible stain, an unthinkable crime, had to be blotted out.[74] In the myth, this too is accomplished by the god

---

[68] Plut. *De def. or.* ἡ διὰ τῆς Δολωνίας ἔφοδος (on the meaning of διὰ see *Num.* 8 θυσίαι δι'ἀλφίτου καὶ σπονδῆς πεποιημέναι). Λαβυάδαι is Pomptow's conjecture (cf. *LS* 77); the Mss. have ΜΗΑΙΟΛΑΔΕ.

[69] Ephoros, *FGrHist* 70 F 31b, criticized by Plut. *De def. or.* 418a.

[70] See II.1.n.14, 3.n.12 above. [71] See p. 120f. above.

[72] Plut. *De def. or.* 418a τοὺς ἔξω Πυλῶν πάντας Ἕλληνας ἡ πόλις κατοργιάζουσα μέχρι Τεμπῶν ἐλήλακεν.

[73] Plut. *Q. Gr.* 293c.

[74] Ἱερὰ ὁδός Hdt. 6.34.2; Plut. *Q. Gr.* 293c. For a list of the stopping-places and sacrifices in Tempe see Ael. *VH* 3.1; cf. Plut. *De def. or.* 418b; Callim. fr. 87, 89; Schol. Pind. *Pyth.* pp. 4.11–14 Drachmann.

Apollo in person.[75] The purificatory god was himself in need of purification, for he had killed. After this, the young boy would break off a laurel branch and carry it back all the way from the valley of Tempe. Accompanied by the music of the flute, he was led through all the lands and was received everywhere with reverence and esteem.[76] When the procession arrived in Delphi, the games could begin[77]—the women had in the meantime apparently performed closing rituals of their own.[78] Apollo himself would return to Delphi at midsummer from the land of the Hyperboreans, as celebrated in the hymn by Alcaeus.[79] Music was the primary mode of experiencing the Delphic god's epiphany, and the musical agon was the most important at Delphi. The violent act at the "place of putrefaction"—the ancient etymology of Pytho[80]—was surmounted and overcome once and for all through luminous order, through the beauty of art. But the order and the art themselves were suspended over an abyss of dread that was continuously torn open in feelings of guilt and sacrificial expiation. Apollo would speak only through the raving woman sitting on top of the covered tripod.

6. *A Glance at Odysseus*

The oldest story of cannibalism in Greek literature is Odysseus' adventure with the Cyclops. The extraordinary popularity of this unforgettable, pithy tale is already attested in the seventh century B.C. through a whole series of vase-paintings. Moreover, the great mass of parallels collected by folklorists—mainly related to the *Odyssey* but in

---

[75] Pind. fr. 249a = Tert. *De cor.* 7.5; Callim. fr. 89; Aristonoos I 17, p. 163 Powell.

[76] Ael. *VH* 3.1; cf. Plut. *De mus.* 1136a; Callim. fr. 194.36.

[77] Before 586, they were ennaeteric: see Schol. Pind. *Pyth.* p. 4.14 Drachmann; Censorinus 18; Schol. *Od.* 3.267. The σεπτήριον took place "shortly before" the Pythian games: see Plut. *De def. or.* 410a with 418a.

[78] Τρεῖς . . . ἐνναετηρίδας κατὰ τὸ ἑξῆς, Septerion, Herois, Charila, see Plut. *Q. Gr.* 293b–f. Plutarch's imprecise statement makes it possible, though not certain, that the Herois and Charila were celebrated before the Pythian games (Fontenrose [1959] 458).

[79] Alcaeus 307 Lobel-Page = Himer. *Or.* 48.10–11.

[80] *Hy. Ap.* 363.

part also exhibiting more primitive features[1]—can hardly be overlooked. One might be tempted to consider the story of the man-eater an almost universal folk motif, and hence not look for close ties with such myths as those of Lykaon, Thyestes, or Tantalos. But more careful consideration uncovers a whole series of strange correspondences, leading us to suspect a specific ritual structure underlying this masterpiece of early Greek song.

First of all, we notice the decisive role played by a ram, a sacrificial animal. Clinging to the ram's fleece and hidden beneath it, Odysseus is able to escape the terrifying cave. The fact that he promptly sacrifices his rescuer to Zeus must gravely offend any animal-lover; but Phrixos acted no differently. The idea of tying men under the bellies of sheep is worthy of the mind that conceived of the wooden horse—and just as impractical. Here, a whole group of those parallel versions seem to offer us something more ancient: threatened by the man-eater, men conceal themselves in the skins of slaughtered animals and thus, disguised as animals, escape the groping hands of the blinded monster.[2] In this case, necessity forced them to kill their rescuers, and it had to be done before the escape. Here, in order to achieve freedom, man must identify himself with the slaughtered animal. If we presume this version behind the adventure of Odysseus, the correspondences with the cult in the cave of Cheiron on Mount Pelion, and with the sheep-sacrifice for Cyprian Aphrodite,[3] are quite close. The fact that Odysseus was named by his grandfather, who in so doing attempted to fix his own nature in words, also becomes significant, for his grandfather was Autolykos, the werewolf from Parnassus.[4]

The poet of the *Odyssey* did not understand it in this way. But even the name *Odysseus, Olytteus,* is clearly non-Greek.[5] The myth of Odysseus leads us back not just to pre-Homeric times but to sources outside Greece. Now, a Greek interpreter once made a strange con-

[1]For the vase-paintings see Schefold (1964) pl. 1 (Eleusinian amphora found 1954); 45 fig. 15 (fragment from Argos, *BCH* 79 [1955], 1–49); pl. 37 (fragment from Aegina). Cf. also the Aristonothos crater in Rome: P. E. Arias and M. Hirmer, *Tausend Jahre griech. Vasenkunst* (1960), pl. 14/15. For the parallels see O. Hackman, *Die Polyphemsage in der Volksüberlieferung* (Helsingfors 1904); K. Meuli, *Odyssee und Argonautika* (1921), 66–78; Cook II (1924), 988–1003; D. L. Page, *The Homeric Odyssey* (1955), 3–16.

[2]Thus by far the majority of variants: see Hackman, *Polyphemsage*, 171–74, 184; cf. the saga of the shipwrecked sailors in the cave of Dionysus in Paus. 2.23.1.

[3]See II.4.nn.22, 32 above. [4]*Od.* 19.406–409.

[5]E. Wüst, *RE* XVII 1909–13.

nection between the *Odyssey* and the Samothracian mysteries: "They say Odysseus was initiated at Samothrace and therefore wore the veil of Leucothea instead of a fillet. For the initiates at Samothrace tie purple fillets around their abdomen."[6] It was commonly believed that the gods of Samothrace would save their initiates from drowning.[7] Although virtually no details of the secret initiation are known, the coins point us toward one fact: the central event was the sacrifice of a ram.[8] Wearing the woolen fillet was linked to a bath. Aside from this, there are only various myths connected with Samothrace. These, however, reveal a series of striking analogies to Odysseus. Just as Dardanus came from an island on a raft (*σχεδία*)[9] at the time of the great flood to found Ilion-Troy, so Odysseus left Calypso's "Ogygian" island—a name still unexplained and enigmatic in the context of the *Odyssey*. Ogygos, however, is elsewhere known as Boeotia's ancestral king, who lent his name to the most ancient Greek flood legend.[10] This makes the parallel between the journeys of Dardanus and Odysseus on the raft even closer. Ever since the most ancient times, the sanctuary of the Cabiri played a central role in Boeotia. One can hardly separate Cadmus from Cadmilus;[11] moreover, his wife Harmonia[12] links the myth directly with Samothrace. Among the grotesque vase-paintings found in the Boeotian Cabirion, scenes from the *Odyssey* crop up with surprising frequency. The best known is a vase on which "Olyteus," driven by "Borias," sails the sea on a primitive raft, with Poseidon's trident in hand.[13] Are Poseidon and Odysseus, the

---

[6]Schol. Apoll. Rhod. 1.917 *καὶ 'Οδυσσέα δέ φασι μεμυημένον ἐν Σαμοθράκῃ χρήσασθαι τῷ κρηδέμνῳ ἀντὶ ταινίας. Περὶ γὰρ τὴν κοιλίαν οἱ μεμυημένοι ταινίας ἅπτουσι πορφυρᾶς*. Schol. P *Od.* 5.381 mentions a "goat island," Αἰγαί, *πλησίον Σαμοθράκης*. According to Aristotle fr. 579 = Schol. Apoll. Rhod. 1.917, Samothrace was called *Λευκοσία*.

[7]See the anecdote of the atheist Diagoras or Diogenes, Diog. Laert. 6.59. On Samothrace see N. Lewis, *Samothrace: The Ancient Literary Sources* (1958); Hemberg (1950), 49–131.

[8]Hemberg (1950), 102, 109.

[9]Lyk. 74–80 with Schol. 73; Schol. Plat. *Tim.* 22a.

[10]*Νήσου ἀπ' 'Ωγυγίης Od.* 6.172, and cf. 1.85, 7.244, 254, 12.448, 23.333; U. v. Wilamowitz-Moellendorff, *Homerische Untersuchungen* (1884), 16–17. On Ogygos see Korinna 671 Page; Paus. 9.5.1; as Cadmus' father see Suda *ω* 12. On the Ogygian flood see Schol. Plat. *Tim.* 22a; Varro in Cens. 21.1; cf. Jacoby in Philochoros, *FGrHist* 328 F 92.

[11]Hemberg (1950) 95, 316–17.

[12]Hellanikos, *FGrHist* 4 F 23; Ephoros, *FGrHist* 70 F 120; cf. *RE* VII 2379–88.

[13]Oxford skyphos, Cook III (1940), 160. R. Stiglitz, "Herakles auf dem Amphorenfloss,"

god and his victim, paradoxically equated here? Since archaic times, Odysseus' iconography has, with strange consistency, included the circular, pointed hat, the pilos, otherwise worn by Hephaestus and his sons, the Cabiri, and further by the Dioscouri, who are themselves Great Gods. Was Odysseus involved in the mysteries of the Cabiri? In any case, the Cyclopes were also among Hephaestus' companions.[14] And the pilos was made "from the wool of a sacrificial animal."[15] The initiate remains clothed in the symbol of the sacrifice.

Whatever these specific parallels prove or make probable, more important yet is the fact that the structure of Odysseus' "sufferings" quite obviously corresponds to the werewolf pattern that turns up again and again from Delphi to Mount Lykaion. Odysseus' life reaches a turning point when he witnesses that "unspeakable" cannibalistic meal in the cave, far from human civilization. In a series of parallel versions, the hero is forced to share in the meal of human flesh.[16] After continuing as a symposium, the gruesome feast is swiftly and violently brought to a close by fire and the invention of man's primordial weapon, the spear hardened by fire.[17] Odysseus escapes beneath the fleece of the ram, but his homecoming is now delayed. Like the Delphic boy, he too must go far away; and like the Arcadian werewolf, he must linger in unknown lands for nine years before being able to return home. The fact that Odysseus' rescue action provokes the Cyclops' curse and Poseidon's anger, an incomprehensible moral paradox, rests on a ritual foundation. The raft carries Odysseus to new shores, and, finally, homeward through the sea. His arrival establishes a new order in place of chaos, "at the waning of the old moon, and the start of the new."[18] The king regains power at

---

Osterr. Jahresh. 44 (1959), 112–41. At Erythrai, Herakles appeared on a σχεδία: Paus. 7.5.5.

[14] Hes. *Th.* 141 portrays the Cyclopes already as smiths; the relationship of these Cyclopes with those of *Od.* 9 is an old ζήτημα. Odysseus already appears with a pilos on the leg of a tripod at Olympia ca. 600 B.C.: see Schefold (1964) fig. 28 p. 71. The man who vanquishes the ogre is, in many parallel versions, a smith (#46, 47, 53, 63, 64, 73, 74 Hackman, *Polyphemsage*), and the blinding is often carried out with molten metal; the Cabiri are smithy-gods.

[15] So with the *pilleus*, sometimes called *galerus*, of the *flamen Dialis*: see Varro in Gell. 10.15.32; Suetonius in Serv. auct. *Aen.* 2.683; Festus *s.v. albogalerus* p. 10 M.; E. Samter, *Familienfeste der Griechen und Römer* (1901), 34–35.

[16] Nos. 20, 68 and cf. #8, 19, 58, 71, 110 Hackman, *Polyphemsage.*

[17] Burkert (1967), 283–85.

[18] *Od.* 14.162, 19.307.

the festival of Apollo,[19] by fighting with his bow. In his transformation, Odysseus journeys between the antitheses of Poseidon's realm and Apollo's. Opposing the wild and far-off lands is the power of justice at home; opposing the man-eater's greed, the cruel but just vengeance; opposing the predator's attack at close quarters, the technology of weapons that can be used at a distance. In either case there is, of course, killing, whether it be that of Poseidon's son or that in the grove of Apollo. Even culture, in its antithesis to anti-culture, is based on sacrifice.

Eduard Meyer[20] demonstrated long ago that a whole series of cultic reminiscences link Odysseus and Penelope with Arcadia. There, too, in the cult, we find the antithesis of Poseidon and Apollo, an antithesis also present in one version of the Delphic legend.[21] The connections that have cropped up simultaneously with the Cabiri, Samothrace, and Troy point to pre-Hellenic cultural levels, remnants of which persisted both in a non-Greek form in Samothrace and Lemnos and in a Greek guise in Arcadia and Delphi. It is hardly feasible to try to determine a more specific national origin, for if we find traces as far back as Çatal Hüyük and beyond, then the patterns themselves must be older than any national differentiation accessible to scholarship. What we find is the antithesis of agriculture and city culture to the society of the predator, which breaks in upon the everyday world on sacred occasions, only to disappear again: humanity asserts itself against the wolves, and civilization rises up out of perversion, as day follows night. For that very reason, daylight presupposes the existence of night. Ritual must constantly reestablish the deadly outdoor realm of the hunting era within the circle of civilization, both to call that civilization into question and to renew it. Both are divine, and perhaps both aspects of sacrifice, the dread of death and the certainty of life, are subject to the same god.

---

[19] *Od.* 20.276; cf. 18.600, 20.156, 250, 21.258–59; Wilamowitz, *Homerische Untersuchungen* (n.10 above), 111–14.

[20] *Hermes* 30 (1895), 263–70; E. Wüst, *RE* XVII 1910–12. Cf. *PR* II 1050–59. For the horses of Odysseus at Pheneos see Paus. 8.14.5, and cf. 8.44.4; in addition see the strange genealogy of Penelope-Pan in Pind. fr. 100.

[21] For the myth of Thelpusa see Paus. 8.25.4–5; there is a corresponding myth of Poseidon (Schol. A *Il.* 23.346) and cult of Apollo (Strabo 9 p. 411; *Hy. Ap.* 244–76, 375–87) at Boeotian Tilphusion; see also Burkert (1979) 125–129. For Poseidon as the patron god of the Delphic oracle, who exchanged Delphi for Kalaureia, *Eumolpia*, see Paus. 10.5.6, 2.33.2; Callim. fr. 593. For an altar of Poseidon at Delphi see Paus. 10.24.4.

III. DISSOLUTION AND NEW YEAR'S FESTIVAL

We have traced the two-sided nature of sacrifice—the encounter with death and the will to live—in a group of rituals characterized on the one hand by the act of cooking a ram in a kettle, and on the other by the oppositions among the participants and the play between exclusion and membership. A similar dramatic structure occurs when the two parts follow sequentially; only the terrifying central act answered by an affirmation of order must be constant. In one group of rituals centering on the sacrifice of a bull, women and girls assume a special role in which they move from lovely to gloomy aspects. Here, the three parts of the sacrificial action—preparation, "act," restitution—are expanded into three related festivals that can be characterized as: (1) a symbolic sacrifice of a girl; (2) an "unspeakable sacrifice"; and (3) a sacrifice of renewal. The rhythm of anticipatory renunciation, followed by the savage "act" and, finally, pleasurable gratification, reflects the age-old situation of the hunter. In the city-culture, however, it is symbolically transformed into a New Year's festival following a period of dissolution, that is, a breakdown of the normal order. The same structure appears in Dionysiac orgies, almost as an atavistic regression. And, further on, we encounter the customs of fishermen who, although situated somewhere between hunting and city cultures, adapted themselves to the same tradition. Through changing economic and social conditions, the fundamental structure of ritual remains.

1. *From Ox-Slaying to the Panathenaic Festival*

DIPOLIEIA

The polis of Athens plays a unique role in Greek literature. This city, with its love of writing, has left us by far the greatest number of inscriptions. For a time, it attracted the best artists, and it dominated the production of painted pottery for centuries. Thus, nowhere are cults so well documented. But the confusing variety of religious phenomena makes us all the more conscious of the limits of our knowledge. People talked about far less than they experienced—either because they thought it self-evident, or because of a certain apprehension. Moreover, those books that dealt specifically with Attic cult survive only in a few fragments. Our picture of festivals in Athens is richer and more varied than that of festivals elsewhere, but for that very reason it is more confused, and it is still only fragmentary.

In Athens, almost every day had its festival or sacrifice.[1] Out of all these sacrifices, one stood out by virtue of its singular, even grotesque, features: the Buphonia, "ox-slaying," for "Zeus of the City" (Διὶ Πολιεῖ). This occurred on the fourteenth day of Skirophorion in midsummer, at the altar of Zeus on the highest spot of the Athenian Acropolis.[2] The festival, though distinguished by its date in the mid-

---

[1]On the Athenian sacral calendar, recorded by Nikomachos at the end of the fifth century B.C., see S. Dow, *Proc. Massachusetts Historical Society* 71 (1953/57), 3–36; *Hesperia* 30 (1961), 58–73.

[2]O. Band, *De Diipoliorum sacro Atheniensium* (1873); Smith (1894) 304–306; H. v. Prott, *RhM* 52 (1897), 187–204; Farnell I (1896) 56–58, 88–93; Nilsson (1906) 14–16; (1955) 152–55; Harrison (1922) 111–13; (1927) 142–50; Deubner (1932) 158–74; Cook III (1940) 570–873; Meuli (1946) 275–77; W. F. Otto, *Paideuma* 4 (1950), 111–26 = *Das Wort der Antike* (1962), 140–61; U. Pestalozza, "Le origini delle Buphonia ateniesi," *Rend. dell'Inst. Lomb.* 89/90 (1956), 433–54; M. Mauss, *Oeuvres* I (1968), 274–83. On the name Διπολίεια (on Διὶ πολιεῖ see Deubner [1932] 158) see *IG* I² 843 = *LS* 17 Ab (taken from the official festival calendar recorded by Nikomachos; cf. J. H. Oliver, *Hesperia* 4 [1935], 32); *IG* I² 188 = *LSS* 10 A 16 (*IG* I² 839 = *LSS* 2 Ac is uncertain; Aristoph. *Pax* 420 should read Διπολίει'; but cf. Διπολιώδη *Nub.* 984). For the date see *LS* 179; Schol. Aristoph. *Pax* 419; *Et. M.* 210.30 = *Et. Gen.* (ις' rather than ιδ' *An. Bekk.* 238.21). The idea that the Buphonia were celebrated τῇ 'Αθηνᾷ, Schol. Aristoph. *Nub.* 985, is a misreading of

dle of the month, by its high location, and by the name of the highest god, was anything but bright and cheerfully devout. Its very name suggests what the ritual subsequently makes tangible: a guilt-laden crime—but one which could not be taken seriously, and so became a farce which seemed to fit neither Zeus, nor the Acropolis, nor the prytaneum, nor yet a glorified picture of the primordial age. Yet people knew and felt that the custom was old. As early as Aristophanes,[3] the epithets "Dipolieia-like" and "full of Buphonia" signified antiquated habits and old-fashioned nonsense that modern youths wished to discard. But (though modified in its details)[4] the Dipolieia survived until the time of the Roman emperors.[5]

Thanks mainly to one report, probably going back to Theophrastus,[6] we can trace the details of this sacrifice in a way that is seldom possible. A whole group of oxen would be driven up to the Acropolis. As always, the procession included water carried by young girls (ὑδροφόροι), sacrificial grain, and the sacrificial knife. At the sacred place, the sacrificial animal would not immediately be placed at the center. Rather, the oxen had to circle the altar[7] on which the grain-sacrifice—a kind of meal or cake—had been set (see Figure 6).[8] One would think the god was being offered the fruits of agriculture. There

---

'Αϑήνησιν Schol. Aristoph. *Pax* 419, just as the puzzling μετὰ τὰ μυστήρια (Deubner [1932] 160.5) in the same scholion comes from *Pax* 419 with its scholion.

[3] *Nub.* 984–85 ἀρχαῖά γε καὶ Διπολιώδη καὶ τεττίγων ἀνάμεστα καὶ Κηκείδου καὶ βουφονίων. The myth attributes the sacrifice to Kekrops (Euseb. Hieron. *chron. a. Abr.* 472; Hsch. Διὸς ϑᾶκοι) or Erechtheus (Paus. 1.28.10). For the oldest inscriptional source see *IG* I² 839 = *LSS* 2 (ca. 500 B.C.).

[4] Cf. n. 8.

[5] Paus. 1.24.4, 28.10; for a calendar frieze see Deubner (1932) 253 pl. 39.

[6] Porph. *Abst.* 2.28–30; traced back to Theophrastus by J. Bernays, *Theophrastos' Schrift über Frömmigkeit* (1866), 121–24; cf. F. Jacoby on *FGrHist* 324 F 16 (Supplement: Notes 129); W. Pötscher, *Theophrastos ΠΕΡΙ ΕΥΣΕΒΕΙΑΣ* (1964), 84–86, 128–32. Following Prott, Deubner (1932), who felt ill at ease with this text, discounted its importance (163–70); "skrupellos fingiert" 169. This skepticism is refuted by newfound evidence or, rather, by evidence that Deubner did not take into account; cf. n. 7 below.

[7] Depicted on a series of black figure vases by the Gela painter (ca. 510/480 B.C.): see Cook III (1940) 581–82; G. Bakalakis, *AK* 12 (1969), 56–60. Further, J. H. Oliver read in a fragment of the Nikomachean calendar (see n. 1 above), *IG* I² 843 = *Hesperia* 4 (1935), 32 ἀπὸ τε̑ς περιελ[άσεος] το̑ν hὲχς το̑ν προτέ[ρον (with doubts, Sokolowski, *LS* 17) to which is now added περι[ε]λ[αύνειν *Hesperia* 37 (1968), 267 = *LS* 179.

[8] Paus. 1.24.4 refers to an altar κριϑὰς . . . μεμιγμένας πυροῖς; Porph. *Abst.* 2.29 to a τράπεζα, ἐπὶ τῆς χαλκῆς τραπέζης πελανὸν καὶ ψαιστά 2.30; πόπανον Schol. (VR) Aristoph. *Nub.* 985; Hsch. βουφόνια; Suda B 474 = Androtion, *FGrHist* 324 F 16; καρποί, πελανός Porph. *Abst.* 2.10. On πελανός see Stengel (1910) 66–72.

was indeed a time "when people shrank from eating oxen, and offered no animals in sacrifice, but, rather, cakes and the fruits of the earth soaked in honey and other such pure sacrifices"[9]—or such was the conclusion drawn already by Plato and more consequently by Theophrastus from the introductory part of the sacrifice. Yet this "pure offering" was merely a prelude, if not actually an excuse or bait for the violent act. By now the axe kept in the shrine would have been polished with the water brought for the occasion. It was simply a question of waiting until one of the animals turned to the altar and, following its instincts, ate the grain. The ox itself thus broke the tabu[10] and sinned against the god and his altar. After this, the "ox-slayer" would swing his axe, the bull would fall. There are several versions of the legend telling how the first "ox-slaying" resulted from the spontaneous rage of a devout farmer when a greedy ox disrupted the sacred act. The killer's name varies—Thaulon, Sopatros, Diomos—but the motivation and the act remain constant, for they are played out in the ritual.[11] To Aratus, this bull-sacrifice marked the close of the Silver Age;[12] the seeming idyll ended in "sacred" bloodshed. We know today that Theophrastus and many other romantics were deluding themselves about the development of mankind: it was far more a question of old hunting instincts breaking through the thin crust of civilization. Aggression had long been held back behind the sacredness of the altar—sacrifice was expected and finally done.

But this new step recoiled at once upon the actors. The "ox-slayer" (*βουτύπος*) who administered the fatal blow then threw away his axe and fled. Pausanias describes this as the normal custom, as

---

[9]Plat. *Leg*. 782c.

[10]The sacrificial bull for Zeus Polieus on Cos is chosen (*κριθείς*) from many which are driven through the marketplace: *SIG* 1025 = *LS* 151 A 19: *θύεται δέ, αἰ μέγ κα ὑποκύψει τᾶι* Ἱστίαι; this is usually understood as though a second sacrifice, for Hestia, were inorganically inserted (E. Farmer Craik, *Par. del Pass*. 22 [1967], 442). But the larger context of the festival for Zeus Polieus suggests the translation "it is sacrificed if it bows its head to Hestia," i.e., turns toward the state hearth at the market. Afterward, "Hestia is reimbursed" (25) for the price of the bull, that is, the sacrificial animal is bought from the goddess (I. 5. n. 38 above). In this interpretation we must accept a doublet, 20–22 + 49–54, in which the *γέρη* are once presented briefly, once in detail.

[11]For Thaulon see Androtion, *FGrHist* 324 F 16 with the parallels cited by Jacoby; for Sopatros see Porph. *Abst*. 2.28–30; for Diomos see ibid. 2.10, repeated in 2.29, which, however, belongs clearly to the cattle-sacrifice for Herakles at the Diomeia (Aristoph. *Ran*. 651; Steph. Byz. *s.v. Kynosarges*). Every sacrifice of a bull is a "primeval crime."

[12]Aratus 131–32. To kill a plow-ox was considered a crime at Athens: Ael. *VH* 5.14; Columella 6 praef. 7; Schol. *Od*. 12.353.

does the legend, whether speaking of Sopatros or Thaulon.[13] Banishment had been the price for spilling blood since ancient times; the Greeks called it "flight," φυγή. Thus, the biological mechanism that makes aggression change to flight was institutionalized as law.[14] At the Buphonia, the one who performed the sacrificial "act" would run away and not return. The remaining participants, happy to be rid of him, could now enjoy the fruits of his action: after the animal had collapsed, the "carvers" would skin it with a knife, cut it up, and remove its bowels. The meat was evidently roasted and eaten at once. In this way, all participants were irrevocably implicated in the sacrifice. The most detailed of the etiological legends, however, was unable to stomach this meal. In this version, Sopatros "buried" the bull whole, but the full offense appears only in what follows: an oracle inserted in the narrative ordered the Athenians not to atone for the crime, but instead to repeat it and, what is more, to eat the sacrificial animal.[15] By making the "act" a collective undertaking, Sopatros could ease his conscience.[16] Thus, everyone now participated according to his group, which represented one of the old Athenian families: the "water-bearers," the "goaders" driving the ox to the altar, the "ox-slayers," and the "carvers."[17] All would work together according to their roles;

---

[13] Paus. 1.24.4; for the legend see Porph. *Abst.* 2.29; Thaulon φυγαδευθείς Schol. T *Il.* 18.483. On ritual flight after the sacrifice see Tenedos, III.4.n.20 below; Delphi, II.5 n.68; Tithorea, Paus. 10.32.17; Tegea, Paus. 8.53.3; Thesmophoria, Hsch. δίωγμα; Crete, Zenob. Ath. 2.7 = Zenob. Par. 5.50 (*Paroem. Gr.* I 141); III. 3/4 below. In paintings, Hephaestus flees at Athena's birth: see Cook III (1940) 656–726. Philoktetes flees after having lit Herakles' pyre: Cook III (1940) 516 = *ARV*[2] 1420.5. For Rome see the Regifugium and Poplifugia. Cf. Meuli (1946) 277; Burkert, *Historia* 11 (1962), 368–69.

[14] Cf. the rites concerning Buzyges and the Palladion procession at Athens: Burkert, *Zeitschrift für Religions- und Geistesgeschichte* 22 (1970), 356–68, reflected in the "flight" and purification of king Demophon.

[15] Porph. *Abst.* 2.29 γευσαμένοις τε τοῦ τεθνεῶτος καὶ μὴ κατασχοῦσιν—"to restrain oneself" (κατασχεῖν) or abstain is explicitly forbidden at this sacrifice. Deubner found this "ungeheuerlich" (167; cf. n. 6 above).

[16] Εἰ κοινῇ τοῦτο πράξειαν πάντες . . . δεῖν κατακοπῆναι βοῦν ὑπὸ τῆς πόλεως Porph. *Abst.* 2.29; 2.10: συνεργοὺς γὰρ λαβὼν τοὺς ἄλλους.

[17] Porph. *Abst.* 2.30 (end) is problematic to the extent that βουτύποι and δαιτροί clearly designate functions, not families; but Kleidemos, *FGrHist* 323 F 5, seems to have attributed these very functions to the Eleusinian Kerykes (cf. Jacoby *ad loc.*); the Κεντριάδαι (Porph. *Abst.* 230) are explained in Phot. as follows: Κεντριάδαι· πατριὰ κηρύκων (on πατριά, "family," see Phot. Εὐμολπίδαι· πατριὰ Ἀθήνησιν). Porphyry's (Theophrastus') reference is thus linked to Atthidographical tradition. In *IG* I[2] 843 = *LS* 17 ΚΗΡΥΧΣΙΝ ΟΙ ΔΙΠΟΛΙΕΙ[Ο]ΙΣ it is uncertain whether it is the family or just some κήρυκες who are participating. There is a competing assertion in Androtion, *FGrHist*

all ate the meat except the one who killed. The bones were subsequently burned on the altar; only the skin remained.

There followed an epilogue emphasizing the event's social relevance. A trial was held at the center of the polis, that is, at the state hearth in the prytaneum, for the crime of having killed at the altar. "Here, the women water-bearers charged that those who had sharpened the axe and the knife were more guilty than they, and these in turn charged him who had handed them the axe, and he charged the man who had cut up the ox, and he who had done this charged the knife which, since it could not speak, was found guilty of murder."[18] The "ox-slayer," who would otherwise have been the first to be blamed, had fled and could not be found. Allegedly, no one knew him. According to Pausanias, the axe was made to stand trial, but acquitted; according to Porphyry, the knife was cast into the sea. These two acts seem more complementary than contradictory. Both the axe and the knife play a part in the sacrifice:[19] the knife alone cannot kill the bull, nor the axe skin it. Because the life-forces seem to ebb away with the blood, it is natural that the knife should be found more guilty than the axe. The knife was, moreover, smaller and more easily obtainable. The axe would presumably have been kept elsewhere, in the shrine, as a primordial symbol of consecrated violence. A plow, the primordial plow of its inventor, was said to be kept in just this way on the Acropolis. The stuffed ox-skin was spread out in front of it, and thus the sacrificial animal had "risen from the dead."[20] Ostensibly, the

---

324 F 16 (cf. Agallis Schol. T *Il.* 18.483; Eust. 1156.59; Hsch. *Θαυλωνίδαι*; Suda *ϑ* 67), which links the *βουτύπος* to the Thaulonidai (cf. Zeus *Θαύλιος* in Thessaly: Cook III [1940], 277–83; Hsch. *Θαύλιος*, Cd. *Θαῦμος*, *ἢ Θαῦλος· Ἄρης Μακεδόνιος. Θαύλια· ἑορτή. Ταραντῖνοι...*). How this competition between the two families is to be smoothed over is still a problem: see A. Mommsen (1898), 521–22; Toepffer (1889), 149–58; Cook III (1940), 596–97. Hsch. *βούτης· ὁ τοῖς Διπολίοις τὰ βουφόνια δρῶν* has probably been confused with *βουτύπος* (Deubner [1932] 162; Cook III [1940] 589). During the Roman Empire, a *ἱερεὺς βουτύπος* Λακρατείδης is attested: *IG* II/III^2 2128.2, 2129.2, 2191a1. For a seat *ἱερέως* Διὸς Πολιέως in the theater, see *IG* II/III^2 5024.

[18] Porph. *Abst.* 2.30, and cf. Ael. *VH* 8.3 (probably taken from Theoprastus); Paus. 1.28.10 *ὁ δὲ πέλεκυς παραυτίκα ἀφείϑη κριϑεὶς καὶ εἰς τόδε ἀνὰ πᾶν ἔτος κρίνεται.* The *βουτύπος* is "not known": see Paus. 1.24.4.

[19] Cook III [1940], 585. Porph. *Abst.* 2.30 mentions both *πέλεκυς* and *μάχαιρα*. Both appear on a relief depicting a sacrifice: Cook III (1940) 28 fig. 7. On the court at the Prytaneion see Demosth. 23.76. For the burying of the sacrificial knife see Eur. *Hik.* 1205–1208.

[20] This only in Porph. *Abst.* 2.29, 30. A *βουζύγης ἐξ ἀκροπόλεως* is mentioned in Aristid. *Or.* 2 I 20 Dindorf. For Athena as inventor of the plow see Serv. auct. *Aen.* 4.402. For spreading out the skin of the sacrificial victim: Scythians, Hdt. 4.72; at the Altaic horse-

pre-sacrificial situation was restored. But even if the famous meals in the prytaneum were essentially vegetarian,[21] nobody could forget that he was no longer living in a Golden Age.

The extraordinary features of this sacrificial festival seem to require extraordinary interpretations: is this bull a totem animal, or a vegetation demon which must be killed at the harvest festival, or perhaps even Zeus himself?[22] There is doubtless some truth in all of these explanations, but by following any one of them, we risk becoming entangled in the religious-historical problem of what something "is"—and is that not simply inventing a new mythology to explain the old? Evidence for the identity of the god and the sacrificial animal can be adduced from the outer limits of the Greek world and, in allusions, even from Greece itself. But in this case, as long as Athenians spoke Greek, they referred concretely to an "ox" that would be "killed" for "Zeus of the City," Διὶ Πολιεῖ.

Karl Meuli lodged a strong protest against isolating the Buphonia ritual and interpreting it in exceptional ways,[23] for he saw that the festival's basic rhythm was absolutely parallel to that of a more straightforward, "normal" sacrifice, from its "beginning" with water and grain to the final "setting-up" and consecration of the remains. The comedy of innocence was merely broader—a fact which incidentally confirms that something very ancient and fundamental is surfacing here, not a "new custom," the creation of a refined sensibility, as Deubner[24] claimed in reaction to the bold theories advanced by historians of religion.

The strange and eccentric character of this ritual remains,[25] but

---

sacrifice, *UdG* IX 287; at the bear festival, Meuli (1946) 229, and cf. Cook I (1914) 185. The Coan *Lex Sacra* dictates that ἔνδορα ἐνδέρεται, on which see Stengel (1910) 85–91. Since *IG* I² 843 (= *LS* 17) mentions wood in connection with ΚΗΡΥΚΕΣ and Dipolieia, the remains were probably burnt.

[21] Ath. 137e, and cf. n. 48 below.

[22] For "the special deity of an ox-clan" see Farnell I (1896) 58. For the vegetation spirit see W. Mannhardt, *Mythologische Forschungen* (1884), 58–71; *GB* VIII 4–7. For the bull = Zeus see Cook III (1940) 605–606, and cf. P. Philippson, *Thessalische Mythologie* (1944), 51–53.

[23] (1946) 275–76.

[24] (1932) 173.

[25] Hunters and nomads too, besides their "ordinary" rituals, have extraordinary sacrificial festivals at which the acts of incurring guilt and making reparation are played out in detail; this applies to the elephant festival among the Pygmies (see I.7.nn.44, 51 above), the bear festival (see I.2.n.5 above), the horse-sacrifice among the Indo-European peoples, the Altaians and the Mongols (see I.7.n.50 above).

we can come closer to understanding it by taking a look at the official Attic calendar. The Buphonia fell on the fourteenth day of Skirophorion, at the full moon in the last month of the year. It was thus the year's last major festival. Since the calendar at Athens, as in many parts of Greece and the Near East, was ordered according to the agricultural year—wherein the New Year comes in the summer, in the interval between harvest and sowing time—the celebration of the Dipolieia presupposes the end of the harvest.[26] But the predominance of such paradoxical, uncanny features at a "harvest festival," where gratification and joy would ordinarily prevail, cannot be explained as agricultural. We must look, rather, to the very serious concept of an "end."

Even for modern man, the end of the year, hovering between transitory past and uncertain future, is a peculiarly stirring experience. Its impact on ancient man as a time of transition, uncertainty, and crisis was far more immediate. Ever since calendars were invented, the beginning that accompanies the New Year has been simultaneously acted out in city government. In Near Eastern monarchies, for instance, the king temporarily abdicated.[27] In the Greek polis, new officials came to power—at Athens, this means the archon, the king, the polemarch, as well as the guardians of the laws and the generals. Trials in criminal court—the most stirring events in the field of law—could not be carried over from one year to the next.[28] There was a caesura. The new archon began by proclaiming that "whatever possessions anyone held before his entry into office, he shall have and keep until he steps down from his office."[29] This proclamation of such continuing security simultaneously curtailed and limited it to the archon's term of office. It almost sounds as though anything was allowed in the break between the old and the new: whatever anyone could quickly snatch up, he could forthwith keep; and the remnants of such customs do indeed exist.[30]

[26]The connection with the harvest is more evident in the sacrifice of a bull for Zeus Sosipolis in Magnesia, *SIG*[3] 589 = *LSAM* 32, inasmuch as the bull is brought before the god "at the start of the sowing" in order to be sacrificed in early summer (after the harvest?); see Nilsson (1955) 155–56.

[27]For the Babylonian New Year's ritual see *ANET* 331–34; S. A. Pallis, *The Babylonian Akitu Festival* (1926).

[28]Antiphon 6.42, 44.

[29]Arist. *Ath. Pol.* 56.2.

[30]Thus, Ptolemy IV absolved all debts and gave amnesty for all crimes on New Year's Day (Oct. 9), 186 B.C., after the victory and birth of the successor to the throne. The

Even when civic life became too stable to permit such legal vagaries, the cleft between the old and the new remained; indeed, it was ritual that marked it out. In the *Laws*, Plato wanted the last month of the year dedicated to Pluto, the god of death. He too had to be honored, for dissolution is no less good or necessary than new life.[31] What in Plato's hands became a belief in individual immortality was first applied primarily to society, which renewed itself through periodic dissolution. Such an act of "dissolution" was performed by the community in the ceremony of slaughtering the ox, where, at the end of the agricultural year, the farmer's animal helper became the victim. Here, far beyond the capacities of normal sacrifice, the ritual illuminates both the horror of killing, from which man tries to escape by fleeing or throwing the blame on others, and the sacred necessity that is ineluctable. All must play their parts until the communal meal, for life can assert itself only through food taken from life: hence the blood spilled on the heights in honor of Zeus of the City.

SKIRA

The context in which the Dipolieia festival is thus set extends yet further. At Athens, the last month of the year was not called Buphonion[32] but Skirophorion, after the Skira festival.[33] It was celebrated on the twelfth day of Skirophorion, i.e., immediately preceding the Buphonia;[34] and, on close inspection it turns out that the Skira is almost the mirror-image of the Buphonia. To be sure, the former refers to Athena, Erechtheus, and Demeter, and the latter to Zeus, but it will

---

new order of law in the ancient monarchies was thought to start with the king's accession to the throne, which was renewed on New Year's Day; cf. L. Koenen, *Arch. f. Papyrusforschung* 17 (1960), 11–16. For five days' ἀνομία at the death of a Persian king, see Sext. *Math.* 2.33; Stob. 4.2.26.

[31] *Leg.* 828c–d.

[32] For the month Buphonion on Delos see *IG* XI 2.203 A 32, 52; on Tenos see *IG* XII 5.842.1, 826; at Karystos see *IG* XII 9.207.39.

[33] C. Robert, "Athena Skiras und die Skirophorien," *Hermes* 20 (1885), 349–79; A. R. van der Loeff, "De Athena Scirade," *Mnemosyne* n.s. 44 (1916), 101–12; "De Sciris," ibid., 322–37; E. Gjerstad, "Das attische Fest der Skira," *ARW* 27 (1929), 189–240; Deubner (1932), 40–50; Burkert, *Hermes* 94 (1966), 23–24; all sources in Jacoby on *FGrHist* 328 F 14 (III B Supplement 286–89). For the date see Schol. Aristoph. *Eccl.* 18.

[34] There is often a free day between consecutive festivals (for this principle at Rome see Latte [1960], 199): the middle day at the Thesmophoria is free—Νηστεία, preparation of the Καλλιγένεια sacrifice (Deubner [1932] 52).

not do to separate the festival rituals according to the individualized names of the gods. Only the ritual's total rhythm can communicate its message, just as it takes the totality of gods to make the world.

The most prominent feature in the Skira is a procession which, in its way, is once again peculiar. Beneath a canopy, "the priestess of Athena and the priests of Poseidon and of Helios set off from the Acropolis toward a place called Skiron. The Eteobutadai carry the canopy."[35] The priests are those of the central gods of the Acropolis: Poseidon-Erechtheus and Athena Polias. Accordingly, the priestess and the priest enjoyed a special position—the latter always belonged to the family of the Eteobutadai. After being destroyed in the Persian Wars, the joint temple of Athena and Erechtheus was finally replaced by the Erechtheum. Already in the *Odyssey*, Athena was said to have entered the "house of Erechtheus."[36] The Skira procession, by contrast, is strangely reversed. It does not go toward this most holy shrine, but away from it to Skiron, on the city limits in the direction of Eleusis. The priests walk beneath a canopy, conspicuous, sheltered, and isolated. The king and the goddess of the city forsake Athens, leaving it abandoned. The fact that the priest of the sun accompanies them may be a Hellenistic innovation, yet it is even more an expression of the idea of departure: the summer solstice is past and Helios begins to decline; the year is gradually drawing to a close. About the same time, the emperor Elagabal, a Syrian sun-priest, celebrated his main festival with a procession in which the sun god departed from his main shrine in the city and moved to one outside it.[37] At Skiron

---

[35]Lysimachides, *FGrHist* 366 F 3 = Harpokr. *s.v.* *Σκίρον*, who found mention of *Σκίρον* in the orator Lykurgos (fr. 47 B.-S.). Schol. (R) Aristoph. *Eccl.* 18 *Σκίρα ἑορτή ἐστιν τῆς* Σκιράδος 'Αθηνᾶς . . . *οἱ δὲ Δήμητρος καὶ* Κόρης. *ἐν ᾗ ὁ ἱερεὺς τοῦ* 'Ερεχθέως *φέρει σκιάδειον λευκόν*. . . . The explanation in both cases that the parasol is called *σκίρον* (because of the association with *σκιερόν*) is not believable, since the festival is called *Σκίρα* (Deubner [1932] 49) and the place name, Skiron, is explained in another way: see Paus. 1.36.4 (named after the dead seer Skiros). Paus. 1.37.2 then mentions a "sanctuary of Demeter and Kore" where "Athena and Poseidon are honored as well"; *ἐπὶ Σκίρῳ ἱεροποιία τις* Strabo 9 p. 393. The (Eteo-)Butadai provide the priest of Erechtheus: see Toepffer (1889) 114–17; for a seat *ἱερέως βούτου* at the Erechtheum see *IG* II/III² 5166.

[36]*Od.* 7.81. The state of things on the Acropolis between the Mycenaean royal palace and the "old temple" of the sixth century, which burned in 480, has not been entirely clarified. Ch. Kardara's conjecture, *Arch. Eph.* (1960), 165–202, that the "house of Erechtheus," including the image of Athena, is to be found in a Mycenaean/post-Mycenaean shrine in the Nike-Pyrgos, must be rejected; the cultic monuments on the height are certainly older than Solon. Cf. n. 98 below.

[37]Herodian 5.6.6 (cf. *Hist. Aug. Eliogab.* 8.3; *Aur. Vict. Caes.* 23.1). For a similar pro-

there was a shrine of Demeter and Kore and one of Athena. There must have been some sort of ram-sacrifice at the Skira like those often attested for the cult of Kore, for those leading the procession, the Eteobutadai, carry the mysterious "ramskin of Zeus," the *Διὸς κῴδιον*, in which the complex of guilt and purification seems to crystallize.[38]

The few remaining descriptions of the festival agree, inasmuch as they point to a dissolution, an inversion of the normal order. Skiron was proverbially the site of dice-games and general license[39]—in this way the men would while away the hours in the period of fasting,[40] for dice is of course a men's game. The Skira was an even more exceptional time for women. It was one of the few days in which they were allowed to leave the isolation of the women's quarters and gather "according to ancestral custom"[41] at one of the special female shrines. They formed their own organization, to preside over which was the greatest distinction possible to a woman. They sacrificed and feasted, all at the men's expense. The fact that they ate garlic in large quantities so as to be odious to the men is, as far as the explanation is concerned, a scurrilous feature, but it fits well in a day when all is reversed: the domestic and the family orders are abolished, marriage suspended.[42] In Aristophanes, the women seize the opportunity provided by this day to hatch their plot for overthrowing male domination with an "assembly of women."[43] The name *Skira* was associated

cession among the Hittites see O. R. Gurney, *The Hittites* (1954²), 155. It could be an old ritual that the king-priest walks backward in front of the wagon of the gods in the procession, and as a comedy of innocence it may be distantly related to the trick of Hermes the cattle-thief.

[38] Paus. Att. δ 18 Erbse (= Suda δ 1210, etc.); cf. Nilsson (1955) 110–13; II.4 above; V.3, p. 267, n. 12 below. Ἐρεχθεῖ ἄρνεως is the dictate of the sacrificial calendar of Nikomachos at an unknown date for the fifth of a month (*IG* II/III² 1357a = *LS* 17 B 5).

[39] Theopompos, *FGrHist* 115 F 228 = Harpokr. Σκιράφια (dice games ἐν Σκίρῳ); Poll. 9.96 (ἐκύβευον ἐπὶ Σκίρῳ ἐν τῷ τῆς Σκιράδος Ἀθηνᾶς νεῴ); Phot. *σκιράφεια*; *An. Bekk.* 300.23; *Et. M.* 717.28; Eust. 1397.24; Steph. Byz. Σκίρος· σκιροφόρος . . . ὃ σημαίνει τὸν ἀκόλαστον καὶ κυβευτήν. Nilsson (*ARW* 16 [1913], 316–17) deduced a dice-oracle from Hsch. *σκειρόμαντις*, Phot. *σκίρον* (Steph. Byz. Σκίρος· πόρναι instead of μάντεις is corrupt), although Hsch. is speaking of augury from the flight of birds.

[40] Hdt. 1.94 on the "invention" of dice-playing among the Lydians.

[41] Συνέρχονται αἱ γυναῖκες κατὰ τὰ πάτρια *IG* II/III² 1177 = *LS* 36.10–12. The meeting-place for women at the Piraeus is the Thesmophorion. Cf. Aristoph. *Thesm.* 834–35; Men. *Epitr.* 522–23; Pherekrates fr. 231 (*CAF* I 206) = Phot. *σκίρον*.

[42] Philochoros, *FGrHist* 328 F 89 = Phot. τρόπηλις· ἐν δὲ τοῖς Σκίροις τῇ ἑορτῇ ἤσθιον σκόροδα ἕνεκα τοῦ ἀπέχεσθαι ἀφροδισίων, ὡς ἂν μὴ μύρων ἀποπνέοιεν.

[43] *Eccl.* 18.

with "white earth."[44] We do not know in what form the "white earth" was "carried," as the name *Skirophorion* indicates; at best, there may be a clue in the etiological legend of how Theseus, when leaving Athens, had a small plaster statue of Athena made, which he carried along with him.[45] The name was already a mystery to the ancient commentators, who hit on the thought that Skiron could mean that striking canopy, or any sort of parasol.[46] Whatever the name means, the function of the Skira is clear: it marks the dissolution in the last month of the year.

The Buphonia continues and supplements the Skira—it virtually inverts the inversion. The priest of Erechtheus and the priestess of Athena, standing, respectively, for the original king and his goddess, would leave the Acropolis. Two days later a sacrifice took place there, though not to Erechtheus or Athena, but to Zeus; and not in "the solid house of Erechtheus," but in the open air. Whereas the priests of the Acropolis would go off in the direction of Eleusis to the Athenian city limits, those who "goaded" the oxen onto the Acropolis two days later belonged to the great priestly family of Eleusis, the Kerykes.

---

[44]In the explanation of the place name, *An. Bekk.* I 304.8 *Σκειρὰς Ἀθηνᾶ . . . ἀπὸ τόπου τινὸς . . . ἐν ᾧ γῆ ὑπάρχει λευκή*, as in the epithet, Athena Skiras, Schol. Aristoph. *Vesp.* 926: *Ἀθηνᾶ Σκιρράς, ὅτι γῇ* (*τῇ* Cdd.) *λευκῇ χρίεται* (cf. n. 45 below); however, Deubner (1932) 46 (with n. 7) in conjunction with van der Loeff ("De Athena Scirade") tries to separate the festival *Σκίρα* (ῐ is certain because of Aristoph. *Eccl.* 18; *Thesm.* 834; Men. *Epitr.* 523; *Et. Gen.* p. 267 Miller) from the place *Σκῖρον* and Athena Skiras. *Σκῖρος* or *σκίρρος* meaning "white stone," "plaster," "stucco" is well attested; *γῆ σκιράς* *IG* II/III[2] 1672.196; Schol. Aristoph. *Vesp.* 926. Long iota, ῑ, according to Herodian, *Gramm. Gr.* III 1.385, 1–4; III 2.581, 22–31; Steph. Byz. *Σκίρος* (p. 576.2 Meineke). But, as in the case of *σιρός* "silo," we may well have to reckon with changes in quantity, especially since even the vowel seems to change: *σκῦρος* "white stone," "paving-stone" (Oros *Et. M.* 720.24 = *Et. Gen.* on the island Skyros), *σκυροῦσθαι, σκυρώδης, σκυρωτὰ ὁδός* Pind. *Pyth.* 5.93. This brings us quite close to Skiron, who hurled travellers from the cliffs, and the Skironic Way. Cf. Brumfield (1981) 156–58, who suggests that *σκίρα* may have been "the preservative lime mixture which was used to line the pits and cover the seed" (173) for storage. Against Deubner, see also Jacoby on Philochoros, *FGrHist* 328 F 14. Jacoby connected the seer Skiros with Athena Skiras, just as Schol. Aristoph. *Eccl.* 18, Phot. *Σκιροφοριών* connected the festival with Athena Skiras. There was another shrine of Athena Skiras at Phaleron, administered by the Salaminioi (*LSS* 19.10, 52.92), who also sacrifice to Skiros (92).

[45]Schol. Paus. 1.1.4 p. 218 Spiro (cf. Wilamowitz, *Hermes* 29 [1894], 243): *Σκιροφόρια παρὰ τὸ φέρειν σκίρα ἐν αὐτῇ τὸν Θησέα ἢ γύψον, ὁ γὰρ Θησεὺς ἀπερχόμενος κατὰ τοῦ Μινωταύρου τὴν Ἀθηνᾶν ποιήσας ἀπὸ γύψου ἐβάστασεν* (*Et. M.* 718.6 = *Et. Gen.* p. 267 Miller: *μετὰ Μινωταύρου* is corrupt, as also then Phot. *Σκίρος* = Suda σ 624, which thereby turns Theseus' departure into his return).

[46]N. 35 above; Poll. 7.174; Attic gloss in Schol. T *Il.* 23.331; Schol. Theocr. 15.38/9b; Phot. *Σκίρος*; Suda σ 624; *An. Bekk.* I 304.3.

And, at least according to one tradition, the Kerykes were connected with the ox-slayers and carvers as well.[47] This reciprocal arrangement between Eleusis and Athens goes yet further. In the myth it is claimed that Celeos of Eleusis founded the prytaneum,[48] and it is a fact that the famous meal there, a vegetarian feast in the spirit of Demeter, was presided over by the Eleusinian hierophant. It was also there that the extraordinary, scurrilous trial took place after the Buphonia. Though the Kerykes traced themselves back to Hermes, the herald of the gods, they considered their human ancestor to be one of the daughters of Cecrops, saying that the god mated with her—thus, once again the Eleusinian family derives from the Acropolis.[49] With the evidence at hand, we cannot tell how old this deep involvement between Athens and Eleusis is, nor whether it developed gradually or was instituted by a conscious act.[50] It already existed, in any case, when Solon codified the sacrificial calendar. Just as the festivals and names of the months antedate Solon considerably, so the interaction between the two neighboring cities may well have stretched back to very early times. The cities united precisely for the strange yet necessary sacrifice through which the "dissolution" at the end of the year came about. Erechtheus set out against Eleusis, and in his place the Eleusinians brought a bull to the heights of the Acropolis for an extraordinary sacrifice. At Skiron itself, there is a coincidence of shrines to Athena and Demeter. It is tempting to assume that the cattle were brought directly from Skiron, after the "sacred plowing at Skiron" was over,[51] but there is no solid evidence. In any case, the Butades, "neatherds," left the Acropolis; the ox-slayers came in their place. Such is the extent of the comedy of innocence.

The exchange of roles between the Acropolis and Eleusis finds mythical expression in the legend of the war between Erechtheus and Eumolpus,[52] the leader of the Eleusinians and first ancestor of the family of hierophants. Erechtheus died in this war, and yet was vic-

---

[47] N. 17 above.

[48] Plut. *Q. conv.* 667d; for the hierophant at the head of the ἀίσιτοι (ἀείσιτοι) see *IG* I² 77, II/III² 678.12, 1773–76, 1781–82, 1788, 1792, 1794–98, 1808; n. 21 above.

[49] Toepffer (1889) 81–85; Hellanikos, *FGrHist* 323a F 24, Androtion, *FGrHist* 324 F 1; Eur. *Erechtheus* fr. 65.113–14 Austin.

[50] On the history of Eleusis see Mylonas (1961); Ch. V below.

[51] For sacred plowing ἐπὶ Σκίρῳ see Plut. *Praec. coni.* 144a.

[52] See Lobeck (1829) 205–14; Engelmann, *RML* I 1298–1300, 1402–1403; Ch. Picard, "Les luttes primitives d'Athènes et d'Eleusis," *Rev. Hist.* 166 (1931), 1–76 (largely hypothetical); as a fixed part of Athenian history see already Thuc. 2.15.1; then Plat. *Menex.* 239b; Isocr. 4 (*Paneg.*) 68; 12 (*Panath.*) 193; "Dem." 60.8. For Erechtheus killing Eu-

torious. To be sure, the ritual could not easily be transformed into a consistent quasi-historical narrative; moreover, details from three separate festivals—the Skira, the Boedromia,[53] and the Mystery procession[54]—were woven together to form a seemingly unified account. But poets and local historians agree that this was the first war that Athens had to win, that the Eleusinians posed a serious threat to the city, and that Erechtheus mysteriously died in battle, rammed into the earth by Poseidon's trident. Athens was victorious, but Eumolpus must have penetrated deep into the city, for the tomb of his son, Imarrhados, was regularly pointed out in the Eleusinion beneath the Acropolis, high on the Panathenaic Way.[55] Could the mark of the trident, that little bit of "sea" in the Erechtheum, perhaps be the place where Erechtheus sank into the earth? There was, however, also a story about the seer Skiros, who, together with Eumolpus, led the Eleusinian attack. His grave was pointed out "at Skiron";[56] thus, the battle must have taken place there, just as the stele of the seer Megistias could be seen at Thermopylae.[57] The place and mythical name *Skiros* point to the procession of the Skira. Erechtheus set out from his "house" on the Acropolis to this place to fight the Eleusinians, and he subsequently disappeared. Euripides described the events leading up to Erechtheus' death in the tragedy *Erechtheus*, the conclusion of which has recently been discovered on a papyrus.[58] Athena herself resolves the play at the end when she addresses Erechtheus' widow, Praxithea, saying, "and for your husband I command a shrine to be constructed in the middle of the city; he will be known for him who killed him, under the name of 'sacred Poseidon'; but among the citizens, when the sacrificial cattle are slaughtered, he

---

molpos see Apollod. 3.203; Schol. Eur. *Phoen.* 854; killing Imarrhados, see Paus. 1.5.2, 27.4, 38.3; cf. Agallis Schol. T *Il.* 18.483, Schol. Eur. *Phoen.* 854.

[53] Philochoros, *FGrHist* 328 F 13; Ael. Aristid. 22.12 Keil; Paus. 1.31.3; *Et. M.* 202.49; *PR* I 263.3.

[54] Paus. 1.38.3; Schol. Eur. *Phoen.* 854. On the other hand, two separate Εὔμολποι have been posited ever since Euripides (*Erechtheus* fr. 65. 100–110; Andron, *FGrHist* 10 F 13; Istros, *FGrHist* 334 F 22); cf. Jacoby on the *Marmor Parium*, *FGrHist* 239 A 15.

[55] Clem. *Pr.* 3.45.1.

[56] Paus. 1.36.4; n. 35 above.

[57] Hdt. 7.228.

[58] Colin Austin, *Recherches de Papyrologie* 4 (1967); *Nova Fragmenta Euripidea* (1968), fr. 65.90–97. On the date of the *Erechtheus* (423 or 422 B.C.) see W. M. Calder, *Greek, Roman and Byz. Studies* 10 (1969), 147–56 and ibid. 12 (1971), 485–95; M. Treu, *Chiron* 12 (1971), 131. On the Erechtheum see n. 98 below. 'Εν *φοναῖσι βουθύτοις* in Euripides (94) can hardly be an allusion to the Buphonia; cf. *ἐν φοναῖς θηροκτόνοις* Eur. *Hel.* 154.

shall also be called 'Erechtheus.' To you, however, since you have rebuilt the city's foundation" (Praxithea had given her assent to the sacrifice of her own daughter before battle), "I grant the duty of bringing in preliminary fire-sacrifices for the city, and to be called my priestess." Thus, the founding of the Erechtheum and the institution of the priestess of Athena coincide.

The marriage of Erechtheus and Praxithea continues in the combination of the cult of Poseidon-Erechtheus and the priestess of Athena. And in fact, the priestess was always a mature, married or widowed woman.[59] Her connection with Erechtheus is manifest above all in the Skira procession. There, the departure from the Acropolis and the journey toward Eleusis repeat Erechtheus' march against the Eleusinians, toward Skiron and death. With the "dissolution" in the last month of the year, there is, mythically speaking, the mysterious yet violent disappearance of the first king—a "king's death." In ritual, this corresponds to the act of killing, the intense, disquieting sacrifice with its inversions, its peculiar assignment of parts, drawing each—if it can—to his particular place in the circle of participants. Thus, inasmuch as sacrifice is an act of killing, it is proper to speak of a king symbolically killed at the end of the year.

That Poseidon and Erechtheus were merely two names for a single god, a fact that is stated by Euripides, is also clearly visible in the cult. In the temple itself one altar stands for both; there is only one priest; consecrations and sacrifice are dedicated to "Poseidon Erechtheus."[60] An historian would say that a Homeric, pan-Hellenic name has been superimposed on an autochthonous, non-Greek name. The myth distinguishes between the two as victor and the vanquished: Poseidon with his trident, against Erechtheus who sank into the depths. Yet in Euripides' play, the conflict produced a paradoxical identity. The victim assumed the god's name, and destruction became a blessing. Whereas the mythographer made a clear distinction between the god and the hero, the tragedian recognized the unity in the polar tension of sacrifice. Here, again, the higher, unambiguous power is the female divinity, the "city goddess, Athena."

---

[59] Plut. *Numa* 9.11; Fehrle (1910) 95; Kerényi (1952) 20–21; from the family of the Eteobutadai, see Drakon, *FGrHist* 344 F 1 = Harpokr. Ἐτεοβουτάδαι; Apollod. 3.196; D. M. Lewis, *BSA* 50 (1955), 1–12.

[60] Paus. 1.26.5; *ἱερεὺς Ποσειδῶνος Ἐρεχθέος* *IG* II/III^2 3538, 4071; "Plut." *Vit. X or.* 843b–c; Athenag. 1; for consecration Ποσειδôνι Ἐρεχθεî see *IG* I^2 580, but *τῷ Ποσειδῶ]νι καὶ τῷ Ἐρε[χθεῖ* II/III^2 1146, and cf. 5058. Hsch. Ἐρεχθεύς· Ποσειδῶν ἐν Ἀθήναις; Cook III (1940) 12.3.

ARRHEPHORIA

The ritual arc extends to yet another festival, indeed, the first attested for the month of Skirophorion, coming right at the start—the Arrhephoria.[61] The preparations for sacrifice, which the myth depicts as the death of the king and father, hint at a drama of sexuality and incest in which the king's daughters become the victims. The Arrhephoria takes its name from two small girls, aged seven to twelve, chosen by the "king" himself from prominent families. During the year, they lived in a house on the Acropolis, playing and starting to weave the peplos of Athena.[62] They would probably have helped in sacrificial duties as well, and in caring for the olive tree. "But when the festival comes round, they perform the following rites during the night. They carry on their heads what Athena's priestess gives them to carry, and neither she who gives it nor they who carry it know what it is she gives them. Not far away in the city is the sacred precinct of 'Aphrodite in the Gardens,' with a natural entrance heading underground: this is where the virgin girls descend. They deposit there what they were carrying and take something else and bring it back covered up. They are then sent away, and other virgins are brought to the Acropolis instead." Pausanias himself, in describing this ritual, states that it is little known and obscure.[63] We can only guess at what was contained in the covered baskets, the *κίσται*, that the girls carried down and what it was they brought back covered. Even if *Arrhephoros* meant "dew-carrier,"[64] this clue does not take us very far. However, the date at the end of the year makes one point clear: in sending these girls, or "virgins," to Aphrodite and under the earth at night, something ended which had endured over the course of a year; an order was broken.

---

[61] Harrison (1922) 131–34; Deubner (1932) 9–17; Cook III (1940) 165–88; Burkert, *Hermes* 94 (1966), 1–25; Brelich (1969) 229–38. The date, the third of Skirophorion "or thereabouts," was deduced by M. Jameson, *BCH* 89 (1965), 157, from the Erchia calendar (*LS* 18); cf. *Hermes* (1966), 5.2; *ἐν Σκιροφοριῶνι μηνί Et. Gen.* (R. Reitzenstein, *Ind. Rostock* [1890/91], 15); *Et. M.* 149.13.

[62] Callim. fr. 520; Harpokr. *ἀρρηφορεῖν*; *Et. M.* 149.18; *An. Bekk.* I 202.3; Suda *α* 3848, *χ* 35; Aristoph. *Lys.* 641 with Schol. The Grammarians note variation in orthography, *ἀρρηφορεῖν* and *ἐρρηφορεῖν*; the dedicatory inscriptions on the Acropolis have, with two exceptions, only *ἐρρηφορήσασαν*; for a detailed treatment see *Hermes* (1966) 3–6.

[63] 1.27.3. The conjecture *οὐκ ἐς ἅπαντα⟨ς⟩ γνώριμα* is confirmed through 5.18.4, 9.25.6 (Hitzig-Blümner *ad loc.*, contrary to *Hermes* [1966], 2.1).

[64] Discussed in *Hermes* (1966), 16–17.

Excavations on the northern slope of the Acropolis have allowed us to follow the path of the Arrhephoroi over a steep stairway that in late Mycenaean times led to a spring, but in historical times led over the slope to a small shrine of Eros nestled among the crags of the northern side.[65] The myth tells how the daughters of Cecrops—Aglaurus, Herse, and Pandrosus—could not restrain their curiosity; one night, by the light of Athena's lamp, they opened the basket the goddess had entrusted to them. Inside they saw the mysterious child Erichthonius and a snake swiftly darting up toward them. In horror, they leapt to their deaths, down the steep northern slope of the Acropolis.[66] In the fall of the king's daughters, the myth obviously mirrors the ending of the Arrhephoroi's duties on the Acropolis, as well as their journey underground. Moreover, the image of the snake and the child Erichthonius points to the contents of the basket. Erichthonius was born in an unheard-of way: he was begotten by Hephaestus, who, while chasing after Athena, discharged his seed on the virgin goddess's thigh. After Athena had wiped off the seed with wool, she hurled the wool to the earth, which subsequently gave birth to the child.[67] The etymology of the name *Erichthonius* given here—"wool" and "earth," ἔρίον and χϑών—likewise points toward cult. Hephaestus, the power of fire, is present in Athena's temple, harnessed in the form of the eternally burning lamp whose woolen wick is kept alive by Athena's oil.[68] The fire is renewed only once, most likely at the end of the year, when the new oil stands ready. Elsewhere, wool and oil were among the sacrificial offerings that were carried solemnly in the kernoi, earthenware vessels with many small cups fitted to the rim.[69] Perhaps there was oil and wool in the kistai,

---

[65] O. Broneer, *Hesperia* 1 (1932), 31–55; 2 (1933), 329–417; 4 (1935), 109–88; 8 (1939), 317–433; G. P. Stevens, *Hesperia* 5 (1936), 489–91.

[66] *PR* I 198–200; II 137–40; B. Powell, *Erichthonius and the Three Daughters of Cecrops* (1906); Jacoby on *FGrHist* 328 F 105 (Supplement 424–27); for depictions in vase-paintings see Brommer (1960) 199–200; M. Schmidt, *AM* 83 (1968), 200–206; Eur. *Ion* 21–26, 1427; Apollod. 3.189.

[67] *Danais* fr. 2 = Harpokr. *αὐτόχϑονες*; cf. the *Tabula Borgiana* p. 4 Kinkel, *Epicorum Graecorum Fragmenta* (1877) = *IG* XIV 1292. For the throne of Amyklai see Paus. 3.18.13; Eur. fr. 925 = Erat. *Cat.* 13; Amelesagoras, *FGrHist* 330 F 1; Callim. fr. 260.19; Nonnus *Dion.* 41.64 *γαμίην . . . ἐέρσην*, clearly alluding to *ἐρρηφόροι*; Apollod. 3.188 *ἐρίῳ ἀπομάξασα τὸν γόνον εἰς γῆν ἔρριψε*; Cook III (1940) 181–237.

[68] Paus. 1.26.6–7; Strabo 9 p. 396; Plut. *Numa* 9.11; Euphorion fr. 9 Powell, followed by Nonnus *Dion.* 13.172–79, 27.114–15, 320–23 with the "mystic lamp" beside "Erechtheus." Cf. R. Pfeiffer, "Die Lampe der Athena," *Ausgew. Schr.* (1960), 1–7.

[69] Polemon in Ath. 478d.

the remnants of the purification of the sacred lamp. Yet both ritual and myth add a terrifying dimension to what would otherwise be harmless—a dimension about which neither Athena's priestess nor the virgins may know. Of course, the life-force of fire is experienced again and again as sexual and phallic, and the snake, that terrifying animal which excites fear even in primates, probably instinctively,[70] also represents phallic impregnation. Fascinating and dreadful at once, this animal belonged to the virgin goddess Athena, and it was both stated and believed that the snake on the Acropolis was actually Erechtheus or Erichthonius; it was also said that Athena made the snake dwell with Cecrops' daughters, or that one of the girls on the Acropolis spent the night with the snake.[71] In the realm of the powerful virgin goddess, sexuality took on a terrifying dimension. But how could the child emerge if the "basket" remained closed? The young girls' way of life had to end, and the priestess herself sent them away to Eros and Aphrodite beneath the earth.

The encounter with death, ending the sheltered life of the "virgin," may be interpreted as an initiation ritual, the exemplary consecration of a maiden in the middle of the polis.[72] The facts that necessary transitions in life are here played up into deadly crises, however, and that the "virgin" faces death derive from the more general function of sacrifice in society. The drama of the maiden's initiation performed as a symbolic maiden-sacrifice[73] opens the great sacrificial festival that embraces the end and the beginning of the year at Athens.

Animal-sacrifice was undoubtedly part of the ritual in the nocturnal festival. Varro mentions a most unusual goat-sacrifice on the Acropolis: it was customary "that no member of the goat family be sacrificed to Athena on account of the olive, because it is said that any olive tree which they bite becomes sterile; for their spittle is poisonous to the fruit. For this reason they are not driven onto the Acropolis at Athens except once a year for a necessary sacrifice."[74]

---

[70] A. Kortlandt and M. Kooij, *Symp. Zool. Soc. London* 10 (1963), 70; Baudy (1980) 29f.

[71] Paus. 1.24.7; Hyg. *Astr.* 2.13; Philostr. *V. Ap.* 7.24; the ancient commentators on δράκαυλος Soph. fr. 643 Radt.

[72] Jeanmaire (1939) 264–67; Burkert, *Hermes* (1966), 13–21; Brelich (1969) 229–38.

[73] See I.7 above.

[74] *R. r.* 1.2.20 . . . *praeterquam semel ad necessarium sacrificium*. For the prohibition, without mention of the sacrifice, see Ath. 587a; Pliny *NH* 8.204. The priestess of Athena does not eat cheese (Strabo 9 p. 395; Ath. 375c), probably because it is made with rennet from a goat's stomach. Horses may not enter the grove of Diana of Aricia (Verg. *Aen.* 7.778–79; Ov. *Fast.* 3.266) precisely because an exceptional horse-sacrifice took place (Ambros. *Virg.* 3.5).

Once again the tabu and its infringement are connected. Because a goat is never otherwise allowed on the Acropolis, the sacrifice assumes a disquieting gravity; its "necessity" is stressed. The olive tree of Athena stands in the Pandroseion,[75] the sanctuary beneath the windows of the Erechtheum, which in mythology was connected with Pandrosus, the daughter of Cecrops. The arrival of the olive tree's enemy, and its death in sacrifice, fits well in the crisis—reflected in the myth of Pandrosus' sisters—that the religious servants on the Acropolis undergo at the Arrhephoria. A goatskin, the aegis, is the terrifying armor of the warlike virgin Athena. It is clear that the memory of a real goatskin, hung after the sacrifice on a sacred tree, or pole, or roughly carved wooden image, is preserved here,[76] even though genuine goatskins were in historical times no longer hung about the ancient wooden image of Athena Polias. At the Plynteria, the "washing festival" a few days before the Arrhephoria, this statue's clothing was removed and washed. Athena got a new cloak (φᾶρος).[77] It would thus have been appropriate to have given her a new aegis as well. In Corinth too, young boys and girls from prominent families served for a year in the temple of Hera Akraia until the sacrifice of a black goat terminated their duties.[78] In the myth, this appears as the death of Medea's children. Everything suggests that—along with the journey beneath the earth—an extraordinary goat-sacrifice occurred at Athens once a year, at the end of the Arrhephoroi's duties. According to one myth Athena, after having killed Gorgon, skinned her and plunged into the battle against the giants wearing the aegis she had thus newly acquired.[79] The goat-sacrifice is a mere prelude to subsequent acts that are greater and more deadly. The first war in early Athenian history was the battle of Erechtheus against Eleusis. Here, too, Erechtheus' death was preceded by sacrifice of a maiden—the sacrifice of his own daughter at his own hands. There is, of course, a great abundance of such myths describing the preliminary death of a girl, and the connection between myth and ritual is flexible. If, for in-

---

[75] Paus. 1.27.2.

[76] See I.7.n.39 above; for the αἰγίς as made of plaited wool (ἐκ τῶν στεμμάτων πλέγμα) see Harpokr. αἰγίς, Suda αι 60.

[77] *LSS* 10 A 5 seemed to establish—against Deubner (1932) 18—the 29th of Thargelion as the date of the Plynteria, but cf. Mikalson (1975) 160ff., and the *Lex Sacra* of Thorikos gives "Skirophorion," *ZPE* 25 (1977), 245 line 52. The Palladion procession to Phaleron is to be kept distinct: see Burkert, *ZRGG* 22 (1970), 356–68.

[78] Phot. ed. Reitzenstein αἰγὸς τρόπον; Zenob. Ath. 2.30 p. 361 Miller; Markellos in Euseb. *Adv. Marc.* 1.3; Burkert (1966) 118.71.

[79] See I.7.n.39 above.

stance, the deaths of Cecrops' daughters became the mythic equivalent of the Arrhephoria, Euripides could shift the deaths of Erechtheus' daughters to the cult of the Hyakinthides, which was located elsewhere.[80] In any case, the anticipatory function of the maiden-sacrifice in guaranteeing victory is certain.[81] Thus, the Arrhephoria points toward a greater "act of killing" through which the dissolution at the end of the year comes to a climax. Perhaps when the girls carried back from the depths something covered like a baby it was meant to signify birth-giving in the mature woman, and so balance the masculine "act of killing."

PANATHENAIA

The Panathenaia celebrate the birth of the polis Athens at the end of the first month of the Attic year.[82] Whereas the previous month had brought dissolution, the Panathenaia reestablished order. To be sure, the period over which this occurred was unusually long: forty-five days separate the Skira from the New Year's festival. Moreover, the dissolution was repeated in another way at the Cronia,[83] on the twelfth day of Hecatombaion, when the order of master and slave was reversed in a lighthearted festival. But it may be that these are compromises between rituals of different origins in an already pluralistic urban society. They could exist side by side so long as they performed a similar function, especially as ritual inherently fosters repetition.

Once again, the complexity of the Panathenaia prevents us from being able to reconstruct it in all its details. Every four years, starting in about 570, the festival would be magnificently enlarged into the Greater Panathenaia with its pan-Hellenic agon.[84] The basic elements

---

[80] See I.7.n.33 above.

[81] The Attic ephebes swear their oath at the shrine of Aglauros: see I.7.n.32 above.

[82] A. Mommsen (1898) 41–159; Deubner (1932) 22–35; Ziehen, *RE* XVIII 2 (1949), 457–93; J. A. Davison, *JHS* 78 (1958), 23–42; 82 (1962) 141–42; H. A. Thomson, *AA* (1961), 225–31.

[83] See Deubner (1932) 152–55.

[84] Pherekydes, *FGrHist* 3 F 2; Euseb. *Chron. a. Abr.* 1451 (566 B.C.); Schol. Aristides p. 323.29 Dind.; dedicatory inscription of the first Agonothetai (. . . *τὸν ἀ]γô[να ϑέσ]αν πρôτο[ι] γλαυ[κ]όπιδι κόρ[ει)*, A. Raubitschek, *Dedications from the Athenian Acropolis* (1949), #326. On the Panathenaic amphoras see J. D. Beazley, *AJA* 47 (1943), 441–65; D. A. Amyx, *Hesperia* 27 (1958), 178–86. The first Lesser Panathenaia were traced back to Erichthonios: see Arist. fr. 637; *Marm. Par.*, *FGrHist* 239 A 10; Hellanikos, *FGrHist* 323a F 2; Androtion, *FGrHist* 324 F 2; Philochoros, *FGrHist* 328 F 8; Erat. *Cat.* 13; Schol. Plat. *Parm.* 127a; Harpokr., Phot., Suda *Παναϑήναια*. Less often they are traced back to Theseus; see Paus. 8.2.1; Plut. *Thes.* 24.3.

of this celebration inaugurating the year must have been appropriate to the Lesser, annual Panathenaia as well. It consisted, naturally, of a sacrificial procession and an agon.

Before this, however, there would be a preparatory festival at night, a Pannychis. By contrast, the main procession, which was enormous, formed "at dawn."[85] In the Parthenon frieze, this great pageant of the polis at its festival was transformed into an enduring work of art.[86] Every member of the community had his place here, from the youthful horsemen to the elders "bearing branches,"[87] from the young girls, who were carrying the sacrificial tools, to the matrons. Above all, even in the Lesser Panathenaia, the procession included over a hundred sheep and cows bound for slaughter at the "great altar."[88] Thus, there was enough meat to give the entire populace a portion, its festival meal, at the marketplace.

It was the beginning of something new. Starting at dawn, a runner would bring new fire in a torch from the grove of Akademos to the Acropolis.[89] The procession was accompanied by a ship on wheels, upon which the now-finished peplos of the goddess was brought, like a sail, to the Acropolis.[90] The coming of something new, the arrival of a goddess in a ship—these are primordial motifs stretching back over thousands of years and echoing even today in song as the theme of advent. A whole series of details shows how the festival sequence—Arrhephoria, Skira, Buphonia—points to the Panathenaia, which in turn corresponds to and fulfills the previous festivals. Even the choice of sacrificial animals was not arbitrary. Neither goats nor rams nor bulls joined in the procession, but, rather, ewes and cows.[91] The proud horse was there as well, as no one who has seen the Parthenon frieze can ever forget, but not as a sacrificial animal. The horse was a living symbol of speed and strength, the essence of ready power. The young men, the ephebes, stood out as those actually sup-

---

[85]For the regulation of the Lesser Panathenaia see *LS* 33 (= *IG* II/III[2] 334 + *Hesperia* 28 [1959], 239) B 32—34.

[86]See Lippold (1950) 148–51.

[87]Philochoros, *FGrHist* 328 F 9 = Schol. Aristoph. *Vesp.* 544; Xen. *Symp.* 4.17. For the armed dance of the *παῖδες* see Aristoph. *Nub.* 988 with Schol.; for the black garments of the ephebes see Philostr. *V. Soph.* 2.1.5 (II 59 ed. Teubn.). See also I.5.n.7 above.

[88]*LS* 33 (n. 85 above) B 16; more than 160 cows could be bought for 41 minai.

[89]Aristoph. *Ran.* 1090–98 with Schol.; the one who comes in last gets beaten.

[90]*Παναθηναϊς σκάφη* *IG* II/III[2] 3198 = *SIG*[3] 894; Strattis fr. 30 (*CAF* I 719); Deubner (1932) 32–34; T.39 #32; Himerios 47.12–17. On the goddess's arrival in the ship see Burkert (1967) 295–96.

[91]Schol. B *Il.* 2.550: *θήλεα τῇ Ἀθηνᾷ θύουσιν*. We do not know what position was occupied by the sacrifice of "bulls and rams" to Erechtheus, *Il.* 2.550, at the Panathenaia.

porting the community. On the peplos begun by the Arrhephoroi (who in the meantime had been dismissed) were woven pictures of the gigantomachy,[92] a triumphant reminder of the crisis for which Athena armed herself with the skin of the Gorgon-goat. Likewise, the myth of Erichthonius spans the two shores that embrace the abyss of "dissolution": it tells of the child Erichthonius who brought death to the Cecropids, and of the adult Erichthonius who established the Panathenaia. Erichthonius had, it was said, invented the four-horse chariot, which he drove in the first Panathenaic agon.[93] It was this that was the most characteristic and distinctive sport at the Panathenaia: chariot-races including the *apobates*, the leap of the armed warrior from his moving chariot.[94] In this way the warrior and king took possession of the land at his advent.

Erechtheus and *Erichthonius* are obviously merely variants.[95] Only *Erechtheus* is used in cult, as it is the original, probably non-Greek, name. *Erichthonius*, who is "peculiarly of the earth," is a Hellenizing neologism, perhaps taken up in Attic epic because of the etymology. The myth then differentiates between the two by telling of Erichthonius' birth, but Erechtheus' death. So, too, the genealogies made Erechtheus king after Erichthonius, who, as the "earth-born" child, had to come at the start. In the festival cycle, the mysterious child and the king's sacrificial death confronted each other in the last month of the year. The new king was inaugurated at the subsequent Panathenaia: Erechtheus is dead, long live Erichthonius! What the Arrhephoria, the Skira, and the Buphonia had dissolved, the act that celebrated the polis's birth restored.

Above the Parthenon frieze, with its Panathenaic procession winding around the cella, above the battle scenes on the metopes, the pedimental sculpture portrays the epiphany of Athena in and for Athens. It is hardly accidental that the depiction of Athena's birth on

---

[92] Eur. *Hec.* 466–74 with Schol.; Arist. fr. 637; Orig. *Cels.* 6.42; F. Vian, *La guerre des géants* (1952), 251–53. Since the establishment of the greater Panathenaia, the peplos was apparently woven only every four years; see Deubner (1932) 30; Davison, *JHS* 78 (1958), 25–26; the custom itself is certainly older.

[93] See n. 84 above.

[94] Dion. Hal. 7.73.2–3; Harpokr. ἀποβάτης; Reisch, *RE* I 2814–17; on the pictorial tradition see Metzger (1951) 359–60; (1965) 71–72; already on late Geometric Attic amphoras, *AA* 78 (1963), 210–25; Philadelphia 30–33–133. The Athenians dedicated the place where Demetrios leaped from the wagon to Zeus Kataibates: Plut. *Demetr.* 10.

[95] *PR* I 198; E. Ermatinger, "Die attische Autochthonensage bis auf Euripides," Diss. Zürich, 1897; Escher, *RE* VI 404–11, 439–46. For Erechtheus and Erichthonios on an Attic bowl (with inscriptions) see Berlin F 2537 = *ARV*^{2} 1268; F. Brommer, *Charites E. Langlotz* (1957), 152–53, pl.21.

the eastern pediment, with the flight of the axe-bearer, looks down on the altar of the Buphonia.[96] The contest between Athena and Poseidon for Attica[97] on the western pediment—the first sight greeting the visitor as he approaches the temple—embodies the same conflict that is acted out in the ritual and marks off its beginning and end. Two cultic monuments made the sanctuary, toward which the procession moved, peculiarly sacred:[98] the first was the bit of "sea," the depression made by Poseidon's trident and filled with salt water. Located in the northern hall of the Erechtheum, yet exposed to the open air, it was the site of "sacrificial libations."[99] The second is Athena's olive tree in the Pandroseion, upon which the western windows of the Erechtheum seem to look out. The "sea" and the olive were the pledges the two great gods offered to the city as proof of their power. Poseidon lost by the decision of Cecrops or Zeus; yet he—or, rather, Erechtheus—was as much a part of Athens as was the goddess Athena herself. In cult, Poseidon was identified with Erechtheus. The myth turns this into a temporal-causal sequence: in his anger at losing, Poseidon led his son Eumolpus against Athens and killed Erechtheus.[100] Even here, the correspondence between Poseidon's defeat and Erechtheus' sinking into the earth was perceived. It was said that Athena expressed her gratitude to her father Zeus for his favorable decision by establishing the Buphonia on the Acropolis[101]—yet another reflection of the sequence Skira-Buphonia. Thus, the mythical contest between Poseidon and Athena merely varies the basic theme—transposed to an Olympian level—that set the tone for the "house of Erechtheus" already in the most ancient tradition: the theme of the goddess juxtaposed with a god or ancestral king who is active as a victim in the bowels of the earth. At the city's highest point, atop the Acropolis, there is also that bit of sea that surfaces in the sanctuary. Likewise, the Babylonian temples contained a bit of Apsu, the primordial Ocean,[102] who was murdered by his son Ea so that Ea could

[96] On Athena's birth and cow-sacrifice see Cook III (1940) 656–62.

[97] *PR* I 202–204; H. Bulle, *RML* III 2861–66; Apollod. 3.177–79.

[98] Hdt. 8.55; Strabo p. 396; Paus. 1.24.3, 26.5; J. M. Paton, ed., *The Erechtheum* (1927), 104–10; N. M. Kontoleon, Τὸ Ἐρέχθειον ὡς οἰκοδόμημα χθονίας λατρείας (Athens, 1949); Bergquist (1967) 22–25.

[99] Βομὸς τô θυεχô IG I^2 372.79, 203; theater seat, *IG* II/III^2 5026: θυηχόου.

[100] Eur. *Erechtheus*; a vase-painting depicts Poseidon and Eumolpos riding toward Athena and the olive tree: L. Weidauer, *AK* 12 (1969), 91–93, T.41.

[101] Hsch. Διὸς θᾶκοι.

[102] E. Dhorme, *Les religions de Babylonie et d'Assyrie* (1949), 32. For a "sea"-basin in the temple at Jerusalem see I Kings 7:23–26, II Chron. 4:2–6. For χάσμα beneath the temple of Hierapolis, see Luk. *Syr. D.* 13.

build his palace and temple on top of him. Ariel's song, "Full fathom five thy father lies,"[103] seems to echo around this temple. Over that bit of sea the olive tree of the goddess grows, eternally green, surviving the course of generations and providing food.

EXCURSUS: THE TROJAN HORSE

According to Attic tradition, Troy fell on the twelfth day of Skirophorion,[104] the day of the Skira. Among the Dorians, the *Iliupersis* was connected with their special festival, the Carneia.[105] These seem no more than arbitrary, unverifiable conceits, but, considering that ancient etiologists could at least begin from personal experience of their festivals, it might be well to ask what these bold assertions could mean.

In point of fact, the Skira is a festival of "dissolution." The city goddess and the king disappear; in their place appear hostile neighbors, the Eleusinians. In the myth, Athens comes to within a hair's breadth of being conquered. And in the ritual, the Eleusinian Kerykes do indeed scale the Acropolis, bringing a bull for sacrifice after Athena's priestess leaves the Acropolis, bound for Eleusis. If a "sacred city" can be conquered at all, it is only during this period of crisis at year's end.

Troy was similarly forsaken by Pallas Athena when Odysseus and Diomedes carried off the Palladion.[106] However, a strange animal went ahead of the Greeks who conquered Troy, a sacrificial animal for Athena, made by the goddess herself: the wooden horse. The Trojans themselves broke through the walls to consecrate the animal to the goddess on their acropolis.[107] Indeed, a priest drew near the horse and struck it with a spear on the side, the priest Laocoön, who quickly

---

[103] W. Shakespeare, *The Tempest*, I.2.

[104] Clem. *Strom.* 1.104. Because this month exists only in Athens (*RE* III A 547; for the cleruchy of Lemnos see *ASAA* 3/5 [1941/43], 76), it must be an Attic tradition.

[105] Evidently already in Alkman 52 Page; Demetrios of Skepsis, in Schol. Theocr. 5.82b, and cf. d; the Carneia was linked to the Doric conquest (Schol. Theocr. 5.82b–c, etc.) and to the founding of Cyrene (Callim. *Hy. Ap.* 2.65–96); see generally Nilsson (1906) 118–29. On the date of Troy's destruction see *PR* II 1288–89.

[106] F. Chavannes, "De Palladii raptu," Diss. Berlin, 1891; *PR* II 1225–27, 1233–37; L. Ziehen, *RE* XVIII 2.171–89.

[107] *PR* II 1227–30, 1237–54. New fragments of Stesichorus' *Iliu Persis* are to be found in *POxy* 2619, M. L. West, *ZPE* 4 (1969), 135–42, with a description of the horse being taken into Troy, πρὸς ναὸν ἐς ἀκρ[όπο]λιν, . . . ἁγνὸν ἄγαλμα θεᾶς 2.6, 10.

paid a dreadful price for his act.[108] His gruesome fate notwithstanding, the Trojans went on to hold a collective feast lasting well into the night. Thereupon, warriors climbed out of an opening in the horse's side and killed the defenseless celebrants.

Ever since the eighth century B.C. the Trojan horse has been depicted as riding on wheels.[109] To this extent, this, one of the most illustrious themes of the oral epic tradition, is quite comparable to the fantastic—and technically impossible—escape of Odysseus beneath the ram. But the relics of other versions remain: according to apocryphal traditions, Odysseus himself was turned into a horse.[110] This looks as though the *πτολιπόρθος*, the sacker of Troy, was actually identical with the Trojan horse. Odysseus died when his son Telegonos stabbed him with an extremely ancient spear of the Upper Palaeolithic type—according to one version,[111] while Odysseus was still a horse. This is clearly the tale of a sacrifice in which a horse was killed with a spear.

Precisely this form of sacrifice was customary in Rome, in the sacrifice of the Equus October,[112] the striking features of which have long fascinated students of religion. But little attention has been paid to the aition of this sacrifice, even though it was already attested by Timaios: stabbing a horse was how the descendants of Troy avenged the fall of their ancestral city, destroyed by a horse. Whatever the real

---

[108] *PR* II 1246–52; Verg. *Aen.* 2.50–56; cf. *Od.* 8.507.

[109] R. Hampe, *Frühe griechische Sagenbilder in Böotien* (1936), pl. 2; Schefold (1964) pl. 6a.

[110] Sextus *Math.* 1.264, 267; Ptolemaios Chennos, Phot. *Bib.* 150a16.

[111] Serv. auct. *Aen.* 2.44; on Telegonos' spear see Schol. HQ *Od.* 11.134; Eust. 1676.45; Burkert (1967) 285–86; A. Hartmann, *Untersuchungen über die Sagen vom Tod des Odysseus* (1917). Ed. Meyer (*Hermes* 30 [1895], 263) saw that the metamorphosis into a horse is connected with the horse-shaped Poseidon in Arcadia (Paus. 8.25.5); Poseidon Hippios and Athena Tritonia were honored on the acropolis of Pheneos; there was a herd of horses, allegedly given by Odysseus, at the sanctuary of Artemis Heurippa: Paus. 8.14.4–6, and cf. the coins in *HN*² 452. F. Schachermeyr, *Poseidon und die Entstehung des griechischen Götterglaubens* (1950), 189–203, thinks that the Trojan horse = Poseidon, the god of the earthquake that destroyed Troy VI; such nature-allegory does not explain the ritual details in the myth.

[112] Timaios, *FGrHist* 566 F 36 = Polyb. 12.4b; the connection with the Equus October is confirmed through the etiological derivation from the Trojan horse; it was still believed by the "vulgus" in the time of Verrius, Festus 178/81 M. Polybius polemicizes against this view by pointing out that many barbarian peoples who had nothing to do with Troy have horse-sacrifice, and precisely when going off to war. U. Scholz, *Studien zum altitalischen und altrömischen Marskult und Marsmythos* (1970), 89–91, wrongly concluded from this that Timaios was likewise speaking of a sacrifice before going off to war in the spring, and not of the October-Horse. See also I.7.n.48 above. At the Taurobolion, the bull is killed with a spear: see Prud. *Peristeph.* 10.1027.

connections behind the old Trojan tradition among the Etruscans and Romans,[113] the fact that Troy's fall, at the fateful feast when the Trojans accepted the wooden horse, was linked to the sacrifice of a horse by means of a spear[114] attests to a deeper understanding. Although, over the course of many generations of singers, literary epic transformed the cultic elements into a mechanical trick, an inkling still remained of what had once been a sacrifice of dissolution—perhaps even at Troy-Ilion—with the stabbing of a horse.

The well-known legend of Gyges[115] also depicts how one who climbed out of a horse seized power: contrary to all custom, the queen removed her clothing in front of Gyges and then aided him in killing the king and wresting his power away. She is obviously a manifestation of the king's divine lover, whom the Greeks called Aphrodite. The Greeks still knew of stories about Gyges' deified hetaera.[116] In Abydus, there was even a shrine of "Aphrodite the whore,"[117] who—in spite of her name—was duly worshipped and had a festival. There was, moreover, a story of how the city was once freed from evil tyrants: these tyrants offered up a sacrifice, feasted, grew drunk, and slept with their hetaerae, one of whom thereupon opened the gates. The armed citizens then rushed in and slew their defenseless oppressors. Normal order and morality could be restored *e contrario* precisely because Aphrodite had dissolved them at her festival.

When Pelopidas murdered the Theban leaders who were loyal to Sparta, thus overthrowing the government in 379, his contemporaries told the story according to the same pattern:[118] the polemarchs

---

[113] A. Alföldi, *Die troianischen Urahnen der Römer* (1957), demonstrated that the tradition goes back at least to the fifth century B.C.

[114] Later, the Greeks occasionally associated δούρειος ἵππος with "spear," Eur. *Tro.* 14; but in the oldest literary source, *Od.* 8.493, 512, the idea of a wooden horse is already long established.

[115] Plat. *Resp.* 359c–60b, on which cf. W. Fauth, *RhM* 113 (1970), 1–42; the horse in the Gyges saga was linked to the Trojan horse by P. M. Schuhl, *RA* 7 (1936), 183–88; G. M. A. Hanfmann, *HSCP* 63 (1958), 76–79; Fauth, op. cit., 22. Cf. also G. Dumézil, *Le problème des Centaurs* (1929), 274; N. Yalouris, *MH* 7 (1950), 65–78.

[116] On Ἑταίρης μνῆμα see Klearchos fr. 29 Wehrli = Ath. 573a; Strabo 13 p. 627; Fauth, *RhM* 113 (1970), 38; cf. W. Fauth, *Aphrodite Parakyptusa* [Abh. Mainz, 1966], 6.

[117] Neanthes, *FGrHist* 84 F 9 = Ath. 572e–f. For Aphrodite Ἑταίρα at Ephesus see Ath. 572e; at Athens see Hsch. Phot. Ἑταίρας ἱερόν.

[118] Xen. *Hell.* 5.4.4–6; not in Plut. *Pelop.* 19, *Gen. Socr.* 577c. It is therefore controversial whether the Theban festival of Aphrodite is historical, and whether it was a private celebration or an established custom; see Nilsson (1906) 374–77. Plut. *Comp. Cim. et Luc.* 1 Ἀφροδίσια τῶν πολέμων καὶ στρατηγιῶν ἄγειν speaks, rather, for an established

were celebrating the Aphrodisia at the end of their term of office when the conspirators smuggled themselves in, disguised as hetaerae. They then unveiled themselves and killed their unsuspecting victims. Another, more realistic, tradition was briefly cited by Xenophon, but he preferred the mythical version which set the calamitous peripeteia in the context of a festival of dissolution.

A particularly strange legend tells of the foundation of Erythrae by conquest through Cnopus, son of Codrus.[119] Cnopus had brought along a priestess of Hecate from Thessaly, who now prepared to sacrifice a bull in full view of the enemy, the former Erythraeans. After its horns had been gilded and its body adorned with fillets, it was led to the altar. However, the bull had been given a drug provoking madness: it tore itself loose and ran toward the enemy, bellowing loudly. The enemy unwittingly seized the bull and sacrificed it themselves, using its meat for their feast. They were thereupon all struck mad, easy prey for the attacking Codrides. Sacrificers and eaters must succumb to those practicing renunciation and aggression. The guilt caused by sacrifice signals an end and a fall—for others; a victory—for one's own triumphant order.

2. *Argos and Argeiphontes*

Nowhere in Greece have traditions survived in such detail as at Athens. For other cities we often have no more than a few scanty, scattered indications about cult, and the literary myths that were able to achieve pan-Hellenic status. But even fragments can be evaluated and classified if we have a fully preserved model. The rhythm of dissolution and a new start, which at Athens leads from the Arrhephoria

---

custom. Even the sailors' revels (Plut. *An seni* 785e; *Non posse* 1097e) have their tradition; cf. the Argonauts on Lemnos (Burkert [1970] 8–9). A quite similar story of a young man who disguises himself as a girl in order to assassinate a tyrant is the aition of a festival at Thessalian Melite: see Nikander in Ant. Lib. 13. There is a similar aition for the *Λύσιοι τελεταί*, the Boeotian festival of Dionysus, in Heraclides fr. 155 Wehrli; cf. III.7.n.24 below.

[119] Polyaen. 8.43; see now Burkert (1979) 59–64, 72–77, where this pattern is discussed under the heading "Transformations of the Scapegoat." To the sending away of the scapegoat on the one side corresponds the festival of dissolution on the other.

through the Skira and the Buphonia and finally to the Panathenaia, is anything but unique. Though greatly expanded, it basically follows the "normal" sacrificial sequence, from the preparatory drama of the maiden, through the uncanny sacrifice of the bull, to the crowning feast in the "hecatombs" of the New Year's festival. The same festival rhythm appears in many other places and in the cults of other city gods. To be sure, we must reckon with different forms, local variants and combinations, but the basic structures are analogous, and details often show a striking correspondence. The myths representing the oldest literary tradition are especially illuminating. Once one has recognized the various stages of sacrifice that organize their peripeteia, they become transparent.

Because of Sparta's superior power, the city of Argos[1] was relegated to a secondary role in the history of Greece, while its cultural significance was overshadowed by that of Athens. Accordingly, the strong development of Argos from the Geometric to the Archaic period contrasts with the stagnation and constant crisis which beset it in historical times. In the Homeric epic, the Greeks are simply called *Argives* or *Danaans*, and a particularly large array of Greek myths focuses on the Argolid. There were three Mycenaean palaces here in close proximity: Mycenae, Tiryns, and Argive Larisa. There are even traces of more ancient, Neolithic traditions here. An important settlement, for instance, was Lerna,[2] site of myths and mysteries, which may have derived its name from Anatolia. Another Neolithic settlement was located on a hill which, in historical times, became the site of the central shrine of the Argolid, forty-five stades from Argos, and actually closer to Mycenae: that is, the Heraion,[3] the major sanctuary of the goddess Hera already in Homer. The goddess is called *Argive Hera*, Ἥρη Ἀργείη, just as Pallas belongs to Athens, Παλλὰς Ἀθηναίη.

The main festival at this shrine[4]—one of the greatest for the city

[1] M. Mitsos, Πολιτικὴ ἱστορία τοῦ Ἄργους (1945); Ἀργολικὴ προσωπογραφία (1952).

[2] J. L. Caskey, *Hesperia* 23 (1954), 3–30; 24 (1955), 25–49; 25 (1956), 147–77; 26 (1957), 142–62; 27 (1958), 125–44; 28 (1959), 202–207.

[3] Ch. Waldstein, *The Argive Heraeum* I/II (1902/5); C. W. Blegen, *Prosymna: The Helladic Settlement Preceding the Argive Heraeum* (1937); A. Frickenhaus, *Tiryns* I (1912), 114–20.

[4] Schol. Pind. *Nem.* 10 inscr.; Schol. Pind. *Ol.* 7.152c–d, 9.132a; Schol. Pind. *Pyth.* 8.113c; Schol. Pind. *Nem.* 10.35, 39; Nilsson (1906) 42–45. A. Boethius, *Der argivische Kalender* (Uppsala Universitets Årsskrift 1922), 1, found it probable that the Heraia occurred in the month Panamos (66). An inscription shows, surprisingly, that this was the first month of the year: see P. Charneux, *BCH* 81 (1957), 200; 82 (1958) 7. In Epidaurus, the month Panamos is preceded by Agrianios: Samuel (1972) 91.

of Argos—was called both *Heraia* and *Hecatombaia*. We know that it included a sacrificial procession, moving from Argos to the shrine, with the priestess of Hera riding in her ancient ox-drawn cart. Our knowledge comes from the story of Cleobis and Biton, who, in place of the oxen, pulled their mother, the priestess of Hera, all the way to the temple.[5] Already by 600 B.C. this example of Argive piety became known throughout Greece, because the Argives dedicated Kouroi, images of the youths, at Delphi. As Callimachus tells us,[6] the Argive maidens also wove a peplos for Hera, and the presentation of this peplos formed a part of the Hecatombaia-Heraia. As at Athens, the procession was followed by an agon that took place inside the city limits. It is mentioned several times by Pindar, even though it never became a pan-Hellenic agon of the first order. The prize was a bronze shield.[7]

This links the agon to the procession, for there a shield was carried along: "Those who had spent their boyhood purely and blamelessly took up a sacred shield and thus led the procession: this was their honor."[8] Boyhood was over; it was time to bear arms. Thus, the festival procession marked an initiation. The ephebes were now capable of bearing arms; the agon repeated the process. It is not known where this shield was stored and from whence it was "taken down" for the procession. The only certainty is that it was sacred to Hera. It became proverbial to call someone "proud as one who has taken on the shield in Argos."[9] According to a myth, Lynkeus gave this shield

---

[5]Hdt. 1.31; for the statues see Lippold (1950) 25; *SIG*[3] 5; cf. Paus. 2.20.3; for coins see Imhoof-Blumer (1885) 37, T. K. XXXIV; M. Guarducci, *Studi U.E. Paoli* (1955), 365–76. Cf. also Palaiphatos 51 and Aen. Tact. 17.

[6]Callim. fr. 66; Agias and Derkylos, *FGrHist* 305 F 4. Demetrios Poliorketes celebrated his wedding at the Heraia: Plut. *Dem.* 25.

[7]*Ὅ τ' ἐν Ἄργει χαλκός* Pind. *Ol.* 7.83; *ἀγὼν ὁ χάλκεος δᾶμον ὀτρύνει ποτὶ βουθυσίαν Ἥρας ἀέθλων τε κρίσιν* Pind. *Nem.* 10.22–23; Schol. Pind. *Ol.* 7.152, and cf. Schol. Pind. *Nem.* 10.39. King Nikokreon gave bronze; see Kaibel *Epigr.* 846 = *IG* IV 583; in the stadium by the Aspis, Paus. 2.24.2. For the myrtle-wreath see Schol. Pind. *Ol.* 7.152c. For coins see Imhoof-Blumer (1885) 41, with shield and wreath. For victory inscriptions see *τὴν ἐξ Ἄργους ἀσπίδα* *IG* II/III[2] 3162, 3169, 3158; IV 589, 590, 591, 597, 611; V 1.658; VII 49; XIV 739, 746, 747, 1102, 1112; *SIG*[3] 1064.9; for a tripod from Vergina see *Proc. Brit. Ac.* 65 (1979), 365. See now P. Amandry, "Sur les concours argiens," *BCH* Suppl. 6 (1980), 212–53.

[8]Plut. 1.44 in *Paroem. Gr.* I 327 and cf. Zenob. Par. 2.3 (I 32); Diog. 1.92 (I 195); Apostol. 3.27 (II 292); Diog. 1.53 (II 9); Macar. 8.23 (II 217).

[9]Callim. fr. 683; Zenob. Par. 6.52 (I 175) = Bodl. 959, Suda ω 245. The shield of Euphorbos was likewise displayed in the Heraion: see Paus. 2.17.3; Nikomachos Porph. *V. Pyth.* 27 = Iambl. *V. Pyth.* 63.

to his son, Abas, when the son announced the death of Danaus.[10] Lynkeus thereby became king of Argos, supported by the armed companies of youths. A new king following the old, a shield transferred from father to son: these reflect the situation of the New Year's festival, which the Heraia shared with the Panathenaia. The coincidence of the names Hecatombaia/Hecatombaion is no accident. The myth makes Lynkeus' wife Hypermestra a priestess of Hera.[11] The new order in the polis Argos came about under the power of Argive Hera.

If the Heraia was a New Year's festival, it must have been preceded by a festival of dissolution, perhaps in the form of the sacrifice of a bull. There is little more than allusions to this in Argos. Pausanias, for instance, mentions a spring called Eleutherion on the road to the shrine of Hera, which the priestesses "use for purification of the sacrifices which are not spoken of."[12] Thus, there were unspeakable sacrifices for which water had to be carried up from this source. Varro mentions an Argive hero who corresponds to the Attic "yoker of oxen," Buzyges. His name is ὁμόγυρος, "he who goes along in the circle,"[13] which recalls the manner in which the bull was "driven around" the altar at the Buphonia, especially as Buzyges was also linked to the sacrifice of an ox. But given the abundance of parallel cults in a city, it is impossible to isolate any combination with certainty. The myth, however, takes us further. Just as the Attic Buphonia was depicted as a primordial crime, ending a Golden, vegetarian age, so, too, the Argive myth included a primordial crime, namely, the first murder among the gods, when Hermes killed Argos, guardian of Io, the beloved of Zeus, who was turned into a cow.[14] Thus, this

---

[10] Hyg. *Fab.* 170 *clipeum quem Danaus consecraverat Iunoni . . . refixit et donavit Abanti ludosque consecravit qui quinto quoque anno aguntur, qui appellantur ἀσπὶς ἐν* Ἄργει (i.e., the foundation myth of the Heraia agon; missing in Nilsson [1906] 42–45); similarly, Hyg. *Fab.* 273. Cf. Serv. auct. *Aen.* 3.286.

[11] Euseb. *Hieron. a. Abr.* 582 following Hellanikos, Jacoby *FGrHist* I a 455.

[12] Paus. 2.17.1. It is uncertain whether Hera's bath in the spring Kanathos, whereby she becomes a virgin again (Paus. 2.38.2–3; Ἥρα Παρθενία Schol. Pind. *Ol.* 6.149g), has anything to do with the Heraion. For Hera Akreia at Argos see Agias and Derkylos, *FGrHist* 305 F 4; Callim. fr. 65; Paus. 2.24.1.

[13] Varro in Aug. *Civ. Dei* 18.6; *R. r.* 2.5.4. Cf. Ζεὺς γυράψιος at Chios, Lycoph. 537 with Schol.

[14] *PR* I 394–97; II 253–66; E. Meyer, *Forschungen zur Alten Geschichte* I (1892), 67–101. F. Wehrli, *Io. Dichtung und Kultlegende* (*AK* Beih. 4, 1967), 196–99. The myth was told already in the old epics at least four times, in the *Danais*, the *Phoronis* (fr. 4–5 Kinkel, and cf. Kinkel p. 211; Phoroneus founds the cult of Hera in Hyg. *Fab.* 274, 143), the Hesiodic *Aigimios* (fr. 295–96 M.-W.) and the Hesiodic *Catalogues* (fr. 124–26 M.-W.); then in Akusilaos, *FGrHist* 2 F 26–27; Pherekydes, *FGrHist* 3 F 67; Aesch. *Hik.* 291–305, etc., and cf. nn.21, 23 below.

Figure 1. Sacrificial procession: goddess Athena (damaged); priestess; altar with wood and fire; sacrificer pouring a libation; maiden carrying basket, attendants with branches driving bull, sow, sheep; flute-player, further participants. Attic black-figure cup, about 560 B.C. Private collection, photo D. Widmer. Münzen- und Medaillen AG, Basel, Auction 18 no. 85. Courtesy, H. A. Cahn. (See p. 4.)

Figure 2. Preparation for sacrifice: fluteplayer, attendant holding ram, sacrificer washing his hands, altar with wood and fire, and with marks of blood, bukranion above, attendant holding water vessel and tray of offerings, dignitary (seer?). Attic red-figure bell crater by the Kleophon painter (*ARV*² 1149.9), 440/30 B.C. Boston, Museum of Fine Arts 95.25, Catherine Page Perkins Fund. Courtesy, Museum of Fine Arts, Boston. (See p. 4.)

Figure 3. Leopard men hunting stag and boar. Wall painting from Çatal Hüyük, about 6000 B.C. From J. Mellaart, *The Neolithic of the Near East,* London 1975, 110 fig. 60. Courtesy, James Mellaart. (See p. 15.)

Figure 4. Sacrificial feast in honor of Dionysus: roasting at an altar and cooking in a tripod kettle. Caeretan hydria, about 530 B.C. Museo Nazionale di Villa Giulia, Rome. Courtesy, Museo Nazionale di Villa Giulia. (See p. 89, n.29.)

Figure 5. Warrior with shield and sword rising from a tripod cauldron (Pelops?). Lion on either side. Bronze mitra from Axos, Crete, about 630 B.C. Courtesy, Museum of Iraklion. (See p. 99.)

Figure 6. Buphonia: bulls strolling around an altar. Attic black-figure oinochoe by the Gela painter (*ABV* 473.185), 510/480 B.C. Munich 1824. Courtesy, Vereinigung der Freunde Antiker Kunst, Basel, and Staatlich Antikensammlungen und Glyptothek, Munich. (See p. 137, n.7.)

Figure 7. 'Lenaia vase': mask of Dionysus fastened to a column, table of offerings with two stamnoi, woman tasting wine. Attic red-figure stamnos by the Villa Giulia painter (*ARV*[2] 621,34), about 450 B.C. Boston, Museum of Fine Arts 90.155, anonymous gift. Courtesy, Museum of Fine Arts, Boston. (See p. 235.)

Figure 8. Mystery initiation: pig sacrifice by Heracles (lion-skin) at a low altar, priest with offering tray pouring a libation. Lovatelli urn, Museo Nazionale delle Terme, Rome. Courtesy, Deutsches Archäologische Institut, Rome. (See p. 257.)

Figure 9. Mystery initiation: purification by a priestess holding a liknon, veiled initiand seated on a ram's fleece (horn beneath his foot). Lovatelli urn, Museo Nazionale delle Terme, Rome. Courtesy, Deutsches Archäologische Institut, Rome. (See p. 267.)

epoch-making act of violence was associated with the Heraion. "When Hermes had killed Argos, the guardian of Io, at Zeus' behest, he was brought to trial. He was arraigned by Hera and the other gods because he was the first god ever to be stained with death. Now when the gods were holding this trial, they were afraid of Zeus, for Hermes had acted on his orders. They wanted both to remove this stain from their presence and acquit the god of murder: agitated as they were, they threw their voting pebbles at Hermes, so that a pile of stones grew at his feet": thus Anticlides following Xanthos the Lydian.[15]

The killer is freed through symbolic stoning. Thus, the pile of stones in which Hermes is present attests to the first bloodshed and how it was overcome.[16] Likewise, in the *Homeric Hymn* bearing his name, Hermes is the inventor of sacrifice and is called βουφόνος.[17] Starting with the Hesiodic *Catalogues*, the Greeks believed that his epithet, Argeiphontes, was won by killing Argos. Modern skepticism concerning this interpretation[18] has arisen partly because of the problem of word formation, but above all because the "killing of Argos" is taken to be insignficant, a minor detail. The myth, however, adds another dimension to this act, surrounding this first divine shedding of blood, i.e., the first sacrifice, with a typical comedy of innocence including trial, sentencing, and apparent stoning. On Tenedos, at the sacrifice of a calf for Dionysus Anthroporrhaistes, the participants shower the killer with stones "in order to remove the stain from themselves."[19] In Aeschylus' metaphor of the ϑῦμα λεύσιμον, the "sacrifice that ends in stoning," there may be a hint that such occurrences were not infrequent.[20] Above all, the courtroom comedy recalls

[15] Xanthos, *FGrHist* 765 F 29; Anticlides, *FGrHist* 140 F 19; Eust. 1809.38–43.

[16] On Hermes, the pile of stones, see Nilsson I (1955), 501–505; I.6.n.29 above. The Argives held trials at a place where, according to the saga, traitors had been stoned: see Deinias, *FGrHist* 306 F 3. Voting with stones at a trial can probably be traced back to stoning rituals.

[17] 436; cf. I.2.n.13 above.

[18] P. Chantraine, *Mél. O. Navarre* (1935), 69–79 (pre-Greek); J. Chittenden, *AJA* 52 (1948), 24–28 ("dog-killer"); A. Heubeck, *Beitr. z. Namenf.* 5 (1954), 19–31 ("Im Glanz prangend"). Argos ("plain", Callim. fr. 299.2; Strabo 8 p. 372) and the eponymous Argos can hardly be distinguished; the fact that the mythical character changes over into the o-declension causes no problem (cf. Αἴολος beside Αἰολεῖς); however, the word formation is problematical. The epic epithet comes perhaps from the locative (*Il.* 6.224, 14.119; *Od.* 4.174) "shining at Argos," then the "killer at Argos." Ever since the *Iliad*, the latter part of the word has, with certainty, been understood as "killer" (like ἀνδρειφόντης, Πολυφόντης).

[19] Ael. *Nat. an.* 12.34; III.4.n.20 below.

[20] Aesch. *Ag.* 1118; Burkert (1966) 119.

the Attic Buphonia. There, in Athens, Hermes' descendants, the Eleusinian Kerykes, are the ones who kill the bull. Correspondingly, the act of Hermes Argeiphontes, "killer of Argos," reflects a Buphonia-rite at Argos.

Moreover, the myth identifies Argos, the "neatherd," as closely as it possibly could with the bull. "Argos killed the bull that ravaged Arcadia, and clothed himself in its skin."[21] In several vase-paintings he can be seen wearing the bullskin. The conqueror of the bull becomes virtually identical with his victim by covering himself with its skin. Hermes, the "ox-slayer," thereupon lulls him to sleep and kills him, as the myth relates,[22] by hitting him with a stone. Thus, the subsequent stoning was payment in kind. To sacrifice a bull, one needs an axe, an instrument once made of stone.

Hermes' act—because it is linked to the myth of Io—is, once again, combined with the preparatory drama of a maiden. Io, the king's daughter and beloved of Zeus, was confined within Hera's sphere of power, guarded in the Argive Heraion, chained to the sacred olive tree.[23] With Argos' death, these chains were broken: and the cow fled into the wide world, goaded to far-off lands by the sting of the gadfly. There seems to be a twofold cultic reality underlying the mythical play between the daughter of the king and the cow: already in Hesiod's *Catalogues*, Io was a priestess of Hera. And the priestess's place is in the sanctuary, tending the eternal flame of the sacred lamp[24]—this, too, is common to the Heraion and the Erechtheum. But if at the Heraia the priestess is led in solemn procession from Argos to the shrine, we must assume that she previously left that shrine in an act of "dissolution." Was the lamp extinguished during her absence? The drama is played out in a more sharply articulated, drastic form on the animal level: when the bull dies in the unspeakable sacrifice, it leaves the cows in its herd without a leader. People at Argos spoke of the "cattle of Argos" which were "sacred to Hera." The hill on which

---

[21] Apollod. 2.4; Schol. Eur. *Phoen.* 1116. For vase-paintings with Argos in a bullskin see the black figure amphora *BM* B 164 = *ABV* 148.2, Cook III (1940) 632; for red figure hydria, Boston 08.417 = *ARV*² 579.84, Cook III (1940) 663; for red-figure-crater from Ruvo, Jatta 1498 = *ARV*² 1409.9, Cook I (1914) 460; for a catalogue of depictions of Argos see R. Engelmann, *JdI* 18 (1903), 37–58.

[22] Apollod. 2.7.

[23] Apollod. 2.6; Pliny *NH* 16.239; cf. black figure amphora, München 573 J. = Cook III (1940) pl. 49.1; red figure stamnos, Wien 3729 = *ARV*² 288.1, Cook III (1940) pl. 49.2. For Io as a priestess of Hera see Hes. fr. 124 M.-W. = Apollod. 2.5; *κλῃδοῦχον* Ἥρας Aesch. *Hik.* 291; Hellanikos, *FGrHist* I a p. 455.

[24] Paus. 2.17.7, and cf. 3.15.6.

the Heraion was set was called Euboea.[25] The cattle were "set free" to be caught for sacrifice. At the bull's death—for thus we may conclude from the myth—a cow would be chased away "as if it were mad." But even the mad cows did not escape the festival of the Hecatombs.

The procession at the Heraia responded in a special way to the sacrifice of the bull in the "dissolution." It does so by means of a singular feature: the act of bearing the sacred shield. In historical times, of course, as we know from Pindar, at least the shields that served as prizes in the agon were made of bronze. They were hoplite shields of the sort common after approximately 700 B.C. Its more ancient predecessor, however, would have been a shield made of cowhide, which thus, in its source, was so directly linked to the cow that in an especially ancient Homeric verse the shield is simply designated by the Indo-European word for cow, *βῶν*.[26] One must kill the bull if one wants the shield. But precisely in this form—as a stretched skin—the *βοῦς* assumes a new existence, becoming the warrior's trustiest comrade-in-arms, a protective skin for his own skin. Thus, the dead bull is security for the living; and thus, in taking up the shield, the young man who has outgrown boyhood enters the shadow and the shelter of the dead. To this extent the armed warrior himself plays the role of Argos, who killed the bull to wear its skin.

In a way, then, the power and order of Argos the city are embodied in Argos the neatherd, lord of the herd and lord of the land, whose name itself is the name of the land. In the myth, Argos is Zeus' opponent, but it has long been seen that he is nonetheless closely identified with Zeus.[27] Just as Argos is called "panoptes," the one who "sees all," so Zeus, the omniscient sky-god, is invoked as Zeus Panoptes. And just as mythographers describe Argos as having four eyes or three, so there was an image of Zeus at Argos with three eyes.[28] In the countless, starlike eyes of Argos,[29] poets saw an image of

---

[25] Paus. 2.17.1. The name Nemea was etymologized from the "grazing" of Argos' cattle: see Arrian, *FGrHist* 156 F 16 = *Et. M.* 176.33 (it would be tempting to connect the altar of Zeus Aphesios mentioned here with *ἄφετα ζῷα*, I.2.n.21 above); Luk. *Dial. Deor.* 3; *Et. M.* 600.23; Schol. Pind. III 3.23 Drachmann. Diod. 4.15.4 mentions a herd of horses sacred to Hera, which existed until the time of Alexander.

[26] *Il.* 7.238; cf. A. Snodgrass, *Early Greek Armour and Weapons from the End of the Bronze Age to 600 B.C.* (1964), 37–68, 170–71.

[27] *PR* I 396.1; E. Meyer, *Forsch. z. alten Gesch.* I (1892), 72, is critical of this view; *ὦ Ζεῦ πανόπτα* Aesch. *Eum.* 1045. For an altar ΔΙϜΟΣ ΠΑΝΟΠΤΑ at Argos see *BCH* 33 (1909), 445; Cook I (1914) 457–62; III (1940) 631.

[28] For Argos with four eyes see "Hes." *Aigimios* fr. 294 M.-W.; two-headed on vase-paintings, see black figure amphora, *BM* B 164 (n. 21 above), bell-crater from Ruvo, Genoa

the universe—just as Zeus himself was the universe. Moreover, this two-faced quality of Argos recalls the myths of double beings who had to be killed and cut up so that our world could come into existence.[30] Indeed, in the context of the city Argos, the mythical Argos was virtually the embodiment of the cosmos, the all-embracing order. This order, so as to endure, had to be secured with a death; it was dissolved for the sake of being reestablished. Argos died in the unspeakable sacrifice of the bull so that the youthful warriors might carry the sacred shield on their shoulders, thus carrying the city's order on into the future, like Aeneas: *attollens umeris famamque et fata nepotum*.[31]

3. *Agrionia*

In the myth, Argos' death causes Io, the king's daughter, to be driven off into distant lands as a mad cow. This pattern of kings' daughters roaming like cows, distracted, through forest and mountain, is better known through a myth from a place directly adjoining Argos—Tiryns, where Proitos was king. Here, too, Hera is active, Hera of Tiryns, whose small seated statue made of wood from the pear tree was reckoned among the most ancient and venerable of Greek statues of the gods. When Argos destroyed Tiryns, the image was brought to the Argive Heraion, where Pausanias still saw it set up

---

1145 = *ARV*[2] 1054.48, Cook II (1924) 380. Marduk has four eyes and four ears: see Enuma Eliš, *ANET* 62. For Argos with three eyes see Pherekydes, *FGrHist* 3 F 66 (the third is on the back of his head). For Zeus with three eyes (the third on his forehead), allegedly Priam's Zeus Herkeios, in the temple of Zeus Larisaios at Argos, see Paus. 2.24.3.

[29] Eur. *Phoen.* 1116–17 *τὰ μὲν σὺν ἄστρων ἐπιτολαῖσιν ὄμματα βλέποντα τὰ δὲ κρύπτοντα δυνόντων μέτα.*

[30] In identifying Janus with Chaos, which had by then been divided, Verrius (Festus 52 M.) and Ovid (*Fast.* 1.103–14) are applying a cosmogonical idea to Janus that was already in the background of the anthropogony in Plato's *Symposium* (189d–193d). At the New Year's festival at Philadelphia, Saturnus appears as a mask with two heads, representing the period of dissolution before the new beginning: see Lydus *Mens.* 4.2 p. 65 Wuensch.

[31] Verg. *Aen.* 8.731.

on a column. The periegete found it "insignificant,"[1] and it was perceived so already in the fifth century, when legend had it that Proitos' daughters had mocked the wretched image and thus incurred the goddess's wrath.[2] Hera's anger was sometimes ascribed to other motivations, but it was always the encounter with Hera in her sanctuary that suddenly wrenched the daughters of the Tirynthian king out of their sheltered existence. The goddess drove them to "frenzied roaming," ἠλοσύνη, according to the Hesiodic *Catalogues*,[3] causing them to break out of the sanctuary and city and to wander the earth. There were stories of "all sorts of indecent behavior,"[4] of shameless nudity and of the madness that caused them to take themselves for cows and roam the Peloponnesus mooing.[5] Our oldest source, the *Catalogues*, presents a somewhat different picture: "because of their loathsome lewdness, the goddess destroyed the tender flower of their youth," "over their heads she poured a dreadful itching substance and spread white leprosy over their whole skin, and now the hair fell out on their scalps and their beautiful heads were bald."[6] This is both lust and the repulsiveness of sickness and old age, a radical antithesis to the image of lovely and modest virgins—redolent of a witch's sabbath. The myth of Pandareos' daughters, to which the *Odyssey* alludes, is comparable: their girlhood, which had stood under the protection of Athena and Artemis, comes to a violent halt when, shortly before

[1]Paus. 2.17.5, 8.46.3. On this image see Akusilaos, *FGrHist* 2 F 28; Demetrios of Argos, *FGrHist* 304 F 1; Simon (1969) 320.29. The fact that the image was made from the wood of the pear tree probably has to do with the festival of the "pear-throwers" and the myth of the pear as the first food after the great flood: see Plut. *Q. Gr.* 303a–b. At Tiryns there was a hero named Argos with a sacred grove, Argos: see Hdt. 6.75–80. For Argos as the donor of the image of Hera see Demetrios, *FGrHist* 304 F 1. Cf. A. Frickenhaus, *Tiryns* (1912), T.2; F. Oelmann, *Bonn. Jbb.* 157 (1957), 18, pl. 1, 3/4.

[2]Akusilaos of Argos, *FGrHist* 2 F 28; cf. Bacchyl. 11.40–58, 82–112; according to Serv. auct. *Ecl.* 6.48, they took the gold of Hera for their own use, i.e., they probably dressed themselves up like Hera. The Arrhephoroi of the goddess at Athens got gold jewelry: see Harpokr. ἀρρηφορεῖν.

[3]Hes. fr. 37.10–15, and cf. fr. 130–33 M.-W.; J. Schwartz, *Pseudo-Hesiodeia* (1960), 369–77, 545–48; cf. *PR* II 246–52; F. Vian, "Melampous et les Proitides," *Revue des Etudes Anciennes* 67 (1965), 25–30.

[4]Μετ' ἀκοσμίας ἁπάσης Apollod. 2.27; γυμναί Ael. *VH* 3.42. The Proitids are perhaps portrayed in the metope from Thermos (seventh century B.C.) in which young girls are baring their breasts: see Schefold (1964) 35 fig. 6; J. Dörig, *AM* 77 (1962), 72–91; doubting, Simon (1969) 320.29.

[5]Serv. and Prob. on Verg. *Ecl.* 6.48; for the metamorphosis into cows see Schol. Stat. *Theb.* 3.453.

[6]Hes. fr. 133. It is clear from Philodemos that Hera is the subject: see M.-W. on fr. 132.

their weddings, they were abducted by the Harpies and given to the "hateful Erinyes" as servants.[7] The daughters of Proitos wandering in the wilderness also became Erinyes-like beings.

Athenian critics found a similarly affected repulsiveness in the gatherings of the garlic-eating women at the Skira.[8] In Aristophanes' *Ecclesiazusae*, the realization of the plot hatched at the Skira is dominated by the image of a lascivious old hag. Old age, repulsiveness, throwing custom to the winds, and deviation of all kinds belong to the period of dissolution both in the Attic ritual and in the myth of the daughters of Proitos. Accordingly, the latter probably reflects the ritual of a *Weiberbund*. The description of the dreadful transformation of the daughters of Proitos is based on the symptoms of real illnesses, and these symptoms are imitated in the ritual, where virgins must actually appear covered with white soot. "Rubbed down with white meal like the basket carriers" is how one comic playwright in Athens describes it, referring to some sacrificial ritual.[9] Likewise, according to the Homeric *Hymn to Hermes*, the prophetic Thriae, servants of Delphic Apollo, are "virgins, their heads besprinkled with white meal."[10] According to the cult-legend of Letrinoi, Artemis of Alpheios and her nymphs masked themselves with clay. The grotesque masks from the shrine of Artemis Orthia at Sparta confirm that this reflects a ritual custom, and similar masks were found in the Heraion of Samos. The oldest representations of the Gorgon are the larger than life-size pot-shaped masks, which were votive offerings to Hera of Tiryns.[11] The transformation of the daughters of Proitos is a ritual masking, forced on the virgins by Hera.

Hera's wrath, however, competed with the power of Dionysus in this myth—and here again the authority cited is a source as early as Hesiod, presumably the *Melampodia*.[12] Melampus, the prophet and

---

[7] *Od.* 20.66–78—an isolated bit of the tradition for this story; the scholion to v. 66 calls the "sickness" of the daughters of Pandareos *κύνα*, which W. H. Roscher (*Das von der Kynanthropie handelnde Fragment des Marcellus von Side*, Abh. Leipzig 17.3 [1897]) connected with Kynanthropy; cf. M. C. van der Kolf, *RE* XVIII 2, 499–504.

[8] See III.1.n.42 above.

[9] Hermippos fr. 26 (*CAF* I 231).

[10] *Hy. Merc.* 553–55. Cf. the Graiai in the myth of Perseus.

[11] For Artemis Alpheiaia see Paus. 6.22.9; cf. Harpokr. *ἀπομάττων, ἤλειφον γὰρ τῷ πηλῷ καὶ τῷ πιτύρῳ τοὺς μυουμένους*. For Artemis Orthia see *JHS* Suppl. 5 (1929), 163, pl. 47–62; Nilsson (1955) 161. For Samos see H. Walter, *Das griech. Heiligtum* (1965), 28. For Tiryns see *RE* VI A 1465; Pickard-Cambridge (1962) pl. XII b.

[12] Hes. fr. 131 = Apollod. 2.26; I. Löffler, *Die Melampodie, Versuch einer Rekonstruktion des Inhalts* (1963), 37–39. The reconstruction on the basis of the various Hesiodic fragments

purifying priest, was also considered to have been the founder of the cult of Dionysus.[13] In this version, Dionysus struck the daughters of Proitos with madness because they were unwilling to accept his orgies. Yet the presence of the Dionysiac element is not radically different here, but is only a slight change of emphasis in structures common to non-Dionysiac rituals as well. The dissolution of the normal order, which otherwise signifies the wrath and alienation of the great goddess, is here transformed into a show of strength by the god of madness. This madness becomes ambivalent: is it a blessing or a curse? The *Melampodia* is probably later than the *Catalogues*, so it permits us to trace the inroads made by the cult of Dionysus in the sixth century. And yet the new interpretation follows the old rhythm of dissolution and new beginning.

Whether caused by Hera or Dionysus, raving goes hand in hand with sacrifice. This is evident only in the Melampus version of the saga, in which the madness is raised to a second level. Proitos refused Melampus' first offer to cure his frenzied daughters, whereupon "the maidens grew even more frantic and were now joined by all the other women as well; for they too forsook their homes, killed their own children, and ran off into the solitude."[14] Thus, once again, an unspeakably gruesome act took place—the murder of one's own children. Dissolution turns into perversion, and in addition to the antithesis of the lovely virgin comes that of the loving mother, for she too has become a witch, murdering and even eating her children. In the "slaughtering of the bull" which we saw reflected in the myth of Argeiphontes, the ancestral king or universal father was the victim. Here, it is the child. Yet this distinction is in fact part of a polar relationship. Patricide and infanticide are the two variants between which the unspeakable sacrifice can shift at any time. Thus, we can postulate even now that a young animal, a bull-calf instead of a bull, could be used as a substitute in the ritual.

Once again, it is the Melampus version that gives a full account of how this dreadful tale could yet end happily: "Melampus took along the strongest youths and pursued the women and girls with battle-cries and a specific ecstatic dance, out of the mountains and on to

---

and testimonia is, however, most uncertain; cf. R. Pfeiffer, *Ausgew. Schriften* (1960), 30–33. In any case, the separation of the myths of the Proitids and Melampus (Nilsson [1955] 613.2) is disproven by Hes. fr. 37.

[13] Hdt. 2.49.

[14] Apollod. 2.28, 3.37 *τοὺς ἐπιμαστιδίους ἔχουσαι παῖδας τὰς σάρκας αὐτῶν ἐσιτοῦντο.* Cf. Paus. 2.18.4; Nonnus 47.484–95.

Sikyon."[15] Strange, how the myth here leaps from Tiryns to Sikyon. In the most common versions, the daughters of Proitos are purified at yet a third place, the sanctuary of Artemis Hemera in Arcadian Lusoi.[16] The myth seems to combine various local traditions; there must also have been a Tirynthian conclusion,[17] or at least a closing rite at Tiryns which, of course, could not have survived the annexation of Tiryns by Argos. In any case, the raving of the maidens and the women is merely an exceptional state followed by the reestablishment of order in the polis, the antithesis of perversion. The women who have gotten out of hand are made to feel the men's superior strength. It is the youths, the ephebes, who prove themselves here, and their leader, Melampus, thereby becomes the new king.[18] He forthwith marries one of the successfully healed daughters; thus Dionysus' priest returns again to Hera's sphere of power, for she is the goddess of marriage. Demetrios Poliorketes celebrated his marriage in Argos at the festival of the Heraia.[19]

But even this last phase did not occur without sacrifice: "Iphinoe, the eldest daughter of Proitos, met her death in the pursuit." Her grave was pointed out in the marketplace at Sikyon.[20] Naturally, there was as little question of an actual human sacrifice in the ritual as there had been in the infanticide. The fact that the raving daughter identifies herself with a cow makes it probable that a cow-sacrifice accom-

---

[15] Apollod. 2.29.

[16] Bacchyl. 11.37–39; Eudoxos fr. 26/7 Gisinger = Steph. Byz. Ἀζανία, Pliny *NH* 31.16 (cf. Theopompos, *FGrHist* 115 F 269; Phylarchos, *FGrHist* 81 F 63; "Arist." *Mir. ausc.* 842b6; Paus. 5.5.10); Callim. *Hy.* 3.235; Paus. 8.18.7–8; R. Stiglitz, *Die grossen Göttinnen Arkadiens* (1967), 101–105. For the purification at Elis see Strabo 8 p. 346; Paus. 5.5.10.

[17] The numerous votive statuettes of women with pigs that were found at Tiryns indicate a rite of purification (cf. V.2.nn. 3–5 below): see A. Frickenhaus, *Tiryns* I (1912), 17. For a sanctuary of Artemis in the Argolis founded by Melampous see Soph. fr. 309 P.; Paus. 2.25.3; Steph. Byz. Οἴνη.

[18] Apollod. 2.29; Schol. Pind. *Nem.* 9.30; Paus. 2.18.4; *PR* II 252. Only Pindar (*Pae.* 4.28–35) has Melampus turn down the kingship.

[19] See III.2.n.6 above.

[20] Apollod. 2.29; for the tomb of Iphinoe with the inscription at the marketplace of Sikyon see *Praktika* (1952), 394–95 = *SEG* 15 (1958), #195. For dramatic pictorial representations of the purification of the Proitids through the sacrifice of a pig, see the crater from Canicattini, *Boll. d'Arte* 35 (1950), 97–107; E. Langlotz and M. Hirmer, *Die Kunst der Westgriechen* (1963), 24; Trendall (1967) 602 #102; *AK* 13 (1970), 67, pl. 30.2; on which cf. a vase from Naples (H. 1760) and a cameo, *RML* II 2573. On purification through Melampus see also Alexis fr. 112 (*CAF* II 337); Diphilos fr. 126 (*CAF* II 577); *θυσίαις τε ἀπορρήτοις καὶ καθαρμοῖς* Paus. 8. 18.7.

panied the rescue and the cure. Thus, the circle of correspondences with the Hecatombaia-Heraia is closed. The ecstatic dance of the ephebes led by Melampus is obviously a ritualized hunt to help catch the wild animals. The hunt is repeated and fulfilled in the animal-sacrifice, which marks and surmounts the crises of society. The myth of Proitos' daughters is the story of an initiation, the path from the virgin to the queen, in the course of which the old order is demolished in a transitional period of madness, and one must pass through death before reaching one's goal. In overcoming perversion, the youths establish themselves and their king.

Our only evidence that the myth of Proitos' daughters was connected with a festival is a gloss in Hesychius: "Agrania, festival in Argos in honor of one of Proitos' daughters." "Honoring" a heroine presupposes her death: the festival was thus for Iphinoe, whom Melampus and his ephebes had killed, nay, sacrificed. In the same breath, Hesychius notes the "Agriania: festival of the dead among the Argives."[21] At a festival of the dead, a Nekysia, the spirits or masks swarm up, demanding their rights for a certain time, but then give way to normal life again. One must propitiate them so that they will leave one in peace. Frequently, various means are used to chase them away.[22] The exceptional period in the myth ends with the death of Proitos' daughter in the wild hunt; and an exceptional period recurs annually "in her honor," only to be overcome. Thus, the antithesis of death must aid in establishing the thesis of life.

Agriania/Agrionia is one of the most widespread of all Greek festival names, in many places even lending its name to a month, Agrionios.[23] The evidence is especially plentiful in Boeotia, and a Boeotian, Plutarch, has provided us with some characteristic details of the

---

[21] Ἀγράνια· ἑορτὴ ἐν Ἄργει, ἐπὶ μιᾷ τῶν Προίτου θυγατέρων. Ἀγριάνια· νεκύσια παρὰ Ἀργείοις καὶ ἀγῶνες ἐν Θήβαις.

[22] See IV.3 below.

[23] Nilsson (1906) 271–74, who would like to make the festival, as a "gathering" of the dead, parallel to the Anthesteria; more likely, however, is the connection with ἄγριος, *Ἀγριάων (Thracian tribe Ἀγριᾶνες, Hdt. 5.16). For the Agrionia at Thebes see n. 21 above; *IG* VII 2447; L. Robert, *BCH* 59 (1935), 193–98 (in honor of Διόνυσος Κάδμειος); at Orchomenos see Plut. *Q. Gr.* 299 f.; at Chaironeia see Plut. *Q. symp.* 717a; *IG* VII 3348; etc. For the month-name Agrianios/Agrionios see Samuel (1972) Index *s.v.*; Ἀγερράνιος at Eresos (cf. Πέρραμος instead of Priamos, Alcaeus 42.2 LP); see *IG* XII 2.527.27, 45; Διόνυσος ὠμηστὴς καὶ ἀγριώνιος Plut. *Anton.* 24.5, and cf. Dionysos Omestes at Lesbos besides Hera and Zeus, Alcaeus 129; Ἀγριώνια καὶ Νυκτέλια Plut. *Q. Rom.* 291a. On Cos, Agrionios is the first month of the year, in late autumn, see R. Herzog, *Abh. Berlin* (1928), nr. 6, 49f.

ritual. At Orchomenos, an accompanying myth directly paralleled the myth of Proitos' daughters. In Boeotia, of course, Dionysus took on the most prominent role. There were stories of a Dionysiac epiphany and frenzy, in keeping with the central role of the priest of Dionysus in the cult.

Orchomenos, the city of Minyas, is yet another place with especially old traditions. Here, it is the daughters of Minyas who are driven to madness and infanticide before their frenzy is calmed in a no less frenzied pursuit.[24] "The only ones to abstain from the Dionysiac dances were the daughters of Minyas, Leukippe, Arsippe, and Alkathoe. . . . But Dionysus was angered. And they were busy at their looms, vying with each other in their work for Athena Ergane, when suddenly ivy and grape vines began to coil around the looms, snakes were nestling in the baskets of wool, and milk and wine dripped from the ceiling."[25] The epiphany of Dionysus brings about Dionysiac madness: "They threw lots into a pot, and the three of them drew lots. And when Leukippe's lot appeared she spoke, vowing to bring the god a sacrifice. And she and her sisters tore her son, Hippasos, apart"[26] "like a fawn,"[27] "and then dashed off to the original maenads, who chased them away, however, because they were polluted with murder. Thereupon they turned into birds"[28]—into owls and bats, animals of the night.

The unspeakable sacrifice (ϑῦμα), offered at the peak of madness, is here in every way a Dionysian sparagmos. Maenads with dismembered fawns were a frequent subject of vase-paintings.[29] The gruesome act causes a rift: in the face of this deed, the Dionysiac horde splits in two, with the "original members," the pure ones, repudiating the polluted ones. The myth closes with a metamorphosis in which the situation of flight and pursuit is forever fixed in an image from nature: the creatures of the night are always hated and pursued by the birds of day.

---

[24] Rapp, *RML* II 3012–16; *PR* I 690. [25] Ael. *VH* 3.42.

[26] Ant. Lib. 10.3 following Korinna (665 Page) and Nikander. [27] Ael. *V.H.* 3.42.

[28] Ibid.; cf. Plut. *Q. Gr.* 299e–f; Ov. *Met.* 4.399–415. The names of the three Minyads are Leukippe (Leuconoe, Ov. 4.168), Alkathoe (Plut., Ant. Lib.) or Alkithoe (Ael., Ov.) and Arsippe (Ant. Lib., Ael.) or Arsinoe (Plut.); Ant. Lib. ends with the transformation into νυκτερίς, γλαῦξ, βύξα (a kind of owl), Ael. with κορώνη, γλαῦξ, νυκτερίς; Ovid speaks only of bats. Aeschylus' *Xantriai* dealt either with the myth of the Minyads or of the Proitids.

[29] E.g., a skyphos, Athens 3442, Harrison (1922) 452; cf. H. Philippart, *Revue Belge de Philologie* 9 (1930), 5–72. For Dionysus tearing apart a deer see a stamnos *BM* 439 = *ARV*² 298, Harrison (1922) 450.

Plutarch explicitly links the myth of Minyas' daughters with a ritual that included pursuit. "The husbands of the daughters of Minyas, because they wore black clothing in grief and sorrow, were called 'sooty,' ψολόεις, but the Minyads themselves were called Oleiae, the 'murderesses.' And even today the people of Orchomenos give this name to the women descended from this family; and every other year, at the Agrionia, there takes place a flight and pursuit of them by the priest of Dionysus with sword in hand. Any one of them that he catches he may kill, and in my time the priest Zoilus killed one of them."[30] Precisely the role that Melampus played in the myth—namely, that of archegete of the Dionysian cult—is played here by the real priest of Dionysus at Orchomenos. Like the armed ephebes, he carries a sword; and the act of killing a woman of the Oleiae corresponds to the death of Proitos' eldest daughter. The serious nature of the ritual is here raised to the highest pitch of intensity. Plutarch subsequently describes how this, our one securely attested instance of human sacrifice, led to a crisis, indeed, to reform of the custom. Zoilus died a painful death, and the people of Orchomenos, after internal disorder, deprived his family of the priesthood. With the fanaticism of a zealot, Zoilus apparently failed to recognize the theatrical, playacting nature of the ritual and thus pursued it *ad absurdum*. In the Dionysian realm, as elsewhere, animal-sacrifice guarantees that the ritual functions sensibly. We can gather from the myth that a mysterious and unspeakable noctural sacrifice for Dionysus—the eater of raw flesh and nocturnal god of the Agrionia—preceded the flight of the "murderesses," and, likewise, that the pursuit culminated in an animal-sacrifice.

The community is divided into two groups at the Agrionia sacrifice, each serving Dionysus. The opposition of the sexes, of women and men, is emphasized by the men being called "sooty," pointing beyond the mourning custom to a ritual masquerade, whereas the leader of the women is named Leukippe, meaning "the white mare." In just this way, Melampus, the "black foot," pursued the daughters of Proitos, who had covered themselves with white meal—a mummery of black soot versus one of white meal. The fact that those with the light color are actually stained, and those who are sooty and black are actually pure inside—an inversion of interior and exterior qualities—reflects the polar tensions that find expression here. The one would be unthinkable without the other; indeed, the one embraces

---

[30] *Q. Gr.* 299e–f. Toepffer (1889) 189–90 defended the text Αἰολεῖαι against Buttmann's conjecture 'Ολεῖαι, which, however, is supported by Plutarch's etymology οἷον ὀλοάς.

the other. Those in white turn into flying creatures of the night, yet the triumphant daytime order still preserves the memory of darkness. The Attic ephebes wore black robes at the Panathenaic festival,[31] and Theseus returned from Crete with a black sail, thus becoming king.

It is always astounding how much light the report of a contemporary can shed on rituals still active in his time. Plutarch speaks briefly of the Agrionia festival in Chaironeia, his home town. "In my own region at the Agrionia, the women search for Dionysus as if he had run away; then they stop and say that he has fled to the Muses and is hidden with them; a bit later, after the meal has ended, they ask each other riddles and conundrums." According to Plutarch, this means that, because of the presence of the logos, "the wild, frenzied behavior is hidden away, kept in the kindly care of the Muses."[32] Here, everything happens between women, and they themselves direct the shift from wild behavior to that controlled by the Muses. Wildness and frenzy have disappeared; the restless searching, as after something lost, has ended, resolved unexpectedly into a "meal," a sacrificial feast in which oppressive anxiety gives way to cheerful sport. We do not know in what way other societal groups took part in this festival, but even Plutarch's brief sketch reveals the same familiar pattern of dissolution followed by the order of the Muses.

In Argos there were tales of king Perseus' deadly pursuit of Dionysus and his female servants. People would point out the graves of the fallen maenads, the "sea-women," sometimes even speaking of the death of the god himself. Yet this event was linked to the founding of Dionysus' temple and his cult.[33] As early as the *Iliad* we find a description of the flight and disappearance of Dionysus. The powerful Lykurgus, son of Dryas, once "drove the nurses of raving Dionysus over the sacred plain of Nysa, and all of them scattered their sacrificial implements on the ground, stricken with an ox-goad by

---

[31] See III.1.n.87 above; also the victory of Melanthios over Xanthos (on which see P. Vidal-Naquet, *Proc. Cambridge Philol. Soc.* 14 [1968], 49–64).

[32] *Q. symp.* 717a.

[33] For the tombs of the Ἅλιαι see Paus. 2.22.1; for the tomb of Χορεία see Paus. 2.20.4; for the temple of Dionysus Kresios with the tomb of Ariadne see Paus. 2.23.7–8, referring to Lyseas (*FGrHist* 312 F 4). The details of what Deinarchos of Delos said are uncertain (*FGrHist* 399 F 1), but the testimonia speak of the god's death (cf. II.5.n.41 above). According to Schol. T *Il.* 14.319, Perseus hurled Dionysus into the lake at Lerna. Nonnus 47.475–741 combined the Perseus and Melampus versions; it is uncertain to what extent he is following Euphorion (fr. 18 Powell).

murderous Lykurgus; while Dionysus in terror dove beneath the ocean waves, and Thetis took him to her bosom, frightened, with strong shivers upon him at the man's threatening shouts."[34] An armed man bursts into a Dionysiac sacrifice prepared by the women who protect and care for the frenzied god. He pursues them to the sea, swinging the axe as one would to kill a cow—later versions depict him pursuing the frenzied god, himself in a frenzy, and, in this state, cutting down his own children with the axe: a victim for a victim. In the logic of the story, Lykurgus is Dionysus' enemy, and Diomedes tells the tale in the *Iliad* to warn of the dangers when men try to fight with gods.

The myth of Lykurgus has often been interpreted as testifying to the resistance met by the expanding cult of Dionysus,[35] but when related, as it surely must be, to the Agrionia ritual at Orchomenos and the myth of Melampus, we find that Lykurgus actually occupies the position of the priest of Dionysus. Thus, it is not an historical conflict that is attested here, but the polar tension between divine madness and human order as acted out in a single ritual. The antagonists are linked to one another by serving the same god,[36] or at least at the same festival, the different stages of which could be named after antithetical gods. The Minyads, who had struggled against Dionysus, became his priestesses, performing the dreadful sacrifice in his honor. Those, in turn, who chased the Minyads away were Dionysian maenads. Pentheus, the enemy of the new god, is himself made to take on the appearance of Dionysus,[37] only to be torn to pieces by the raving Bakchai. In one version of the myth, Lykurgus too is torn to

---

[34] *Il.* 6.130–40; Eumelos *Europia* fr. 10 Kinkel = Schol. A *Il.* 6.131; thereafter the *Lykurgia* by Aeschylus, fr. 69–100 Mette; Soph. *Ant.* 955–65; Hyg. *Fab.* 242, 132; Apollod. 3.34–35; hymn to Dionysus in Page, *Literary Papyri* (1941), 520–25 = fr. 56 Heitsch, *Die griech. Dichterfragmente der röm. Kaiserzeit* (1963); *PR* I 688. For vase-paintings see Brommer (1960) 355; for mosaics see P. Bruneau and C. Vatin, *BCH* 90 (1966), 391–427; for a new mosaic from Trikka, see *BCH* 92 (1968), 867–88. It was disputed whether *βουπλήξ* *Il.* 6.135 was an axe (Leonidas *Anth. Pal.* 9.352) or a whip: see Schol. T.

[35] Wilamowitz (1932) 65f.; Nilsson I (1955) 565, 611–12; Harrison (1922) 369; Rohde (1898) II 39–43 interprets the myths of the Proitids and the Minyads in this way, but wants to leave out Lykurgus (40.2). Besides this, it was fashionable to interpret the myth in terms of nature, with Lykurgus representing winter (*PR* I 687–88) or the heat of summer (Rapp, *RML* II 2203) in opposition to the vegetation spirit.

[36] See W. F. Otto (1933) 100 on the sacrifice at Tenedos (III.4.n.20 below): "Der Sinn des Mythos ist, dass der Gott das Furchtbare, das er tut, selbst erleidet."

[37] Eur. *Bacch.* 821–35, and cf. E. R. Dodds, *Euripides Bacchae* (1960²) on 854–55.

bits as a victim for Dionysus. In the ritual, the roles are variable. As Strabo says, some actually identified Lykurgus with Dionysus.[38] And as late as the Roman Empire we still find a Dionysian mosaic with Lykurgus in the middle, striking his daughter with the axe,[39] for this act of violence is also a Dionysian sacrifice.

Dionysus' nurse being pursued with the axe, and the leap into the sea, are the motifs that determine the other Dionysus-myth known to the Homeric epic, the myth of Ino-Leukothea. Formerly the mortal daughter of Cadmus but "now" honored as a goddess in the sea, she saves Odysseus with her veil.[40] The transformation of the king's daughter into a goddess is always linked to the birth of Dionysus in Thebes: Ino took care of the young Dionysus and brought him up. To avenge herself for this, Hera struck Ino and her husband Athamas with madness. The story normally goes on to tell of a double infanticide, through which the family of Athamas was annihilated. Athamas slew his own son, Learchos, "hunting him down like a stag."[41] Ino then fled with her second son, Melikertes—alternately, she killed Melikertes herself in the boiling water of a tripod kettle and fled Athamas' rage with her dead child;[42] in any case, she finally threw herself with her son down a steep cliff into the sea.

Once again, a child is sacrificed in a moment of madness, with flight and pursuit coming after. The motif of the tripod, the stag comparison, even the names Athamas and Ino establish a close link with the werewolf motif from Lykaon to Phrixos.[43] "Wolf's madness," λύσσα, is at work here, as it was with Lykurgus. And as with him, Athamas wields the double axe in his pursuit. Moreover, as before, the nurse and child leap into the sea.

There can be no doubt that there is cultic action underlying the

---

[38] Strabo 10 p. 471; Arabia: Nonnus 21.160 f. For dedications ϑεῷ Λύ]κούργῳ see D. Sourdel, *Les cultes d'Hauran à l'époque romaine* (1952), 81–88; for an altar of Λυ]κοῦργος from Cotiaeum (Phrygia) see *Journal of Roman Studies* 15 (1925), 163–64, pl. 22.

[39] Cuicul (Algeria), in Nilsson (1957) 114.

[40] *Od.* 5.333–35; Alkman 50b Page; Eur. *Med.* 1282–89 with Schol. Hyg. *Fab.* 2; Ov. *Met.* 4.539–42; Apollod. 3.28; *PR* I 601–605; Schirmer, *RML* II 2011–17; Eitrem, *RE* XII (1925) 2293–2306.

[41] Ὡς ἔλαφον ϑηρεύσας Apollod. 3.28, and cf. Schol. *Od.* 5.334; Schol. Luk. p. 266.13; Ov. *Fast.* 6.481–98; Serv. *Aen.* 5.241; vase-paintings, *AK* 23 (1980), 33–43.

[42] Apollod. 3.28, and cf. Eur. *Med.* 1284–89; Schol. Pind. III p. 192.8, 194.22 Drachmann. A peculiar dedication is that of one Menneas ϑεᾷ Λευκοϑέᾳ Σεγείρων with reference to his great-grandfather, τοῦ ἀποϑεωϑέντος ἐν τῷ λέβητι, δι' οὗ αἱ ὁρταὶ ἄγωνται *OGI* 611: the lebes, as a funerary urn, signifies both death and deification.

[43] See II.1–4 above.

myth of Leukothea. Leukothea was a goddess worshipped in many temples,[44] but precisely because her cult was so widespread, stretching far beyond the Greek world, its contours are indistinct. It is hard to say for which local cult the most common version of the myth was intended. (Of the return of Melikertes-Palaimon at the Isthmian sanctuary, more later.)[45] Xenophanes mentions what seemed to him a strange combination of sacrifice and mourning in the Elean cult of Leukothea,[46] which was perhaps taken over from Phocaea. He mocks this paradoxical combination, although in its tension between killing and surviving it is the direct successor to the hunter's comedy of innocence. On Delos we find the sanctuary of Leukothea combined with phallagogy.[47] Above all, Megara laid claim to Leukothea: Ino's corpse was said to have been found and buried there, and that was where she first received her divine name, Leukothea.[48] The rocks from which she leapt were pointed out not far away. Moreover, there was a "white plain" through which Athamas had pursued her.[49] From the standpoint of the story, setting the pursuit within a fixed area is paradoxical, but it makes sense if we are dealing with a ritual analogous to the Agrionia of Orchomenos, where the release of aggression is kept within set bounds. The pursuit across the "white plain," projected into the cult of the "white goddess," provides the link to the daughters of Proitos, to Leukippe—perhaps indeed to the Skira.

4. *Tereus and the Nightingale*

The abomination of a mother killing her own child, projected into the bird world, as with the Minyads, is the subject of the myth of the

---

[44]See Eitrem, *RE* XII 2293–2306. Nilsson does not discuss Leukothea, even though *cuncta Graecia* (Cic. *Nat. deor.* 3.39) worshipped her.

[45]See III.7.

[46]*VS* 21 A 13 = Arist. *Rhet.* 1400b6.

[47]See I.7.n.54 above.

[48]Paus. 1.42.7; Zenob. Par. 4.38. *Μολουρὶς πέτρα* Paus. 1.44.7–8; Schol. Pind. III p. 194.9 Drachmann; Schol. Lyk. 229.

[49]*Λευκὸν πεδίον* Schol. *Od.* 5.334; Eust. 1543.26; Nonnus 10.76; *Et. M.* 561.44; Steph. Byz. *Γεράνεια*; probably = *Καλῆς δρόμος* Plut. *Q. conv.* 675e.

nightingale, which, like those of Lykurgus and Leukothea, already appears in the Homeric epic. The nightingale mourns incessantly for Itylos or Itys, the son whom she killed with her own hands. Nightingale poems have appeared in an unbroken stream from Homer up until modern literature. And since they have in large part shaped our conceptions, no one has had any difficulty imagining that "the beautiful but sad song of the nightingale" "could stir one to thoughts of the bird's heavy guilt and deep sorrow."[1] Nonetheless, it requires only a little objectivity to realize what a misunderstanding, indeed, what a perverse supposition this is on the part of the human fantasy with respect to the song of the bird. This conception was not drawn from the reality of nature, but from the human tradition of horror in a nocturnal ritual.

In the *Odyssey*, Penelope turns to the myth of the nightingale as the primordial image of mourning: "As when Pandareos' daughter, the greenwood nightingale, perching in the deep of the forest foliage, sings out her lovely song, when springtime has just begun; she varying the manifold strains of her voice, pours out the melody, mourning Itylos, son of the lord Zethos, her own beloved child, whom she once killed with the bronze when the madness was on her."[2] Pherekydes supplements the story, expanding it to include Zethos' brother Amphion of Thebes and his wife Niobe.[3] Seething jealousy over Niobe's greater number of children drove Aedon, the wife of Zethos, to murder. One night she took up a weapon to kill one of her nephews, but in the dark she struck her own and only child. Her flight after the deed and her transformation into a bird was presupposed in her name, Aedon, "nightingale."

The form of the myth that joins the swallow to the nightingale is yet richer in characters and relationships. It became the canonical version at Athens, though it had already been part of a work ascribed to Hesiod,[4] presumably the *Ornithomantia*. As early as the seventh century B.C., the metopes in the temple at Thermos depicted Aedon and Chelidon with the child, Itylos, between them.[5] Hesiod and Sappho knew the swallow as the daughter of Pandion,[6] and "many poets" called the nightingale Daulias, as Thucydides attests.[7] In his *Tereus*,

---

[1]Roscher, *RML* I 85, and cf. ibid. II 569–73; Höfer, *RML* III 2344–48, V 371–76; *PR* II 154–62; Sophocles, *Fragments*, ed. A.C. Pearson II (1917), 221–38; for vase-paintings see Brommer (1960) 372, esp. *ARV*[2] 456.10.

[2]*Od.* 19.518–23; translation by R. Lattimore. [3]*FGrHist* 3 F 124.

[4]Fr. 312 M.-W. = Ael. *VH* 12.20. [5]Schefold (1964) 33–34, T.20.

[6]Hes. *Erga* 568; Sappho 135 LP. [7]Thuc. 2.29.

which influenced most of the later sources, Sophocles probably did not introduce many innovations.[8] Tereus, king of Daulis and a Thracian by birth, was the son-in-law of Pandion, king of Attica, having married his daughter Procne. The fateful tale begins with a maiden's tragedy and a king's guilt. Procne's virgin sister, Philomela, came under the power of Tereus, who raped her and cut out her tongue so that his deed would remain secret. He imprisoned her on an isolated farm.[9] There Philomela wove a peplos in which she depicted the story of her sufferings. When she was finished, the peplos was brought to the queen. In this way Procne learned of the crime, which led to an uprising of all women and a reunion of the wife and the dishonored maiden. Their victim, however, was not the father, but the son. Itys—his usual name in this version—was torn to pieces, partially boiled, partially roasted, and set before his father for supper. When Tereus afterward discovered what had been done to him, he grabbed a double axe and pursued the dreadful sisters—at this moment, the story shifts to the bird realm: Procne becomes the sorrowing nightingale, Philomela the swallow which, because of its maimed tongue, can only twitter. Tereus, however, the wielder of the axe, turns into an "epops," the woodpecker-like bird that can split wood[10] and which is usually somewhat incorrectly translated as the "hoopoe."

It is patent that flight and pursuit are being staged here, as in the Agrionia ritual. And in fact, the myth is rooted in the Dionysian realm: Ovid describes how the women's nocturnal rising occurs on the pretext of being a festival of Dionysus. Procne comes to Philomela as a maenad.[11] The horrible meal corresponds to a Dionysian sacrifice in the detail that the meat is "partially roasted, partially boiled."[12] This is just what the Titans did to the child Dionysus after they had killed him. Thus, among Dionysiac-Orphic initiates it is forbidden to

[8] Fr. 581–95 Pearson. Cf. Aesch. *Hik.* 60–68; fr. 609 Mette; Apollod. 3.193–95; Hyg. *Fab.* 45. Among the Romans (Philokles? see Radke, *RE* XXIII 249–50), Philomela turns into the nightingale. A peculiar version of the Aedon myth is found in Ant. Lib. 11, quoted from Boio.

[9] Ἐπὶ τῶν χωρίων Apollod. 3.194; ἵδρυσεν ἐν κώμῃ φυλακήν τινα παρακαταστήσας Liban. *Narr.* 18 (VIII 45 Foerster); *stabula* Ov. *Met.* 6.521, 573, 596.

[10] D'Arcy Thompson, *Glossary of Greek Birds* (1936²), 95–100.

[11] Ov. *Met.* 6.587–605. The Dionysian element is certainly there already in Sophocles; cf. Acc. trag. 642. L. Koenen, in *Studien zur Textgeschichte und Textkritik* (*Festschr. G. Jachmann* [1959], 83–87), accordingly conjectures ὄρνις ἐγένετ' ἐκ τῶν ὀργίων Aristoph. *Av.* 16.

[12] Ov. *Met.* 6.645–46 calls it a "sacrifice according to ancestral custom" (648); see II.1.n.29 above.

"roast that which has been boiled." The same motif accompanied the unspeakable sacrifices of Lykaon, Thyestes, and Harpagos.

Precisely because of the myth's wide circulation, it is difficult to localize the corresponding rituals. Pandareos belongs in Miletus, Zethos in Thebes, Pandion in Athens, and Tereus in Daulis. But the tradition clings to this last place with particular doggedness. This was where the gruesome meal took place, Pausanias assures us,[13] and his reference to the ornithological miracle that swallows do not nest at Daulis indicates local tradition. When he adds that this meal "started the defilement of the table among men," he raises the Daulian meal to the status of a primordial crime, to the very first meal of meat. This thus competes with the myth of the Attic Buphonia, of Lykaon and Tantalos, of the killing of Argos as the first murder, and probably reflects a local Daulian claim. Further, Pausanias mentions[14] a sanctuary of Athena at Daulis where the most ancient cultic image had been brought by Procne from Athens. Procne, the queen, thus appears as a priestess of Athena at Daulis, just as queen Praxithea had in Athens. Philomela's work on the peplos belongs to the realm of Athena Ergane, to whom the Minyads had likewise been so exclusively dedicated. The Arrhephoroi worked on a peplos as well, and the end of their duties in the encounter with the snake of the Acropolis corresponds to Philomela's fall.

Through his connection with the family of king Pandion, Tereus is also linked to Athens.[15] Admittedly, virtually nothing is known of the Attic festival, the Pandia, except that it followed close on the heels of the Great Dionysia.[16] This could just be coincidence, especially as there is a sacrifice to "Epops" attested for the fifth day of Boedromion, in the fall.[17] There is an even closer connection of the cult of Pandion and Tereus with Megara, about which Pausanias provides us with a few details. There was a memorial to Pandion at Megara,[18] and he was

---

[13] 10.4.8; cf. Strabo 9 p. 423; *Et. M.* 250.1; Steph. Byz. Δαῦλις; Apollod. 3.195. On the other hand, δαῦλον is explained as a "thicket" (Paus. 10.4.7). Hsch. Δαῦλις· ἑορτὴ ἐν Ἄργει, μίμημα τῆς Προίτου πρὸς Ἀκρίσιον μάχης indicates a sacrifice with mock combat.

[14] 10.4.9.

[15] There was a statue of Procne with Itys by Alkamenes on the Acropolis: Paus. 1.24.3; G. P. Stevens, *Hesperia* 15 (1946), 10–11.

[16] Phot. Πάνδια; Deubner (1932) 176.

[17] In the sacrificial calendar of Erchia, *LS* 18 Δ 20, E 12.

[18] Paus. 1.5.3, 39.4, 41.6 at the cliff of Athena Aithyia, who in the shape of a waterfowl carried an Attic king under her wings to Megara (Hsch. Ἐν δ'Αἴθυια). Cf. I.7.n.54 above; III.6.n.8 below.

the object of a cult there. The grave of Tereus was likewise located there, and it was connected with an especially odd sacrifical ceremony: "every year they offer him a sacrifice using pebbles instead of barley-grains."[19] We are ignorant as to how, and on what sort of sacrificial animal, these pebbles were thrown, but this much is clear: although rendered harmless, this is a symbolic stoning ceremony, showing that guilt was incurred and pardoned. In just this way, by symbolically stoning Hermes, the gods extricated themselves from any guilt for the killing of Argos. In Megara, too, Tereus is linked to an unspeakable sacrifice that appears in the myth as the primordial guilt that established killing and the eating of meat among men.

At Tenedos, a newborn calf was sacrificed to Dionysus Anthroporrhaistes, the man-destroyer, after cothurnoi were put on its feet, apparently in order to identify it as closely as possible with the god of tragedy. The sacred double axe was used to slaughter it. The sacrificer, however, then fled to the sea, pursued by the participants, who hurled stones at him, thus purifying themselves of guilt.[20] For Plutarch, Dionysus Omestes is identical with Dionysus Agrionios.[21] The circle of comparable rituals thus comes to a close.

According to the myth, Tereus was a Thracian. But the names become transparent from the perspective of Greek: Epops, the "overseer," is certainly the name of a bird, but it cannot be set apart from such similar forms as Epopetes and Epopeus. All these names appear as epithets of Zeus[22] and indicate an "overseeing" universal god or sky god. At Erchia, sacrifices were made to Zeus Epopetes in exactly the same way that they were to the Epops. Thus, from the standpoint of the name, Tereus the Epops becomes the exact equivalent of Argos Panoptes. Even the name *Tereus* begins to sound so Greek that it could be taken for a translation or paraphrase of Epops. He is the "watcher," guarding Philomela as Argos did with Io. He is the custodian of power who, like Argos, is nonetheless destined to fall victim to an uprising, a dissolution. Does the name *Philomela* point to an in-

---

[19] Paus. 1.48.8–9, and cf. I.1.n.16 above. Strabo 9 p. 423 knows of a Megarian Tereus tradition, which he incorrectly ascribes to Thucydides (2.29).

[20] Ael. *Nat. an.* 12.34; Nilsson (1906) 308–309; (1955) 156; Cook I (1914) 659; II (1924) 654–73. Euelpis of Karystos spoke of human sacrifice at Tenedos: Porph. *Abst.* 2.55.

[21] Plut. *Anton.* 24.5.

[22] Hsch. Ἐπόπτης· Ζεύς, and cf. Stesichorus 280 Page; Hsch. Ἐπόψιος· Ζεὺς καὶ Ἀπόλλων and cf. Hom. *Hy. Ap.* 496; cf. Callim. *Hy.* 1.82; Apoll. Rhod. 2.1123; for sacrifice Διὶ Ἐπωπετεῖ see *LS* 18 Γ 20; Hsch. Ἐπωπετής· Ζεὺς παρὰ Ἀθηναίοις. Cf. *PR* I 117.2. Hsch. ἔποψ· ἐπόπτης . . . On Τηρεύς–τηρεῖν see Schol. Aristoph. *Av.* 102; *Et. M.* 757.45, and cf. ἐπόπτας καὶ τηρητάς *Et. M.* 65.44.

troductory sheep-sacrifice, just as a preliminary sheep-sacrifice was linked to Pandrosus, the daughter of Cecrops?[23] There can be no peplos without wool. And *Itylos*, this more anciently attested form of the name, was already connected with the Latin *vitulus*, "calf," ἰταλός, "bull," the word that gave Italy its name. The boy's name would then be an indication of the animal used in the unspeakable sacrifice, the bull-calf. Admittedly, if this is so, we cannot clear up the question of which non-Greek language forms the background for the myth.[24]

We have seen how the rituals of the Agrionia correspond to the rhythms of the New Year's festival in the cities of Athens and Argos. In the myth of Proitos' daughters, as in that of the nightingale, the Dionysian element is present only in the later versions. Here we can probably grasp the growth of the cult of Dionysus starting in the seventh century B.C., which followed in the footsteps of the old ritual. We now find the private group, the familial order, rather than the community as a whole, coming to the fore, just as we saw the bull-calf replace the bull; private groups could also more easily afford a smaller victim. Although the festivals of the polis seem older, this does not exclude the possibility that cultic societies revived the clan traditions of the pre-polis era.

What sets Dionysus apart, even in a predetermined framework, is the "frenzy," the individual experience of ecstasy—which, of course, is not clearly distinguished from drunkenness. It occurred in the sacrificial ritual, during the transitional period when the normal order was inverted and there were wild outbursts. The god here desires the rupturing of the establishment: it is his epiphany.[25] It is still linked with sacrifice, but this appears as an initial step to ignite the frenzy which is then experienced for its own sake.

In the private sphere, marriage is the principal order that is overturned. This is repeatedly stressed in the myths. Out of loyalty to their husbands, the Minyads refused to follow the horde of mae-

---

[23] Harpokr. ἐπίβοιον = Philochoros, *FGrHist* 328 F 10.

[24] The gloss ἰταλός, οὐίτουλος was known to the Greeks at least since Hellanikos (*FGrHist* 4 F 111). Timaios said that the word was Greek (*FGrHist* 566 F 42), others that it was Etruscan (M. Pallottino, *Testimonia linguae Etruscae* [1954], #839); cf. M. Leumann, *Glotta* 27 (1938), 90. The version in Ant. Lib. 11 suggests Lycia, whereas there may be a Phrygian variant in the βέκκος story (Schol. Aristid. III 361.13 Dind.; Egyptianized Hdt. 2.2), inasmuch as the mute nurse at the isolated farm recalls Philomela.

[25] D. Sabbatucci, *Saggio sul misticismo greco* (1965), 55–68, also brings out the distinction between possession that is perceived as an illness and "mystical" possession that is perceived as salvation. The identification of Orphic with "mystic" (65) is, however, questionable.

nads.[26] Aedon, the nightingale, incurred the wrath of Hera in boasting that her marriage was happier than that of the queen of the gods.[27] Whenever the human order is considered so stable, it will all the more certainly be broken by a higher power and changed into its opposite. Dionysus provides the antithesis to the family: whereas a wife must tend the house, the maenads roam the wilderness; whereas a wife is modestly dressed, the Dionysiac mob raves in wild, lascivious, shameless nudity; whereas a wife must work, especially at the loom, Dionysus scares women and girls "away from the looms and the spindle"; whereas a wife must love her husband and provide for her children, in the night of the Agrionia the mother kills her child to wound her husband. Hate and murder, instead of affectionate union, rule the night, which reveals what the day suppresses and hides. In precisely this way, the frenzied outburst leads to a purification. "Madness delivers him who was maddened aright and possessed from his troubles."[28] If Hera and Dionysus become antagonists, they are nonetheless mutually determinant. The maiden's tragedy becomes an initiation, a preparation for marriage. The battle between men and women at the Dionysia on Chios ended in a marriage which, according to the legend, produced the most famous of all Chians, Homer.[29] The festival room at the Villa dei Misteri at Pompei was adjacent to the matrimonial bedroom.[30]

5. *Antiope and Epopeus*

At Sikyon, the mythical king Epopeus, whose name so clearly recalls that of Epops and Zeus Epopetes, was worshipped as a hero. His grave was in the sacred precinct of Athena, beside the goddess's al-

---

[26] Ael. *VH* 3.42. Priests of Dionysus and Hera were not allowed to speak with each other at Athens: see Plut. fr. 157 Sandbach, and cf. *Q. Rom.* 291a.

[27] Ant. Lib. 11.3.

[28] Plat. *Phdr.* 244e.

[29] Seleukos in Harpokr. *Ὁμηρίδαι* (missing in Nilsson [1906] 306): . . . *αἱ γυναῖκές ποτε τῶν Χίων ἐν Διονυσίοις παραφρονήσασαι εἰς μάχην ἦλθον τοῖς ἀνδράσι, καὶ δόντες ἀλλήλοις ὅμηρα νυμφίους καὶ νύμφας ἐπαύσαντο.*

[30] On the Bacchic rites of the Villa as an initiation into *matrona* status see O. Brendel, *JdI* 81 (1966), 206–60, esp. 258–60. The Corinthian saga of Medea, which belonged to a

tar.[1] The combination of the goddess's cult and the grave of the hero is reminiscent of the relationship of Attic Athena to Erechtheus. The ancestral king who was killed stands beside the victorious Olympian goddess, as the act of propitiating the dead is juxtaposed to the Olympian fire-sacrifice. Erechtheus is largely identical with Poseidon. In the myth, however, Epopeus of Sikyon is virtually the double of Zeus, thus confirming the unity of the series: Epops, Epopsios, Epopetes, Epopeus.[2]

In the common version, however, Sikyon is linked to Boeotia through the marriage of Epopeus and Antiope, a king's daughter from Boeotian Hyria, whose sons, Zethos and Amphion, built the walls of Thebes.[3] Whether this indicates an historical connection between Hyria-Thebes and Sikyon or whether epic singers combined these stories and names according to their own fantasies is impossible to say. In our oldest sources, the connection between Boeotia and Sikyon is not present. Thus, in the catalogue of women in the Odyssean *Nekyia*,[4] Antiope is the daughter of Asopos, wife of Zeus and mother of Zethos and Amphion, in a purely Boeotian setting. A digression in the *Cypria*[5] tells how "Epopeus lost his city in war because he had seduced the daughter of Lykos." The fragment does not even mention the daughter's name. In the Hesiodic *Catalogues*, by contrast, Antiope was the subject of her own *Ehoie*, which, along with the play by Euripides, presumably determined Apollodorus' summary.[6] Here, Boeotian and Sikyonian elements are linked, as is assumed by the sixth-century poet Asios.[7] There Antiope, daughter of Asopos, bore Zethos and Amphion, "pregant both by Zeus and Epopeus, the peo-

festival of Hera Akraia, also depicted a woman's revolt, with the killing of a virgin, regicide, infanticide and finally the woman's flight: see Burkert (1966) 117–19, and cf. III.1.n.78.

[1] Paus. 2.11.1, 6.3. Cf. P. Odelberg, *Sacra Corinthia Sicyonia Phliasia* (Uppsala, 1896), 185; H. Skalet, *Ancient Sikyon* (1928), 173.

[2] See III.4.n.22 above.

[3] *PR* II 114–19; Cook I (1914) 734–39.

[4] *Od.* 11.260–65. The two versions of the founding of Thebes—Zethos and Amphion on the one hand, Cadmus on the other—were reconciled in different ways: see Pherekydes, *FGrHist* 3 F 41; Apollod. 3.40; F. Vian, *Les origines de Thèbes* (1963), 69–75.

[5] Prokl. *Chrest.* p. 103.20 Allen.

[6] Hes. fr. 181–82; Eur. *Antiope*; H. v. Arnim, *Supplementum Euripideum* (1913), 9–22; Apollod. 3.41–44, and cf. Hyg. *Fab.* 8; Schol. Apoll. Rhod. 4.1090. The Paestan calyx-crater, Berlin F 3296, *RML* II 2186, Trendall (1967) 203, was inspired by Euripides. For Hellenistic relief cups see U. Hausmann, *AM* 73 (1958), 50–72.

[7] Fr. 1 Kinkel = Paus. 2.6.4.

ple's shepherd." Euripides is the first source in which the Dionysiac atmosphere plays a part in the myth of Antiope, and it was perhaps invented by him in honor of the god of tragedy.

In spite of the story's complex layers, the familiar basic structure is preserved intact. At the start is the maiden's tragedy: Antiope loses her virginity in Zeus' arms and then marries Epopeus of Sikyon. In the Dionysian version, Zeus himself appears on Mount Kithairon in the shape of a satyr.[8] The realistic epic has Epopeus, unattended by any divine double, as the seducer. Whether seducer or savior, the male partner who seizes the maiden thereby seals his own fate. Antiope's relative—either the father Lykurgos, the father Nykteus, or the uncle Lykos[9]—marches against Sikyon and conquers it. Epopeus falls, and Antiope falls into the hands of the "wolvish" powers. She secretly gives birth to twins and exposes them. All that is left for her is slavery, dishonor, and abuse. At this stage in the story her life is governed by a witchlike stepmother, Dirke, the queen, who in the Dionysian interpretation is seen as an initiated maenad[10] whose duty it is to lead the young, uninitiated woman through a course of sufferings to a final goal. Antiope's passion ends with a dramatic inversion of roles: just as Dirke tries to kill her with a wild bull, Zethos and Amphion, now grown into youths, storm the farm. Now Dirke in turn is chained to the bull and dragged to her death. Lykos then abdicates and, with the kingship now falling to them, the twins take power and build the walls of Thebes.[11]

Whereas in the Agrionia myths the maidens and women banded together to rise up against the men—Proitos' daughters with the women of Argos, Philomela with Procne—here, the wild women, with Dirke as their leader, direct their aggression toward a young girl, a slave. Similar things occurred in ritual. A slave would be led by women into the shrine of Mater Matuta; they would "box her ears and beat her with rods."[12] A beating with a rod is depicted in the Villa dei Misteri. In this way a young woman would be introduced into the cir-

[8] Euripides according to Malalas p. 49 ed. Bonn. (*TGF* p.410); Schol. Apoll. Rhod. 4.1090; Ov. *Met.* 6.110. For two mosaics from the Roman Empire see Cook III (1940) 467 pl. 469; rationalized in Kephalion, *FGrHist* 93 F 5.

[9] Antiope's father is called Lykurgos in the *Cypria*, Nykteus in Euripides. The latter makes Lykos the cruel king in the interregnum.

[10] Hyg. *Fab.* 7 *baccha fuerat*; 8: Dirke comes *per bacchationem* to Antiope's refuge (according to Euripides); Paus. 9.17.6.

[11] For the closing scene of the Euripidean drama see *PPetr.* 1 = p. 21 von Arnim, and cf. n. 6 above.

[12] Plut. *Q. Rom.* 267d. On the Villa dei Misteri see III.4.n. 30 above.

cle of matrons. In the myth of Antiope, this abuse, which can also be an initiation, occurs at an exceptional time. Nykteus and Lykos, "the nocturnal one" and "the wolf," are in power, but in the time of the wolf, the woman Dirke is likewise active and dangerous. Her end, the end of the reign of women or witches, leads to the foundation of the city and reestablishment of the daytime ruler. The sons of Zeus are called "those of the white horses," Λευκοπώλω.[13] Opposed to them is the bull, as the agent of the last sacrifice in the intermediate period. The transition to the new stage is marked once more in the opposition of bull and horse.

A passing remark by the Boeotian Plutarch gives us some insight into just how closely the myth of the young, warlike riders taking power corresponds to the military organization of the polis of Thebes. The grave of Dirke is, he reports, "unknown to any Theban who has not served as hipparch. For the retiring hipparch takes his successor alone and shows him the grave at night; and after performing certain sacrifices there in which no fire is used, they cover up and obliterate all trace of them and return their separate ways in the dark."[14] A secret sacrifice at the secret grave of Dirke is the act through which the old hipparch hands on his office to the new. What had been covered up must be exposed; there must be bloodshed; an animal is torn to pieces and buried. This nocturnal killing repeats the violent act by means of which "those of the white horses" seized power.

Nothing else is known of the rites of this period of transition, except perhaps for a remnant transformed into magic. Pausanias mentions the grave of Amphion and Zethos before Thebes—a not particularly large burial mound surrounded by stones that have barely been worked.[15] At the beginning of summer, when the sun was in the constellation of Taurus, the men of Tithorea would try to steal earth from the mound. During that time, the Thebans stood guard there in order to prevent this from happening, for it was said that this earth would bring fertility to either Tithorea or Thebes. Thus, two groups were at odds, the alien Tithoreans and the native Thebans, robbers and guards, almost certainly at night, at the grave of the mythical riders

---

[13] Τὼ Λευκοπώλω Eur. *HF* 29; *Phoen.* 606; Hsch. Διὸς κοῦροι. Λευκὼ πώλω Eur. *Antiope; PPetr.* 1.71, p. 22 v. Arnim.

[14] *Gen. Socr.* 578b. The method for covering up the traces of a sacrifice is described in *Hy. Merc.* 140. Oedipus' tomb at Kolonos Hippios at Athens was known only to Theseus and his followers (Soph. *OC* 1518–32), and that of Sisyphus at the Isthmus was also secret (see III.7.n.39 below).

[15] 9.17.4–7, and cf. J. G. Frazer, *Pausanias* V (1898), 57; Cook I (1914) 736.

before the city, in the sign of the bull. This can hardly be unrelated to that other solitary nocturnal rite, the hipparch's inauguration at the tomb of Dirke, who was killed by Amphion and Zethos. So, too, in all likelihood, at Lemnos digging up earth with curative powers was part of a festival of renewal.[16] At Athens, the Skirophoria seems to have involved "carrying white earth." None of these associations, however, can be conclusively proven.

The cultic situation at Sikyon is perhaps clearer. Epopeus dedicated the temple of Athena, which "surpassed all other temples of the time in size and ornamentation,"[17] with a victory sacrifice. The valiant Sikyonians saw a reflection of themselves in the image of the armed goddess. But next to Athena's altar is the tomb of the founder, Epopeus, and close at hand the "gods who ward off," the *ϑεοὶ ἀποτρόπαιοι*, were worshipped. "In front of them, they perform the rites that are thought among the Greeks to ward off evil,"[18] gloomy sacrifices, apparently, expressing vexation and anxiety. Danger and death were signalled beside victory and immortality. The cult would have performed its function of renewing life and vital energies by stressing the sequence from the king's death and warding off of evil to the triumphal sacrifice for Athena. The analogy with Athens, with the festivals involving Erechtheus and Athena Polias, bears up under analysis. Whereas at Athens the myth split up a single figure into Erechtheus, the dead king, and Erichthonius, the founder of the Panathenaia, the Sikyonian story is somewhat more complex, accommodating both stages in the life of Epopeus: first he was mortally wounded, then he celebrated his triumph and died of his wound thereafter.[19] Epopeus could be at once the victim and the founder of the cult.

There was a statue of Antiope at Sikyon in the temple of Aphrodite,[20] a temple so important that in the Classical era a chryselephantine statue of the goddess was made for it. Only one priestess, an elderly woman, was allowed to enter the temple itself, with a maiden chosen annually and given the title of *Lutrophoros*. This recalls the cult of Zeus Sosipolis at Olympia,[21] and perhaps the statue of Antiope

---

[16] Burkert (1970) 10; III.6.nn.21, 22 below; III.1.n.44 above.

[17] Paus. 2.11.1. For a Sikyonian coin of Athena see Imhoof-Blumer (1885) 31.

[18] Paus. 2.11.1.

[19] Paus. 2.6.3. Sikyon is the son of Erechtheus in Hes. fr. 224, but he is the nephew of Epopeus in another genealogy (Paus. 2.6.5).

[20] Paus. 2.10.4.

[21] See II.2.n.49 above.

is an indication that there was a similar polarity at Sikyon between Antiope/Aphrodite and Epopeus/Athena, i.e., the feminine realm against the masculine. The sacrifices of the men, establishing the order of the warlike goddess, obviously could not exist without the power of Aphrodite constantly creating new life. The end of the virgin's duties, the advent of an exceptional period, the death of the king: these were the conditions for the younger generation's accession to power.

6. *The Lemnian Women*

Just as, in the figure of Leukothea and in the name Skira, the festivals and myths of dissolution pointed beyond the borders of Greece, so the most famous myth of a female uprising takes us back to a city in which the pre-Greek population and culture remained independent until the sixth century B.C. and continued even longer in the cult, that is, in Hephaestia on Lemnos, the city of Hephaestus and the Cabiri. The Greeks called the inhabitants *Tyrsenoi*. They spoke and wrote an unknown language, presumably of the Anatolian type. Even their defeat at the hands of Miltiades and the colonization by Attic kleruchs was not sufficient to break all continuity.[1]

"Of all legendary evils, that of Lemnos comes first": so sang the chorus of *Choephoroi* in Aeschylus.[2] But the story of the man-killing Lemnian women had long been known through the legend of the Argonauts. It starts in the typical way, with adultery. This time, how-

---

[1]On the history of Lemnos see C. Fredrich, *AM* 31 (1906), 60–86, 241–55; F. L. W. Sealey, *BSA* 23 (1918/19), 148–74; C. Fredrich, *IG* XII 8 pp. 2–6; *RE* XII 1928–30. The Italian excavations brought to light important new information: see the preliminary report in *ASAA* 15/16 (1932/33), but they were interrupted in 1939; cf. *EAA* III 230–31, IV 542–45. On the Athenian conquest see Hdt. 6.137–40; cf. Philochoros, *FGrHist* 328 f 100/101.

[2]*Cho.* 631; cf. *PR* II 849–59. On reconstructing the ancient Argonaut myth see P. Friedlaender, *RhM* 69 (1914), 299–317 = *Studien zur antiken Literatur und Kunst* (1969), 19–34; K. Meuli, *Odyssee und Argonautika* (1921); U. v. Wilamowitz-Moellendorff, *Hellenistische Dichtung* II (1924), 232–48. For the myth as related to the festival see F. G. Welcker, *Die aeschylische Trilogie Prometheus und die Kabirenweihe zu Lemnos* (1824), 155–304; G. Dumézil, *Le crime des Lemniennes* (1924); Burkert (1970).

ever, the entire male population is implicated. The wrath of Aphrodite—here taking the place of Hera, the goddess of marriage—falls upon the women, who develop a sickening body odor that drives away the men.[3] They, in turn, take up with Thracian slave-girls, unaffected by the goddess's anger. The women then form a conspiracy that erupts in a nocturnal uprising. In a single bloody night they murder the entire male population of the island, not just the husbands but fathers and sons as well,[4] an act more radical than Procne's. The island henceforth belongs to the women, who govern it like Amazons. Yet, this can only be a transition, an intermediary period.

Only one man has a special fate, the one who actually represents the patriarchal society, king Thoas. He is saved by his daughter Hypsipyle, who hides him in a wooden, coffinlike chest (λάρναξ), which Hypsipyle—alone, or with the aid of those trying to discover her secret—pushes into the sea.[5] Valerius Flaccus fills in the detail that the king was first hidden in the temple of Dionysus, beneath the god's robes, and then led to the sea, in the mask of the god, by the Bakchai under Hypsipyle's guidance.[6] It is impossible to say how much of this reflects the more ancient local tradition, but as early as Euripides, Thoas is intimately linked to Dionysus—indeed, he is the god's son.[7] Curiously, the death of Osiris is told in precisely the same way: Seth locks him up in a larnax and the Nile carries him out to sea.[8] By the fifth century B.C., the Greeks considered Osiris and Dionysus identical. Things both sacred and evil disappear mysteriously in the vast reaches of the sea.

As the king disappeared at sea, so from the sea new life returned

---

[3]Kaukalos? *FGrHist* 38.2; Apollod. 1.114; Schol. Apoll. Rhod. 1.609 (Apollonios himself is silent concerning the δυσωδία); Schol. Eur. *Hec.* 887; Zenob. Ath. 1.19 p. 351 Miller; Eust. 158.17; Dio. Chrys. *Or.* 33.50; see at n. 14 below.

[4]Πᾶν ἄρσεν ὁμοῦ γένος Apoll. Rhod. 1.618; "fathers and husbands" Apollod. 1.115; for the most detailed account see Stat. *Theb.* 5.85–334; Val. Flacc. *Arg.* 2.107–427.

[5]Apoll. Rhod. 1.620–26; Theolytos, *FGrHist* 478 F 3, Xenagoras, *FGrHist* 240 F 31, and Kleon of Kurion, Schol. Apoll. Rhod. 1.623/6a; cf. Eur. *Hypsipyle* fr. 64, 74–87, 105–111 Bond (1963); Schol. Pind. III p. 2.8–13 Drachmann. For the λάρναξ on the red figure bowl Berlin 2300 = *ARV*[2] 409.43, see G. M. A. Richter, *The Furniture of the Greeks, Etruscans and Romans* (1966), 385. This is not the place to deal further with the widespread motif of the ark (Danae, Auge, Tennes, Osiris, etc.).

[6]*Arg.* 2.242–302, and cf. Immisch, *RML* V 806.

[7]*Hypsipyle* fr. 64.111, and cf. H. Lloyd-Jones in G. W. Bond, *Euripides Hypsipyle* (1963), 157ff.; *AP* 3.10. For the *Euneidai*, priests of Dionysus Melpomenos, at Athens as descendants of Jason and Hypsipyle see Toepffer (1889) 181–206.

[8]Plut. *Is.* 356c. Osiris = Dionysus in Hdt. 2.42 and probably already in Hekataios.

to Lemnos. One night, the ship of the Argonauts—the primordial ship—on which the most valiant men of Greece were united, appeared on the coasts of Lemnos.[9] Its arrival transformed the would-be Amazons' hatred of men into its opposite. According to Aeschylus, they made the Argonauts, even before landing, swear to help them revive the work of Aphrodite.[10] An agon in honor of the dead was held to test the strength of the living successors. The Lemnian women provided a prize for the winner—a cloak.[11] The attire is linked with marriage or, rather, a disorganized mass celebration of the nuptials, ending *e contrario* the period of hate between the sexes and the lack of men. Already in the *Iliad* we hear of Euneos, lord of the "good ship," son of Jason and Hypsipyle and ruler of Lemnos.[12]

Once again, it is only by a coincidence of locality—and that in late antiquity—that we are informed about a ritual celebrated annually "because of the crime of the Lemnian women against the men," a festival of purification and new fire. The myth gives the aition of the rite and reflects the details of this festival. Philostratus of Lemnos provides us with an eyewitness account—for at Hephaestia, he himself or a close relative was "the priest of Hephaestus, after whom the city is named"—"Lemnos is purified at a certain time in the year and the fire on the island is extinguished for nine days. A sacred ship brings fire from Delos, and if it arrives before the funerary sacrifices are over, it may not be brought to anchor on Lemnos; rather, it rides on the open sea before the promontories, till, according to sacred custom, it is permitted to sail in. For at this time they call upon subterranean and secret gods, and thus, as I think, they keep the fire pure on the sea. But when the sacred ship has sailed in and they have distributed the fire for all other necessities of life and especially for the crafts that need fire, they say that from then on a new life begins for them."[13]

---

[9] Apoll. Rhod. 1.630–52; Stat. *Theb.* 5.335–47.

[10] Fr. 40 Mette, and cf. Pind. *Pyth.* 4.254; Herodoros, *FGrHist* 31 F 6. Thence Λήμνιαι as a title and theme in comedy: Aristoph. fr. 356–75; Nikochares fr. 11–14 (*CAF* I 772); Antiphanes fr. 144–45 (*CAF* II 70), and cf. Alexis fr. 134 (*CAF* II 345); Diphilos fr. 54 (*CAF* II 558); Turpilius 90–99 Ribbeck.

[11] Simonides 547 Page; Pind. *Pyth.* 4.253 with Schol.; cf. Apoll. Rhod. 2.30–32, 3.1204–1206, 4.423–34.

[12] *Il.* 23.747; cf. 21.41, 7.468–69, 14.230; n. 7 above.

[13] *Her.* p. 232 Boissonade (Paris 1806) = p. 325 Kayser (Zürich 1844 = 1853^2) = ed. Teubn. (1871) II 207 = L. de Lannoy, ed. Teubn. (1977) p. 67.7. On the corrupt passage *καὶ καϑ' ἕνα τοῦ ἔτους* against A. Wilhelm (*καϑ' ἐνάτου ἔτους*, *Anz. d. Ak. d. Wiss. Wien* [1939], 41–46), see Burkert (1970) 3: *καιρὸν καϑ' ἕνα τοῦ ἔτους* (?); cf. *καθ' ἕνα καιρόν*

This is one of the clearest, most impressive descriptions of a time of dissolution and exception, in which normal life almost comes to an end: there is no fire, no normal food, no sacrifices to the gods, and no funeral pyre; the bakers and smithies lay down the tools of their trades, and the family breaks apart. The Hellenistic historian Myrsilus of Lesbos claimed that Medea cast a spell on the Lemnian women out of jealousy of Hypsipyle, "and to this very day, there is a certain day every year on which the women keep away from their husbands and sons on account of their sickening smell."[14] The fantastic stench that broke up all the marriages on Lemnos returns regularly every year; the most grotesque feature in the myth becomes reality. This is clearly a ritual that belongs to that exceptional period. We can gather how that sickening smell came about by turning to the parallel of the Attic Skira: there, when the women gathered together they chewed on garlic "in order not to smell of salves."[15] Whatever their Lemnian sisters did to produce the same effect,[16] they too disgusted the men and drove them away, the wives their husbands, the mothers their sons. In the myth this is raised to the level of a man-killing hatred, transforming a day on which the sexes are separated into a transitional period of matriarchy.

This links the Lemnian festival to the Skira; and what the myth of Thoas implies is attested in ritual at Athens—that is, the departure of the king.[17] To be sure, the road to Skiron is less dramatic than the coffinlike chest on Lemnos. We do not know what actually happened at Lemnos, but perhaps the phallagogy at the Delian Dionysia[18] presents another possible way in which a disappearance could be ritually enacted at a Dionysiac sacrificial festival. In any case, sacrifice was clearly a part of the exceptional period at Lemnos, sacrifice without fire, so that one could eat at most only raw pieces of meat, burying the rest or throwing it into the sea. Subterranean powers seem to rise up out of the sacrificial pits into which the blood flows, powers that take

---

Plut. *Is.* 380d (= Manetho, *FGrHist* 609 F 22). Cf. Nilsson (1906) 470–71. For the priest of Hephaestus called Philostratos see *IG* XII 8.27.

[14] *FGrHist* 477 F 1.

[15] Philochoros, *FGrHist* 328 F 89: see III.1.n.42 above.

[16] A marginal gloss in Antig. *Mir.* 118 = Myrsilos, *FGrHist* 477 F 1b mentions πήγανον, an herb whose smell repels snakes (Arist. *Hist. an.* 612a28) and causes sexual abstinence (Schol. Nik. *Alex.* 410); perhaps this herb was used in the Lemnian ritual, just as according to Schol. Nik. *Alex.* 410 it was used in the mysteries.

[17] See III.1.n.35 above.

[18] See I.7.n.54 above.

over the island. A pacing ram is often depicted on the coins of Hephaestia;[19] it may be assumed, then, that sacrifice of a ram formed a part of the city's main festival. Erechtheus, too, is offered a ram.[20]

The act of digging sacred "Lemnian earth," as performed by the priestess of Artemis at Mount Mosychlos, where Hephaestus fell to earth, played a special role in Lemnos. "Lemnian earth," slabs of reddish clay stamped with the picture of a goat, was reputed to have medicinal properties useful for many different ailments, and continued to be so viewed in the Near East until the twentieth century.[21] Galen personally travelled to Lemnos to observe the mining of Lemnian earth.[22] In modern times this took place on the twenty-eighth of August, under the supervision of the local priest. Dioskourides mentions a goat-sacrifice at this occasion,[23] but by the time of Galen the Lemnians no longer had anything to do with such a practice. The connection between the digging at Hephaestus' mountain and the festival of fire in Hephaestus' own city is indisputable. The fact that a priestess of Artemis participates, instead of Hephaestus, indicates the absence of the god, the transitional period in which the subterranean powers are conjured up. Moreover, the festival occurs in August, at virtually the same time as the Attic Skira. Even the name *Skira* denotes a special white earth that is carried.

When the intermediary period ended, the men crowded at the shore to keep watch for the ship bringing back new life, the new, pure fire: thus, Hephaestus returned to his city. So, too, Argo, the primordial ship, brought new life back to the land of women. Above all, it was the fire-using artisans, as Philostratus stresses, the bakers and the smithies, who got a share of the new flame. According to myth, the Cabiri, the children or grandchildren of Hephaestus, were themselves artisans.[24] Their shrine, the Cabirion, has been excavated on Lemnos not far from Hephaestia, and the continuity of cult from the pre-Greek to the Greek era is astounding. A community of initiates

---

[19] Königliche Museen zu Berlin, *Beschreibung der antiken Münzen* (1888), 279–83; *HN*[2] 262–63; Cook III (1940) 233–34; Hemberg (1950) 161, and cf. 102, 284 on Samothrace.

[20] See III.1.n.38 above.

[21] C. Fredrich, *AM* 31 (1906), 72–74; F. W. Hasluck, *BSA* 16 (1909/10), 220–30; Cook III (1940) 228–34.

[22] XII 169–75 Kühn.

[23] 5.113.

[24] Akusilaos, *FGrHist* 2 F 20; Pherekydes, *FGrHist* 3 F 48. For the excavation report see *ASAA* 1/2 (1939/40) 223–24; 3/4 (1941/43), 75–105; 15/16 (1952/54), 317–40; D. Levi in *Charisterion A.K. Orlandos* III (Athens, 1966), 110–32; Hemberg (1950) 160–70.

would gather there for secret celebrations in which wine played a major role. As worshippers of the mythical smithies, they were probably a *Männerbund* which modeled itself on a smithy guild. According to the myth, the Cabiri fled from Lemnos in horror at the women's abominable deed.[25] But if their cult survived, they must have returned when the fire was brought back and the artisans could go back to work. The Dioskouroi were among the Argonauts, and as Great Gods they have been compared to the Cabiri time and again, even to the point of identification.[26] Hephaestus, the Cabiri, the Dioskouroi—and Odysseus—wear the circular peaked cap (πῖλος). The leader of the Argonauts is Jason, whose name can hardly be distinguished from Iasion, the husband of Demeter, and Iasion, the brother of Dardanos on Samothrace.[27] The Argonauts' goal was to retrieve the fleece of a ram mysteriously sacrificed in the land of the sun. Just as the herald who conducts the negotiations between the Argonauts and the Lemnian women is called Aithalides,[28] the "sooty one," so Lemnos, as the island of Hephaestus, is called Aithale. Such are the intimate links between the details of the Argonaut saga and Lemnos. From the standpoint of the cult and the pre-Greek perspective, the Argo is the ship of the Cabiri bringing new fire and new life. According to Pindar, the Lemnian agon was won by the white-haired Erginos, the "worker," at whom the others had laughed.[29] Here, though in Greek guise, is a hint of Hephaestus' victory in his own city to the accompaniment of ritual laughter such as was required by medieval custom at Easter.[30]

In spite of the similarities between the Lemnian festival and the corresponding festivals at Athens, Argos, Thebes, and Sikyon in the rhythm of dissolution and starting anew, there is a characteristic difference. At Lemnos, the masculine order was not reestablished by shield-carriers or white riders—i.e., not by a military organization—but by an artisan society. Perhaps this was why Lemnos fell to the Greeks. Yet there were powers at work in the lower classes—as seen from the perspective of the Greek aristocracy—that found a certain resonance even among the Greeks and played a part in the social cri-

---

[25] Phot. Κάβειροι.

[26] Hemberg (1950) passim; F. Chapoutier, *Les Dioscoures au service d'une déesse* (1935), passim.

[27] Cf. also the Carian city Iasos.

[28] Apoll. Rhod. 1.641–51; Pherekydes, *FGrHist* 3 F 109 = Schol. *ad loc.*; Αἰθαλία Polyb. 34.11.4; Steph. Byz. Αἰθάλη.

[29] *Ol.* 4.19–23; cf. Schol. 32c; Callim. fr. 668.

[30] P. Sartori, *Sitte und Brauch* III (1914), 167. Cf. Mannhardt (1875) 502–508; *GB* X 121–31.

sis and reform of the polis. Besides the ram mentioned above, the coins of Hephaestia display the felt caps of the Cabiri, the herald's staff of Hermes Aithalides, and grapes and vines as well.[31] That the Cabiric element is closely related to the Dionysian, indeed, that it overlaps with it smoothly, is shown by the drinking cups from the Cabirion at Thebes,[32] and also by the Lemnian myth which so closely connects Thoas with Dionysus-Osiris. Hephaestus' return in the Dionysiac procession was one of the most popular themes in vase-painting,[33] starting when the aristocratic government at Corinth gave way to tyranny. Alcaeus of Lesbos introduced the theme into literature, echoing in a characteristically Greek fashion a theme from the non-Greek island of Hephaestus.

7. *The Return of the Dolphin*

Again and again the path from destruction to a new beginning leads through the sea, perhaps most clearly on the island of Lemnos, but also in Leukothea's leap into the sea and Lykurgus' pursuit of Dionysus. The Attic etiological writers even thought that the Skira reflected Theseus' departure for Crete.[1] This connection is quite natural for those who live by the sea: so many things disappear into its vastness never to return again; other things wash ashore, bringing unforeseen benefits. The fear of death and happy deliverance, loss and recovery, are closely related. Whenever the sea receives the unspeakable sacrifice, purity and innocence seem to be reestablished. And yet there must be consequences: the sea is just; it receives and it gives. The return from the sea was almost stereotypically accompanied by the image of the most beautiful, the nimblest, the most nearly human of all the inhabitants of the sea—the dolphin.

Although they were only fourth in importance, the Isthmian games at Poseidon's sanctuary near Corinth achieved pan-Hellenic

---

[31] See n. 19 above; mentioned already by Welcker, *Aeschylische Trilogie*.

[32] P. Wolters and G. Bruns, *Das Kabirenheiligtum bei Theben* (1940); *Neue deutsche Ausgrabungen* (1959), 237–48; Hemberg (1950) 184–205; G. Bruns, *AA* (1967), 228–73.

[33] F. Brommer, *JdI* 52 (1937), 198–212; A. Seeberg, *JHS* 85 (1965), 102–109; Alcaeus 349 L.-P.

[1] See III.1.n.45 above.

status.[2] For the most part, its cult legend was linked to Leukothea's leap into the sea: here, at the Isthmus of Corinth, the body of young Melikertes had been brought ashore by a dolphin. Sisyphus, the shrewd founder of Corinth—and coincidentally the "inventor" of the burial ritual—buried the dead boy, who was henceforth known as Palaimon, and established the Isthmian games in his honor.[3] The boy on the dolphin was a frequent subject in sculpture, and he appeared on Corinthian coins as the emblem of the Isthmian games—sometimes as a limp corpse, sometimes as a merry rider.[4] Was it possible that a hero worshipped in his own shrine, the Palaimonion, could really have died?

As often, there are two cult centers that give the sanctuary at the Isthmus its shape: that of Palaimon and that of Poseidon, the hero and the god, chthonic versus Olympian ritual, the tholos and the temple. Between the two, the stadium for the foot-race began and ended. To be sure, the tholos in the Palaimonion which Pausanias saw, and which was depicted on the coins of the Roman Empire, was first built in Roman times,[5] and in the process a new stadium was constructed over the old. Thus, it is not known what the original precinct of Palaimon looked like. But we can trace the cult of Palaimon at least as far back as the etiological legend in Pindar, and it is likely that it appeared as early as the ancient epic of Eumelos.[6] Perhaps at first a simple sacrificial pit was enough for the nocturnal sacrificial ritual.

For a black bull was slaughtered at night for Palaimon. And to Plutarch this seemed more a mystery initiation (τελετή) than an athletic and folk festival.[7] Philostratus mentions an ecstatic dirge like

---

[2]K. Schneider, *RE* IX 2248–55, superseded by O. Broneer's excavation of the sanctuary, *Hesperia* 22 (1953), 182–95; 24 (1955), 110–41; 27 (1958), 1–37; 28 (1959), 298–343; 31 (1962), 1–25; Roux (1958) 91–103.

[3]Pind. fr. 56; Arist. fr. 637; Prokles (a student of Xenokrates) in Plut. *Q. conv.* 677b; Musaios, *FGrHist* 455; Aristid. *Or.* 6.32–35 Keil; Apollod. 3.29; Schol. Pind. III pp. 192–94 Drachmann; Schol. Eur. *Med.* 1284; probably already in Eumelos, Jacoby ad *FGrHist* 451 F 4, A. Barigazzi, *Riv. di Filol.* 94 (1966), 129–48, on "Dion" *Or.* 37.11–14.

[4]Paus. 2.1.8, 3.4. For coins see Imhoof-Blumer (1885) 10–12, T. B I–XIII; cf. Philostr. *Im.* 16 (II 362.24 ed. Teubn. 1871).

[5]Paus. 2.2.1; Imhoof-Blumer (1885) T. B XI–XIII; *Hesperia* 27 (1958), 15–17; F. Robert, *Thymélè* (1939), 156–59; Roux (1958) 100–102, fig. 11; O. Broneer, *Isthmia* II (1973), 101f.; *IG* IV 203. Philostratos (II 362.27) has Poseidon himself dig up the subterranean ἄδυτον for Palaimon.

[6]See n. 3 above.

[7]*Thes.* 25; cf. μυστήρια Liban. *Or.* 14.5.67; ταῦρον μέλανα Philostr. *Im.* 363.1; ταυροφόνῳ τριετηρίδι Pind. *Nem.* 6.40. For coins on which a bull moves toward the Palaimonion see Imhoof-Blumer (1885) pl. B. XI, XIII; Philostratos II 363.1 mentions a herd of cattle belonging to Poseidon.

those in the mysteries,[8] and Aelius Aristides speaks of "initiations" and orgies and, prior to that, an "oath."[9] Pausanias refers to the Palaimonion as the site of sacred oaths;[10] the oath that the contestants had to take before the games most probably occurred right there—an encounter with Palaimon at night in the underground vault preceded the days of competition. Here, too, the path leads from grief to vitality, from death to the order of life, from Palaimon's sacrificial pit to the altar of Poseidon.

The god of the sea presided over the place where sea routes and land routes cross. The dolphin and the dead youth came from the sea. The myth, then, makes the Isthmian games only the last step in a tragedy whose gruesome central act it locates elsewhere, in the house of Athamas and at the Molurian cliff near Megara.[11] As in the case of Antiope and Epopeus, the wandering bards presumably combined various local traditions. In that case, we should postulate an unspeakable sacrifice at the Isthmus itself on the shore, to which the return of the dolphin-boy would then correspond.

And in fact, on the beach below the sanctuary, next to the altar of Melikertes, a spruce would be pointed out which was linked to the story of Sinis, the "spruce-bender," *pityokamptes*.[12] This Sinis killed his sacrificial victims by tying them to a spruce on either side and then letting the trees snap back up, thus tearing the victim apart or smashing him. This went on until one day Theseus did the same to Sinis, and "because of" this bloody victory, this killing of Sinis, Theseus founded the Isthmian games, at least according to a tradition with Attic bias.[13] A victim torn apart and hung on a tree that bears no fruit is a terrifyingly clear image of an unspeakable sacrifice. Indeed, such a sacrificial ritual using two recoiling trees is actually attested in Gaul.[14] (Poets and interpreters, of course, preferred to substitute another story at the start, the story of Leukothea.) The victor's prize at the Isthmian games was a spruce wreath. Following the example of Ne-

---

[8] *Her.* II 207.21 ed. Teubn. (1871) = p. 325 ed. Zürich (1844 = 1853²).

[9] *Or.* 46.40 Keil.

[10] 2.2.1.

[11] See III.3.nn.40–42 above.

[12] Paus. 2.1.3–4; cf. Bacchyl. 17.19; Eur. *Hipp.* 977–78; Diod. 4.59; Schol. Pind. III 193.3, 195.3 Drachmann. On the pictorial tradition see Wörner, *RML* IV 921–34; Joh. Schmidt, *RE* III A 238–44; Brommer (1960) 189–90.

[13] *Marm. Par.*; *FGrHist* 239 A 20; Plut. *Thes.* 25; Schol. Nik. *Alex.* 605.

[14] *Comment. Lucan.* 1.445; E. Thevenot, *Hommages à W. Deonna* (1957), 442–49. Alexander had Bessos killed this way: Plut. *Alex.* 43. Cf. the fir tree of Pentheus, Eur. *Bacch.* 1064 ff.; for images of Dionysus made from this fir tree see Paus. 2.2.7.

mea, the spruce wreath was replaced by a celery wreath from Classical until Hellenistic times.[15] Later, the spruce wreath, the wreath from the sacrificial tree, was restored. The "mystery-like" dirge for Palaimon always remained part of the Isthmian festival.

Released from this gloomy background, the cheerful and liberating legend of the sixth century further developed the image of the dolphin-rider under the colors of the renewed cult of Dionysus, even using almost the same location. In this version, Arion, the Dionysiac poet, is saved by a dolphin and comes ashore at the sanctuary of Poseidon. Corinthian sailors had wanted to rob him of gold and his life while he was travelling with them from Tarentum to Corinth. In full singer's garb, Arion played his last song on the cithara and sprang into the sea, where a dolphin suddenly appeared and carried him to Tainaron. There—surely in the famous sanctuary of Poseidon—Herodotus saw the statue of a dolphin-rider. The story actually ends, however, in Corinth, where Arion goes to the palace of the tyrant Periander and provides testimony to convict the criminals. According to Herodotus, this story was told by both Corinthians and Lesbians.[16]

It has long been recognized that this pretty tale has a most specific meaning.[17] As Herodotus attests in this context and as even Pindar already knew, Arion is the "inventor of the dithyramb."[18] This introduction of Dionysiac choral songs cannot be separated from the emergence of Dionysiac motifs, of the thiasoi of padded dancers on Corinthian pottery starting precisely at the time of Periander.[19] After the fall of the aristocratic regime of the Bakchiadai, who claimed that they were the direct descendants of Dionysus,[20] the cult of the god

[15] Plut. *Q. conv.* 677b; Callim. fr. 59; Schol. Apoll. Rhod. 3.1240. Temporarily replaced by the σέλινον: Pind. *Ol.* 13.33; *Nem.* 4.88; *Isthm.* 2.16, 8.64; Nik. *Alex.* 604–606 with Schol. 605; Schol. Pind. III p. 193.11.

[16] Hdt. 1.24; cf. the alleged song of thanksgiving by Arion, *Poetae Melici Graeci* 939 Page.

[17] C. M. Bowra, "Arion and the Dolphin," *MH* 20 (1963), 121–34 = *On Greek Margins* (1970), 164–81.

[18] Pind. *Ol.* 13.18–19 with Schol.; Hellanikos, *FGrHist* 4 F 86; Arist. fr. 677 = Procl. *Chrest.* 320a31; Dikaiarchos fr. 75 W.; Schol. Plat. *Resp.* 394c; Tzetz. ad Lyk. p. 2.15 Scheer.

[19] H. Payne, *Necrocorinthia* (1931), 118–24; F. Brommer, *Satyroi* (1937), 20–22; L. Breitholz, *Die dorische Farce im griech. Mutterland* (Göteborg, 1960); Webster in Pickard-Cambridge (1962) 100–101, 171–73. For padded dancers at Athens see A. Greifenhagen, "Eine attische schwarzfigurige Vasengattung und die Darstellung des Komos im 6. Jh.," Diss. Königsberg, 1929; H. Seifert, "Dithyrambos und Vasenmalerei in Athen," Diss. Würzburg, 1970. For the picture of Dionysus on the amphoriskos with the return of Hephaestus, Athens N.M. 1092, see G. Loeschcke, *AM* 19 (1894), 510; Payne #1073; Brommer 21; Webster in Pickard-Cambridge (1962), List of Monuments #38.

[20] Satyros *POxy* 2465 fr. 3 col. II; H. Lloyd-Jones, *Gnomon* 35 (1963), 454.

had to develop new and more democratic forms. It is quite conceivable that a Lesbian poet and musician established the musical form for these crude folk-dances. On one of these vases, the dancers are busy with a dolphin. Is it wine that they are pouring into the water?[21] In any case, the association of Dionysiac dances and dolphins is thus attested to virtually within Arion's lifetime. A bit later, in the early forms of Dionysiac comedy, dolphin-riders and dolphin-masks became popular at Athens as well.[22]

Whereas the Lesbians and the Corinthians told of the adventure of Dionysus' poet, the *Homeric Hymn* makes the hero the god Dionysus himself. He is seized by Tyrrhenian pirates who want to enchain him while at sea. But the chains fall off, vines start to sprout and wind around the mast and sail, and the mast is covered with ivy. The sailors leap into the sea in terror and are transformed into dolphins. Only the pilot is spared by the god, for he alone had spoken against the pirates; indeed, the god makes him "entirely happy" by putting him in the god's own service.[23]

Our earliest source for the accompanying ritual dates to the Roman Empire: in Smyrna "in the month of Anthesterion, a trireme is raised up and carried to the marketplace. The priest of Dionysus steers it like a pilot as it comes from the sea, having cast off."[24] The image of the ship of Dionysus, carried or driven on wheels, is known

[21] Paris, Louvre MNC 674; Payne #989; Webster in Pickard-Cambridge (1962) 172, List of Monuments #43.

[22] See a black figure skyphos, Boston 20.18, in M. Bieber, *The History of the Greek and Roman Theatre* (1961), fig. 125a; black figure bowl, Louvre CA 1924, *AA* 1942, 71 pl. 3; black figure lekythos, Kerameikos, ibid. pl. 4/5; red figure psycter, New York, Norbert Schimmel Collection: G. M. Sifakis, *BICS* 14 (1967), 36–37, pl. VI—he suspects that the inscription ΕΠΙ ΔΕΛΦΙΝΟΣ is the beginning of a choral song. For satyrs and dolphins see, e.g., the black figure cylix, Louvre F 138 = *ABV* 635.34.

[23] *Hy. Dion.*, esp. 53–54; then Pind. fr. 236; Eur. *Cyclops* 11; Aglaosthenes, *FGrHist* 499 F 3; Apollod. 3.37–38; Ov. *Met.* 3.582–691, etc.; cf. the Lysikrates monument at Athens: H. Herter *Archaiognosia* 1 (1980), 101–34.

[24] Philostr. *V. Soph.* 1.25.1, II 42.24–27, and cf. II 54.8 ed. Teubn. (1871); Aristid. *Or.* 17.6 Keil = I 373 Dindorf (with a characteristic aition: the hostile Chians intended to conquer the city while the people of Smyrna were celebrating on the mountain, but they themselves were destroyed together with their ships by the returning Smyraeans: for the Dionysia as the retaking of the city see III.1. Excursus above, esp. p. 160); *Or.* 21.4 Keil = I 440 Dindorf. Nilsson (1906) 268. On coins from Magnesia, four men are depicted carrying the bow of a ship with the child Dionysus (?): M. Bernhart, *Jb. f. Numismatik u. Geldgesch.* 1 (1949), 22. Καταγώγια of Dionysus are attested at Miletus, *LSAM* 48, at Priene: *SIG*[3] 1003 = *LSAM* 37, at Ephesus: *Acta S. Timothei* ed. Usener (*Progr. Bonn* [1877]; Nilsson [1906] 416.5 with ritual combat). For the arrival of the dolphin-rider and the founding of the city in the Tarentine tradition of Phalantos-Taras, especially on Tarentine coins, see *RE* IV A 2286–87. For Dionysia at Tarentum see Plat.

to us already from the sixth century B.C., from a Clazomenian vase found in Egypt,[25] with men dressed in strangely Egyptian-like aprons carrying the ship, and from three Attic vases, dated to between 500 and 480 B.C. In the latter, the ship has a very ancient kind of wheel.[26] The sacrificial bull that is led along in the procession suggests a dithyramb at the festival of Dionysus. The Greater Dionysia were founded at Athens in the course of the Dionysiac reforms around 560, and were subsequently expanded.[27] Ultimately, the dithyramb acquired its classical form near the end of the sixth century, through Lasos of Hermione. To be sure, the god of the Dionysia is Dionysus of Eleutherai in Kithairon, and to begin the festival his image would be carried in once again from the direction of Eleutherai. But the advent of new life, with all its high spirits and voluptuousness, is so graphically embodied in the image of the ship that, at least on occasion, the central place in the procession was held by the wagon-ship, which was even introduced into the Panathenaic procession.[28] Indeed, the image of the god surrounded by dolphins on his ship of vines is the epiphany of the "god who comes from afar" par excellence, an image most beautifully depicted on the eye-cup by Exekias.[29]

Leg. 637b; for Tarentum = Satyrion see Diod. 8.21; Verg. *Aen.* 7.801; Prob. *Georg.* 2.197; Steph. Byz. Σατύριον.

[25] Oxford 1924.264; J. Boardman, *JHS* 78 (1958), 2–12; Pickard-Cambridge (1962) 84, List of Monuments #82. For men carrying a boat in Egyptian art see, e.g., *AOB* 494, 497; for the wagon-ship see, e.g., *AOB* 199; E. Panofsky, *Grabplastik* (1964), fig. 8. For the god's arrival on the ship see also *ANEP* 676, 677, 686; Burkert (1967) 295–96.

[26] Black figure skyphos, *Acr.* 1281a. Pickard-Cambridge (1968) fig. 12; black figure skyphos, *BM* B 79, Pickard-Cambridge (1968) fig. 13, Deubner (1932) T.14.2; black figure skyphos, *Bologna* 130, C. H. E. Haspels, *Attic Black-Figured Lekythoi* (1936), 253 #15, Pickard-Cambridge (1968) 13, Deubner (1932) pl. 11.1; cf. also the black figure amphora "in Corneto," *JdI* 27 (1912), 76–77 = *Tarquinia* 678, Simon (1969) 284 fig. 276, where the same statuesque, seated, outsized Dionysus is depicted travelling in the ship. Because of the parallel from Smyrna (n. 24 above), the procession with the wagon-ship is usually assigned to the Anthesteria (Nilsson [1906] 269; [1955] 572, 583; Deubner [1932] 102–103; hesitantly, Pickard-Cambridge [1968] 12–13), even though the festival at Smyrna is called Dionysia and the Dionysia at Priene (*SIG*^{3} 1003.20–24) do not take place in the month Anthesterion; A. Frickenhaus, *JdI* 27 (1912), 61–69, and E. Bethe, *Hermes* 61 (1926), 463, argue in favor of the Greater Dionysia. On the primitive "crossbar-wheel" see H. L. Lorimer, *JHS* 23 (1903), 132–51; G. Childe in C. Singer, E. J. Holmyard, and A. R. Hall, *A History of Technology* I (1954), 214; Burkert (1967) 295.

[27] On the Dionysia see Deubner (1932) 138–42; Pickard-Cambridge (1968) 57–101; on Lasos see Pickard-Cambridge (1962) 12–15.

[28] See III.1.n.90 above. On Pegasos of Eleutherai see I.7.n.53 above.

[29] München 2044 = *ABV* 146.21; cf. n. 26 above; Hermippos fr. 63 (*CAF* I 243); Nilsson (1906) 270; A. Lesky, *Gnomon* 26 (1954), 211. On Dionysus as the "god who comes from afar" see Otto (1933) 75–81.

Arion came from Lesbos, and a myth located in Lesbos describes how, after a bloody catastrophe, new and consecrated life arose from the sea. According to the story, after Orpheus had been torn apart by the Thracian maenads, his head and his lyre floated across the sea to Lesbos. There, fishermen fished it out of the water and deposited it in an underground cave at Antissa, "there where now there is a sanctuary of Bakchos."[30] Upon burying the head, which had been torn off in Dionysiac frenzy, there was a celebration in which the dead man's lyre would sound anew. The story of Terpander, who brought Aeolic music to the Greek mainland in the seventh century, was linked to Antissa.[31] And, as the vase-paintings show, the Lesbian tale of Orpheus was known at Athens starting at least as early as the fifth century B.C.[32]

A parallel legend reflecting a neighboring ritual leads us to Lesbian Methymna. There, fishermen netted a strange statue of the god made of olive wood—a phallus and a head at once. With an oracle's approval, it was given a cult and sacrificial festivals as Dionysus Phallen. A bronze copy of the log was seen by Pausanias at Delphi.[33] "Carrying the god's image at the Dionysia" is mentioned in a Methymnian inscription.[34] Did they fish it out of the sea every year? Although the idea of a head or phallus, the personality or fructifying force of the dead man, raised to the core of new life, is cruder and less sublimated than the Antissan tradition of Orpheus, the two are nonetheless most

---

[30] Luk. *Adv. ind.* 109 = *OF* T.118; Phanokles fr. 1 Diehl/Powell = Stob. 4.20.47 = *OF* T.77; for the district of Antissa see Myrsilos, *FGrHist* 477 F 2, and cf. Philostr. *Her.* 5.3 (II 172.12 ed. Teubn.), 10.7 (II 181.17); *V. Ap.* 4.14; Aristid. *Or.* 24.55 Keil = I 841 Dindorf; Hyg. *Astr.* 2.7; Procl. *Resp.* I 174 Kroll = *OF* T.119; Nik. *Harm. Exc.* 1 pp. 266.8–12 Jan = *OF* T.163. On the motif of the prophesying head see W. Deonna, *REG* 38 (1925), 44–69; in a secret cult in New Zealand (1864) see *Globus* 7 (1865), 149. See generally *PR* II 406–408; Ziegler, *RE* XVIII 1242, 1293.

[31] Phot. *μετὰ Λέσβιον ᾠδόν* = Arist. fr. 545.

[32] See two red figure vases, *ARV*² 1174.1 (Cook III [1940] pl. 16) and *ARV*² 1401.1 (Cook III [1940] 101), Brommer (1960) 358; a red figure hydria in Basel, *AK* 15 (1972), 128–37. Cf. Cook III [1940] 101–102, pl. 17, 18.

[33] Paus. 10.19.3 (*Διόνυσον Κεφαλῆνα* Mss., *Φαλλῆνα* Lobeck [1829] 1087); cf. Nilsson (1955) 593.6; Oinomaos of Gadara in Euseb. *Praep. Ev.* 5.36.1–3 = Parke and Wormell (1958) #337: *Φαλληνὸν τιμῶσι Διωνύσοιο κάρηνον*. On fantasies where phallus = head see Herter, *RE* XIX 1727–28. For an image of Dionysus coming from the sea at Dionysopolis (Pontos) see Skymnos 753–54; yet there are other divine images that come from the sea: see Nilsson (1906) 226.3 Cf. J. Kroll, "Das Gottesbild aus dem Wasser," *Festschr. F. von der Leyen* (1966), 251–68; G. Beccatti, *Boll. d. comm.* 67 (1939), 37–60.

[34] *IG* XII 2.503; Nilsson (1906) 282–83; on coins from Methymna and Antissa see *HN*² 560–61; Imhoof-Blumer, *Zeitschr. f. Numism.* 20 (1897), 285, pl. X 23/4.

intimately related on a structural level. Inversely, a legend at Ainos speaks of an image of Hermes driven across the sea from the Troad to Thrace.[35] It is found by fishermen who toss it back into the sea, only to catch it a second time. They thereupon sacrifice the first fruits of their catch to the image while passing it around from man to man. Finally, they "set it up" in a temple in the city. The act of "carrying around" seems to provide an especially close link with the Phallen of Methymna. The cult's lower-class milieu extends to Ainos as well, and precisely this prompted Callimachus to use the legend.

The story of the death of Hesiod leads us back to the realm of high poetry and to a gloominess comparable to the myth of Palaimon. His death in a sanctuary of Zeus Nemeios, not far from Oineon and Naupaktos, was already known to the Athenians at the time of the Peloponnesian War.[36] Transferred to the sacral sphere, the story of his death becomes part of the pattern of sacrificial ritual. It starts with a maiden's tragedy. The poet was accused of having disgraced a virgin; her brothers slew him in the temple of Zeus and hurled him into the sea. On the third day following, however, just as the Locrians were going toward the sea at Rhion to celebrate the festival of Ariadne, a school of dolphins brought the corpse ashore.[37] Hesiod's body was then deposited in the sanctuary of Zeus Nemeios—though the location of his grave was known only to initiates.[38] The murderers fled but did not escape punishment. Whereas Pausanias speaks of a festival of Poseidon at Rhion, the festival of Ariadne suggests Dionysus: the legends of Palaimon and Arion were likewise shaped by the polarity

---

[35] Callim. fr. 197, above all the Diegesis; for Ainos as *κτίσμα Μιτυληναίων καὶ Κυμαίων* see Strabo 7 p. 331 fr. 52. On coins from Ainos see H. A. Cahn, *Schweiz. numismat. Rundschau* 31 (1944), 59–63; cf. Nilsson (1955) 81–82.

[36] Thuc. 3.96.1.

[37] *Certamen Homeri et Hesiodi* 14, p. 42 Wilamowitz = p. 234 lines 224–53 Allen, following Alkidamas (M.L. West, *CQ* 17 [1967], 446) and Eratosthenes (fr. 17–21 Powell); Plut. *Conv. sept. sap.* 162d; Paus. 9.31.6. On the fate of the murderers see Plut. *De soll. an.* 969e, 984d; Poll. 5.42. The festival of Ariadne is mentioned in the *Certamen*, p. 42.11 Wil. = l. 234 Allen; Plut. 162e speaks of *ἡ τῶν Ῥίων θυσία*, a festival for Poseidon (Paus. 10.11.6; *Διονύσια* of the *Ναυπάκτιοι* are attested in Schol. Aristoph. *Ach.* 195). On Poseidon-Dionysus see also Taras (son of Poseidon, Arist. fr. 590, and "Satura," Coel. Antipater fr. 35 Peter, *Historicorum Romanorum Reliquiae*). Cf. Nilsson (1906) 383–84; U. v. Wilamowitz-Moellendorff, *Die Ilias und Homer* (1916), 406–13; E. Vogt, *RhM* 102 (1959), 199–203; R. Merkelbach, *Miscellanea A. Rostagni* (1963), 519–21. In contrast to Thucydides, Plutarch, and Pausanias, the locale in the *Certamen* is the land of the Opuntian Lokrians across from Euboea.

[38] Plut. 162e–f. A tomb of Hesiod was, however, displayed at Orchomenos: see Arist. fr. 565, *Certamen* p. 42.23 Wil. = 1.247–53 Allen.

of Dionysus and Poseidon. At the Isthmus, too, there were secret graves.[39] Thus, the death of the poet who with his *Theogony* gave the Greeks their gods was subsumed into the structure of the sacred and of sacrifice with its ambivalence. In the end he found pardon and permanence in the sanctuary. Indeed, his fall assured him of a successor, for the product of that deadly union was, according to the story, Stesichorus, the next great molder of myth.[40]

8. *Fish Advent*

In Greek myth, the dolphin of Poseidon is a symbolic emblem: it is the sea-god's attribute, an expression of playful, elegant beauty and friendly companionship. At a deeper level it perhaps symbolizes the mother's womb, receiving and bringing to birth.[1] The fish has a far more concrete significance as fish in the Anatolian-Phoenician counterpart to the myth of Leukothea, the myth of Atargatis and Ichthys. Already in the fifth century, Xanthus the Lydian told of how the evil queen Atargatis "was captured by Moxos the Lydian and because of her haughtiness was drowned together with her son, Ichthys, in the lake of Askalon, and eaten up by the fish."[2] Just as Athamas had

---

[39] Paus. 2.2.2 = Eumelos, *FGrHist* 451 F 4 on the tombs of Sisyphus and Neleus; cf III.5.n.14 above, the tombs of Dirke and Oedipus.

[40] Philochoros, *FGrHist* 328 F 213. The dead man's return from the sea as a sign of Dionysus' favor appears also in the legend of Alexander of Pherai, who was killed in 358: see Theopompos, *FGrHist* 115 F 352—Alexander especially honored Dionysus Pelagios of Pagasai; following the god's instructions, a fisherman fished the bones of the dead man out of the sea so that they could be buried. According to a cult legend from Brasiai (Lakonia), Semele was washed ashore there in a larnax and was given a solemn burial; Dionysus, however, was brought up by Ino in a cave (Paus. 3.24.3–4 without details concerning rites); for the cult of Myrtilos, washed ashore at Pheneos, see Paus. 8.14.11; for Knopos at Erythrae, see Hippias, *FGrHist* 421 F 1.

[1] E. B. Stebbins, "The Dolphin in the Literature and Art of Greece and Rome," Diss. Baltimore, 1929; M. Rabinovitch, *Der Delphin in Sage und Mythos der Griechen* (1947).

[2] *FGrHist* 765 F 17 = Ath. 346e. The form of the name, Moxos, going back to Xanthos, cf. *FGrHist* 90 F 16, fits with the Hittite Muksus/Muksas; cf. H. J. Houwink Ten Kate, *The Luwian Population Groups of Lycia and Cilicia Aspera* (1961), 44–50. On Atargatis see P. Perdrizet, *Mélanges Cumont* (1936), 885–91; P. Lambrechts and P. Noyen, *Nouv. Clio* 6 (1954), 258–77.

driven Leukothea and Melikertes into the sea, so here the king had both mother and son thrown into the sea. And like Leukothea, Atargatis subsequently became a goddess because of her sufferings: she became the Great Goddess of Askalon. The Greeks also called her Derketo. Her sanctuary is located by the lake of Askalon, and every fish it contains is sacred to the goddess.[3] Ktesias further hellenized the myth and rendered it harmless: Derketo was not eaten by the fish, but was instead saved by them when she hurled herself into the waters in shame and despair after the birth of her illegitimate daughter, Semiramis. Since she was carried ashore by a fish, all fish are sacred to her: the Syrians may not eat them. In this context, Ktesias attests—as Lukian did later—that the goddess was portrayed as half-fish, half-human.[4]

The Syrian fish-tabu was noted by the Greeks time and again.[5] The detailed report given by Mnaseas of Patara proves that this was not just a simple prohibition but, rather, the typical ambiguity of sacred ritual. "Every day the priests" of Atargatis "bring to the goddess real fish and set it before her on a table, nicely cooked, both boiled and roasted, and then the priests of the goddess consume the fish themselves."[6] For, according to Antipater of Tarsus, "Gatis the queen of the Syrians was such a gourmet that she issued a proclamation forbidding anyone to eat fish without Gatis";[7] or, as Mnaseas put it, she decreed "that no one might eat fish, but, rather, must bring it to her in the temple." Thus, it is not that one may not eat fish because they are holy; rather, they are holy because they are eaten in a sacred sacrificial meal in the company of Atar-Gatis, the Great Goddess, the mother of the "fish," Ichthys, herself. Mnaseas even goes on to say that her son's descendants were the fish Galene, Myraina, and the Elakatenes—large fish, prized for eating.[8] They were presumably kept in the sacred lake.

In the temple of the Syrian Goddess at Bambyke-Hierapolis, too, there was a pond with sacred fish.[9] Their astonishing tameness with

---

[3]Diod. 2.4.3.

[4]Ktesias, *FGrHist* 688 F 1 = Diod. 2.4; Strabo 16 p. 785; Luk. *Syr. D.* 14.

[5]Ever since Xen. *Anab.* 1.4.9; *LSS* 54; Wächter (1910) 97–98; cf. R. Eisler, *Orpheus the Fisher* (1921) passim; F. J. Dölger, *Ichthys* I (1910), 120–42; II (1922), 175–447.

[6]In Ath. 346d–e. [7]In Ath. 346c–d.

[8]In Ath. 301d.

[9]Luk. *Syr. D.* 14, 45–48; Ael. *Nat. an.* 12.2; Pliny *NH* 32.17. Diod. 2.4.2, referring to Ktesias (*FGrHist* 688 F 1), speaks of the lake at Askalon, "Eratosth." *Catast.* 38 p. 180 Robert of the lake at Bambyke. There are fish that come to sacrifice to the sound of the

the priests—did they press up willingly for the sacrificial meal?—was famous. Sacrifices were brought down to the lake, and it was told that Hera led the way, holding back Zeus so that he wouldn't see the fish, since otherwise they would die.[10] Thus, for the king of the gods this sacrifice is hidden, it is a sacrifice of aversion, frightening yet necessary, the domain of the divine wife. Nonetheless, we can still clearly make out the pattern of the unspeakable sacrifice, here performed at the lake of the sacred fish. The Greeks equated the Syrian Goddess with Aphrodite. It was said that an egg fell from heaven into the Euphrates and that it was carried ashore by fishermen and hatched by doves. Inside the egg was Aphrodite.[11] There was also a story, elaborating on Hesiod, that dolphins and escorting fish, *πομπίλοι*, "were born together with Aphrodite from the blood of Uranos":[12] the epiphany of the goddess thus coincides with the arrival of the sacred fish.

There is almost no need to call attention to the structural identity between the Syrian fish tabu and the normal bloody sacrificial meal: that which is consecrated is used for food, and thus the meal itself is a strictly regulated, sacred act. For the Syrians, every meal of fish becomes a sacrificial meal, just as each act of killing is a sacrifice. And just as every dinner of meat is preceded by the bloody business of killing, so the ostensibly bloodless act of catching fish presupposes violence and death, above all in the plunge into the watery depths. The myth of Uranos reflects the castration of a sacrificial animal whose genitals one would throw over one's shoulder into the water

---

flute at the sanctuary of Apollo at Sura near Myra in Lycia: see Polycharmos *FGrHist* 770 F 1/2 = Ath. 333d–f; Plut. *Soll. an.* 976c; Pliny *NH* 32.17; Ael. *Nat. an.* 8.5, 12.1. For "Lydia" see Varro *R.r.* 3.17.4. The well-known fable of the piper and the fish comes from a related district: see Hdt. 1.141; Ennius *Sat.* 65 Vahlen. For a pond with sacred fish at Smyrna see *SIG*³ 997.

[10] Luk. *Syr. D.* 47.

[11] Nigidius Figulus fr. 100 Swoboda = Schol. Germ. pp. 81, 145 Breysig; Hyg. *Fab.* 197. Others told of how Aphrodite leapt into the Euphrates while fleeing Typhon (cf. Pind. fr. 91), and changed into a fish: see Diognetos of Erythrai, *FGrHist* 120 F 2 = Hyg. *Astr.* 2.30; Ov. *Met.* 5.331; *Fast.* 2.459; Manil. 4.579–82. At Aphaka by the Libanon, there was a sanctuary of Aphrodite with a sacred lake in which sacrificial offerings were submerged (Zosimos 1.58; those offerings which are pleasing to the goddess sink, as in "Ino's water," Paus. 3.23.8); on the festival day fire falls from the mountain into the river Adonis, "this is Aphrodite Urania" (Sozomen. 2.5.5; Zosimos speaks of a fire-ball in the air). The mention of the mountain instead of the sky reveals the true character of the rite: a fire-wheel would be rolled down the mountain (see Mannhardt I [1875] 507–508).

[12] Epimenides, *FGrHist* 457 F 22 = Ath. 282e–f. On the birth of Aphrodite see I.7.n.56 above.

without turning around to look. At Bambyke, the sacrificial animals were led to the lake. In the myths of Askalon, too, submersion is presupposed. When rationalized, this appears to be nothing but feeding the fish, but the sacred, festival character of the action cannot be derived from this function. Rather, in this fishing we see the projection of something developed in another sphere: the unbroken tradition of hunting and sacrificing ritual in which the prerequisite for acquiring food is the guilt-ridden act of killing. And in fact, in the history of mankind, fishing is far more recent than hunting big game,[13] even though it is already prominent in the Upper Palaeolithic, and of great importance by the Neolithic. As a rule, only a meal of meat was considered sacral by the Greeks. Fish was the everyday, profane garnish for Demeter's bounty. While this reflects the tradition of immigrant peoples who originally lived far from the sea,[14] the coastal inhabitants around the Mediterranean sacralized the meal of fish itself. As fishing supplanted the hunt, hunting customs turned into fishing customs. Preparatory maiden-sacrifices are documented in fishing cultures: a girl would be thrown into the sea at the start of the season,[15] and the terrifying act of symbolic parricide or infanticide is found here as a preparatory event. (There is no analogy, however, to the peculiar structure of the "exceptional" period.) Mother and son unite in the catastrophe, throwing themselves to the fish, but the mother of animals herself responds by sending forth the blessing of nourishment, to which she herself gives birth, for Atargatis is the mother of the fish.

What we have encountered at Bambyke and Askalon leads us to the high civilizations of the ancient Near East, but also to various customs among the fishermen of Greece. In the Babylonian temple of Marduk, sacred fish were brought as offerings to the god. The "Weidner Chronical" relates how "the fishermen of Esagila" set forth to catch fish "for the table of Bel"; an evil king tried to prevent them, but Ku-Ba'u "gave the fishermen bread, gave them water," and therefore Marduk made Ku-Ba'u queen.[16] Whether queen Ku-Ba'u, the fishermen's friend, has something to do with the goddess Kubaba, Kybebe-

---

[13] Müller-Karpe (1966) 162. [14] A. Lesky, *Thalatta* (1947), 1–37, esp. 17–20.

[15] See I.7.n. 24 above.

[16] For translation and commentary see H. G. Güterbock, *Zeitschr. f. Assyriol.* 42 (1934), 54–55. For pictures of the sacrifice of the sacred fish on cylinder seals see F. J. Dölger, *Ichthys* I (1910), 428–29; III (1922) pl. 18; R. Eisler, *Orpheus the Fisher* (1921), pl. 22; for the feeding of the fish see ibid., pl. 20. For priests dressed as fish see Dölger III pl. 18.7 = Eisler pl. 16; Dölger III pl. 17.1/2. Cf. Dölger I 425–31.

Kybele, is a matter for debate.[17] In any case, at Babylon catching and offering fish in the temple was a central act of piety without which no government could endure. A bit later in the "Chronical," another fisherman who catches a "fish as a gift" for the "great lord Marduk" becomes king himself.

A similar system is presupposed in the myth of Adapa for the temple of Ea at Eridu.[18] Adapa, created by Ea as "guardian of the rites," "went fishing for Eridu as prescribed"; "he caught fish in the middle of the lake for the household of his lord." He then did battle with the South Wind and broke his wings, for which he had to defend himself before the court of Anu. In mourning robes he did penance, until finally, newly attired and anointed, he became the priest of Ea at Eridu. Here, though abstract speculation is combined with poetry to produce a complex and ambiguous epic, it seems that the theme of the fisherman as priest, of the priest as fisherman in the context of guilt incurred and expiation, points back to the sacrificial rites of the temple and to the theme of sacrifice as a whole.

In Ugaritic, Athirat is called "mistress of the sea," and her servant Qds-w-Amrr is a fisherman, the "fisherman of mistress Athirat of the sea."[19] Nothing is known of the appertaining ritual. But even the title links the goddess both to the sanctuaries of the Syrian Goddess and to the temple systems of Mesopotamia.

Among the Greeks, corresponding customs are to be found not in the great temples but in the geographical and social fringes of the Greek world. Just as the fishermen of Methymna or Ainos pulled their Dionysus- or Hermes-log out of the sea, there was another place where Dionysus was annually immersed in the sea. This place may have been Halai Aixonides in Attica[20] where, when tuna-fishing began, the first tuna would be sacrificed to Poseidon, that is to say, eaten by the priest and distinguished citizens in the sanctuary.[21]

---

[17] Cf. W. F. Albright, *Arch. f. Orientforsch.* 5 (1928/29), 229–31; Th. Jacobsen, *The Sumerian King-List* (1939), 104–105; E. Laroche, in *Eléments orientaux dans la religion grecque ancienne* (1960), 113–28; R. Gusmani, *Kadmos* 8 (1969), 158–61.

[18] *ANET* 101–103 (the quotes: A 9, 15; B 50) = *AOT* 143–46; cf. *ANET* Addenda 671–72: the possibility of identifying Adapa with the fish-man Oannes in Berossos, *FGrHist* 680 F 1.4, is discussed.

[19] M. H. Pope and W. Röllig in *Wörterbuch der Mythologie*, ed. H. W. Haussig, I (1965), 246–49; M. C. Astour, *Hellenosemitica* (1965), 206.

[20] Oracle in Philochoros, *FGrHist* 328 F 191 = Schol. T *Il.* 6.136 and Plut. *Aet. phys.* 914d; cf. Jacoby *ad loc.* (ἁλιεύειν Schol., ἁλιεῦσιν Plut., Ἁλαιεῦσιν Wilamowitz and Maass, and cf. Jacoby *ad loc.*; but Ἁλιεῖς at Argos should also be considered, see Steph. Byz. *s.v.*); K. Tümpel, "Διόνυσος Ἁλιεύς," *Philologus* 48 (1889), 681–96.

[21] Krates, *FGrHist* 362 F 2; cf. Antigonos of Karystos in Ath. 297e. The tunafish hunt

A report by Hegesandros about Apollonia, on the peninsula of Chalcidike by Lake Bolbe, exhibits a strange correlation of funerary sacrifice and fishing. The lake was named after Bolbe, the mother of Olynthos by Herakles. Olynthos' tomb is on the Olynthiac River, which flows into Lake Bolbe. In the months of Anthesterion and Elaphebolion, in spring, the people of Apollonia sacrifice to their dead, including their Hero, at his tomb by the river. Then, they say, "Bolbe sends a 'broiler' to Olynthos and at this time countless fish go up from the lake into the Olynthiac River . . . , and all the inhabitants from the surrounding area can put up as much preserved fish as they need."[22] The goddess of the lake will send the people ample food if they honor her dead son with sacrifice. The gloomy ritual on shore is answered by the advent of the fish.

The people of Lesbos, in legend, sacrificed a maiden to Poseidon, Amphitrite, and the Nereids. A youth, providentially called Enalos, "man of the sea," jumped down with her into the sea; he survived, and later, when he went to the shore, a huge wave brought forth a crowd of big octopuses who willingly followed him to the sanctuary of Poseidon[23]—to serve for a meal, no doubt.

In Classical Greek literature we encounter Dictys, the "net-man," the fisherman on the island of Seriphos who one day netted a chest in which Danae and the young Perseus were hidden. Mother and child had been hurled into the sea, just like Ino and Melikertes, just like Atargatis and Ichthys—except that here the coffin-chest, which also appeared in the Lemnian myth, becomes the ark that saves them.[24] In his *Diktyoulkoi*, the "net-drawers," Aeschylus translates Danae's arrival into a Dionysian milieu: wine-growers and coal burners surrounded by satyrs draw the net out of the water.[25] The arrival of the god's bride and the divine child in the ark has been taken simply as a story motif, but the myth of Perseus had a more concrete significance for the fishermen of Seriphos. According to Aelian, they made it a point never to catch a specific kind of fish, the *τέττιξ ἐνάλιος*, and if it

---

begins with a prayer, as it still does today in Sardinia: Ael. *Nat. an.* 15.3–6. The trident was used for hunting tuna: see Diog. 5.22 (*Paroem. Gr.* I 255); Apost. 8.96 (*Paroem. Gr.* II 459); II.l.n.30 above. For a vase-picture of a tuna-sacrifice see Detienne and Vernant (1979) 179 with fig. 16.

[22] Hegesandros in Ath. 334e; the word *ἀπόπυρις* for fish-sacrifice appears in the Coan inscription *SIG*[3] 1106 = *LS* 177.42, 62.

[23] Plut. *Conv. sept. sap.* 163a–d; cf. Myrsilos, *FGrHist* 477 F 14; Anticlides, *FGrHist* 140 F 4.

[24] On Danae see Hes. fr. 135.3–5; *RML* I 946–49; III 1986–2060; *PR* II 229–33; Brommer (1960) 205–206.

[25] Fr. 464–74 Mette.

got caught in their nets, they threw it back into the sea: "they say that the fish are the playmates of Perseus, Zeus' son."[26] A special renunciation distinguished the fishermen of Seriphos from any common fishermen, and this tabu was linked to Perseus, who played among the fish, a fish-prince among the denizens of the sea. It is surely no coincidence that fish-sacrifice is attested for the cult of Hekate,[27] the daughter of Perses or Perseus. To be sure, this leads us once more to the fringes of the Greek world: Themistokles himself would have languished in obscurity had he been born on Seriphos.[28]

Pankrates, a poet of the second century A.D., narrates a legend about the sacred "escort-fish," *πομπίλος*, who was especially honored among the Samothracian gods.[29] During the golden age, Epopeus, a fisherman from the island of Ikaros, caught these sacred fish, and he and his sons ate them in a festive meal. Shortly thereafter, a sea monster swam up to the old man's ship and devoured Epopeus before the eyes of his sons. He who eats the sacred fish is himself eaten by a sea monster—this is an inversion of what, in the recurrent cycle of ritual, is understood the other way around: because the old man sank into the sea, fish can be caught and eaten. Once again, the mention of the Samothracian gods takes us beyond the limits of the Greek world. Already Hipponax combined the Cabiri, soot, a period without fire, and a particular fish, *ἀθερίνη*, although we cannot make sense of all the fragment's details.[30] And judging by pictorial representations, fish-sacrifice played a special role in the mystery cult of the Thracian riders,[31] which seems, in turn, to be related to the Great Gods of Samothrace.

Among the Greeks themselves we find the remnants of a leap

---

[26] *Nat. an.* 13.26. Cf. Paus. 2.18.1: Perseus *ἔχει . . . τιμὰς . . . μεγίστας ἔν τε Σερίφῳ* . . . . For a fish called Περσεύς in the Red Sea see Ael. *Nat. an.* 3.28. The pictures on the coins of Tarsos are peculiar: for Perseus with a statue of Apollo Lykeios facing a fisherman, see F. Imhoof-Blumer, *JHS* 18 (1898), 177–78; *RML* III 2059; P. R. Franke, *Kleinasien zur Römerzeit* (1968) #127. For Perseus with a tuna on the coins of Kyzikos see *RML* III 2058.

[27] Eust. 87.31, 1197.23; Apollod., *FGrHist* 244 F 109 = Ath. 325a–b. For Hekate Περσηίς see Hes. according to Schol. *Od.* 10.139; Apoll. Rhod. 3.467, etc., *Περσέως παρθένος* Lyk. 1175. For the fish-sacrifice of a masked woman to Artemis or Bendis on an Etruscan stamnos see G. Schneider-Hermann, *AK* 13 (1970), 52–70. For a phlyax player eating a fish on an altar see A. D. Trendall, *Phlyax Vases* (1967²) pl. 4c.

[28] Plut. *Them.* 18.

[29] In Ath. 283a.

[30] Fr. 78 Masson-West, and cf. fr. 4.

[31] F. J. Dölger, *Ichthys* I (1910), 143–50, 443–46; II (1922) 420–47; D. Tudor, *Corpus monumentorum religionis equitum danuvinorum* (1969/76).

into the water, though in humorous guise. At Hermione,[32] people spoke of a diving competition in the cult of "Dionysus of the black goatskin," Melanaigis. The expression "Delian diver"[33] suggests a similar situation on the island of Apollo—on the François vase, a swimmer or diver accompanies Theseus' ship as it lands. The myth of Theseus' leap into the sea to retrieve the ring reflects such a diving test.[34] At the Maiuma in Ostia,[35] a boisterous festival celebrated by provincials but attended by genteel Romans as well, participants threw each other into the water.

Analogous motifs frequently surface in Greek myths. Skiron fell from the Skironic rocks into the sea and was eaten by an enormous tortoise[36]—indeed, the tortoise was so important to the coastal inhabitants that Aegina took it as its emblem. Andromeda and Hesione were set out almost like bait to lure the great sea beast, the Ketos, whom the hero then slew.[37] At Tanagra, the women's procession down to the beach provoked an attack by the sea monster, the Triton, who was subsequently caught with wine and killed in a Dionysiac hunting ceremony.[38] The image of the Ketos was presumably inspired by seal- and whale-hunts, hunts for a sea mammal with red, warm blood.[39] This brings us back to the dolphin's realm. Of course, the

---

[32]Paus. 2.35.1, and cf. 2.34.10–11: cult of Poseidon and Aphrodite *Ποντία καὶ Λιμενία* at Hermione.

[33]Sokrates-Apophthegma Diog. Laert. 2.22, 9.12; Herondas 3.51. Cf. the picture on the François vase (*ABV* 76.1), e.g., in Schefold (1964) pl. 51a.

[34]Bacchyl. 17; Brommer (1960) 165, 185. The sea-god Glaukos is, in the myth, the metamorphosis of a fisherman who leapt into the sea: *PR* I 610–13; *RML* I 1678–86.

[35]*Cod. Iust.* 11.46; Lydos, *Mens.* 4.80 p. 133 Wuensch; Suda *μ* 47; *Piscatorii ludi* Festus 238 M.

[36]Apollod. *Epit.* 1.2; Diod. 4.59; in vase-paintings, with Theseus overthrowing Skiron (Brommer [1960] 160–62, 190–91). At Elis, Aphrodite Urania sets her foot on a turtle: Plut. *Praec. coni.* 142d; *Is.* 381e; Paus. 6.25.1. It was said that Lais was beaten to death with "turtles": Ath. 598a; Schol. Aristoph. *Plut.* 179. For the turtle as the enemy of and sacrifice for Re in Egypt see H. G. Fischer, *Bull. Metr. Mus.* 24 (1966), 193.

[37]*PR* II 237–42; 549–58. The myth of Andromeda, set near Jaffa in Palestine (Konon, *FGrHist* 26 F 1.40; Strabo 16 p. 759; Jos. *Bell. Jud.* 3.420; Paus. 4.35.9; Pliny *NH* 5.69, 128) has an Egyptian counterpart in *PAmh.* (A. Erman, *Die Literatur der Ägypter* [1923], 218–20; Th. H. Gaster, *Bibliotheca Orientalis* 9 [1952], 82–85; S. Morenz, *Forschungen und Fortschritte* 36 [1962], 307–309): Yam, the sea, demands tribute; Astarte goes down to the sea; Seth fights for her—evidently an Egyptian version of a Caananite myth (cf. n. 19 above). For a Hittite counterpart see J. Friedrich, *Archiv Orientální* 17 (1949), 230–54.

[38]Paus. 9.20.4–5; cf. Demostratos in Ael. *Nat. an.* 13.21; Ephoros, *FGrHist* 70 F 225; Ath. 551a. For Tritons on an ancient clay figurine from Tanagra see *RML* V 1164.

[39]Cf. the mother of the seals and the Eskimo myth of the sacrifice of the virgin, I.8.n.27 above.

Greek myths and a large share of major Greek cults have become characteristically detached from the fisherman's everyday pragmatism and needs, playing out their socio-psychological function in a purely symbolic fashion. However, such culturally refined developments are always in danger of growing anemic.

We have seen that the same structure of sacrificial ritual presents itself at different levels. The most detailed picture of the New Year's festival of the polis, with its dissolution in the unspeakable sacrifice and its restoration of order in the festive feast and agon, was provided by Athens and Argos, but we were able to detect hints of it at Sikyon and Thebes as well; in the non-Greek realm, there was the parallel of the Lemnian fire festival, where an artisan guild supplanted the customary Greek military organization. The same structures were given a new emphasis in the expanding cults of Dionysus, in the Agrionia type on the one hand, where the period of exception became the setting for ecstasy and the sacrificial sparagmos outdoors, and in the type of the Dionysian advent on the other, where the god entered the city from the sea. Fishing rituals and legends came into play here too, especially in non-Greek areas. The sacrifice of the maiden and the plunge into the sea are answered by the arrival of food from the sea. It is impossible to trace just how the rituals of hunters, fishermen, nomadic animal-breeders, and city dwellers grew apart, influenced each other, and overlapped. We may therefore wonder all the more at the structural unity that rendered that reciprocal exchange possible. The basic structure of sacrifice, with its preparations, bloody central act, and restitution, grows into a great arc of myth embracing the maiden's tragedy, regicide/parricide or infanticide, and the younger generation's accession to power. Nourishment, order, and civilized life are born of their antithesis: the encounter with death. Only *homo necans* can become *homo sapiens*.

IV. ANTHESTERIA

1. *Testimonia and Dissemination*

The importance of the Anthesteria, celebrated in the spring in honor of Dionysus, is immediately shown by the fact that it lent its name to a month, and not only at Athens; the name of the month Anthesterion is attested for the entire Ionian region, for Eretria on Euboea, for the island Tenos, from Miletus to Priene on the coast of Asia Minor, Ephesus, Teos, from Erythrai to Smyrna, and in the Ionic colonies of Thasos, Kyzikos, and Massalia.[1] This agreement was noted already by Thucydides, who drew the conclusion, still irrefutable, that this festival and the name of this month must antedate Ionian colonization of Asia Minor.[2] That makes the Anthesteria one of the earliest attested of all Greek festivals. And inasmuch as the festival deals with Dionysus and wine, one may conclude that the wine-god Dionysus must already have been long familiar by 1000 B.C. The Linear B texts from Pylos that refer to Dionysus[3] before 1200 B.C. make this

[1]See Samuel (1972) Index *s.v.*; for the festival at Teos, see *SIG*[3] 38.33; *SEG* 4.598; Thasos, *LSS* 69; Smyrna, Philostr. *V. Soph.* 1.25.1 (II 42.24 ed. Teubn.); Iasos, *Bull. epigr.* 1973 nr. 70; Massalia, Just. 43.4.6 (IV.3.n.12 below). For Syracuse, see Timaios, *FGrHist* 566 F 158; Diog. Laert. 4.8; Antigonos in Ath. 437e. Cf. Farnell V (1909) 214–24, 317–20; Nilsson, *Studia de Dionysiis Atticis* (Lund, 1900), 115–38; idem (1906) 267–71. For the Anthesteria and the Aiora see *Eranos* 14 (1916), 181–200 = *Opuscula* I (1951), 145–65; (1955), 582–84, 594–98; Foucart (1904) 107–63; Harrison (1922) 32–74; (1927) 275–94; Deubner (1932) 93–123; van Hoorn (1951); Pickard-Cambridge (1968) 1–25.

[2]Thuc. 2.15.4 with the Scholia *POxy* VI p. 124 #853; Deubner (1932) 122–23.

[3]PY Ya 102; Xb 1419; Gérard-Rousseau (1968) 74–76; L. R. Palmer, *The Interpretation of Mycenaean Greek Texts* (1963), 250–58. Of no less importance is the excavation of the temple at Agia Irini on Keos: since 1500 B.C. it was continuously used as a cult site, and

conclusion easier to accept, even if it is conceivable that the god's name may be a secondary accretion to the wine festival. The Greeks always connected the name *Anthesteria* with "blossoming," in particular with the blossom of the vine,[4] and there is no reason to deviate from this simple interpretation of the name.

Once again, only Athens provides us with enough material to form a comprehensive, detailed picture of the festival. Here, in addition to accounts by local historians and allusions by Attic poets, we have the evidence of a clearly delineated type of pottery, the Choes pitcher.[5] There can be no doubt that it was used on the main day of the festival, whose very name was Choes, the day of the "pitchers." The paintings on these pitchers are also related to the festival events. Most of the evidence is concentrated in the fifth and fourth centuries B.C., but there are isolated documents in Hellenistic and later times as well, so we know that this festival spanned over 1,000 years.

Thucydides tells us that the main day of the festival fell on the twelfth day of Anthesterion.[6] This was the day of the Choes, the most

---

since Archaic times the cult was certainly that of Dionysus: see J. L. Caskey, *Hesperia* 33 (1964), 326–35; Simon (1969) 289.

[4]Istros, *FGrHist* 334 F 13 = Harpokr. Ἀνθεστηριών; cf. Macr. *Sat.* 1.12.14; *Et. M.* 109.12; *An. Bekk.* I 403.32; translated "Floralia" by Just. 43.4.6; Διόνυσος Ἄνθιος *IG* II/III^2 1356 and Paus. 1.31.4. Δ. Εὐάνθης Phanodemos, *FGrHist* 325 F 12, and cf. Euanthes as the father of the giver of wine, Maron, *Od.* 9.197; Hes. fr. 238; Ἀνθιστήρ Thera *IG* XII 3.329 ("Bekränzer," Wilamowitz [1932] 77.2). Unconnected with Dionysus are Ἥρα Ἀνθεία, Ἡροσάνθεια, ἀνθεσφόροι at Argos (Nilsson [1906] 357), ἀνθεσφόροι in Sicily (Poll. 1.37), Ἀνθεστρίδες in Rhodes (*LSS* 96, and cf. Hsch. ἀνθεστηριάδες, *An. Bekk.* 215.16), Ἄνθεια at Paiania (*LSS* 18). The derivation from *ἀνα-θέσσασθαι (A. W. Verrall, *JHS* 20 [1900], 115–17; Harrison [1922] 47–49) must be rejected already because of the apocope, which is precisely not Attic-Ionic. Τήρια as the suffix for festival names goes back to Mycenaean times: *λεχεστρωτήρια Gérard-Rousseau (1968) 201–203.

[5]Studied by Deubner (1932) 238–47, and comprehensively by van Hoorn (1951); see J. R. Green, *BICS* 8 (1961), 23–27. Cf. S. P. Karouzou, "Choes," *AJA* 50 (1946), 122–39; H. R. Immerwahr, "Choes and Chytroi," *TAPA* 77 (1946), 245–60; E. Simon, "Ein Anthesterien-Skyphos des Polygnotos," *AK* 6 (1963), 6–22; Metzger (1965) 55–76; E. Simon, *Gnomon* 42 (1970), 710–11. For a skeptical view see A. Rumpf, "Attische Feste—Attische Vasen," *Bonn. Jbb.* 161 (1961), 208–14. Many, though by no means all, depictions on Choes pitchers refer to the Anthesteria. This is often confirmed by a Choes pitcher being depicted again in the painting itself: one chous even has a graffito ΧΟΕΣ (Blech [1982] 307 n.179). There are depictions of the Anthesteria on other sorts of vases as well. Typical Choes pitchers indicate that there was also an Anthesteria in southern Italy: see van Hoorn (1951) 50–52; I. McPhee, *AK* 22 (1979), 38f. Cf. n.1 above; IV.5.n.11 below.

[6]2.15.4; τῇ δωδεκάτῃ is deleted as an interpolation by Torstrik, Hude, and Jacoby (*FGrHist* III b Suppl., Notes pp. 160–61), but appears already in *POxy* 853 and thus represents an ancient tradition; the received text is defended by A. W. Gomme, *A Historical Commentary on Thucydides* II (1956), 52–53. "Demosth." 59.76.

popular, and often the only part of the festival that is mentioned. It was preceded by the day of "opening the casks," the Pithoigia, on the eleventh day of Anthesterion, and it was followed by the day of the "pots," the Chytroi, on the thirteenth day of the month.[7] One must recall that, according to the old religious chronology, sundown signaled the end of a day and that evening and night were reckoned as the eve of the following day. Thus, the Pithoigia and the Choes meet on the evening of the eleventh, the Choes and the Chytroi on the evening of the twelfth. Already in antiquity, this hazy distinction occasionally caused confusion.

"Casks," "pitchers," "pots"—the earthy, popular character of this festival may be seen in these designations. Indeed, this festival was a *quantité négligeable* for the finances of the polis[8] when compared with, say, the Panathenaia, the Mysteries, or the Greater Dionysia. It occurred largely on the level of folk custom, in contrast to the more recent Dionysia, which were established in the sixth century by the tyrants and the polis. Moreover, the sanctuary of Dionysus in the Marshes,[9] which Thucydides considered to be one of the oldest in Athens, was apparently untouched by the monumental building program at Athens. It has not been identified with certainty and had apparently already disappeared in the time of Pausanias—perhaps it was replaced by the private cult site of the Iobakchoi. It probably languished due to an especially sacred commandment that was enjoined upon it: it could be opened only on a single day in the year, the day

[7] Philochoros, *FGrHist* 328 F 84 (cf. Jacoby *ad loc.*); Callim. fr. 178; Apollod., *FGrHist* 244 F 133; Schol. Thuc. p. 121.20 Hude; cf. Nilsson (1955) 594. Aristoph. *Ach.* 1076 *ὑπὸ τοὺς Χοᾶς γὰρ καὶ Χύτρους* led Didymos (Schol. *ad loc.*, Suda χ 622) to claim that the Choes and Chytroi were on the same day.

[8] In the account of sales of sacrificial hides, *IG* II/III² 1496, the Lesser Dionysia brings in 311 Dr., the Greater Dionysia 808 Dr., the Anthesteria nothing.

[9] Called *τὸ ⟨τοῦ⟩ ἐν Λίμναις Διονύσου* Thuc. 2.15.4; Isaios 8.35; "Demosth." 59.76; Philochoros (?), *FGrHist* 328 F 229; Callim. fr. 305; Strabo 8 p. 363; Schol. Aristoph. *Ran.* 216 (*ἐν ᾧ καὶ οἶκος καὶ νεὼς τοῦ θεοῦ*); Steph. Byz. *Λίμναι*. Not mentioned by Pausanias, who describes the shrine at the theater of Dionysus as the oldest shrine of Dionysus: 1.20.3. Philostr. *V. Ap.* 3.14 also mentions an *ἄγαλμα τοῦ Διονύσου τοῦ Λιμναίου*; cf. van Hoorn, *RA* 25 (1927), 104–20. The fact that there were no marshes at this sanctuary is discussed by Strabo 8 p. 363 and Schol. Thuc. *POxy* VI #853. W. Dörpfeld excavated a small shrine between the Areopagus and the Pnyx, which was later the cult site of the Iobakchoi (*IG* II/III² 1368 = *SIG*³ 1109 = *LS* 51). It has been hypothetically identified with the Limnaion: see *AM* 20 (1895), 161–76; 46 (1921) 81–96; Judeich (1931) 291–96; Pickard-Cambridge (1968) 21–25. G. T. W. Hooker, *JHS* 80 (1960), 112–17, pleaded for the area around the Ilissos; Guépin (1968) 283 seeks to locate the Limnaion in the Ilissos temple (V.3.n.2 below). There may be a picture of the temple on the Chous: München 2464; van Hoorn (1951) #699 pl. 61.

of the Choes. Another riddle is posed by the name *Dionysus in the Marshes*: in historical times, marshes and swamps could scarcely be found in Athens. If it corresponds so poorly to Athenian conditions, it must have come from a more ancient, alien tradition. There is no such thing as an autochthonous origin for religion.

2. *Pithoigia and Choes*

The Anthesteria has long attracted attention for three reasons. The first is as a children's festival.[1] On the day of the Choes, all three- and four-year-old children were given presents. The depictions on the little Choes pitchers of the children, their offertory tables, and toys are a unique record of Athenian private life. Second, for the historian of religion, the Anthesteria was fascinating as a festival of the dead: it was said that ghosts or spirits of the dead emerged from the underworld on these days and entered the city, only to be chased away at the end of the festival.[2] Third, references to a "sacred marriage" at this festival have provoked great curiosity: the "queen" of Athens, wife of the archon basileus, was presented to Dionysus in marriage.[3] Thus, animism and fertility magic both came into play, overshadowing that which, judging by the names of the days as well as by the statements of the Athenians, was fundamentally the central event: opening the casks and drinking the new wine. These simple actions were here given a set, ritualized form, and in interpreting the Anthesteria, our main goal must be to understand this ritual.

"At Athens, the people start with the new wine on the eleventh day of the month Anthesterion, calling the day Pithoigia." So Plutarch, who adds a pious interpretation: "And since long ago they have apparently poured a libation of the wine before drinking and prayed that the use of this draught would not harm them, but, rather, be good for them."[4] Thus, it is the wine casks which are opened on this

---

[1] See n.27–29 below.

[2] See IV.3 below. The interpretation of the Anthesteria as a festival of the dead was advanced mainly by Harrison (1922) 32–49; cf. Nilsson (1955) 594–97, who assumes an extrinsic but very old connection between Dionysus and the festival of the souls (597).

[3] See IV.4 below.

[4] *Q. conv.* 655e. For the month Πιθοιγιών at Peparethos see *IG* XII 8.645.5.

day, or, more precisely, the great clay jars (πίθοι), which were sealed after the wine had fermented. The rule that the wine must then lie untouched for several months until spring is certainly strange and artificial, but it was observed even outside of Greece, among the Romans.[5] Drinking the wine is not left to the whim of the individual; the community comes together and celebrates the god. The beginning seems bound up with danger: it was possible that this drinking could "do harm." Even today, the growers of wine follow set customs, starting the harvest together, pressing their wine together.

Here, tasting the new wine is a collective celebration within the sanctuary. The report of the Atthidographer Phanodemos can only refer to the Pithoigia: "At the temple of Dionysus in the marshes, the Athenians mix the new wine which they bring from their casks for the god, and then drink it themselves. Hence Dionysus was called the god of the marsh, because the new wine was mixed with water and drunk on that occasion for the first time. . . . Delighted then with the mixture, the people celebrated Dionysus in song, dancing and calling upon him with the names Flowery, Dithyrambos, the Frenzied One, the Roarer."[6]

It is unthinkable that wine would be mixed and poured out to the wine-god at a closed temple. For this reason alone, Phanodemos must be referring to the Anthesteria. However, the temple ἐν Λίμναις was open only on the Choes, on the twelfth day of the month.[7] The fact that the eleventh day was already called "the opening of the casks" is due to the sacral chronology. In the evening, the day of the Pithoigia passes over into the Choes, so that the casks would have been opened just before nightfall, and the temple would have opened at sundown. Plutarch attests that, in his native Boeotia, the new wine would be

---

[5]The Vinalia on the twenty-third of April are *degustandis vinis instituta*: Pliny *NH* 18.287, and cf. Varro 1.1.6.16; Festus 65 M.; Ov. *Fast.* 4.863–900; Wissowa (1912) 115.8.

[6]*FGrHist* 325 F 12 = Ath. 465a: πρὸς τῷ ἱερῷ φησι τοῦ ἐν Λίμναις Διονύσου τὸ γλεῦκος φέροντας τοὺς Ἀθηναίους ἐκ τῶν πίθων τῷ θεῷ κιρνάναι, εἶτ' αὐτοὺς προσφέρεσθαι. Πρὸς τὸ ἱερόν Jacoby, with the consequence that the date of the opening, "Demosth." 59.76, has to be changed (III b Suppl. Notes p. 161). If Dörpfeld's identification of the Limnaion is correct (see IV.1.n.9 above), only a few people could enter the shrine at the same time. K. Kerényi, *Symb. Oslo* 36 (1960), 5–11, concludes from the word γλεῦκος, "must," that Phanodemos is describing an autumn festival. But Plut. *Q. conv.* 655e–656b evidently identifies γλεῦκος with νέος οἶνος: τὸ γλεῦκος ἥκιστα μεθύσκει 655f; εἰκότως ὁ νέος οἶνος οὐ μεθύσκει 656a; cf. *sapa* Ov. *Fast.* 4.780. Γλεῦκος of course also means grape juice (νεοθλίπτῳ ὑπὸ γλεύκει Nik. *Alex.* 299); the change brought about through fermentation is not marked in the language. For depictions of the opening of the cask see van Hoorn (1951) #613 pl. 81, #196 pl. 82.

[7]"Demosth." 59.76. The shrine of Dionysus at Thebes (Paus. 9.16.6) is likewise open only on one day; cf. Paus. 2.7.5 (Dionysus at Sikyon), 7.20.1 (Patrai).

opened in honor of the Agathos Daimon "after the evening wind."[8] Throughout the day, people flocked together from vineyards all over Attica: freeholders who seldom entered the city, slaves and laborers of the landowners who lived in the city—a colorful crowd of strangers and friends with great *πίθοι* loaded on clattering carts drawn by donkeys: they gathered at the place in front of the temple, waiting for it to open at sunset, and to pour the first libation to the god from the newly opened casks. After holding out for months, despite longings and anxious curiosity, they finally broke the resinated seals. The tension of testing the results of a year's work dissolved into pleasure—reason enough to praise the god of wine.

The fact that the wine-tasting grew into a drinking competition on the following day of the pitchers, and that everyone got his own jug—slaves and laborers, too, indeed, even children—seems to be such a simple form of collective merriment as to require no explanation.[9] In Aristophanes' *Acharnians*, the good fortune of the peace-making anti-hero, Dikaiopolis, culminates in a drinking bout at the Choes. Here too, Dikaiopolis wins and gets a wineskin as a prize, enough to fill dozens of Choes pitchers. Thus, the guzzling is self-perpetuating—no wonder scholars have been satisfied to state that the Choes was an undeniably merry festival.[10] Yet the background for this day's merriment seems strange and even uncanny.

There is unambiguous testimony that the day of the Choes was a "day of pollution" (*μιαρὰ ἡμέρα*).[11] People would start the day by chewing—contrary to all natural predilection—on leaves of a particular hawthorn variety, *ῥάμνος*, which were otherwise used to ward off ghosts.[12] Doors would be painted with pitch—a normal way to water-

---

[8]On the sixth day of the month Prostaterios: Plut. *Q. conv.* 655e.

[9]Procl. Schol. Hes. *Erga* 368, on Pithoigia: *οὔτε οἰκέτην οὔτε μισθωτὸν εἴργειν τῆς ἀπολαύσεως τοὺ οἴνου θεμιτὸν ἦν* . . . Cf. Antigonos of Karystos, Ath. 437e. That is why the "black" day of the Choes is a "white" day for slaves: see Callim. fr. 178.2. On the children see nn. 27–29 below. For expenditures for state slaves at the Χόες see *IG* II/III^2 1672.204.

[10]Aristoph. *Ach.* 1000–1234. "The Anthesteria . . . plainly a cheerful feast": Pickard-Cambridge (1968) 15.

[11]Phot. *μιαρὰ ἡμέρα· ἐν τοῖς Χουσὶν Ἀνθεστηριῶνος μηνός*. More concisely Hsch. *μιαραὶ ἡμέραι· τοῦ Ἀνθεστηριῶνος μηνός* (cf. Eust. 456.6). There is a tendency, contrary to Photios' clear indication, to treat the Chytroi as the actual *μιαρὰ ἡμέρα*: see Farnell V (1909) 216; Pickard-Cambridge (1968) 14.

[12]Phot. *ῥάμνος· φυτὸν ὃ ἐν τοῖς Χουσὶν ὡς ἀλεξιφάρμακον ἐμασῶντο ἕωθεν*; Phot. *μιαρὰ ἡμέρα*. On *ῥάμνος* see Nik. *Ther.* 861–62: *μούνη γὰρ νήστειρα βροτῶν ἄπο κῆρας ἐρύκει* (862) with Schol. 860 = Sophron fr. 166 Kaibel, Euphorion fr. 137 Powell;

proof the wood;[13] but when all the doors of the city shone, sticky and black, so that a door could be opened only with care, it was a most striking expression of a *dies ater*. All temples were shut on this day,[14] so that normal life was largely paralyzed: since there could be no oaths sworn in the temple, no important business could occur, no marriage be settled on. There could be no "normal" sacrifice at any of the altars. Nevertheless, the temples were not barricaded, just surrounded with ropes. Each individual had to construct the symbolic boundary in his mind: on this day access to the gods was interrupted. Only that temple which was otherwise shut was now open—the temple of Dionysus ἐν Λίμναις.

In observance of the *dies ater*, far from the gods, people gathered behind doors freshly covered with pitch to eat together and, above all, to drink.[15] The family, including all relatives—though probably without women—assembled at the house of the head of the family. Officials gathered at the office of the archons, the Thesmotheteion near the Areopagus.[16] The "king," basileus, would preside. The people probably came together at the usual mealtime, in the late afternoon. What followed, however, was the clear antithesis of the usual festival meal. Each participant had his own table,[17] and whereas wine and water were normally served in a great mixing bowl out of which the wine-pourers would fill the cups all around, each participant at the Choes was given a pitcher that would be his forever, the Chous, which held about two and a half liters of mixed wine.[18] This is the pre-

Dioskor. 1.90; Ov. *Fast.* 6.129–68 on *spina alba*; Rohde (1898) I 237.3; Harrison (1922) 39–40.

[13] Phot. ῥάμνος· . . . καὶ πίττῃ ἐχρίοντο τὰ δώματα (σώματα Cd.); Phot. μιαρὰ ἡμέρα· . . . καὶ πίττῃ τὰς θύρας ἔχριον. On the use of pitch see the building account from Eleusis, *IG* II/III² 1672.170 πίττης κεράμια πέντε ἀλεῖψαι τὰς ὀροφὰς τοῦ Ἐλευσινίου . . . καὶ τὰς θύρας. The priest at the Babylonian New Year's festival paints the doors of the shrine with cedar-resin: *ANET* 333.

[14] Poll. 8.141 περισχοινίσαι; περισχοίνισμα Alkiphr. 4.18.11; in the etiological myth see Phanodemos, *FGrHist* 325 F 11; for vase-paintings see K. Friis Johansen, *Acta archaeologica* 38 (1967), 175–98 (who incorrectly speaks of the "Chytroi").

[15] The guests brought food in baskets; see Aristoph. *Ach.* 1085–1142, Schol. ad 961; for a different view see Eratosthenes, *FGrHist* 241 F 16.

[16] Plut. *Q. conv.* 613b; Alkiphr. 4.18,11; cf. Arist. *Ath. Pol.* 3.5; Aristoph. *Ach.* 1203, 1224 with Schol.

[17] Eur. *Iph. Taur.* 949; Plut. *Q. conv.* 643a; Eratosthenes, *FGrHist* 241 F 16.

[18] Eur. *Iph. Taur.* 953, 960; Phanodemos, *FGrHist* 325 F 11; Apollod., *FGrHist* 244 F 133. On the pitchers see Krates in Ath. 495b. At Athens they were sold at the Choes: see Skylax 112. On a sacrificial animal, 5 κεράμια and wine for the state slaves εἰς Χόας see *IG* II/III² 1672.204.

requisite for the notorious drinking competition: crowned with ivy wreaths,[19] the people would wait for the trumpet signal[20] blown from the Thesmotheteion at the king's order to initiate the drinking. Then all those assembled would drink "in silence,"[21] without a word or a song—indeed, apparently, without prayer—filling and refilling their cups till the Chous was empty. Out of all the odd customs on this "day of pollution," the silence while drinking probably seemed the most peculiar to the loquacious Athenians. To them, wine and song went together, and drinking to one another with song and speech was a highly refined social game. On the day of the Choes, people sat together under one roof but as if enclosed by invisible walls: separate tables, separate jugs, and all surrounded by a general silence known otherwise only at sacrifice when the herald calls out his *εὐφημεῖτε*.

The language of the ritual is clear: the so-called drinking competition bears the stamp of a sacrifice. The peculiarities of the Choes-drinking are the norm at the bloody sacrifice: not just the silence,[22] but the individual tables[23] and the distribution in portions as equal as possible;[24] above all, the atmosphere of pollution and guilt. From this perspective, the drinking competition reveals its original function: everyone starts together so that no one can say another started first.[25] Likewise, when the day begins, the act of chewing the leaves to avert evil, rather than carrying them or hanging them up, is a cathartic preparation for the sacred meal, handed down from hunting rituals.[26]

---

[19] Alkiphr. 4.18,11; frequently depicted on the Choes pitchers—cf. IV.4.n.2 below.

[20] Aristoph. *Ach.* 1001; cf. IV.5.n.15 below.

[21] Plut. *Q. conv.* 613b, 643a; Eur. *Iph. Taur.* 951. The prize, according to Phanodemos, *FGrHist* 325 F 11, was a cake (*πλακοῦς*); Aristoph. *Ach.* 1002, 1225 has a wineskin—a comic exaggeration of the drinking competition: besides the Chous, Dikaiopolis immediately drinks a bowl of unmixed wine (1229); he thereupon receives a whole *ἀσκός*. For Nike with a Chous—i.e., victory in the drinking competition—depicted on a Chous see Würzburg 4937 = *ARV*² 871.95; E. Simon, *Gnomon* 42 (1970), 711.

[22] Εὐφημεῖν: see Stengel (1920) 111; among the Romans see G. Mensching, *Das Heilige Schweigen* (1926), 101–102.

[23] Μονοφάγοι in the cult of Poseidon at Aegina, *καθ' αὑτοὺς ἐφ' ἡμέρας ἑκκαίδεκα μετὰ σιωπῆς ἑστιῶνται* Plut. *Q. Gr.* 301d–e (cf. Ath. 588e); *ἀνδρακὰς καθήμενος* Aesch. *Ag.* 1595 at the feast of Thyestes—the text, however, is fragmentary and corrupt (cf. E. Franekel *ad loc.*).

[24] *Διόνυσος ἰσοδαίτης* Plut. *De E* 389a, Harpokr., Hsch. *Ἰσοδαίτης*.

[25] For "dividing up the guilt" in sacrificial ritual see Meuli (1946) 228; at executions, see K. v. Amira, "Germanische Todesstrafen," *Abh. München* 31.3 (1922), 226, 228; at a plot of murder, Hdt. 5.92γ4.

[26] For laxatives and the like, see *GB* VIII 83; before the "festival of the first fruits" (Indians) see *GB* VIII 73, 75–76.

By eating food, one incurs guilt which must be distributed equally among all. And only those who receive their share can belong, bound together by the act they have committed.

For precisely this reason, the meaning of the Choes touches the lives of children. When a child was no longer a baby, at the age of three, it would be presented to the family clan, the phratry, and it participated in the Choes festival for the first time that same year.[27] "Birth, Choes, adolescence, and marriage"[28] are the basic stages in the development of a young Athenian. The child was given a wreath of blossoms, his own table, and his own pitcher, of a size appropriate to his age. Sharing in the wine signified the first step toward sharing in the life of the society, in adult life. A little Choes pitcher was placed in the grave of any child who died before it was three, so that it could at least reach the goal symbolically in the next life which it had failed to reach in this one.[29] This was analogous to the placement of the Loutrophoros, the water jug for the bridal bath, on the tomb of one who had died before marriage.[30] Most of the Choes pitchers that have survived come from such grave offerings, a custom which appears to have been especially fashionable for a time in the second half of the fifth century.

This interpretation of the Choes ritual as an initiation, a bond made by symbolically incurring guilt, is confirmed by the etiological myths told by the Athenians to explain the customs. Though varying in detail, they agree in speaking of a murder and blood guilt that left its mark upon the drinking of wine. And they forged a link with

---

[27] Philostr. *Her.* 12.2 (II 187.21 ed. Teubn. 1871) Ἀθήνησιν οἱ παῖδες ἐν μηνὶ Ἀνθεστηριῶνι στεφανοῦνται τῶν ἀνθέων τρίτῳ ἀπὸ γενεᾶς ἔτει. For membership in the phratry in the "third or fourth year" see Procl. *In Tim.* I 88.18 Diehl; Deubner (1932) 116, 234.

[28] Γάμων, γεννήσεως, χοῶν, ἐφηβείας: see *IG* II/III^2 1368.130; cf. the relief, Koumanoudes 3509, Deubner (1932) pl. 16.1 with the epigram ἡλικίης χοικῶν, ὁ δὲ δαίμων ἔφθασε τοὺς Χοῦς (#157 Kaibel = *IG* II/III^2 13139). On the wreath of blossoms and offertory table see van Hoorn (1951) passim. The oft-depicted little cart was given to Pheidippides at the Diasia (Aristoph. *Nub.* 864), but an Athenian terracotta has a silenus pulling it: F. Eckstein, and A. Legner, *Antike Kleinkunst im Liebieghaus* (Frankfurt, 1969), pl. 41. The inscription Ἀκρύπτωι ὁ πατήρ on a Chous in Baltimore, *CV* USA 306.3, shows that it was a present for a child. For teachers receiving presents on the day of the Choes see Eubulides fr. 1 (*CAF* II 431). On Keos, one could only drink wine once one had married: see Arist. fr. 611.28.

[29] S. Karouzou, *AJA* 50 (1946), 126, 130; A. Rumpf, *Bonn. Jbb.* 161 (1961), 213–14; van Hoorn (1951) #118, for instance, comes from the tomb of a child; #115; fig. 35 portrays a grave-stele; cf. the stone Chous, Deubner (1932) pl. 15. The "good nurse" ΠΥΡΑΙΧΜΗ ΤΙΘΗΝΗ ΧΡΗΣΤΗ is shown holding a Choes pitcher on her grave-stele: see E. Simon, *AK* 6 (1963), pl. 3.2.

[30] Demosth. 44.18, 30; Eust. 1293.8; Cook III (1940) 370–96.

heroic epic by introducing Orestes: after killing his mother, Clytaemnestra, Orestes came to Athens pursued by the Erinyes, in search of expiation. Demophon, the Athenian king, did not dare turn the suppliant away, but he had to avoid polluting himself and his fellow citizens through contact with one who was himself polluted. Hence the curious solution: Orestes might enter the house, but was given his own table and jug of wine, and no one said a word to him. Both included and excluded at once, Orestes celebrated the first Choes festival together with the Athenians.[31] All behaved as though they had been stained with murder, and on this day all Athenians are Oresteioi.[32] As artificial as the inclusion of Orestes in the Athenian custom may be, the ritual's inner tension is appropriately expressed in the conflict of duties and the shrewd solution found by the king: a communal meal in which community is simultaneously abolished; the murderer's tabu, paradoxically extended to all Athenians. The murderer may not enter the temples—on the day of the Choes, the temples are closed; the murderer must be kept away from hearth and table—at the Choes, people eat at separate tables; it is forbidden to speak with the murderer—the Athenians empty their pitchers in silence. The day of the Choes is a "day of pollution," *μιαρὰ ἡμέρα*—above all, the murderer is the one who is "polluted," *μιαρός*.[33]

The new wine is imbibed as though it carried blood guilt. This is expressed even more forcefully in another etiological myth about the Choes festival, in which the wine is brought to Athens by Aetolians. They were killed, and the oracle ordered the Choes festival to be established in atonement.[34] Aetolia was a center of viticulture, or at least of myths about wine: the ruler there was Oineus, the wine-man,

---

[31] Eur. *Iph. Taur.* 947–60. Phanodemos, *FGrHist* 325 F 11 = Ath. 437c–d is the one who mentions Demophon; cf. Plut. *Q. conv.* 643a, 613b. Apollod., *FGrHist* 244 F 133 = Schol. Aristoph. *Ach.* 961, *Eq.* 95 speaks of Pandion; cf. Jacoby on 325 F 11, III b Suppl. p. 184. For Orestes' trial at Athens see also Hellanikos, *FGrHist* 323a F 22; *Marm. Par.*, *FGrHist* 239 A 25. For the connection with the Anthesteria see also Schol. Lyk. 1374. It is assumed that the Orestes-aition for the Choes goes back to the sixth century and that Aeschylus, *Eum.* 448–52, 474–75, implicitly rejects it: see Jacoby III b Suppl., Notes pp. 28–29; cf. R. Pfeiffer, *Kallimachosstudien* (1922), 104–12.

[32] Callim. fr. 178.2.

[33] Wächter (1910) 64–76; L. Moulinier, *Le pur et l'impur dans la pensée et la sensibilité des grecs* (1950), 81–92; esp. Soph. *OT* 236–43; Plat. *Euthyphr.* 4b; on the silence see Aesch. *Eum.* 448; Eur. *HF* 1219; *Or.* 75; fr. 427; *LSS* 115 B 54 (Cyrene).

[34] Ael. fr. 73 Hercher = Suda φ 428, χ 364; cf. Schol. Aristoph. *Ach.* 961. There is a similar story about the death of a priest of Dionysus as the aition of a goat-sacrifice at Potniai: see Paus. 9.8.2 "Slaves and Aetolians" are excluded from the sanctuary of Leukothea at Chaironeia: see Plut. *Q. Rom.* 267d.

whose grandfather, Orestheus, planted the first vine, the offspring of a bitch.[35] It has rightly been suspected that the Attic myth of the Choes festival confused Orestheus and Orestes.[36] Beyond the similarity in names, however, they are linked by the theme of bloodshed. In the version of the myth that points toward Aetolia, the Athenians are not just Orestes' companions, but the murderers' descendants, sharing the guilt for his act.

There was a parallel myth from Ikaria, the modern Dionyso, an Attic village famous for its vineyards and the customs of its vinegrowers. Dionysus himself came to the house of Ikarios, bringing him the vine and instructing him in cultivation, harvesting, and pressing of the wine. Ikarios happily loaded the casks full of the god's new gift onto his cart and brought it to his fellow villagers. But the "opening of the casks" turned into a disaster: when the revellers, unfamiliar with wine, grew drunk and sank to the ground, Ikarios was suspected of having poisoned them. The angry crowd thereupon killed their benefactor with clubs, and his blood mixed with the wine. His daughter, Erigone, led by her dog Maira, searched desperately for her lost father till she found his body in a well; she subsequently hanged herself.[37] Thus, in the land of wine, in Attica, the myth of the wine overflows with gruesome details: this wine is a very special juice and anything but harmless.

What we found expressed in the ritual is confirmed in the myths of violence and murder surrounding the first wine: drinking the new wine fulfills the function of a sacrificial meal, consecrated as something bizarre, a disastrous inversion of the norm, on this day when

---

[35] Hekataios, *FGrHist* 1 F 15; Apollod. 1.64.

[36] F. G. Welcker, *Nachtrag zu der Schrift über die Aeschylische Trilogie* (1826), 186, 211; S. Wide, *Lakonische Kulte* (1893), 82–83.

[37] The later authors (esp. Hyg. *Astr.* 2.4 = *"Eratosth." Catast.* pp. 77–81 Robert; Nonnus 47.34–264) depend for the essentials on Eratosthenes' *Erigone* (fr. 22–26 Powell; R. Merkelbach, *Miscellanea di Studi Alessandrini in memoria di A. Rostagni* [1963], 469–526). Dionysus' visit is depicted on black figure vases (Brit. Mus. B 149 = *ABV* 245.60; B 153 = *ABV* 243.45) without names being inscribed; the host could thus also be called Amphiktyon (Philochoros, *FGrHist* 328 F 5; Paus. 1.2.5) or Semachos (Philochoros, *FGrHist* 328 F 206; Euseb. *Hieron. chron. a. Abr.* 523). It then appears on a series of Attic reliefs in the late Hellenistic age (Ch. Picard, *AJA* 38 [1934], 137–52; M. Bieber, *The Sculpture of the Hellenistic Age* [1955], 154; *EAA* III 114; interpretation disputed). According to Paus. 1.2.5, when the cult of Dionysus Eleuthereus (cf. I.7.n.53) was introduced, the oracle of Delphi (#545 Parke and Wormell [1958]) referred to the god's arrival at the home of Ikarios; this was thus taken as the oldest and decisive epiphany. For a new mosaic with ΔΙΟΝΥΣΟΣ· ΑΚΜΗ· ΙΚΑΡΙΟΣ and ΟΙ ΠΡΩΤΟΙ ΟΙΝΟΝ ΠΙΟΝΤΕΣ from Paphos see *Archaeology* 21 (1968) 48–53.

the normal order is inverted. The association of wine and blood, especially around the Mediterranean where red wine predominates, is natural and is attested outside of Greece, in the Semitic realm.[38] This is clearly not just a metaphor: the drinking of wine became sacred when a whole complex ritual of bloody sacrifice was transferred to the labors and pleasures of the wine-grower.[39] For it is certain that the sacrificial rites, rooted in the life of the hunter, are far older than these, even though the history of the origin and dissemination of intoxicating beverages in the Neolithic and in the early civilizations is still unclear. Various kinds of beer, the fermented drink made from barley, probably existed before wine; and we must consider that other kinds of narcotics may have served similar functions in the religious ritual.[40] Here, the male society discovered a new, overpowering area of experience in which the burdens of reality were swept away by the flood of something utterly different. And just as groups had always found their identity and inner solidarity through a sacrificial ritual, so this new pleasure was acted out as a secret, unspeakable sacrifice. By simultaneously liberating and binding, the god of wine offered a new and stable form of community.

Among the Indo-Aryans, the sacred intoxicating drink is called *Soma*, a god who descended from heaven, was mashed, trampled, and squeezed—a sacrificial victim, but still a god, regardless of his form—and leads the pious back to heaven.[41] The Greeks tended to equate Dionysus and the wine already in Classical times.[42] Conse-

---

[38] "Blood of the vine" in Ugaritic: Baal II iv 37, *ANET* 133; Gen. 49:11; Sir. 50.15. "Blood of the earth," Androkydes, Pliny *N.h.* 14.58.

[39] Above all, pressing the grapes turns into the bloody sacrificial act of tearing apart, already among the Egyptians: see S. Schott, "Das blutrünstige Keltergerät," *Zeitschr. f. ägypt. Sprache u. Altertumskunde* 74 (1938), 88–93; D. Wortmann, *ZPE* 2 (1968), 227–30; Eudoxos in Plut. *Is.* 353b–c; Israel, Isaiah 63:2; then via the Apoc. of John 14.18–20 up through late medieval depictions of wine-pressing; cf. Eisler (1925) esp. 226–35, 246–48, 269–79, 334–44. The Greek "eye-cups" are possibly a continuation of the Palaeolithic "skull-cups" (Müller-Karpe [1966] 241; Maringer [1956] 123–28, 125: still present at Pompei).

[40] For conjectures concerning beer and Dionysus see Harrison (1922) 413–25; for wine made from sadar-fruit at Çatal Hüyük see Mellaart (1967) 269. R. G. Wasson, *Soma, Divine Mushroom of Immortality* (1968), tries to prove that "soma" was an hallucinogenic mushroom (fly-agaric); he is criticized by J. Brough, *Bull. School Or. Afr. Stud.* 34 (1971), 331–62. For a detailed discussion of drugs and ecstasy especially in America, see La Barre (1970) 143–49.

[41] *Rig-Veda* IX (for German transl. see K. F. Geldner III [1951], 1–120).

[42] Eur. *Bacch.* 284; *Cyclops* 519–28; Plat. *Leg.* 773d (wine as μαινόμενος θεός); Phanodemos, *FGrHist* 325 F 12; Philochoros, *FGrHist* 328 F 5. "Der Wein ist Dionysos," K. Schefold, *MH* 27 (1970), 119.

quently, the drinker of the wine would be drinking the god himself, and the myths about the death of the inventor of wine came to be descriptions of the sufferings, death, and transformation of the god himself. In this regard, the Classical Greeks had virtually insurmountable inhibitions: ever since Homer, gods had been immortal by definition. How, then, could a god die or become the victim of a cannibalistic meal? Such myths become themselves "unspeakable," ἄρρητος. But there was a single god of whom this story was told: Dionysus. The Titans lured the child Dionysus away from his throne, tore him apart, and ate him. As we can gather from allusions,[43] this myth, apparently handed down in the Orphic mysteries, was known in the fifth century, even if it was officially ignored. To be sure, it describes not the preparation of the wine[44]—regardless of later allegorizing interpretations—but, rather, a bloody initiation sacrifice with boiling and roasting. The rite of the Anthesteria implies a somewhat different, though largely analogous, myth of the god torn apart, whose blood is represented in the sacramental drinking of the wine.[45] Of course, this hypothetical myth may always have existed only in allusions and disguises, whereas the story once again made distinctions between the god and the victim. Nevertheless, Philostratus claimed

---

[43]The oldest certain source known for the myth of Dionysus' death is Callim. fr. 643 (see II.5.n.41 above); cf. Jacoby on Philochoros, *FGrHist* 328 F 7. It was argued by Wilamowitz (1932) 378–80 and, after him, L. Moulinier, *Orphée et l'orphisme à l'époque classique* (1955), 46–60, that this myth was invented in the early Hellenistic age. But there are earlier allusions to it: (1) Pind. fr. 133.1 ποινὰν παλαιοῦ πένθεος; cf. P. Tannery, *Rev. Philol.* 23 (1899), 129; H. J. Rose, *HThR* 36 (1943), 247. (2) The identification with Osiris, and Herodotus' emphatic silence concerning the πάθη of Osiris—which were by no means secret in Egypt, 2.61, 132, 179, and cf. G. Murray in Harrison (1927) 342–43. (3) Plat. *Leg.* 701c Τιτανικὴ φύσις and 672b διεφορήθη τῆς ψυχῆς τὴν γνώμην. (4) Isocr. 11 (Bus.) 39. (5) Xenokrates fr. 20 Heinze, and cf. Plat. *Crat.* 400c. Ancient philologists conjectured that the myth could be traced back to Onomakritos (Paus. 8.37.5, probably following Arist. fr. 7); a sixth-century poem could perhaps underlie this conjecture. The Derveni papyrus, which has decisively changed the situation concerning sources for Orphism, has preserved nothing about Dionysus. See also K. Kerényi, *Dioniso* 14 (1951), 139–56; *Mythos, Scripta in hon. M. Untersteiner* (Genoa, 1970), 171–78.

[44]For the πάθη of Dionysus as an allegory of wine-preparation see Diod. 3.62.7 = *OF* 301, and cf. 4.5.1; Skolion in Plut. *Q. conv.* 676e; for a pressing-song see Schol. Clem. Pr. 4.4 p. 297.4 Stählin; Cornutus 30; Himer. *Or.* 45.4 = *OF* 214. For wine as αἷμα βακχίου see already Timotheos 780 Page. See also H. Herter, *RhM* 100 (1957), 109–10 on a Pompeian painting; E. Simon, *Hommages A. Grenier* III (1962), 1418–27, on Campana reliefs.

[45]So also Guépin (1968) 294: "Sacramental drinking of Dionysus as wine." Foucart (1904) 138–48 tried to derive the Anthesteria from the cult of Osiris, without seeing the special function of the drinking of the Choes.

that the Athenians performed masquerades at the Anthesteria, and presented Bakchai, nymphs, and horai "amid the Orphic theology";[46] that is, he was thinking of recitations or performances of the Orphic Dionysus myth on the day of the Choes. Admittedly, this evidence comes from late antiquity, but even the drinking competition of Classical times was an "initiation," τελετή, a symbolic reprise of a bloody rite performed in sacred silence, incurring guilt for death, to establish the order of life.

3. *Carians or Keres*

When men became rambunctious and tried to claim as their due what had been granted simply as an exception, one could rebuff them with the verse quoted from a comedy, "Get out, you . . . ! The Anthesteria is over."[1] However, our sources do not agree as to precisely which vocative designation accompanied that "get out!" Some speak of "Keres," "as though dead souls haunt the city at the Anthesteria";[2] others of "Carians," slaves who were allowed to participate in the Anthesteria by way of exception, or else were considered the aboriginal inhabitants of Attica and hence entitled to take part. Either way, our sources are agreed that they were intimately linked to the Anthesteria.

Influenced by the theory of animism, both Otto Crusius and Erwin Rohde strongly advocated the "dead souls" explanation.[3] There was the immediate parallel of the Roman Lemuria,[4] but soon a whole

---

[46] *V. Ap.* 4.21. Cf. Luk. *De salt.* 39.

[1] Zenob. Ath. 1.30 p. 352 Miller = Zenob. Par. 4.33, *Paroem. Gr.* I 93 ἐπὶ τῶν τὰ αὐτὰ ἐπιζητούντων πάντοτε λαμβάνειν. Proverbs, as quotations from drama, often appear in verse, above all in trimeter, e.g., Zenob. Par. 1.50, 70, 75, 81, 83, 86, 90, 92, 96, etc.; by overlooking the function of the verse as a proverb, scholars were over-hasty in making it into a ritual cry (see Deubner [1932] 113–14; Pickard-Cambridge [1968] 14).

[2] Mentioned second in Phot. θύραζε κᾶρες, Suda ϑ 598 = Paus. Att. ϑ 20 Erbse; it is an addition in some manuscripts at Zenob. Par. 4.33. Cf. Hsch. κήρ· ψυχή . . . κῆρες· ψυχαί.

[3] O. Crusius in *Allgemeine Encyclopädie der Wissenschaften und Künste* II 35 (1884), 265–67; *RML* II 1136–66, esp. 1148, 1162; Rohde (1898) I 239.2; Harrison (1922) 34–36, 42–49; Deubner (1932) 113; cf. Malten, *RE* Suppl. IV 883–900.

[4] Varro in Nonnus p. 135; Ov. *Fast.* 5.442. For parallels see E. B. Tylor, *Primitive Culture* II (1871; 1913[5]), 40; Rohde, Crusius, Deubner opp. cit.; cf. G. Dumézil, *Le problème des Centaurs* (1929), 3–52.

group of related folk-customs were marshalled and it was found that festivals of the dead appeared time and again in which the dead were invited in, entertained, and finally, more or less drastically, chased away again. Thus, the Anthesteria became an All Souls festival; even the name was seen to reflect a "conjuring up" of the souls,[5] and the cask opened at the Pithoigia was thought to contain the souls. In this view, wine and drinking became strangely unconnected accessories, and doubt arose whether to consider Dionysus here as the god of wine or as "lord of the souls."

Against this, there were philological misgivings that the souls of the dead were ever Keres, or the Keres souls of the dead, among the Greeks. Rather, they were thought to be independent, "harmful demons," or at most "spirits,"[6] for whom no connection with any dead ancestors was attested. Moreover, it was pointed out that the "Carian" explanation, which had been set aside with scorn, reflected an ancient and secure tradition, the only one to appear in the old version of Zenobius' collection of sayings.[7] Crusius traced it back to the Athenian Demon, who was writing before Philochoros, in the fourth century B.C.[8] The "Keres" version, by contrast, was a late addition which, according to Crusius, was a polemic against Demon by Didymus. Thus, the Athenians themselves were speaking of Carians, and it is hard to explain how such a misunderstanding, if it is such, could have arisen there.

The Paroemiographers' claim that there was an especially large number of Carian slaves at Athens[9] is, of course, unsatisfactory. According to all other testimony, Thracian and Getan slaves were far more numerous. But this approach too comes from the perspective of the Choes ritual: this "black day" is a "white day" for slaves[10]—a sign that all is topsy-turvy—when they too may celebrate and participate in drinking. Still stranger is the story attributed to Demon: "Once, the Carians inhabited part of Attica and, when the Athenians celebrated

---

[5]See IV.1.n.4 above.

[6]Wilamowitz (1931) 272.

[7]Zenob. Ath. 1.30 p. 352 Miller = Zenob. Par. 4.33 (n.11 below).

[8]*Analecta critica ad Paroemiographos Graecos* (1883; reprinted in *Corpus Paroemiographorum Graecorum, Supplementum* [1961], II), 48–49, 146 "Demonis mira inventa" (49). On Demon see *FGrHist* 327. The fact that the older tradition speaks of Carians was stressed by R. Ganszyniec, *Eranos* 45 (1947), 100–113; M. H. A. L. H. van der Valk, *REG* 76 (1963), 418–20, tried to show that Demon was wrong. Pickard-Cambridge (1968) 14–15 and J. Brunel, *RPh* 41 (1967), 98–104, are undecided.

[9]Paus. Att. ϑ 20 (n. 2 above); Zenob. Par. 4.33 mentioned first.

[10]See IV.2.n.9 above.

the Anthesteria, they made an agreement with them, taking them into the city and into their homes. If, however, after the festival, someone should meet such Carians still lingering in Athens, he would say jokingly: "Get out, you Carians! The Anthesteria is over!"[11]

More important than the astounding claim that Carians ever inhabited Attica is the information concerning a custom which clearly underlies this report: during the festival, aliens, "aboriginal inhabitants," come to the city, indeed, they enter the houses as entitled by an agreement. But they may stay no longer than the duration of the festival. Precisely such a custom is attested for the Anthesteria in the city of Massalia.[12] On this day, in accordance with the "right of guest-friendship," many Gauls living in the surrounding areas could enter the city, and others smuggled themselves in on carts driven into the city from outside and clearly used for transporting casks. As it turned out, this open-door policy very nearly proved the ruin of Massalia.

The motif of allegedly aboriginal inhabitants appearing on certain days only to be chased away afterward is found especially in one area of folklore—the masquerade.[13] By approaching the problem from this perspective, we can resolve the contradictions of the tradition. In mask customs such as those practiced in isolated Alpine valleys well into the twentieth century, the grotesquely masked beings that invaded a village had, above all, the right to be entertained as guests. The respect accorded to them was explained by their status as the ancestors of the human race or as earlier inhabitants of the country. The belief in spirits is intimately and reciprocally related to mask customs. In the case of Athens, this prompts the hypothesis that the "spirits," Κῆρες, and the "aboriginal inhabitants," Κᾶρες, who filled the city on the day of the Choes were identical. They were mummers—probably called Κᾶρες in Attic. It has been suggested that there may have existed an old inflection Κήρ, Καρός, but this is doubtful,[14] though there

[11] Zenob. Ath. 1.30 p. 352 Miller has only this version, which appears second in Zenob. Par. 4.33.

[12] Justin. 43.4.6; J. Brunel, "D'Athènes à Marseille," *Revue des Etudes Anciennes* 69 (1967), 15–30, recognized the structural correspondence with the visit and expulsion of the Carians, and also compared the legend of the murdered Aetolians (IV.2.n.34 above).

[13] K. Meuli, *Schweizer Masken* (1943), 13–64; *Schweiz. Arch. f. Volkskunde* 28 (1927/28), 23–29, esp. 27; on the "Schurtendiebe" in the Lötschental see L. Rütimeyer, *Ur-Ethnographie der Schweiz* (1924), 364.

[14] E. Schwyzer, *Glotta* 12 (1923), 17–18; *ἐν καρὸς αἴσῃ Il.* 9.378, the meaning of which was disputed in antiquity (see Schol. AB, Eust. 757.16–56; Hsch. Κάρ); criticism by R. S. P. Beekes, *MSS* 36 (1977), 5–8. As one meaning for Κάρ, Hesychius has *πρόβατον*, thus forging a link with *κάρνος*, Κάρνεια.

may have been dialect variants even within Attica. At any rate, "harmful demon" and "bogeyman" would fit the mummers equally well. The association with the barbarous Carians, however, was always easy to make. It is hard to say which way we should, for instance, explain a Zeus Karios[15] or the aboriginal Megarian, Kar.[16]

The Attic Κᾶρες correspond at least in part to the Ionic Κῆρες, if only because both are "chased away." On the day of the "Carians," the people chew on hawthorn, which keeps away the Keres.[17] The festival now becomes comprehensible: during the Anthesteria, masked and menacing mummers invade the city and its homes, coming from outlying areas together with the new wine—perhaps even riding on the wagons that carry the casks. At any rate, it is attested that on the day of the Choes, mummers would ride around in the city on carts, pursuing, with lewd jests, anyone they met.[18] The Choes pitchers often contain depictions of grotesque masks in various forms that induced reactions of terror and even aggression.[19] Whereas the more artistic masquerade became centered at the Greater Dionysia, in comedy and tragedy, the Anthesteria remained a more primitive, improvisational, parodistic form of mummery.

The mixture of merriment and seriousness is particularly striking in the masquerade: wild laughter is acted out against the backdrop of terror and fright. To this extent, driving away the alien "Carians" fits

---

[15] Hdt. 5.66; for Apollo Κάρειος at Hierapolis see G. Pugliese Carratelli, *ASAA* 41/2 (1963/64), 351–70; for a ἱερὸν τοῦ Καρίου at Torrebis/Lydia see Nikolaos, *FGrHist* 90 F 15.

[16] Paus. 1.39.5; Steph. Byz. Καρία; for Apollo Καρινός in the form of a pyramidal stone see Paus. 1.44.2.

[17] See IV.2.n.12 above.

[18] Phot. τὰ ἐκ τῶν ἁμαξῶν, Suda τ 19 = Paus. Att. τ 4 Erbse: *ἐν τῇ τῶν χοῶν ἑορτῇ οἱ κωμάζοντες ἐπὶ τῶν ἁμαξῶν τοὺς ἀπαντῶντας ἔσκωπτόν τε καὶ ἐλοιδόρουν. τὸ δ' αὐτὸ καὶ τοῖς Ληναίοις ὕστερον ἐποίουν.* Harpokr. (Phot., Suda π 2023) *s.v.* πομπείας speaks generally of Διονυσιακαὶ πομπαί, thence ἐν τοῖς Διονυσίοις App. Prov. 4.80 (*Paroem. Gr.* I 453), Schol. Luk. pp. 77.28, 202.15. *Μεθυσθέντες κωμάζουσιν τῆς ἡμέρας* Zenob. Ath. 1.74 p. 358 Miller, App. Prov. 4.80. For ἐξ ἁμάξης as the model of lewd mockery see Aristoph. *Eq.* 464; Demosth. 18.122; Plat. *Leg.* 637b; Men. *Perinthia* fr. 4; Philemon fr. 43 (*CAF* II 489); Numenios fr. 2 p. 121 Leeman = Euseb. *Praep. Ev.* 14.6.13; Dion. Hal. *Ant.* 7.72.11; Luk. *Iup. trag.* 44; Philostr. *V. Ap.* 4.20; Schol. Aristoph. *Nub.* 296: *τὴν τρύγα χριόμενοι, ἵνα μὴ γνώριμοι γένωνται, οὕτως τὰ αὑτῶν ᾖδον ποιήματα . . . ἁμάξης ἐπικαθήμενοι.*

[19] For a child frightened by a mask see van Hoorn (1951) #918 fig. 84, and cf. #117 fig. 148; #505 fig. 240; for a child warding off a grotesque being see #102 fig. 26, and cf. #256 fig. 15; #102 recalls the type of the Herakles κηραμύντης: see the pelike Berlin 3317, Harrison (1922) 166, *EAA* IV 347 (similarly Herakles against ΓΕΡΑΣ, pelike Louvre G234 = *ARV*^{2} 286.16, and cf. 284.1, 653.1, 889.160; *RML* III 2083).

in with the sacrificial character of drinking at the Choes. It is precisely in sacrifice, in the central moment of the unspeakable action, that one finds the intrusion of aliens, integrated as part of the comedy of innocence, who seize a portion for themselves and must therefore withdraw again. We may recall the bands of werewolves, the people of Delphi at sacrifice, and the hirpi Sorani.[20] Just so at the sacramental drinking of the wine, unfamiliar, uncanny guests were present beside the friends and family who had been invited. On this day, no one might be turned away, each received his pitcher of wine; yet each man sat alone at a separate table, behind pitch-covered doors. Thus, one encountered the sacred through that which is uncanny.

A pan-Hellenic myth tells of another opening of a cask which likewise attracted wild guests: Herakles stopped at the house of Pholos in the Pholoe Mountains, and in his honor, his host opened the big old cask that was sunk in the floor. Thereupon the centaurs stormed down from the mountains. They grew drunk and started the fight that ended in their bloody defeat.[21] This was a favorite theme in Archaic vase-painting: centaurs come from outside to taste the wine and are subsequently driven away. This myth is a Peloponnesian version of the Attic Pithoigia and Choes on a heroic level.

4. *Sacred Marriage and Lenaia-Vases*

Even though the topsy-turvy order of the day of the Choes, with its license, its drunken mockery, was enjoyed to the full, the goal

[20] See Ch. II above.

[21] Apollod. 2.83–85; *PR* II 499–502; Brommer (1960) 135–38. Dumézil (1929) tried to show that centaurs existed as masks: see his pl. 1. This sort of animal masquerade, with the animal's hind part fastened on, is now already attested through the wall-paintings of Çatal Hüyük (see I.2.n.19, I.8.n.28 above). The picture on the lekythos from Jena (*ARV*² 760.41; Harrison [1922] 43) in which the *ψυχαί*, which have been conjured by Hermes, swarm out of the pithos can be explained through the function of the funerary vases, or round clay rings, at libations for the dead; cf. the black figure conical stand from Frankfurt in H. V. Herrmann, *Omphalos* (1959), pl. 5; A. Furtwängler, *Antike Gemmen* (1900), pl. 20.32; *pace* Harrison, this has no direct connection with the Dionysian *πιθοίγια*.

must always have been to overcome the "day of pollution," to end the period of godlessness: the Chytroi follows the Choes. Sundown on the twelfth of Anthesterion signaled the end of the "day of pollution." By this time, the Choes pitchers were empty, but they could not be simply put away. At other festivals, after the drinking was over, pious revellers would bring the wreaths that they had worn to a temple and deposit them on a statue.[1] On this day, however, the temples were closed, except for that of Dionysus "in the Marshes." Hence the peculiar ritual that closed the day of the Choes. According to the tale, it was once again begun by king Demophon when he was entertaining Orestes: "He ordered that after the drinking was over, they should not deposit in the temples the wreaths which they had worn, since they had been under the same roof with Orestes. Rather, each should lay his wreath around his Choes pitcher and take it to the priestess at the temple 'in the marshes,' and then perform the further sacrifices in the sanctuary."[2] Thus, on the evening of the day of the Choes, the streets and alleys of Athens came to life with people flocking to the temple "in the marshes," holding their empty pitchers, crowned with wreaths. After drinking two and a half liters of wine, not every reveller was quite steady on his feet, and there could be no more question of sacred silence. Aristophanes has his watery chorus of croaking frogs sing of the events at the temple "in the marshes": "Let us strike up the hymn to the sound of the flute, my lovely sounding song, ko-ax, ko-ax, which we sing in the water to the Nysaean son of Zeus, Dionysus, when the drunken crowd staggers in procession to my sacred precinct at the sacred festival of pots."[3] The word *κραιπαλόκωμος*, "rambling in drunken revelry," captures the mood of the evening. On a visual level, it is brought to life in the depictions on the Choes pitchers.[4] There we see the somewhat unsteady figures, their

---

[1]See Timaios, *FGrHist* 566 F 158.

[2]Phanodemos, *FGrHist* 325 F 11; Deubner (1932) 99, 100 paraphrases the last words, *ἔπειτα θύειν ἐν τῷ ἱερῷ τὰ ἐπίλοιπα*, as "die Neige zu spenden"—but *ϑύειν* is not *σπένδειν*.

[3]*Ran.* 211–19.

[4]Deubner (1932) 244; H. R. Immerwahr, *TAPA* 77 (1946), 247–50; cf. van Hoorn (1951) #762 fig. 173; #385 fig. 85; #328 fig. 503; #633 fig. 95; #40 fig. 97; #838 fig. 88; pelike Basel fig. 109; #602 fig. 107; #651 fig. 168; #581 fig. 527, etc.; #842 fig. 87 = Deubner (1932) pl. 9.2 = Metzger (1965) 68.26: a "priestess" receiving wreaths (or Basilinna awaiting Dionysus; cf. E. Simon, *AK* 6 [1963], 21?). Plato *Critias* 120b says that in Atlantis the bowls out of which people drink at the sacrifice for an oath are consecrated in the shrine. For the breaking of pots in funerary cult see W. Helbig, *SB München* (1900), 2, 247–51 (against this cf. *LS* 97.9; [*τὰ δὲ ἀ*]*γγεῖα ἀποφέρεσϑαι*); in Hebraic sin-offering, see at Lev. 6:21.

wreath-covered pitchers (obviously long empty) in hand or even hung on the lyre, striding along by the light of torches, reeling and capering. According to Aristophanes, this occurred at the Chytroi, for with the evening the new phase had already begun.

Just as the drinking at the Choes corresponded to the central act of the bloody sacrifice, we recognize the closing ritual of the hunting and sacrificing complex in this evening assembly. Killing and eating were followed by gathering the remains[5] in order to make a symbolic restitution and a permanent order. The sacred wine was distributed in the Choes pitchers in equal portions: everyone had the same amount to drink. Now all these jugs were gathered together at a consecrated place. Time and again in myth the remnants of a victim torn apart are collected, deposited, brought back to life in just this way. Such was the story of Dionysus torn apart,[6] regardless of whether the events were said to occur at Delphi or were moved to Crete. Perhaps this perspective helps clarify the name *Dionysus in the Marshes*, which seems so inappropriate to the local conditions at Athens: marshes and swamps—or, for the coastal inhabitant, the sea—are the places where things disappear and surface again miraculously. This is where victims are submerged. This is where stories appear of the god's return from the depths.[7] This is the place where Dionysus reveals himself as god, beyond bloodshed, death, and the sacral meal.

The temple was administered by a priestess—not a priestess exclusively its own, for this temple was normally closed, but by a woman who assumed the priestly duties for this day. Fourteen women were appointed by the "king" for the temple "in the marshes." They were called simply "the venerable ones."[8] At their head was the "queen,"[9]

---

[5]See I.2 above.

[6]Philodem. *De piet.* 2 p. 16 col. 44 Gomperz Ῥέας τὰ μέλη συνθείσης ἀνεβίω; Diod. 3.62.6 πάλιν δ'ὑπό τῆς Δήμητρος τῶν μελῶν συναρμοσθέντων; cf. II.5.n.41 above. Cf. the myths of Aktaion (II.4.n.18 above), Hippolytus (Sen. *Phaedra* 1247–48, 1256–79), Pentheus (Eur. *Bacch.* 1299–1300), Orpheus ("Erat." *Cat.* 24 pp. 140–41 Robert), Osiris (Plut. *Is.* 358a).

[7]Thus, at the spring in Lerna Dionysus sinks and reappears, and is "called up" (Plut. *Is.* 364 f., and cf. III.3.n.33 above); cf. also III.8 above.

[8]The form γέραιρα (feminine of γεραρός; cf. χίμαιρα/χιμαρός) is confirmed through inscriptions (*IG* II/III² 6288; XII 3.420) and was read by Aristarchus at *Il.* 6.270 (Schol. A); it is transmitted (with different accentuation) at *Et. Gen.* = *Et. M.* 227.35 and *An. Bekk.* I 231.32, and cf. 228.9 (= Ael. Dion. γ 7 Erbse), it should be so read at Harpokr. *s.v.* (Cd. γεραιαί or γεραραί); "Demosth." 59.73, 78; Poll. 8.108; Hsch. (incorrectly classified) has γεραραί; Deubner (1932) 100 n.5.

[9]The tradition in Demosthenes (59.74) is split between βασίλισσα, which Phrynichos (p. 225 Lobeck), Aelius Dionysius (β 5 Erbse), and Pollux (8.90) recognize, and βασίλιννα, which also appears in the context of a child's game: Men. fr. 652.

the wife of the archon basileus himself. She was responsible for swearing in the "venerable ones," and she herself had the most spectacular role to play in the program of the festival: she was given to the god as his bride. In a building in the marketplace, the Bukolion, the god and the mortal woman came together in love.[10]

On which day of the Anthesteria this occurred is not recorded. Yet it should be clear that the "day of pollution" at least would be out of the question, and since the "queen" was formally delivered to the god as his bride, there is no possibility of shameless coupling by daylight. Marriage processions belong to the night, as do the works of Aphrodite. Now, because the Pithoigia is clearly preliminary in nature, the only possible time left in the festival is the night of transition from the Choes to the Chytroi.[11] This is confirmed by vase-paintings, especially a Choes pitcher in New York on which the marriage of Dionysus and Ariadne is shown, framed by the revellers from the day of the Choes.[12] The torch and the dangling Choes pitcher clearly mark the time as night, at the start of which the "tipsy crowd" marched to the Limnaion to celebrate the "sacred Chytroi."

---

[10] "Demosth." 59.73, 76; Arist. *Ath. Pol.* 3.5; Hsch. Διονύσου γάμος. That this act was part of the Anthesteria (E. Buschor, *AM* 53 [1928], 102–103, considered it to be of the Lenaea) is clear from the fact that the νόμος stating what was required of the "queen" was written on a stele kept in the Limnaion, which was open only on the day of the Choes: see "Demosth." 59.75–76; likewise, the altar, for the oath of the γέραιραι mentioned thereafter (79), can only be the one in the Limnaion. The Eleusinian Hierokeryx (ibid.) assists the women at the (bloody) sacrifice for the oath. On the θεοίνια mentioned in the oath see Jacoby on *FGrHist* 334 F 3.

[11] Thus also E. Simon, *AK* 6 (1963) 11; Pickard-Cambridge (1968) 11, *contra* Deubner (1932) 109, who suggests "den Vormittag und vielleicht den Beginn des Nachmittags" of the day of the Choes. For μεθημερινοὶ γάμοι as scandalous see Demosth. 18.129; cf. *LSS* 115 A 11–14.

[12] New York Metr. Mus. 06.1021.183 = van Hoorn (1951) #745 fig. 105 = Metzger (1965) 62–63, pl. 27.2. E. Simon, *AK* 6 (1963), 12, correctly comments: "Es gibt Szenen, in denen die Entscheidung: Ariadne oder Basilinna, nicht gefällt werden darf." For Dionysus and Ariadne in the bower see Chous Leningrad 2074 St. = van Hoorn #579, Metzger (1951) pl. XIII, 1. For revellers with Chous beside Dionysus, Ariadne, Eros, see fr. calyx-crater Tübingen 5439 = *ARV*² 1057.97, *AK* 6 (1963), pl. 5.1. The wedding of Dionysus also appears on an oinochoe from the Villa Giulia: see L. Curtius in *Vermächtnis der antiken Kunst* (1950), fig. 37–41; H. Marwitz, *Antike und Abendland* 12 (1966), fig. 2. For Dionysus stepping toward a woman on a throne see the oinochoe (not the normal form of the Chous) in the Brit. Mus., Deubner (1932) 101–102, pl. 10. For Dionysus, escorted by torchbearers with Chous, moving toward a door behind which a woman waits, see calyx-crater Tarquinia *RC* 41.97 = *ARV*² 1057.96, *AK* 6 (1963), pl. 5.3 (of the Komos-scene type, see van Hoorn [1951] #761 fig. 117, Immerwahr, *TAPA* 77 [1946], 250). For a satyr-child next to a recumbent couple on a South Italian Chous at Brindisi see K. Kerényi, *Römische Mitteilungen* 70 (1963), 98, pl. 43. An Italic vase portraying Dionysus with the horns of a bull beside Ariadne (E. M. W. Tillyard, *The Hope*

The details of the sacred marriage were kept a secret, "unspeakable." Our sources are uniformly silent and offer no assistance in deciding between the two possible explanations: was there a symbolic union with a statue, a herm,[13] or did a mortal represent the god—most likely the "king" himself?[14] Even in one of the surviving speeches of Demosthenes, that of the prosecution against Neaira, which deals with the scandal that the daughter of a hetaera—herself not blameless—rose to the status of "queen," we are provided with little more than vague indications. "This woman offered up the unspeakable sacrifice on behalf of the city; she saw that which a non-Athenian should not have seen; such a woman entered the room that none of the many other Athenians enters, but only the 'king's' wife; she administered the oath to the 'venerable women,' who assist in the sacred acts; she was given to Dionysus as a bride; she performed the ancestral customs before the gods on behalf of the city, many sacred secret customs."[15] In spite of its lack of clarity in the details, this report gives us the outline of a set program. Entering a place that may not be entered: next to the temple in the sanctuary "in the marshes" there was a subterranean "house"[16] which obviously came into play here. Whatever was carried down into it and whatever was then taken out of it—we recall the night of the Arrhephoroi—it was followed by a sacrificial oath by which the "venerable ones" were bound together; the oaths were taken "over the sacrificial baskets." There were fourteen "venerable ones," corresponding to the fourteen Athenian altars of Dionysus.[17] This indicates a large number of sacrifices to Dionysus. The

Vases [1923], pl. 31.218; van Hoorn [1951] p. 51; Kerényi, op. cit.) has been linked with the marriage in the Bukolion. H. Marwitz, *Antike und Abendland* 12 (1966), 97–110, tries to explain the "Aldobrandic wedding" as referring to the Attic Hieros Gamos.

[13] H. Goldmann, *AJA* 46 (1942), 64–67.

[14] Farnell V (1909) 217 (with doubts); Deubner (1932) 107–109, 116–17; cf. *GB* II 148. Against this cf. E. Simon, *AK* 6 (1963), 12 with reference to the myth of Theseus: the king must defer when Dionysus appears. In a similar way Oineus leaves Deianeira to Dionysus: Hyg. *Fab.* 129. The myth of Kephalos and Prokris (Pherekydes, *FGrHist* 3 F 34), however, contains the motif that the king departs but comes back in disguise. For coupling with a statue of Leukippos before the wedding at Phaistos see Ant. Lib. 17.6.

[15] 59.73, and cf. 85.

[16] See IV.1.n.9 above.

[17] *An. Bekk.* 231.32; Ael. Dion. γ 7 Erbse (n. 8 above); it is not stated nor is it probable that all of these altars were in the Limnaion. Foucart (1904) 138–41 brought out the strange correspondence that Osiris was torn into fourteen parts (Plut. *Is.* 358a; for 26 parts, cf. Diod. 1.21.2), and that accordingly there were tombs of Osiris in equal number. For two komasts—a woman at an altar, beside her a man with two torches on a Chous—see van Hoorn (1951) #870 fig. 69; for a man with Chous and sacrificial basket,

climax came when the "queen" was presented to the god and the rite was accomplished—precisely what Aristotle unabashedly calls the sexual act.

If the sacramental drinking on the day of the Choes symbolized a bloody sacrifice, the sacred marriage that followed the gathering of the remains must likewise belong in the context of ritual restitution. And this is several times attested in myth and custom. The victim is appeased by being given a woman;[18] indeed, he is revitalized in the embrace and obtains new regenerative powers. Thus, Isis conceives Horus after Osiris' scattered remains have been gathered together;[19] and the god enters the Pythia sitting on the tripod.[20] Here, too, of course, the "sacred" in the sacred marriage carries the greatest danger: just as the woman can revive her dead partner, he can kill the woman.

These outlines would have to suffice, were it not for the pictorial tradition which in all probability provides us with a precise indication of the form in which Dionysus appeared on that night. Dozens of Attic vases exhibit an utterly primitive form of Dionysiac statue that has sparked the curiosity of religious historians for a long time. This was no anthropomorphic god. There was simply a mask suspended on a column. Sometimes there are two masks peering in either direction, like Janus. A robe was hung around the column, the crude indication of a body, though lacking arms and legs. Instead of these, we see cakes skewered onto it; branches sprout from the body; a three-legged sacrificial table is set up in front of the statue, covered with all sorts of food, but, most importantly, two jugs of wine, the stamnoi. With measured steps, women move about the whole scene, drawing wine and drinking it—at least when the painter restrains his fantasy and leaves out the usual horde of intruding satyrs and maenads (see Figure 7).[21]

---

a statue (of Dionysus?), and a man in front of an altar see a fragment from the Agora P 5270, L. Talcott, *AJA* 49 (1945), 526–27.

[18] See I.7.n.40–42, 51 above.

[19] Indicated in Plut. *Is.* 358e, and cf. 357d; H. Bonnet, *Reallexikon der ägyptischen Religionsgeschichte* (1952), 569–70.

[20] See II.5.nn.55, 56 above.

[21] A. Frickenhaus, *Lenäenvasen* (72. Winckelmannsprogr. 1912), described twenty-nine vases; for a supplement see Pickard-Cambridge (1968) 30.2. The depiction on the black figure lekythos München 1871, in which R. Hackl, *ARW* 12 (1909), 195, saw Egyptian "mummy worship," and cf. J. Boardman, *The Greeks Overseas* (1980^2), 151, Beazley *ABV* 470.103, and Simon (1969) 274, however, saw "Dionysus," is closely related to this iconographical type. The iconographical parallels from Egypt adduced by Hackl are not to

It is impossible to decide which Attic festival of Dionysus this mask-worship reflects. August Frickenhaus, who made the most comprehensive survey of these vases, called them "Lenaia-vases." Since next to nothing is known of the Lenaia, his theory cannot be conclusively refuted. But the Choes vases have recently yielded up some evidence that speaks for a connection with the Anthesteria.[22] A similar depiction has appeared on a Choes pitcher,[23] and another Choes pitcher clearly exhibits an earlier stage in the ritual: here we see the mask of the god in the Liknon, flanked by two women with the wine-kantharos and a tray containing fruits.[24] This is not, in any case, part of the Pithoigia, for the wine has already been poured into the stamnoi[25] where it was stored for daily use. For the Greeks, a wine-drinking woman was scandalous, but the women on the Lenaia-vases are evidently performing a solemn, sacred duty. It is likely, then, that they represent—as the mortal counterpart of the mythical maenads—the society of the "venerable ones," administering their office on the night of the Chytroi. There is a text listing the rituals of the Anthesteria which mentions, between the "tying" of the temple with ropes and the Chytroi itself, a "setting-up," *ἵδρυσις*.[26] This word could just

---

be taken lightly: the depiction thus becomes a further example for the syncretism of Osiris/Dionysus at the time of Hekataios (cf. III.6.n.8 above). The main argument for the attribution to the Lenaia is the name of the festival itself, which is linked to *Λῆναι* = *βάκχαι* (Frickenhaus 27–28). There is literary evidence for Dionysus Περικιόνιος at Thebes: see Mnaseas Schol. Eur. *Phoen.* 651; as a column, *στῦλος*, encircled by ivy, see the oracle and Eur. fr. 203 *TGF* in Clem. *Strom.* 1.24.163.

[22] Besides Frickenhaus, those advocating the Lenaia were Deubner (1932) 127–32; Simon (1969) 276; hesitantly, Pickard-Cambridge (1968) 30–34; undecided, Metzger (1965) 66–68. Those arguing for the day of the Choes, with reference to Phanodemos, *FGrHist* 325 F 12 (see IV.2.n.6 above), were Nilsson, *JdI* 31 (1916), 329 = *Opuscula* I (1951), 198, etc.; (1955) 587; W. Wrede, "Der Maskengott," *AM* 53 (1928), 81–95; Webster in Pickard-Cambridge (1962) 80. The votive offering by two women of a masklike image of Dionysus—which recurs in a similar form on herms—is not decisive: see J. Frel, *AA* (1967), 28–34; E. Simon (1969) 271.12 connected it with Lenaios.

[23] Leningrad 19893, van Hoorn (1951) #603 fig. 53, but preferably in Metzger (1965) pl. 27.3, pp. 66–67. In contrast to the other Lenaia-vases, there are men portrayed here next to the idol and the offertory table. There is a bull's skull in the picture.

[24] Athens, Coll. Vlasto, van Hoorn (1951) #271 fig. 38 = *ARV*² 1249.13, Nilsson (1955) pl. 38.1.

[25] *Κατεσταμνισμένος* Theophr. *Caus. Pl.* 2.18.4.

[26] Alkiphr. 4.18.11 (*αἵρεσιν* Cdd.; *ἵδρυσιν* conj. Meineke). (Hock [1905] 62 argues for a link with the setting-up of the fourteen altars, but altars "set up" in older times normally continue to exist.) For the setting-up of a Dionysus herm on a sarcophagus at Princeton see F. Matz, *Die dionysischen Sarkophage* III (1969), #202 pl. 211, 218, and cf. *Abh. Mainz* (1963), 15, 1428–43 also for the connection with the "god of masks"; see also Hock (1905) 56.

as well refer to the strange statue of Dionysus as to the two stamnoi in which the wine is set up before the god of wine. In either case, that which had previously been dismembered and destroyed in an unspeakable sacrifice was now given shape again.

The statue betrays its origins. It is not a permanent temple-statue but is simply improvised for an annual ceremony. We can virtually see how it was done: the most important thing was the mask, which was brought and raised up, fixed and adorned. The table would then be brought and food and wine set on it. The "queen" had to enter a room which no one otherwise ever entered. One of the oldest Lenaia-vases depicts a woman dancing in front of a great mask of Dionysus set up in a cave.[27] Did the "queen" carry it up out of the subterranean Oikos in the Limnaion? And what was the source of the regenerative power so important for the subsequent marriage? It is curious how the statue of Dionysus on Lesbos combines the head and the phallus.[28] Yet at Athens we find nothing more to illuminate the dark abyss of the unspeakable. Only this much is clear, that amid prayer and sacrifice, running blood and flickering fire, the mask was raised, clothed, and adorned, that amid the singing of hymns, the drinking of wine and dancing with ever greater frenzy around the column, the god would suddenly appear in the middle of the night to celebrate his sacred marriage with unparalleled vital power.

We recognize here too the enduring elements of those prehistoric restitution rituals. Just as the animal's bones—most importantly, its skull—had been deposited at a specific site—or, rather, raised and consecrated—so here the mask, the equivalent of the skull,[29] was set up after the sacred wine had been consumed: the deity was present. In this way, the ritual attempted to document the restoration of order after its violation, the continuance of life through death. The Greeks did not subject this phenomenon to any sort of sociological-psychological analysis, nor in Classical times did they speak directly of the god's death and resurrection. Rather, they told the simple myth that Dionysus disappeared and returned from afar. One of the Lenaia-vases depicts the arrival of Dionysus, led by Hermes, at the altar of the "venerable women."[30]

We can surmise the course of the nocturnal celebration only in vague steps. The god and the bride must have been led in a double

[27] Berlin 1930, Frickenhaus #1 p. 3; *BCH* 87 (1963), 319; *EAA* IV 1104.

[28] See III.7.n.33 above.

[29] See I.6.n.16 above; H. Baumann, *Paideuma* 4 (1950), 205.

[30] Akr. 325 = *ARV*^{2} 460.20, Frickenhaus p. 22, Cook I (1914) 707 (cf. 708), B. Graef and E. Langlotz, *Die antiken Vasen von der Akropolis zu Athen* II (1933), pl. 20.

bridal procession from the Limnaion, whose gates would thereupon close for another year, to the Bukolion in the Agora.[31] Who took the mask down from the column, perhaps to put it on and embody the god for a night, is unknown.[32] The doors of the Bukolion likewise closed after the god's bride went in. Of course, the revellers' merry-making and turmoil continued in the streets long into the night, just as the Pannychis would accompany a wedding until sleep finally brought this long and many-faceted day to a close.

5. *Chytroi and Aiora*

The "day of the pots" took its name from the special festival food prepared for it: grains of all sorts were cooked together in a pot until they were soft, and then sweetened with honey.[1] This meal, which

---

[31] Both the skyphos Berlin F 2589 = *ARV*² 1301.7, Deubner (1932) pl. 18.2, *AK* 6 (1963), pl. 3.3, and the skyphos in Basel, E. Simon, *AK* 6 (1963), 6–22, pl. 2, have been linked to the procession of the "queen"; see also the bell-crater Louvre G 422 = *ARV*² 1019.77, *AK* 6 (1963), pl. 7.5; the volute-crater Vatican, *ARV*² 590.5, *AK* 6 (1963), pl. 6.1, etc. A πομπή beginning alongside Dionysus, i.e., perhaps in the Limnaion, is allegorically depicted on the Chous, New York 25.190, Deubner (1932) pl. 9.4; Metzger (1965) 66, O. Brendel, *AJA* 49 (1945), 519–25; cf. van Hoorn (1951) #273 fig. 23 = *ARV*² 1323.36. The wagon-ship belongs in the Dionysia rather than in the night of the Chytroi: see III.7.n.26 above. The little Choes pitcher to which Deubner (1932) 104–107, pl.11, attached such importance must be reevaluated in light of the bell-crater Copenhagen *NM* 13829: see K. Friis Johansen, "Eine Dithyrambos-Aufführung in Athen," *Meded. Da. Vid. Selsk.* 4/2 (1959), Pickard-Cambridge (1962) pl. 1, in which festively attired men sing while standing around a three-legged "maypole." If the identification of the dithyramb is correct, then the festival is probably the Dionysia. The procession of Dionysus underneath the ivy-canopy on the wagon recurs at Alexandria, σκιὰς ἐκ κισσοῦ καὶ ἀμπέλου, Kallixeinos, *FGrHist* 627 F 2 (p.169.20), cf. Eust. 857.36; Hsch. σκιάς; Poll. 7.174.

[32] See nn.13,14 above.

[1] Πᾶν σπέρμα εἰς χύτραν ἑψήσαντες Didymos Schol. Aristoph. *Ach.* 1076; χύτραν πανσπερμίας Theopompus, *FGrHist* 115 F 347a. Cf. Sosibios in Ath. 648b ἐστὶ δὲ τό πυάνιον . . . πανσπερμία ἐν γλυκεῖ ἡψημένη. On the panspermia see Nilsson (1955) 127–29; among modern Greeks see B. Schmidt, *Das Volksleben der Neugriechen* (1871), 60; E. Gjerstad, *ARW* 26 (1928), 154–70; among Serbians and Bohemians see J. Lippert, *Christentum, Volksglaube und Volksbrauch* (1882), 421, 635; among Russians see *Wörter und Sachen* 2 (1910), 100. Even today at a funeral in Russia: "Dann bekam jeder in seine Schüssel ein klein wenig Honiggrütze, die wir, der Seele zum Gedenken, ohne jede Zutat auslöffelten," A. Solschenizyn, *Im Interesse der Sache* (1970³), 52.

plays a significant role in folk custom outside Greece as well, has been called "a supper for the souls,"[2] and it certainly does reappear in the cult of the dead as well, though only because it is part of an especially ancient tradition. Simply put, it represents the most primitive of all festival meals, coming from a time when the arts of grinding grain into flour and baking bread or cakes were as yet unknown: all edible grains that could be found in nature were put together to allay hunger, prepared with honey, the one seasoning found whole in nature: this is the "panspermia."

The historian Theopompus has a report on this in a passage transmitted in two versions. The shorter one claims that "no one ate" from these pots,[3] and this gave rise to the theory of a meal for the dead from which the living were excluded, the more so because it was accompanied by talk of sacrifices for Chthonic Hermes—at the Choes. The more comprehensive version, however, says that "it is their (the Athenians') custom at the Choes to sacrifice to none of the Olympian gods, but, rather, to Chthonic Hermes; and none of the priests eats from the pot which everybody in the city cooks."[4] Thus, the food in the pot was eaten on this day by everyone in the city except the priests. They, for their part, sacrificed to Hermes, not to the Olympian gods, whose temples, as we recall, were closed on the day of the Choes. On the one hand, then, we have the priests and bloody food; on the other, a vegetarian meal. The antithesis is maintained all the way through. Hermes is the mediator between this world and the next, the god who carries Dionysus away and brings him back. Whereas his sacrifice would probably occur in the night between the Choes and the Chytroi, the "food in the pot" conclusively established the daytime order.[5]

As the etiology of the Chytroi, Theopompus tells the myth of the

---

[2]Harrison (1922) 37; cf. Deubner (1932) 112; Nilsson (1955) 595.

[3]Schol. Aristoph. *Ach.* 1076, Suda χ 622 = Theopompus, *FGrHist* 115 F 347a, *τῆς δὲ χύτρας μηδένα γεύσασθαι*. Accordingly, Harrison (1922) 37 writes "no man tasted"; Deubner (1932) 112–13, "natürlich durfte niemand von dem Opfer essen"; Nilsson (1955) 595, "davon kostet niemand."

[4]Schol. R (the source for Schol. M) Aristoph. *Ran.* 218 = Theopompus, *FGrHist* 115 F 347b: *θύειν αὐτοῖς ἔθος τ*(*οῖς*) Χουσίν (*ἔχουσιν* Cd., em. A. Wifstrand in Nilsson [1955] 595n.; *τοῖς* Χουσίν is also in the parallel text F 347a) *τῶν μὲν* 'Ὀλυμπίων *θεῶν οὐδενὶ τὸ παράπαν*, 'Ἑρμῇ *δὲ* Χθονίῳ· *καὶ τῆς χύτρας ἣν ἕψουσιν πάντες οἱ κατὰ τὴν πόλιν, οὐδεὶς γεύεται τῶν ἱερέων*. It is arbitrary to call *τῶν ἱερέων* an "interpolation" (Jacoby III b Notes p. 88.5, and cf. Harrison [1927] 291.1). A. Mommsen (1898) 398 was correct.

[5]Pots and the "setting-up" (*ἵδρυσις*) of a statue and of a temple go together: see Aristoph. *Pax* 923 with Schol., *Plut.* 1198 with Schol., Phot. *ὄμπνην*; Hsch. *ἱδρύεσθαι*; Hock (1905) 59–64; cf. I.5.n.17 above.

flood. The few men who were able to save themselves cooked that meal of grains in a pot into which everything which could be found was thrown together. In this way they regained their strength and "named the whole festival after the name of the day on which they regained their courage." At the same time, "those who then survived tried to appease Hermes on behalf of the dead," by means of the sacrifice to Hermes mentioned above.[6] Thus, the Chytroi is indeed linked with the dead, but our sources are unambiguous in calling the Choes "the day of pollution." According to Theopompus, the Chytroi signified the recovery of the solid earth after the flood, the return to a normal way of life. The memorial to the dead is like a departure, a turning away: *θύραζε* Κᾶρες. The slaves and laborers are sent back to work; the masqueraders no longer have rights. The story of Orestes can also be concluded in this way: Orestes was purified during the night—the Areopagus met at night[7]—and after being given one last sacrifice, the "venerable" Erinyes disappeared.

The story of the flood complicates the picture because it brings in an entirely new myth. Yet the flood is not infrequently linked to an unspeakable sacrifice, which functions as its cause. In just this way the flood began after Lykaon's cannibalistic meal[8] or after the killing at Samothrace.[9] In the great flood that covers all, both the crime and criminals go down into permanent oblivion, and new life can begin on new shores. Thus, even if it was a later addition in Attica, the saga of the flood provides a structurally appropriate caesura between the sacramental sacrifice at the Choes and the new start on the day of the pots.

Just as an agon ends a sacrifice, so there are agons attested for the Chytroi.[10] In spite of occasional attempts to make them more

---

[6]Theopompus, *FGrHist* 115 F 347 b: *διασωθέντας οὖν τοὺς ἀνθρώπους, ἧπερ ἐθάρρησαν ἡμέρᾳ, τῷ ταύτης ὀνόματι προσαγορεῦσαι καὶ τὴν ἑορτὴν ἅπασαν . . . τοὺς τότε περιγενομένους ὑπὲρ τῶν θανόντων ἱλάσασθαι τὸν* Ἑρμῆν. Sacrifices to herms are often depicted on Choes pitchers: see van Hoorn (1951) 26–27; it has long been a matter of dispute whether or not herms can also portray Dionysus (cf. IV.4.nn.13, 22, 26 above). At Cyzicus, tombs are garlanded with wreaths on the twelfth and the thirteenth of Anthesterion: *SEG* 28 (1978), 953.52.

[7]Luk. *Hermot.* 64; *De domo* 18.

[8]See II.1.n.15 above.

[9]See II.6.nn.9, 10 above. Cf. Guépin (1968) 287.

[10]Philochoros, *FGrHist* 328 F 57, and cf. F 84; "Plut." *Vit. X or.* 841 f.: restitution through Lykurgos; Ath. 130d; Diog. Laert. 3.56; *IG* II/III^2 2130.69 (ephebic inscription 192/93 A.D.): *ἐπετέλεσαν τοὺς* Κύθρους. Agons are frequently represented on Choes pitchers (van Hoorn [1951] 33–39); they are, however, by no means all connected with the *ἀγῶνες* Χύτρινοι.

prominent, they remained hopelessly overshadowed by the Dionysia and the Panathenaia. But even so, the evidence continues up through the second century A.D. It was, of course, the ephebes who played the most prominent role here. The newly won order is, after all, the business of the younger generation.

The day of the Chytroi contained a special delight for children, girls, and virgins: that is, swinging on a swing. For us, this is unproblematic fun, but, as the Choes pitchers show us, it had a solemn side for the Athenians. A throne was set up and covered with elegant clothes; a fire was lit; an open *πίθος* stood beside it in the ground—whether it was seen as an opened wine-cask or meant to receive libations for the dead is uncertain.[11] Here, too, the encounter with death and the joy of life permeate one another: sometimes we see a satyr, or even Eros himself, energetically swinging a girl.

The myth that the Athenians told in connection with this custom is surprisingly gloomy: a "wandering" maiden hanged herself; to propitiate her, the maidens and women of Athens must likewise "swing,"[12] though of course just on a swing, thereby replacing anxi-

---

[11] *Et. M.* 42.3 *Αἰώρα· ἑορτὴ 'Αθήνησιν* (*'Αθηνᾶς* Cdd., *'Αθηναῖς* [*sic*] Gaisford) *ἣν καλοῦσιν εὔδειπνον*; Hsch. *εὐδείπνοις· θυσία τις* [*παρὰ*] *'Αθήνησιν +καὶ ἡ τριτογενής* (*ἐπὶ 'Ηριγόνης* Meursius); Hsch. *'Αλῆτις· ἑορτὴ 'Αθήνησιν ἡ νῦν αἰώρα* (*'Εώρα* Cd.) *λεγομένη*. That it occurred on the third day of the Anthesteria is shown by Callim. fr. 178.4, the Orestes-Erigone aition, by the association *εὔδειπνος/χύτροι* and by depictions on Choes pitchers, above all. (1) Chous, Coll. Vlasto, van Hoorn (1951) #270 fig. 10 = *ARV*² 1249.14, Pickard-Cambridge (1968) fig. 9: a garlanded man sets a garlanded little boy on a swing; to the left is an opened pithos in the ground, to the right a throne with woman's clothing and a wreath. (2) Chous, New York 75.2.11, van Hoorn (1951) #744 fig. 12 = *ARV*² 1313.11: "women perfuming clothes"; the sacral character of the scene was pointed out by E. Buschor, *AM* 53 (1928), 100.3; Deubner (1932) 113.3, and cf. Immerwahr, *TAPA* 77 (1946), 256–58: robes on a swing above a fire, garlanded women, to the right the same throne as in #1. (3) Hydria, Berlin 2394 = *ARV*² 1131.172; *FR* III 28: a girl swinging, a woman, a fillet hung up as a sign of festivity, a pithos in the ground as in #1. (4) Hydria, Louvre CA 2191 = *ARV*² 1131.173, *CV* France 635: Eros swings a girl; fillet; pithos. (5) Skyphos, Berlin 2589 = *ARV*² 1301.7, Deubner (1932) pl. 18, Nilsson (1955) pl. 37.2: satyr swinging a girl. The inscription is legible: *Εὐά*[*ν*]*θεια* [*κ*]*αλή*, Immerwahr, *TAPA* 77 (1946), 259. (6) Lekythos, München 234, Metzger (1951) pl. 5.1: ΠΑΙΔΙΑ swings ΙΜΕΡΟΣ. Cf. an Apulian lekythos, New York 13.232.3, Cambitoglou and Trendall (1961) 59.5, *Bull. Metr. Mus. of Art* 36 (1941) 235: woman letting a little girl swing; boy with strigil on the altar; Hermes. On South Italian Choes, see IV.1.n.5 above. The pictures of swinging girls on black figure amphoras by the "swing painter," Boston 98.918 = *ABV* 306.41; Louvre F 60 = *ABV* 308.74, refer to the festival, as is indicated by the richly adorned clothing. Cultic background has also been surmised in the case of the Minoan terracotta group of the swinging girl from Hagia Triada: see Nilsson (1950) 332n.; S. Marinatos, *Antichthon* 2 (1968), 1–34.

[12] Hyg. *Astr.* 2.4 = Erat. *Cat.* p. 79 Robert (the festival "Aletis"); Hyg. *Fab.* 130 (*oscillatio* = *αἰώρα*); cf. Ael. *Nat. an.* 7.28.

ety with high spirits. There were various explanations as to who Aletis, "the wanderer," was. According to one version she was Erigone, the daughter of Aegisthus, who pursued her father's murderer, Orestes, all the way to Athens to accuse him. When he was acquitted, however, she took her own life.[13] In another version, Erigone was the daughter of that Ikarios who was visited by Dionysus and given the first wine, which, however, caused his dreadful death. When she found her father dead, she hanged herself. It was this version that dominated Hellenistic and Roman literature through Eratosthenes' poem *Erigone*.[14] The other version was presumably used by Sophocles, but goes back to the sixth century. Another version, though half-incomprehensible, perhaps preserves the most authentic tradition. Here, the "wanderer" was the daughter of a tyrant-king who invented the trumpet[15]—the Tyrrhenian trumpet played a part in the drinking at the Choes. Finally, she was sometimes equated with Medea or Persephone.[16]

Thus, the name *Erigone* is solidly attested and evidently used in the cult. There is mention of songs about the "wanderer," Aletis,[17]

---

[13] *Marm. Par.*, *FGrHist* 239 A 25; Apollod. *Epit.* 6.25, 28; Schol. Eur. *Or.* 1648; Accius *Erigona*, perhaps following the model of Sophocles' *Erigone*, and cf. Pearson on Soph. fr. 235–36. According to Kinaithon (Paus. 2.18.6), Orestes married Erigone; according to Hyg. *Fab.* 122, she became a priestess in Attica.

[14] See IV.2.n.37 above.

[15] Hsch. Αἰώρα· ἑορτὴ Ἀθήνησιν, ἣν οἱ μὲν ἐπὶ τῇ Μάλεω Τυρρηνοῦ (τυράννου Cd.) θυγατρί φασιν; *Et. Gen.* = *Et. M.* 62.7 *s.v.* Ἀλῆτις· . . . οἱ δὲ τὴν τοῦ Μαλεώτου τοῦ Τυρρηνοῦ θυγατέρα; Schol. Stat. *Theb.* 4.224 *Maleus Tuscorum rex, qui tubam primus invenit* (cf. 6.382); Cape Malea and Apollo Maleotas (see *RE* XIV 875–881) were named after him. Strabo 5 p. 225 explains Regisvilla near Pyrgi as βασίλειον Μάλεω τοῦ Πελασγοῦ, ὅν φασιν . . . ἀπελθεῖν ἐνθένδε εἰς Ἀθήνας. Malea is linked to Silenus-dances, Poll. 4.104; Pind. fr. 156. Cf. the Tyrrhenians as the opponents of Dionysus in the *Homeric Hymn*, III.7.n.23 above. The Etruscan Mezentius claims the wine of Latium for himself: see Varro in Pliny *N.h.* 14.88; Fasti Praenestini, *CIL* I² 316; Dion. Hal. *Ant.* 1.65.2; Plut. *Q. Rom.* 275e; Ov. *Fast.* 4.863–900; Cato fr. 12 *HRR* I² 59. For the Tyrrhenian trumpet see already Aesch. *Eum.* 567; Paus. 2.21.3; Schol. Aristoph. *Ran.* 133; Clem. *Strom.* 1.74.6 with reference to τραγῳδίαι. Hyg. *Fab.* 274.20–21 is peculiar: the sounding of the trumpet signifies the rejection of cannibalism.

[16] *Et. Gen.* = *Et. M.* 62.9. As the wife of Aegeus, Medea was temporarily the queen of Athens. Aletis = Persephone, διότι τοὺς πυροὺς ἀλοῦντες πέμματά τινα προσέφερον αὐτῇ. οὕτω Μεθόδιος. We may ask whether the Diasia as well (on which see Deubner [1932] 155–57), ten days after the Chytroi, was related to the Anthesteria. Apollonios, *FGrHist* 365 F 5, links it too to the flood aition; according to Plut. *Sulla* 14.10, there were ὑπομνήματα πολλά to the flood in this month; it is therefore uncertain whether the ὑδροφορία (Apollonios, *FGrHist* 365 F 4; Hsch., *Et. M. s.v.*) is connected with the Chytroi (thus Deubner [1932] 113; Nilsson [1955] 595); cf. Jacoby *ad loc.*

[17] Arist. fr. 515 = Ath. 618e; Poll. 4.55; Plat. Com. fr. 212 (*CAF* I 659) = Hsch. ἀλῆτις.

which perhaps were sung at the swinging festival. The association between swinging and suffocating is likewise solidly attested.[18] Even this amusement symbolizes an act of violence, a sacrifice. The father's death driving his daughter to despair is a motif that the two familiar Erigone myths have in common: murdering the father leads to the death of the maiden. Thus we see the sacrificial pattern of the Anthesteria confirmed one last time: the maiden's sacrifice—of the Polyxena type[19]—is a final ceremony of propitiation for what happened on the day of the Choes. Erigone, the daughter of Ikarios, was made the bride of Dionysus when he visited her father.[20] She is thus the mythic counterpart of the "queen" who, as the most preeminent of Athenian women, was given to the god on the night before the swinging festival. The terror retained by the myth is transformed into something charming in the ritual: in honor of Erigone, the "one born early," the act of swinging in the morning breeze, rising and falling, no longer tied to the earth, removes the final impurities still to be overcome from the "day of pollution." After having passed through the unspeakable, one can rejoice in the flowers of spring, which gave the Anthesteria their name.

6. *Protesilaos*

As early as the Iliadic "Catalogue of Ships" we find a story, present also in the *Cypria* at the beginning of the Trojan War, of how the first Greek leaped from the ships onto the Trojan shore and immediately became the first Greek slain. This was Protesilaos,[1] whose very

---

[18] Paus. 10.29.3 on Polygnotos' picture of Phaedra swinging; Serv. *Aen.* 6.741; Serv. *Georg.* 2.389; see also G. Devereux, *Mélanges C. Lévi-Strauss* (1970), 1246 n.55: "certains Eskimos pendaient leurs enfants par le col de leur vêtement, 'pour leur donner du plaisir' (ivresse d'anoxémie)."

[19] See I.7.n.40 above.

[20] This only in Ov. *Met.* 6.125. Cf. E. Panofsky, *A Mythological Painting by Poussin in the Nationalmuseum Stockholm* (Stockholm, 1960), 23–28.

[1] *Il.* 2.695–702; *Cypria* fr. 17 Allen = 15 Bethe = Paus. 4.2.7; cf. Hes. fr. 199.6; Türk, *RML* III 3155–71; *PR* II 60–64; L. Radermacher, "Hippolytos und Thekla," *SB Wien* 182.3 (1916), 99–111; G. Herzog-Hauser, *Mélanges Boisacq* (1937), 471–78; T. Mantero in *Mythos: Scripta in Honorem Marii Untersteiner* (1970), 187–226.

name reflects his fate, "the first of men." It is only in the fifth century that we learn that Protesilaos' influence by no means ceased with his death. In Euripides' tragedy *Protesilaos*,[2] the young widow Laodameia is unable to reconcile herself to her husband's death. With slight variations, the later sources all tell the same story: Laodameia sets up in her bedroom an image of the dead man, made either of wax or wood. She talks to him, cries in front of him, even flies into a Bacchic frenzy, crowned with a wreath in front of the image. Her agony is enough to compel the dead man up out of Hades. Protesilaos appears to her and shares her bed for one night. According to one version,[3] the image is burned the next morning; in all the sources, Laodameia takes her own life.[4]

This vampire-story, also told by Phlegon[5] with the male and female roles reversed—the inspiration for Goethe's *Braut von Korinth*—is generally held to be a folk-tale motif. However, Protesilaos was more than an epic hero. A sacred precinct at Phylake in Thessaly was dedicated to him, and agons (mentioned by Pindar)[6] were held there in his honor. Most important was the great and rich sanctuary of Protesilaos in Elaius on the Thracian Chersonnesus, where his tomb was displayed. He was worshipped as a god.[7] Of course, by the time of Philostratus nothing was left but the foundations with a statue rising up out of them, still worshipped by the populace. In the time of Xerxes' invasion, by contrast, the Persian governor Artayktes carried off great treasures from among the votive offerings, for which act his gruesome demise after the victory of the Greeks was considered a just punishment. The story stressed above all that he brought women into

---

[2] *TGF* p. 563; Schol. Aristid. p. 671.30 Dindorf.

[3] Hyg. *Fab.* 104, and cf. 103.

[4] Apollod. *Epit.* 3.30; Eust. 325.22–26; Philostr. *Im.* 2.9.5; Luk. *Dial. mort.* 23; cf. Ov. *Her.* 13. For ΠΡΟΤΕΣΙΛΑΣ as a rider on a Corinthian pyxis in the Louvre, see *Arch. Zeitg.* (1864), pl. 184, *RML* III 3163; according to K. Schauenburg, Protesilaos is depicted in Hades on an Apulian pottery sherd in Mainz: see *JdI* 73 (1958), 68–70; *Bonn. Jb.* 161 (1961), 216.

[5] O. Keller, *Rerum naturalium scriptores Graeci minores* (1877), 57–62 = *FGrHist* 257 F 36 I.

[6] Pind. *Isthm.* 1.58–59 with Schol.; Philostr. *Her.* 2.3 (II 143.19 ed. Teubn.); 2.8 (II 148.24 ed. Teubn.); cf. Konon, *FGrHist* 26 F 1.13 on Skione. For coins of Phthiotian Thebes see *RML* III 3166.

[7] Hdt. 7.33, 9.116, 120; Thuc. 8.102; Lyk. 532–34; Strabo 7 p. 331, 13 p. 595; Pliny *NH* 4.49, 16.238; Arr. *Anab.* 1.11.5; Philostr. *Her.* 2.1 (II 140–41 ed. Teubn.): only a foundation-wall and a statue, deformed by time and worship, survive. See also coins: W. Drexler, *Zeitschr. f. Numism.* 14 (1887), 130–32. For Protesilaos honored as a god see Paus. 1.34.2; Tzetz. ad Lyk. 533.

the holy of holies for sexual orgies;[8] for the Greeks, sex in a temple was the abomination par excellence.[9] But there must have been some sort of arrangement that gave the Persians the idea of turning the temple into a harem. Artayktes' sacrilegious marriage presupposes some kind of custom or at least a fantasy of a sacred marriage in the temple of Protesilaos. In that case, Protesilaos' tomb and Laodameia's fatal night of love would not merely stand within a novelistic context. The miracle that confronted the sinner is most significant: pickled fish, τάριχοι, came back to life—a dangerous force, burst forth from the dead and "embalmed."

The rite that we saw reflected in the Lenaia-vases with their depictions of wine-drinking women marching around a mask of Dionysus entailed a statue being set up, with a woman dancing in front of it in ever-greater agitation until the statue came to life. This same act is presupposed in the myth of Laodameia. In both cases the setting-up of an image is an act of restitution preceded by a sacrifice. Likewise, the death of Protesilaos belongs to a specific type with ritual equivalents: in order to reach a new stage or win a new land, there must be a victim.[10] Death itself establishes permanent worship equal to that enjoyed by the gods. Similar stories of restoring the dead man by means of a statue were told of Aktaion, Attis, and, of course, Dionysus.[11]

It is no surprise that the cult of Protesilaos thereby takes on a somewhat Dionysiac complexion. Protesilaos' father, Iphiklos, was linked to the story of Melampus. And in the *Cypria* his wife was the granddaughter of Aetolian Oineus.[12] Philostratus, moreover, made him the wine-grower's most faithful friend. A sarcophagus from the Roman Empire depicts the return of Protesilaos following directly upon a sacrifice to Hermes Chthonios. On another, the dead man departs, as Laodameia breaks down in front of a mask of Dionysus.[13]

In the third century B.C. Phylarchus told a curious story about

---

[8] Hdt. 9.116–20 (followed by Paus. 3.4.6; Philostr. *Her.* 2.1 [I 141.11 ed. Teubn.])

[9] See I.7.n.11 above.

[10] See I.5.n.22 above, and cf. n.17.

[11] Aktaion: Apollod. 3.31; II.4.n.18 above. Attis: Diod. 3.59.7. Dionysus: Firm. *Err.* 6.4.

[12] *PR* II 58–60; n.1 above.

[13] See the sarcophagus from S. Chiara, Naples, *Wiener Vorlegeblätter* B 11.4, *RML* III 3167, and the sarcophagus, Vatican, *Wiener Vorlegeblätter* B 11.3, *RML* III 3170; C. Robert, *Die antiken Sarkophag-Reliefs* III 3 (1919), 496–500, pl. 132. For Protesilaos as the Thracian Dionysus see M. Mayer, *Hermes* 20 (1885), 123–29. For a demonic image coming to life during a song sung by women in a medieval story from Denmark ("Canta Bovi"), see R. Wolfram, *Zeitschr. f. Völkerkunde* 42 (1932), 145.

this same city, Elaius. He did not fail to mention that it was the site of Protesilaos' tomb. In this city, a virgin had to be sacrificed annually to the Penates. A dispute between the king and a father, over whose daughter should die, ended in a particularly gruesome sacrifice. Matusios "killed the daughter of the king and, having mixed her blood with wine in a mixing bowl, offered it to the king to drink on his arrival." When the deed was discovered, Matusios was hurled into the sea along with the mixing bowl. This was the origin of the name "the Matusian foothills"; the crater was translated to heaven as a constellation.[14] In this way the memory of the gruesome act was made permanent and sacred.

Drinking wine from the sacred crater of Dionysus is here seen as drinking blood and is linked to the sacrifice of a girl. Precisely this is the will of the gods, here called *Penates* in the Latin translation, but evidently the Great Gods or Cabiri, as associated with Samothrace, Lemnos, and Troy.[15] The drinking of wine played a major role in the mystery rites of the Cabiri. Phylarchus' horror-story reflects analogous mysteries for the Great Gods. Further, the plunge into the sea after an unspeakable sacrifice belongs to the set type of the Leukothea myth.[16]

There is no simple way to connect the cult of Protesilaos with the ritual underlying the story of Matusios, even though both individually reveal striking correspondences to the Attic Anthesteria: the one in the setting-up of the statue, the sacred marriage, and the death of a young woman, the other in the drinking of wine as blood in connection with the sacrifice of a girl. But whereas in the story of Matusios the girl's death comes first, in the myth of Protesilaos it comes afterward. Moreover, we cannot associate Protesilaos' death with the drink from the crater. Additional myths that have come down to us thirdhand are too distorted for us to form any secure judgment, but there is a strange bridge from Protesilaos to the Cabiri: an inscribed vase from the Cabirion of Thebes portrays *Pratolaos*[17] beside the Dionysus-like *Kabiros* and his *pais*. The "first man" is the first mortal altogether,

[14] *FGrHist* 81 F 69 = Hyg. *Astr.* 2.40; Μαζουσία (ἄκρα) Lyk. 534; Strabo 7 p. 331 fr. 52. For Matusia, see Pliny *NH* 4.49.

[15] See generally Hemberg (1950), who does not discuss this source; cf. II.6, III.6 n.24 above.

[16] See III.7 above.

[17] Nilsson (1955) pl. 48.1; *AM* 13 (1888), 421, pl. 9; O. Kern, *Hermes* 25 (1890), 7. For Protesilaos as an epic modification of *Protolaos see A. Fick and F. Bechtel, *Die griechischen Personennamen* (1894²), 408.

the first to die—transposed into the heroic milieu, he is Protesilaos, the first to fall at Troy. Dionysus dismembered was likewise connected with man's origins. These are, of course, only conjectural associations, but in any case the ritual of the Anthesteria leads us once again into the grey area between the Greek and the pre-Greek world. Whether we must reckon with Thracian or pre-Thracian material, imported by way of Asia Minor, is yet another question.

V. ELEUSIS

1. *Documentation and Secret*

The words *mystical, mystery, mysterious* are still common today. Their origins are in the ancient Greek cult, in particular the most famous one, the Eleusinian mysteries. Yet, the modern usage of these terms is misleading.[1] If *mysticism* means personal introspection, the opening of a deeper dimension in the soul until a light shines forth within, then the Eleusinian mysteries were precisely *un*-mystical. They were celebrated in front of thousands of participants in a sealed initiation hall. The light, the fire that was to be seen there, was doubtless real. Our concept of *mysticism* first arose when Plato, appropriating the metaphors of the mysteries, used them in the *Phaedrus* and *Symposium* to express the spiritual contemplation of the philosopher, a concept which then was handed down through Neoplatonism and Monasticism. The celebrations were mysterious only to outsiders. Initiates were given explanations, but a holy oath prevented them from revealing anything to the outside world. The basic phenomenon addressed in the words *μύστης*, "the initiate," *μυεῖν*, "to initiate," *μυστήριον*, "ceremony or place of initiation," is this: by means of specific ritual ceremonies, a man was made a new member of a cult group, the main function of which was this very initiation ceremony. The Romans rendered the word *μυστήρια* as *initia*, *μύησις* as *initiatio*.[2] Thus, when we speak of the Greek mysteries as *initiations* we are simply fol-

---

[1] On the concept of mysticism see H. Schloetermann, *Mystik in den Religionen der Völker* (1958); R. C. Zaehner, *Mysticism, Sacred and Profane* (1957); D. Sabbatucci, *Saggio sul misticismo greco* (1965)—who, however, postulates a genuine mystical experience underlying the exoteric testimonies (155–61).

[2] *Initia*: Cic. *Leg*. 2, 36; Varro *R.r.* 2, 4, 9; *initiari*: Trag. inc. 43 Ribbeck; Cic. *Tusc*. 1, 29; *Samothracum initia*: Varro *L.L.* 5.58; *initiatio* in Eleusis: Suet. *Nero* 34.4.

lowing this ancient translation. The esoteric element, the secrecy, is a correlate of the fact that admission depends on individual initiation (*μύησις*, *initiatio*). In Christianity, too, a consecration, the first communion or confirmation, is the condition for admission to holy communion; indeed, the early Christian authors found it natural to describe baptism and holy communion as the "mysteries" of their faith.[3] But Christians, except for those of the Gnostic sect, gave up the secrecy.

There is no lack of documents for the cult of Eleusis; on the contrary, no other local cult in Greece is so richly attested. The sanctuary itself, which Pausanius demurred to describe,[4] is there for all to see, thanks to careful excavations. The great hall of initiation, the Telesterion, and its development from the Peisistratean to the Parthenon era are particularly well known, as are the strange, asymmetrically placed holy of holies and the throne of the hierophant.[5] We have votive offerings from the sanctuary, reliefs and vase-paintings that, together with analogous pictures found elsewhere, yield up a copious Eleusinian iconography.[6] Whole inventories of Attic vases exported especially to southern Russia portray Eleusinian gods and heroes. A large number of inscriptions, including governmental decrees, accounting reports, and honorary and funerary inscriptions, familiarize us with the details of administration, priesthood, financial conduct of the sanctuary, and even, in a few lucky cases, the mystery celebration itself. A plebiscite from ca. 220 A.D.[7] records the entire festival program as it was

---

[3]Already in the New Testament, the Gospel is a *μυστήριον*: Matt. 13:11; Rom. 16:25; Coloss. 1:26–27; Ephes. 6:19, 3:9; cf. I Cor. 14:2; II Thess. 2:7. Cf. Bornkamm, *Kittels Theol. Wörterbuch* IV 809–34. On Clement see at n.12, 13 below. Ambrosius *De mysteriis* (Migne *Patrologia Latina* XVI 389–410) deals with baptism and holy communion; see also J. C. M. Fruytier, "Het woord ΜΥΣΤΗΡΙΟΝ in de Catechezen van Cyrillus van Jerusalem," Diss. Nijmwegen, 1947.

[4]1.28.7.

[5]The thorough, comprehensive study by Foucart (1914) was written before the more recent excavations; F. Noack, *Eleusis, die baugeschichtliche Entwicklung des Heiligtums* (1927), has also been superseded by subsequent findings, on which see Mylonas (1961) for a summary description; an important step was J. N. Travlos, "Τὸ *ἀνάκτορον τῆς* 'Ἐλευσῖνος," *Ephem.* (1950/51), 1–16. The most important surveys are Deubner (1932) 69–91; O. Kern, *RE* XVI (1934), 1211–63; Kerényi (1962) and (1967).

[6]Pringsheim (1905); B. Grossmann, "The Eleusinian Gods and Heroes in Greek Art," Diss. Washington Univ., Saint Louis (Missouri), 1959 (microfilm); Kerényi (1962); E. Simon, "Neue Deutung zweier Eleusinischer Denkmäler des 4. Jh. v. Chr.," *AK* 9 (1966), 72–92; Metzger (1951) 231–65; (1965) 1–53.

[7]*IG* II/III^2 1078 = *SIG*^{3} 885 = *LS* 8. For other important inscriptions see plebiscite on the greater and lesser mysteries before 480 (*Hesperia* 17 [1948], 92 = *SEG* 12 [1955], #2 =

determined "according to ancient custom," right up to the procession to Eleusis on the nineteenth of Boedromion, and that night was the night of the mysteries.

In addition, we have the literary evidence. The ancient *Homeric Hymn to Demeter* already weaves an Eleusinian episode into the myth, doubtless referring to some aspect of the ritual.[8] Local historians even wrote books about the Eleusinian mysteries, without, of course, violating the secret; "speakable" details were plentiful enough.[9] To speak of the mysteries in allusions, while avoiding the secret itelf, became almost a sport for the orators. Sopatros' fictitious speech for the friend of a man who had experienced the whole initiation in a dream was the culmination of this trend.[10] More important still is the appropriation of the mystery language and images to philosophy, above all in Plato and his successors.[11] The philosophical path is conceived of as an initiation, and the contemplation of the pure mind is compared to the epopteia of the mysteries. It should not be entirely impossible to retranslate the metaphor into the reality from which it was taken.

Christian Platonism, then, described Christianity as a mystery

---

LSS 1); cult statutes ca. 460 (*IG* I² 6 = *SIG*³ 42 = *LSS* 3); fourth-century regulation of the mysteries, esp. announcement and selection of the *παῖς ἀφ' ἑστίας* (*Hesperia* 49 [1980], 260–66; part of this in *LSS* 12); regulation of the procession, first century B.C. (*Hesperia* 10 [1941], 64–72 = *LSS* 15); accounts (*IG* I² 311–13; II/III² 1671–81, and cf. the honorary decree *IG* II/III² 847 = *SIG*³ 540); building accounts (*IG* I² 81, a bridge; II/III² 1666, 1668; cf. the "Koirobos Inscription," K. Kourouniotis, *Eleusiniaka* I [Athens, 1932], 177 = *SEG* 10 [1949] #24); funerary epigrams for hierophants (*IG* II/III² 3639 = Kaibel add. 97a; 3661 = Peek 879; 3811; hierophantis: 3709); plebiscites concerning grain taxes (*ἀπαρχαί*), (*IG* I² 76 = *SIG*³ 83 = *LS* 5, ca. 423; *IG* II/III² 140 = *SIG*³ 200 = *LSS* 13, 352 B.C.); a sacrificial calendar from Eleusis (*IG* II² 1363 = *LS* 7; S. Dow and R. F. Healey, *HThR* 21 [1966], 1–58); on the Eleusinian agon see *IG* I² 5 = *LS* 4, ca. 500 B.C.. On the entry in the calendar of Nikomachos see *IG* II/III² 1357 = *LSS* 10 A 60–76; III.1.n.1 above.

[8] *Hy. Dem.* 96–302; F. Wehrli, "Die Mysterien von Eleusis," *ARW* 31 (1934), 77–104; G. E. Mylonas, *The Hymn to Demeter and Her Sanctuary at Eleusis* (University of Washington Publications 12, 1942).

[9] Philochoros, Περὶ *μυστηρίων τῶν* 'Αθήνησιν, *FGrHist* 328 T 1; Melanthios Περὶ *τῶν ἐν* 'Ελευσῖνι *μυστηρίων*, *FGrHist* 326 F 2–4; Theodorus 'Ο Παναγὴς *προσαγορευόμενος*, Περὶ *τοῦ* Κηρύκων *γένους*, *FGrHist* 346 F 1. It cannot be determined to what extent Stesimbrotos Περὶ *τελετῶν* (*FGrHist* 107 F 12–20, 26–28), Neanthes Περὶ *τελετῶν* (*FGrHist* 84 F 14), and Hikesios, Περὶ *μυστηρίων* (Clem. *Pr.* 5.64.5) touched upon Eleusis.

[10] *Rhet. Gr.* VIII 110–24 Waltz; [*λόγοι* 'Ηρ]*ακλέους μὴ ἐωμέ*[*νου τελ*]*εῖσθαι τὰ* 'Ελευσίνια, *Pap. d. R. Univ. Milano* (1937), #20 (V.4.n.58 below).

[11] P. Boyancé, "Sur les mystères d'Eleusis," *REG* 75 (1962), esp. 464–73. E. Des Places, "Platon et la langue des mystères," *Annales de la fac. des lettres et sciences hum. d'Aix* 38 (1964), 9–23; above all *Symp.* 209e–212a; *Phdr.* 249c, 250b–c. Cf. J. Pascher, *H ΒΑΣΙΛΙΚΗ ΟΔΟΣ. Der Königsweg zu Wiedergeburt und Vergottung bei Philon von Alex-*

and Christ as the hierophant;[12] the "false" heathen mysteries were naturally the more vehemently attacked. Clement of Alexandria, above all, set himself the task in his *Protrepticus* of tearing the veil away from the secret. He would expose what the night of the mysteries had hidden[13] and set it out in all its wretchedness: murder, indecency, sex, and crime. Scholarship has been justly skeptical of these accounts presented by a hostile party *cum ira et studio*;[14] yet, effective polemics must contain at least a kernel of the truth, and besides, Clement's hatred is combined with a Platonic sympathy for the mystery language. The situation is different—which oddly is almost always overlooked[15]—in a document preserved by Hippolytus of Rome in his *Refutation of All Heresies*. It is not the Christian bishop speaking here; he quotes the sermon of a Gnostic, a "Naassenian," who claims the basic identity of all mysteries with Gnostic Christianity. The mysteries of Attis have a decisive influence in this case. Presumably such a Gnostic, like other *homines religiosi* of late antiquity, had himself initiated in as many mysteries as possible; at the same time, conscious of the "freedom of god's children," the Gnostic felt himself above all traditional commandments and prohibitions.[16] Although it is almost inconceivable that an initiate, sympathetic to the rite, would tell about it, such seems to have been the case here. Since that time, "the great, wonderful, most perfect epoptic secret" of Eleusis has been openly known—the hierophant displayed an ear of cut wheat.[17] Was that, then, all there was to it?

Clearly this secret is a special case. It is surely more devout prop-

---

andreia (1931), who, however, attempts to trace Philo's mystery language all too directly back to the actual mysteries.

[12] Clem. *Pr.* 120.1 *δᾳδουχοῦμαι τοὺς οὐρανοὺς καὶ τὸν θεὸν ἐποπτεῦσαι, ἅγιος γίνομαι μυούμενος· ἱεροφαντεῖ δὲ ὁ κύριος καὶ τὸν μύστην σφραγίζεται φωταγωγῶν*. . . . cf. 120.5, 1.10.3.

[13] *Pr.* 2.12.1, 14.1, 22.4, 7.

[14] The most radical skepticism about Clement and Hippolytus is exercised by Mylonas (1961). The position that Clement's statements can refer only to Alexandria is defended by Kerényi as well: (1962) 107–12; (1967) 116–19. For the rest, he stresses the uniqueness of the Eleusinian mysteries and does not question the significance of *Hippolytus*: (1962) 98–99, (1967) 92–93.

[15] The text is discussed as "Hippolytus," for example, by Foucart (1914) 420, 433, and cf. 479; Deubner (1932) 85; Kern, *RE* XVI 1236, 1240; Mylonas (1961) 305–10; Kerényi (1962) 98; Des Places (1969) 212. The "Naassenian's" sermon as a Gnostic document is dealt with thoroughly by R. Reitzenstein, *Poimandres* (1904), 81–102; *Studien zum antiken Synkretismus* (1926), 105–109, 161–73.

[16] On the pathos of the Gnostic's "freedom" see Porph. *Abst.* 1.42 *βυθὸς ἐξουσίας*. . . .

[17] Hippol. *Ref.* 5.8.39; cf. V.4.n.77 below.

aganda than fact that the secret of the mysteries was never violated. Indeed, how could something be kept a secret when it was shown to thousands every year? At the time when the great Telesterion was being built, the secret of Eleusis was flagrantly and provocatively violated by the first atheist, the philosophizing poet Diagoras of Melos. He "told everyone the mysteries, thus making them vulgar and mean, and dissuaded those who wished to be initiated."[18] Told on the street, then, the secret of the mysteries is no blessing, no gain; rather, it is a nothing, like faerie-gold that turns to charcoal by daylight. The Athenians condemned Diagoras to death and pursued him throughout their realm. The Eleusinian mysteries, however, continued to be celebrated until eight hundred years after Diagoras. Diodorus reports that the same mysteries found in the Eleusinian, Samothracian, and Orphic rites "are handed down openly to all, according to ancient custom, in Cnossos on Crete. What others transmit under the seal of secrecy is hidden there from none who wants to learn."[19] Nevertheless, it was to Eleusis, not to Cnossos, that the people went.

Opinions differed about the extent of the Eleusinian secret. The poet Aeschylus was brought to trial for profaning the mysteries because a stage prop had recalled the rites. He claimed in his defense that he had not known that this was secret.[20] In the course of time, scruples became even greater. Pausanias, for instance, claims that a dream prevented him from describing the sanctuary of Eleusis,[21] and the Neopythagorean Numenius dreamt that he had seen the Eleusinian goddesses dressed as prostitutes standing in front of a brothel. They told him that he had prostituted the secrets of Eleusis in a book of "interpretations," that is, philosophical explications like those of Plato.[22] Numenius surely had not gone as far as the "Naassenian."

---

[18] Krateros, *FGrHist* 342 F 16 = Schol. Aristoph. *Av.* 1073, and cf. Melanthios, *FGrHist* 326 F 2–4; F. Jacoby, *Diagoras ὁ Ἄθεος* (Abh. Berlin, 1959, 3).

[19] Diod. 5.77.3.

[20] *Οὐκ εἰδέναι ὅτι ἀπόρρητα ἦν* Arist. *EN* 1111a9; for tumult and accusation *ἐπὶ τῷ τῶν μυστικῶν περιφέρειν τινὰ δοκεῖν* see Heraclides *Fr.* 170 Wehrli = *Comm. in Arist. Gr.* XX 145; *ἐκρίνετο ἀσεβείας ἐπί τινι δράματι* Ael. *VH* 5.19. Together with Clem. *Strom.* 2.60.3 (who, vulgarizing Heraclides, speaks of a trial on the Areopagus when actually it was only a special court of initiates for a mystery trial: Andoc. 1.31) we may, on the whole, understand Aristotle's statement to mean that Aeschylus proved he was not an initiate (differently, Aristoph. *Ran.* 886–87); it is possible, however, that there were differences of opinion among initiates regarding the limits of *ῥητά* and *ἀπόρρητα*. Cf. Lobeck (1829) 76–84; Kern, *RE* XVI 1249.

[21] 1.38.7.

[22] Fr. 39 Leemans = Macr. *Somn. Sc.* 1.2.19.

More and more the rule obtained that the hierophant was "hieronymous," that his private name should not be mentioned.[23] The heightened secrecy veiled the sinking power of the mysteries.

It is in this absolute observance of a secrecy no longer related to its content that one of the secret's fundamental characteristics is betrayed: a secret is not very significant when seen by the light of day. It is essential that it be kept a secret. The *mystes* is distinguished by the fact that non-mystai, the uninitiate, live alongside him. The inner circle of initiates contrasts with those who stand outside, and man reacts to this dichotomy of "in" and "out" with an almost instinctive urge toward the inner circle. Even children discover again and again spontaneously how keeping a secret evokes respect and a feeling of power: blessed is he who belongs. Thus, presumably since the most ancient times, groups that have separated themselves from society and its culture have invariably established themselves as secret societies. There is no *imperium* without the *arcana imperii*; there is no exclusive society without its secret. This determines who belongs to the group and who is to be driven away; exclusiveness on the inside corresponds to aggression on the outside.

A group can endure only so long as it continues to admit new members; the harder and more irrevocable the admission, the more strong and durable the society. Construction and penetration of barriers through the ritual of initiation are mutually determinant: secret and initiation are features of one of the most successful structural forms in the human community. By referring themselves to the superhuman authority of the holy, such groups have survived for thousands of years.

As a closed group, the community of mystai could be virtually identical with the polis. In Mykonos, female inhabitants and initiated foreigners were considered equals in a cult of Demeter,[24] and in Athens the polis stood in the closest relationship with Eleusis. The mysteries were supervised by the king, basileus,[25] who had always, therefore, to be an initiate. The same was true for the ephebes who organized the festival procession. The story that Herakles was adopted by Pylios

---

[23] Clinton (1974) 9f.; Luk. *Lexiph*. 10; Eunap. p. 52 Boiss; *IG* II/III^2 3811; first applied in *IG* II/III^2 1934 (ca. 300 B.C.), but there are many exceptions to the rule down to Roman times.

[24] *SIG*^{3} 1024 = *LS* 96.20–22. The meaning of *τετελεσμένος, ἀτελής, τελίσκεσθαι* *LSS* 115 B 40–43 (Cyrene) is disputed. After the liberation of Messene, the mysteries of Andania were renewed as the "heritage of Aristomenes": Paus. 4.26.8.

[25] Arist. *Ath. Pol.* 57.1.

before being initiated at Eleusis[26] closely relates adoption into the family-structured polis with initiation into the mysteries. With the exception of one boy at each celebration, only adults were initiated.[27] Thus, the celebration still marked the transition into the adult world. The Athenians were, as a rule, mystai. Demonax the Cynic struck people as disagreeable because he exempted himself from the mysteries.[28] And yet the mystical community of Eleusis was sufficiently detached from the polis that it could be effective outside it: women, too, were initiated, as were slaves and foreigners. In Rome, Eleusis became fashionable for a time, and the emperors from Hadrian to Commodus brought the sanctuary its last period of grandeur.[29]

The festival, for all its international appeal, remained bound to its setting and to the families of the Eumolpidai and Kerykes, the traditional providers of hierophants and dadouchoi. Eleusis owed much of its character to this carefully poised balance between worldwide and local ties. Because it offered access to all, it could spread through the whole ancient world, yet, thanks to its local tradition, it could maintain its identity through all the changes in time and fashion without relying on books, that is, on philosophically formulated dogma. Trade had long brought many peoples to the market at Eleusis, for there the three roads met from Attica, Boeotia, and the Peloponnesus.[30] The educative power of Athens[31] then did its part by frequently portraying the gods of Eleusis in its philosophy and poetry.

The sociological and structural description of the Eleusinian festival as the self-renewal of a secret society through initiation describes only a superficial function. Of course, not just any password or token could become a secret of the mysteries, but only that which could release, shape, and guide the force of the human soul. In the tradition, the gifts of the goddess Demeter make up a two-part Eleusinian

---

[26] Plut. *Thes.* 33.2; Apollod. 2.122 (interpolation); Luk. *Scyth.* 8. Jul. *Or.* 7.238b *τὸν μυούμενον ἐχρῆν πολιτογραφηθῆναι πρότερον καὶ Ἀθηναῖον γενέσθαι* could not generally have held true: Lobeck (1829) 20, 38–39; Hdt. 8.65. The emperors Verus and Commodus were adopted into the family of the Eumolpidae: *IG* II/III² 3592 = *SIG*³ 869.25; *IG* II/III² 1110 = *SIG*³ 873.

[27] *LSS* 3 C 20–22 *μ]ύστεμ μὲ ἐνέ[λικα μυεῖν μεδέ]να πλὲν τô ἀφ' ἑ[στίας μυομέν]ο* (cf. V.4.n.31 below); cf. F. Sokolowski *HThR* 52 (1959), 3.

[28] Luk. *Dem.* 11.

[29] See *RE* XVI 1255–58; cf. V.5.n.2 below.

[30] The market in Eleusis is brought to life in the *Sikyonios* of Menander, Act 4.

[31] See Wilamowitz (1932) 59.

theme:[32] on the one hand, the nourishment from grain turning crude cannibalism into tame custom, and, on the other, the "better hope" for the life after death. In the *Homeric Hymn to Demeter* it is said that "whoever on this earth has seen these is blessed, but he who has no part in the holy rites has another lot as he wastes away in murky darkness." These lines are echoed by Sophocles: "Thrice blessed are those that have seen these rites and then come to Hades: there is life there for them alone; for the others, everything there is evil." The dichotomy of "in" and "out" is quite naturally projected into the afterlife. Scholarship has been tempted to divide these two gifts of Demeter, viewing the nourishment from grain as primitive agrarian magic, the victory over death as the later hope for the next life.[33] Indeed, emphasis shifted in the course of history between the introduction of agriculture into Greece in the sixth millenium and the "discovery of the individual" around 600 B.C. Nonetheless, even agriculture is "young" in terms of human history, and the themes of nourishment, death and survival are found already in Palaeolithic rituals, in the complex of hunting and sacrifice. Similarly, the secret male society is very ancient. Sacrificial rites, indeed, animal-sacrifices, punctuate the mysteries of Demeter. As elsewhere, symbolism presupposes a programmed scheme of action that has become transferable: the symbolism of the grain grows out of the sacrificial ritual, just as the Great Goddess seems to have sprung out of the Palaeolithic.[34]

For the time being this may stand as an anticipatory conjecture. In any case, we shall not attempt to isolate the phenomenon of Eleusis but, rather, see it in historical perspective, with reference to related mystery cults. Mysteries of Demeter were among the most widespread rituals in Greece: those in the towns of Andania in Messenia and Lykosura in Arcadia are, by chance, known with some precision;[35] southern Italy and Sicily furnish rich material, though little clarification in the details.[36] Beneath all the local differences we can

---

[32] Isocr. 4 (*Paneg.*) 28, and cf. Cic. *Leg.* 2.36; *Hy. Dem.* 480–82; Soph. fr. 837 Pearson; Krinagoras, *AP* 11.42.

[33] See, e.g., Nilsson (1955) 661.

[34] See I.8 above.

[35] *LS* 65 = *SIG*[3] 736 = *IG* V 1.1390, and *LS* 68 = *SIG*[3] 999 = *IG* V 2.514; Paus. 4.33.4–6, 8.37; Nilsson (1955) 478; Stiglitz (1967) 30–46.

[36] Frequently reproduced are the golden ears of wheat from a Sicilian tomb—Nilsson (1955) pl. 42.2; P. Wolters, *Festschr. J. Loeb* (1930), 111–29—and the temple with ears of wheat on an Apulian funerary vase—Nilsson (1955) pl. 42.3; Kerényi (1962) 158.

assume a common structural base stretching out beyond Greece to the Meter cult of Asia Minor. Since it was discovered that agriculture came to Greece from Asia Minor and that Kybele is a continuation of the Great Goddess of Çatal Hüyük, historico-religious studies have had to take such matters into consideration. The ancient world saw the special quality of Eleusis in the unique seriousness and purity of its divine services,[37] characteristics that modern realists dismiss as Athenian cultural propaganda. In whatever way merits and chance came together, Eleusis is for us the most prominent and impressive example of a more comprehensive complex.

The existence of the secret gives the skeptic almost unlimited power over the mysteries. Whatever can be learned from testimony is, he can argue, not the secret, precisely because it is known.[38] No critic, of course, can be prevented from claiming ignorance. But if one patiently collects the surviving fragments from the larger context, adding the diverse reflections in myth and philosophy, then in the convergence of lines one can recognize forms that yield a sociological, historical, and psychological sense. Such an endeavor is to be preferred to the *ars nesciendi*: the reconstruction attempt is worthwhile even if only a torso becomes visible.

2. *The Myth of Kore and Pig-Sacrifice*

All who celebrated the initiation of Eleusis had to bring a sacrificial pig (χοῖρος). This was not a part of the secret and even gave rise to jokes. Thus the Aristophanic antihero answers a threat of death with some nimble panhandling: "Lend me three drachmas for a little pig.

G. Giannelli, *Culti e miti della Magna Grecia* (1963²), 31–35, 48, 65–67, 118, 127–28, 154–55; 187–204; G. Zuntz, *Persephone: Three Essays on Religion and Cult in Magna Graecia* (1971).

[37] Diod. 5.4.4.

[38] E.g., Mylonas (1961) 229, 275; P. Roussel, *BCH* (1930), 65, and cf. Kerényi (1962) 39, 62, 67–68, who, however, gives a different formulation: "durch den Mythos in Wort und Bild führt der Weg über das Wort und das Bild hinaus" (40).

Before I die I have to get initiated."[1] A slave gets a tantalizing whiff of roast pig when he hears the Iakchos-song of the approaching mystai,[2] and pictures show how the little pigs are brought by worshippers, especially by Herakles, the mythical archetype of the Eleusinian initiate (see Figure 8).[3]

The pig-sacrifice for Demeter was the most common feature of all forms of the Demeter cult. Votive statuettes of worshippers with sacrificial pigs or pig statuettes appear in sanctuaries of Demeter throughout the Greek world, from Asia Minor, over Crete, to Sicily.[4] Pig-sacrifice was above all part of the Thesmophoria, the widespread form of the Demeter festival in which women celebrated among themselves apart from the men. Here, though, there was no roast pig. Instead, the pigs were thrown into underground chambers or pits (μέγαρα). There is literary evidence for this in Athens and Potniai, and a sacrificial pit of this kind was excavated in Priene.[5]

The pig was the cheapest sacrificial animal and the easiest to raise in quantity, but for this very reason it was not the final perfect sacrifice. The megarismos occurred on the first introductory day of

---

[1]Aristoph. *Pax* 374 with Schol.; cf. Plat. *Resp.* 378a; Epicharmus fr. 100 Kaibel. The full price of myesis was 15 drachmas: *IG* II/III[2] 1672, 207; 1673, 24.

[2]Aristoph. *Ran.* 337—the mystai apparently also ate the pig, i.e., tasted it (cf. n. 10 below).

[3]Relief-hydria from Cumae, Leningrad 51659, Metzger (1965) pl. 21, Nilsson (1955) pl. 47; Lovatelli urn (cf. V.3.n.12 below). For a παῖς ἀφ' ἑστίας see J. Leipoldt, *Bilderatlas zur Religionsgeschichte* 9–11 (1926), fig. 190 (restored), and cf. 187; Clinton (1974) 103. For Demeter with a pig, see the terracotta statuette from Eleusis, *RML* II 1368; for votive pigs, see *Antike* 18 (1942), 25, Mylonas (1961) pl. 66. For a pig and the bunch of twigs on coins, see Svoronos (1924) pl. 103; *HN*[2] 391. Cf. Athenian votive relief 1016, Metzger (1965) 38 #24; Nilsson, *Opuscula* II (1951), 554.39. For an adult pig sacrificed to the Eleusinian goddesses, see the votive relief Louvre 752; J. Charbonneaux, *La sculpture grecque et romaine au Musée du Louvre* (1963), 121.

[4]E.g., votive statuettes of worshippers with pigs or the goddess herself with a pig, found in sanctuaries of Demeter: see F. Winter, *Die Typen der figürlichen Terrakotten* I (1903), 92–93, 115–18; for Corinth, see *Hesperia* 34 (1965), 22 pl. 11a.

[5]The μεγαρίζειν is described by Clem. *Pro.* 2.17.1 and more thoroughly in Schol. Luk. pp. 275.23–276.24; otherwise the sources give only indications of the θέσις τῶν θεσμοφορίων, Schol. Aristoph. *Thesm.* 585, and cf. Phot. μέγαρον; Ael. Dion. μ 2 Erbse. Counter to Clement's explicit statement, Deubner (1932) 40 mistakenly connected the statement of the Lukian Scholion to the Skira, which is there compared to the Thesmophoria: see Burkert, *Hermes* (1966), 7–8. For Potniai see Paus. 9.8.1; for Priene see Th. Wiegand and H. Schrader, *Priene* (1904), 154–55; M. Schede, *Die Ruinen von Priene* (1964[2]), 93–94, fig. 107, 110. For the Thesmophoria as "the most widespread festival of Greece" (Nilsson [1955] 463) we may in addition refer to Nilsson (1906) 313–25, (1955) 463–66; for the Thesmophorion in Thasos see *BCH* 89 (1965), 470–71.

the Thesmophoria. At other times as well, the rite of casting-down had the function of compelling a greater fulfillment through self-denial and submission. There is no evidence that pigs were taken along on the great procession of the mystai on the nineteenth of Boedromion; they would have been bothersome on the long march. Thus, the pig-sacrifice belonged to the preliminary ceremonies of the myesis, performed "for those initiated in Eleusis, in the courtyard of the sanctuary and, for those initiated in the city, in the Eleusinion," above the Agora.[6] But "as long as you have not reached the Anaktoron, you have not been initiated."[7] The fulfillment of the initiation first came in the great procession to Eleusis. The pig-sacrifice at Eleusis was a preliminary.

The mystery sacrifice distinguished itself from "normal" sacrificial rites in that the sacrificial animal was individually assigned to the initiate, that is, everyone had to provide his own sacrificial pig. A passage in Plutarch even depicts an initiate bathing in the sea together with his pig.[8] We do not know if this was the rule on that day of preparation, the sixteenth of Boedromion, when the mystai were called "to the sea,"[9] but we do know that the pig had to be as clean as the initiate who was to approach the sacred. The Greeks mentioned explicitly that the initiate surrendered the animal to death "in his stead" and that a life was exchanged for a life.[10] This, too, was no secret. The pig-sacrifice as a substitution is very widespread in initiation festivals among the agrarian cultures of the South Seas;[11] a distant historical connection with the Demeter mysteries is altogether possible.

Among the Greeks, the word and image of the *χοῖρος* had defi-

---

[6] *LSS* 3 C 39–42, according to Sokolowski's admittedly uncertain restoration. An *ἐσχάρα, Ἐλευσῖνι ἐν τῇ αὐλῇ* is mentioned by "Demosth." 59.116.

[7] Max. Tyr. 39.3k; *μυεῖσθαι* in the Telesterion: Dio Chrys. *Or.* 12,33; *ἔξω τοῦ νεὼ τὰ προτέλεια μυήσας* Themist. *Or.* 5.71a.

[8] Plut. *Phoc.* 28,6.

[9] *Ἅλαδε ἔλασις* *IG* II/III² 847.20; the gate *ἐ[ι] ἅλαδε ἐ[χ]σελαύνοσιν οἱ μύσται* *IG* I² 94.35 = *SIG*³ 93; *ἅλαδε μύσται* Hsch.; Polyaen. 3.11.2; Schol. Aeschines 3.130; *Et. M.* 469.18 (confused with the *ἱερὰ ὁδός*). The reference is to the sixteenth of Boedromion (Polyaen.).

[10] Schol. Aristoph. *Ach.* 747 *ἕκαστος δὲ τῶν μυουμένων ὑπὲρ ἑαυτοῦ ἔθυεν*, and cf. Porph. *Abst.* 2.28 concerning the Pythagoreans: *ὅτε δὲ εἰς ἀπαρχήν τι τῶν ζῴων ἀνθ' ἑαυτῶν μερίσειαν τοῖς θεοῖς* (hence Aristoxenos could prove that Pythagoras ate pig: fr. 25 = Gell. *NA* 4.11 and fr. 29a = Diog. Laert. 8.20). Each initiand must be individually initiated: *IG* I² 6 = *LSS* 3 C 22–26.

[11] H. Nevermann, "Die Religionen der Südsee," in *Die Religionen der Menschheit* V 2 (1968), 54, 57, 97; A. E. Jensen, *Beschneidung und Reifezeremonien bei Naturvölkern* (1933), 90–91.

nite associations that Aristophanes could not resist: χοῖρος is slang for the female genitals; the naked pig and the sexual object merge. Thus, in the *Acharnians*, the Megarian sells his daughters in a sack as "mystery piggies."[12] Here, associative undercurrents surface in laughter. The animal that is to die in the preliminary sacrifice in place of the initiate himself was experienced as a female entity: the pig-sacrifice had the character of an anticipatory sacrifice of a maiden.

Greek mythology in fact explains the pig-sacrifice as the maiden's descent into the underworld, that is, as the rape of Kore by Hades. When the Lord of the Dead sank into the earth with his stolen bride, the pigs of the shepherd Eubuleus were pulled along into the depths. The women in the Thesmophoria therefore throw pigs into the underground μέγαρα.[13] In another version, Demeter could no longer find the tracks of her stolen daughter, because a herd of pigs had run over them.[14] Kore had disappeared and in her place pigs were rooting about, therefore pigs had to die in the sanctuary of Demeter, just as Persephone had fallen to the god of the dead.

The rape of Kore-Persephone is one of the best-known and most widespread of the Greek myths.[15] It is by no means specifically Eleusinian. A fig tree where Kore had descended was shown at Eleusis,[16] but there were far more famous places where Hades was thought to have driven into the earth with his bride, as, for instance, the Ennian Lake[17] or the spring of Kyane near Syracuse.[18] Like the pig-sacrifice, this myth is one of the general features of Demeter-worship throughout the Greek world and even beyond it.

Since antiquity, the myth of Kore has been regarded as especially

---

[12] Aristoph. *Ach.* 729–817; for "mystery pigs," see 747, 764; for the word-play on χοῖρος, see 767–75; cf. Aristoph. *Vesp.* 1353, 1364 with Schol.; Varro *R.r.* 2.4.10. See also the so-called "Baubo" statuettes (a woman on a pig): e.g., Cook II (1924) 132; O. Rubensohn, *AA* (1929), 195–204.

[13] Schol. Luk. pp. 275.23–276.24; Clem. *Pr.* 2.17.1; cf. n.5. above.

[14] Ov. *Fast.* 4.465–66, following Callimachus; the pig as enemy of the sown field: Hyg. *fab.* 277; Serv. *Georg.* 2.380; Schol. Aristoph. *Ran.* 388. There is a strange tradition in Porph. *Abst.* 2.9, in which Klymene (a name that recalls Persephone) "mistakenly" kills the first pig.

[15] The most thorough discussion is in R. Foerster, *Der Raub und die Rückkehr der Persephone* (1874). Cf. *PR* I 747–806; L. Bloch, *RML* II 1284–1379. The oldest and most important testimony is the *Homeric Hymn to Demeter*: see V.1.n.8; on Orphic versions, see Graf (1974) 151–81. On the versions of the myth in Callimachus and Nicander, as they can be reconstructed from Ovid, see H. Herter, *RhM* 90 (1941), 236–68.

[16] Paus. 1.38.5, and cf. Phanodemos, *FGrHist* 325 F 27.

[17] Firm. *Err.* 7.3, and cf. Ov. *Fast.* 4.445–50.

[18] Diod. 5.4; Cic. *Verr.* 4.107; Ov. *Met.* 5.412–24. Cf. *PR* I 758–59; *RML* II 1313–15.

transparent and comprehensible as a description of the agricultural cycle: Kore is the grain that must go under the earth[19] so that, from this seeming death, the new fruit can appear. Hunger threatens when Kore disappears, but to the delight of gods and men, she returns, and with her the blessing of grain from Demeter. In Athens there was even a popular metonymy that allowed grain and flour to be addressed as Persephone.[20] Yet the details, as they occur for instance in the *Homeric Hymn*, do not agree with the agricultural interpretation.[21] Kore is said to spend four months in the underworld, eight months in the sunlight; the grain, however, sprouts just a few weeks after sowing. Around the Mediterranean it does not stay in the earth for four months: it sprouts in autumn, not in spring. The Eleusinian mysteries, on the other hand, were celebrated neither at sowing time, nor sprouting time, nor harvest time, but about one month before sowing in the autumn.

Martin P. Nilsson therefore advocates an interpretation more in accord with nature.[22] Kore's path into the underworld is the storage of the grain, specifically, the seed grain, in subterranean granaries during the summer months. At this point in the Mediterranean summer all vegetable life seems to die. Then during the first autumn rains the stocks of the state are brought from their underground containers: Kore returns to the upper world and the vegetation cycle starts anew. The great and very probably sacral role of the granary in Neolithic towns[23] accords with this interpretation, as does the connection between storage vessels and the concept of the underworld as seen in the great buried pithoi[24] of Minoan-Mycenaean times. The four

---

[19] Varro in Aug. *Civ.* 7.20, and cf. Kleanthes, *SVF* I #547 = Plut. *Is.* 377d; Cic. *Nat. deor.* 2.66; Plut. *Is.* 378f; Schol. Aristoph. *Vesp.* 1438; Cornutus 28; Porph. *Περὶ ἀγαλμάτων* fr. 7 p. 9* Bidez = Euseb. *Praep. Ev.* 3.11.9; Arnob. 5.32, 5.43; *Hymn. Orph.* 29.13–14; assumed in Epigenes, *OF* 33 = Clem. *Strom.* 5.49.3.

[20] Eubulos fr. 75.10 (*CAF* II 191); Antiphanes fr. 52.9 (*CAF* II 31). Vase-painters make the ears of wheat cross over Persephone's head, e.g., Hydria Athens 1443, Metzger (1951) pl. 34.3, Hydria Tyskiewitz (Lyon), Metzger (1951) pl. 33.1.

[21] Lines 339–403, 445–47; Apollod. 1.33; half a year in each: Ov. *Fast.* 4.614; *Met.* 5.567; Hyg. *Fab.* 146.

[22] *ARW* 32 (1935), 106–14 = *Opuscula* II (1952), 577–88, and cf. (1955) 472–74; opposed by K. Kourouniotis, *Deltion* 15 (1933/35), 6–15; L. Malten, *Gnomon* 20 (1944), 121; Brumfield (1981) 211–16; preceding Nilsson was F. M. Cornford, *Essays and Studies W. Ridgeway* (1913), 153–66. In fact Schol. Arat. 150 puts the rape of Kore in summer, with reference to Egypt.

[23] See I.5.n.40 above.

[24] See also IV.3.n.21, IV.5.n.11 above.

months can be explained thus. There is no evidence, however, that the Greeks of historical times understood the myth in this way. The *Homeric Hymn* explicitly sets Kore's return in the spring.[25] Thus, Nilsson's thesis has been generally, although perhaps too generally and hastily, rejected.

The myth can, as we have seen, be related to the actual events of the year in two or more ways, gaining thereby each time a particular relevance and transparency. On the whole, however, it cannot be derived from natural conditions. What actions of the farmer could give rise to such essential and penetrating features as, on the one hand, Kore's flower-picking in the meadow and, on the other, the wanderings of Demeter in search of her daughter? The myth is shaped not by natural phenomena but by purely human themes: marriage and death, grief and anger, and final reconciliation. It is certain, in any case, that the festivals of the cult of Demeter-Kore were in accord with these themes. Festivals of flower-picking, "the journey down," and "the journey up" (Kathodos and Anodos), are frequently attested in the Greek world[26] and are only loosely connected with the seasons. The Thesmophoria could be held immediately before the sowing, as in Athens, but they could also occur in the middle of the summer.[27] Wherever they were held, the festivals were set according to a calendar. Even those fixed "four months" would correspond better to a sacral calendar than to a vegetation period. The rituals were established by tradition as self-sufficient in their interpersonal function; thus the myth, although aiming both at festival rituals and natural events, preserved at its core a human drama.

For, contrary to all vegetation interpretations, the myth does not tell of a cycle. What occurs proves to be irrevocable. There is no victory over death: Hades accomplished his goal. The opposition of Hades and Zeus justifies a double existence between the upper and lower world in which the latter's rights are not infringed upon. Life has gained the dimension of death, but this also means that death contains a dimension of life.

To be raped by Hades, to enter into a marriage with him, means

---

[25] Line 401.

[26] Κόρης . . . *ἀνθεσφόρια* Pollux 1.37 (Sicily); Strabo 6 p. 256 (Hipponion); Paus. 2.35.5 (Hermione); *Χρυσάνθεια* Κόραια in Sardis, *BMC* Lydia pp. cix–x. Ἡ *ἀνάβασις τῆς θεοῦ—ἡ δύσις τῆς θεοῦ* (sc. of Kore) in Dardanos (?) *IG* XII Suppl. 29 = *LS* 128 in intervals of 9 months. For Κόρης *καταγωγή* (corresponding to the Dionysiac *καταγώγαί*, this is an "entry" rather than a "descent") in Sicily, see Diod. 5.4.6, at harvest-time.

[27] Nilsson (1955) 465–66.

simply to die.[28] The Kore myth relates a maiden's death that has the approval of Zeus: it describes the sacrifice of a maiden. As almost always in sacrificial myths, the tragedy of the maiden is only a preparation for what is to follow: for the hunter, it is the great hunt, the dreadful and liberating act of killing; among fishermen, it is the arrival of the fish and the great haul. If Demeter is the goddess of grain, then, for her, the nourishment from grain is the goal answering to the surrender of the maiden. The myth and cult of Demeter are a symbolizing transformation of the older sacrificial ritual into agrarian terms; accordingly, the harvest festival took the place of the sacrificial meal. The new themes functioned, of course, only as substitutes within preestablished structures and, for this very reason, the connection with practical agriculture is only partial and loose. The festival rituals could sever themselves again from the seasons and accomplish on their own strength what they had always accomplished, that is, order and renewal of society; with the development of personal initiation, they could even shape the faith of the individual confronted with the problem of death.

There are, significantly, variants of the Kore myth in which the agricultural connection completely disappears. A strange form of the "rape" appears on some votive reliefs from Lokroi Epizephyrioi in Southern Italy. A young man (a local hero?) abducts the maiden but then hands her over to a solemn, bearded old man, the god of the underworld.[29] The character of renunciation in the maiden-sacrifice is quite clear: the maiden, whom the young man was already holding in his arms, is surrendered to the god of death. In Lokroi there was a strange rite of maiden-sacrifice. In the magnificent temple of Aphrodite, the young women of the town had to give themselves to foreigners. This too signifies a renunciation, an exchange of roles in the critical transition from virginity to womanhood. Naturally the foreigners' nighttime privilege was limited; the daytime order lay in the hands of the Lokrians. Accordingly, in Abydos they told of the defeat and expulsion of those who had enjoyed the pleasures of Aphrodite in the temple of Aphrodite Porne.[30] The Lokrians believed they owed their military victories to their Aphrodite. Here, then, the sacrifice of

---

[28] See Eur. *Heracl.* 484; *Tro.* 307–41; *Or.* 1109; *Iph. Aul.* 461; Soph. *Ant.* 816, 891, 1204, 1240; *AP* 7.13, 182, 186, 221, 489, 507b, 599.

[29] P. Zancani Montuoro, "Il rapitore di Kore nel mito Locrese," *Rend. Acc. di Archeol. Napoli* 29 (1954), 79–86; H. Prückner, *Die lokrischen Tonreliefs* (1968), 72–74. Cf. on Lokroi I.7.n.21 above.

[30] See III.1.n.117.

a maiden, accomplished in the form of an initiation, was again an anticipatory sexual renunciation guaranteeing great success.

In the Sumerian myth of Inanna's journey to the underworld, the oldest literary example of a Kathodos, there is no direct tie to grain, yet it is not unrelated to the Kore myth.[31] When, in 1951, the end of this myth became known, it was a great surprise. Until then scholars had connected Ištar's descent into hell with the conjectured resurrection of Dumuzi-Tammuz and had seen therein once again a reflection of the vegetation cycle. Now, however, the myth takes a far more aggressive turn, the main part describing a ritual leading to death, a sacrifice of a maiden. The "pure Inanna" decides of her own free will to go to the underworld. She adorns herself and sets off for the Land of No Return. The seven gates of the underworld open for her and, as she passes through each gate, a piece of her attire is removed: the crown, the staff, the necklace, the chain about her chest, the ring, breastplate, loincloth. The seven judges of the underworld gaze at her with the eyes of death, after which she is hanged upon a beam. In the upper world, her servant carries the lament for Inanna from town to town, to Ekur, Ur, and Eridu. Then magical beings created by Enki call Inanna back to life. The words "Inanna ascends from the underworld" are repeated over and over like a password, and she rises, accompanied by the Gallu, dangerous armed underworld beings who neither eat nor drink but only destroy. Before them, all men prostrate themselves in the dust. Only Dumuzi stays seated on his throne, whereupon the Gallu seize him and carry him off to the underworld.

In this case there is no mother-daughter drama, only the death, transfiguration, and return of the one "pure goddess." Until now no ritual has been adduced that could correspond to this myth, and yet the bridge to the Greek world seems to be forged by the Anatolian Mother, Kybele, and her retinue of maddened Galloi.[32] It is she who

---

[31] *ANET* 52; S. N. Kramer, *Journ. Cuneif. Stud.* 5 (1951), 1–17. In addition, the pursuit of Dumuzi by the Gallu; B. Alster, *Dumuzi's Dream* (1972). All versions now in S. N. Kramer, *The Sacred Marriage Rite* (1969), 107–132. Cf. O. R. Gurney, "Tammuz Reconsidered," *Journ. Sem. Stud.* 7 (1962), 147–60; A. Falkenstein, "Der sumerische und der akkadische Mythos von Inannas Gang zur Unterwelt," *Festschr. W. Caskel* (1968), 96–110; Th. Jacobsen, *The Treasures of Darkness* (1976), 55–63. The parallel to the myth of Kore was drawn by Guépin (1968) 120–27. At the beginning of the Sumerian poem "Gilgamesh, Enkidu and the Underworld" are the words: "After Ereshkigal had been carried off into Kur as its prize" (S. N. Kramer, *Sumerian Mythology* [1961[2]], 37; *History Begins at Sumer* [1956], 171), i.e., the queen of the underworld is a maiden who was abducted from the upper world.

[32] See Hepding (1903); Burkert (1979) 99–111; cf. III.8.n.17 above. Perhaps the Greek

brings castration and death to the unfaithful Attis. The mother of the gods, storming through the mountains with her wild attendants, is still more the huntress than the giver of grain. Her wrath abates only when she receives the tympanon that comes from the sacrifice of a bull (in Babylon, the kalu-priests were entrusted with the knowledge of how to make the tympanon in secret sacrificial ceremonies).[33] As with Demeter, the mother's fury and the wild hunt are motivated by the loss of the daughter: the virgin-sacrifice is, now as before, a preparation, freeing ferocious powers and pressing toward a sacrifice through which upper and lower worlds reach a tension-filled equilibrium.

When the American Indians tell of the death of the maiden, the mother's wrath, the unsuccessful return from the underworld, the successful establishment of death and, at the same time, certain tambourine dances among the men;[34] when a theme of Japanese and Polynesian myth is the death of a goddess as a condition for the gift of nourishment;[35] when already in Neolithic Çatal Hüyük the two goddesses seem to appear as mother and daughter, the former connected with grain[36]—one begins to sense the dimensions of a theme that has survived only in isolated indications, islands like the peaks of sunken mountain ranges. Eleusis, for all its peculiarities, is not alone in the theme of death, pain, and expectation; seeking, failing to find, and discovery. And, for the receptive initiate, the routine sacrifice of the "mystery pig" could always assume a deeper dimension: standing there at the edge of death, he destroys a life in his stead; the act of killing is irrevocable and yet must provoke an answer. The scales of life's equilibrium have been tipped and, if an equilibrium exists at all at the center of being, the scales must swing back again. It is the hope of the initiate that the path into death will lead to life.

Κοράγια, a procession of men (Mantineia: *IG* V 2.265.16, 27, 266.41; *κοραγωγός* in Athens, *IG* II/III² 1247.20; Hsch. *κοραγεῖν τὸ ἀνάγειν τὴν Κόρην*) should be taken as a demonic procession similar to that of the Gallu with Inanna. Against this, the independence of Dumuzi is stressed by C. Colpe, "lišān mitḫurti," *Festschr. W. v. Soden* (1969), 23.

[33] See I.1.n.44. On Meter and Tympanon: Eur. *Hel.* 1346–52; *Bacch.* 123–29; Epidaurian *Hymn IG* IV 1² 131, *Poetae Mel. Gr.* 935 Page.

[34] A myth of the Cherokees in C. Lévi-Strauss, *Mythologiques* III (1968), 229.

[35] Japan: K. Florenz, *Die historischen Quellen der Shinto-Religion* (1919), 41–42, 144–47. On Polynesia see I.5.n.43 above.

[36] Mellaart (1967) 236, 238; (1970) I 170–71; cf. V.4.n.75 below.

3. *Myesis and Synthema*

The few indications that we have concerning the Eleusinian mystery rituals are the more problematical because there were various sites and various stages in the mysteries. The community permitted to participate in the festival at Eleusis is broken up into mystai and epoptai. One could become an epoptes[1] by participating in the great festival for a second time one year later. A distinction was also made between the Lesser and Greater Mysteries. They were divided according to time, place, and sanctuary. The Lesser Mysteries occurred "in the city," in the precinct of Agra by the banks of the Ilissos, where a small temple of Meter, the mother of the gods, stood until modern times. The date on which they were celebrated was the twentieth of Anthesterion, seven months before the Greater Mysteries.[2] Virtually no details have come down to us about what took place by the Ilissos; there are only general statements concerning a "purification," a "preliminary consecration."[3] Though the story of Herakles' initiation at

---

[1] *'Επώπτευον δὲ τοὐλάχιστον ἀπὸ τῶν μεγάλων ἐνιαυτὸν διαλείποντες* Plut. *Demetr.* 26; Philochoros, *FGrHist* 328 F 69/70; Schol. Aristoph. *Ran.* 745. *Μύσται—ἐπόπται* already *IG* I² 6.49 = *LSS* 3 B 5. Cf. Plat. *Symp.* 209e; *Phdr.* 250c; Plut. *Alc.* 22; Sen. *Q. nat.* 7.30.6 *Eleusis servat quod ostendat revisentibus*. Of course, Cicero only lived at Athens for half a year (*RE* VII A 838; Lobeck [1829] 37), and Romans thereafter would rarely have gone to Eleusis twice. Theon Smyrn. pp. 14–15 Hiller mentions the following steps: *καθαρμός, τελετῆς παράδοσις* (= *μύησις*?), *ἐποπτεία, ἀνάδεσις καὶ στεμμάτων ἐπίθεσις, ὥστε καὶ ἑτέροις παραδοῦναι δύνασθαι*, just as Plut. *An seni* 795d mentions *μυσταγωγῶν* as the conclusion, *μυούμενος* as the beginning. The *μύησις* was accomplished on a specific day of the *μυστήρια*, as is shown by Plat. *Meno* 76e, and cf. V.2.n.7 above. Crassus came too late: see Cic. *De or.* 3.75; for an emperor, of course, the mysteries could be repeated: *IG* II/III² 3592 = *SIG*³ 869.24.

[2] *Μυστήρια τὰ μέζονα–τὰ ὀλέζονα* *LSS* 1; *LSS* 3 B 32. Since the time spans mentioned here for the *σπονδαί* at the Lesser and Greater Mysteries correspond to each other exactly (mid-Gamelion until the tenth of Elaphebolion, and mid-Metageitnion until the tenth of Pyanopsion), the actual festival day in both cases must also come on the twentieth of the intermediate month (A. Mommsen [1898] 406, ignored by Deubner). *Τὰ μεγάλα–τὰ πρὸς Ἄγραν μυστήρια* *IG* II/III² 661.9.21; 847.22, 1231; *ἐν Ἄγρας* *An. Bekk.* 326.24, and cf. Steph. Byz. *Ἄγρα*, Suda *α* 339. For the temple of Meter see *IG* I² 310.132; F. Studniczka, *JdI* 31 (1916), 169–230; H. Möbius, *AM* 60/61 (1935/36), 234–57 = *Studia Varia* (1967), 108–37.

[3] Schol. Aristoph. *Plut.* 845 *ὥσπερ προκάθαρσις καὶ προάγνευσις*; Jul. *Or.* 5.173b–c: *προτέλεια; παρὰ τὸν Ἰλισσὸν . . . καθαρμὸν τελοῦσιν* Polyaen. 5.17.1. Athena pu-

Eleusis is very common, it is sometimes said that the Lesser Mysteries were established especially for Herakles.[4] In Classical times the festival was administered by the Eleusinian personnel. The hierophant, the dadouchos, the hierokeryx, and the priestess of Demeter each got their fee.[5] Slaves needed to clean the shrine could be hastily initiated at the Lesser Mysteries for this purpose.[6] By the fourth century at least, initiation in the Lesser Mysteries was mandatory before proceeding to the Greater.[7] Yet in later times this requirement was obviously no longer observed. In Agrai there was neither a Telesterion nor Epopteia; but there was a cult of Artemis Agrotera, the Huntress, and this is hardly coincidental,[8] since Meter, in Anatolia and elsewhere, has stronger connections with hunting than Demeter. The association with the Eleusinian mysteries may also represent a balancing between the municipal Athenian cult and the far more extravagant neighboring cult. For the Athenians, "the Mysteries" were and always remained primarily those celebrated at Eleusis.

We can say with certainty that the Greater Mysteries included an initiation, a myesis, and that there was a pig-sacrifice associated with Eleusis.[9] A further preparatory act belonging to the Eleusinian myesis is mentioned in a gloss by Hesychius: "*ϑρόνωσις*, introductory cere-

---

rified herself at the Ilissos with *mystica lampas*: Stat. *Theb.* 8.765. *μίμημα τῶν περὶ τὸν Διόνυσον* Steph. Byz. Ἄγρα. The allegorical interpretation of the Lesser and Greater Mysteries given by the "Naassenian," Hippol. *Ref.* 5.8.42–44, contaminates Plat. *Gorg.* 497c (Greater/Lesser Mysteries) with Plat. *Symp.* 209e (Myesis/Epopteia). The statement that the Lesser Mysteries were held for Persephone, the Greater for Demeter (Schol. Aristoph. *Plut.* 845) comes from associating *ἐλάττονα/μείζονα μυστήρια* with *ϑεὰ ἡ πρεσβυτέρα–ἡ νεωτέρα* (*IG* II/III² 1673.300, and cf. 3546, 3585).

[4] Diod. 4.14.3; Schol. Aristoph. *Ran.* 501; *Plut.* 845, 1013; see also the relief from Ilissos, Athens 1778, *Ephem.* 1894 pl. 7, Kerényi (1962) 65 pl. 6. Cf. n. 11 below.

[5] *LSS* 1, 3 C.

[6] *IG* II/III² 1672.207, 1673.24, after the Anthesteria (*εἰς Χοᾶς* 1672.204).

[7] Plat. *Gorg.* 497c with Schol. (the first part of the Scholion follows Atthidographic tradition; see Schol. Aristoph. *Plut.* 845; the second part is an abbreviated paraphrase of Clem. *Pr.* 15); Plut. *Demetr.* 26. The Lesser Mysteries are no longer attested in Roman times.

[8] Kerényi (1962) 64 interprets the designation of the locale *ἐν Ἄγρας* (e.g., *IG* I² 310.132, 324.96; *LS* 18 A 39) as "auf dem Gebiet der Göttin namens Jagdbeute"; for a different interpretation see P. Chantraine, *Classica et Mediaevalia* 17 (1956), 1–4; *RPh* 40 (1966), 37–39. Apollodoros obviously refers to Agra in *FGrHist* 244 F 142 = Clem. *Pr.* 2.13.1, the *μυστήρια* are named *ἀπὸ Μυοῦντός τινος Ἀττικοῦ, ὃν ἐν κυνηγίᾳ διαφϑαρῆναι.*

[9] There is explicit reference to the mysteries in Boedromion at Plut. *Phoc.* 28; cf. V.2.n.8, V.3.n.3 above; for the Iakchos-song and the aroma of roast pig see Aristoph. *Ran.* 338. Kerényi (1962) 68–69, (1967) 55–56 discusses the pig-sacrifice only in connection with Agrai.

mony for those to be initiated." Plato relates the term to the Korybantes in the cult of Meter.[10] The pictorial tradition, however, portrays such an act of "sitting on a seat" precisely in connection with the initiation of Herakles.[11] This mythical initiation appears in three scenes on two reliefs made during the Roman Empire, on the sarcophagus from Torre Nova and on the so-called Lovatelli urn (see figures 8 and 9). These echo a common model from which individual scenes were reproduced on Roman architectural, or so-called Campana, reliefs.[12] The preliminary sacrifice of a pig is followed by the *θρόνωσις* in the central scene: the initiand sits veiled and barefoot, on a strangely shaped stool covered with a skin. One of the copyists misunderstood it as the lion's skin of Herakles,[13] but a ram's head or horn underneath the initiand's foot clearly shows that a ramskin is meant. A priestess approaches the veiled candidate from behind. On the urn she is holding a winnowing fan over him; on the sarcophagus she passes a burning torch very close to his hand. The ancient name for such rituals is

---

[10] Plat. *Euthyd.* 277d (cf. *Leg.* 790d–e; Dio Chrys. *Or.* 12.33; for *θρονισμοὶ* Μητρῷοι as a work of "Orpheus" see Suda o 654). The finds in the "Anaktoron" at Samothrace may indicate a corresponding rite there; see A. D. Nock, *AJA* 45 (1941), 577–81.

[11] Herakles' initiation at Eleusis is now attested already in Pindar, *POxy* 2622 and *PSI* 1391; H. Lloyd-Jones, *Maia* 19 (1967), 206–29; thereafter Eur. *Heracl.* 613; Kallias in Xen. *Hell.* 6.3.6; Diod. 4.25.1; "Plat." *Axioch.* 371e; *Pap.d. R. Univ. Milano* 20 (1937), 20 (V.4.n.58 below); Apollod. 2.122; on Agra see n. 4 above. See also Attic vases of the fifth and fourth centuries: "Skyphos Somzée" Brussels A 10 = *ARV*² 661.86, Metzger (1965) pl. 13; *CV* Belgique 71.1. Pelike, Leningrad 1792 = *ARV*² 1476.1, Nilsson (1955) pl. 46, Kerényi (1962) pl. 38. Pelike, Brussels R 235 = *ARV*² 1121.11, *CV* Belgique 72.4. "Pourtalès-Vase," bell-crater *BM* F 68 = *ARV*² 1446.1, Metzger (1951) pl. 33.3, 17; cover for a bowl, Tübingen E 183 = *ARV*² 1477.7, Nilsson (1955) pl. 45.1; Kerényi (1962) pl. 43. Cf. D. Feytmans, *ACl* 14 (1945), 285–318.

[12] For the sarcophagus (more exactly, an ossuary, length 130 cm; Asia Minor second century A.D.) see G. E. Rizzo, *Römische Mitteilungen* 25 (1910), 89–167; Deubner (1932) pl. 7.1; Mylonas (1961) fig. 84; Kerényi (1962) pl. 7. For the urn (Museo Nazionale Romano, Rome) see E. C. Lovatelli, *Boll. d. Comm.* 7 (1879), 5–18, pl. 1/3; Deubner (1932) pl. 7.2; Nilsson (1955) pl. 43.2; the best reproductions are in Kerényi (1962) pl. 8–11. For the Campana reliefs see H. von Rohden and H. Winnefeld, *Architektonische röm. Tonreliefs der Kaiserzeit* (1911), 7–8. The thronosis (as on the sarcophagus) also appears on a marble relief in Naples: see Cook I (1914) 426; *RM* 25 (1910), 104; cf. *Ephem.* 1911, 44–45. On the interpretation see Pringsheim (1905) 9–12; P. Roussel, *BCH* 54 (1930), 58–65; Mylonas (1961) 205–208 (hypercritical); Kerényi (1962) 68–71 (in reference to Agrai). A figure on the side of the sarcophagus corresponds to a figure on the relief from the Ilissos temple (n. 2 above): see F. Studniczka, *JdI* 31 (1916), 172–73; for this reason, H. Möbius, *AM* 60/61 (1935/36), 250 = *Studia Varia* (1967), 119–20, considers whether the model for the whole series of pictures might not come from there—a variation of the Eleusinian version on the urn.

[13] On the Lovatelli urn: see Figure 9.

clear: purification by air—just as the grain in the winnowing fan is purified by the wind—and purification by fire.[14] The psychological effect is also at once clear. The recurrent binding or veiling of the eyes in initiation is not fortuitous. Blind, helpless, and abandoned, the candidate must suffer the unknown. He is captive and ignorant, surrounded by those who are active and knowing. Having previously been isolated, made insecure, and frightened, he must now experience the unveiling, his new sight, as a blissful liberation. His new contact with reality prepares him for contemplation of the divine.

The connection of the Thronosis with the Eleusinian rather than the Lesser Mysteries is attested by the *Homeric Hymn to Demeter*. Here, on coming to Eleusis, the goddess Demeter herself performs this act. Her conduct, which appears unmotivated both psychologically and artistically, is the model for those who enter her mysteries. As she entered the hall of king Keleos, "she refused to sit on the shining seat, but, rather, remained silent, with downcast eyes, until Iambe, knowing her duty, set up a stool and over this she spread a shimmering ramskin. Then she sat down, holding the veil over her face in her hands. And she sat silently on the stool for a long time in sorrow."[15] Here, too, there is a seat, a ramskin, the bowed head, and the veil; the only difference is that whereas the representations depict the mystai, the myth speaks of the god.

Aristophanes parodies this act by having Socrates as a false priest initiate the novice, Strepsiades, into his newfangled meteorological mysteries. "Sit down on the sacred seat," "take this wreath"—"But please don't sacrifice me!" cries the mistrusting candidate worriedly —"Be quiet!" Dust trickles down on him, a festive prayer is sung, and Strepsiades hastily pulls his cloak up over his head in order not to get wet, for now the gods—the clouds—appear.[16] A few years later, after the great Mystery scandal, Aristophanes would presumably not have

---

[14] Serv. *Aen.* 6.741; *Georg.* 1.166.

[15] 192–98; F. Wehrli, *ARW* 31 (1934), 78–79.

[16] A. Dieterich, *RhM* 48 (1893), 275–83 = *Kl. Schr.* (1911), 117–24, recognized that Aristoph. *Nub.* 254–68 was a parody of a ritual; to be sure, he spoke of "Orphism" (following him cf. Pringsheim [1905] 26; Harrison [1922] 511–16), since a parody of the Eleusinian rite seemed unthinkable to him. But a precisely corresponding rite seems to be attested only at Eleusis; cf. the use there too of the Διὸς κῴδιον (*χρῶνται . . . καὶ ὁ* δᾳδαῦχος ἐν Ἐλευσῖνι Paus. Att. δ 18 Erbse; III.1.n.38 above); W. K. C. Guthrie, *Orpheus and Greek Religion* (1952²), 210–12. The comic poet would, however, have left open the possibility that he could deny any reference; the Eleusinian rituals were not unique. The singeing of the Kedestes in Aristoph. *Thesm.* 236–48 may parody the torch-purification.

dared to write such a scene. Yet this veiled sitting was still only the beginning of the initiation, coming before the secret. It could be seen as a general, outer form of initiation revealing nothing of its content, and for this reason it could be portrayed in the visual arts.

The third and last scene of this initiation frieze is a different matter:[17] the initiate approaches Demeter. He is splendidly dressed, his bundle of twigs showing that he is a participant in the Iakchos procession. The goddess sits on a plaited basket (*κίστη*), about which a snake may be seen winding. Demeter looks back in the direction of a young woman hurrying toward her with a torch: this is Persephone coming back from the underworld. The divine myth is presented here in connection with a ritual instrument, the kiste, and a very general symbol, the snake. These hints for those with knowledge betray nothing to the uninitiated. The basket remains covered. The snake arouses both a fear of death and a secret sexual fascination. For the initiate, however, the snake is no longer dangerous. He can touch it without fear. Approaching Demeter, experiencing Kore's return, transforming the fear of death into quiet confidence—these are the themes of the night of the mysteries at Eleusis. But what actually happened is hidden behind the glorious artistic facade of Greek mythology.

We know that the encounter with the kiste, the *cista mystica*,[18] was part of the initiation, because of a much-discussed saying transmitted by Clement of Alexandria. He describes it as the "watchword" (*σύνθημα*) of the Eleusinian Mysteries: "I have fasted, I have drunk the kykeon, I have taken from the 'kiste,' worked, deposited into the basket and out of the basket into the 'kiste.'"[19] It has been objected

---

[17] It is widely assumed that the frieze, taken in this order from right to left, portrays the sequence of steps in the initiation: e.g., Dieterich, *RhM* 48, 276; Harrison (1922) 546; Kerényi (1962) 70. The identification of the initiate in the third scene with Herakles in the first has been disputed, e.g., by Pringsheim (1905) 23–24 and Mylonas (1961) 207, who wrongly identifies the candidate on the urn and on the Campana-reliefs (Kerényi [1962] pl. 12) with the iconographically completely different "Iakchos." The latter is added on the left of the sarcophagus, whereas the candidate is left out. On the snake see III.1.n.70 above.

[18] On the *κίστη* at Eleusis see Pringsheim (1905) 49–64; Metzger (1965) 33–36; 41–44; see generally O. Jahn, *Hermes* 3 (1869), 317–34. The *κίστη* is connected mainly with mysteries of Demeter and Dionysus (see Nilsson [1957] 57), but also with those of Attis (Hepding [1903], 195.1; Cumont [1930] pl. I.3), Isis (V. Tran Tam Tinh, *Essai sur le culte d'Isis à Pompei* [1964], 107, 153), Ma Bellona (Cumont [1930] pl. II 1).

[19] Clem. *Pr.* 2.21.2 (followed by Arnob. 5.26) *κἄστι τὸ σύνθημα* Ἐλευσινίων *μυστηρίων· ἐνήστευσα, ἔπιον τὸν κυκεῶνα, ἔλαβον ἐκ κίστης, ἐργασάμενος ἀπεθέμην εἰς κάλαθον καὶ ἐκ καλάθου εἰς κίστην*; cf. Pfeiffer on Callim. fr. 21.10. *Σύνθημα* "Parole"

that Clement was unfamiliar with Athens and could hardly have obtained such specialized information. The mention of the "basket" (κάλαθος) seems more suggestive of Demeter celebrations in Alexandria.[20] However, Demeter mysteries there are unattested and Clement could hardly have expected his Alexandrian public to accept something Alexandrian as "Eleusinian." The saying, however, seems to be a genuine "watchword" precisely because it really discloses nothing. The initiate is only telling someone with knowledge that he has accomplished all the prescribed rites in the proper order. Precisely what rites these were is hidden behind the most general, unspeaking words: a covered basket, an open basket, taking, "working," putting back. For generations scholars have tried to puzzle out what the kiste and the kalathos could have contained. Clement's indignant tone suggests sexual objects. Symbolic intercourse or birth, male, female or both, are thus the possibilities that have been played out in all combinations.[21]

Hdt. 9.98; etc.; meaning the same, σύμβολον Eur. *Rhes.* 572/3. For a parody of the *signum* of the Bacchus Mysteries see Plaut. *Mil.* 1016; cf. Plut. *Ad. ux.* 611d. For *signa* and *responsa* as the mutual signs of recognition for initiates see Firm. *Err.* 18.1. For the most part, scholars have sought a specific part of the ritual in which the synthema had to be spoken (e.g., Deubner [1932] 80; Kerényi [1962] 77). But the Acarnanians came unasked into the Telesterion, and paid with their lives (Livy 31.14); Arnob. 5.26 *quae rogati in sacrorum acceptionibus respondetis* uses the concept of the σύμβολον following the model of the Christian symbolon: see Delatte (1955) 12–23.

[20] Pringsheim (1905) 49, 300–301; Nilsson (1955) 659 assumes an Alexandrian elaboration of the Eleusinian synthema. The kalathos is connected not only with the Demeter procession at Alexandria (Callim. *Hy.* 6.1–7; for coins see *ACl* 20 [1951], 359, 361), but with the mysteries of Demeter on Paros (Apollod., *FGrHist* 244 F 89); for a goddess sitting on the kalathos see the Thesmophorion on Thasos, *BCH* 89 (1965), 469; the Chalkis Museum (ca. 280 B.C.). For a large kalathos flanked by blades of wheat on a South Italian lekanis see Trendall (1967) 552.882, pl. 215.5. In the myth, the kalathos is present when Persephone is picking flowers: Clem. *Pr.* 2.17.1; see also the sarcophagus reliefs, C. Robert, *Die antiken Sarkophag-Reliefs* III 3 (1919), #362–63, 373–74, 377–78, 383–84, 387, 389, 393–94, 399, 405–406, 412–13, 415, 419. The grave-stele of Nikarion (*IG* II/III^2 9796) in the museum at Eleusis depicts a large kalathos in its pediment. The objects on coins which Deubner (1932) 79.9 identified as kalathoi are bakchos-rings: see J. D. Beazley, *Numism. Chron.* VI 1 (1941), 1–7. Epiphanios *Expos. Fidei* 10 (*OF* p. 110), who mentions the kalathos in the context of Eleusis, is evidently paraphrasing Clem. *Pr.*

[21] A. Dieterich, *Eine Mithrasliturgie* ([1903; 1923^2], 124–26) suspected that the kiste contained a phallus on the analogy of the θεὸς διὰ κόλπου in the mysteries of Sabazios, and cf. Clem. *Pr.* 2.16.2; Firm. *Err.* 10, and cf. Kerényi (1962) 78, (1967) 66. A. Körte, *ARW* 18 (1915), 16–26, inferred from Theodoret *Gr. aff. cur.* 7.11 that a rebirth occurred by means of coming into contact with a κτείς (in an earlier passage, however, in which Theodoret first explains the word κτείς, he speaks of Thesmophoria, 3.84); agreeing

One can marshal support for all these interpretations. Intercourse as a mystery is a common metaphor, or more than a metaphor. Aphrodite Mysteries were intimately connected with marriage preparations.[22] There is a tradition in which the reproductive organ of the dismembered Dionysus is hidden in a kiste.[23] The unveiling of the phallus in a winnowing fan is a central event in the mysteries of Dionysus.[24] Eleusis, however, was famous for its special purity and the celebrations took place under the aegis of the divine powers of the female. Thus a late authority speaks of the female genitals, *κτείς*, as the emblem of Eleusis, and an almost over-obvious allusion in Aristophanes points to such associations with the kiste: when the women make peace with the men, Lysistrata says to the sexually afflicted representatives of the opposite sex, "Now keep yourselves nice and clean so that we women can then entertain you in the city with the contents of our *κίσται*."[25] The religious metaphor of self-purification and abstinence points to the marvelous festival to come. Genital symbols are least appropriate for the representation of a birth. Since no one experiences his birth consciously, a rebirth likewise does not lend itself to impressive symbolization.

The controversy surrounding the interpretation reflects how uncertain the interpreters are as to what degree of explicitness they must assume in ritual symbolism. For a puritan, naked sexuality is overwhelming and transforming, something like a mystery secret. Repetition, however, quickly exhausts its fascination. The phallic herms on the streets of Athens became a matter of concern only after they had been mutilated. A far longer-lasting effect results from something indirect, allusive, and ambiguous. In one case, Clement found out the

---

with Körte cf. Kern, *RE* XVI 1239; disagreeing, cf. Deubner (1932) 81–83. Ch. Picard, *RHR* 95 (1927), 220–55, suggested a phallus in the kiste, a *cunnus* in the kalathos; cf. M. J. Lagrange, *Rev. Bibl.* 38 (1929), 71–81; L. Ziehen, *Gnomon* 5 (1929), 152–54; S. Eitrem, *Symb. Osl.* 20 (1940), 140–44.

[22] On the mysteries of Dionysus and marriage see III.4 above. For *μυεῖσθαι*, etc., used of a wedding see Alicphr. 1.4.3; Charito 4.4.95; Helidorus 1.17, etc. For marriage rites in the mysteries see Firm. *Err.* 2.1; Dieterich (1923) 121–34; R. Merkelbach, *Roman und Mysterium* (1962), 16–18.

[23] Clem. *Pr.* 2.19.4 with Schol., in reference to the Cabiri. The *αἰδοῖα* of the Galloi are kept in *θαλάμαι* after having been cut off: see Schol. Nik. *Alex.* 8; there is a *θαλάμη* in a Meter ritual in Polemon, Ath. 478c (Pringsheim [1905] 72–73). Cf. Meuli (1946) 256, the genitals of a butchered reindeer buried in a box made of bark; and cf. I.7 above.

[24] Best known from the painting in the Villa dei Misteri; F. Matz, ΔΙΟΝΥΣΙΑΚΗ ΤΕΛΕΤΗ (Abh. Mainz, 1963, 15) 7–21.

[25] Aristoph. *Lys.* 1182–84; G. W. Elderkin, *ClPh* 35 (1940), 395.

contents of a *cista mystica*—in the mysteries of Dionysus Bassaros.[26] They consisted of sesame cakes, pyramid cakes, globular cakes, polyomphalos cakes, lumps of salt, pomegranates, fig branches, a narthex, ivy, round cakes, poppyseed cakes, and on top of it all, of course, a snake. Thus too Theocritus portrays the Bakchai taking all manner of baked goods out of their kistai and depositing them on the altar.[27] The contents of the kiste are thus related to food and to sacrifice; the function of the kiste itself is to store and conceal. It is, as it were, a primeval receptacle, older even than the invention of pottery.[28]

The contents of the Eleusinian kiste were probably also many-shaped and ambiguous. The only specific indication may, perhaps, be contained in the word ἐργασάμενος, "I worked." Spinning or weaving comes to mind, since both often appear as preparatory contrasts prior to a departure from the everyday to the mythic world. Kore worked at a loom before the snake attacked her.[29] Aristotle's student Theophrastus suggests another interpretation, more plausible with respect to Demeter as a goddess of grain. In his cultural-historical work *On Piety*, Theophrastus writes that when men discovered agriculture and the grinding of grain, "they hid the tools with which they worked [sc. the grain] as a secret and encountered them as something sacred."[30] In talking of things hidden yet encountered, sacred things

---

[26] *Pr.* 2.22.4: σησαμαῖ . . . καὶ πυραμίδες καὶ τολύπαι καὶ πόπανα πολυόμφαλα χόνδροι τε ἁλῶν καὶ δράκων, ὄργιον Διονύσου Βασσάρου.

[27] Theocr. 26.7. In Dionysios' *Bassarika*, the remains of the omophagy are hidden in κίσται before daybreak, 9 v. 39 (D. L. Page, *Literary Papyri* [1950], 540; E. Heitsch, *Die griech. Dichterfragmente der röm. Kaiserzeit* [1963²], 66).

[28] Burkert (1967) 292–93.

[29] Epigenes in Clem. *Strom.* 5.49.3 = *OF* 33; Diod. 5.3.4; Porph. *Antr.* 14; Nonnus 6.123–64. For kalathos, ἱστός, ἔργα Περσεφόνης in Parian myth see Apollod., *FGrHist* 244 F 89; for ἔριον ἄπλυτον in the kernos see Polemon in Ath. 478d.

[30] Theophr. in Porph. *Abst.* 2.6 (W. Pötscher, *Theophrastos* ΠΕΡΙ ΕΥΣΕΒΕΙΑΣ [1964], p. 148): τὰ μὲν τῆς ἐργασίας ὄργανα θείαν τοῖς βίοις ἐπικουρίαν παρασχόντα κρύψαντες εἰς ἀπόρρητον ὡς ἱεροῖς αὐτοῖς ἀπήντων. Cf. Theophrastus Περὶ εὑρημάτων Schol. A *Il.* 1.449, Schol. *Od.* 3.441, Eust. 132.25, Suda o 907. The significance of Theophrastus' testimony was recognized by Delatte (1955) 5–8, but cf. already F. Speiser *Zeitschr. f. Ethnol.* 60 (1928), 370. Delatte referred also to Diod. 5.5.2 (Demeter invented the κατεργασία of the grain) and above all to Pliny *NH* 7.191 (the invention of *molere et conficere* in Attica). Cf. the activities of the Vestal Virgins, Serv. *Ecl.* 8.82. Grinding stones and mortars have been found in Neolithic tombs: see J. Makkay, *Act. Arch. Hung.* 30 (1978), 13–36. For a female shaman in Japan who, at her initiation, must beat rice cakes until she faints, see M. Eder, *Paideuma* 6 (1958), 373–74. For mortars in the cannibalistic τέλειον πάσχα of the Gnostics see Epiphanios *Pan.* 26.5.5. At the festival of Tammuz, the Ssabians mourn the god, who was ground up in a mill: see D. Chwolson, *Die Ssabier und der Ssabismus* II (1856), 27; Gese (1970) 73 f.

connected with grain, Theophrastus can only mean the mysteries of Demeter and, because he is writing in Athens, the allusion must be to Eleusis. "The tools with which they worked" are, in their simplest form, the mortar and pestle. The grain, once ground and cooked in water with a seasoning, produces the kykeon which the initiate drinks, just as Demeter did in the house of Keleos after sitting veiled and in silence.[31] Accordingly we may presume that some ears of wheat and a mortar and pestle were among the objects to be found in the covered and uncovered baskets. The initiate had to grind the wheat, at least symbolically, in order to help in producing the next kykeon. This may seem rather banal by the light of day, but this too is an act of destruction—necessary nonetheless for nourishment. The sexual associations of stamping and grinding are obvious. Here again the basic human themes of aggression, the need for food and sexuality are addressed. In proper frame of mind one can experience what would otherwise be simple as something fundamental. The rite performed by the priest as the highest mystery of Christianity is very similar to that which can be traced back far into Anatolian-Hittite culture—that is, the breaking of the bread.[32]

A curious parallel to the Eleusinian myesis comes from a Roman initiation custom, that of the most solemn form of marriage contract, the *confarreatio*. This rite was performed "through a kind of sacrifice offered to Jupiter Farreus, for which spelt-bread was used."[33] A sheep was slaughtered as the sacrificial animal, and it was customary "to set up two seats connected by the skin of the sheep that had been the sacrificial animal, and there the marriage couple, the *flamen* and *flaminica*, were permitted to sit during the *confarreatio* with their heads veiled."[34] Here, too, we encounter the sitting on the sheepskin and veiling of the head, and it is followed by a communal rite with a bread made from the most ancient Neolithic grain; the bread is broken, then eaten communally; thus, collective sacrifice brings about social cohesion. The correspondence with Eleusis is yet greater if we consider Varro's comments on pig-sacrifice: "As a prelude to the marriage, the

[31] *Hy. Dem.* 206–11; for the Orphic version see Clem. *Pr.* 2.20–21 = *OF* 52. With the scoffer's transformation into a lizard (Askalabos), see Nikander in Ant. Lib. 24 and *Ther.* 484–87 with Schol. 484; Ov. *Met.* 5.446–61; Delatte (1955) 30–35.

[32] See I.5.n.42 above.

[33] Gaius 1.112; *κοινωνία τοῦ φαρρός* Dion. Hal. *Ant.* 2.25.2–3, *κοινωνοὺς τῆς ἱερωτάτης τε καὶ πρώτης τροφῆς γενέσθαι*. This presumes—counter to the skepticism of Wissowa (1912) 387.3—a communal meal. On the Attic sesame cake at weddings see I.5.n.42 above.

[34] Serv. auct. *Aen.* 4.374, and cf. Festus 114 M., Plut. *Q. Rom.* 271 f.

ancient kings and nobles in Etruria, both bride and groom, used to sacrifice a pig to seal the bond; the ancient Latins and the Greeks who lived in Italy appear to have celebrated it in the same way."[35] The marriage contract and the mystery initiation thus have the following sequence in common: a preliminary pig-sacrifice, sitting on a sheepskin, and the collective meal of grain. Varro does not neglect to refer to the *initia Cereris*. In Greece, too, the polarity between Demeter and Hera, between transforming and maintaining the societal status quo, is firmly attested.[36] In the Neolithic, establishment of the community through sacrifice assumed various basic forms. The marriage bond and the mystery community are two related products of the ritual that elevates the individual into a new, social existence.

4. *The Sacrifice in the Telesterion*

The goal of initiation is the path to Eleusis and to seeing what occurred in the great chamber of initiation on the sacred night. It is hard to say how the individual myesis and preparations, including mythological and philosophical-allegorical instruction,[1] were related to this mass ceremony. The pig-sacrifice and the thronosis belong to the individual's purification and accordingly preceded the procession of the mystai. If, on the other hand, the synthema, once consummated, is supposed to guarantee an initiation, then the gestures involving the basket and kiste must come at the end of the celebration. There is no evidence to suggest when the kykeon was drunk[2]—an in-

[35] Varro *R.r.* 2.4.9.

[36] Serv. auct. *Aen.* 4.58 *cum Eleusine Cereris sacrum fit, aedes Iunonis clauditur; item cum Iunoni Eleusine fit, templum Cereris clauditur, nec sacerdoti Iunonis licet gustare unde Cereri sit libatum.*

[1] Τῆς *τελετῆς παράδοσις* Theon p. 14.26 Hiller; *διδακτικόν–τελεστικόν* Arist. Περὶ *φιλοσοφίας* fr. 15 Ross. The uninitiated Aetolians betray themselves in the Telesterion *absurde quaedam percunctantes*, Livy 31.14.8.

[2] Kerényi (1962) 77, (1967) 65 places the drinking of the kykeon immediately after the *γεφυρισμοί* (n. 19 below); on the vessels in which the kykeon was perhaps carried see

dication that it probably belonged to the secret central portion of the festival.

The juxtaposition of mystai and epoptai complicates the reconstruction even more. It should be emphasized that the step that was the decisive one in a man's life was his myesis, which occurred only once. All promises refer to the mystai. The Epopteia repeats, renews, and deepens that which had been laid as a foundation in the myesis. Already the mystai were permitted to see the blissful "sight."[3] The epoptai may simply have seen more or, more importantly, differently. For whereas the mystai must "suffer" and were passively affected by the events, the epoptai were "observers" with a broader, calmer view. No evidence has survived to tell us how this juxtaposition of myesis and epopteia was organized. It is conceivable, on the one hand, that the mystai had to leave the Telesterion before a second act in the ceremony, but being sent out would make one all too aware of one's deficient status; an Eleusinian initiate was no longer a katechoumenos. Only one possibility seems to remain: during a specific central ceremony, the mystai had to be veiled and allow the priests to do to them whatever it was they did. The epoptai, on the other hand, could view the sacred events freely for the first time. The initiate was accompanied into the Telesterion by his sponsor, the mystagogue,[4] who would direct him in conducting himself properly.

Instead of too few, there are almost too many indications of what went on at Eleusis. What is missing is the relationship among the parts and their inner cohesion. The myth is an essential aid to our understanding. Demeter came to Eleusis searching for her daughter; the mystai, following in her footsteps, do the same. The departure from the everyday world in the great procession to Eleusis corresponds to the search for Kore. This is followed by the act of finding: Demeter found her daughter again at Eleusis;[5] "Proserpina is sought with burning torches in the night; when she is found, the entire cere-

---

Kerényi (1967) 181–86 and *Initiation, Numen* Suppl. 10 (1965) 62–63. *Tempus habent mystae sidera visa cibi*, Ov. *Fast*. 4.536—which cannot follow the *γεφυρισμοί*; *῞Εσπερος, ὅς τε πιεῖν Δαμάτερα μῶνος ἔπεισεν* Callim. *Hy*. 6.8—Ovid's aition mentions not the kykeon, however, but the poppy (531–54).

[3]The "sight" (*Hy. Dem*. 480; Pind. fr. 137; Soph. fr. 837 Pearson) is identified with the Epopteia by, e.g., Deubner (1932) 83; but *ὁρᾶν* does not equal *ἐφορᾶν*. Cf. *δεῖ γὰρ μυηθῆναί με πρὶν τεθνηκέναι* Aristoph. *Pax* 375; *ὅσοι μεμνήμεθα* Aristoph. *Ran*. 456.

[4]*LSS* 15, esp. 40–41.

[5]*Δήμητερ . . . αὐτόθι τὴν κόρην εὗρες* Aristid. *Or*. 22.11 Keil (I 422 Dind.), and cf. 22.4 (I 417 Dind.); Himer. *Or*. 6.5 Colonna; Tzetz. ad Hes. *Erga* 32; *Hymn. Orph*. 18.14: Pluton brought Kore *ὑπ' 'Ατθίδος ἄντρον*.

mony is ended with rejoicing and waving of torches."[6] Anxious wandering is transformed, through the terror of death, into blissful joy.

Moreover, it is certain that this transformation went hand in hand with the transition from night to light. The hierophant completed the initiation in the Telesterion "amid a great fire."[7] It must have been here that the permanent little room, located just off center in the great hall, played its part. The more precise writers called it the *Anaktoron*, a name which in the more imprecise usage was applied to the whole Telesterion.[8] There was an entrance at the side, next to which stood the throne of the hierophant. He alone was allowed to go inside it.[9] And the mystai then saw him "emerge from the Anaktoron,

---

[6]Lact. *Inst. epit.* 18(23).7 *facibus accensis per noctem Proserpina inquiritur, et ea inventa ritus omnis gratulatione ac taedarum iactatione finitur*; stated more briefly in Lact. *Div. Inst.* 1.21.24. Cf. Varro in Aug. *Civ.* 7.20; Fulgent. *Myth.* 1.11.

[7]*Νυκτὸς ἐν Ἐλευσῖνι ὑπὸ πολλῷ πυρὶ τὰ μεγάλα καὶ ἄρρητα μυστήρια* Hippol. *Ref.* 5.8.40; *σκότους τε καὶ φωτὸς ἐναλλὰξ αὐτῷ φαινομένων* Dio Chrys. *Or.* 12.33; *σὺ δ' ὦ πυρὸς δέσποινα Δήμητρος κόρη* Eur. *Phaëthon* (fr. 781 *TGF* = Suppl. Euripideum [1913] p. 77) 59, and cf. *πυρφόρους θεάς* Eur. *Phoen.* 687 with Schol. 683; *πῦρ τὸ μυστικόν* Himer. *Or.* 60.4, 8.8 *οὐ πατρὸς μυσταγωγοῦντος . . . οὐ τὸ δᾳδούχων πῦρ βλέπει*, 29.1 *ὁ τοῦ πυρὸς τοῦ κατ' Ἐλευσῖνα πόθος. Ὁ δ' ἐντὸς γενόμενος καὶ μέγα φῶς ἰδών, οἷον ἀνακτόρων ἀνοιγομένων* Plut. *De prof. virt.* 10.81d–e. Clem. *Pr.* 2.22.1 *ἄξια μὲν οὖν νυκτὸς τὰ τελέσματα καὶ πυρός*. Schol. Soph. *OC* 1048 *ὑπὸ τῆς μυστικῆς φλογὸς καὶ τῶν ἱερῶν δᾴδων*.

[8]On the remains of the building see Mylonas (1961) 69, 83–88, 111, 120–21 following J. N. Travlos, *Ephem.* 1950/51, 1–16; cf. Kerényi (1967) 86–87; O. Rubensohn, "Das Weihehaus von Eleusis und sein Allerheiligstes," *JdI* (1955), 1–49; L. Deubner, *Zum Weihehaus der eleusinischen Mysterien* (Abh. Berlin, 1945/46, 2), argued the thesis that *ἀνάκτορον* designates the whole *τελεστήριον* (for this word see Plut. *Pericl.* 13; *μυστικὸς σηκός* Strabo 9 p. 395; *οἶκος* Aristid. *Or.* 22.9 Keil), and cf. already Deubner (1932) 88–90 citing Noack, whose findings have been superseded by Travlos and Mylonas. *Ἀνάκτορον* denotes the chamber of initiation when the reference is to initiation "inside the Anaktoron"—Jul. *Or.* 7.239a; Sopatros pp. 114.24, 121.24, 123.24; Themist. *Or.* 5.71a—but Deubner's interpretation falls with Plut. *De prof. virt.* 81e *ἐντὸς γενόμενος καὶ μέγα φῶς ἰδών, οἷον ἀνακτόρων ἀνοιγομένων*. We must, then, connect the epigram to the hierophant (*ὦ μύσται, τότε μ' εἴδετ' ἀνακτόρου ἐκπροφανέντα νυξὶν ἐν ἀργενναῖς*, *IG* II/III² 3811) and hierophantis (*ἣ τελετὰς ἀνέφαινε θεοῖν παρ' ἀνάκτορα Δηοῦς*, *IG* II/III² 3764) with the high point of the celebration, the fire shining from the holy of holies; the throne of the hetaera of Demetrius stood *παρὰ τὸ ἀνάκτορον* (Hegesandros in Ath. 167f.) near the throne of the hierophant as reconstructed by Travlos. The ambiguity comes from the expression "to reach the Anaktoron" as the goal of initiation: see Max. Tyr. 39.3k, Sopatros p. 118.20.

[9]Ael. fr. 10 = Suda ε 3604, ι 195, μ 381; *μέγαρον = ἀνάκτορον* Hsch. *ἀνάκτορον*; cf. Suda α 1924. For a different view see Kerényi (1967) 109–110. Poll. 1.9 *χωρίον ἄβατον = ἀνάκτορον* (but cf. 1.17 *ἀνάκτορον–χρηστήριον*); see *IG* II/III² 3811, n. 8 above.

in the shining nights of the mysteries."[10] A "great light" would become visible "when the Anaktoron was opened."[11] This was, then, the location of the great fire; the smoke escaped through a hole in the roof above it.[12] In other places people referred to Demeter's *Megaron*—an ancient word for "palace"—and this was likewise primarily the site of a great fire. Such a Megaron was found in the open air at Lykosura.[13] Burn marks are the most ancient evidence for the cult at Eleusis,[14] and there too the celebration occurred at first in the open air, though, as at Lykosura, it was certainly screened off from the outside world by walls. At Lykosura, moreover, we have evidence of something that was natural to all Greek cults, but unattested (and hence unconsidered)[15] for Eleusis alone: i.e., that the great fire at a festival for the gods does not burn for its own sake but for its purificatory and its destructive powers. Offerings for the gods, sacrificial remains, corpses are purified and dispensed with by fire. Thus, the fire in the Eleusinian Telesterion must likewise have formed the center of a sacrificial ritual. And if our sources do not mention it, this must be because it was an *ἄρρητος θυσία*. With this hypothesis, the Eleusinian ritual falls into place in the larger context of Greek cult and gives us a further clue by which to grasp the rhythm of the nighttime events.

The great procession marching the more than thirty kilometers between Athens and Eleusis on the thirteenth of Boedromion[16] follows the path of the enraged Demeter. Here, too, the enthusiasm for

---

[10] *IG* II/III[2] 3811, n. 8 above.

[11] Plut. 81e, n. 8 above; n. 82 below.

[12] Τὸ *ὀπαῖον ἐπὶ τοῦ ἀνακτόρου* Plut. *Pericl.* 13.7; Mylonas (1961) 119–20. There is no certainty regarding an *ὀπαῖον* in the older Telesterion (Mylonas [1961] 70.38, 112); yet from the oldest times, *ὀπαῖα* served as openings for smoke—see G. S. Korres, *Atti e memorie del I Congresso Int. di Micenologia* I (1968), 81–86, on *Od.* 1.320. There is no mention of daylight breaking in; it is a nocturnal light.

[13] K. Kourouniotes, *Ephem.* 1912, 142–61; Paus. 8.37.3; Ammonios 113 *τὸ δὲ μέγαρον περιῳκοδομημένη ἑστία, ἔνθα τὰ μυστικὰ τῆς Δήμητρος.*

[14] Mylonas (1961) 57–58; Kerényi (1967) 93.

[15] Kerényi did associate the Eleusinian fire with the burning of the dead on a pyre, and referred to the self-immolation of the Brahman Zarmanochegas at Eleusis (Strabo 15 p. 720; Dio Cass. 54.9.10), and cf. (1962) 102–103, (1967) 101; and Ch. Picard, *RHR* 107 (1933), 137–54, saw a connection between the cremation at Eleusis portrayed in Euripides' *Hiketides* and the mysteries; *Δήμητερ ἑστιοῦχ' Ἐλευσῖνος χθονός* Eur. *Hik.* 1.

[16] *Ἄιδουσιν γοῦν τὸν Ἴακχον* Aristoph. *Ran.* 320 with Schol. 395, 399, 408; Polemon of Ilion *Περὶ τῆς ἱερᾶς ὁδοῦ*, and cf. Harpokr. *ἱερὰ ὁδός*. For the program of the preceding days (*IG* II/III[2] 1078 is the main source) see Kerényi (1962) 73–75, (1967) 60–66; for the sacred *εἰκάδες* see already Eur. *Ion* 1076.

the collective undertaking is based on aggression. The emblem of the mystai, depicted time and again on the monuments, is a bundle of branches perhaps called βάκχος.[17] Such carrying and waving of branches is found with great frequency at festivals of the gods and basically reflects the most primitive, virtually pre-human kind of weaponry: a branch broken off from a tree greatly enhances the strength of one's bare hands, and even more so the impression made by a threatening gesture. It gives one superior standing.[18] This aggressive posture is turned against the novices who, frightened, are led about by the nose by those long initiated. The place for vulgar mockery was the bridge across the Kephisos at Athens. There is mention of a prostitute who stood on the bridge, a custom evidently parodied by Aristophanes when he has the drunken Philokleon station a scantily clad hetaera with two torches, to joke with as "before the mysteries."[19] This has often been linked to that part of the myth in which Baubo, by exposing herself obscenely, made the grieving Demeter laugh.[20] But perhaps we must reckon with a variety of references in the myth here too. The joking on that first bridge (γεφυρισμός) does not serve to liberate; it is, rather, a contrast to what is to follow; one must tear oneself loose from this in order to cross the mountain and reach the plain of Eleusis.

---

[17] Hsch. *βάκχος . . . καὶ κλάδος ἐν ταῖς τελεταῖς*; Schol. Aristoph. *Eq.* 408 *βάκχους ἐκάλουν . . . καὶ τοὺς κλάδος οὓς οἱ μύσται φέρουσιν* (citing Xenophanes, *VS* 21 B 17, who, however, does not refer to Eleusis); Serv. *Aen.* 6.136. Cf. Pringsheim (1905) 16–19; H. Seyrig, *BCH* 51 (1927), 203–205; J. D. Beazley, *Num. Chron.* VI 1 (1941), 1–7; K. Kourouniotes, *Ephem.* 1937, 242–43. For corresponding objects in other cults cf. a woman with a bundle of branches raised in the air before Priapos, "Cameo Morgan," *EAA* VI 389; the berešma of the Magi, reproduced, e.g., in Cumont (1930) pl. V 5, Strabo 15 p. 733.

[18] See I.3.n.3 above; Burkert (1979) 43.

[19] Aristoph. *Vesp.* 1363 and Schol. 1361: *τοὺς γὰρ μέλλοντας μυεῖσθαι προλαβόντες δεδίττονται*, and cf. J. S. Rusten, *HSCP* 81 (1977), 157–61; Strabo 9 p. 400 on the Kephisos: *ἐφ' οὗ καὶ ἡ γέφυρα καὶ οἱ γεφυρισμοί*; Hsch. *γεφυρίς· πόρνη τις . . . ἄλλοι δὲ οὐ γυναῖκα, ἀλλὰ ἄνδρα ἐκεῖ καθεζόμενον . . .συγκαλυπτόμενον . . . σκώμματα λέγειν*; for *γεφυρίζειν* in the transferred sense "to mock" see Plut. *Sulla* 2.2, 6.18, 13.1. There was also a bridge over the Ῥειτοί (*IG* I² 81.5, and cf. Paus. 1.38.1) and the Eleusinian Kephisos (*IG* II/III² 1191 = *SIG*³ 1048; *AP* 9.147). It is uncertain what the verses cited by Plutarch (fr. 60 Sandbach; *Carmina popularia* 877 Page) refer to: *πάριθι Κόρη γέφυραν· ὅσον οὔπω +τριπολεονδε* (*τρίπολον δή* or *τριπολεῖν δεῖ* Wilamowitz [1932] 51.3; referring to the way home, according to Kerényi [1967] 127).

[20] Wilamowitz (1932) 53; Kerényi, *Symb. Osl.* 36 (1960), 11–16; Wehrli, however (*ARW* 31 [1934], 80–82), links the scene to "der eigentlichen Mysterienfeier."

The rhythmic cry of Ἴακχ᾽ ὦ Ἴακχε[21] united the crowd of young and old, slave and free, Athenian and foreigner. Priestesses accompanied the procession carrying "the sacred" objects in the covered *κίσται* on their heads.[22] "Iakche" is merely a cry with which the departing crowd would whip itself into ever greater excitement. In Classical times Iakchos was considered a divine or demonic personage, frequently identified with Dionysus.[23] In later times, an Iakchos-statue was evidently brought along as well.[24] By the time the procession reached Eleusis, the sun would be going down. Torches would flare up. The people entered the sanctuary "together with Iakchos."[25] We do not know the details of what happened at the spring, at the gate, at the grotto of Pluto. "The wanderings" mentioned[26] suggest a

---

[21] Aristoph. *Ran.* 316–17; Hdt. 8.65.1 *τὴν φωνὴν εἶναι τὸν μυστικὸν ἴακχον*; cf. metaphorically, Himer. *Or.* 69.7 *ὅστις μὲν ἀκούει καὶ πείθεται, πολὺν ἠχήσει τὸν Ἴακχον.* See I.4.n.2 above.

[22] *IG* I² 81.9–11 hoς *ἂν* hι*ερὰ φέροσι* hαι hι*έρεαι ἀ[σ]φαλέστατα.* For the statues of the Kistophoroi from the inner Propylaea see, for instance, Kerényi (1962) pl. 20/1.

[23] *Τῆς Δήμητρος δαίμονα* Strabo 10 p. 468; as son of Persephone, see Schol. Aristoph. *Ran.* 324; of Demeter or of Dionysus, see Schol. Aristid. p. 648.15; 21–23 Dindorf; for Iakchos = Dionysus, see Soph. *Ant.* 1119, 1151; fr. 959 Pearson; Eur. *Ion* 1075–86; *Bacch.* 725; Philodamos 27–36 p. 166 Powell; Schol. Aristoph. *Ran.* 343, 395, 399, 404; therefore, probably, Dionysus' increased prominence at Eleusis in the fourth century (on which see Metzger [1951] 248–57; [1965] 21, 53; G. Mylonas, *Ephem.* 1960, 68–118; G. Daux, *BCH* 88 [1964], 433; *Διονύσιον IG* II/III² 1672.67; dedication 4604).

[24] There is an Ἰακχαγωγός, *IG* II/III² 1092 B 31, theater seat *IG* II/III² 5044, Poll. 1.35; *τοῦ Ἰάκχου ὑποδοχή IG* II/III² 847.21, and cf. 1672.8. Paus. 1.2.4 mentions a statue of Iakchos by Praxiteles. Scholars have identified the figure of the youth with the two torches and hunting boots—typical of Eleusinian pictures—as Iakchos (Pringsheim [1905] 67–68, 78–89; Metzger [1951] 157–58; idem [1965] 52; Mylonas [1961] 211; etc.). But the inscription on the fragmentary stamnos by the Meidias Painter, Boston 03.842 = *ARV*² 1315.2, was read [ΕΥΜΟΛ]ΠΟΣ, i.e., the mythical hierophant; contra, H. Metzger, *REG* 91 (1978), 512. Yet confirmation came from a votive relief with a hierophant in the same costume: *AJA* 64 (1960), 268, pl. 73; Graf (1974) 60–66; Clinton (1974) 32–35. In cases where two such figures are portrayed, as on the bell-crater, *BM* F 68 = *ARV*² 1466.1 (Kerényi [1962] T.2, "Pourtalès-Vase"), they may represent Eumolpos and Eubuleus (combined with Eumolpos in the Orphic version: Clem. *Pr.* 2.20.2), or rather hierophant and daduchos. Cf. *FR* II 56; E. Simon, *AK* 9 (1966), 89–90.

[25] Ἐν Ἐλευσῖνι τῷ Ἰάκχῳ *συνεισελαύνειν LSS* 15.42.

[26] Plut. fr. 178 Sandbach: *πλάναι τὰ πρῶτα καὶ περιδρομαὶ κοπώδεις καὶ διὰ σκότους τινὲς ὕποπτοι πορεῖαι καὶ ἀτέλεστοι*; cf. Plat. *Phaedo* 108a: the path to Hades *ἔοικε σχίσεις τε καὶ τριόδους πολλὰς ἔχειν· ἀπὸ τῶν θυσιῶν τε καὶ νομίμων τῶν ἐνθάδε τεκμαιρόμενος λέγω.* On the labyrinthine path into the next world see F. Layard, "Totenfahrt auf Malekula," *Eranos Jb.* 4 (1937), 242–91; D. C. Fox, "Labyrinth und Totenreich," *Paideuma* 1 (1940), 381–94; K. Kerényi, *Labyrinthstudien* (1950²).

lengthy route leading this way and that. Finally the celebrants would reach the end of their journey: the "house that received the mystai"—i.e., the Telesterion—opened its doors.[27] In the pressing crowds, the torches must have been extinguished. Darkness enveloped the multitude of many thousands and only a few small flames provided a bit of light, in front of which the priests—hierophant, dadouchos, priestess of Demeter—now played their parts. The journey into the underworld suggested in some literary sources[28] was not realized in any concrete sense at Eleusis. Yet the darkness of the sealed room may well have evoked a sense of nearness to Hades.

It was what occurred in that room, however, that was truly frightening. Demeter's wrath demanded a victim. The myth tells how Demeter took the son of the Eleusinian king—in the hymn his name is Demophon, in later tradition, Triptolemus[29]—and held him in the fire. According to the myth, she wanted to purify him for immortality, and religious studies have gathered much corroborative evidence for such beliefs in fire-magic.[30] However, the boy's mother has an unerring sense of reality: this way lies certain death. The goddess rebukes her "lack of understanding" because she shrinks from this path.

The notion that the myth corresponds to something in the mystery celebration finds support in the fact that a child, usually a young boy, had a special role at Eleusis: among all the adult mystai, there was always one child chosen for initiation. He was subsequently called the boy "who was initiated from the hearth."[31] Being thus

---

[27] Μυστοδόκος δόμος . . . ἀναδείκνυται Aristoph. *Nub.* 302.

[28] Luk. *Katapl.* 22, and cf. Foucart (1914) 401. But Lukian is only referring to the complete darkness out of which the terrifying daduchos—here Teisiphone—appears.

[29] *Hy. Dem.* 226–91, Ov. *Fast.* 4.529–60 following Callimachus; Hyg. *Astr.* 2.14; cf. Soph. fr. 604 Pearson; Hyg. *Fab.* 147. In his *Triptolemos* (468 B.C.), Sophocles may have portrayed Demeter as his nurse; at approximately this time, Triptolemos' iconography changes from a bearded type to one more like an ephebe. For a compilation of 122 Triptolemos-vases see *Recueil Charles Dugas* (1960), 132–39. According to Pringsheim (1905) 21, the Eleusinian relief with the so-called "baptism" (e.g., Deubner [1932] pl. 6.3; Nilsson [1955] pl. 45.2; Kerényi [1962] pl. 13), which is broken off on the left, portrays Triptolemos as an initiate between the "two goddesses"; according to E. Simon, *AM* 69/70 (1954/55), 45–48, however, it depicts a boy as a sacrificial servant at the head of a procession of worshippers to the goddess.

[30] J. G. Frazer, *Apollodorus* II (1921), 311–17, and cf. M. Delcourt, *Pyrrhos et Pyrrha: Recherches sur les valeurs du feu dans les légendes helléniques* (1965).

[31] *IG* I² 6 = *LSS* 3.108; Isaios fr. 84 Baiter-Sauppe = Harpokr. ἀφ' ἑστίας; *An. Bekk.* 204.19. There are many inscriptions from statue-bases and some surviving statues: see now Clinton (1974) 98–114; Mylonas (1961) fig. 80. New evidence on the form of selection in *Hesperia* 49 (1980), 264.

chosen was a great distinction, and proud parents often set up statues of their children in the sanctuary if they were honored in this way. The "hearth" "from which" the child was initiated was probably the state hearth of the Prytanes at the marketplace.[32] This shows that the child represents the community, and makes it very probable that he was meant to correspond to the mythical Demophon, whose very name reflects the "people." The child must pay close attention to what he is told, for he must "appease the gods in place of all those who are being initiated."[33] A relief (which, unfortunately, is severely damaged) depicts two figures next to Demeter on her throne, holding torches very close to a child cowering between them.[34] Thus, a torch ritual reminiscent of the depiction of Herakles' initiation is here superimposed on the mythical image of Demophon-Triptolemos in the fire. Such is the reality of the child's "initiation in the fire," which was, then, not without danger. What Callimachus and Ovid said that Demeter did to the child Triptolemos was perhaps actually part of the rite: she put him to sleep with poppy juice.[35] The tranquilizing opiate could thus be used to still the children's fear. At Eleusis, too, the poppy is an emblem of Demeter.[36]

---

[32] Foucart (1914) 279.

[33] Porph. *Abst.* 4.5 *ἀντὶ πάντων τῶν μυουμένων ἀπομειλίσσεται τὸ θεῖον, ἀκριβῶς δρῶν τὰ προστεταγμένα.* Cf. *IG* II/III² 4077; children *οἳ τὸ πρὸ μυστῶν ἄλλων ἐν τελεταῖς στέμμα κόμαισι θέσαν.*

[34] Sammlung Este, Vienna 1095; O. Walter, *Osterr. Jahresh.* 30 (1936/37), 50–70; Nilsson, *Opuscula* II (1952), 624–27; (1955) pl. 44.2, "Feuerreinigung des Demophon"; Metzger (1965) 38. "Fire magic" can be done with heated wine and a torch: see Hippol. *Ref.* 4.31, O. E. v. Lippmann, *Beiträge zur Geschichte der Naturwissenschaften und der Technik* (1923), 60–66; this could explain the fire in Eur. *Bacch.* 757–78; the Eleusinian wine tabu (*Hy. Dem.* 206–208) may correspond to a secret use of the wine.

[35] Ov. *Fast.* 4.547–48. There is a peculiar lekythos from Kerch (Louvre *CA* 2190; Metzger [1965] pl. 15; Kerényi [1962] pl. 42, [1967] pl. 54) on which an exhausted initiate is leaning against a rock while Triptolemos is flying above him. Iconographically, the initiate corresponds to the Attis on the marble tray in the Cabinet des Médailles: see P. Friedlaender, *Studien zur antiken Literatur und Kunst* (1969), 527 pl. 16.

[36] For the bundle of branches and the poppy on a frieze from the Eleusinion, see Kerényi (1962) pl. 1a; for a poppy stalk and blade of wheat on coins from Athens/Eleusis see Svoronos (1924) pl. 104.38–45; for poppies (?) on the sacrificial tray of the priest on the Lovatelli urn, see Kerényi (1962) pl. 8. The poppy was interpreted as *τῆς πολυγονίας σύμβολον*: Porph. *De cultu simulacr.* fr. 6 Bidez = Euseb. *Praep. Ev.* 3.11.7; Cornut. 28, however, knew of the special effect of the *soporiferum papaver* (Verg. *Aen.* 4.486; Ov. *Fast.* 4.531, and cf. 4.661). Nyx or Hypnos is depicted holding poppies over Endymion on sarcophagi: see C. Robert, *Die antiken Sarkophagenreliefs* III 1 (1897), # 50, 58, 65, 83 = New York 47.100.4, and cf. *Bull. Metr. Mus. Art* 15 (1956), 124. For a Minoan goddess with poppies see S. Marinatos, *Ephem.* 1937, 287; *Kreta und das mykenische*

Thus, though sublimated in the myth and symbolized in ritual, the theme of infanticide[37] is present in the mysteries. This is the theme that forms the core of so many other sacrificial festivals—the Lykaia, Pelops at Olympia, the Agrionia rituals, and Procne: the mother or the nurse kills the young boy in order to hurt a man, or does so simply in madness. This tale is repreated time and again as the explanation and counterpart of the unspeakable sacrifices. At Eleusis, too, a second sacrifice appeases the wrath provoked by the preliminary maiden-sacrifice.

This was of course accomplished through an animal-sacrifice, leaving human beings untouched yet maintaining the seriousness of the ritual. It is here that the realm of the *ἄρρητον*, the unspeakable, begins, but we can make an educated guess as to what occurred. The ramskin upon which Demeter and the mystai would sit could only have come from a sacrifice.[38] The candidate for initiation was thus confronted first of all with a fait accompli. What had happened would become clear during the Epopteia at the latest: a ram would be killed, skinned[39]—the job of the Kerykes, who followed the example of Hermes—and finally burned in the "great fire" in the Telesterion. In another context, but also at Eleusis, the ram is attested as a sacrificial victim for Kore.[40] We know from sources as early as the *Odyssey* that the sacrifice of a ram was used to establish communication with the

---

Hellas (1959), fig. 130–31. For the Neolithic evidence see G. R. Levy, *The Gates of Horn* (1948), 105–106 (a human sacrificial victim lulled to sleep?).

[37] See I.8.n.4 above. In Egypt, the corresponding myth is that of the burning child Horus—the fire is extinguished by the Nile: see L. Koenen, *Chronique d'Egypte* 37 (1962), 167–74. On the identification of Isis and Demeter see Plut. *Is.* 357b–c.

[38] So also Kerényi (1962) 69–70, (1967) 60, and cf. V.3.n.16 above.

[39] On the daduchoi and the *Διὸς κῴδιον* see Paus. Att. δ 18 Erbse (cf. III.1.n.38 above). Perhaps Xenokrates fr. 99 Heinze = Plut. *De es. carn.* 996a (*Ἀθηναῖοι τῷ ζῶντα τὸν κριὸν ἐκδείραντι δίκην ἐπέθηκαν*) refers to a rite (elaborated as an anecdote by Helladios: Phot. *Bibl.* 534b38); see also II.5.n.45 above on Marsyas. For a bloody sacrifice with castration in initiation see J. von Ins, "Ekstase, Kult und Zeremonialisierung," Diss. Zürich, 1979, 237f., following J. Jahn, *Muntu, Umrisse der neoafrikanischen Kultur* (1958), 74–81, on the Nánigos in Latin America.

[40] See the account of the epistates, *IG* II/III^2 1673.72 *τοῖς δημοσίοις . . . προθύματα δοθέντα εἰς μύησιν οἶς . . . Δήμητρι οἶς . . .* Κόρηι *κριός*. There was also a sacrifice at the Eleusinia: see the calendar of Nikomachos, *LSS* 10.63 Φερρεφάττῃ *κριός*, and cf. *Inschriften von Erythrai und Klazomenai* (1973), 207.47.78. According to the Eleusinian-Orphic myth, Clem. *Pr.* 2.20.2, Eubuleus was a swineherd, Eumolpos—ancestor of the hierophants—a shepherd, Triptolemos a neatherd: su/ove/taurilia. There is a statue of Demeter with a pig, a kiste, an altar covered with a fleece and tympanon, and an ox (or cow): M. C. Vermaseren, *Corpus Cultus Cybelae Attidisque* VII (1977), nr. 65.

world of the dead. The decorations at the corners of the Telesterion were rams' heads.[41] It would not occur to the uninitiated why rams' heads were gazing down on them rather than lions'; the initiate, however, understood.

In connection with the Anatolian mysteries of Demeter, Clement relates a myth reflecting certain ritual details:[42] Demeter was enraged at Zeus for having raped her—the same reason that Arcadian Demeter had been angry at Poseidon[43]—thus supplication ceremonies were called for in which branches hung with wool were carried (a familiar sight to the Greeks). Then "bile would be drunk," "a heart torn out," followed by "unspeakable touching." Evidently a priest would make gestures of supplication and drink a bitter drink; thereafter the sacrificial animal was killed and its heart was torn out. Then came the unspeakable act, which Clement lays bare: "Zeus tore off a ram's testicles. He brought them to Demeter and threw them into the folds of her dress, thus doing false penance for his rape, as if he had castrated himself."[44] It is clear that the very thing done to the sacrificial animal in ritual is here raised to the sphere of the gods in the myth. In the process, guilt and expiation are played out on two levels at once: the aggressive act is motivated as punishment for a sexual crime but, because the genitals fall into the goddess's lap, it turns into a sacred marriage.

Nothing compels us to make similar assumptions for Eleusis, but the mysteries of Meter and Demeter are related, and there are parallels in detail that go beyond the sacrifice of the ram. On the day of the mysteries at Eleusis, for instance, the supplicant's branch is the symbol that seals his death.[45] And it was not only the "Naassenian" who

---

[41] Mylonas (1961) fig. 21, p. 80.

[42] *Pr.* 2.15.1–2. Clement (15.1–17.1) tells the myth of Demeter and Kore in a continuous narrative, inserting intermittent references to the cults: *ταῦτα* (*ταὐτὰ* Mondésert) *οἱ Φρύγες τελίσκουσιν Ἄττιδι καὶ Κυβέλῃ καὶ Κορύβασιν* 15.1; *τὰ σύμβολα τῆς μυήσεως ταύτης* 15.3; *Σαβαζίων γοῦν μυστηρίων σύμβολον* 16.2; *ταύτην τὴν μυθολογίαν . . . ἑορτάζουσιν* 17.1. The first explicit reference to Eleusis is in 20–21. Arnob. 5.20–21 follows Clement, but gives additional details, e.g., the metamorphosis of Zeus into a bull. He too mentions *mysteria, quibus Phrygia initiatur atque omnis gens Ilia.*

[43] Paus. 8.25.5–7, Schol. Lyk. 153 (Demeter Erinys, Thelpusa), and cf. Callim. fr. 652; Paus. 8.42.1 (Phigalia).

[44] *Pr.* 2.15.2 (Arnob. 5.20). Pausanias clearly alludes to a parallel version (2.3.4): *τὸν δὲ ἐν τελετῇ Μητρὸς ἐπὶ Ἑρμῇ λεγόμενον καὶ τῷ κριῷ λόγον ἐπιστάμενος οὐ λέγω* (Lobeck [1829] 151); see also Hdt. 2.42. On "tearing the heart out," see I.1.n.22 above.

[45] Andoc. 1.113–16; I.5.n.47 above. The murder of the suppliant, which is demanded by the hierophant at the mysteries, is evidently a sacred form of sacrilege, a type of *ἄρρητος θυσία.*

claimed that the hierophant became a eunuch by drinking hemlock.[46] On the other hand, a much-disputed passage in Bishop Asterios mentions a "sacred marriage": at Eleusis there were "sacred encounters between the hierophant and the priestess, each alone with the other; are not the torches extinguished and does not the crowd believe that its salvation depends on what these two do in the dark?"[47] A much earlier example of sexual innuendo surrounding the Eleusinian priesthood was Andokides' cutting accusation against the dadouchos Kallias that he had seduced his own stepdaughter, thus becoming in truth "the priest of the mother and the daughter."[48] The contradiction between the sexual fantasies and the idea of becoming a eunuch cannot be removed but must, rather, be seen as a polarity. For precisely this reason a sacred marriage is not a normal marriage, but something unheard-of and impossible that occurs in the context of the sacrifice.

We can make out only the bare outlines of what happened after the unspeakable sacrifice: gruesomeness and sexual outbursts finally overcome in the establishment of a divine order. We know nothing of how this was accomplished in practice. The sacred ritual acquires its stability precisely by symbolizing and sublimating that which is all too

---

[46]Hippol. *Ref.* 5.8.40 *εὐνουχισμένος δὲ διὰ κωνείου*; Serv. *Aen.* 6.661 *qui maxima sacra accipiebant . . . herbis . . . quibusdam emasculabantur*; Hieron. *Adv. Iov.* 1.49, Migne *Patrologia Latina* 23.295f. *Hierophantas quoque Atheniensium usque hodie cicutae sorbitione castrari, et postquam in pontificatum fuerint allecti, viros esse desinere*; Jul. *Or.* 5.173c–d; Orig. *Cels.* 7.48 *κωνειασθεὶς τὰ ἄρσενα μέρη*; Schol. Pers. 5.145 *Sacerdotes Cereris Eleusiniae . . . hoc liquoris genere* (sc. *cicuta*) *unguebantur, ut a concubitu se abstinerent*, and cf. Pliny *NH* 25.95. It follows from Paus. 2.14.1 that the Eleusinian hierophant was not allowed to marry, yet there were married hierophants: see Isaios 7.9; Hypereides fr. 230 Baiter-Sauppe; *IG* II/III² 3628; Clinton (1974) 44f. Their marriages were evidently consummated before they took office: see Paus. 7.25.13.

[47]Asterios *Hom.* 10, Migne *Patrologia Graeca* 40.324 (new ed. by C. Datema, Leiden, 1970). It has been argued against his testimony that the "two temples" he mentions were in Alexandria (Kerényi [1962] 109, [1967] 117) and that there was no *καταβάσιον* at Eleusis (Mylonas [1961] 314); but as to the former objection, his comments start applying to Eleusis only in the next sentence, and, as to the latter, the Anaktoron, where none could enter, could with some imagination be depicted as a gate to the underworld.

[48]Andoc. 1.124 *ἱερεὺς ὢν τῆς μητρὸς καὶ τῆς θυγατρός*; L. Koenen in *Studien zur Textgeschichte und Textkritik* (1960), 87. Further evidence for a sacred marriage at Eleusis has been sought in the imitation by Alexander of Abonuteichos (Luk. *Alex.* 38–39), and cf. Harrison (1922) 550, Deubner (1932) 85; disputed by Mylonas (1961) 315. Schol. Plat. *Gorg.* 497c is based on Clement: see V.3.n.7 above. Synes *Calv. laud.* 7 (on the ripened blade of wheat) presupposes Demeter's wedding: *ἐπὶ τούτοις Ἐλευσὶς ἄγει τὰ Δήμητρος ἀνακαλυπτήρια*. Tert. *Ad. nat.* (*cur rapitur sacerdos Cereris, si non tale Ceres passa est*) seems to associate what Asterios describes with the myth of Kore's abduction.

direct. At the Thesmophoria, the women's festival, the dark red juice of the pomegranate evidently represents blood.[49] At Eleusis, a peculiar role is played by the bean as the antithesis to the "precepts" of Demeter. Of course, Pausanias tells us only "that the Athenians were unable to attribute the invention of beans to Demeter; he who has seen an initiation at Eleusis or read the so-called works of Orpheus will know what I mean."[50] Some abstruse details on the symbolism and fantasies related to beans have been preserved in the Pythagorean tradition: beans were associated with human flesh and male semen, the female womb and a child's head; eating beans was considered cannibalism.[51] But beans belonged to the world of the dead as well.

The bean fantasies recall the Orphic tale of Baubo, who exposed her genitals to Demeter in such a way that they looked like the face of a child—Iakchos.[52] We find this illustrated in statuettes from Demeter sanctuaries in Asia Minor, on which a female abdomen appears as a face between two upward-pointing torches.[53] Such, scoffed Gregory of Nazianus, were the gestures used by Demeter to initiate her mystai.[54] It must be said that no Baubo statuettes have been found at Eleusis; on the other hand, there is the strange remark that the small shark (γαλεός) was considered impure for the mystai of the "two goddesses" "because it gave birth with its mouth."[55] The interchangeability of the oral and sexual spheres—also reflected among the Greeks in

[49] The θεσμοφοριάζουσαι eat pomegranate seeds: see Clem. *Pr.* 2.19.3; Deubner (1932) 58. On ῥοιά, blood, see Paus. 9.25.1; Artemidoros 1.73; cf. Cook III (1940) 831–18; Kerényi (1962) 126–34, (1967) 133–44.

[50] Paus. 1.37.4

[51] Hippol. *Ref.* 1.2.14; Antonios Diogenes in Porph. *V. Pyth.* 44, Lydus *Mens.* 4.42; A. Delatte, *Serta Leodiensia* (1930), 41–49; M. Marcovich, *Philologus* 108 (1964), 29–39; M. Detienne, *Archives de Sociologie des Religions* 29 (1970), 153–55.

[52] *OF* 52 = Clem. *Pr.* 2.21.1; H. Diels, "Arcana Cerealia," *Miscellanea A. Salinas* (1907), 3–14. Cf. *OF* 49; Asklepiades, *FGrHist* 12 F 4; Hsch. Βαυβώ = Empedokles, *VS* 31 B 153. Baubo is attested epigraphically on Paros: *IG* XII 5.227 beside Δημήτηρ Θεσμοφόρος, Κόρη, Ζεύς Εὐβουλεύς. For one of the Theban maenads in Magnesia see O. Kern, *Die Inschriften von Magnesia am Maeander* (1900), #215. "Babo," the old woman in Thracian folk-custom (R. M. Dawkins, *JHS* 26 [1906], 196–97) is Slavic (Russ. "babushka," "grandmother"), but the word is evidently baby talk, so we must be careful in assuming influences (cf. Sumerian *Kubaba, Baba*).

[53] Diels, "Arcana Cerealia"; F. Winter, *Die Typen der figürlichen Terrakotten* II (1903), 223; Th. Wiegand and H. Schader, *Priene* (1904), 161–63; Nilsson (1955) pl. 45.3.

[54] In Jul. 1.115, Migne *Patrologia Graeca* 35.653 ἃ καὶ νῦν ἔτι τελεῖ τοῖς σχήμασιν; this is Gregory's addition to his source, Clement.

[55] Ael. *Nat. an.* 9.65 οἱ μυούμενοι τοῖν θεοῖν οὐκ ἂν πάσαιντο γαλεοῦ φασιν· οὐ γὰρ αὐτὸν εἶναι καθαρὸν ὄψον, ἐπεὶ τῷ στόματι τίκτει. This fish is therefore a symbol of regeneration in Egypt: E. Hornung, *Eranos Jb* 46 (1977), 444f.

a specialized sense of "unspeakable touching"—thus seems to have played a part at Eleusis after all. And a variation of the myth points in this direction as well.[56] The prerequisite for Demeter's *θεσμοί*, her "thesis," is an "antithesis" which borders on the perverse. To be sure, in the context of the pure ritual, a symbolic gesture is enough, for example, exhibiting or eating a bean.

The "unspeakable" was acted out in semi-darkness, sometimes in total darkness. But the uncanny atmosphere led to an epiphany. Kore's return from the underworld was a high point in the celebrations. Apollodorus of Athens wrote: "When Kore is called up, the hierophant strikes the bronze gong"[57]—in his view, this was clearly not yet a part of the secret ritual—and the call did not go unheard. Walter F. Otto and Karl Kerényi compared the text of a rhetorical exercise from Hadrianic times in which Herakles argued with the hierophant. Herakles no longer needed the Eleusinian mysteries, for he had been supremely initiated through his journey to the underworld. "Lock up Eleusis and the sacred fire, dadouchos. I have experienced far truer mysteries. . . . I have seen Kore."[58] Walter F. Otto took this for a confirmation of his fundamental conviction that the Greeks were able to experience their gods directly as personal entities. Here is no trace of touching crude sexual symbols: seeing the goddess is the high point of the mysteries. Karl Kerényi made this the heart of his interpretation of Eleusis, postulating a genuine vision, a ghost-like

---

[56] Schol. Aristid. p. 53.15 Dind. (Demeter gives the grain) *πρῶτον ἀθέσμως συγγενομένη* Κελεῷ. Luk. *Lexiph.* 10 (δᾳδούχῳ *τε καὶ τοῖς ἄλλοις ἀρρητοποιοῖς*) is meant obscenely. See also *Hymn. Orph.* 41.6 (Demeter) Εὔβουλον *τέξασα θεὸν θνητῆς ὑπ' ἀνάγκης*. Iambe (*Hy. Dem.* 202) and Baubo are often associated with the Gephyrismoi (n. 19 above), but if the drinking of the kykeon or the giving of the grain follows immediately thereafter, it cannot be just an incidental preparation that accounts for Demeter's anger being assuaged; *ὁσίης ἕνεκεν* (*Hy. Dem.* 211) points to the desacralization after the *ἄρρητον*. A harvest custom in Normandy gives us an inkling of what really occurred in the rite (W. Mannhardt, *Mythol. Forsch.* [1884], 186): at the threshing feast a ram is slaughtered, the tail is cut off and specially roasted, and every young girl in the company is given a piece of it "mit vielem Gelächter." A. Heusler, *Zeitschr. f. Volkskunde* 13 (1903), 29–30; cf. I.7.nn.44–50 above.

[57] Apollod., *FGrHist* 244 F 110; cf. Pind. *Isthm.* 7.3 Dionysus *χαλκοκρότου πάρεδρον* Δαμάτερος; *χαλκοῦ τ' αὐδὰν χθονίαν* in the song to Meter, Eur. *Hel.* 1346; Vell. Pat. 1.4.1 *nocturno aeris sono, qualis Cerealibus sacris cieri solet*; Schol. Aristoph. *Ach.* 708. For Kore's coming in the visual arts see V.3.n.17; cf. the lekythos from Sofia, Metzger (1965) pl. 23.1/2, where Kore appears on Demeter's lap, between Hermes and Eumolpos.

[58] *Pap. d. R. Univ. Milano* (1937), #20 pp. 176–77 *ἀπόκλει[σον τὴν* 'Ε]*λευσεῖνα καὶ τὸ πῦρ* [*τὸ ἱερὸν*], δᾳδοῦχε, . . . *μυστήρια* [*πολλῷ ἀ*]*ληθέστερα μεμύημαι . . . τὴν* Κόρην *εἶδον*; W. F. Otto, *Eranos Jb.* 1939, 83–112 = *Die Gestalt und das Sein* (1955), 315–37; Kerényi, *Paideuma* 7 (1959), 76–77; (1962) 90; (1967) 83–84.

apparition on the night of the mysteries. However, in order to explain a vision repeated annually by the mystai, he was forced to consider whether the seasoning in the kykeon might be a hallucinogen[59]—a dubious borrowing from chemistry.

Lobeck, on the other hand, pointed out long ago that Christian songs and sermons speak of the unmitigated presence of the god in the mass as if it were a foregone conclusion.[60] Yet on the surface there is nothing there but the priest and his ministers, bells and candles, water, bread and wine. So too at Eleusis we need expect no more than the presence of the hierophant and dadouchos, who were seen "together"[61] at the gong and the fire, performing with the kiste and the wheat, the implements and containers. An individual's willingness to undergo an experience varies, yet it can be heightened by such means as fasting and keeping vigil through the night. The collective ritual which, in the history and tradition of man, has become associated with the soul is able to pull that soul into its rhythm so that many actually experience what is expected of them, and the remainder feel ashamed in their isolation.

Realists have suggested that a divine image, perhaps an especially old, primitive, and hence sacred one, would be displayed. Similar things did indeed occur in the mysteries.[62] Yet in the year 415 B.C., when aristocratic clubs were accused—not entirely without cause, as it seems—of having "performed the mysteries" in secret meetings, it occurred to no one to ask about a statuette as a corpus delicti.[63] In playing the part of the hierophant, there was no need of special instruments.

We cannot guess what appeared—perhaps only for an instant—in the flickering firelight. Orpheus, who was himself a hierophant,

---

[59] Kerényi (1962) 100, (1967) 96. On *γλήχων* in the initiation see *Numen* Suppl. 10 (1965), 63–64; (1967) 179–80; "the epiphany of a divine Phantom" (1967) 119.

[60] Lobeck (1829) 119.

[61] Sopatros *Rhet. Gr.* VIII 114.24 *ἐπεὶ οὖν εἴσω τῶν ἀνακτόρων γεγένημαι καὶ μύστης ὢν ἱεροφάντην ἅμα καὶ δᾳδοῦχον τεθέαμαι.*

[62] Lobeck (1829) 57; there is evidence for mysteries in which the images of the gods were stripped naked, in the metaphorical language of Themistios, who praises his father as follows: *σὺ . . .ἐγύμνους τὰ ἀγάλματα* (*Or.* 20.235a). Mylonas (1961) 273–74: "small relics from the Mycenaean age."

[63] See Kerényi (1967) 111. The majority of sources on the Mystery scandal of 415 refer not to an "imitation" but to a "performance" of the mysteries: *τὰ μυστήρια ποιοῦντα* Andoc. 1.11, and cf. 12, 16, 17; *τὰ μυστήρια . . . ὡς ποιεῖται ἐφ' ὕβρει* Thuc. 6.28.1; *ἀπομιμούμενον τὰ μυστήρια καὶ δεικνύοντα* in the *eisangelia* of Thessalos, Plut. *Alc.* 22.4; Lys. *Or.* 6.51 (concerning Andocides): *οὗτος γὰρ ἐνδὺς στολήν, μιμούμενος τὰ ἱερὰ ἐπεδείκνυ τοῖς ἀμυήτοις*; the imitation here probably refers to a gesture.

was only able to see Eurydice, the "far-ruler" from the underworld, for an instant before she vanished.[64] Perhaps it was itself only a sign, a gesture. A series of sources mentions secret "figures," *σχήματα*, of the mysteries—gestures or dance steps. Mysteries can be revealed as clearly in deeds as in words; one can "dance" them.[65] There are vase-paintings on which the mythical hierophant Eumolpos appears to be dancing.[66] As indicated in the rhetorical exercise of Sopatros, the Eleusinian mysteries consisted of "figures" and "calls."[67] Much earlier, the Stoic Cleanthes compared the cosmos to a chamber of the mysteries in which the sun gives off light as the dadouchos, but the gods are "mystical figures and sacred calls."[68] The author of the *Epinomis* expected philosophical piety to insure a proper attitude toward sacrifices and purifications "not by making subtle use of figures, but by truly honoring virtue."[69] Like Cleanthes, he wrote at Athens.

Besides the "figures," there were the "sacred calls." Only the "Naassenian" relates how the hierophant "at Eleusis, when performing the great, unspeakable mysteries amid great fire, calls out at the

---

[64] There are numerous allusions to *φάσματα* which were seen in the mysteries, cf. Plat. *Phdr.* 250c *εὐδαίμονα φάσματα μυούμενοί τε καὶ ἐποπτεύοντες*; Plut. fr. 178 Sandbach *σεμνότητας ἀκουσμάτων ἱερῶν καὶ φασμάτων ἁγίων*; Aristid. *Or.* 22.3 Keil (I 416 Dind.) *ἐν τοῖς ἀρρήτοις φάσμασιν*; Procl. *Resp.* II 185.4 Kroll *φάσματα . . . γαλήνης μεστά*, and cf. I 39.1–17. For *φάσματα καὶ δείματα* in the mysteries of Dionysus see Orig. *Cels.* 4.10. For a priestess as the spirit Ἔμπουσα in the mysteries of Sabazios, *ἀπὸ σκοτεινῶν τόπων ἀνεφαίνετο τοῖς μυουμένοις*, see Idomeneus, *FGrHist* 338 F. 2.

[65] Sopatros *Rhet. Gr.* VII 115.11 *μὴ λόγον εἰπών, μὴ σχήματι δηλώσας τὴν τελετήν*, and cf. 115.30. Τὰ *μυστήρια ἐξορχεῖσθαι*: see Luk. *Pisc.* 33; *Salt.* 15; Epict. 3.21.16; Clem. *Pr.* 2.12.1; etc.

[66] On Eumolpos see n. 24 above; portrayed dancing, see, for instance, the bell-crater *BM* F 68 = *ARV*[2] 1446.1, Kerényi (1962) pl. 2; a hydria from Istanbul, Metzger (1951) pl. 32, Kerényi (1962) pl. 37.

[67] *Rhet. Gr.* VIII 123.26 *ἂν δᾳδουχίαν θεάσωμαι καὶ σχῆμά τι περὶ τοῦ ἀδελφοῦ γιγνόμενον . . . ἂν τῶν ἱεροφάντου ῥήσεων αἴσθωμαι . . . ἀδελφός*. The fellow initiand is here referred to as "brother": see the oath of the Isis mystai, *PSI* 1162, *ZPE* 1 (1967), 73; on the procedure see the transferral into the Christian milieu in Clem. *Pr.* 12.120.1 *ἱεροφαντεῖ δὲ ὁ κύριος καὶ τὸν μύστην σφραγίζεται φωταγωγῶν*. Contrary to Kerényi's suggestion—(1962) 100, (1967) 94—the text of Sopatros should not be altered. Cf. Luk. *Alex.* 40 *δᾳδουχίαις καὶ τοῖς μυστικοῖς σκιρτήμασι*; Greg. Naz. n. 54 above; Clem. *Pr.* 12.120.5, where Christ, as the hierophant, says *γυμνὸν δικαιοσύνης ἐπιδείξω τὸ σχῆμα, δι' οὗ πρὸς τὸν θεὸν ἀναβαίνετε*. For a different perspective (images) see Procl. Eucl. p. 141.22 Friedlein *τὰ ἐν τοῖς ἀγγείοις τῶν θεῶν καὶ ἀδύτοις κρύφια καὶ ἄρρητα σχήματα*; cf. 138.7.

[68] *SVF* I #538 = Epiphan. *De fide* 9.41; *τοὺς θεοὺς μυστικὰ σχήματα ἔλεγεν εἶναι καὶ κλήσεις ἱεράς*.

[69] Plat. *Epin.* 989c *οὐ σχήμασι τεχνάζοντες*. . . .

top of his voice: the mistress has given birth to a sacred boy, Brimo to Brimos. That is," he adds, "the strong to the strong."[70] The name *Brimo* is used for Demeter, for Hekate, and for an independent goddess.[71] It is otherwise unattested at Eleusis, and it is even harder to say who the boy may have been to whom the mistress gave birth. Even among initiates there seem to have been various interpretations. We hear the name Iakchos-Dionysus, son of Persephone,[72] or Plutos, son of Demeter.[73] Or were the "two goddesses"—who in pictorial representations were intentionally made to resemble each other, almost to the extent that they cannot be told apart—in fact identical?[74] The difference in their names proves nothing: mythological systematizations are secondary. "A child is born." Side by side with the peril of death and blood we find the miracle of new life in birth. This is

[70]Hippol. *Ref.* 5.8.40 *νυκτὸς ἐν Ἐλευσῖνι ὑπὸ πολλῷ πυρὶ τελῶν τὰ μεγάλα καὶ ἄρρητα μυστήρια βοᾷ καὶ κέκραγε λέγων· "ἱερὸν ἔτεκε πότνια κοῦρον, Βριμὼ Βριμόν", τουτέστιν ἰσχυρὰ ἰσχυρόν.* The hierophant chanted his proclamation, as indicated already in the name *Eumolpos;* cf. *Εὐμόλπου προχέων ἱμερόεσσαν ὄπα* on the funerary epigram of a hierophant, *IG* II/III[2] 3639; *τὰς ἐξ ἀνακτόρου φωνάς, εὐφωνία,* Philostr. *V. Soph.* 2.20, II 103.15–20 ed. Teubn. (1870).

[71]For the angered Demeter identified with Brimo see Clem. *Pr.* 2.15.1; Euseb. *Praep. Ev.* 2.2.41; Theodoret *Gr. aff. cur.* 1.22. For Brimo = Hekate see Apoll. Rhod. 3.1210, and cf. 861; Lyk. 1175–76. For Brimo = Persephone, raped by Hermes at Lake Boibe, see Schol. Lyk. 1176, 698; Prop. 2.2.12. Cf. *PGurob VS* 1 B 23.19 = *OF* 31.5; for a parody see Luk. *Menipp.* 20. Hsch. *βρίμη· ἀρρητοποιία γυναικεία.*

[72]*Ἀθηναῖοι Διόνυσον τὸν Διὸς καὶ Κόρης σέβουσιν . . . καὶ ὁ Ἴακχος ὁ μυστικὸς τούτῳ τῷ Διονύσῳ ἐπᾴδεται* Arr. *Anab.* 2.16.3; Cic. *Nat. deor.* 2.62 on Ceres-Libera-Liber: *quod quale sit, ex mysteriis intellegitur; τῆς Κελεοῦ καὶ Τριπτολέμου καὶ Κόρης καὶ Δήμητρος καὶ Διονύσου ἐν Ἐλευσῖνι τελετῆς* Hippol. *Ref.* 5.20.5; Eur. *Or.* 964 *Περσέφασσα καλλίπαις θεά,* Schol. *ἡ γεννήσασα τὸν Ἴακχον.* Cf. the birth of Dionysus on a pelike from Kerch as a counterpart to the birth of Plutos, Leningrad 1792 = *ARV*[2] 1476.1, Nilsson (1955) pl. 46, Kerényi (1962) pl. 38/9, E. Simon, *AK* 9 (1966), 72–86, Graf (1974) 67–75. For Ceres as the nurse of Iakchos see Lucr. 4.1168, Arnob. 3.10; cf. the bell-crater from Al Mina, Oxford 1956–335, Metzger (1965) pl. 25.2; Nilsson (1967) pl. 53.1. For Dionysus as the son of Demeter see Diod. 3.64.1. Cf. also n. 23 above.

[73]Hes. *Th.* 969, cf. *Hy. Dem.* 489; Skolion 885.1 Page = Ath. 694c; Aristoph. *Thesm.* 296; for the child Plutos with the horn of plenty in the circle of Eleusinian divinities on fourth-century vases see the pelike from Kerch, n. 72 above; a lid, Tübingen E 183, V.3.n.11 above; pelike Sandford Graham, Metzger (1965) pl. 14.1; the hydria, Istanbul, n. 66 above; he is portrayed in an especially beautiful way, between growing blades of wheat, on a fragment from Fethiye Djami, *Deltion* 17 (1961/62), pl. 35, Metzger (1965) pl. 16.2. Deubner (1932) 86 raised the possibility that Plutos and the blade of wheat were identical.

[74]See Kerényi (1962) 46–47, (1967) 32–33 on P. Roussel, *Les cultes égyptiens à Délos* (1916), #206 = *Inscriptions de Délos* 2475 *Δ]ήμητρος Ἐλευσινίας καὶ κόρης καὶ γυναικός* (cf., however, Roussel 199).

the sacrificial ritual's necessary supplement, which makes the cycle of life a possibility. In just this way at Mount Lykaion, in Olympia, on Mount Parnassus, the birth of the child stands side by side with sacrificial killing, the woman's achievement next to the man's. Already in the domestic shrines of Çatal Hüyük it was customary to depict the Great Goddess as giving birth. For the most part, she appears as mother of the animals, but a statuette found in a grain bin represents her sitting on a throne between leopards, giving birth to a human child.[75] Is this already the grain-mother? The Mexicans portrayed the Great Goddess giving birth to the corn-god in a frontal posture much like that of the statues at Çatal Hüyük.[76] Whether this reflects an historical connection or mere coincidence, the image, the appurtenant thought, experience, and ritual action all serve the same necessary function in the balance of human life. "Plutos," wealth in the form of grain, is the primary yield of the agricultural year, the source of people's food. Following in the footsteps of the more ancient hunting festivals, this process is dramatized in the sacrifice.

The blade of cut wheat was made visible at Eleusis, displayed by the hierophant amid general silence.[77] The "Naassenian's" explanation that the blade corresponded to Attis, who was called by his mystai the "sprouting, cut blade of wheat," has rarely been taken seriously, has at most been used to call the report's authenticity into question. But—unbeknownst to the Gnostic—already Dumuzi, the victim of Inanna who rose from the underworld, was represented as a blade of wheat.[78] And when Hesiod tells the well-known myth of Uranos' castration, he uses the word "he mowed." Kronos wields a sickle, just like Meter-Demeter.[79] Historically seen, the seemingly far-

---

[75]Mellaart (1967) 234, pl. 67–68 and pl. IX; cf. I.8.n.26 above.

[76]K. Th. Preuss. *Bilderatlas zur Religionsgeschichte* 16 (1930), XII, fig. 64. In the Egyptian Book of the Dead 78.30 it says "ich wurde in die heiligen verborgenen Dinge . . . eingeführt, als man mich die Geburt des Gottes, des Grossen sehen liess": see J. Bergmann, *Ich bin Isis* (Uppsala, 1968), 230 n.2.

[77]Hippol. *Ref.* 5.8.39 Ἀθηναῖοι μυοῦντες Ἐλευσίνια καὶ ἐπιδεικνύντες τοῖς ἐποπτεύουσι τὸ μέγα καὶ θαυμαστὸν καὶ τελειότατον ἐποπτικὸν ἐκεῖ μυστήριον, ἐν σιωπῇ τεθερισμένον στάχυν. Mylonas (1961) 275 assumes that the Phrygian and Eleusinian cults have been confused; he notes that blades of cut wheat are often depicted. Nobody would deny this. The secret is hidden in what is familiar. For Attis and the blade of cut wheat see Jul. *Or.* 5.168d (ἄρρητον θέρος); Firm. *Err.* 3.2, and cf. 2.7; Porph. p. 10* Bidez = Euseb. *Praep. Ev.* 3.11.12.

[78]E. D. van Buren, *Symbols of the Gods in Mesopotamian Art* (1945), 13; *Anal. Or.* 12 (1935), 327–35; cf. V.3.n.30 above.

[79]*Th.* 181. Cf. Apoll. Rhod. 4.986–90: Corcyra was called *Drepane* after the sickle of Demeter, who taught the Titans how to reap—or after the castration of Uranos. For the

fetched fantasy, equating the cutting of the blade with castration, is merely a transposition of hunting behavior onto agriculture—which also explains why an animal sacrifice is still included in the harvest festival. Of course, this was long past by the time the hierophant displayed the blade, which attested to a liberating transformation: for what had appeared in the darkness as the castration of a ram is disclosed in the gleaming fire as the cutting of the grain. The uncanny, provocative source of reproduction is transformed into the fruit of the earth, which itself holds the power of perpetuating life. A regular feature of the Mithras reliefs is the bull dying in the sacrifice, its tail turning into a blade of wheat.[80] Even "domesticated" food must reach man by way of the unspeakable sacrifice. And to be eaten, a blade must once more go through fire.[81]

The virgin's return, the birth of the child, and the blade are, in three gradations, symbols of the restoration and renewal of life. It grew light in the middle of the night when "the Anaktoron was opened" and the hierophant came from the door,[82] with the "great fire" blazing inside. Of course, the sequence of events is uncertain, and we are surely missing many details. Perhaps the kykeon was only drunk now, and now the mystai would touch the kalathos and the kiste. But as soon as the objects were returned to the kiste, a seal of secrecy fell once again on that which had happened. The collective experience that life and nourishment result from terror, the encounter

---

island named after the castration of Kronos by Zeus see Timaios, *FGrHist* 566 F 79. For lamentation for Osiris while reaping in Egypt see Diod. 1.14 (Foucart [1914] 441, 443). Mesomedes Εἰς τὴν Ἶσιν indicates the stages of the mysteries of Isis-Demeter: an underground wedding (*χθόνιος ὑμέναιος*, 11) and the birth of a child (*νηπιάχου γονά*, 14), *πῦρ τέλεον ἄρρητον* (15), *ὅ τε* Κρόνιος *ἄμητος* (17), *πάντα δι' ἀνακτόρων* Ἴσιδι *χορεύεται* (19/20). The cutting of the wheat is given a poetic/universalizing guise in the words of comfort for the child's death in Euripides' *Hypsipyle*, fr. 757.5–7 *TGF* = fr. 60.93–95 Bond: *ἀναγκαίως δ'ἔχει βίον θερίζειν ὥστε κάρπιμον στάχυν καὶ τὸν μὲν εἶναι, τὸν δὲ μή.*

[80]F. Cumont, *Textes et monuments relatifs aux mystères de Mithra* I (1899), 186–88; L. A. Campbell, *Mithraic Iconography and Ideology* (1968), 86–87; see also W. Mannhardt, *Mythol. Forschungen* (1884), 187–88.

[81]This is also indicated in the myth of the child in the fire: *ζέα*, *far*, can be threshed only after having been toasted in the fire. For Triptolemos as the inventor of threshing see Callim. *Hy.* 6.20 f. (where *ἀπέκοψε*, "cut," alludes to castration). For the *ἅλως* Τ*ριπτολέμου* see Paus. 1.38.6. The myth of Ino and Phrixos combines the toasting of the grain with the sacrifice of a child and that of a ram: see *PR* II 42 and *Nova fragmenta Euripidea*, ed. C. Austin (1968), pp. 101–102; II.4.n.27 above.

[82]Plut. *De prof. virt.* 81 (n. 8 above). For "opening" and "closing" of the Anaktoron see also Poseidonios, *FGrHist* 87 F 36 #51 = Ath. 213d; Himer. *Or.* 69.7 Colonna; Themistios *Or.* 20.235 ff.; Synesios Dion 6.44c.

with death and destruction, binds the mystai together and adds a new dimension to their lives.

The nighttime festival was brought to a close outside the Telesterion, perhaps even outside the sanctuary. The narrow confines were too small to hold in such an experience. The waving of torches and the exultant dancing of the mystai, so impressively evoked in Aristophanes' choral song, occurred on the "meadow."[83] The crowd perhaps flocked to the field called Rharion, where the first grain was sown and harvested. In Hermesianax, Eumolpos' mother, the mythic model for the priestess of Demeter, "performs the powerful cry of joy of the mystai, panting through Rharion, site of the orgies, according to the custom."[84] The dance was possibly still set off by the gestures of the hierophant, but one had to be careful at this point not to "dance out" the mysteries themselves. The waning moon would by now have risen and could illuminate this festival until dawn, as a celestial torch. Large sacrifices with ample meals of meat would still take place—the normal form of cult was reestablished with the return to normal life. The ephebic inscriptions mention bull-sacrifices in Eleusis "at the mysteries"[85]—this was no longer secret and must have occurred after the initiation was over: one could not be a proper "spectator" on a full stomach. The ephebes would show off their youthful strength by "lifting up" the bull for sacrifice, a custom that virtually developed into an agon, a bullfight.[86] The role of the younger generation within the framework of the ancient custom was likewise part of the festival's conclusion. Those who had won special honors were given the same portion as the Eumolpidai when it came to distributing the meat.[87] In worldly pleasures, it is hard to be content with only

[83] Soph. fr. 891 P = Schol. Aristoph. *Ran.* 344; Aristoph. *Ran.* 340–53, 372–76; Eur. *Ion* 1074–86 *καὶ Διὸς ἀστερωπὸς ἀνεχόρευσεν αἰθήρ . . . τόποι καθαροὶ καὶ λειμῶνες ἐδέξαντο* Plut. fr. 178.11 Sandbach; Lact. *Inst. epit.* 23.7, n. 6 above.

[84] Hermesianax fr. 7.17 Powell on Antiope, mother of Eumolpos, *ἥ τε πολὺν μύστησιν Ἐλευσῖνος παρὰ πέζαν εὐασμὸν κρυφίων ἐξεφόρει λογίων Ῥάριον ὀργειῶνα νόμῳ διαποιπνύουσα* (διαποιπνωιουσα A, *διαπομπεύουσα* Powell) *Δημήτρᾳ*. . . .

[85] *Hesperia* 24 (1955), 220–39 = *SEG* 15 (1958), #104 (127/26 B.C.) 11–12 [*ἤραντο . . . τοὺς β*]*οῦς δι' ἑαυτ*[*ῶν*] *τοῖς Μυστηρίοις ὡσαύ*[*τως ἐν Ἐλευσῖνι*; cf. *IG* II/III² 1006.10 *ἐν Ἐλευσῖνι τῇ θυσίᾳ*; 1008.9 *ἐβουθύτησαν ἐν τῷ* [*περιβόλῳ*]; 1028.11 *ἐν τῷ περιβόλῳ τοῦ ἱεροῦ*; 1011.8, 1029.7, 1030.7; *Hesperia* 34 (1965), 255–72 = *SEG* 22 (1967) #111.7. For Bukrania on vases in the midst of the Eleusinian divinities see, for instance, the lid, Tübingen V.3.n.11 above; the hydria, Athens 1443, Metzger (1965) pl. 19.1.

[86] See Stengel (1910) 105–12; L. Ziehen, *Hermes* 66 (1931), 227–34; a red figure vase-painting, Cook I (1914) 505; Artemidoros 1.8.

[87] *IG* II/III² 1231.9–13, and cf. 1078.33–36.

the gift of Demeter. And thus the sacrificial cycle ended with the familiar group of three: Su/ove/taurilia.

A solemn libation is the last ritual, performed by daylight. Two specially shaped jugs, plemochoai, are filled and poured out, the one toward the east, the other toward the west[88]—a gesture embracing the whole world. Demeter's gift is indeed spread across the whole world, as told in the myth of Triptolemos. Perhaps in the process, the people called out "Rain!" to the heavens, and "Conceive!" to the earth, ὕε–κύε.[89] Those things that had been experienced in their essence during the night of the mysteries continued to affect the cycle of life. Even grain comes from the dead.[90] Without this supplement, life would be incomplete: the initiation is a consummation, a τέλος.

5. *Overcoming Death and Encountering Death: Initiation and Sacrifice*

Now as before, the secret of Eleusis leaves room for many conjectures and hypotheses in its details, but we can survey its basic dimensions. Even if we could make a film that exhaustively documented the celebration in the Telesterion, we would still be no closer to explaining the "thrice blessed," the basis of the initiate's hopes for the other world.[1] The way in which men mold themselves into a community by means of tradition is a basic phenomenon, easier to reproduce than to illuminate rationally.

---

[88] Ath. 496a; Deubner (1932) 91; Kerényi (1962) 135, (1967) 141.

[89] Kerényi (1962) 135, (1967) 141; Hippol. *Ref.* 5.7.34 τὸ μέγα καὶ ἄρρητον Ἐλευσινίων μυστήριον· ὕε κύε. Procl. *In Tim.* III 176.28 Diehl ἐν τοῖς Ἐλευσινίοις ἱεροῖς εἰς μὲν τὸν οὐρανὸν ἀναβλέποντες ἐβόων "ὕε", καταβλέψαντες δὲ εἰς τὴν γῆν τὸ "κύε" (the same gestures occur in the Roman devotion: see Macr. *Sat.* 1.9.12); in the time of Proclus, the mysteries were already part of the past. Cf. the inscription from a well at the Dipylon gate, *IG* II/III^2 4876 Ὁ Πᾶν· ὁ Μήν· χαίρετε Νύνφαι καλαί· ὕε κύε ὑπέρχυε, not, however, "open to the public view" (Mylonas [1961] 270), but on the inside, "invisible" (*BCH* 20 [1896], 80).

[90] Hippokr. *De victu* 4.92.

[1] See V.1.nn.32–33 above; see also Epictetus 3.21.13–16.

We tend to assume that there must have been a specific Eleusinian message, a secret but distinct declaration of death overcome. But no matter how surprising it may seem to one Platonically influenced, there is no mention of immortality at Eleusis, nor of a soul and the transmigration of souls, nor yet of deification. Roman emperors identified themselves with Triptolemos, Gallienus even with Demeter herself;[2] yet during the Greek period at Eleusis the distinction between the immortal gods and mortal man was apparently maintained. Eleusis had already been shaped before Pythagoras[3] and Plato.

All attempts to reconstruct a genuine Eleusinian belief have been thwarted by the diversity of ancient interpretations, reflecting a genuine ambiguity in the events that took place at Eleusis. One could cite Varro for the belief that Eleusinian mysteries were concerned "only" with the invention of grain;[4] one could understand the myth of Demeter's arrival in the manner of Euhemerus, saying that it contains the recollection of the transition from culturelessness to culture in the festival.[5] Those philosophically educated could offer a spiritualizing explanation, arguing that the vital force, the pneuma, in the grain, was the actual divinity revealed at Eleusis.[6] The Platonists went further, setting nature aside to seek the drama of spirit and matter, its rise and fall, within the mystery celebration; thus too the "Naassenian" in Hippolytus.[7] The explanations given to the mystai through oral instruction probably underwent greater changes in the course of time than did Christian theology or religious instruction in the church. There was no dogma at Eleusis.

---

[2]Ch. Picard, "La patère d'Aquileia et l'éleusinisme à Rome aux débuts de l'époque impériale," *ACl* 20 (1951), 351–81; cf. the cameo, Paris, Cab. Med. 276, Cook I (1914) 228; an onyx vessel, Braunschweig, A. Furtwängler, *Antike Gemmen* III (1900), 338–39; GALLIENA AUGUSTA, A. Alföldi, *Zeitschr. f. Numism.* 38 (1928), 174–94.

[3]The Doxographers trace the teachings about immortality back to Thales (*VS* 11 A 1.24, A 22a) or Pherekydes (*VS* 7 A 5); on the transmigration of souls and Pythagoreanism see W. Burkert, *Lore and Science in Ancient Pythagoreanism* (1972), 120–36.

[4]Aug. *Civ. Dei* 7.20: *multa in mysteriis eius* (sc. *Cereris*) *tradi, quae nisi ad frugum inventionem non pertineant*. See also the interpretation of Proserpina–Moon, Varro *L. l.* 5.68 = Ennius, Epicharmus 59 Vahlen², and cf. Plut. *De fac.* 942d, etc.

[5]Varro interprets the secret concerning the gods of the mysteries, *ut homines eos fuisse taceretur*, Aug. *Civ. Dei* 18.5, and cf. 4.31; Cic. *Tusc.* 1.29; Epictetus 3.21.15; Serv. *Aen.* 4.58.

[6]Kleanthes *SVF* I #547 = Plut. *Is.* 377d, and cf. 367c.

[7]Hippol. *Ref.* 5.8.41–44, and cf. Sall. 4.7–9 on the myth of Attis; Plat. *Symp.* 209e–212a is in the background. Plutarch, *De Iside et Osiride*, and Iamblichus, *De mysteriis*, generally argue for the Platonic/transcendental interpretation of the mysteries, and against the nature interpretation. Cf. also Numenios at V.1.n.22 above.

Indeed, even the pre-philosophic formation of Greek religion, the anthropomorphic, "Homeric" mythology, seems to provide only a superficial account of the point of the mysteries at Eleusis. There were indeed gods at work here, but what they were called and in what relationship they stood to one another remained undetermined and ambiguous. Eubuleus, Daeira, Iakchos[8]—there may well have been secret myths, but the essential element apparently lay beyond myth, or, rather, did not reach the level of spoken language, nor that of philosophical thought.

The place, tradition, priestly families, and ritual as the characteristic communication and formative experience remained constant. Everything revolved around the encounter with death, which was celebrated in the sacrifice. Even for the mystai, death was a fact and could not be shrugged off. The hope of the initiate was that in that self-same death he would be "blessed"; he had learnt that, as a funerary epigram from the Imperial epoch puts it, both simply and memorably, "for mortals, death is no evil, it is, rather, the good."[9] Surprisingly, the dreadful gods of the underworld put on a friendly face. The mysteries effected a reconciliation with death; hence that "blessed" with which the mystai mutually reinforced their faith.

The festival bond is archaic, as is the concept of an elite group that sees the "bliss" of the initiate only in contrast to the uninitiate, who "will lie in the mire."[10] Ironically objective, Herodotus gives a similar description of the belief in immortality among the Getai, who were convinced by Zalmoxis "that he and his drinking companions and their descendants would not die":[11] membership in the tribe and participation in festive eating and drinking guaranteed one's hopes for the next world. Examples can be adduced from primitive societies showing how initiation, puberty rites or induction into a secret society determine one's status both in the here-and-now and after death.[12] After all, cohesive archaic societies naturally conceive of

---

[8]See V.4.n.23–24 above; on Daeira see Nilsson, *Opuscula* II (1951), 545–47; Kerényi (1962) 171, 368, (1967) 213, 160. See also Kerényi (1962) 136–51, (1967) 144–69.

[9]*IG* II/III² 3661.5–6 *οὐ μόνον εἶναι τὸν θάνατον θνητοῖς οὐ κακόν, ἀλλ' ἀγαθόν.*

[10]Plat. *Phd.* 69c; *Resp.* 363c–d; Diog. Laert. 6.39; Plut. fr. 178.17 Sandbach; cf. V.1.n.32 above.

[11]Hdt. 4.95.

[12]So especially in the initiations and "Totenfahrt" in Malekula (Melanesia): cf. J. Layard, *Stone Men of Malekula* (1942); "Totenfahrt auf Malekula," *Eranos Jb.* 4 (1937) 242–91. This is not the place to describe in detail the development of initiation, kingship, and funerary ritual.

themselves as living among their own dead, who play a determinant role in their lives. In order to reach a new plane of existence in the initiation ritual, one must normally undergo "sufferings,"[13] an encounter with death, through which death is overcome: in sacrifice, in the act of killing, the will to live rises triumphant over the fallen victim.[14] After this, a real death seems no more than a repetition, anticipated long ago. The ritual shifts anxiety in such a way that the resultant formative forces work toward the continuance of our societal forms in the present.

Interpretations on these lines that proceed from initiation ritual have deeper foundations than those based only on agricultural magic. Neolithic agriculture was, after all, shaped by older traditions. For the cultivated, city-dwelling Greeks or Romans, the path to Eleusis was a regression to the goddess of grain, to the growing forces of the plant world. At its core, this regression went back yet further, beyond agriculture to the hunting and sacrificing ritual. If we use the word *primitive* in this regard, it is not in the sense of "imperfect," "silly," or "defective," but, rather, "basic." It connotes simple, self-evident suppositions: that an individual cannot live in isolation, that he is dependent on the societal grouping from which he came; that the death of the individual is an integral part of communal life, for which reason the encounter with death is unavoidable. This, in turn, can elicit both the triumphant ecstasy of survival and the willingness to die. The fact that, in the course of life, one can take the other's place, feeding itself, begetting and dying, is unalterable—indeed, to the Greeks it is "divine";[15] one can only hope that the gods will be merciful in the process.

The amazing variety of rituals and cult sites, myths and names which we have examined may seem confusing, but the same dynamic structures recur with almost monotonous regularity. Sacrifice as an encounter with death, an act of killing that simultaneously guarantees the perpetuation of life and food, grew up out of the existence of the Palaeolithic hunter and remained the formative core of the sacred ritual. It was, moreover, a point of reference and a moving force behind stories of myth. This core finds expression in the cannibalistic fan-

---

[13] Cf. I.5.nn.44–45 above.

[14] Such is the teaching of the ancient *Acheruntici libri* of the Etruscans: *certorum animalium sanguine numinibus certis dato divinas animas fieri . . . et ab legibus mortalitatis educi* (Arnob. 2.62).

[15] Nilsson (1955) 675–76 rightly cites Plat. *Symp.* 207d, 208b.

tasies, or even practices, of werewolf societies, in "murdering" the bull at the end of the year and also in the sacred yet uncanny drinking of the wine and in the sacrifices that accompany the night of the mysteries. This core likewise determines the prelude and the conclusion, the hesitant beginning and the painstaking ending, preliminary renunciation and joyous, victorious gratification. Included in the prelude and renunciation is the maiden's tragedy—Kallisto and Io, Philomela and Ino, but above all Kore–Persephone. The closing confirmation occurs in the procession of armed ephebes, and in the agon from the Lykaia and the Olympics, through the Panathenaia to the Chytroi and the Eleusinian "bullfight." This, in turn, is linked to eating the food now happily secured, whether it be manifested in hecatombs of cattle, in a haul of fish, or in the gift of Demeter. The differentiations are old and significant, and yet all encompassed by the overarching span of the ritual, which is neither self-evident nor banal, but frightening and yet incomparably powerful.

The modern world, whose pride is in the full emancipation of the individual, has gradually allowed the ritual tradition to break down. At the same time, it has relegated death to the fringes of existence and thought. As the idealistic tradition deteriorates, however, secret societies, ecstatic behavior, love of violence and death spring up all the more wildly and destructively amid seemingly rational orders. Ritual cannot be produced artificially, much less its transcendent orientation, which is no longer shrouded in superstition and secrets. The ideal of a new, non-violent man is a protest of hope against the tradition of violence and anxiety. But it is hard to foresee how the individual, egocentric intelligence can be subordinated to the collective need in order to make possible the continuance of mankind over the breach between the generations. In the end, societal forms in which man's archaic psyche will be granted its rights will presumably assert themselves. We can only hope that primitivism and violence will not be released unbridled. In any case, our knowledge of the traditions that proved themselves in the past and thus survived in the various experiments of human development should not be lost as we proceed, by trial and error, toward an uncertain future.

Abbreviations and Bibliography

AA	*Archäologischer Anzeiger*
ABV	J. D. Beazley, *Attic Black-Figure Vase-Painters*. Oxford, 1956.
ACl	*L'Antiquité Classique*
AJA	*American Journal of Archaeology*
AK	*Antike Kunst*
AM	*Athenische Mitteilungen*
ANEP	*The Ancient Near East in Pictures Relating to the Old Testament*, ed. J. B. Pritchard. Princeton, 1954. Supplement 1968.
ANET	*Ancient Near Eastern Texts Relating to the Old Testament*, ed. J. B. Pritchard. Princeton, 1955^2. Supplement (pp. 501–710), 1968.
AOB	*Altorientalische Bilder zum Alten Testament*, ed. H. Gressmann. Berlin, 1927^2.
AOT	*Altorientalische Texte zum Alten Testament*, ed. H. Gressmann. Berlin, 1926^2.
ARV^2	J. D. Beazley, *Attic Red-Figure Vase-Painters*. Oxford, 1963^2.
ARW	*Archiv für Religionswissenschaft*
ASAA	*Annuario della Scuola archeologica di Atene*
BCH	*Bulletin de Correspondance Hellénique*
bf.	black figured
BICS	*Bulletin of the Institute of Classical Studies of the University of London*
BMC	British Museum, Catalogue of Greek Coins
BSA	*Annual of the British School at Athens*
CAF	*Comicorum Atticorum Fragmenta*, ed. Th. Kock. Leipzig, 1880–1888.
CAG	*Commentaria in Aristotelem Graeca*
CIG	*Corpus Inscriptionum Graecarum*
CIL	*Corpus Inscriptionum Latinarum*
ClPh	*Classical Philology*
CQ	*Classical Quarterly*
CR	*Classical Review*
CRAI	*Comptes Rendus de l'Académie des Inscriptions et Belles-lettres*
CV	*Corpus Vasorum*
EAA	*Enciclopedia dell'Arte Antica Classica e Orientale*
FD	*Fouilles de Delphes*
FGrHist	F. Jacoby, *Die Fragmente der griechischen Historiker*. Berlin–Leiden, 1923–1958.

FR	A. Furtwängler and K. Reichhold, *Griechische Vasenmalerei*. Munich, 1904–1932.
GB	J. G. Frazer, *The Golden Bough*. London, 1911–1936^3 (13 vols., cited by numerals as indicated in the Index, XII 147).
GDI	H. Collitz, *Sammlung der griechischen Dialektinschriften*. Göttingen, 1884–1915.
HN^2	B. V. Head, *Historia Numorum*. Oxford, 1911^2.
HRR	*Historicorum Romanorum Reliquiae*, ed. H. Peter. Leipzig, 1883–1906; I^2, 1914.
HSCP	*Harvard Studies in Classical Philology*
HThR	*Harvard Theological Review*
IG	*Inscriptiones Graecae*
JdI	*Jahrbuch der [kaiserlich] deutschen archäologischen Instituts*
JHS	*Journal of Hellenic Studies*
JNES	*Journal of Near Eastern Studies*
JRAS	*Journal of the Royal Asiatic Society*
LGS	I. v. Prott and L. Ziehen, *Leges Graecorum Sacrae e titulis collectae*, vols. I, II. Leipzig, 1896–1906.
LS	F. Sokolowski, *Lois sacrées des cités grecques*. Paris, 1969.
LSAM	F. Sokolowski, *Lois sacrées de l'Asie Mineure*. Paris, 1955.
LSS	F. Sokolowski, *Lois sacrées des cités grecques*. Supplement. Paris, 1962.
MH	*Museum Helveticum*
MSS	*Münchner Studien zur Sprachwissenschaft*
NGG	*Nachrichten der Gesellschaft der Wissenschaften zu Göttingen*
NJb	*Neue Jahrbücher für Philologie und Pädagogik* (1831–1897); *Neue Jahrbücher für das klassische Altertum, Geschichte und deutsche Literatur und für Pädagogik* (1897–1924)
OF	*Orphicorum Fragmenta*, ed. O. Kern. Berlin, 1922 (reprint 1963).
OGI	*Orientis Graeci Inscriptiones Selectae*, ed. W. Dittenberger. Leipzig, 1903–1905.
PR	Ludwig Preller, *Griechische Mythologie*, 4. Revised edition by C. Robert, I–III. Berlin, 1894–1926.
PSI	*Papiri greci e latini (Pubbl. d. Società Italiana per la ricerca dei papiri greci e latini in Egitto)*
RA	*Revue Archéologique*
RAC	*Reallexikon für Antike und Christentum*
RE	*Realencyclopädie der klassischen Altertumswissenschaft*
REG	*Revue des Etudes Grecques*
rf.	red figured
RFIC	*Revista di Filologia e d'Istruzione Classica*
RGG^3	*Die Religion in Geschichte und Gegenwart*, 3. Revised edition by K. Galling. Tübingen, 1957–1965.
RhM	*Rheinisches Museum*
RHR	*Revue d'histoire des religions*
RML	*Ausführliches Lexikon der griechischen und römischen Mythologie*, ed. W. H. Roscher. Leipzig, 1884–1937.
RPh	*Revue de Philologie*
SEG	*Supplementum epigraphicum Graecum*

SIG[3] *Sylloge Inscriptionum Graecarum*, ed. W. Dittenberger. Leipzig, 1915–1924[3].

SMSR *Studi e materiali di storia delle religioni*

SVF *Stoicorum Veterum Fragmenta*, ed. H. v. Arnim, vols. I–IV. Leipzig, 1903–1921.

TAPA *Transactions and Proceedings of the American Philological Association*

TGF *Tragicorum Graecorum Fragmenta*, ed. A. Nauck. Leipzig, 1889[2] (reprint Hildesheim, 1964, with Supplement, ed. B. Snell).

UdG W. Schmidt, *Der Ursprung der Gottesidee* I–X. Münster, 1908–1952.

VS H. Diels, *Die Fragmente der Vorsokratiker*, 6. Revised edition by W. Kranz. Berlin, 1951 (=1971[15]).

ZPE *Zeitschrift für Papyrologie und Epigraphik*

ZRGG *Zeitschrift für Religions- und Geistesgeschichte*

Astour (1965) M. C. Astour. *Hellenosemitica: An Ethnic and Cultural Study in West Semitic Impact on Mycenaean Greece.* Leiden, 1965.

Baudy (1980) G. J. Baudy. *Exkommunikation und Reintegration. Zur Genese und Kulturfunktion frühgriechischer Einstellungen zum Tod.* Frankfurt, 1980.

Bergquist (1967) B. Bergquist. *The Archaic Greek Temenos: A Study of Structure and Function.* Lund, 1967.

Blech (1982) M. Blech. *Studien zum Kranz bei den Griechen.* Berlin, 1982.

Brelich (1969) A. Brelich. *Paides e Parthenoi.* Rome, 1969.

Brommer (1960) F. Brommer. *Vasenlisten zur griechischen Heldensage.* Marburg, (1956) 1960[2].

Brumfield (1981) A. Chandor Brumfield. *The Attic Festivals of Demeter and Their Relation to the Agricultural Year.* New York, 1981.

Burkert (1966) W. Burkert. "Greek Tragedy and Sacrificial Ritual." *Greek, Roman and Byzantine Studies* 7 (1966), 87–121.

Burkert (1967) ———. "Urgeschichte der Technik im Spiegel antiker Religion." *Technikgeschichte* 34 (1967), 281–99.

Burkert (1968) ———. "Orpheus und die Vorsokratiker." *Antike und Abendland* 14 (1968), 93–114.

Burkert (1970) ———. "Jason, Hypsipyle, and New Fire at Lemnos." *CQ* 20 (1970), 1–16.

Burkert (1979) ———. *Structure and History in Greek Mythology and Ritual.* Berkeley and Los Angeles, 1979.

Burkert (1980) ———. "Griechische Mythologie und die Geistesgeschichte der Moderne." In *Les études classiques aux XIXe et XXe siècles, Entretiens sur l'antiquité classique* 26 (1980), 159–99.

Burkert (1981) ———. "Glaube und Verhalten: Zeichengehalt und Wirkungsmacht von Opferritualen." In *Le sacrifice dans l'antiquité, Entretiens sur l'antiquité classique* 27 (1981), 91–125.

Cambitoglou and Trendall (1961) A. Cambitoglou and A. D. Trendall. *Apulian Red-Figured Vase-Painters of the Plain Style*. Archaeological Institute of America, 1961.

Casabona (1966) J. Casabona. *Recherches sur le vocabulaire des sacrifices en Grec des origines à la fin de l'époque classique*. Aix-en-Provence, 1966.

Clinton (1974) K. Clinton. *The Sacred Officials of the Eleusinian Mysteries*. Philadelphia, 1974 (Transactions of the American Philosophical Society 64.3).

Cook (1914, 1924, 1940) A. B. Cook. *Zeus*, vols. I, II, III. Cambridge, 1914, 1924, 1940.

Cumont (1930) F. Cumont. *Die orientalischen Religionen im römischen Heidentum*. Leipzig, 1930[3] (reprint Darmstadt, 1959; *Les religions orientales dans le paganisme romain*, Paris, 1906; 1929[4]).

Delatte (1955) A. Delatte. *Le cycéon, breuvage rituel des mystères d'Eleusis*. Paris, 1955 (= Bulletin de l'Académie Royale de Belgique, Cl. d. Lettr. 5. sér. 40, 1954, 690–751).

Des Places (1969) E. Des Places. *La religion grecque*. Paris, 1969.

Detienne (1977) M. Detienne. *Dionysos mis à mort*. Paris, 1977.

Detienne and Vernant (1979) M. Detienne and J.-P. Vernant. *La cuisine du sacrifice en pays grec*. Paris, 1979.

Deubner (1932) L. Deubner. *Attische Feste*. Berlin, 1932.

Dieterich (1923) A. Dieterich. *Eine Mithrasliturgie*. Leipzig, (1903) 1923[3] (reprint Darmstadt, 1966).

Dodds (1951) E. R. Dodds. *The Greeks and the Irrational*. Berkeley, 1951.

Dumézil (1929) G. Dumézil. *Le problème des Centaurs*. Paris, 1929.

Eibl-Eibesfeldt (1970) I. Eibl-Eibesfeldt. *Liebe und Hass. Zur Naturgeschichte elementarer Verhaltensweisen*. München, 1970.

Eisler (1925) R. Eisler. *Orphisch-Dionysische Mysteriengedanken in der christlichen Antike*. Leipzig, 1925 (Vorträge der Bibliothek Warburg, 1922/23, part two; reprint Hildesheim, 1966).

Eitrem (1915) — S. Eitrem. *Opferritus und Voropfer der Griechen und Römer.* Kristiania, 1915.

Eitrem (1917) — ———. *Beiträge zur Religionsgeschichte* II. *Skrift.* Videnskapsselskap Kristiania, 1917, 2.

Farnell I, II (1896) III, IV (1907) V (1909) — L. R. Farnell. *The Cults of the Greek States.* Vols. I, II, III, IV, V. Oxford, 1896, 1907, 1909.

Fehling (1974) — D. Fehling. *Ethologische Überlegungen auf dem Gebiet der Altertumskunde.* München, 1974.

Fehrle (1910) — E. Fehrle. *Die kultische Keuschheit im Altertum.* Giessen, 1910 (Religionsgeschichtliche Versuche und Vorarbeiten 6, reprint Berlin, 1966).

Fontenrose (1959) — J. Fontenrose. *Python: A Study of Delphic Myth and Its Origins.* Berkeley, 1959.

Foucart (1904) — P. Foucart. *Le culte de Dionysos en Attique.* Paris, 1904 (Mémoires de l'Académie des Inscriptions et Belles Lettres 37).

Foucart (1914) — ———. *Les mystères d'Eleusis.* Paris, 1914.

Gérard-Rousseau (1968) — M. Gérard-Rousseau. *Les mentions religieuses dans les tablettes mycéniennes.* Rome, 1968 (Incunabula Graeca 29).

Gese, Höfner, and Rudolph (1970) — H. Gese, M. Höfner, and K. Rudolph. *Die Religionen Altsyriens, Altarabiens und der Mandäer.* Stuttgart, 1970 (Die Religionen der Menschheit 10.2).

Girard (1972) — R. Girard. *La violence et le sacré.* Paris, 1972 (*Violence and the Sacred*, Baltimore, 1977).

Graf (1974) — F. Graf. *Eleusis und die orphische Dichtung Athens in vorhellenistischer Zeit.* Berlin, 1974.

Guépin (1968) — J. P. Guépin. *The Tragic Paradox: Myth and Ritual in Greek Tragedy.* Amsterdam, 1968.

Harrison (1922) — J. E. Harrison. *Prolegomena to the Study of Greek Religion.* Cambridge, (1903), 1922[3] (reprint 1955).

Harrison (1927) — ———. *Themis: A Study of the Social Origins of Greek Religion.* Cambridge, (1912), 1927[2] (reprint 1962).

Hemberg (1950) — B. Hemberg. *Die Kabiren.* Uppsala, 1950.

Hepding (1903) — H. Hepding. *Attis, seine Mythen und sein Kult.* Giessen, 1903 (Religionsgeschichtliche Versuche und Vorarbeiten 1, reprint Berlin 1967).

Hock (1905) — G. Hock. *Griechische Weihegebräuche.* Diss. München, 1905.

Höfler (1934)	O. Höfler. *Kultische Geheimbünde der Germanen. I.* Frankfurt, 1934.
van Hoorn (1951)	G. van Hoorn. *Choes and Anthesteria.* Leiden, 1951.
Imhoof-Blumer (1885, 1886, 1887)	F. Imhoof-Blumer and P. Gardner. *Numismatic commentary on Pausanias,* vols. I–III. London (reprinted from the Journal of Hellenic Studies), 1885, 1886, 1887.
Jeanmaire (1939)	H. Jeanmaire. *Couroi et Courètes: Essai sur l'éducation spartiate et sur les rites d'adolescence dans l'antiquité hellénique.* Lille, 1939.
Judeich (1931)	W. Judeich. *Topographie von Athen.* München, (1905), 1931[2] (Handbuch der Altertumswissenschaft).
Kerényi (1952)	K. Kerényi. *Die Jungfrau und Mutter in der griechischen Religion. Eine Studie über Pallas Athene.* Zürich, 1952.
Kerényi (1962)	———. *Die Mysterien von Eleusis.* Zürich, 1962.
Kerényi (1967)	———. *Eleusis: Archetypal Image of Mother and Daughter.* New York, 1967.
Kirk (1970)	G. S. Kirk. *Myth: Its Meaning and Functions in Ancient and Other Cultures.* Berkeley and Los Angeles, 1970.
Krämer (1966)	W. Krämer. "Prähistorische Brandopferplätze." In *Helvetia antiqua, Festschr. E. Vogt* (Zürich, 1966), 111–22.
La Barre (1970)	W. La Barre. *The Ghost Dance: The Origins of Religion.* New York, 1970.
Latte (1960)	K. Latte. *Römische Religionsgeschichte.* München, 1960. (Handbuch der Altertumswissenschaft).
Lippold (1950)	G. Lippold. *Die griechische Plastik.* München, 1950 (Handbuch der Altertumswissenschaft).
Lobeck (1829)	C. A. Lobeck. *Aglaophamus sive de theologiae mysticae Graecorum causis.* Königsberg, 1829 (reprint Darmstadt, 1961).
Lorenz (1963)	K. Lorenz. *Das sogenannte Böse: Zur Naturgeschichte der Aggression.* Wien (1963), 1970.[25]
Mannhardt (1875)	W. Mannhardt. *Wald- und Feldkulte* I: *Der Baumkultus der Germanen und ihrer Nachbarstämme: Mythologische Untersuchungen.* Berlin, 1875 (1905[2] with minor amendments; reprint Darmstadt, 1963).
Maringer (1956)	J. Maringer. *Vorgeschichtliche Religion.* Einsiedeln, 1956.
Megas (1956)	G. A. Megas. Ἑλληνικαὶ ἑορταὶ καὶ ἔθιμα τῆς Λαϊκῆς λατρείας. Athens, 1956.

Mellaart (1967) J. Mellaart. *Çatal Hüyük: Stadt aus der Steinzeit.* Bergisch Gladbach, 1967 (Çatal Hüyük: A Neolithic Town in Anatolia. London, 1967).

Mellaart (1970) ———. *Excavations at Hacilar.* Vols. I, II. Edinburgh, 1970.

Metzger (1951) H. Metzger. *Les représentations dans la céramique attique du IVe siècle.* Paris, 1951.

Metzger (1965) ———. *Recherches sur l'imagérie athénienne.* Paris, 1965.

Meuli (1946) K. Meuli. "Griechische Opferbräuche." In *Phyllobolia* (Festschrift Peter Von der Mühll) (Basel, 1946) 185–288.

Meuli (1967) ———. "An Karl Schefold. In *Gestalt und Geschichte (Festschr. K. Schefold).* Bern, 1967 (*AK* Beiheft 4) 159–61.

Mikalson (1975) J. Mikalson. *The Sacred and Civil Calendar of the Athenian Year.* Princeton, 1975.

A. Mommsen (1898) A. Mommsen. *Feste der Stadt Athen im Altertum.* Leipzig, 1898.

Morris (1967) D. Morris. *The Naked Ape: A Zoologist's Study of the Human Animal.* New York, 1967.

Müller-Karpe (1966) H. Müller-Karpe. *Handbuch der Vorgeschichte.* I: *Altsteinzeit.* München, 1966.

Müller-Karpe (1968) ———. *Handbuch der Vorgeschichte.* II: *Jungsteinzeit.* München, 1968.

Mylonas (1961) G. E. Mylonas. *Eleusis and the Eleusinian Mysteries.* Princeton, 1961.

Nilsson (1906) M. P. Nilsson. *Griechische Feste von religiöser Bedeutung mit Ausschluss der attischen.* Leipzig, 1906 (reprint Darmstadt, 1957).

Nilsson (1950) ———. *The Minoan-Mycenaean Religion and Its Survival in Greek Religion.* Lund, (1927), 1950[2].

Nilsson (1955) ———. *Geschichte der griechischen Religion.* Vol. I. München, (1940), 1955[2] (=1967[3], with supplements S. 848–70 and pl. 53) (Handbuch der Altertumswissenschaft).

Nilsson (1957) ———. *The Dionysiac Mysteries of the Hellenistic Age.* Lund, 1957.

Nilsson (1967) See Nilsson (1955).

Otten (1958) H. Otten. *Hethitische Totenrituale.* Berlin, 1958.

Otto (1933) W. F. Otto. *Dionysos: Mythos und Kultus.* Frankfurt, 1933 (1948[2], with minor changes in pagination).

Parke and Wormell (1956) H. W. Parke and D. E. W. Wormell. *The Delphic Oracle*, vols. I, II. Oxford, 1956.

Pickard-Cambridge (1962) A. Pickard-Cambridge. *Dithyramb, Tragedy, and Comedy.* Oxford, (1927), 1962[2], revised by T. B. L. Webster.

Pickard-Cambridge (1968) ———. *The Dramatic Festivals of Athens*. Oxford, (1952), 1968[2], revised by J. Gould and D. M. Lewis.

Pringsheim (1905) H. G. Pringsheim. *Archäologische Beiträge zur Geschichte des Eleusinischen Kultes*. Diss. Bonn. München, 1905.

Pritchett (1979) W. K. Pritchett. *The Greek State at War.* III: *Religion*. Berkeley and Los Angeles, 1979.

Rohde (1898) E. Rohde. *Psyche: Seelencult und Unsterblichkeitsglaube der Griechen*. Freiburg, (1894), 1898[2] (= 1929[9, 10]; reprint Darmstadt, 1961).

Roux (1958) G. Roux. *Pausanias en Corinthie*. Paris, 1958.

Roux (1971) ———. *Delphi. Orakel und Kultstätten.* München, 1971.

Rumpf (1961) A. Rumpf. "Attische Feste—Attische Vasen." *Bonner Jahrbücher* 161 (1961), 208–14.

Samuel (1972) A. E. Samuel. *Greek and Roman Chronology.* München, 1972 (Handbuch der Altertumswissenschaft).

Schefold (1964) K. Schefold. *Frühgriechische Sagenbilder.* München, 1964.

Schwenn (1915) F. Schwenn. *Die Menschenopfer bei den Griechen und Römern*. Giessen, 1915 (Religionsgeschichtliche Versuche und Vorarbeiten 15, 3, reprint Berlin, 1966).

Simon (1969) E. Simon. *Die Götter der Griechen*. München, 1969.

Smith (1894) W. R. Smith. *Lectures on the Religion of the Semites*. London, 1894[2].

Stengel (1910) P. Stengel. *Opfergebräuche der Griechen*. Leipzig, 1910.

Stengel (1920) ———. *Die griechischen Kultusaltertümer.* München, (1890), 1920[3] (Handbuch der Klassischen Altertumswissenschaft).

Stiglitz (1967) R. Stiglitz. *Die grossen Göttinnen Arkadiens. Der Kultname ΜΕΓΑΛΑΙ ΘΕΑΙ und seine Grundlagen*. Wien, 1967.

Straube (1955) H. Straube. *Die Tierverkleidungen der afrikanischen Naturvölker.* Wiesbaden, 1955.

Svoronos (1924) J. N. Svoronos. *Les monnaies d'Athènes*. Athens, 1924.

Toepffer (1889) J. Toepffer. *Attische Genealogie*. Berlin, 1889.

Trendall (1967) A. D. Trendall. *The Red-Figured Vases of Lucania, Campania and Sicily*, vols. I, II. Oxford, 1967.

Vermeule (1979) E. Vermeule. *Aspects of Death in Early Greek Art and Poetry.* Berkeley and Los Angeles, 1979.

Wächter (1910) Th. Wächter. *Reinheitsvorschriften im griechischen Kult.* Giessen, 1910 (Religionsgeschichtliche Versuche und Vorarbeiten 9, 1).

Wilamowitz (1931) U. v. Wilamowitz-Moellendorff. *Der Glaube der Hellenen* I. Berlin, 1931.

Wilamowitz (1932) ———. *Der Glaube der Hellenen* II. Berlin, 1932.

Wissowa (1912) G. Wissowa. *Religion und Kultus der Römer.* München, (1902), 1912[2] (Handbuch der Klassischen Altertumswissenschaft).

Yavis (1949) C. G. Yavis. *Greek Altars: Origins and Typology.* Saint Louis, 1949.

Index of Cult Sites and Festivals

Index of Names of Gods and Heroes

Index of Persons and Things

Index of Greek Words

Designer: Rick Chafian
Compositor: G&S Typesetters, Inc.
Printer: Vail-Ballou Press
Binder: Vail-Ballou Press
Text: 10/12 Palatino
Display: Palatino & Italic